Illinois SCHOOL LAW SURVEY

Sixth Edition

Brian A. Braun

ILLINOIS ASSOCIATION
OF SCHOOL BOARDS

430 East Vine Street
Springfield, Illinois 62703-2236

One Imperial Place
1 East 22nd Street
Lombard, Illinois 60148-6120

March, 2000

ISBN: 1-880331-11-X

CAUTIONARY NOTE

Illinois School Law Survey provides answers to general questions regarding statutes, case law, and administrative rules in force as of January 1, 2000. It is not intended to provide advice in the handling of specific situations. Because the law is in a state of continual change, the reader should treat this publication as a source of instruction in the basic principles of school law and as a guide to matters meriting further study or the assistance of legal counsel.

Finally, *Illinois School Law Survey* generally excludes laws that are unique to Chicago Public School District 299.

Comments and suggestions for improvements in *Illinois School Law Survey* may be addressed to either the author or to the Publications Department of the Illinois Association of School Boards.

SPECIAL THANK YOU

The Illinois Association of School Boards is extremely grateful to **David L. Franklin**, who played an invaluable role in developing the original edition of *Illinois School Law Survey*. A longtime teacher and writer in the fields of school law and school finance, Professor Franklin retired from the educational administration department at Illinois State University.

AUTHOR

Brian Braun, of Champaign, has been an attorney with the firm of Miller, Tracy, Braun, Funk & Paisley, Ltd. since January 1983. He was an attorney on the staff of the Illinois Association of School Boards from 1977 to 1983 and a language arts teacher in DuPage County from 1969 until 1977. He was born in Chicago and raised in Glencoe, Illinois, where he attended the Glencoe Public Schools and New Trier High School. He is a graduate of the University of Illinois College of Communications and the DePaul University College of Law.

Mr. Braun has lectured on school law and labor relations at a number of Illinois colleges and universities, was a member of the Board of Directors of the National Council of School Attorneys (1991-1995) and is a past chairman of the executive committee of the Illinois Council of School Attorneys (IASB). In November 1996, Brian Braun received the Harold P. Seamon Award from IASB for distinguished service to public education.

Mr. Braun and his wife, Terre, a kindergarten teacher at Westview Elementary School, in Champaign, have three children: David 18, Aaron 17 and Max 8. Mr. Braun's interests include golf, gardening and genealogy.

AUTHOR'S ACKNOWLEDGEMENTS

Many thanks to those who have been mentors, colleagues and friends. A special thank you to Jerry Glaub without whom this project would have been impossible at its inception.

For Terre, David, Aaron and Max who will always mean everything to me.

Brian A. Braun
Champaign, Illinois
March 1, 2000

HOW TO USE
ILLINOIS SCHOOL LAW SURVEY

In addition to simply reading the text from front to back, the user of *Illinois School Law Survey* has two ways to locate information. The Table of Contents on pages vii through xi lists the broad topics covered in each chapter. In many cases, these topic headings will get the reader to the desired information.

However, any legal question probably relates to several topics, and information can show up under any number of different headings. (Seniority rights of teachers, for example, may be discussed under teacher employment as well as under collective bargaining.) Moreover, broad topic headings often will not describe or suggest a particular question or narrow point of law. The user interested either in a narrow topic or in one with multiple facets should use the Quick Reference Index beginning on page 586. This alphabetical list of topics includes references too narrow to be listed in the Table of Contents and shows whether the topic is discussed at more than one place in the text.

The reader also will find a table of court cases arranged in alphabetical order by name of plaintiff beginning on page 548. All court decisions cited in this book are listed in the table with a full legal reference. At the end of each case citation is listed the question(s) where the case is cited in the text.

The table of case law serves at least two purposes. The user who knows only a case name will be able to find a full citation and a list of applicable questions and answers. Also, where an answer carries a case law citation, the reader can use the table to find other questions and answers related to the same case.

QUESTION NUMBERS

The number to the left of the colon in each question number reflects the chapter number, 1 through 27. Questions within each chapter are numbered to the right of each colon; that is, 1:10, 1:20, 1:25, 2:10, 2:15, and so on.

While questions are presented in numerical sequence, intervals between numbers are variable. Questions in the first edition were numbered at intervals of 10, leaving room for the insertion of new questions as needed in subsequent editions.

CONTENTS

UNDERSTANDING LEGAL REFERENCES   xiii

1: CONTROL OF ILLINOIS PUBLIC SCHOOLS   1

Federal Government, 1; State Government, 1; School Districts, 3; School Boards, 4; State Board of Education, 6; Regional Governance, 9; Local-Municipal Government, 11; State Academic Standards, 12; Waiver of State Requirements, 15; Charter Schools, 16

2: SCHOOL BOARDS   23

School Board Structure, 23; Vacancies, 27; School Board Powers and Duties, 30

3: SCHOOL BOARD MEMBERSHIP   36

Qualifications, 36; Incompatibility, 37; Compensation and Expenses, 38; Disclosure of Economic Interests, 40; Interest in Contracts, 42; Resignations, 45; Removal and Forfeiture, 46; Gift Ban Act, 48

4: SCHOOL ELECTION PROCEDURES   53

General Election Laws, 53; Election Authority, 56; Election of School Board Members, 58; Candidate Nominations, 58; Candidate Withdrawal, 61; Objections to Nominating Petitions, 61; Certification of Candidates, 63; Public Policy Elections, 66; Advocacy and Electioneering, 70; Determining Election Results, 72; Voting, 74

5: SCHOOL BOARD OFFICERS   76

Elected Officers, 76; Treasurers, 78

6: SCHOOL BOARD MEETINGS   82

Public Meetings, 82; Calling Meetings, 85; Notice
of Meetings, 88; Closed Meetings, 89; Conducting
Meetings, 93; Minutes, 97

7: SCHOOL DISTRICT RECORDS   100

Applicable Statutes, 100; Personnel Records, 101;
Student Records, 105; Freedom of Information Act,
116

8: CHANGING SCHOOL DISTRICT
BOUNDARIES AND TERRITORY   127

District Consolidation, 127; Boundary Changes,
131; Non-Charter District Detachment and
Annexation, 132; Detachment and Annexation
Petitions, 135; Regional Board of School Trustees,
137; Charter District Detachment and Annexation,
142

9: CONTROL AND USE OF SCHOOL PROPERTY   145

Acquisition and Ownership, 145; Disposing of
School Property, 148; School Buildings, 152; State
Construction Aid, 153; Building Contractors, 158;
Safety, 159; Use of School Facilities, 165

10: THE EDUCATIONAL PROGRAM   167

Curricular Authority, 167; The School Year and
Day, 178; Testing and Reporting, 180; Grades and
Grading, 184; Educational Materials, 185

11: STUDENTS AND PARENTS 188

Compulsory Attendance, 188; Home Schooling, 190; Truancy, 191; Right to Attend School, 194; Student Residency and Tuition, 195; Homeless Child, 200; Health Examination and Immunization, 201; Student Fees, 202; Student Insurance, 203; Status of Minors, 203; Child Abuse and Neglect, 204; Student Transportation, 206; Academic Clubs and Extra-curricular Activities, 208; Sexual Harassment of Students, 210

12: STUDENT DISCIPLINE 216

Disciplinary Authority, 216; Parent and Student Protections, 219; Student Expression and Dress, 220; Student Publications, 223; Prohibited Behaviors, 225; Corporal Punishment, 228; Student Searches, 229; Police Searches and Arrests, 233; Suspension and Expulsion, 237; Alternative Schools, 245

13: CHILDREN WITH DISABILITIES AND SPECIAL EDUCATION 248

Special Education Defined, 248; Eligibility for Special Education, 252; Special Programs and Services, 257; Evaluation and Placement, 262; Rights of Children and Parents, 264; Financial Obligations, 269; Discipline of Students with Disabilities, 271; Special Education Facilities, 274; Special Education Joint Agreements, 275; Special Education Due Process Hearings, 276

14: RELIGION AND RACE AND THE PUBLIC SCHOOLS 285

A. Religious Issues: Constitutional Principles, 285; Prayer, 287; Parochial School Services, 290; School Facilities, 291; Curricular Issues, 295

B. Racial Issues: School Desegregation, 297; Segregation Remedies, 298; Employment, 300

15: TERMS AND CONDITIONS OF TEACHER EMPLOYMENT 303

State Certification, 303; Certificate Renewal, 309; Additional Teacher Qualifications, 314; Teaching Assignments and Workloads, 315; Probationary Employment, 318; Substitute Teachers, 320; Evaluating Teachers, 321; Teacher Compensation, 324; Retirement System Contributions, 327; Leaves, 329; Teacher Resignations, 331

16: TEACHER TENURE AND SENIORITY RIGHTS 333

Teacher Tenure, 333; Acquisition of Tenure, 335; Part Time Teachers, 339; Seniority and Reduction in Force, 339; Seniority and Bumping, 344

17: SCHOOL EMPLOYMENT IN GENERAL 348

Employment Standards, 348; Compensation, 351; Salary Deductions, 352; Holidays and Leaves, 353; Workers' Compensation, 357; Unemployment Insurance, 359; Americans with Disabilities Act, 360; Employee Speech, 363; Sexual Harassment, 367; Employment Rights and Employee Discipline, 370

18: TEACHER DISMISSAL FOR CAUSE 377

Dismissal of the Probationary Teacher, 377; Dismissal of the Tenured Teacher, 380; Causes for Dismissal, 382; Remediability, 385; Due Process and Teacher Dismissal, 389; Teacher Suspension, 396

19: SCHOOL ADMINISTRATORS 398

Duties of Administrators, 398; Administrator Qualifications, 400; Employment Contracts, 402; Tenure, 405; Reclassification of Principals, 406; Dismissal Rights, 408

20: NONCERTIFICATED EMPLOYEES 409

Duties of Noncertificated Employees, 409; Wages and Hours, 411; Benefit Programs, 413; Dismissal, 414; School Bus Drivers, 418

21: COLLECTIVE BARGAINING 420

Illinois Educational Labor Relations Act, 420; Covered Employers and Employees, 422; Statutory Obligations of Employers, 424; Bargaining Units, 430; Exclusive Bargaining Representative, 431; Nonunion Employees, 434; Unfair Labor Practices, 436; Impasses and Strikes, 439; Grievance Resolution, 443; Contractual Provisions, 444

22: SCHOOL DISTRICTS AND LIABILITY FOR INJURIES 447

Tort Immunity Concepts, 447; Tort Immunities, 449; Liability of Individuals, 451; Injuries to Employees, 452; Injuries to Students, 453; Safety Requirements, 456; Judgments, 458

23: PROPERTY TAX INCOME 460

Authority to Levy Taxes, 460; Property Assessments, 461; Tax Levies, 464; Levy Hearings, 466; Property Tax Rates, 467; Referendum to Increase Tax Rates, 472; Tax Abatements, 474

24: STATE AID AND OTHER SCHOOL INCOME 475

Sources of Income, 475; State Mandates, 476; State Aid, 478; State Aid Computations, 479; State Aid Penalties, 482; State Aid Distribution System, 482; Investment Income, 483; Gifts, 486; Other Sources of Income, 487

25: BUDGETING AND MANAGING SCHOOL FUNDS   488

The Budget, 488; Accounting Procedures, 491; Fund Accounts, 492; Other Funds, 495; Financial Reports and Audits, 497; Purchasing and Bidding Requirements, 498; Installment Purchases and Contracts, 503

26: SCHOOL BOARD BORROWING AND DEBT   506

Interfund Transfers and Loans, 506; Working Cash Fund, 508; Authority to Borrow, 510; Short Term Borrowing, 510; Bond Issues, 514; Debt and Financial Difficulty, 518

27: ILLINOIS HIGH SCHOOL ASSOCIATION   521

Standards for Schools, 522; Sportsmanship, 525; Student Eligibility, 526; Boys and Girls Teams, 537; Coaching and Practicing, 539; Recruitment, 543; Non-School Events, 545; Student Awards, 547

TABLE OF CASE LAW   548

An alphabetical list of court cases with each case keyed to the questions where it is cited in the text.

QUICK REFERENCE INDEX   586

An alphabetical subject index.

UNDERSTANDING LEGAL REFERENCES

All legal references in this book are cited in standard forms that employ numerous abbreviations. In order to retrieve legal source materials, therefore, the lay reader must (a) understand the abbreviations used in the legal citations and (b) know where to find the legal publications cited.

An explanation of abbreviations used in this book is provided on page xvi.

Citations involving statutes may be the easiest for the lay reader to locate. Law libraries and most attorneys and court houses will have current statutes available—the *United States Code* and the *Illinois Compiled Statutes*. Numbering of chapters and sections are relatively easy to comprehend.

Administrative regulations may be the most difficult materials to locate. The *Illinois Administrative Code* is a publication that is not always found in a law office or court house, but it may be purchased on CD ROM from the Illinois Secretary of State's Administrative Code Division. Or check a law library or consult the administrative agency that issued the regulation in question.

Federal rules are found in *Federal Rules Digest* and *Code of Federal Regulations*.

READING CASE CITATIONS

Publications that report court decisions are found in law libraries. In Illinois, law libraries are maintained by most universities and colleges and can be found in most county court houses. Small law libraries are maintained by many lawyers.

Court cases are cited by case name, which is printed in italics. Case citations following each case name reveal which court decided the case and in what year. Case citations also tell where to find the case cited. The format for each case citation is the same:

• The first number refers to the volume of the set of books in which the case can be found.

• The second reference is to the set of books in which the case can be found.

• The next reference is to the edition of that set of books.

- The final reference is to the page on which the case cited can be found in the volume and set.

For example, 23 Ill.App.3d 196 means the case referred to can be found in volume 23 of *Illinois Appellate Reports, Third Edition* on page 196.

Knowing the edition is important, because cases are reported chronologically. New editions of various reporters are issued randomly whenever the publishers think the volume numbers have gotten too high. Thus, when the publishers thought the volume numbers were getting too high in *Illinois Appellate Reports*, they simply went from volume 351 Ill.App. to volume 1 Ill.App.2d. Thus, knowing the volume and page number is not enough to find a case easily unless you know the edition number, too.

Cases are frequently reported in more than one set of books. Thus, the same case may be found in *Supreme Court Reporter*, in *United States Reports* and in *Lawyers' Edition*. Wherever possible we have given multiple citations for each case.

STATE COURTS

Cases which have been tried in the Illinois state court system are identifiable by their citations. There are three levels of courts in Illinois. The lowest is the circuit court, which is the trial level. Circuit court decisions are not generally reported, have very little precedential value, and are not referred to anywhere in this text.

A party may appeal an adverse circuit court decision to the appropriate Illinois appellate court as a matter of right. There are five geographically-determined Illinois appellate courts, which are designated by district numbers one through five. The First District Appellate Court hears Cook County appeals and the Second District Appellate Court covers Lake County and the northwestern part of the state. The Third and Fourth Districts hear north central and south central appeals, and the Fifth District hears cases originating in circuit courts located in the southern third of the state.

All Illinois appellate court citations are cited to one of the three editions of *Illinois Appellate Reports* — Ill.App. or Ill.App.2d or Ill.App.3d. Each appellate court citation also gives the reader information in a parenthetical notation about which appellate court decided the case cited and when it was decided. For example, (5th Dist. 1990) means the Fifth District Appellate Court decided the case in 1990.

A party may ask the Illinois Supreme Court to review an adverse appellate court decision. The Illinois Supreme Court may accept or reject most appeals at its pleasure. The reader can determine whether the Illinois Supreme Court has rendered a decision in a case, because all such cases are cited to *Illinois Reporter*. If a case has a citation to Ill. or Ill.2d, the reader will know the decision referred to was rendered by the Illinois Supreme Court.

FEDERAL COURTS

The federal court system is also three-tiered. Usually, in education law, lawsuits dealing with federal Constitutional questions are brought in federal court and questions which deal with state law are brought in state court.

The federal court system starts with a federal district court. There are three federal district courts in Illinois which are designated as the Northern District, Central District and Southern District. Federal District Court decisions are reported in a set of books called *Federal Supplement*. If the reader sees a citation to F.Supp., it means the case cited was decided by the lowest federal court, a federal district court.

A party may appeal an adverse federal district court decision to the appropriate federal circuit court of appeals as a matter of right. There are eleven federal circuit courts of appeals across the nation. All Illinois cases are heard by the Seventh Circuit Court of Appeals. All federal court of appeals cases are cited in this text to *Federal Reporter*. Therefore, if the reader sees a citation to F. or F.2d, this means the case cited was decided by a federal appeals court. Each court of appeals citation includes a parenthetical notation designating the court of appeals which rendered the decision and the year the decision was rendered. For example, (7th Cir. 1990) means the Seventh Circuit Court of Appeals decided the case in 1990.

A party may ask the United States Supreme Court to review an adverse decision rendered by a court of appeals. In most cases, the Supreme Court may review a decision or deny the right to review at its pleasure. All cases referred to in this text decided by the Supreme court are cited to *Supreme Court Reporter*. Therefore, if the reader sees a citation to S.Ct., this means the case was decided by the United States Supreme Court.

ABBREVIATIONS USED IN LEGAL CITATIONS

2d—second edition

3d—third edition

A.—*Atlantic Reporter*

ALR—*American Law Reporter*

aff'd.—affirmed

app.—appeal

art.—article

BNAC—Bureau of National Affairs

c.—chapter

C.D. Ill.—Central District of Illinois, refers to the federal district court in Illinois in which the case was tried. Federal district courts are identified in parentheses by state and region within the state; i.e., M.D. Pa. for Middle District of Pennsylvania, and year (M.D. Pa. 1992).

cert.—certiorari (the word is used in this text to describe a request to the United States Supreme Court to review an adverse court of appeals decision)

cert.den.—certiorari denied (means the U.S. Supreme Court declined to review the case)

C.F.R.—*Code of Federal Regulations*

Cir.—circuit

C.J.S.—*Corpus Juris Secundum* (a legal encyclopedia)

Cmwlth.—Commonwealth

Const.—Constitution

D.C.—District Court or District of Columbia

D.C. Cir.— U. S. Court of Appeals for the District of Columbia Circuit

den.—denied

E.D.—Eastern District

eff.—effective

et al.—in the name of a case, "et al." means there are other parties who are referred to collectively

et seq.—et sequentes (and the following)

et ux.—and wife

ex rel.— on behalf of, for the use of, or on the relation of

F.—*Federal Reporter*

F.E.P.—*Fair Employment Practice Cases*

Fed.R.Civ.P.—*Federal Rules of Civil Procedure*

F.R.D.—*Federal Rules Digest*

F.Supp.—*Federal Supplement*

IELRB—Illinois Educational Labor Relations Board

ILCS—*Illinois Compiled Statutes*

Ill.—*Illinois Reports*

Ill. Admin. Code—*Illinois Administrative Code*

Ill. App.—*Illinois Appellate Reports*

Ill. Const.—*Illinois Constitution*

Ill. Dec.—*Illinois Decisions*

in re—in the matter of, petition of, or application of

Ind.—*Indiana Reports*

La.App.—*Louisiana Courts of Appeal Reporter*

L.Ed.—*Lawyers' Edition*

M.D.—Middle District

Minn.Sup.Ct.—Minnesota Supreme Court

N.D.—Northern District

N.E.—*Northeastern Reporter*

N.J.—*New Jersey Reports*

no.— number

N.W.—*Northwestern Reporter*

N.Y.—*New York Reporter*

N.Y.S.—*New York Supplement*

Ohio Misc.—*Ohio Miscellaneous*

op.—opinion

P.—*Pacific Reporter*

P.A.—Public Act

Pa. Super.—Pennsylvania Superior Court

Pa.Cmwlth.—*Pennsylvania Commonwealth Court Reports*

PERI—*Public Employee Reporter for Illinois*

reh.—rehearing

rem.—remand or remanded (returned to a lower court)

rev.—reversed

S.Ct.—*Supreme Court Reporter*

S.D.—Southern District

continued

S.E.—*Southeastern Reporter*

So.—*Southern Reporter*

sec.—section

Slip op.—Slip opinion (an opinion which is so new it is not yet published in law reporters)

sub nom.—sub nominee (in the name of)

sugg.— suggestion

supp.—supplemented

S.W.—*South Western Reporter*

Tex.Ct.App.—Texas Court of Appeals

U.S.—*United States Reports*

U.S.C.—*United States Code*

U.S.L.W.—*United States Law Week*

Va.App.—*Virginia Court of Appeals Reports*

vac.—vacated

Wash.—*Washington Reports*

W.D.—*Western District*

WL — *Westlaw*

1: CONTROL OF ILLINOIS PUBLIC SCHOOLS

FEDERAL GOVERNMENT

1:10   Is education a state or federal function?

Early in the nineteenth century there was little state involvement in education. Later, education became almost entirely a function of state or local government. In the twentieth century, the state has assumed responsibility for the regulation of education. The Illinois State Constitution establishes a system of public schools, whereas the U.S. Constitution makes no mention of education. Ostensibly, therefore, education is a responsibility of the state.

Since the 1950s, however, the federal government has assumed a more aggressive role in the regulation of the schools by imposing requirements upon the states. Federal laws, such as the 1964 Civil Rights Act and its amendments and the Individuals with Disabilities Education Act, have greatly changed education in the last thirty years.

1:20   What federal agency is responsible for the administration of federal programs for public schools?

The U.S. Department of Education is the principal federal agency which regulates public schools.

20 U.S.C. 3411

STATE GOVERNMENT

1:30   Are public school districts governmental entities?

The Illinois Constitution provides:

"A fundamental goal of the People of the State is the educational development of all persons to the limits of their capacities.

"The State shall provide for an efficient system of high quality public educational institutions and services. Education in public schools through the secondary level shall be free. There may be such other free education as the General Assembly provides by law.

"The State has the primary responsibility for financing the system of public education."

Ill. Const. art. X, sec. 1

Board of Education of Community Consolidated School District 606, Tazewell County v. Board of Education of Community Unit District 124 of Mason and Tazewell Counties, 11 Ill.App.2d 408, 137 N.E.2d 721 (3rd Dist. 1956)

O'Connor v. Board of Education of School District No. 23, 645 F.2d 578 (7th Cir. 1981) cert. den. 102 S.Ct. 641, 454 U.S. 1084, 70 L.Ed.2d 619 (1981), on rem. 545 F.Supp. 376

1:40   Are all the laws which govern Illinois public schools found in The Illinois School Code?

The laws of Illinois are published in a six volume set titled Illinois Compiled Statutes. Many of the laws affecting education are contained in Chapter 105, which is commonly called "The School Code." The laws of Illinois were reorganized in 1993. Before January 1, 1993, Illinois laws were organized as Illinois Revised Statutes. In Illinois Revised Statutes, the School Code was Chapter 122.

There are many chapters in addition to Chapter 105 of the Illinois Compiled Statutes which directly affect or regulate schools. For example, elections are administered by laws contained in Chapter 10. The Educational Labor Relations Act and other labor matters are found in Chapter 115, The Open Meetings Act is included in Chapter 5, pensions laws are in Chapter 40, and various laws relating to records are contained in Chapter 50.

There are many other chapters of Illinois Compiled Statutes which are relevant to schools. Various state agencies have rules and regulations which are found in the Illinois Administrative Code. There are also numerous federal laws which apply to schools.

1:50   What is the difference between the terms "common schools," "free schools," and "public schools?"

The terms common schools, free schools, and public schools are used interchangeably in the School Code.

105 ILCS 5/1-3

SCHOOL DISTRICTS

1:60   What are "county school units?"

The territory in each county, exclusive of charter districts which are required to appoint their own school treasurers, constitute county school units. County school units of less than two million inhabitants are known as Class I county school units, and county school units of two million or more inhabitants are known as Class II county school units.

105 ILCS 5/5-1

1:70   What types of school districts are there in Illinois?

The numerous school district designations in Illinois vary mostly in name and reflect, not important legal distinctions, but different statutory terminology in use at the time different school districts were organized. Many of the statutes under which Illinois school districts were first organized have since been repealed. Among the variations in district type that reflect important legal distinctions:

1) Unit districts, which were created under various designations, provide education for kindergarten through grade 12. Elementary districts (grades K-8) and high school districts (grades 9-12) create a dual structure.

2) Charter districts, originally created under charters granted by the state, typically are governed by special sections of the School Code. Schools in the City of Chicago, for example, are governed by article 34 of the School Code.

105 ILCS 5/11A-1
105 ILCS 5/11B-1
105 ILCS 5/12-1
105 ILCS 5/12-10
105 ILCS 5/32-1.1
105 ILCS 5/33-1
105 ILCS 5/34-2

SCHOOL BOARDS

1:80   What is a school board?

The term "school board" refers to the governing body of any school district created under the authority of the School Code, including boards of school directors and boards of education. The majority of school boards are governed by Article 10 of the School Code. However, the boards of some larger school districts and some special charter districts are governed by Articles 32, 33 and 34 of the School Code.

> 105 ILCS 5/10-1 et seq.
> 105 ILCS 5/32-1 et seq.
> 105 ILCS 5/33-1 et seq.
> 105 ILCS 5/34-1 et seq.

1:90   Are school boards created by the state Constitution?

No, the Illinois Constitution does not refer to local school boards. They are creations of state statutes.

1:100   Do school districts or their governing bodies have inherent powers?

A school board is a creation of the state, and creations of the state are without inherent power. A school board may exercise only those powers which the legislature has specifically granted, or those powers which are reasonably implied from a specified power, to achieve the purposes which the legislature has assigned to them.

> *Goedde v. Community Unit School District No. 7, Macoupin County*, 21 Ill.App.2d 79, 157 N.E.2d 266 (3rd Dist. 1959)

1:110   What kinds of school boards are there in Illinois?

The majority of school boards are governed by Section 10-10 of the School Code, which requires each to have seven members elected for terms of four years. There are numerous exceptions allowed or required by law, however:

1) Section 10-3 provides for a three member board of school directors in school districts with fewer than 1,000 inhabitants,

except that a consolidated district must have a board of seven directors;

2) Section 32-1.1 authorizes school boards of charter districts with 100,000 to one million inhabitants to expand from seven members to 11 members unless the district's original charter or other special law provides otherwise;

3) Article 34 provides for a seven-member board of education appointed by the mayor in Chicago;

4) Section 32-1.5 authorizes the voters of special charter districts to elect a school board of three, five or seven members;

5) Section 32-3.2 requires certain special charter districts in cities of more than 45,000 inhabitants to have 11 members appointed by the mayor;

6) Section 33-1 authorizes special charter districts in cities of 100,000 to 500,000 inhabitants to elect seven-member boards of education, with members serving five-year terms. The same boards are authorized by Section 33-1a to adopt an alternative arrangement, subject to voter approval at a referendum, electing three board members at large and four members from school board districts that are substantially equal in population.

The school boards of special charter districts, which predate most of the laws creating school boards, operate under provisions of their own state charters unless they have chosen to adopt Article 10 of the School Code or have selected one of the other options available in Articles 32 or 33.

105 ILCS 5/10-1
105 ILCS 5/10-10
105 ILCS 5/31-1.2
105 ILCS 5/32-1 et seq.
105 ILCS 5/33-1
105 ILCS 5/34-3

1:120 May citizens claim that an improper type of school board exists in a given school district?

When a petition signed by 10 percent or 1,500 legal voters, whichever is less, is submitted to a regional superintendent of schools, the regional superintendent must take a special census of the school district to determine if the district has the proper type of school board, a board of school directors or a board of education. The expenses of this census are to be borne by the school district involved.

If the census shows that the proper type of board does not exist, then the regional superintendent is required to immediately notify the school district and to certify to the proper election authorities that an election shall be held at the next general election in order to select the appropriate and entirely new board of the type legally required for a given school district.

105 ILCS 5/3-14.16

STATE BOARD OF EDUCATION

1:130   How was the State Board of Education created?

The State Board of Education was created by the Illinois Constitution, which provides in part:

"There is created a State Board of Education to be elected or selected on a regional basis. The number of members, their qualifications, terms of office and manner of election or selection shall be provided by law. The Board, except as limited by law, may establish goals, determine policies, provide for planning and evaluating education programs and recommend financing. The Board shall have such other duties and powers as provided by law.

"The State Board of Education shall appoint a chief state educational officer."

Ill. Const. art. X, sec. 2

1:140   How are members of the Illinois State Board of Education selected?

Members of the State Board of Education are appointed by the Governor with the advice and consent of the Senate. The State Board consists of nine members. Members are appointed pursuant to statutorily defined geographic areas of representation.

At no time may more than five members of the State Board be from one political party. Party membership is defined as having voted in the primary of the party in the last primary before appointment. Members of the State Board serve for six-year terms.

105 ILCS 5/1A-1 et seq.

1:150 What are the qualifications for membership on the State Board of Education?

The members of the State Board of Education must be citizens of the United States and residents of the State of Illinois and are selected on the basis of their knowledge of or interest and experience in problems of public education. No member of the State Board may be gainfully employed or administratively connected with any public school system nor have any interest in or benefit from funds provided b the State Board of Education to an institution of higher learning, public or private, within Illinois nor shall they be members of a school board or board of school trustees of a public or nonpublic school, college, university, or technical institution within Illinois.

105 ILCS 5/1A-2
Hoskins v. Walker, 57 Ill.2d 503, 315 N.E.2d 25 (1974)

1:160 Are State Board of Education members compensated?

State Board of Education members are reimbursed for all ordinary and necessary expenses incurred in performing their duties as members of the Board. They receive no other compensation. Expenses must be approved by the State Board and must be consistent with the laws, policies, and requirements of the State of Illinois regarding such expenditures. Any member may include in his claim for expenses $50 per day for meeting days.

105 ILCS 5/1A-2

1:170 How is a vacancy on the State Board of Education created?

A vacancy on the State Board of Education is created when a member:

1) dies;

2) files a written resignation with the Governor;

3) is adjudicated to be a person under legal disability under the Probate Act or a person subject to involuntary admission under the Mental Health and Developmental Disabilities Code;

4) ceases to be a resident of the judicial district from which he or she was appointed;

5) is convicted of an infamous crime, or of any offense involving a violation of his or her legal duties;

6) fails to maintain the qualifications for membership required by law.

105 ILCS 5/1A-2.1
405 ILCS 5/1-100 et seq.
755 ILCS 5/1-1 et seq.

1:180   How may a member of the Illinois State Board of Education be removed from office?

The Governor may remove a member of the State Board of Education for incompetence, neglect of duty, or malfeasance in office.

Ill. Const. art. V, sec. 10

1:190   What are the qualifications for the office of State Superintendent of Education?

The State Board of Education determines the qualifications of and appoints the State Superintendent of Education. The State Superintendent of Education serves at the pleasure of the State Board and pursuant to a performance contract linked to statewide student performance and academic improvement within Illinois schools.   No employment contract for a State Superintendent of Education may exceed three years and the contract cannot contain a rollover provision which contains an automatic extension. The State Superintendent cannot be a member of the State Board. The State Board establishes the compensation for the State Superintendent and establishes the duties, powers, and responsibilities of the office.

105 ILCS 5/1A-4(B)

1:200   What are the duties and authorities of the State Superintendent of Education?

The State Superintendent of Education is the chief administrative officer of the State Board of Education. As such, he is responsible for the supervision and evaluation of all public schools, for enacting and enforcing rules governing the operation of public schools, and for carrying out the policies of the State Board of Education.

105 ILCS 5/2-2 et seq.

1:210 What types of school district recognition does the State Board of Education grant?

There are three types of recognition status:

1) Full Recognition is granted to a school district or attendance center which meets the minimal standards required of public elementary and secondary schools and has submitted an annual application for recognition.

2) Probationary Recognition is given to a school district or attendance center which has not met minimal standards. Probationary Recognition is a warning the school must make certain improvements.

3) Non-recognition is given to a school district or attendance center which fails to submit an Annual Application for Recognition, fails to meet legal requirements, or fails to give evidence of meeting minimal standards. A school district which fails for any school year to maintain a recognized school shall not be eligible to file for such year any claim upon the common school fund or collect tuition from another school district.

School districts assigned Probationary Recognition or Non-recognition may request re-evaluation by the State Board of Education to substantiate corrections of the areas of noncompliance previously cited.

105 ILCS 5/18-8.05
23 Ill. Admin. Code 1.50

REGIONAL GOVERNANCE

1:220 What is an educational service region?

An educational service region is a county or a group of counties administered for educational purposes by a regional superintendent of schools.

105 ILCS 5/3A-1 et seq.

1:222 What is the difference between an educational service region and a regional office of education?

There is no difference. The terms are synonymous.

105 ILCS 5/3-0.01

1:230   How are regional superintendents of schools selected?

Regional superintendents of schools are elected pursuant to general election laws by popular vote from all counties comprising the educational service region served.

105 ILCS 5/3A-6

1:240   What is the difference between a county superintendent of schools, a regional superintendent of schools, and a regional superintendent?

These terms refer to the same elective office and are interchangeable.

105 ILCS 5/3-0.01

1:250   What are the qualifications for regional superintendent of schools?

No one is eligible to file a petition of candidacy for the office of regional superintendent of schools at any primary or general election, or to enter into the duties of this office either by election or appointment, unless he possesses the following qualifications:

1) is of good character;

2) has a master's degree;

3) has earned at least 20 semester hours of credit in professional education at the graduate level;

4) holds a valid all-grade supervisory certificate, limited supervisory certificate, life supervisory certificate, or an administrative certificate with superintendent endorsement;

5) has had at least four years experience in teaching; and

6) was engaged for at least two years of the previous four years in full-time teaching or supervising in the common public schools or serving as a county or regional superintendent of schools for an educational service region in Illinois.

A candidate for office must file a statement of economic interests. If elected he must take an oath of office, post a bond of no less than $12,000, and may not practice any other profession during the term of office.

5 ILCS 420/1-101
105 ILCS 5/3-1 et seq.
105 ILCS 5/3A-6

LOCAL-MUNICIPAL GOVERNMENT

1:260   May any other unit of local government regulate a school district?

The operation of public schools is a state function and not a function of local government. Local governmental entities may not regulate the operation of a school district.

Ill. Const. art. VII, sec. 1
Ill. Const. art. VII, sec. 10
Board of Education of Minooka Community High School District No. 111 Grundy, Kendall and Will Counties v. Carter, 119 Ill.App.3d 857, 458 N.E.2d 50, 75 Ill.Dec. 882, (3rd Dist. 1983)
Board of Education of School District No. 150 v. City of Peoria, 76 Ill.2d 469, 394 N.E.2d 399, 31 Ill.Dec. 197 (1979)
Board of Education of the City of Rockford v. Page, 33 Ill.2d 372, 211 N.E.2d 361 (1965)
Board of Education of School District 33 v. City of West Chicago, 55 Ill.App.2d 401, 205 N.E.2d 63 (2nd Dist. 1965)

1:270   May school districts enter into cooperative agreements with units of local government?

The Illinois Constitution allows intergovernmental cooperative agreements, providing in part:

"Units of local government and school districts may contract or otherwise associate among themselves, with the State, with other states and their units of local government and school districts, and with the United States to obtain or share services and to exercise, combine, or transfer any power or function, in any manner not prohibited by law or by ordinance. Units of local government and school districts may contract and otherwise associate with individuals, associations, and corporations in any manner not prohibited by law or by ordinance. Participating units of government may use their credit, revenues, and other resources to pay costs and to service debt related to intergovernmental activities.

"Officers and employees of units of local government and school districts may participate in intergovernmental activities authorized by their units of government without relinquishing their offices or positions.

"The State shall encourage intergovernmental cooperation

and use its technical and financial resources to assist intergovernmental activities."

Ill. Const. art. VII, sec. 10(a) et seq.

5 ILCS 220/1 et seq.

Village of Elmwood Park v. Forest Preserve District of Cook County, 21 Ill.App.3d 597, 316 N.E.2d 140 (1st Dist. 1974)

1:280   How is fire protection for school sites provided?

If the location of any public school building is not within any municipality or fire protection district, fire protection service is provided by the municipality or fire protection district which maintains the facility for fire fighting equipment which is closest to the school site. The school district must pay to the municipality or fire protection district the reasonable cost of such service.

105 ILCS 5/16-10

STATE ACADEMIC STANDARDS

1:300   What factors are considered in the establishment of state recognition standards for student performance and school improvement?

The standards include, but are not necessarily limited to, state assessment of student performance, local assessment results, student attendance rates, retention rates, expulsion rates and graduation rates.

105 ILCS 5/2-3.25

1:310   Does the State Board of Education have authority to collect school information from a school district to determine its level of recognition?

The State Board is authorized to collect information, data, test results, student performance and school improvement indicators with respect to school recognition standards, student performance and school improvement.

105 ILCS 5/2-3.25b

1:320   What is the state academic watch list?

Schools that are not meeting standards of academic performance and improvement may be placed on a State Superintendent of Education academic watch list. An on-site visitation is held to determine whether extenuating circumstances exist as to why a school or schools should not be placed on the list.

105 ILCS 5/2-3.25d

1:330   What is required of a school district which has a school or schools placed on the academic watch list?

A school district with a school or schools on the academic watch list must submit a revised school improvement plan listing the district's expectations for removing each school in the district from the watch list and for improving student performance in the school. The improvement plan must be developed in consultation with the staff of the affected school and must be approved by the board of education. The revised improvement plan must be submitted to the State Board of Education for approval and must have specific measurable outcomes for improving student performance so that performance equals or exceeds standards set for the school by the State Board.

105 ILCS 5/2-3.25d

1:335   Are any school districts relieved of quality review and school improvement plan requirements?

If a school district has completed school improvement plans in all required curricular areas and if in any two if the three most recent school years the composite assessment test scores of the students at a school within the district places the school in the "exceeds standards" category or within the top 15 percent of the "meets standards" categories established by the State Board of Education, that school is exempt for the next two succeeding school years from all requirements relating to the school improvement plan and from quality review visits.

105 ILCS 5/2-3.25k

**1:340   How soon may a school placed on the academic
          watch list get off the list?**

A school or schools once placed on the academic watch list
must remain on the list for at least one full school year. During
the year, the school is evaluated and assessed by the State
Board of Education as to whether it is meeting the outcomes
identified in its school improvement plan.

105 ILCS 5/2-3.25d

**1:350   What happens if a school remains on the
          academic watch list after two years?**

The State Superintendent of Education appoints a school
improvement panel for such schools. The panel:

1) assists the school in the development and implementation
of a revised school improvement plan;

2) makes progress reports and comments to the State
Superintendent of Education; and

3) has authority to review and approve or disapprove all
actions of the board of education that pertain to implementation
of the revised school improvement plan.

105 ILCS 5/2-3.25e
Texas v. United States, 118 S.Ct. 1257, 523 U.S. 296, 140 L.Ed2d 406
(1998)

**1:360   What may happen to a school district that fails
          to make reasonable efforts to implement an
          approved school improvement plan?**

The school district may suffer loss of state funds by school
district, attendance center, or program as the State Board of
Education deems appropriate.

105 ILCS 5/2-3.25f

**1:370   What penalties may the State Board of
          Education impose on a school or school district
          that has been on the academic watch list for
          more than four years?**

School board members may be removed from office, and an
independent authority may be appointed to operate the school or
school district for purposes of improving pupil performance and

school improvement or the State Board of Education may non-recognize the school or school district and reassign its students and administrative staff. If a school district is non-recognized in its entirety, it is automatically dissolved under a procedure established by law. There are constitutional questions about certain aspects of this legislation because it may not be consistent with provisions of the federal Voting Rights Act.

105 ILCS 5/2-3.25f 2
105 ILCS 5/3-14.28
Texas v. United States, 118 S.Ct. 1257, 523 U.S. 296, 140 L.Ed2d 406 (1998)

WAIVER OF STATE REQUIREMENTS

1:380   May the State Board of Education grant waivers from the requirements of the School Code or from State Board administrative rules and regulations?

A school district may petition the State Board of Education for a waiver or modification of the mandates of the School Code or from the administrative rules and regulations of the State Board. Waivers or modifications may be requested when a school district demonstrates that it can address the intent of the rule or mandate in a "more effective, efficient, or economical manner or when necessary to stimulate innovation or improve student performance."

105 ILCS 5/2-3.25g

1:382   Are there rules, regulations or laws from which waivers cannot be requested or granted?

Waivers cannot be requested and will not be granted from laws, rules, and regulations pertaining to special education, teacher certification or teacher tenure and seniority.

105 ILCS 5/2-3.25g

1:384   How does a school district request a waiver?

A request for a waiver must be approved by the school board requesting it following a public hearing on the application and plan. The waiver request must be submitted to the State Board of Education within 15 days of approval by the school board. The hearing must give educators, parents and students an opportunity to provide testimony to the school board.

The hearing must be preceded by at least one notice published in a newspaper of general circulation in the school district that sets forth the time, date, place and general subject matter of the hearing. The published notice must appear at least seven days prior to the hearing.

The school district must provide written notice to the affected exclusive bargaining agent at least seven days before the hearing of the district's intent to seek approval of a waiver or modification and of the hearing.

105 ILCS 5/2-3.25g

1:386 How are waivers approved?

Following the receipt of waiver request, the State Board of Education has 45 days to review the request. If the State Board fails to disapprove a request, the request is deemed granted. Any request disapproved by the State Board may be appealed to the General Assembly by the requesting school district.

105 ILCS 5/2-3.25g

1:388 For how long are approved waivers effective?

An approved waiver or modification may remain in effect for a period not to exceed five school years and may be renewed upon application by the school district.

105 ILCS 5/2-3.25g

CHARTER SCHOOLS

1:500 What is a charter school?

A charter school is a public, nonsectarian, nonreligious, non-home based, non-profit school. A charter school is organized and operated as a nonprofit corporation or other discrete, legal, nonprofit entity authorized under the laws of the state of Illinois. A charter school may be established by creating a new school or converting an existing public school or attendance center to charter school status. Charter schools are exempt from some, but not all, School Code requirements otherwise applicable to public schools.

105 ILCS 5/27A-5

1:510 How is a charter school created?

A proposal to establish a charter school may be initiated by individuals or organizations meeting certain statutory requirements. The proposal is submitted to the local school board for consideration. The school board is required to convene a public meeting within 45 days of receipt of a charter school proposal and to evaluate the proposal in relation to statutory guidelines. The school board must file a report with the State Board of Education granting or denying the proposal. If the school board approves the proposal, a contract is developed and submitted to the State Board of Education for certification.

A charter school may also be created if a charter school proposal has been certified by the State Board of Education and thereafter a petition of five percent or more of the voters of a school district or districts is circulated. Certification and properly completed petitions results in a referendum on the question of the establishment of a charter school. If the referendum question carries, the State Board of Education is required to approve the charter within seven days after certification by the State Board that the proposition received a majority of the votes cast.

105 ILCS 5/27A-6
105 ILCS 5/27A-6.5
105 ILCS 5/27A-7
105 ILCS 5/27A-8

1:520 Is an appeal available if the local school board denies a charter school proposal?

The State Board of Education may reverse a local board's denial if it finds that the charter school proposal is in compliance with statutory requirements and is in the best interests of students. If the State Board reverses the local board, the State Board shall act as the authorized chartering entity for the charter school, performing all functions under the charter school statute otherwise performed by the local school board.

The State Board will withhold from funds otherwise due the

school district any funds authorized for the charter school and pay those amounts to the charter school.

105 ILCS 5/27A-9

1:530   With which laws must a charter school comply?

A charter school must comply with the School Code requirements for:

1) criminal background checks;
2) Section 24-24 of the School Code regarding the discipline of students;
3) The Tort Immunity Act;
4) Section 108.75 of the General Not For Profit Corporation Act of 1986 regarding indemnification of officers, directors, employees and agents;
5) The Abused and Neglected Child Reporting Act;
6) The Illinois School Student Records Act;
7) state goals, standards and assessments established in Section 2-3.64 of the School Code;
8) the Illinois Educational Labor Relations Act.

In addition, a charter school must comply with all federal laws which would be otherwise applicable to a public school and all federal and state laws and constitutional provisions prohibiting discrimination on the basis of disability, race, creed, color, gender, national origin, religion, ancestry, marital status, or need for special education services.

105 ILCS 5/10-21.9
105 ILCS 5/24-24
105 ILCS 5/27A-4 (a)
105 ILCS 5/27A-5 (g)
105 ILCS 10/1 et seq.
115 ILCS 5/1-1 et seq.
325 ILCS 5/1 et seq.
745 ILCS 10/1-101 et seq.
805 ILCS 105/108.75

1:540   Is there a limit on the number of charter schools which may operate in the state at any one time?

The total number of charter schools operating at any one time may not exceed 45. Not more than 15 may operate in Chicago, not more than 15 in DuPage, Kane, Lake, McHenry, Will and Cook county outside Chicago with not more than one charter school that has been initiated by a school board or by intergovernmental agreement between or among school boards operating at any one time in the school district where the charter school is located, and not more than 15 in the remainder of the state with not more than one charter school that has been initiated by a school board or by intergovernmental agreement between or among school boards operating at any one time in the school district where the charter school is located.

105 ILCS 5/27A-4(b)

1:550   May an existing private, parochial or non-public school be approved as a charter school?

No.

105 ILCS 5/27A-4(c)
105 ILCS 5/27A-6.5(a)

1:560   May two or more school boards issue a charter to a single shared charter school?

Yes.

105 ILCS 5/27A-4(e)

1:570   Who may enroll in a charter school?

Enrollment is open to any pupil who resides within the geographic boundaries of the area served by the local school board.

105 ILCS 5/27A-4(d)

1:580   May children be assigned and required to attend a charter school?

No.

105 ILCS 5/27A-4(g)

1:590   May teachers or non-certificated employees be assigned to a charter school?

A school board may not require any employee to be employed in a charter school.

105 ILCS 5/27A-4(f)

1:600   What elements must be included in a charter school proposal?

The following elements must be included in a charter school proposal:

1) The name of the proposed charter school which must include the words "Charter School."

2) The age or grade range, areas of focus, minimum and maximum numbers of pupils to be enrolled in the charter school and any other admission criteria that would be legal if used by a school district.

3) A description of and an address for the physical plant in which the charter school will be located.

4) The mission statement of the charter school, which must be consistent with the General Assembly's declared purposes.

5) The goals, objectives, and pupil performance standards to be achieved by the charter school.

6) In the case of a proposal to establish a charter school by converting an existing public school or attendance center to charter school status evidence that the proposed formation of the charter school has received the required approval from certified teachers, from parents and guardians.

7) A description of the charter school's educational program, pupil performance standards, curriculum, school year, school days, and hours of operation.

8) A description of the charter school's plan for evaluating pupil performance, the types of assessments that will be used to measure pupil progress towards achievement of the school's pupil performance standards, the time line for achievement of those standards, and the procedures for taking corrective action in the event that pupil performance at the charter school falls below those standards.

9) Evidence that the terms of the charter as proposed are economically sound for both the charter school and the school district, a proposed budget for the term of the charter, a description of the manner in which an annual audit of the financial and administrative operations of the charter school including any services provided by the school district are to be conducted, and a plan for the displacement of pupils, teachers, and other employees who will not attend or be employed in the charter school.

10) A description of the governance and operation of the charter school, including the extent and nature of parental, professional educator and community involvement in the governance and operation of the charter school.

11) An explanation of the relationship that will exist between the charter school and its employees, including evidence that the terms and conditions of employment have been addressed with affected employees and their recognized representative, if any. However, a bargaining unit of charter school employees shall be separate and distinct from any bargaining units formed from employees of the school district in which the charter school is located.

12) An agreement between the parties regarding their respective legal liability and applicable insurance coverage.

13) A description of how the charter school plans to meet the transportation needs of its pupils, and a plan for addressing the transportation needs of low income and at-risk pupils.

14) The proposed effective date of the charter; provided that the first day of the first academic year and the first day of the fiscal year of the charter school shall be no earlier than August 15 and no later than September 15.

15) Any other information reasonably required by the State Board of Education.

105 ILCS 5/27A-7

1:610   For what term is a charter granted?

A charter may be granted for a period of not less than five nor more than ten school years and is renewable thereafter for periods not to exceed five years if the charter school meets certain statutory requirements.

105 ILC 5/27A-9

1:620   Who may teach in a charter school?

A charter school teacher is not required to meet every certification condition otherwise required of teachers in Illinois public schools.

Charter school teachers must either be fully certificated or have:

1) a bachelors degree from an accredited institution of higher learning;

2) been employed for at least five years in an area requiring application of the person's education;

3) passed the tests of basic skills and subject matter knowledge required in the School Code;

4) demonstrated continuing evidence of professional growth which includes but is not limited to successful teaching experience, attendance at professional meetings, membership in professional organizations, additional credits earned at institutions of higher learning, travel specifically for educational purposes, and reading of professional books and periodicals.

105 ILCS 5/27A-10(c)

1:630   When may a charter school teacher resign?

A charter school teacher may resign only if notice of resignation is given to the charter school's governing body at least 60 days before the end of the school term and the resignation must take effect immediately upon the end of the school term.

105 ILCS 5/27A-10(d)

1:640   Is a school board required to grant a leave of absence for a teacher to teach in a charter school?

Yes. A school board must grant a teacher who requests one a leave of absence for up to five years if the teacher accepts employment in a charter school. At the end of the authorized leave of absence the teacher must return to the district or resign. If the teacher returns to the district he must be assigned to a position which requires teacher certification and qualification. The tenure and retirement benefits of a teacher who is granted a leave of absence to teach in a charter school may not be affected by the leave of absence.

105 ILCS 5/27A-10(b)

2: SCHOOL BOARDS

SCHOOL BOARD STRUCTURE

2:10 How is the membership of an Illinois school board structured?

Most Illinois school boards consist of seven members elected at large. School districts with less than 1,000 inhabitants are governed by three-member boards of school directors unless the voters in the district petition the board and vote in a general election to increase the number of board members to seven. Charter district boards also may have more or fewer than seven members, depending upon the section of the School Code that governs.

There also are exceptions to the at-large provision. The boards of many school districts must guarantee representation to unincorporated areas or ensure that congressional townships have proper representation. The constitutionality of these provisions has not been tested and these requirements vary with type of district, when the district was created, and how resident population is distributed.

105 ILCS 5/10-1
105 ILCS 5/10-10
105 ILCS 5/11A-8
105 ILCS 5/11B-7

2:20 Are all school boards elected?

The Chicago Board of Education is appointed by the mayor of Chicago. Special charter districts may have an appointed school board if such a procedure is set forth in the original charter and the charter has not been amended.

105 ILCS 5/9-1 et seq.
105 ILCS 5/32-1.5 et seq.
105 ILCS 5/34-3 et seq.
Latham v. Board of Education of Chicago, 31 Ill.2d 178, 201 N.E.2d 111 (1964)

**2:25   What are the territorial representation require-
          ments that apply to Illinois school boards?**

The requirement for territorial representation applies to
community unit districts and consolidated districts created
prior to January 1, 1975, and to combined districts created prior
to July 1, 1983. A district may remove itself from the territorial
representation requirements by vote of the electorate in an election as provided by law.

Where such a district is smaller than two congressional
townships or 72 square miles, but includes more than one congressional township or 36 square miles of unincorporated areas,
not more than five members may be selected from incorporated
areas.

Where such a district's territory is greater than two congressional townships or 72 square miles, not counting congressional townships of fewer than 100 inhabitants, not more than
three board members may be selected from any one township
unless:

• 75 to 90 percent of the population reside in one township,
in which case four members must be selected from that township and three must be selected from the remaining townships,
or

• more than 90 percent of the population reside in one township, in which case all board members may be selected from any
one or more townships.

105 ILCS 5/11A-8
105 ILCS 5/11B-7

**2:26   Do territorial representation requirements
          change as the geographic distribution of a school
          district's population changes?**

Illinois statutes do not provide guidance and there is no case
law defining how, if at all, school board membership and territorial representation should change as population changes
occur. Presumably, the legislature intended that territorial representation changes should be made, when appropriate, for the
election following each decennial census. However, there is no
statutory scheme whereby such changes are implemented.

2:27   How does a school board subject to representation requirements become an at-large board?

A unit school district formed prior to 1975 or a combined school district formed before July 1, 1983 may elect its school board at-large and without regard to intra-district representation requirements if the matter is submitted to voters and a majority of those voting in the election in each congressional township, including any township of less than 100 inhabitants, vote in favor of the proposition. The school board may cause the matter to be placed on the ballot, or the matter may be placed on the ballot by petition of the lesser of 2,500 or 5 percent of the school district's registered voters.

105 ILCS 5/11A-8(c)
105 ILCS 5/11B-7(c)

2:30   May a school board be elected from representative districts rather than at-large?

A school board may, by resolution, or must if petitioned by the lesser of 2,500 or 5 percent of the district's registered voters, submit to election the question of electing school board members by representative districts rather than at-large.

105 ILCS 5/9-22

2:40   If the voters approve the election of school board members by representative districts, how are the representative districts formed?

The at-large school board must divide the school district into seven school board districts, each of which must be compact and contiguous and substantially equal in population to each other district. The terms of office of the board members incumbent at the time the proposition to elect from representative districts is adopted expire on the day of the next regular school election, at which time one member is elected from each school board district.

In districts which have four-year terms, those members first elected from representative districts must, by lot, determine three to serve for two years and four to serve for four years. Their successors serve four-year terms.

In school districts which have six-year school board terms, those members first elected from representative districts must, by lot, determine three to serve two-year terms, two to serve

four-year terms, and two to serve six-year terms. Their successors serve six-year terms.

105 ILCS 5/9-22

2:45   How are representative districts altered to reflect changes in population patterns?

The school board must reapportion the representative districts to reflect the results of each decennial census. The reap-
portionment plan must be approved by a majority of the board
not less than 90 days before the last date for filing nominating
petitions for the next board election in the year following the
census. The school board also must, publicly by lot, divide the
representative districts into two groups providing staggered
terms. Board members from one group of districts will be elected for terms of four years, four years and two years, while those
from the other group will be elected for terms of two years, four
years and four years.

105 ILCS 5/9-22

2:50   What is a school board member's term of office?

The standard term of office for a school board member is
four years. A school board may, by resolution, submit to the voters the question of increasing the term of office to six years.

Under certain circumstances a school board member's term
of office may be less than four years. During the transition period from November to April elections in 1999 and 2001, some
school board members will serve less than four-year terms of
office.

A school board member also may be appointed and/or elected to less than a full term to fill a vacancy on the board.

105 ILCS 5/9-5
105 ILCS 5/10-10

2:60   How many times may a school board member be elected?

There is no limit to the number of terms to which a school
board member may be elected.

105 ILCS 5/9-1

VACANCIES

2:70   What acts create a vacancy on a school board?

Elective offices become vacant within the meaning ot the School Code, unless the context indicates otherwise, on the happening of any of the following events before the expiration of the term of the office:

1) death of the incumbent;

2) resignation in writing filed with the secretary or clerk of the board;

3) becoming a person under legal disability;

4) ceasing to be an inhabitant of the district from which the member was elected;

5) conviction of an infamous crime, or of any offense involving a violation of official oath;

6) removal from office;

7) the decision of a competent tribunal declaring the election void;

8) ceasing to be an inhabitant of a particular area from which the member was elected, if the residential requirements are violated.

105 ILCS 5/10-10 et seq.
105 ILCS 5/11A-8
105 ILCS 5/11B-7

2:74   What are the infamous crimes which would prevent a person from holding public office in Illinois?

Illinois courts have defined infamous crimes as felonies involving conduct which is inconsistent with commonly accepted principles of honesty and decency or which involve moral turpitude. Generally, the courts have held that if the crime is one for which a penitentiary sentence could be imposed it is an infamous crime. Certain misdemeanors of sufficient seriousness or import may be infamous crimes.

The vacancy occurs upon the public official's conviction in a trial court whether or not an appeal is filed or pending.

People ex rel. Keenan v. McGuane, 13 Ill.2d 520, 150 N.E.2d 168 (1958)

2:80   If a school board member's conviction of an infamous crime is reversed, is the member's school board seat restored to him?

Any elected official of any school district convicted in any court of the State of Illinois or of the United States of a felony, bribery, perjury or other infamous crime is, upon conviction, ineligible to continue in office. If a final order reverses the conviction, eligibility to hold the office is restored, and the officer is reinstated for the duration of the term of office remaining.

Upon the conviction and ineligibility of any person, a successor is chosen to fill the vacancy. The successor holds office for the remainder of the term or until a final order reversing the conviction is entered, whichever occurs first.

5 ILCS 280/1

2:85   Which public body has authority to determine whether or not a vacancy exists on a school board?

The school board has authority to determine whether or not the facts occasioning a vacancy exist.

10 ILCS 5/25-3

2:90   How is a board of school directors vacancy filled?

When a vacancy occurs on a board of directors, the remaining directors must, within 30 days, fill the vacancy by appointment until the next regular school election. If they fail to do so, the regional superintendent must fill the vacancy by appointment within 30 days. If the regional superintendent fails to fill the vacancy, it is filled at the next regularly scheduled election.

105 ILCS 5/10-4

2:100   How is a vacancy on a board of education filled?

Whenever a vacancy occurs on a board of education, the remaining members must notify the regional superintendent of the vacancy within five days of its occurrence. The school board then fills the vacancy by appointment until the next regular school election, at which election a successor is elected to serve the remainder of the unexpired term.

However, if the vacancy occurs with less than 868 days

remaining in the term, or if the vacancy occurs less than 88 days before the next regularly scheduled election for the vacant office, then the person so appointed serves the remainder of the unexpired term, and no election to fill the vacancy is held.

Should a board of education fail to act within 45 days after the vacancy occurs, the regional superintendent must, within 30 days after the remaining members have failed to fill the vacancy, fill the vacancy by appointment.

105 ILCS 5/10-10

2:110   What qualifications must a person have to be appointed to fill a school board vacancy?

To be appointed to fill a school board vacancy, a person must have the same qualifications as the person he was appointed to replace. On the date of appointment he must be at least 18 years of age, a resident of the state and the district for at least one year preceding appointment, a registered voter and not a school trustee or school treasurer.

Whether elected or appointed by the remaining members or the regional superintendent, the successor must be an inhabitant of the particular area from which his predecessor was elected if residential requirements apply.

105 ILCS 5/10-4
105 ILCS 5/10-10
105 ILCS 5/10-11
105 ILCS 5/11A-8
105 ILCS 5/11B-7

2:115   Where a school board's membership must include representation of particular congressional townships or unincorporated areas, must the person selected to fill a vacancy live in the same township or unincorporated area as the predecessor?

The answer to this question turns on which ballot format applies. If ballot format 5 is applicable, a person filling such a board vacancy must live in the same congressional township as his predecessor. Ballot format 5 is for school boards that must have four members from the district's most populous township and three members from the rest of the district.

If ballot format 4 applies, the successor need not be from the same township as his predecessor, but the successor's residency must not cause the board to have more than three members from any one township. Format 4 is for boards that may have no more than three members from any one township.

105 ILCS 5/10-10
105 ILCS 5/10-11
105 ILCS 5/11A-8
105 ILCS 5/11B-7

SCHOOL BOARD POWERS AND DUTIES

2:130   Who holds the authority to establish rules and regulations in school districts?

School boards. Illinois law provides that school boards are to adopt and enforce all necessary rules for the management and government of the public schools of their district. The rules adopted by a school board are to be filed for public inspection in the administrative office of the district.

105 ILCS 5/10-20.5
Board of Education of City of Chicago v. Chicago Teachers' Union, Local 1, 89 Ill.App.3d 861, 412 N.E.2d 587, 45 Ill.Dec. 236 (1st. Dist. 1980), rev. on other grounds 88 Ill.2d 63, 430 N.E.2d 1111 58 Ill.Dec. 860
Beck v. Board of Education of Harlem Consolidated School District No. 122, 27 Ill.App.3d 4, 325 N.E.2d 640 (2nd Dist. 1975) aff'd. 63 Ill.2d 10, 344 N.E.2d 440

2:135   What is the distinction between "school board powers" and the powers of a school board member?

A school board has powers set forth in the law. A school board member acting as an individual has none of those powers.

2:140   May a school board member acting alone exercise the powers granted to a school board?

A school board may act only at a legal meeting when a quorum is present and after a requisite number of "yea" votes is counted on a properly presented and seconded motion on an issue properly within the powers of the board.

105 ILCS 5/10-12
Bunsen v. County Board of School Trustees of Lake County, 48 Ill.App.2d 291, 198 N.E.2d 735 (2nd Dist. 1964)

2:144   Is a school board member who acts or speaks as an individual about school district matters vulnerable to a defamation suit?

A school board member who acts or speaks as an individual about school district matters probably has no protection from suit. School board members are protected from liability when acting "during the formal legislative process" at school board meetings, but may not have protection when speaking in other contexts.

Meyer v. McKeown, 266 Ill.App.3d 324, 641 N.E.2d 1212, 204 Ill.Dec. 593, (3rd Dist. 1994)

2:150   May a board member visit schools of the district to ensure their proper functioning?

A board of education is directed by law to "visit, inspect and maintain" schools. Although boards lawfully delegate this duty to employees, it also is lawful for a board to include school visits as part of a properly convened meeting.

Unless so directed by official action of the board, however, the individual board member is free to visit and inspect schools only in accordance with board policies regulating public visitation. The individual board member may not assume powers or duties belonging to the full board, and has only the same rights and powers as other citizens when the board is not in session.

105 ILCS 5/10-20.6
105 ILCS 5/24-25

2:160   Where are the powers of a school board enumerated in the law?

School board powers are enumerated in the School Code at Sections 10-20 et seq., Sections 10-22 et seq. and 10-23 et seq. The listing of school board powers is not exclusive and a school board may "exercise all other powers not inconsistent with this Act that may be requisite or proper for the maintenance, operation and development of any school or schools under the jurisdiction of the board."

105 ILCS 5/10-20 et seq.
105 ILCS 5/10-22 et seq.
105 ILCS 5/10-23 et seq.

2:163   May the school board delegate its powers?

A school board is responsible for exercising its powers in accordance with the law. A school board is empowered to decide who is entitled to attend school, employ teachers, select textbooks, approve contracts, dismiss teachers, expel students, and to make numerous other decisions. In each case, the board's decision must be recorded in the minutes of a meeting as a motion or resolution adopted by a formal vote.

A school board may delegate to the superintendent the authority necessary to exercise certain of the board's powers. Some powers of the board are not delegable, including the powers to dismiss teachers or expel students, for example. When powers are delegated, the person to whom they are delegated may be held responsible for the reasonable use of that authority.

A board that wishes to give its superintendent authority for the exercise of board powers needs to (a) be sure the superintendent understands the board's aims and standards, (b) devise a means for periodically checking to see that its powers are being used reasonably, and (c) be prepared to take formal action supporting the superintendent's decisions on these matters when they come to the board in the form of recommendations.

105 ILCS 5/10-22.1 et seq.
105 ILCS 5/10-23 et seq.
Board of Education of Rockford School District No. 205, v. The Illinois Educational Labor Relations Board, 165 Ill.2d 80, 649 N.E.2d 369, 208 Ill.Dec. 313 (1995)

2:165   What is the difference between school board policies and administrative procedures?

School board policies are the pronouncements of the school board that govern the school district. Policies may be broad and general or narrow and specific.

Administrative procedures describe how the school district will go about adhering to board policies. Administrative procedures must be consistent with board policy, picking up where the policies leave off and filling in the specific details not contained in the policies. Policies are usually rules that are adopted by the board; administrative procedures are rules created by administrators.

2:167 Must a school district's administrative procedures be adopted by the school board in order to have legal effect?

No, although the administration must have some authority from the board to create rules, regulations or procedures. The safer practice would be for a board to specifically empower its administrators to act. Such authority might be specific to the task at hand, or it might be a general grant of authority. In the absence of a specific board authorization, an administrative rule, regulation or procedure probably binds the board and the district when the board has knowledge of the rule, regulation or procedure and fails to take action to amend or repeal it.

2:170 May a school board reverse a previously adopted official act?

In most cases a school board may revoke or rescind a previous action. Excepted are situations when the prior act has vested rights in third parties which would be prejudiced if the board's original action were reversed.

City of Kankakee v. Small, 317 Ill. 55, 147 N.E. 404 (1925)
People ex rel. MacMahon v. Davis, 209 Ill.App. 117 (1st Dist. 1918), rev.
284 Ill. 439, 120 N.E. 326
People v. Trustees of Schools, 42 Ill.App. 60 (2nd Dist. 1891)

2:180 Are the actions of a prior school board binding on a successor school board?

A school board is a continuing entity. While the individual membership of the board may change, the board itself is on-going. The lawful acts of a prior school board bind a successor school board unless the act of the prior board is reversible and the successor board votes to reverse.

City of Kankakee v. Small, 317 Ill. 55, 147 N.E. 404 (1925)
Illinois ex rel. MacMahon v. Davis, 209 Ill.App. 117 (1st Dist. 1918), rev.
284 Ill. 439, 120 N.E. 326

2:190   What happens if a local school board fails to forward reports required by law?

If the trustees of schools of any township in Class II county school unit, or any school district which forms a part of a Class II county school unit but which is not subject to the jurisdiction of the trustees of schools of any township in which the district is located, or any school district in the case of any Class I county school unit fail to prepare and forward, or cause to be prepared and forwarded, to the regional superintendent of schools reports required by the School Code, the regional superintendent is required by law to furnish such information or to employ a person to furnish such information as far as is practicable. Such a person shall have access to the books, records, and papers of the school district to enable him or her to prepare the reports required by law, and the school district is required to permit such person to examine their books, records, and papers at a time and place that may be desired for this purpose.

The regional superintendent is authorized by law to bill the district for such services in an amount to cover the cost of the preparation of the reports if an external person is employed to prepare them.

105 ILCS 5/3-7
105 ILCS 5/3-15.1

2:200   Are school boards authorized to pay membership dues to professional organizations or associations?

A school board is authorized to pay both state and national association membership dues to school associations which benefit students.

A school board may also form, join and provide for the expenses of associations of Illinois school boards formed for the purpose of conducting county or regional school board institutes and otherwise disseminating and interchanging information regarding school board problems, duties and responsibilities. There are statutory requirements which must be met by any such organization in order to qualify to receive financial support from school districts.

105 ILCS 5/10-22.40
105 ILCS 5/23-1 et seq.

2:210   May a school board appoint committees?

A school board may appoint committees to research and make recommendations to the board. A school board may not give up its non-delegable decision-making authority to a committee.

Thomas v. Board of Education of Community Unit School District of Pope County, 117 Ill.App.3d 374, 453 N.E.2d 150, 721 Ill.Dec. 845 (5th Dist. 1983)

Elder v. Board of Education of School District 127 1/2 of Cook County, 60 Ill.App.2d 56, 208 N.E.2d 423 (1st Dist. 1965)

Lindblad v. Board of Education of Normal School District, 221 Ill. 261, 77 N.E. 450 (1906)

3: SCHOOL BOARD MEMBERSHIP

QUALIFICATIONS

3:10 What are the qualifications for school board membership?

In order to qualify for school board membership, an individual must be, in each case as of the date of election: a United States citizen, a resident of the State of Illinois and of the school district for at least one year preceding election, at least 18 years of age, a registered voter, and neither a school trustee nor a school treasurer.

A school board member may not hold an incompatible office. Certain types of school districts have additional residency requirements. Additional residential requirements apply to persons appointed to fill school board vacancies.

105 ILCS 5/10-1
105 ILCS 5/10-3
105 ILCS 5/11A-8
105 ILCS 5/11B-7

3:15 May a postal employee run for election to a school board?

Federal law prohibits postal employees from running in partisan elections. School board elections once were, but are no longer, explicitly non-partisan.

5 U.S.C. 7324a(2)

3:20 What does residence mean in the context of qualification for school board membership?

Residence is physical presence in a particular place with intention to remain permanently.

Stein v. County Board of School Trustees of DuPage County, 40 Ill.2d 477, 240 N.E.2d 668 (1968)

INCOMPATIBILITY

3:30 What is meant by the term "incompatibility of offices?"

When two public offices are deemed incompatible under the law, it means that an individual may not hold those two offices simultaneously. Offices are incompatible when because of the duties of either office a conflict of interest may arise; or when the duties of one office are such that the holder cannot in every instance faithfully perform the duties of the other. A public official who accepts a second office that is incompatible constructively resigns or vacates the first office.

Ill. Const. art. IV, par. 2(e)
Ill. Const. art. VI, par. 13(b)
105 ILCS 5/3-2
105 ILCS 5/5-3
105 ILCS 5/8-1
People ex rel. Black v. Dukes, 108 Ill.App.3d 965, 439 N.E.2d 1305, 64 Ill.Dec. 497 (3rd Dist. 1982) vac. 96 Ill.2d 273, 449 N.E.2d 856, 70 Ill.Dec. 509 (1983)
People ex rel. Myers v. Haas, 145 Ill.App. 283 (1st Dist. 1908)

3:40 What public offices are incompatible with school board membership?

The following offices are incompatible with school board membership by reason of the listed authority:

1) By reason of state Constitutional prohibition, certain elective offices in the judicial, executive or legislative branches of government are incompatible with membership on a school board. These incompatible offices include all classes of judges, such elected statewide officers as governor, attorney general and secretary of state, and members of the General Assembly. Other offices must be examined case by case.

2) By reason of statutory prohibitions, a school board member may not serve simultaneously as a school trustee, Cook County school treasurer, regional superintendent of schools, or member of the State Board of Education. A school board member elected to the board of a community college district may serve only the remainder of the unexpired school board term while serving on the community college board.

In addition, the Illinois Attorney General's office has at various times issued opinions that the following offices are incompatible with school board membership: board of review member, county zoning board of appeals member, township assessor, township school trustee, and village president. Many other elective offices are incompatible with school board membership.

In a city, village or unincorporated town with fewer than 2,500 inhabitants, an alderman of the city or a member of the board of trustees of a village or incorporated town, during the term of office for which he is elected may also serve on a school board, regional board of school trustees, board of school directors or board of school inspectors.

Ill. Const. art. IV, par. 2(e)
Ill. Const. art. VI, par. 13(b)
50 ILCS 105/1
50 ILCS 105/1.3
50 ILCS 105/2
50 ILCS 105/2a
105 ILCS 5/3-2
105 ILCS 5/5-3
105 ILCS 5/8-1
110 ILCS 805/3-7

People ex rel. Black v. Dukes, 108 Ill.App.3d 965, 439 N.E.2d 1305, 64 Ill.Dec. 497 (3rd Dist. 1982) vac. 96 Ill.2d 273, 449 N.E.2d 856, 70 Ill.Dec. 509 (1983)

People ex rel. Myers v. Haas, 145 Ill.App. 283 (1st Dist. 1908)

COMPENSATION AND EXPENSES

3:50   May a school board compensate its members for services rendered?

No member of a school board may be compensated for services rendered except the secretary or clerk of the board, who may be paid an amount to a limit specified by statute.

105 ILCS 5/10-10
105 ILCS 5/10-22.32
105 ILCS 5/22-1

3:60   May a school board member be advanced expenses to attend meetings?

A school board may advance its members the actual and necessary expenses incurred in attending the following meetings:

1) meetings sponsored by the State Board of Education or the Regional Superintendent of Schools;

2) meetings sponsored by the Illinois Association of School Boards; and

3) meetings sponsored by a national organization in the field of public school education.

Authorized expenses are those reasonably anticipated to be incurred on the days necessary for travel to and from, and for attendance at, such meetings including meals, lodging, transportation, parking and tips. Entertainment expenses (plays or concerts, for example) are not generally reimbursable.

If moneys are so advanced, the member to whom money is advanced must submit an itemized verified expense voucher showing the amount of his actual expenditures, with receipts attached where possible. When moneys are advanced but not required for such actual reasonable expenses, the member must refund the excess amount. The member may be reimbursed if the actual reasonable expenses exceed the amount advanced.

105 ILCS 5/10-22.32
105 ILCS 5/23-1

3:61   May a newly elected school board member be reimbursed for expenses before he is seated on the board?

A person elected at the consolidated election held in April 1999 or April 2001 can receive expenses to attend school board association training after the person is elected but before the person is seated, provided such reimbursement is authorized by the school board.

105 ILCS 5/10-22.32

3:70   May a school board member receive reimbursement for actual expenses incurred by a non-member spouse who accompanies him to a school board function?

No.

105 ILCS 5/10-22.32

3:80   May a school board member receive lost wages as a school board expense?

No.

105 ILCS 5/10-22.32

DISCLOSURE OF ECONOMIC INTERESTS

3:90   Which school district personnel are required to file economic interest statements?

Each school board member must file annually an economic interest statement. Each person employed by the school district who holds administrative certification (whether employed as an administrator or not) must file and each school employee who functions as the head of a department and who exercises similar authority and has direct supervisory authority over or direct responsibility for the formulation, negotiation or execution of contracts in the amount of $1,000 or greater, or who has authority to issue or promulgate rules and regulations within areas under the authority of the school district, or who has supervisory authority for 20 or more employees is also required to file an economic interest statement each year.

In order to be placed on the ballot at a school board election, each candidate must have filed an economic interest statement with the county clerk and filed the county clerk's receipt with the school board secretary during the time period for filing nominating papers.

Anyone working for the school district as an independent contractor need not file an economic interest statement.

5 ILCS 420/4A-101 (f)
5 ILCS 420/4A-101 (i)
5 ILCS 420/4A-105
105 ILCS 5/9-10
Havens v. Miller, 102 Ill.App.3d 558, 429 N.E.2d 1292, 57 Ill.Dec. 929 (1st. Dist. 1981)

3:100   When must an economic interest statement be filed?

A person required to file an economic interest statement must do so upon initial appointment or employment and by May 1 of each year unless he has already filed a statement in that calendar year.

A candidate for elective office must file his economic interest statement not later than the end of the period during which he can file nominating papers if he has not already filed a statement in relation to the same unit of government within a year preceding such action.

5 ILCS 420/4A-105

Miceli v. Lavelle, 114 Ill. App.3d 311, 448 N.E.2d 989 (1st. Dist. 1983)

Allen v. Love, 112 Ill.App.3d 338, 445 N.E.2d 514, 68 Ill.Dec. 66 (1st Dist. 1983)

3:110   What are the penalties for failure to file an economic interest statement?

Persons who fail to meet the May 1 filing deadline are subject to late filing penalties ranging from a late filing fee of $15 until May 15, to $100 per day from May 15 until May 31. Failure to file by May 31, or willful filing of a false or incomplete economic interest statement, is a class A misdemeanor and may cause forfeiture of office or employment. However, any filing within 30 days of actual notice of failure to file bars forfeiture of office or employment. If the failure to file resulted from not being included for notification by the school district and a statement is filed within 30 days of actual notice of the failure to file, no fine or forfeiture of office results.

5 ILCS 420/4A-101

5 ILCS 420/4A-107

Miceli v. Lavelle, 114 Ill. App.3d 311, 448 N.E.2d 989 (1st. Dist. 1983)

Allen v. Love, 112 Ill.App.3d 338, 445 N.E.2d 514, 68 Ill.Dec. 66 (1st Dist. 1983)

3:115   How is notice given regarding failure to file or obligation to file the statement of economic interests?

The county clerk notifies elected officials who fail to meet the May 1 filing deadline.

In addition, the superintendent of each school district must certify to applicable county clerks, no later than February 1 of each year, the names and addresses of employees who are required to file the statement of economic interests. Certification must include a separate alphabetized list of the covered employees by the county in which the employees reside. The county clerk notifies no later than April 1 those persons whose names are included on the lists that they must file the statement of economic interests by May 1.

5 ILCS 420/4A-101 et seq.

3:120   Must a school board candidate disclose campaign contributions?

If a school board candidate accepts campaign contributions of any kind or makes campaign expenditures of any kind in an aggregate amount exceeding $1,000 during any 12 month period, he is subject to disclosure and filing requirements. The provisions of the applicable statutes include keeping a detailed account of every contribution in excess of $20, including the name and address of the person making the contribution and the date on which it was made.

10 ILCS 5/9-1 et seq.

INTEREST IN CONTRACTS

3:130   What is the Corrupt Practices Act?

The Corrupt Practices Act provides in part:

"No person holding any office, either by election or appointment under the laws or Constitution of this State, may be in any manner financially interested, directly in his own name or indirectly in the name of any other person, association, trust or corporation, in any contract or the performance of any work in the making or letting of which such officer may be called upon to act or vote."

The Act contains exceptions similar in type to those contained in the School Code conflict of interest provisions applicable to school board members.

50 ILCS 105/3
105 ILCS 5/10-9
Brown v. Kirk, 33 Ill.App.3d 477, 342 N.E.2d 137 (5th Dist. 1975), rev. on other grounds 64 Ill.2d 144, 355 N.E.2d 12 (1975)

3:140   What interest may a school board member have in a school contract?

A school board member is prohibited from having any interest directly or indirectly in any contract, work, or business of the school district or in the sale of any article to the school district. A school board member is prohibited from purchasing any school district property, except a school board member may purchase a house constructed by the school district's vocational education students if the property is to be used as the board member's primary residence and if the sale is as otherwise provided for in the law.

These prohibitions are subject to certain limited exceptions. The exceptions permit certain small contracts to be let ($1,000 or less), and allow a limited business relationship with the school district if certain procedures are followed and the school board member owns less than a 7 1/2 percent interest in the company desiring to do business with the school district. If materials, merchandise, property, services or labor to be provided under a contract are not available from any other person, firm, association, partnership, corporation or cooperative association in the district, a contract may be let in which a school board member would otherwise have an impermissible interest if the aggregate amount of all such contracts let to the school board member does not exceed $5,000 in any fiscal year.

105 ILCS 5/5-22
105 ILCS 5/10-9

3:145   Is it a conflict of interest for an elected public school official to be employed as a substitute teacher in the same school district in which he is an elected official?

Whether or not service as a substitute teacher results in a conflict depends upon the amount of salary earned by the board member. The statute provides the amount "of the contract" must be less than $1,000. However, because there are appearances of impropriety inherent in any situation wherein a school board member appears to personally benefit from his service on the board and practical conflicts are inevitable when a principal or other mid-level administrator is called upon to supervise or direct his employer, service by a board member in any capacity as an employee of the school district is very unwise.

105 ILCS 5/10-9

3:150 May a school board member avoid conflict of interest by abstaining on the vote to award a contract in which he is interested?

If the award of a contract would otherwise result in a conflict of interest, the conflict is not cured by a school board member's abstention on the vote or absence from the meeting when the vote is taken.

105 ILCS 5/10-9

3:160 Is it a conflict of interest for a school board member to be married to a person employed by the district which the school board member serves?

This has been a controversial area of the law. It is probably not a conflict of interest if the employee was hired by the school district before the school board member was seated. A conflict of interest may result if the spouse of a school board member is hired during the school board member's term of office and the school board member influences the hiring decision.

30 ILCS 505/1
50 ILCS 105/3
105 ILCS 5/10-9
Hollister v. North, 50 Ill.App.3d 56, 365 N.E.2d 258, 8 Ill.Dec. 20 (4th Dist. 1977)
Illinois v. Simpkins, 45 Ill.App.3d 202, 359 N.E.2d 828, 3 Ill.Dec. 969 (5th Dist. 1977)
Shoresman v. Burgess, 412 F.Supp. 831 (N.D. Ill. 1976)

3:170 May a school board member or school employee have a financial interest in the books, apparatus, or furniture used in the district?

No state, county, township, or school officer or teacher may be interested in the sale, proceeds, or profits of any book, apparatus, or furniture used or to be used in any school with which such officer or teacher may be connected, except when the interest of the teacher is based upon authorship or development of instructional materials listed with the State Board of Education and adopted for use by a school board. Each teacher having an interest in instructional materials must file an annual statement so certifying with the secretary of the school board.

No employee or officer of a school district, special education joint agreement, office of a regional superintendent of schools or the State Board of Education may have a direct or indirect financial interest in any agreement between the entity of which the person is an employee or officer and any corporation, organization or other entity that collects or participates in the collection of payments from private health care benefit plans or federally funded health care programs.

105 ILCS 5/14-7.04
105 ILCS 5/22-5

RESIGNATIONS

3:180 When a school board member resigns, when is the resignation effective?

A school board member's resignation, once tendered, is final and is effective when filed with the school board secretary or clerk.

105 ILCS 5/10-11
Cole v. McGillicuddy, 21 Ill.App.3d 645, 316 N.E.2d 109 (1st Dist. 1974)
Allen v. Powell, 42 Ill.2d 66, 244 N.E.2d 596 (1969)

3:185 When does the resignation of a public official take effect?

Although a resignation once tendered is effective on receipt and may not be thereafter withdrawn, a resignation specifying a future effective date does not take effect until the date specified. A vacancy does not exist in the office resigned until the future effective date contained in the resignation, although for certain purposes a time period triggered by the resignation may begin at the time the resignation is tendered no matter when the resignation may be effective.

10 ILCS 5/25-1
105 ILCS 5/10-11
Cole v. McGillicuddy, 21 Ill.App.3d 645, 316 N.E.2d 109 (1st Dist. 1974)
Allen v. Powell, 42 Ill.2d 66, 244 N.E.2d 596 (1969)

REMOVAL AND FORFEITURE

3:190   May a regional superintendent of schools remove a school board member from office?

A regional superintendent of schools may remove a school board member from office for willful failure to perform official duties. A regional superintendent may not remove a school board member from office for any other cause.

105 ILCS 5/3-15.5
Texas v. United States, 118 S.Ct. 1257, 523 U.S. 296, 140 L.Ed2d 406 (1998)
East St. Louis Federation of Teachers Local 1220, American Federation of Teachers, AFL-CIO v. East St. Louis District Financial Oversight Panel, 178 Ill.2d 399, 687 N.E.2d 1050, 227 Ill.Dec. 568 (1997)
People ex rel. Kolker v. Blair, 8 Ill.App.3d 197, 289 N.E.2d 688 (5th Dist. 1972)
People ex rel. Howard v. Harris, 164 Ill.App. 136 (3rd Dist. 1911)

3:193   May a school board member be removed from office for failure to attend meetings?

The regional superintendent of schools is empowered to remove a school board member from office for "willful failure to perform official duties." Regional superintendents have seldom exercised this power.

105 ILCS 5/3-15.5

3:195   May voters remove a school board member from office by recall petition or election?

No.

5 ILCS 420/4A-107
105 ILCS 5/3-15.5
105 ILCS 5/10-10 et seq.
720 ILCS 5/33-3

3:196   What course of action is available to a citizen who believes a member of a school board is not legally qualified to hold office?

The citizen may ask the school board to investigate and declare a vacancy or the citizen may petition the court challenging the board member's right to hold office. A school board has the power to determine whether or not there is a vacancy on the board.

10 ILCS 5/25-3

3:200 Under what circumstances does a school board member forfeit office?

A school board member forfeits office if convicted of official misconduct.

Official misconduct occurs when a board member, acting in his official capacity, intentionally or recklessly fails to perform any mandatory duty as required by law; knowingly performs an act he knows he is forbidden by law to perform; intends to obtain a personal advantage for himself or another by performing an act in excess of his lawful authority; or solicits or knowingly accepts for the performance of any act a fee or reward that he knows is not authorized by law.

A school board member also forfeits office when he willfully violates any of the laws governing a school district's working cash fund. Board members may also lose their seats under a number of other circumstances, including conviction of certain crimes, failure to maintain residency in the district or failure to perform certain required acts.

105 ILCS 5/20-1 et seq.
720 ILCS 5/33-3

3:210 May a school board member be subject to a fine for willfully violating any laws governing the operation of Illinois public school districts?

Under some conditions, fines against school board members may be assessed. For example, Illinois law provides that any member of a board of school directors or board of education of any school district, or any other person holding any office, trust, or employment under any school district, who willfully violates any of the provisions of the School Code governing a working cash fund shall be guilty of a business offense and fined not exceeding $10,000, and shall forfeit his right to his office, trust or employment and shall be removed therefrom.

Any member or other person is liable for any sum that may be unlawfully diverted from the working cash fund or otherwise used, to be recovered by a school district or by any taxpayer in the name and for the benefit of the school district in an appropriate civil action.

105 ILCS 5/20-6
105 ILCS 5/22-1 et seq.

GIFT BAN ACT

3:300   What is the State Gift Ban Act and to whom does it apply?

The State Gift Ban Act is a 1998 addition to Illinois Compiled Statutes which restricts receipt of gifts by public officials and employees. The Act applies to school board members, administrators, teachers and all other full or part-time certified and full or part-time non-certified employees of the school district.

5 ILCS 425/1 et seq.

3:310   What is a gift as defined by the State Gift Ban Act?

The definition of gift is broad. A gift is any "gratuity, discount, entertainment, hospitality, loan, forbearance, or other tangible or intangible item having monetary value including but not limited to, cash, food and drink, and honoraria for speaking engagements related to or attributable to government employment or the official position" of a school employee or member of a school board.

5 ILCS 425/5

3:320   Who is a gift giver under the State Gift Ban Act?

The statute defines gift givers as prohibited sources. Prohibited source is defined as a person or entity who is registered or is required to be registered as a lobbyist; or is seeking official action; or does business or seeks to do business; or conducts activities regulated by; or has interests that may be substantially affected by the performance or non-performance of a school board member or employee of the school district.

5 ILCS 425/5

3:330   What gifts are not prohibited by the State Gift Ban Act?

There are 23 types of gifts which are permitted under the Act. They are:

1) Anything for which market value is paid or anything not used and promptly disposed of.

2) A contribution as defined in the Election Code that is lawfully made under that Act or attendance at a fund-raising event sponsored by a political organization.

3) A gift from a relative, meaning those people related to the individual as father, mother, son, daughter, brother, sister, uncle, aunt, great aunt, great uncle, first cousin, nephew, niece, husband, wife, grandfather, grandmother, grandson, granddaughter, father-in-law, mother-in-law, son-in-law, daughter-in-law, brother-in-law, sister-in-law, stepfather, stepmother, stepson, stepdaughter, stepbrother, stepsister, half brother, half sister, and including the father, mother, grandfather, or grandmother of the individual's spouse and the individual's fiance or fiancee.

4) Anything provided by a person on the basis of a personal friendship unless the member, officer, or employee has reason to believe that, under the circumstances, the gift was provided because of the official position or employment of the member, officer, or and not because of the personal friendship. In determining whether a gift is provided on the basis of personal friendship, the member, officer, or employee shall consider the circumstances under which the gift was offered, such as:

• the history of the relationship between the individual giving the gift and the recipient of the gift, including any previous exchange of gifts between those individuals;

• whether to the actual knowledge of the member, officer, or employee the individual who gave the gift personally paid for the gift or sought a tax deduction or business reimbursement for the gift; and

• whether to the actual knowledge of the member, officer or employee or the individual who gave the gift also at the same time gave the same or similar gifts to other members, officers or employees.

5) A commercially reasonable loan evidenced in writing with repayment due by a date certain made in the ordinary course of

the lender's business.

6) A contribution or other payments to a legal defense fund established for the benefit of a member, officer or employee that is otherwise lawfully made.

7) Intra-office and inter-office gifts. For the purpose of this Act, "intra-office gifts" means any gift given to an officer or employee of a school district, from another employee of that school district;

8) Food, refreshments, lodging, transportation, and other benefits:

• resulting from the outside business or employment activities (or outside activities that are not connected to the duties of the member, officer, or employee as an office holder or employee) of the member, officer, or employee, or the spouse of the member, officer, or employee if the benefits have not been offered or enhanced because of the official position or employment of the member, officer, or employee and are customarily provided to others in similar circumstances;

• customarily provided by a prospective employer in connection with bona fide employment discussions; or

• provided by a political organization in connection with a fund-raising or campaign event sponsored by that organization.

9) Pension and other benefits resulting from continued participation in an employee welfare and benefits plan maintained by a former employer.

10) Informational materials that are sent to the office of the member, officer or employee in the form of books, articles, periodicals, other written materials, audiotapes, videotapes, or other forms of communication.

11) Awards or prizes that are given to competitors in contests or events open to the public, including random drawings.

12) Honorary degrees (and associated travel, food, refreshments, and entertainment provided in the presentation of degrees and awards).

13) Training (including food and refreshments furnished to all attendees as an integral part of the training) provided to a member, officer, or employee if the training is in the interest of the school district.

14) Educational missions, including meetings with government officials either foreign or domestic, intended to educate

public officials on matters of public policy, to which the member, officer, employee, or judge may be invited to participate along with other federal, state, or local public officials and community leaders.

15) Bequests, inheritances, and other transfers at death.

16) Anything that is paid for by the federal government, the State, or a governmental entity, or secured by the government or governmental entity under a government contract.

17) A gift of personal hospitality of an individual other than a registered lobbyist or agent of a foreign principal, including hospitality extended for a nonbusiness purpose by an individual, not a corporation or organization, at the personal residence of that individual or the individual's family or on property or facilities owned by that individual or the individual's family.

18) Free attendance at a widely attended event permitted under number 20 below.

19) Opportunities and benefits that are:

• available to the public or to a class consisting of all employees, officers, or members whether or not restricted on the basis of geographic consideration;

• offered to members of a group or class in which membership is unrelated to employment or official position;

• offered to members of an organization such as an employee's association or credit union, in which membership is related to employment or official position and similar opportunities are available to large segments of the public through organizations of similar size;

• offered to any group or class that is not defined in a manner that specifically discriminates among government employees on the basis of branch of government or type of responsibility, or on a basis that favors those of higher rank or rate of pay;

• in the form of loans from banks and other financial institutions on terms generally available to the public; or

• in the form of reduced membership or other fees for participation in organization activities offered to all government employees by professional organizations if the only restrictions on membership relate to professional qualifications.

20) A plaque, trophy, or other item that is substantially commemorative in nature and that is extended for presentation.

21) Golf or tennis; food or refreshments of nominal value and catered food or refreshments; meals or beverages consumed on the premises from which they were purchased.

22) Donations of products from an Illinois company that are intended primarily for promotional purposes, such as display or free distribution, and are of minimal value to any individual recipient.

23) An item of nominal value such as a greeting card, baseball cap, or T-shirt.

5 ILCS 425/15

3:340   What is the penalty for violation of the Gift Ban Act?

A person who is a member, officer or employee is subject to penalties which include the possibility of a reprimand; an order to cease and desist; an order to return the money or other items or make restitution; dismissal or removal from office; donation to a charity of an amount equal to the gift and or a fine up to $5,000. A person who is not a member, officer or employee and who violates the Act is subject to a fine up to $5,000.

5 ILCS 425/65
5 ILCS 425/70

4: SCHOOL ELECTION PROCEDURES

GENERAL ELECTION LAWS

4:10 What types of elections involve public school districts?

Elections conducted by public school districts include the election of school board members and various public policy propositions, such as to increase authorized property tax rates, issue bonds, consolidate districts, create single-member school board districts, or deactivate a high school. A school election also may involve an advisory question placed before the voters.

4:20 What laws govern the election of school board members?

School board elections except those involving school districts which have adopted Article 33 of the School Code are consolidated elections governed by the general election laws of the state. Provisions peculiar to school boards are found in the School Code.

10 ILCS 5/1-1 et seq.
105 ILCS 5/9-1 et seq.
105 ILCS 5/33-1 et seq.

4:30 When are school board members elected?

From 1981 until 1998, school board members were elected in odd numbered years in a nonpartisan election held on the first Tuesday after the first Monday in November. Beginning in 1999, school board members will be elected in odd-numbered years on the first Tuesday in April.

School districts that have adopted Article 33 of the School Code elect school board members on the first Tuesday in April

in odd-numbered years and on the third Tuesday in March in
even-numbered years.

10 ILCS 5/2A-1.1(b)
10 ILCS 5/2A-1.2 (4)
10 ILCS 5/2A-1.2 (12)
105 ILCS 5/33-1 et seq.

4:31   What are the terms of office for school board members elected during the transition from nonpartisan November elections to April elections?

Board members elected in November 1997 will serve from
November 1997 until November 2001.

Board members elected in 1999 and 2001 will be elected in
the spring (April) and seated in November when the terms of
their predecessors expire. That is, board members elected in
April 1999 will serve from November 1999 until April 2003;
board members elected in April 2001 will serve from November
2001 until April 2005.

Board members elected in April 2003 will be seated in April
2003 and serve until April 2007.

10 ILCS 5/2A-51
10 ILCS 5/2A-54

4:40   What laws govern the holding of a school district referendum on a public policy issue, such as a proposition to increase tax rates, issue bonds or consolidate districts?

Article 28 of The Election Code sets forth the general election laws governing all public policy referenda. Article 9 of The
School Code addresses some specific requirements of school district referenda.

However, school boards may place on the ballot only those
public policy questions authorized by statute. Such authorization is found at several locations in the School Code, including
Article 17 (increases in authorized tax rates), Article 19
(issuance of building bonds), and Article 20 (working cash fund
bonds). Authority for elections on school district reorganization
and consolidation are found in Articles 7, 7A, 11A, 11B and 11D.

To place a proposition on the ballot at a referendum, a

school board must adopt a resolution citing the specific author-izing statute.

10 ILCS 5/28-1
105 ILCS 5/9-1

4:50 When may public policy issues be placed on the ballot?

A public policy referendum may be held only on any of the four scheduled election dates in each two-year election cycle. In even-numbered years, those dates are the third Tuesday in March (General Primary) and the first Tuesday after the first Monday in November (General Election).

In odd-numbered years, regular election dates are the last Tuesday in February (Consolidated Primary) and the first Tuesday in April (Consolidated Election).

There are three exceptions to this schedule that may apply in different circumstances:

1) A proposition may not be placed on the ballot at any reg-ular election where there is no contest for a public office on the ballot in at least one precinct within the school district.

2) A school board may petition the circuit court for an emer-gency election where the board believes it cannot reasonably wait until the next regular election date.

3) Not more than three propositions (other than propositions submitted by backdoor referendum) may be submitted to the voters of a school district at the same election.

10 ILCS 5/2A-1.1
10 ILCS 5/2A-1.2(f)
10 ILCS 5/2A-1.4
10 ILCS 5/28-1

4:55 When must a school board submit a public policy advisory referendum to vote at a regularly scheduled election?

Whenever 10 percent or more of the registered voters of a school district submit a valid written petition regarding a ques-tion of public policy to a school board, the board must cause the question to be submitted to the voters. The result of an adviso-ry referendum is not binding on the school board.

10 ILCS 5/28-6

ELECTION AUTHORITY

4:60   Who is in charge of conducting elections?

The Illinois State Board of Elections has general supervision over the administration of registration and election laws of the state.

Local elections are conducted by an election authority designated by statute. In most locales, the election authority is the county clerk. In a number of cities, a Municipal Board of Election Commissioners is the election authority. In DuPage County, a County Board of Election Commissioners is the election authority.

The election authority is responsible for voter registration, determining polling places, publishing notices, printing ballots, absentee voting, and other mechanics of running the election.

10 ILCS 5/1-3
10 ILCS 5/1A-1 et seq.

4:70   Does the school board have any duties related to the conduct of school elections?

The school board has no duties directly relating to the conduct of any election. However, certain duties and actions of the board relate to the election:

1) The board, by proper resolution, may place public policy propositions on the ballot at an election.

2) Members of the board make up an electoral board to hear and rule on objections to candidate nominating petitions and voter petitions.

3) The board must canvass the precinct returns and declare the results following each election of board members and school district referendum.

4) The school board secretary or clerk serves as the local election official, assisted by designated representatives appointed by the board.

10 ILCS 5/1-3
10 ILCS 5/10-9
10 ILCS 5/22-17
105 ILCS 5/9-1.1
105 ILCS 5/9-2(d)
105 ILCS 5/9-10

4:80 What are the election duties of the school board secretary?

Duties of the school board secretary, in the capacity of local election official, are set out in Article 9 of the School Code and various sections of the Election Code. Those duties include:

1) Publish a legal notice of the time and place for filing nominating papers for the biennial school board election (an optional duty that is not required);

2) Receive and file the nominating papers of school board candidates;

3) Conduct a lottery to establish the order of names on the ballot in the event of simultaneous filings;

4) Provide each candidate with a notice of obligations under the Illinois Campaign Financing Act;

5) If any formal objections to a candidate's nominating papers are filed, forward the objections to the chairman of the local electoral board;

6) Receive voter petitions and school board resolutions calling for propositions to be placed on the ballot at a regular election;

7) Certify to the election authority the ballot to be used at the school board election, including the names of candidates in the manner and order they are to appear on the ballot;

8) Certify to the election authority any public policy propositions that are to appear on the ballot, including the wording of the proposition as taken from the school board resolution or voter petition;

9) Following the election, forward precinct results received from the election authority to the school board, which will canvass results.

10 ILCS 5/10-1 et seq.
10 ILCS 5/17-22
105 ILCS 5/9-1 et seq.

ELECTION OF SCHOOL BOARD MEMBERS

4:90   What effect does consolidation of school districts have on the election of board members?

When a school district will cease to exist by consolidation, annexation or otherwise within six months after a regular school board election date, no election of school board members is held on that date and any board member whose term would otherwise terminate is continued until the old district ceases to exist.

Under certain circumstances relating to the consolidation, creation and/or combination of school districts, a new school board may be elected at the same election as the district's structural change is being voted on.

105 ILCS 5/10-10
105 ILCS 5/11A-3
105 ILCS 5/11A-5
105 ILCS 5/11A-8
105 ILCS 5/11B-3
105 ILCS 5/11B-6
105 ILCS 5/11D-2
105 ILCS 5/11D-6

4:100   Is the procedure for running for the school board in a newly organized school district's first election the same as when running for an existing school board?

The procedures are the same except that in a newly created district's first election, the regional superintendent of schools, rather than the school board secretary, performs all of the duties of the local election official.

105 ILCS 5/9-10

CANDIDATE NOMINATIONS

4:110   How does a school board candidate acquire a place on the ballot?

To be placed on the ballot, a candidate must cause to be filed a nominating petition and a statement of candidacy with the secretary of the school board or such other person as the school board may designate. The statement of candidacy must include a receipt showing that a statement of economic interests has been timely filed with the county clerk.

5 ILCS 420/1-101 et seq.
105 ILCS 5/10-10

4:120   When may a school board candidate circulate a nominating petition to gather signatures?

A school board candidate may cause to be circulated a petition no earlier than 90 days preceding the last day for the filing of the petition (161 days before the election).

10 ILCS 5/10-4

4:130   During what time frame must a school board candidate file his nominating petition?

A candidate for school board must cause his nominating petition and statement of candidacy to be filed no more than 78, nor less than 71 days before the date of election.

10 ILCS 5/10-6(2)
105 ILCS 5/9-10

4:140   With whom does a school board candidate file a nominating petition?

A school board candidate must cause his nominating petition to be filed with the secretary of the school board or a person designated by the board to receive nominating petitions. The school board secretary must, within seven days of filing the nominating petition or on the last day for filing the petition, whichever is earlier, acknowledge to the petitioner in writing the secretary's acceptance of the nominating petition.

If the school board secretary is an incumbent school board member seeking re-election, a disinterested person must witness the filing of his petition.

105 ILCS 5/9-10

4:150   What information is required on a petition of candidacy for school board?

A petition must include:

1) a statement of candidacy;
2) the name of the school district;
3) the name and place of residence of the candidate with specified street and number;

4) whether the candidate is seeking a full term or is seeking to fill a partial term caused by a board vacancy;
5) the date of the election;
6) the number of voter signatures required;
7) the notarized signature of the petition circulator;
8) a receipt from the county clerk showing the candidate has timely filed a statement of economic interests.

School board nominating petitions must be on sheets of uniform size, and must contain the circulator's affidavit and a statement of an individual's candidacy.

10 ILCS 5/10-5
105 ILCS 5/9-10
Klingelmueller v. Haas, 111 Ill.App.3d 88, 443 N.E.2d 782, 66 Ill.Dec. 856 (3rd Dist. 1982)

4:160   How many signatures are required on a school board candidate nominating petition?

Nominating petitions for board of education candidates must be signed by at least 50 registered voters who reside in the school district or 10 percent of the registered voters who reside in the school district, whichever is less. Nominating petitions for school directors must be signed by at least 25 registered voters who reside in the school district or 5 percent of the voters who reside in the school district, whichever is less.

105 ILCS 5/9-10

4:170   Must a candidate for school board declare a political party affiliation?

School board candidates are not required to declare political party affiliation.

4:180   May a school board candidate be required to sign a loyalty oath in order to file a nominating petition?

While a signed loyalty oath is required by the Election Code for filing a school board candidate's nominating petition, this requirement is unconstitutional and is, therefore, unenforceable. A school board candidate's nominating petition may not be refused for a candidate's failure or refusal to sign a loyalty oath.

Communist Party of Illinois v. Ogilvie, 357 F.Supp. 105 (N.D. Ill. 1972)

CANDIDATE WITHDRAWAL

4:190   May a school board candidate run for both a full term and a partial term created by a board vacancy?

No. A candidate for either a board of education or board of school directors who has filed nominating petitions for both a full term and a partial term at the same election must withdraw one petition or the other, in writing, within five business days following the last day for filing petitions.

10 ILCS 5/10-7
105 ILCS 5/9-10

4:200   How may a school board candidate withdraw his candidacy and have his name removed from the ballot?

A candidate may withdraw by filing a written request signed by the candidate and acknowledged before an officer qualified to take acknowledgment of deeds not later than the date for certification of candidates for the ballot. Filing is to be made at the principal office of the school district.

10 ILCS 5/10-7

OBJECTIONS TO NOMINATING PETITIONS

4:210   Who determines whether a candidate's nominating papers meet legal requirements?

The local election official who receives and files nominating papers makes an initial determination as to whether the papers are in apparent conformity with the law. The school board secretary must receive and file only those petitions which include a statement of candidacy, the required number of voter signatures, the notarized signature of the petition circulator and a receipt from the county clerk showing that the candidate has filed a statement of economic interests on or before the last day to file.

105 ILCS 5/9-10

4:220 Is it possible to challenge a school board candidate's nominating petitions on the grounds that signatures are invalid or were improperly gathered or that other information contained in the petition is incorrect?

The local election official has no authority to question the accuracy or truthfulness of information contained in a nominating petition. However, candidate nominating petitions are open to public inspection and any legal voter of the district may file a written objection with the board secretary within five days after the last day for filing nominating petitions. The objector's petition must state fully the nature of the objection, the interest of the objector and the relief requested.

10 ILCS 5/10-7
10 ILCS 5/10-8

4:230 Who hears objections to school board candidate nominating petitions?

The Education Officers Electoral Board (EOEB) hears challenges to school board candidate nominating petitions. The EOEB is composed of the president of the school board (who is designated as chairperson), the school board secretary, and the school board member with the longest continuous service. The composition of the EOEB is altered to include the school board member with the second longest continuous service when one of the persons who would otherwise sit on the EOEB is a candidate for the office with relation for which a petition is being challenged.

10 ILCS 5/10-9

4:240 What procedures are used by the Education Officers Electoral Board for hearing objections to nominating petitions?

When a school board secretary receives an objection to a nominating petition, the secretary must send a copy of the objection to the candidate. The original objection is sent to the chairperson of the Education Officers Electoral Board (EOEB) by registered mail, noting the day and hour the objector's petition was received.

The chairperson of the EOEB must call a meeting of the EOEB to hold a hearing on the objector's petition. The hearing must be held not less than three nor more than five days after the chairperson receives the secretary's notice of objection. A hearing notice must be sent to the objector and to the candidate(s) named in the objection by registered mail and the chairperson of the EOEB must cause the sheriff to serve the parties with notice.

Following a hearing to consider the objection, the EOEB must render a timely decision in writing. The decision of the Education Officers Electoral Board is subject to appeal to the circuit court within 10 days of the EOEB's decision. If no court challenge is filed within the 10-day period, the EOEB must send a copy of its decision to the school board secretary by registered or certified mail.

10 ILCS 5/10-8 et seq.

Schumann v. Kumarich, 102 Ill.App.3d 454, 430 N.E.2d 99, 58 Ill.Dec. 157 (1st Dist. 1981)

Gilbert v. Municipal Officers' Electoral Board of Deerfield, 97 Ill.App.3d 847, 423 N.E.2d 952, 53 Ill.Dec. 283 (2nd Dist. 1981)

People ex rel. Talerico v. Lata, 96 Ill.App.2d 34, 238 N.E.2d 217 (1st Dist. 1968)

CERTIFICATION OF CANDIDATES

4:250   When does the board secretary certify school board candidates to the election authority?

The board secretary must certify candidates to the election authority not less than 61 days before the election, directing the election authority to place the names of candidates on the official ballot in the same manner as presented on the certification.

10 ILCS 5/10-15

4:260   What determines the format of the school board election ballot?

Ballots for school board elections are prescribed in the School Code, which provides for differing formats that conform to differing residential restrictions on school board membership. Ballot formats include those for boards with members elected entirely at large, as well as for those with restrictions on the number of members that may be elected from less populous congressional townships and unincorporated areas.

105 ILCS 5/9-12 et seq.
105 ILCS 5/9-22
105 ILCS 5/11A-8
105 ILCS 5/11B-5
105 ILCS 5/11B-7

4:270   What determines the order of names on a school board election ballot?

Candidates' names appear on the ballot in the order filed with the school board secretary. The secretary must conduct a lottery to establish the order of candidates' names in the event of simultaneous filings. Simultaneous filings are those petitions filed by persons standing in line at the normal opening hour of the office on the first day for filing and those petitions received in the first mail delivery of the day.

Where residency restrictions call for a ballot format that groups candidates by area of residence, the order in which petitions are filed or selected by lottery establishes the order in which candidates groupings appear on the ballot.

105 ILCS 5/9-11.1 et seq.

4:275   Is the school board secretary required to use any particular lottery procedure in determining the order of candidates' names in the event of simultaneous filings?

By law the lottery must be conducted within nine days after the last day for filing nominating petitions and must be open to the public. The board secretary must give written notice to the candidates who filed simultaneously no later than seven days before the lottery. Notice of the lottery also must go to any citizen or organization entitled to have poll watchers on the day of the election. A notice giving the time and place of the lottery must be posted at the entrance of the board secretary's office.

Although the School Code is silent on the matter of lottery procedure, the Election Code requires other election officials to use a lottery approved by the State Board of Elections. Board of

Elections Rule 201.40 describes an approved lottery procedure which, summarized briefly, provides the following:

a) The names of all candidates who filed simultaneously for the same office shall be listed alphabetically and shall be numbered consecutively commencing with the number one, which is assigned to the candidate whose name is listed first on the alphabetic list. For example, if five candidates by the names of Downs, Brown, Edwards, Cook and Adams have filed simultaneously, they will be arranged alphabetically and assigned the numbers as follows: Adams, one; Brown, two; Cook, three; Downs, four; and Edwards, five.

b) All ties will be broken by a single drawing. A number is placed in a container representing each number assigned to each candidate as provided for above. For example, if there are five candidates involved in the lottery, the numbers one through five are placed in a container.

c) Numbers in the container are thoroughly shaken and mixed and then withdrawn one at a time. The candidate whose position on the alphabetical list corresponds to the first number drawn is certified ahead of the other candidates. The candidate whose position on the list corresponds to the second number drawn is certified second, and so on.

A separate but identical procedure is used in the event of simultaneous filings for a separate election to fill an unexpired term.

10 ILCS 5/10-6.2
105 ILCS 5/9-11.1
26 Ill. Admin. Code 201.40

4:280   Are write-in candidates permitted at a school board election?

Voters may write in and cast votes for persons not listed on the ballot. However, write-in votes are not counted unless the candidate has filed with the election authority a declaration of intent to run as a write-in candidate no later than 5:00 p.m. on the Tuesday immediately preceding the election.

10 ILCS 5/17-16.1
10 ILCS 5/18-9.1

PUBLIC POLICY ELECTIONS

4:290   How does a school board get a public policy issue on the ballot?

A school board must pass a proper resolution at an official board meeting that a question be submitted to the voters in a referendum at a regularly scheduled election. The resolution must be adopted at least 65 days prior to the date of the regularly scheduled election. The resolution must state the regular election at which the referendum will be submitted to the voters.

The school board secretary is responsible for certifying the question to be submitted at the referendum to the county clerk at least 61 days before the election. This certification must include the form of the referendum question, the date the school board adopted the resolution, and a certified copy of the resolution passed by the school board.

10 ILCS 5/28-1 et seq.

4:300   How many separate propositions may a school board have placed on the ballot at any one election?

Not more than three public policy questions other than back door referenda may be submitted to referendum at the same election.

105 ILCS 5/28-1 et seq.

4:310   How are voter-initiated petitions, including backdoor referenda and advisory referenda, placed on the ballot?

Except under certain conditions specified in statute, a voter-initiated petition must be filed with the school board secretary at least 78 days before the regularly scheduled election. The board secretary must certify the question to be placed on the ballot to the county clerk at least 61 days prior to the regularly scheduled election.

10 ILCS 5/28-2
10 ILCS 5/28-5
Ayers v. Martin, 233 Ill.App.3d 397, 584 N.E.2d 1028, 165 Ill.Dec. 594 (4th Dist. 1991)

4:313 What information must be provided in the publication of a notice of a resolution which may be subject to backdoor referendum?

The publication of the resolution must include a notice of the specific number of voters required to sign a petition requesting that the public question be submitted to the voters, the time within which the petition must be filed, and the date of the prospective referendum.

In addition, when a resolution for issuing working cash fund bonds is published, the recording officer of the district (presumably the board secretary) must provide a petition form to any individual requesting one.

10 ILCS 5/28-2(f)
105 ILCS 5/20-7

4:315 Is it possible to challenge a voter-initiated petition on the grounds that signatures are invalid or were improperly gathered or that other information contained in the petition is incorrect?

The local election official has no authority to question the accuracy or truthfulness of information contained in a voter-initiated petition.

The school board lacks standing to challenge the accuracy or truthfulness of information contained in a voter-initiated petition. However, such petitions are open to public inspection and any legal voter of the district may file a written objection with the board secretary within five days after the last day for filing voter-initiated petitions. The objector's petition must state fully the nature of the objection, the interest of the objector and the relief requested. Such objections frequently challenge whether the petitions contain the required number of valid signatures by identifying some signatures as forgeries, those of non-residents, unregistered voters, or identify technical errors in the execution of the petitions.

The objections are heard and ruled upon by the Education Officers Electoral Board in generally the same manner as objections to candidate nominating petitions.

10 ILCS 5/10-8 et seq.
10 ILCS 5/28-3

4:320   What is an emergency referendum?

An "emergency referendum" is a referendum conducted on other than a regularly scheduled election date. Whenever any public question is to be submitted pursuant to law, whether by action of the governing body of a school district, by petition, or by court order, the governing body of the school district whose powers or duties are directly affected by the result of the vote on the public question may petition the circuit court for an order declaring such proposition to be an emergency and fixing a date other than a regularly scheduled election date on which a special referendum election shall be held for the submission of the public question.

The petition must set forth the public question and the action taken which requires the submission of the question, the next regularly scheduled election at which the proposition could otherwise be placed on the ballot, the estimated costs of conducting a separate special election, and the reasons why an emergency exists to justify the special election prior to the next ensuing regular election. The petition must be approved by a majority of the members of the school board.

The court must conduct a hearing on the petition. Any resident of the area in which the referendum is to be conducted may oppose the petition. The court may approve the petition for an emergency referendum only upon a finding, supported by the evidence, that the referendum is necessitated by an imminent need for approval of additional authority in order to maintain the operations or facilities of the school district and that such need is due to circumstances beyond the control of the governing body.

10 ILCS 5/2A-1.4

4:330   What information must be provided on the ballot and in a notice of election increasing a district's tax rate?

In addition to the notice requirements of the general election law, whenever a proposition to increase a school tax rate is submitted to be voted upon by the voters of any district, the notice of such election must include an estimate of the approximate amount of taxes extendible under the maximum rate then in force and an estimate of the approximate amount of taxes extendible under the proposed increased rate, such amounts being computed upon the last known full, fair cash value; provided that any error, miscalculation or inaccuracy in computing the amounts does not invalidate or affect the validity of any rate so increased.

The school board must make such estimate, and the secretary must certify such amount to the election authority as part of the certification of the proposition as required by the general election law. The estimate must appear on the ballot on which the proposition is printed but must not appear as a part of the proposition.

In addition, where the proposition is to authorize or increase a tax rate, the notice of election and the form of ballot must include:

1) the geographic or other common name of the school district by which that is commonly known and referred to, as well as the number of the district;

2) the maximum rate at which such tax may be levied if the proposition is approved;

3) the total dollar amount of the most recently approved annual budget of the district, what the total dollar amount of that budget would be if increased by the amount of additional tax which may be levied if the proposition is approved, and what the percentage increase in that annual budget would be if the total dollar amount were increased by that amount of additional tax; and

4) if the proposition is to increase the annual rate of an existing tax levied by the district, then the annual rate at which the tax is currently levied and the percentage of increase between the maximum rate at which such tax may be levied if the proposition is approved and the annual rate at which such tax currently is levied.

105 ILCS 5/9-11
105 ILCS 5/17-3.4

ADVOCACY AND ELECTIONEERING

4:340 May a school board use school district funds to inform voters of its reason for seeking a tax rate increase, bond issue, or other public policy question?

The school board has an obligation to present voters with the facts so they might arrive at informed judgments. On the other hand, public funds belong to all the electorate—opponents as well as proponents—and cannot be used to represent just one side or to finance a campaign to influence the outcome of the referendum.

Public funds must not be used to urge any elector to vote for or against any candidate or proposition or be appropriated for political campaign purposes. This does not prohibit the use of public funds for dissemination of factual information relative to any proposition appearing on an election ballot.

10 ILCS 5/9-25 et seq.
Citizens to Protect Public Funds v. Board of Education of Parsippany-Troy Hills, 13 N.J. 172 (1953)
Elsenau v. City of Chicago, 334 Ill. 78, 165 N.E. 129 (1929)

4:350 May a school board use district funds to disseminate printed information regarding a public policy question on the ballot?

Yes, so long as the printed information presents the facts, both pro and con, and does not urge voters to vote for or against the issue.

10 ILCS 5/9-25 et seq.
Citizens to Protect Public Funds v. Board of Education of Parsippany-Troy Hills, 13 N.J. 172 (1953)
Elsenau v. City of Chicago, 334 Ill. 78, 165 N.E. 129 (1929)

4:360 May supporters of a school board referendum urge voters to support the ballot proposition?

Yes, provided that:

1) no public funds are used by supporters of such an effort;

2) any individual or organization which accepts or expends $3,000 or more in supporting or opposing a school referendum organizes as a "local political committee" under the Election Code;

3) the school board and school employees, in their official capacities, treat proponents and opponents with an equal hand.

10 ILCS 5/9-1 et seq.

10 ILCS 5/9-25 et seq.

Citizens to Protect Public Funds v. Board of Education of Parsippany-Troy Hills, 13 N.J. 172 (1953)

Elsenau v. City of Chicago, 334 Ill. 78, 165 N.E. 129 (1929)

4:370   What is required of a local political committee?

Such a committee must file a statement of organization and must report contributions and expenditures. Forms are obtained from and filed with the county clerk. Obligations are set forth in Manual of Instructions, Illinois Campaign Financing Act, issued by the State Board of Elections.

10 ILCS 5/9-1 et seq.

4:380   What legal requirements apply to the literature of a political committee?

Any literature issued by the school board should be clearly identified as to source and purpose. It should be made clear that the political literature of a citizens committee was not financed with public funds.

People v. White, 116 Ill.2d 171, 506 N.E.2d 1284, 107 Ill.Dec. 229 (1987)

4:385   May a candidate for public office distribute anonymous campaign literature?

Campaign literature need not contain the name and address of the person who published and distributed it.

People v. White, 116 Ill.2d 171, 506 N.E.2d 1284, 107 Ill.Dec. 229 (1987)

4:390   May a local political committee of citizens assign poll watchers to polling places on election day?

Yes, each organization of proponents and opponents of a ballot proposition which has registered with the election authority at least 40 days before the election is entitled to have one poll watcher per precinct. Each poll watcher must be registered to vote from a residence in the county where the proposition is being voted on and must have obtained necessary credentials from the election authority. Credentials shall be available for distribution at least two weeks before the election.

10 ILCS 5/17-23

DETERMINING ELECTION RESULTS

4:400   How does a school board canvass election votes?

The county clerk must send the school board secretary an original sealed tally sheet and certificate of result for each school district voting precinct. The school board secretary must, within 24 hours, give these documents to the school board which, acting as a whole, functions as a canvassing board. The school board must canvass the returns within seven days of the election. The school board thereafter transmits a signed copy or original duplicate of its canvass to the county clerk and to the Illinois State Board of Elections.

10 ILCS 5/17-22
10 ILCS 5/22-17 et seq.

4:405   Where candidates for the school board must be grouped into residential areas, may the canvassing school board select winners in a manner that ensures all seats are filled?

Generally, the canvassing school board must seat candidates in order from the highest vote getter on the ballot to the lowest vote getter. Where seating a high vote getter would exceed the maximum number of board members who may be elected from a particular geographic area, the board must skip that candidate and go to the next highest vote getter. However, where a ballot includes an unexpired term, the unexpired term must be filled first and independently of the full terms.

10 ILCS 5/22-17
105 ILCS 5/9-12
105 ILCS 5/10-10

4:410   What steps must be taken by a successful write-in candidate and by the canvassing school board prior to seating a winning write-in candidate?

Election statutes are silent with respect to the seating of successful write-in candidates in a school board election. However:

1) Every school board member must have a statement of economic interests on file with the county clerk. Therefore, as soon as possible after the canvass, a successful write-in candidate should file a statement of economic interests with the county clerk.

2) Statutes governing the seating of successful write-in candidates at primary and consolidated elections call for the filing of a statement of candidacy. Because a canvassing school board has no practical means of determining whether the write-in candidate meets legal qualifications, the board might reasonably require that a statement of candidacy and a receipt from the county clerk for the economic interests statement be filed with the secretary before seating a successful write-in candidate. The statement of candidacy provides a notarized affirmation that legal qualifications are met.

 5 ILCS 420/4A-101 et seq.
 10 ILCS 5/7-60 et seq.

4:415   What steps must be taken to determine the winner in the event of a tie vote among two or more school board candidates?

The canvassing board has the duty of breaking the tie in order to declare a winner. However, the law is unclear as to how such ties are to be broken. Presumably any lottery method would be acceptable if it is a fair and impartial method of random selection. The lottery prescribed by the State Board of Elections for determining ballot order of names in the event of simultaneous filings would be such a method.

 10 ILCS 5/10-6.2
 10 ILCS 5/22-17 et seq.
 105 ILCS 5/9-11.1
 26 Ill. Admin. Code 201.40

4:420   On what bases are school board elections invalidated?

The mandatory requirements of the election laws must be met or an election will be set aside. Whether a provision of election law is mandatory or not is subject to the following analysis:

1) Does the statutory scheme expressly or impliedly provide that the failure to follow the provision will render an election void?

2) Does the failure interfere with the result of the election?

3) Was any person legally eligible to vote not permitted to vote?

4) Was any person voting not a resident of the territory sought to be organized?

5) Were the polling places chosen for any improper motive?

6) Was there fraud in, or resulting from, the selection of the polling places?

Jones v. Municipal Officers Electoral Board, 122 Ill.App.3d 926, 446 N.E.2d 173, 61 Ill.Dec. 684 (1st Dist. 1983).

Madden v. Schumann, 105 Ill.App.3d 900, 435 N.E.2d 173, 61 Ill.Dec. 684 (1st Dist. 1982)

Schumann v. Kumarich, 102 Ill.App.3d 454, 430 N.E.2d 99, 58 Ill.Dec. 157 (1st Dist. 1981)

Havens v. Miller, 102 Ill.App.3d 558, 429 N.E.2d 1292, 57 Ill.Dec. 929 (1st Dist. 1981)

Goble v. Board of Education of Iuka Community Consolidated School District No. 7, Marion County, 83 Ill.App.3d 284, 404 N.E.2d 343, 38 Ill.Dec. 919 (5th Dist. 1980)

Menssen v. Eureka Unit District No. 140, 70 Ill.App.3d 9, 388 N.E.2d 273, 26 Ill.Dec. 649 (4th Dist. 1979)

Gibson v. Kankakee School District No. 111, 34 Ill.App.3d 948, 341 N.E.2d 447 (3rd Dist. 1975)

Gann v. Harrisburg Community Unit School District, 73 Ill.App.2d 103, 218 N.E.2d 833 (5th Dist. 1966)

VOTING

4:500   Who is eligible to vote in elections of school board members and on public policy issues placed on the ballot by a school board?

To vote in a school board election or public policy referendum presented by a school board, an individual must be registered to vote from a residence within the boundaries of the school district.

In school board elections where board membership is at-large, the voter may vote for as many seats as are up for election. The same is true where the number of board members elected from particular townships or incorporated areas is regulated by law. In the latter case, a voter may vote for more candidates than may be lawfully elected from a particular geographic area.

In a school district where board members are elected from board member districts, the school district is divided into seven voting districts of substantially equal population. Voters living within each voting district elect one school board member from among candidates running from residences within that voting district.

10 ILCS 5/6-27
105 ILCS 5/9-12 et seq.
105 ILCS 5/9-22
105 ILCS 5/11A-8
105 ILCS 5/11B-7
105 ILCS 5/12-2

5: SCHOOL BOARD OFFICERS

ELECTED OFFICERS

5:10 What officers must a school board elect?

The School Code requires boards of school directors to elect a president and a clerk. Boards of education must elect a president, vice president and a secretary. The secretary need not be a member of the school board, but all other board officers must be members.

No other officers are required by the School Code, but additional offices may be created by vote of the school board.

105 ILCS 5/10-5
105 ILCS 5/10-13 et seq.

5:20 May school board officers be elected by secret ballot?

The Open Meetings Act requires the election of school board officers by open vote at a public meeting. The voting may not be done by any form of secret ballot.

5 ILCS 120/1
People ex rel. Hopf v. Barger, 30 Ill.App.3d 525, 332 N.E.2d 649 (2nd Dist. 1975)

5:30 For how long are school board officers elected?

Officers of boards of education serve two-year terms unless the school board adopts a resolution and policy fixing the term at one year. Illinois law does not specify a term of office for officers of boards of directors. In such districts, officers' terms may be fixed by board resolution.

As school board elections are moved ahead from November to April of odd-numbered years, the terms of officers at some point will necessarily be for less than one or two years during the transition period.

105 ILCS 5/10-5
105 ILCS 5/10-13 et seq.

5:35   When are school board officers elected?

Officers are elected at the school board's organizational meeting following the seating of members elected at each biennial election. Boards that opt for one-year terms must also elect officers in the even-numbered years.

105 ILCS 5/10-5
105 ILCS 5/10-16

5:40   Who serves as the president of the school board in the absence of the elected president?

The vice-president of the school board performs the duties of the president if there is a vacancy in the office or in the president's absence or inability to act.

105 ILCS 5/10-13 et seq.

5:50   May school board officers be paid for their services?

Only the secretary of a board of education may be compensated. Other officers of the board may not be paid for their services.

105 ILCS 5/10-14

5:60   Are there limitations on compensation of the board secretary?

The secretary of the board of education, whether a member of the board of education or not, may be paid. The rate of pay must be set by the board of education before the secretary is elected.

If the secretary is a member of the board, the rate of pay may not exceed the statutory limit set forth in the School Code. There is no statutory limit on the compensation for a secretary who is not a member of the board.

105 ILCS 5/10-14

5:70   Who serves as board secretary or clerk in the absence of the elected secretary or clerk?

If a clerk or secretary is absent from a board meeting or refuses to perform the duties of the office, a secretary or clerk pro tempore must be appointed by the remaining board members.

105 ILCS 5/10-14

5:75   May a school board officer be removed from office for failure to attend meetings?

No. However, the statutes which provide for the election of school board officers also allow the appointment of pro tempore officers in the absence, inability to act, or incapacity of the elected officer.

105 ILCS 5/10-13 et seq.

TREASURERS

5:80   What is a school treasurer?

The school treasurer is the only lawful custodian of school funds, is responsible for all receipts, disbursements and investments of school funds, and pays orders issued by the school board.

105 ILCS 5/8-1 et seq.

5:90   How is a school treasurer elected or appointed?

In Class I county school units (all counties other than Cook), each school board either:

1) elects one of its members to serve as treasurer without salary for a period of one year, or

2) appoints a non-member as treasurer and fixes compensation. The appointed treasurer (non-member of the board) serves at the pleasure of the board.

In Class II county school units (Cook County), the trustees of schools appoint a township treasurer unless the Class II county school unit is no longer subject to the jurisdiction and authority of the trustees of schools, which may occur in a number of different ways pursuant to a complicated statutory scheme.

105 ILCS 5/5-1
105 ILCS 5/8-1 et seq.

5:95   What qualifications are required of a school district treasurer?

Illinois statutes provide various sets of qualifications for school treasurers, depending upon the source and manner of appointment:

1) A treasurer who is a member of the school board has no required qualifications other than election by vote of the board for a term of one year. This option of electing a board member as treasurer is available to school boards in all counties other than Cook, as well as to any Cook County school board that has withdrawn from the jurisdiction of the township trustees and township school treasurer under Section 5-1(b) of the School Code.

2) A treasurer who is not a member of the school board must be at least 21 years old, of approved integrity and, if appointed for the first time after October 1, 1977, must have a financial background or related experience or 12 semester hours of credit of college level accounting. This option of appointing a treasurer who meets these qualifications is available to school boards in all counties other than Cook, as well as to any Cook County school board that has withdrawn from the jurisdiction of the township trustees and township school treasurer under Section 5-1(b) of the School Code.

3) A township school treasurer appointed by township trustees in Cook County must be a resident of the township and neither a trustee nor member of a school board. If appointed for the first time after August 14, 1989, the individual must be a certified public accountant or certified school business official or have experience as a Cook County township school treasurer prior to July 1, 1989.

4) A treasurer appointed by a Cook County school board that was under the jurisdiction of a township treasurer at the time that office was abolished in the township under Section 5-1(c) of the School Code must be neither a school board member nor district superintendent and, if appointed for the first time after August 14, 1989, must be a certified public accountant or certified school business official or have experience as a Cook County township school treasurer prior to July 1, 1989.

105 ILCS 5/5-1(b)
105 ILCS 5/5-1(c)
105 ILCS 5/8-1

5:100   May the county treasurer be designated the treasurer of a school district?

Yes.

Ill. Const. art. VII, sec. 4(e)

5:110   How is a vacancy in the office of school treasurer filled?

In Class I county school units and Class II county school units no longer within the jurisdiction of the trustees of schools and township treasurer, when a vacancy occurs in the office of school treasurer by death, resignation, or removal from office, the school board appoints a new treasurer.

In Class II county school units still within the jurisdiction of the trustees of schools, the trustees of schools elect a treasurer to fill the unexpired term.

105 ILCS 5/8-1

5:120   How is the school treasurer paid?

In Class I county school units, a school board may elect one of its members as school treasurer to serve without compensation or appoint a non-member and fix compensation.

In Class II county school units no longer within the jurisdiction of the trustees of schools and township treasurer, the school board appoints the treasurer and fixes compensation.

In Class II county school units still within the jurisdiction of the trustees of schools, the trustees appoint a school treasurer and fix compensation. The treasurer so appointed cannot be a trustee or school board member.

Compensation for a school treasurer must be fixed prior to the appointment of the treasurer and may not be decreased during the treasurer's term of office.

105 ILCS 5/5-1
105 ILCS 5/8-1
105 ILCS 5/8-3

5:130   Who is responsible for checking a school treasurer's books?

The regional superintendent of schools is required to examine all books, accounts, and vouchers of every school treasurer in the region at least once each year. If any irregularities are found, the regional superintendent is required to report the irregularities at once in writing to the trustees of Class II county school units or to the respective school boards of those school districts which form a part of a Class II county school unit but which are not subject to the jurisdiction of the trustees of schools of any township in which any such district is located or to the respective school boards of districts in Class I county school units. The trustees or the school board is required to take immediate action as the case demands.

The regional superintendent is also required to examine all notes, bonds, mortgages, and other evidence of indebtedness which the township or school treasurer holds officially, and if any of the papers are found not to be in proper order or the securities are insufficient, the regional superintendent is required to report the problem in writing to the board of trustees.

105 ILCS 5/3-14.11

5:140   When may a school treasurer be removed from office?

In Class I county school units (all counties except Cook) and in Class II county school units (Cook County) which are no longer subject to the jurisdiction of the trustees of schools and township treasurer, an appointed school treasurer serves at the pleasure of the school board and may be removed by the board at any time for cause. The School Code does not provide a method to remove an elected school treasurer from office during the treasurer's one-year term.

In Class II county school units still within the jurisdiction of the trustees of schools, the trustees of schools may remove a school treasurer from office for cause

105 ILCS 5/8-1
Hertel v. Boismenue, 229 Ill. 474, 82 N.E. 298 (1907)

6: SCHOOL BOARD MEETINGS

PUBLIC MEETINGS

6:10   What is a meeting under Illinois law?

The Open Meetings Act defines a meeting as any gathering of a majority of a quorum of the members of a public body held for the purposes of discussing public business.

The definition of "public body" includes committees and sub-committees of the school board, an ethics commission, ethics officer or ultimate jurisdictional authority acting under the State Gift Ban Act, as well as the school board itself.

The provisions of the Open Meetings Act do not apply to collective bargaining negotiations or grievance arbitrations.

5 ILCS 120/1.02
115 ILCS 5/18
Board of Regents of the Regency University System v. Reynard, et al., 292 Ill.App.3d 968, 686 N.E.2d 122, 227 Ill.Dec. 66 (4th Dist. 1997)
Nabhani v. Coglianese, 552 F.Supp. 657 (N.D. Ill. 1983)
People ex rel. Difanis v. Barr, 83 Ill.2d 191, 414 N.E.2d 731, 46 Ill.Dec. 678 (4th Dist. 1980)
People ex rel. Cooper v. Carlson, 28 Ill.App.3d 569, 328 N.E.2d 675 (2nd Dist. 1975)

6:15   Must a school board comply with the Open Meetings Act?

School boards are governed by the notice and conduct of meeting provisions of the Open Meetings Act.

5 ILCS 120/1 et seq.
105 ILCS 5/10-6
105 ILCS 5/10-16

6:20   Are school board meetings open to the public?

A school board meeting must be open to the public unless:

1) the purpose of the meeting is collective bargaining negotiations or grievance arbitration; or

2) the school board excludes the public by voting to convene in closed session for one or any combination of the permissible reasons for closed session.

The provisions for exceptions to open meetings requirements are strictly construed against closed meetings.

5 ILCS 120/1
5 ILCS 120/2 et seq.
115 ILCS 5/18

6:30 May school boards or school board members hold unofficial meetings to discuss school business?

No. It is public policy in Illinois that public business is to be conducted in public, and both the actions and deliberations of public bodies are to be conducted in public. The conduct of school business is limited to official meetings of the school board or its committees.

A discussion of school business by a majority of a quorum—three members of a seven-member school board—would be a violation of the Open Meetings Act as would a meeting held by a majority of a quorum of a committee of a public body at which school business was discussed.

5 ILCS 120/1
105 ILCS 5/10-6
105 ILCS 5/10-16
Board of Regents of the Regency University System v. Reynard, et al., 292 Ill.App.3d 968, 686 N.E.2d 122, 227 Ill.Dec. 66 (4th Dist. 1997)
Illinois News Broadcasters Association v. City of Springfield, 22 Ill.App.3d 226, 317 N.E.2d 288 (4th Dist. 1974)

6:35 Does the Open Meetings Act apply to school board committee meetings?

The Open Meetings Act applies to all school board committees. Committees composed of faculty or administration are not generally school board committees and, therefore, are not subject to the Open Meetings Act. Whether any particular school board created or endorsed committee is or is not subject to the Open Meetings Act is a fact question which requires an analysis of the duties, purpose and structure of the committee.

5 ILCS 120/1.02
115 ILCS 5/18
Board of Regents of the Regency University System v. Reynard, et al., 292 Ill.App.3d 968, 686 N.E.2d 122, 227 Ill.Dec. 66 (4th Dist. 1997)
People ex rel. Difanis v. Barr, 83 Ill.2d 191, 414 N.E.2d 731, 46 Ill.Dec. 678 (1980)

Rockford Newspapers, Inc. v. Northern Illinois Council on Alcoholism and Drug Dependence, 64 Ill.App.3d 94, 380 N.E.2d 1192, 21 Ill.Dec. 16 (2nd Dist. 1978)

Pope v. Parkinson, 48 Ill.App.3d 797, 363 N.E.2d 438, 6 Ill.Dec. 756 (4th Dist. 1977)

6:37   Are meetings of persons who have been elected to a school board but not yet seated subject to the Open Meetings Act?

No. Persons who have been elected to a public body are not members of the public body and cannot conduct business until they are seated.

5 ILCS 120/1.02
105 ILCS 5/10-16

6:40   Are school staff meetings subject to the Open Meetings Act?

Staff meetings involving teachers, administrators or other employees are not subject to the Open Meetings Act even when such meetings are held to prepare presentations for the school board.

People ex rel. Cooper v. Carlson, 28 Ill.App.3d 569, 328 N.E.2d 675 (2nd Dist. 1975)

6:50   May citizens make audio or video tape recordings of school board meetings?

Citizens may tape, film, or use other means of recording the activities at open school board meetings. School boards may adopt reasonable rules to govern the making of such recordings.

5 ILCS 120/2.05

6:60   What is the penalty for violation of the Open Meetings Act?

Any person, including the state's attorney of the county in which the school district is located, may bring a civil action in circuit court alleging a violation of the Open Meetings Act. Circuit courts are authorized to award attorney fees and costs to a successful complainant. The court may provide such other relief as it may deem appropriate. The school board may be ordered to open a future meeting or meetings to the public or to make available to the public all or parts of the minutes of the improperly closed session.

The court has the power to declare null and void any final action taken at an illegal meeting, and may enjoin the school board from future violations of the Open Meetings Act.

5 ILCS 120/3

Bromberek School District No. 65 v. Sanders, 174 Ill.App.3d 301, 528 N.E.2d 1336, 124 Ill.Dec. 228 (1st Dist. 1988) app. den. 124 Ill.2d 553, 535 N.E.2d 912, 129 Ill.Dec. 147 (1989)

6:70 Are individuals subject to criminal charges for Open Meetings Act violations?

Violation of the Open Meetings Act by an individual is a Class C misdemeanor, punishable by a fine of up to $500 and/or 30 days in jail.

5 ILCS 120/3

CALLING MEETINGS

6:80 When must a newly-constituted board of education first meet?

Within seven days after each election of members, a school board must organize by electing its officers and fixing a time and place for regular meetings.

When school board members are elected at the consolidated elections held in April of 1999 and April of 2001, the school board must organize within seven days of the first Tuesday after the first Monday in November.

105 ILCS 5/10-16

6:90 When may a school board hold meetings?

Meetings of school boards must be public and held at times and places convenient to the public.

A school board may hold regular meetings at such times as it designates in the annual notice of its regular meetings. Special meetings may be called by the president or any three members of a board of education or any two members of a board of school directors.

Public notice of all meetings must be given and no official business may be transacted except when a quorum of members is present at a regular or a special meeting. For a three-member board of directors, two members constitute a quorum. For a seven-member board, a quorum consists of four members.

Meetings subject to the Open Meetings Act may not be held on legal holidays except when a regular meeting date falls on a legal holiday.

5 ILCS 120/2.01 et seq.
105 ILCS 5/10-16

6:100   How must a school board give notice of its regular meetings?

A school board is required to give notice of all regular meetings of the board. At the beginning of each calendar or fiscal year, the school board must give public notice of the schedule of all its regular meetings for the year. The schedule must state the times, dates, and places of the meetings and must be posted at the principal office of the district, or, if there is no such office, at the building in which the meeting is to be held.

5 ILCS 120/2.02 et seq.
105 ILCS 5/10-16
Argo High School Council of Local 571, I.F.T., A.F.T., A.F.L.-C.I.O. v. Argo Community High School District 217, 163 Ill.App.3d 578, 516 N.E.2d 834, 114 Ill.Dec. 679 (1st Dist. 1987)

6:102   Is a school board required to post an agenda before its meetings?

Except for meetings held in the event of a bona fide emergency, or with respect to open meetings to be reconvened within 24 hours, or when the time and place of a reconvened meeting is given at the original meeting and there is no change in the agenda, a school board must post an agenda at least 48 hours in advance of the holding of a meeting. The agenda must be posted at the principal office of the school board and at the location where the meeting is to be held.

5 ILCS 120/2.02

6:104 May a school board hold a closed session at a meeting for which its agenda does not include notice of closed session?

Yes, provided the meeting is otherwise in compliance with the provisions of the Open Meetings Act.

5 ILCS 120/2a

6:110 How does a school board change its schedule of regular meeting dates?

A school board may change the dates of its regularly scheduled meetings by giving 10 days notice in a manner set forth by statute.

5 ILCS 120/2.02
105 ILCS 120/2.03
Argo High School Council of Local 571, I.F.T., A.F.T., A.F.L.-C.I.O. v. Argo Community High School District 217, 163 Ill.App.3d 578, 516 N.E.2d 834, 114 Ill.Dec. 679 (1st Dist. 1987)

6:120 How does a school board call a special meeting?

Special meetings may be called by the president or by any three members of a board of education or any two members of a board of school directors.

Board members must be given notice of special meetings in writing, stating the time, place and purpose of the meeting.

Public notice must be given and an agenda of the meeting posted at least 48 hours in advance of a special meeting. Notice also must be given to any news medium that has provided necessary information in the same manner as is given to members of the board.

Special meeting notices must include an agenda.

5 ILCS 120/2.02
105 ILCS 5/10-6
105 ILCS 5/10-16
Argo High School Council of Local 571, I.F.T., A.F.T., A.F.L.-C.I.O. v. Argo Community High School District 217, 163 Ill.App.3d 578, 516 N.E.2d 834, 114 Ill.Dec. 679 (1st Dist. 1987)

6:130 May a school board adjourn a meeting to another meeting?

A meeting may be adjourned to another meeting as many times as the school board deems necessary so long as the school board complies with the provisions of the Open Meetings Act with respect to each reconvened meeting.

Public notice, including an agenda, must be given for each reconvened meeting unless the original meeting was open to the public and is to be reconvened within 24 hours. Public notice also is not required when an announcement of the time and place of the reconvened meeting was made at the original public meeting and there is no change in the agenda.

5 ILCS 120/1 et seq.

NOTICE OF MEETINGS

6:140   How must public notice of school board meetings be given?

Public notice must be given by posting a copy of the notice at the principal office of the school board or, if no such office exists, at the building in which the meeting is to be held. The board must supply copies of the notice of its regular meetings, and of the notice of any special, emergency, rescheduled, or reconvened meeting, to any news medium which has filed an annual request for notice. Any such news medium must also be given the same notice of all special, emergency, rescheduled, or reconvened meetings in the same manner as is given to members of the school board provided such news medium has given the school board an address or telephone number within the territorial jurisdiction of the school board at which such notice may be given.

Public notice must include an agenda in the case of a regular, special, rescheduled, or reconvened meeting. An agenda for a regular meeting must be posted at the principal office of the school board and at the location where the meeting is to be held.

5 ILCS 120/2.02

6:150   May a school board hold an unscheduled emergency meeting without notice?

Yes. In a bona fide emergency, notice requirements may be waived. However, notice must be given as soon as practicable prior to such meeting to any news media that have filed annual requests for meeting notices.

5 ILCS 120/2.02

6:160   What must a school board include in its meeting agenda?

The contents of a school board meeting agenda is at the discretion of the board. The Open Meetings Act requires only that an agenda be included with the public notice of special meetings, rescheduled regular meetings, and reconvened meetings for which public notice is required and that an agenda be posted 48 hours prior to a regular meeting.

5 ILCS 120/2.02

6:165   May a school board conduct business not listed on its agenda at a regular, special, rescheduled or reconvened meeting?

At a special meeting or a rescheduled or reconvened meeting that requires an agenda, the school board may transact only the business that is germane to items listed on the agenda. Action taken on any item not identified on the agenda may be held invalid by a court. At a regular meeting the school board may consider items not specifically listed in its agenda.

5 ILCS 120/2.02

CLOSED MEETINGS

6:170   When may a school board hold a closed meeting?

The Open Meetings Act requires all meetings of school boards to be open meetings. Meetings or portions of regular or special board meetings may be closed to the public only under the exceptions provided for in the Act. The only exceptions are for collective bargaining negotiations and grievance arbitrations which are exempt from the provisions of the Open Meetings Act. The closed meeting exceptions are:

1) The appointment, employment, compensation, discipline, performance, or dismissal of specific employees of the public body, including hearing testimony on a complaint lodged against an employee to determine its validity;

2) Collective negotiating matters between the public body and its employees or their representatives or deliberations concerning salary schedules for one or more classes of employees;

3) The selection of a person to fill a public office, as public

office is defined in the Open Meetings Act or to fill a vacancy in a public office when the public body is given the power to appoint under law or the discipline, performance or removal of the occupant of a public office when the public body is given power to remove the occupant under law;

4) Evidence or testimony presented in open hearing or in closed hearing where specifically authorized by law, to a quasi-adjudicative body as defined in the Open Meetings Act, provided that the body prepares and makes available for public inspection a written decision setting forth its determinative reasoning.

5) The purchase or lease of real property for the use of the public body;

6) The setting of a price for the sale or lease of property owned by the public body;

7) The sale or purchase of securities, investments, or investment contracts;

8) Emergency security procedures and the use of personnel and equipment to respond to actual danger to the safety of employees, students, staff or public property, provided that a description of the actual danger must be made a part of the motion to close the meeting;

9) Student disciplinary cases;

10) The placement of individual students in special education programs and other matters relating to individual students;

11) Litigation, when an action against, affecting or on behalf of the particular public body has been filed and is pending before a court or administrative tribunal, or when the public body finds that an action is probable or imminent, in which case the basis for the finding must be recorded and entered into the minutes of the closed meeting;

12) The establishment of reserves or settlement of claims as provided in the Local Governmental and Governmental Employees Tort Immunity Act, if otherwise the disposition of a claim or potential claim might be prejudiced, or the review or discussion of claims, loss or risk management information, records, data, advise or communications from or with respect to any insurer of the public body or intergovernmental risk management association or self insurance pool of which the public body is a member;

13) Self evaluation, practices and procedures or professional ethics, when meeting with a representative of a statewide association of which the public body is a member;

14) Discussion of minutes of meetings lawfully closed under the Open Meetings Act, whether for purpose of approval by the body of the minutes or semi-annual review of the minutes.

5 ILCS 120/2
115 ILCS 5/18
People ex rel. Ryan v. Villa Park, 212 Ill.App.3d 187, 570 N.E.2d 882, 156 Ill.Dec. 406 (2nd Dist. 1991)

6:180   What final actions of a school board may be taken in closed session?

None. All final actions of a school board must be taken in open session.

5 ILCS 120/2

6:190   May a school board poll it members or take a straw vote in closed session?

A school board may poll its members in closed session so long as the final vote is taken in open session.

Jewell v. Board of Education DuQuoin Community Unit Schools, 19 Ill.App.3d 1091, 312 N.E.2d 659 (5th Dist. 1974)

6:200   What procedure is required to enter closed session?

A school board must, by roll call vote in open session, pass a motion to go into closed session. The motion to close must include a legally sufficient reason for the closed session and must be entered in board minutes. Only those topics specified in the vote to close may be deliberated during the closed session.

5 ILCS 120/2a

6:210   If a school board meeting is to consist entirely of a closed session, must a board give notice?

Yes. Such a meeting presumably would be either a special meeting or a reconvened meeting stemming from a formal vote of the board at an earlier public meeting. Notice requirements for special or reconvened meetings would apply.

A public vote to go into closed session is required at the

opening of the special or reconvened meeting or during the original adjourned meeting.

5 ILCS 120/2.02

6:220   With respect to the term "employment," what may a school board discuss in closed session?

A school board may meet in closed session to consider the employment of individual employees. A school board may also meet in closed session to consider the performance of specific employees. The term "employment" does not include matters of policy or matters involving classifications of employees. Such matters that relate to collective bargaining may fall under the collective bargaining exception.

Even when discussion of employment may be held in closed session, final action must be taken in open session.

5 ILCS 120/2
People v. Board of Education of District 170 of Lee and Ogle Counties, 40 Ill.App.3d 819, 353 N.E.2d 147 (2nd Dist. 1976)

6:225   May a school board insist that complaints against employees be heard only in closed session?

Yes. A school board may vote to meet in open or, on a permissible subject, in closed session. A permissible subject for a closed meeting is for the school board to hear testimony on complaints lodged against an employee to determine its validity. With respect to any alleged right to criticize an employee in public at a school board meeting, the School Code allows a school board to establish reasonable rules governing public comment at its meetings.

5 ILCS 120/2
105 ILCS 5/10-16
Stachura v. Truszkowski, 763 F.2d 211 (6th Cir. 1985)

6:226   What effects are there to public disclosure of the causes for an employee's dismissal?

Public employees have constitutionally protected liberty interests in personal reputation, integrity and the right to have access to future employment opportunities. When a school board seeks to dismiss an employee for causes which may impugn his reputation or character, and makes the stigmatizing charges public, the employee must be provided a hearing at which he has the opportunity to refute the charges. If a school district places stigmatizing charges in an employee's personnel record, it has publicized the charges. If the employee disputes the accuracy of the charges, the employer must provide the employee with a "name-clearing" hearing.

Donato v. Plainview-Old Bethpage Central School District, 96 F.3d 623 (2nd Cir. 1996) cert. den. 117 S.Ct. 1083, 519 U.S. 1150, 137 L.Ed.2d 218

Hayes v. Phoenix Talent School District, 893 F.2d 235 (9th Cir. 1990)

Brandt v. Board of Co-op Educational Services, Third Supervisory District, Suffolk County, New York, 820 F.2d 41, app. after rem. 845 F.2d 416 (2nd Cir. 1988)

Bishop v. Wood, 96 S.Ct. 2074, 426 U.S. 341, 48 L.Ed.2d 864 (1976)

Board of Regents of State Colleges v. Roth, 92 S.Ct. 2701, 408 U.S. 564, 33 L.Ed.2d 548 (1972)

6:227   May a school board censure one of its members for disclosing confidential information from a closed meeting?

A school board has no explicit power to censure or otherwise sanction one of its members. Neither is a school board explicitly prohibited from doing so. A censure resolution has no legal or practical effect except to publicly embarrass the censured party.

Swanson v. Board of Police Commissioners, 197 Ill.App.3d 592, 555 N.E.2d 35, 144 Ill. Dec. 138 (1990), cert. den., 133 Ill.2d 874 (1990)

CONDUCTING MEETINGS

6:230   What rules of procedure must a school board follow with respect to the conduct of school board meetings?

School boards are not required to follow any particular rules of procedure in the conduct of their meetings. The School Code authorizes school boards to adopt rules and regulations for the management and governance of the schools. Rules adopted by a school board must be made available for public inspection in the administrative office of the school district.

105 ILCS 5/10-20.5

6:233   Must a school board's rules of procedure be in writing?

In order to have any legal effect, rules must be in writing and available for public inspection. Moreover, written rules of procedure increase the likelihood that all members of the public body will understand and abide by them and decrease the opportunity for misunderstanding and legal challenges to board actions.

105 ILCS 5/10-20.5

6:235   Must a school board abide by any rules of procedure that it has adopted?

A public body may formally change its own rules or may temporarily suspend them. Decisions regarding rules and whether they are changed or suspended are made by majority vote of the public body. Rules which are required by law (for example, the minimum number of votes required to discharge a tenured teacher) may not be changed.

6:240   Must a school board allow time for public comment at a school board meeting?

At each public meeting of the school board, employees and members of the public must be afforded time, subject to reasonable constraints, to comment or ask questions of the board.

105 ILCS 5/10-6
105 ILCS 5/10-16

6:250   What is a quorum of a school board?

For a seven-member board, a quorum is four and a majority of a quorum is three. For a three-member board or board committee, two members is a quorum and two members is also a majority of a quorum.

105 ILCS 5/10-6
105 ILCS 5/10-12

6:260   May a school board adjourn a meeting when a quorum is not present?

If a quorum is not present at a special or regularly scheduled meeting, those members present, by a majority vote, may adjourn the meeting to a specific time and place, provided the date to which the adjournment is taken is prior to the date of the next regularly scheduled board meeting.

5 ILCS 120/2.02

6:270   May school board officers vote on motions?

Any school board member, including the president, vice president, secretary or clerk (provided they are members of the board), may make motions, second motions, participate in debate, and vote.

On any motion requiring a record of the voting, the vote of the president and each other officer should be recorded as yes, no, abstain, or absent.

105 ILCS 5/10-7

6:280   How many members of a school board must vote for a measure in order for it to carry?

A quorum of the school board must be present to have an official meeting and to conduct business. No vote, except a vote to adjourn, has any weight and effect without a quorum present.

Unless otherwise provided by law, a motion is decided by a majority of the votes cast. Notable exceptions are:

1) a motion to dismiss a tenured teacher requires an affirmative vote by a majority of the entire school board (four of seven members);

2) the sale of school real estate or improvements thereon must be approved by at least two-thirds of the school board (five of seven members), as must a lease agreement for a term longer than 10 years.

A tie vote defeats the motion.

105 ILCS 5/5-22
105 ILCS 5/10-12
105 ILCS 5/10-22.11
105 ILCS 5/10-22.12
105 ILCS 5/24-12

6:290   How is a vote of present or abstain counted?

When a statute requires concurrence of a majority of the members of a decision-making body and a member passes, abstains or does not vote, that member is deemed to have concurred with the majority of those who voted. If the statute requires an affirmative vote of a majority, then nothing less than a majority of yeas or nays is required.

Lake County Forest Preserve District v. Northern Trust Bank, 207 Ill. App.3d 290, 565 N.E.2d 715, 152 Ill.Dec. 182 (2nd Dist. 1990)

Prosser v. Village of Fox Lake, 91 Ill.2d 389, 438 N.E.2d 134, 63 Ill.Dec. 396 (1982)

6:295   May a member of a public body cast a vote by proxy?

The Open Meetings Act requires that public business be conducted openly. A proxy vote is in conflict with the legislative purpose of the Act.

5 ILCS 120/1 et seq.
105 ILCS 5/10-12

6:297   May a school board hold a meeting via telephone conference call?

A meeting may be conducted by telephone provided that:

1) the school board complies with the notice and procedural requirements of the Open Meetings Act, and

2) the meeting is open to the public so that the voices of the members of the public body can be heard and members of the public can speak to the members of the public body (e.g., a two-way speaker phone announced and set up at the offices of the public body).

The physical presence of board members is not required to constitute a "gathering" for purposes of obtaining a quorum and taking action on issues.

5 ILCS 120/1 et seq.
Freedom Oil Company v. Illinois Pollution Control Board, 275 Ill.App.3d 508, 655 N.E.2d 1184, 211 Ill.Dec. 801 (4th Dist. 1995)

6:298   Can one member of a school board participate in a public school board meeting by telephone?

The requirements of the Open Meetings Act are met if the voice of the absent board member is made audible to everyone in the meeting room and if the voices of other board members are audible to the absent board member.

5 ILCS 120/1 et seq.
Freedom Oil Company v. Illinois Pollution Control Board, 275 Ill.App.3d 508, 655 N.E.2d 1184, 211 Ill.Dec. 801 (4th Dist. 1995)

MINUTES

6:300   How should minutes be recorded?

The secretary or clerk must keep a record of the official acts of the school board in a punctual, orderly, and reliable manner. The minutes must be signed by the president and the secretary or clerk of the board.

The minutes, whether of open or closed session, must minimally include the date, time, and place of the meeting; list board members present or absent; and give a summary of discussion on all matters proposed, deliberated or decided and a record of any votes taken. The minutes must record all motions, identify the board members making the motion and the second, and show the result of the voting.

On matters requiring a roll call vote, the yeas and nays must be recorded.

5 ILCS 120/2.06
105 ILCS 5/10-7
105 ILCS 5/10-14
Davis-El v. O'Leary, 626 F.Supp. 1037 (N.D. Ill. 1986)

6:305   Must a public body give official approval to the minutes of its meetings?

No law specifically requires a public body to approve the minutes of its meetings. For all practical purposes, minutes are official as soon as the secretary types them into a readable form. In fact, the secretary's handwritten notes or tape recordings may be considered official for some purposes if that is all that is available, or if a court orders an investigation of what actually happened at a meeting.

However, Illinois law recognizes that the approval process

gives the public body an opportunity to correct any errors that the secretary might have made in recording what happened at the meeting. The Open Meetings Act provides "the minutes of meetings open to the public shall be available for public inspection within seven days of the approval of such minutes by the public body."

The School Code requires that a school district maintain a mailing list of persons requesting to be included thereon and mail them certain documents, including, "within 10 days of each board meeting, a copy of the approved meeting minutes."

   5 ILCS 120/2.06(b)
   105 ILCS 5/10-21.6

6:307   Must the minutes be read aloud at a public meeting before the public body approves them?

No. An acceptable and more common practice is to provide each member of the public body with a copy of the minutes for review and to adopt a motion to "approve the minutes as written and distributed."

6:310   May a school board amend its minutes after official approval?

A school board may amend its minutes or other official record after approval in order to make the minutes or record conform to the facts. This may be done at any time by formal board action.

However, alteration of the minutes will not suffice to change the outcome of a vote or otherwise reverse or alter a previous act. Rather, a legally sufficient vote of the school board reversing the previous act or vote is required.

   Menssen v. Eureka Unit School District 140, 70 Ill.App.3d 9, 388 N.E.2d 273, 26 Ill.Dec. 649 (1979)

6:315   Must a public body make the minutes of its public meetings available for public inspection and copying?

Yes. The Open Meetings Act provides "the minutes of meetings open to the public shall be available for public inspection within seven days of the approval of such minutes by the public body."

The School Code requires a school district to maintain a mailing list of persons requesting to be included thereon and mail them certain documents, including, "within 10 days of each board meeting, a copy of the approved meeting minutes." A subscription fee approximating actual costs may be charged.

The Freedom of Information Act provides that public records, including the minutes of public meetings, must be made available to the public for copying as well as inspection.

5 ILCS 120/2.06(b)
5 ILCS 140/3(a)
105 ILCS 5/10-21.6

6:320   Must a school board keep minutes of its closed sessions?

A school board must keep minutes of each closed session. Closed session minutes may be kept confidential, but the board must review the entire body of its closed session minutes at least every six months to determine if there is a continuing need for confidentiality as to all or any part of those minutes.

5 ILCS 120/2.06
105 ILCS 5/10-7

6:330   Can a board of education be required to release the minutes of a closed session?

Courts have authority to examine closed session minutes in camera (privately) in deciding litigable issues. Courts also have authority to require school board members to testify about what occurred in closed session, and may order the release to the public of closed session minutes.

5 ILCS 120/3(b) et seq.
5 ILCS 140/11(d), (f)
Bobkoski v. Board of Education of Cary Consolidated School District 26, 141 F.R.D. 88 (N.D. Ill. 1992)
Illinois Educational Labor Relations Board v. Homer Community Consolidated School District No. 208, 160 Ill.App.3d 730, 514 N.E.2d 465, 112 Ill.Dec. 802, aff'd. 132 Ill.2d 29, 547 N.E.2d 182, 138 Ill.Dec. 213 (1989)

7: SCHOOL DISTRICT RECORDS

APPLICABLE STATUTES

7:10 Which statutes govern access to school district records?

School district records which were prepared or received prior to July 1, 1984, are governed by the Local Records Act; reports and records prepared or received on or after July 1, 1984, are governed by the Freedom of Information Act.

Student records are regulated by the Illinois Student Records Act and the federal Family Educational Rights and Privacy Act.

The records of school employees are regulated by the state Personnel Records Review Act.

20 U.S.C. 1232g
5 ILCS 140/1 et seq.
50 ILCS 205/15
105 ILCS 10/1 et seq.
820 ILCS 40/2 et seq.
Spinelli v. Immanuel Evangelical Lutheran Congregation, Inc., 144 Ill.App.3d 325, 494 N.E.2d 196, 98 Ill.Dec. 269 (2nd Dist. 1986), aff'd. in part, rev. in part 118 Ill.2d 389, 515 N.E.2d 1222, 113 Ill.Dec. 915

7:20 Which school district records covered by the Local Records Act are available for public access and inspection?

The Local Records Act requires the maintenance of certain school district financial records and allows public access and inspection of those records. The Local Records Act applies to records prepared or received by a school district before July 1, 1984.

50 ILCS 205/3a

7:30 For how long must a school board keep state aid records?

A school board must keep records to substantiate its state aid claims for at least three years.

105 ILCS 5/10-20.1

PERSONNEL RECORDS

7:40   Do school district employees have a right to inspect their school district personnel records?

School employees may have the right to access their personnel records if a collective bargaining agreement so provides or pursuant to the Illinois Personnel Records Review Act. The Act applies to school districts having five or more employees. Under the Act, an employee may inspect most personnel documents dated July 1, 1984 or later which have been or are intended to be used for employment, promotion, transfer, additional compensation, discharge, or discipline.

820 ILCS 40/0.01 et seq.
Spinelli v. Immanuel Evangelical Lutheran Congregation, Inc., 144 Ill.App.3d 325, 494 N.E.2d 196, 98 Ill.Dec. 269 (2nd Dist. 1986), aff'd. in part, rev. in part 118 Ill.2d 389, 515 N.E.2d 1222, 113 Ill.Dec. 915

7:50   What procedures govern the inspection of personnel records?

The procedures governing the inspection of employee records may be covered in a local employee collective bargaining agreement. Rules regarding inspection of personnel records are subject to bargaining when a recognized bargaining unit is involved.

In other cases, the procedures which may be used are contained in the Personnel Records Review Act.

820 ILCS 40/0.01 et seq.

7:60   What parts of an employee's personnel record may a school board withhold from inspection?

Provided an applicable collective bargaining agreement does not provide to the contrary, a school board may withhold from inspection and copying:

1) letters of reference;

2) any portion of a test document, except that the employee may see a cumulative total test score for either a section or the entire test document;

3) materials which are used by the school board for management planning including, but not limited to, judgments, external peer review, documents, or recommendations concerning future salary increases and other wage treatments, school board bonus plans, promotion and job assignments, or other comments or ratings used for a school board's planning purposes;

4) information of a personal nature about a person other than the employee if disclosure of the information would constitute a "clearly unwarranted invasion of the other person's privacy;"

5) any records relevant to any pending claim between the school board and the employee which might be discovered in a legal proceeding;

6) investigatory or security records maintained by the school board to investigate criminal conduct by an employee or other activity by the employee which could reasonably be expected to harm school property, operations, or business, or could by the employee's activity cause the school board financial liability unless and until the school board takes adverse personnel action based on information in that record.

820 ILCS 40/7
820 ILCS 40/10

7:70   May an employee copy the contents of his personnel file?

An employee may obtain copies of non-confidential information contained in his personnel file. A school board may charge a copying fee not to exceed the cost of duplication.

820 ILCS 40/3

7:80   Are employee personnel records subject to public access and inspection?

Employee personnel records are exempt from the requirements of laws granting public access to and inspection of school district records. The exemption is permissive, however, and may be waived by the employee.

5 ILCS 140/7

7:90 May a school board make employee disciplinary records public over the employee's objections?

A school board may not divulge a disciplinary report, letter of reprimand, or other disciplinary action to a third party other than the employee's labor organization or the employee's representative unless advance written notice is provided to the employee by first class mail to the employee's last known address.

However, advance written notice to the employee is not required under any of these conditions:

1) the employee has specifically waived the requirement of written notice as part of a written and signed employment application,

2) the disclosure is ordered in a legal proceeding or arbitration;

3) the information is requested by a government agency as a result of a claim by an employee or in connection with a criminal investigation by a governmental agency.

820 ILCS 40/7(1)

7:100 Are school boards restricted in what information may be collected and inserted in employee personnel records?

An employer may not gather or keep records of employee associations, political activities, publications, communications, or nonemployment activities unless the employee submits the information in writing or authorizes the employer in writing to keep or gather the information.

These prohibitions do not apply to activities which occur on the employer's premises or during working hours which interfere with the performance of the employee's duties or the duties of other employees or activities, regardless of when and where occurring, which constitute criminal conduct or may reasonably be expected to harm the employer's property, operations, or business, or could, by the employee's action, cause the employer financial liability.

The employer must purge from an employee's file records relating to a Department of Children and Family Services investigation which results in an unfounded report.

820 ILCS 40/9
820 ILCS 40/13

7:120   What is meant by the prohibition against keeping records as to employee associations?

A school board is prohibited from keeping records of employee activities or associations when these activities or associations are not related to the employee's job. The prohibition is intended to prevent the accumulation and retention of information as to non-job related employee politics, religion, affiliation and belief.

820 ILCS 40/9

7:130   Under what circumstances must a school board delete disciplinary information from an employee personnel file?

Disciplinary reports, letters of reprimand, or other disciplinary records which are more than four years old must be deleted from a personnel file when the contents of the personnel file are provided to third parties except in conjunction with a legal proceeding or arbitration.

820 ILCS 40/8

7:140   May an employee remove material from his personnel file?

Except in the case of Department of Children and Family Service investigations which have been returned unfounded, an employee does not have a statutory right to remove material from his employer-maintained personnel file.

820 ILCS 40/6
820 ILCS 40/13

7:150   What are the employee's rights if the employee disagrees with information contained in his personnel file?

In the event an employee disagrees with some portion of the contents of his personnel file, the employee may submit a written statement and the employer is required to attach the statement to the disputed portion of the file.

820 ILCS 40/6

STUDENT RECORDS

7:160   What is the purpose of the Student Records Act?

The purpose of the Student Records Act is to establish a degree of privacy and confidentiality with regard to student records. It gives parents and students limited access to student records, the right to inspect and copy the contents of the records, and the right to challenge material contained in them. The Act restricts who may have access to student records and what may be disclosed from them.

105 ILCS 10/1 et seq.

7:170   What are student records within the meaning of the Student Records Act?

A student record is any writing or other recorded information created on or after January 1, 1975 concerning a student and by which a student may be individually identified, maintained by a school or at its direction or by an employee of a school, regardless of how or where the information is stored. The Student Records Act applies to the records of current students and students previously enrolled.

Records maintained by a school employee for his personal use are not covered by the Act if those records are destroyed no later than the student's graduation or permanent withdrawal from school.

105 ILCS 10/1 et seq.
Sieck v. Oak Park-River Forest High School District No. 200, 807 F.Supp. 73 (N.D.Ill. 1992)

7:172   Are the records of a police officer who works at school student records?

Student records do not include information maintained by law enforcement professionals working in the school.

105 ILCS 10/2(d)

7:180   What is a student records custodian?

Each public school must designate an official records custodian who is responsible for the maintenance, care, and security of all student records regardless of whether or not the records are in his personal custody or control. The custodian must take all reasonable measures to prevent unauthorized access to, or dissemination of, student records. School boards must take reasonable measures to assure persons affected by the Student Records Act are informed of their rights and obligations.

105 ILCS 10/3 et seq.
Human Rights Authority of the State of Illinois Guardianship and Advocacy Commission by Aune v. Miller, 124 Ill.App.3d 701, 464 N.E.2d 833, 79 Ill.Dec. 929 (3rd Dist. 1984)

7:190   Does federal law govern student records?

The federal Family Educational Rights and Privacy Act regulates student records. Its provisions are similar to those of the Illinois Student Records Act.

20 U.S.C. 1232

7:200   Who has the right to access, inspect and copy student records?

Parents and any person designated a representative by a parent have rights of access, inspection, and copying with regard to both permanent and temporary student records. Students have a right to access, inspect, and copy their permanent records and may be permitted access to their temporary records. The following categories of persons are also permitted access:

1) employees or officials of the school district or the State Board of Education who have a current educational or administrative interest in the student;

2) the records custodian of another school in which the student has enrolled or will enroll;

3) any person for research, statistical reporting or planning purposes, provided no student or parent can be identified from the records;

4) persons designated by court order;

5) persons required by state or federal law;

6) in connection with an emergency to appropriate persons if the knowledge of such information is necessary to protect the health or safety of the student or other persons; or

7) a governmental agency or social service agency contracted by a governmental agency in furtherance of an investigation

of a student's school attendance pursuant to the compulsory student attendance laws provided that the records are released to the employee or agent designated by the agency.

105 ILCS 10/5 et seq.
23 Ill. Admin. Code 375.20

7:204   May law enforcement officers or the state's attorney gain access to student records without a court order?

The relevant statutes are unclear as to the answer to this question. It was probably the legislative intent of a 1998 amendment to the Student Records Act that law enforcement officers and officers of the court have access to permanent and temporary student records without a court order. However, the express language of sections 5 and 6 of the Act prevent the disclosure of temporary records without a court order.

105 ILCS 10/4 (f)
105 ILCS 10/6(a)(6.5)

7:206   May school officials disclose student records in response to a subpoena?

It is common for school officials to receive requests for student records in connection with civil suits and in custody disputes. Student records cannot be disclosed (even in response to a subpoena) by school officials except under circumstances authorized by the Student Records Act. Usually, disclosure requires either a consent from one parent or the adult student, or if consent cannot be obtained, a court order.

105 ILCS 10/6

7:210   When do parental rights to access student records end?

All rights and privileges held by the parent with respect to accessing student records become exclusively those of the student on the student's eighteenth birthday, when the student is legally emancipated, upon graduation from high school, marriage, or entry into military service.

105 ILCS 10/2(g)

**7:220   When a parent, representative or student
           requests to inspect and copy student records,
           how promptly must the records be produced?**

Access must be granted within a reasonable time, but in no
case later than 15 school days after the date of receipt of the
request by the official records custodian.

105 ILCS 10/5(c)

**7:230   What student records may be withheld from
           parental or student access?**

A parent or student may be denied access to confidential letters and statements of recommendation furnished in connection
with applications for employment or admission to a post-sec-
ondary educational institution, or the receipt of an honor or honorary recognition, provided that the letters and statements are
not used for purposes other than those for which they were
specifically intended and were either:

      1) placed in a school student record prior to January 1, 1975;
or

      2) the student waives access after being advised of the right
to obtain the names of persons making the confidential recommendations.

Communications otherwise protected by law as privileged or
confidential, including but not limited to information communicated in confidence to a physician, psychologist, or other psy-
cho-therapist, or information which is communicated by a student or parent in confidence to school personnel may also be
withheld.

105 ILCS 10/5(e)
John K v. Board of Education for School District No. 65, Cook County, 152
Ill.App.3d 543, 504 N.E.2d 797, 105 Ill.Dec. 512 (1st Dist. 1987) app. den. 115
Ill.2d 542, 511 N.E.2d 429, 110 Ill.Dec. 457 (1987)

**7:240   May a student's school records or report card be
           withheld from the student or parent as a
           disciplinary measure?**

No.

105 ILCS 10/8

7:250 What must be contained in a parent and student notification of student records rights?

School districts must notify students and parents of their rights to inspection and copying under the Student Records Act. The notification must contain the following information:

1) the types of information contained in the permanent and temporary records of students;

2) the right to inspect and copy permanent and temporary records;

3) the cost of copying such records;

4) the right to control access and release of student records;

5) the right to request a copy of information released;

6) the rights and procedures for challenging the contents of student records;

7) the persons, agencies, or organizations having access to student records without parental consent;

8) the right to copy student records or information contained in a student record which is proposed to be destroyed or deleted and the school's schedule for reviewing and destroying such information;

9) the categories of information the school has designated as "directory information" and the right of parents to prohibit the release of such information;

10) a statement informing the parents that no person may condition the granting or withholding of any right, privilege, or benefits or make as a condition of employment, credit, or insurance the securing by any individual of information from a student's temporary record which such individual may obtain through the exercise of any right secured under the Act or these regulations;

11) the right of parents to inspect and challenge the information contained in a student record forwarded to another school district; and

12) the student record policies of the school district which are not included in the Act.

105 ILCS 10/3
23 Ill. Admin. Code 375.30

7:260   What are student permanent records?

Student permanent record means the "minimum personal information necessary to a school in the education of the student and contained in a school student record." A permanent record must include the student's name, birth date, address, grades and grade level, parents' names and addresses, attendance records, gender, place of birth, class rank, graduation date, scores on college entrance examinations, accident reports, health records, and the records pertaining to any release of permanent record information.

Honors and awards received, information about participation in school-sponsored activities or athletics, or offices held in school-sponsored organizations may be included in the student's permanent record. No other information may be included in a student's permanent record.

105 ILCS 10/2(e)
23 Ill. Admin. Code 375.10

7:270   What are student temporary records?

Student temporary record means all information contained in a school student record but not contained in the student permanent record. A temporary record may include family background information; intelligence test scores; aptitude test scores; reports of psychological evaluations including information on intelligence, personality and academic information obtained through test administration, observation or interview; elementary and secondary achievement level test results; participation in extra curricular activities including any offices held in school sponsored activities; honors and awards received; teacher anecdotal records; disciplinary information; special education files including the report of the multi-disciplinary staffing on which placement was based and all records relating to special education placement, hearings and appeals; and other information of clear relevance to the education of the student.

A student's temporary record must include information regarding serious disciplinary infractions that resulted in expulsion, suspension or "the imposition of punishment or sanction." Serious disciplinary infraction for purposes of this section means infractions involving drugs, weapons or bodily harm to another.

105 ILCS 10/2(f)
105 ILCS 10/4 (c), (d)
23 Ill. Admin. Code 375.10
John K v. Board of Education for School District No. 65, Cook County, 152
Ill.App.3d 543, 504 N.E.2d 797, 105 Ill.Dec. 512 (1st Dist. 1987) app. den. 115
Ill.2d 542, 511 N.E.2d 429, 110 Ill.Dec. 457 (1987)

7:280 For how long must a school preserve a student's permanent record?

A student's permanent record must be maintained by a
school for a minimum of 60 years after the student has transferred, graduated or otherwise permanently withdrawn from
school.

105 ILCS 10/4(e)

7:290 For what period may a school retain a student's temporary record?

A student's temporary record must be maintained for not
less than five years after the student has transferred, graduated or otherwise withdrawn from school.

105 ILCS 10/4(f)

7:300 What directory information contained in student records may be made public by a school district?

A school district may publish directory information such as
student names; addresses; gender; grade level; birth date; birth-
place; parents' names and addresses; academic awards; degrees
and honors; information related to school-sponsored activities,
organizations, and athletics; major field of study; period of
attendance in school; and other identifying information and similar publications so long as such publications comply with the
regulations of the State Board of Education.

This information may be released to the general public,
unless a parent requests that the information not be released.
Each school is required to provide notice of which information it
considers to be directory. Non-directory information may not be
disclosed without prior written consent of the parent or student.

105 ILCS 10/6(e)
23 Ill. Admin. Code 375.80

7:310   What notice must be given to parents before a school releases student records to another school district?

No information from student records may be released to another school unless otherwise permitted by the Student Records Act or unless the parents receive prior written notice of the nature and substance of the information proposed to be released. Also, prior to the release of school records, the parents must be given an opportunity to inspect and copy the records and challenge their contents.

105 ILCS 10/5(b)
23 Ill. Admin. Code 375.70

7:320   Does the Illinois Freedom of Information Act provide public access to student records?

The Freedom of Information Act provides that information prohibited from disclosure by state or federal law is exempt from access under the Act. Therefore, access to student records is not possible under the Act.

5 ILCS 140/7
105 ILCS 10/6
Bowie v. Evanston Community Consolidated School District No. 65, 165 Ill.App.3d 101, 522 N.E.2d 669, 119 Ill.Dec. 7 (1st Dist. 1988) app. allowed 122 Ill.2d 570, 530 N.E.2d 239, 125 Ill.Dec. 211, aff'd. 128 Ill.2d 373, 538 N.E.2d 557, 131 Ill.Dec. 182 (1989)

7:330   Must a school maintain a record of the information which is released from a student record?

A record of any information released from a student record must be made and kept as a part of the student record. The record of release must be maintained for the life of the student record and is available only to the parent, student, and the official records custodian. Each record of release must include:

1) the nature and substance of the information released;

2) the name and signature of the official records custodian releasing the information;

3) the name of the person requesting the information, the capacity in which the request has been made, and the purpose of the request;

4) the date of the release; and

5) a copy of consent to the release.

Except for parents and students, no person to whom information is released, and no person designated a representative by a parent, may permit any other person to have access to information without a prior consent of the parent.

105 ILCS 10/6(c), (d)

7:340 May a school district restrict parental access to student psychological reports or do parents have a right to review raw material?

Parents may review any material contained in student records, including material upon which further conclusions are drawn and any raw psychological data. The school or the parent may elect to have present at the time of review a qualified professional to assist in the interpretation of raw data.

105 ILCS 10/5(a), (b)

John K v. Board of Education for School District No. 65, Cook County, 152 Ill.App.3d 543, 504 N.E.2d 797, 105 Ill.Dec. 512 (1st Dist. 1987) app. den. 115 Ill.2d 542, 511 N.E.2d 429, 110 Ill.Dec. 457 (1987)

7:350 May parents challenge the contents of a student's records?

Parents may challenge the accuracy, relevance, or propriety of any entry in a student record except:

1) academic grades;

2) references to expulsions or out of school suspensions if the challenge is made at the time the student's records are forwarded to another school to which the student is transferring. There are hearing procedures by which disputed information may be removed from a student record as a result of parental challenge.

Parents may insert in their child's school student record a statement of reasonable length setting forth their position on any disputed information contained in the record. The school must include a copy of this statement in any subsequent dissemination of the information in dispute.

105 ILCS 10/7
23 Ill. Admin. Code 375.90

7:360   What are the hearing procedures for student record challenges?

Each school board must establish administrative procedures for parents to challenge the content of student records. The procedural aspects of the policy must include at minimum:

1) A method by which a challenge may be initiated by a request for hearing. The request must be submitted in writing to the school record custodian and must contain notice of the specific entry or entries to be challenged and the basis of the challenge.

2) Upon receipt of a challenge, an initial informal conference must be held within 15 days. If the conference does not resolve the challenge, the following procedures are utilized.

3) A hearing officer must be appointed by the school. The hearing officer may not be an employee assigned to the attendance center where the student is enrolled.

4) A formal hearing must be conducted within 15 days after the informal conference, unless the parties mutually agree to an extension. A verbatim record of the hearing must be kept. The conduct of the hearing must include the right to present evidence and to call witnesses, the right to cross-examine witnesses, the right to counsel, and the right to a written statement of decision and the reasons therefor.

5) The decision of the hearing officer must be rendered no later than 10 school days after the conclusion of the hearing. A copy of the decision must be transmitted to the parents or student and the school. Any decision must be based solely upon the information presented at the hearing. The hearing officer may require the challenged contents in the school record be maintained, removed, changed, clarified, or added to.

6) The results of the hearing may be appealed to the appropriate regional superintendent of schools within 20 days after the decision is transmitted. If a parent appeals, the school must be notified by the parent within 10 school days of the appeal, and the school must forward all documents regarding the hearing to the regional superintendent.

7) The regional superintendent must render a decision within 20 school days of receipt of the hearing record.

8) Either party may appeal the decision of the regional superintendent to the circuit court of the county in which the school is located.

105 ILCS 10/7
23 Ill. Admin. Code 375.90

7:370   What are a school board's duties with respect to maintenance of the records of students not enrolled in school on or after the enactment of the Student Records Act (March 24, 1976)?

Schools are not required to separate permanent and temporary records, or to destroy records according to any statutorily established schedule for students not enrolled in school on or after the effective date of the Student Records Act (March 24, 1976).

However, the parents of a student not enrolled in school on or after March 24, 1976, may request a school board to comply with the Student Records Act with respect to their child's records, and the school board must honor this request.

105 ILCS 10/4(i)

7:380   How often must a school district review the contents of student records?

Each school district is required to review student records periodically as necessary, but not less than once every four years or upon a student's change in attendance center, whichever occurs first.

The purpose of review is to verify entries and eliminate or correct out-of-date, misleading, inaccurate, unnecessary, or irrelevant information.

105 ILCS 10/4(g)
23 Ill. Admin. Code 375.40 (b)

7:390   What is the penalty for violation of the Student Records Act?

Any person who is aggrieved by any violation of the Student Records Act may seek injunctive relief. Any person who is injured by a willful or negligent violation of the Act may sue for damages. Costs and attorneys fees are available to a successful plaintiff in either cause.

The State Board of Education or designated state's attorneys also may seek injunctive relief to secure compliance with the Act.

Willful failure to comply with any provision of the Act is a petty offense, except that willful or malicious falsification of student records is a Class A misdemeanor.

Absent proof of malice, no cause of action or claim for relief, civil or criminal, is possible against any school, employee, or official of a school, or person acting at the direction of a school for any statement made or judgment expressed in any entry to a school student record of a type which does not violate the Act or the regulations issued by the State Board of Education.

105 ILCS 10/9

John K v. Board of Education for School District No. 65, Cook County, 152 Ill.App.3d 543, 504 N.E.2d 797, 105 Ill.Dec. 512 (1st Dist. 1987) app. den. 115 Ill.2d 542, 511 N.E.2d 429, 110 Ill.Dec. 457 (1987)

FREEDOM OF INFORMATION ACT

7:400   What are records within the meaning of the Freedom of Information Act?

The Freedom of Information Act defines public records broadly. It includes all records, reports, forms, writings, letters, memoranda, books, papers, maps, photographs, microfilms, cards, tapes, recordings, electronic data processing records, recorded information and all other documentary materials regardless of physical form or characteristics. It includes, but is not limited to:

1) administrative manuals, procedural rules, and instructions to staff, except those covered by a statutory exemption;

2) final opinions and orders made in the adjudication of cases, except adjudication of student or employee grievance or disciplinary cases;

3) substantive rules;

4) statements and interpretations of policy which have been adopted;

5) final planning policies, recommendations, and decisions;

6) factual reports, inspection reports, and studies;

7) all information in any account, voucher, or contract dealing with the receipt or expenditure of public or other funds;

8) the names, salaries, titles, and dates of employment of all employees and officers;

9) materials containing opinions concerning the rights of the state, the public, a subdivision of state or a local government, or of any private persons;

10) the name of every official and final records of voting in all proceedings of the school board;

11) applications for any contract, permit, grant, or agreement, except where covered by a statutory exemption;

12) each report, document, study, or publication prepared by independent consultants or other independent contractors for the school board;

13) all other information required by law to be made available for public inspection or copying; and

14) information relating to any grant or contract made by or between the school board and another public body or private organization.

5 ILCS 140/2(c)
Kenyon v. Garrels, 184 Ill.App.3d 28, 540 N.E.2d 11, 132 Ill.Dec. 595 (4th Dist. 1989)

7:410 Who has the right to inspect and copy school board records under the Freedom of Information Act?

Any person may access, inspect, or copy school board public records. A person is any "individual, corporation, partnership, firm, organization, or association, acting individually or as a group."

5 ILCS 140/2(b)

7:415   May a member of the public request public records from a school board member?

The Freedom of Information Act requires the disclosure of the records of public bodies, not the records of individual members. School board records, including information pertaining to an individual board member, must be obtained by filing a request with the school district, not with the individual member.

5 ILCS 140/3(a)

Quinn v. Stone, 211 Ill.App.3d 809, 570 N.E.2d 676, 156 Ill.Dec. 200 (1st Dist. 1991) app. den. 141 Ill.2d 559, 580 N.E.2d 133, 162 Ill.Dec. 507 (1991)

7:420   May a school board limit public access to school board records to residents of the school district?

No. Access to public records may not be limited based on residency or any other criterion.

5 ILCS 140/2

7:430   What must be contained in Freedom of Information Act notice to the public?

A school board must prominently display at each of its administrative or regional offices, make available for inspection and copying, and send through the mail if requested to do so, the following:

1) A brief description of the school district, including but not be limited to, a short summary of its purpose, a block diagram giving its functional subdivisions, the total amount of its operating budget, the number and location of all of its separate offices, the approximate number of full and part-time employees, and the identification and membership of any board, commission, committee, or council which operates in an advisory capacity relative to the operation of the school board, or which exercises control over its policies or procedures, or to which it is required to report; and

2) A brief description of the methods whereby the public may request information and public records, a directory designating by titles and addresses those employees to whom requests for public records should be directed, and any fees allowable under the Act.

5 ILCS 140/4

7:435 Must a school board maintain a list of records it maintains?

A school board must maintain and make available for inspection and copying a reasonably current list of all types or categories of records under its control which were prepared or received after July 1, 1984. The list must be reasonably detailed in order to aid persons in obtaining access to the public records. A school board must also furnish upon request a description of the manner in which public records stored by means of electronic data processing may be obtained in a form comprehensible to persons lacking knowledge of computer language or printout format.

5 ILCS 140/5

7:440 May a school board adopt rules regulating the time and place at which citizens may have access to public records?

A school board may promulgate rules regulating the times and places where publicly accessible records will be made available, the person from whom the records may be obtained, and rules or regulations pertaining to both the availability of district records and the procedures to access the records.

5 ILCS 140/3(g)

7:450 What records are exempt from public access and inspection under the Freedom of Information Act?

The Freedom of Information Act exempts numerous records from public access and copying. Some of the most common categories of records which are exempt are:

1) All records if compliance with the request would be unduly burdensome, the request cannot be narrowed, and the burden on the school board to comply would outweigh the public interest in the information requested.

2) Records which are in immediate use by persons exercising official duties which require the use of the records.

3) Information prohibited from disclosure by federal or state law or by rules or regulations adopted pursuant thereto.

4) Information which, if disclosed, would constitute a clearly unwarranted invasion of personal privacy, unless such disclosure is consented to in writing by the individual subjects of the information. The disclosure of information that bears on the public duties of public employees and officials shall not be considered an invasion of personal privacy. Material exempted under this section includes:

a) files and personal information maintained with respect to clients, patients, residents, students or other individuals receiving social, medical, educational, vocational, financial, supervisory or custodial care or services directly or indirectly from federal agencies or school boards;

b) personnel files and personal information maintained with respect to employees, appointees or elected officials of a school board or applicants for such positions;

c) files and personal information maintained with respect to any applicant, registrant or licensee by any public body cooperating with or engaged in professional or occupational registration, licensure or discipline;

d) information required of any taxpayer in connection with the assessment or collection of any tax unless disclosure is otherwise required by state statute; and

e) information revealing the identity of persons who file complaints with or provide information to administrative, investigative, law enforcement or penal agencies.

5) Preliminary drafts, notes, recommendations, memoranda and other records in which opinions are expressed, or policies or actions are formulated, except that a specific record or relevant portion thereof shall not be exempt when the record is publicly cited and identified by the president of the school board.

6) Minutes of closed sessions of school board meetings which are closed to the public as provided in the Open Meetings Act, until such time as the board makes such minutes available to the public.

7) Test questions, scoring keys and other examination data used to administer an academic examination or determine the qualifications of an applicant for a license or employment.

8) Library circulation and order records identifying library users with specific materials.

9) Information received by a primary or secondary school, college or university under its procedures for the evaluation of

faculty members by their academic peers.

10) Information concerning any school board's adjudication of student or employee grievances or disciplinary cases, except for the final outcome of such cases.

11) Course materials or research materials used by faculty members.

12) Investigatory records compiled for state or local administrative law enforcement purposes or for internal matters of a school board under certain conditions.

13) Proposals and bids for any contract, grant, or agreement, including information which, if it were disclosed, would frustrate procurement or give an advantage to any person pro posing to enter into a contract or agreement with the board, until an award or final selection is made and information prepared by or for the board in preparation of a bid solicitation until an award or final selection is made.

14) Valuable formulae, designs, drawings and research data obtained or produced by any school board when disclosure could reasonably be expected to produce private gain or public loss.

15) Architects' and engineers' plans for buildings.

16) Communications between the school board and an attorney or auditor representing the board that would not be subject to discovery in litigation, and materials prepared or compiled by or for a board in anticipation of a criminal, civil, or administra tive proceeding upon the request of any attorney advising the board, and materials prepared or compiled with respect to internal audits of school boards.

17) Administrative or technical information associated with automated data processing operations, including, but not limited to, software, operating protocols, computer program abstracts, file layouts, source listings, object modules, load modules, user guides, documentation pertaining to all logical physical design of computerized systems, employee manuals, and any other information that, if disclosed, would jeopardize the security of the system or data contained therein or the security of materials exempt under the Act.

18) Documents or materials relating to collective negotiat-

ing matters between school boards and their employees or representatives, except that any final contract or agreement is subject to inspection and copying.

19) Drafts, notes, recommendations, and memoranda pertaining to the financing and marketing transactions of the board and the records of ownership, registration, transfer, and exchange of municipal debt obligations, and of persons to whom payment with respect to such obligations is made.

20) The records, documents, and information relating to real estate purchase negotiations until those negotiations have been completed or otherwise terminated; with regard to a parcel involved in a pending or actually and reasonably contemplated eminent domain proceeding under Article VII of the Code of Civil Procedure, records, documents, and information relating to that parcel shall be exempt, except as may be allowed under discovery rules adopted by the Illinois Supreme Court; the records, documents, and information relating to a real estate sale shall be exempt until a sale is consummated.

21) Any and all proprietary information and records related to the operation of an intergovernmental risk management association or self-insurance pool or jointly self-administered health and accident cooperative or pool.

22) Information related solely to the internal personnel rules and practices of a school board.

23) Information which is prohibited from disclosure under the State Gift Ban Act.

There are numerous other categories of information which are exempted from disclosure under the Act.

5 ILCS 140/1
5 ILCS 140/3(f)
5 ILCS 140/7
50 ILCS 205/3a
105 ILCS 10/1 et seq.
Illinois Educational Labor Relations Board v. Homer Community Consolidated School District No. 208, 160 Ill.App.3d 730, 514 N.E.2d 465, 112 Ill.Dec. 802, aff'd. 132 Ill.2d 29, 547 N.E.2d 182, 138 Ill.Dec. 213 (1989)
Bowie v. Evanston Community Consolidated School District No. 65, 165 Ill.App.3d 101, 522 N.E.2d 669, 119 Ill.Dec. 7 (1st Dist. 1988) app. allowed 122 Ill.2d 570, 530 N.E.2d 239, 125 Ill.Dec. 211, aff'd. 128 Ill.2d 373, 538 N.E.2d 557, 131 Ill.Dec. 182 (1989)

7:460 What is disclosed if a requested record includes both exempt material and records which may be disclosed?

When any public record that is exempt from disclosure under the Freedom of Information Act contains any material that is not exempt, the school board must separate the exempt material from the non-exempt material and make the non-exempt available for inspection and copying.

5 ILCS 140/8
Hamer v. Lentz, 132 Ill.2d 49, 547 N.E.2d 191, 138 Ill.Dec. 222 (1989)

7:470 Must a school board comply with a request to make public the names and salaries of its employees?

The names and salaries of school board employees are public record and available for public inspection.

5 ILCS 140/2(c)
People ex rel. Recktenwald v. Janura, 59 Ill.App.3d 143, 376 N.E.2d 22, 17 Ill.Dec. 129 (1st Dist. 1978)
Stein v. Howlett, 52 Ill.2d 570, 289 N.E.2d 409 (1972)

7:480 How quickly must a school board respond to a Freedom of Information Act request?

A school board must either comply with the request or deny the request for public records within seven working days after the request has been received. A request may be either fully or partially fulfilled or denied.

If a school board fails to respond to a written request within seven working days after it is received, the request is deemed denied.

5 ILCS 140/3(c)

7:490 May a school board extend the time to respond to a Freedom of Information Act request beyond seven days?

A school board may extend the time limit to respond to a request to access or copy school records for not more than an additional seven working days for any of the following reasons:

1) The requested records are stored in whole or in part at other locations than the office having charge of the requested records.

2) The request requires the collection of a substantial number of specified records.

3) The request is couched in categorical terms and requires an extensive search for the records responsive to it.

4) The requested records have not been located in the course of routine search and additional efforts are being made to locate them.

5) The requested records require examination and evaluation by personnel having the necessary competence and discretion to determine if they are exempt from disclosure or should be revealed only with appropriate deletions.

6) The request for records cannot be complied with by the school board within the time limits prescribed without unduly burdening or interfering with the operation of the school.

7) There is a need for consultation, which shall be conducted with all practicable speed, with another public body or among two or more components of a public body having a substantial interest in the determination or in the subject matter of the request.

When additional time is required for any of the above reasons, the school board must notify the person making the request by letter within the seven-day time limit fixed for responding to the request of the reasons for the delay and the date by which the records will be made available or that a denial will be forthcoming.

5 ILCS 140/2(d)

7:500 What appeal is available to the public following denial of a request to inspect and copy public records?

Any person denied access to inspect and copy any school district record may appeal the denial by sending a written notice of appeal to the school board president or superintendent of schools. Upon receipt of the appeal, the public record must be reviewed to determine whether the record is open to inspection and copying. The person who has requested the appeal must be notified of the determination within seven working days after the appeal has been received.

5 ILCS 140/2(e)
5 ILCS 140/10

7:510 What are the procedural requirements necessary to deny a request to inspect and copy records?

A school board may refuse a request to inspect and copy records when an exemption is provided in the law or when responding would be unduly burdensome. When a request is denied, the school board must notify the person making the request in writing of the decision to deny, the reasons for the denial, and the name and title or position of each person responsible for the denial.

The notice also must inform the person of his right to appeal to the president of the school board, and each notice of denial must inform the person of his right to seek judicial review in a circuit court of proper jurisdiction.

When a request for school district records is denied on the grounds the records are exempt under the Freedom of Information Act, the notice of denial from the school board must specify the exemption claimed.

Copies of each denial issued by a school board must be retained in a single, central office file which is open to the public. The file must be indexed according to the type of exemption and, to the extent feasible, according to the type of records which have been requested.

5 ILCS 140/9

7:520 Is any further appeal available to an individual denied access to public records following appeal to the school board president?

Any person who has been denied access to inspect or copy public records and who has exhausted administrative remedies may file suit in the circuit court of the county where the school district is located.

5 ILCS 140/11

**7:530   Does the Freedom of Information Act require a
            school board to create or maintain any specific
            records?**

The Act does not require a school board to create or maintain any record not otherwise required by law, rule or regulation, or maintained at the discretion of the school board.

5 ILCS 140/1

8: CHANGING SCHOOL DISTRICT BOUNDARIES AND TERRITORY

DISTRICT CONSOLIDATION

8:10 May two or more entire elementary districts or two or more entire high school districts combine to form a new district?

Yes. Any contiguous territory having an equalized assessed valuation of at least $5,000,000 and a population of not less than 1,500 and not more than 500,000 may be formed into a combined school district. A petition calling for the combination of districts must be filed by the school boards of each district affected or by 10 percent of the legal voters residing in each district affected. The petition must be filed with the regional superintendent of the region in which the greater portion of the equalized assessed valuation of the territory described in the petition is located.

The petition must be approved by the regional superintendent after a hearing on the petition and by the State Superintendent of Education and thereafter (only after approval has been obtained) the proposal placed on the ballot at an election in the affected territory. The proposed combination of districts must be approved by a majority of voters of each district who vote on the proposition in the election.

105 ILCS 5/7-1
105 ILCS 5/7-2
105 ILCS 5/7-4
105 ILCS 5/7-7.7
105 ILCS 5/11B-2 et seq.

8:15 What is a "committee of ten?"

A petition calling for the creation of a combined school district or unit school district must provide for a committee of ten petitioners to represent the interests of all petitioners. The committee is authorized, for example, to amend the petition within certain parameters.

A committee of ten also is called for in detachment and

annexation petitions.

105 ILCS 5/7-2b
105 ILCS 5/11A-3
105 ILCS 5/11B-3
105 ILCS 4/11D-2

8:20   May new community consolidated or community high school districts be formed?

All statutory references to the creation of community consolidated school districts were removed from the School Code by the General Assembly. It is possible for two or more contiguous unit school districts—or one or more unit school districts and one or more high school districts—all of which are contiguous, to dissolve and form a single new high school district and one or more new elementary districts. It is not possible under other circumstances to form a new high school district.

A single unit school district may not, for example, divide into high school and elementary districts. Almost all the existing community consolidated and township high school districts were formed before statutory restrictions were enacted limiting the formation of such districts.

105 ILCS 5/7A-1 et seq.
105 ILCS 5/10-21.5
105 ILCS 5/11D-1 et seq.
Board of Education of Hamilton County Community Unit School District No. 10, Hamilton County v. Regional Board of School Trustees of Jefferson and Hamilton Counties, 121 Ill.App.3d 848, 460 N.E.2d 100, 77 Ill.Dec. 241 (5th Dist. 1984)

8:30   What kind of school district may be newly created under current law?

Any type of school district except a community consolidated district may be newly created, although some types of school districts may be newly created only under very limited circumstances.

105 ILCS 5/7-1 et seq.
105 ILCS 5/7A-1 et seq.
105 ILCS 5/11A-1 et seq.
105 ILCS 5/11B-1 et seq.
105 ILCS 5/11D-1 et seq.

8:33 What is a unit school district?

A unit school district is one that offers education for all children in grades kindergarten through 12 who live within the territory of the district.

8:36 What is a dual district?

A dual district is an area served by two separate school districts, one an elementary district providing education through grade 8 and the second a high school district providing education from grades 9 through 12. Boundaries of the elementary district and high school district may be coterminous but often are not. One high school district may cover all or some of the same geographic area as two or more elementary districts. Or an elementary district may serve portions of the same area served by two or more high school districts.

8:40 How is a community unit district created?

Creation of a community unit school district begins with the filing of a petition with the regional superintendent of schools and concludes with approval of the voters and election of a new school board. The petition may be filed by the boards of education of each of the school districts wholly or partially included in the territory described in the petition, or the petition may be filed by a specified number of voters residing in the affected school districts. The petition must be approved by the regional superintendent and State Superintendent of Education.

At the election, the proposition must be approved by a majority of the votes cast in each of the affected school districts. (The proposition loses if it is defeated by a majority of the votes cast in any one of the affected school districts, even if it receives a majority of the votes in all of the districts combined.)

The School Code sets forth specific requirements for: (a) the territory to be included in the proposed unit district; (b) signatures required on the petition; (c) the filing of the petition; (d) hearing procedures; (e) the referendum on the proposal, and (f) the election of a new school board.

105 ILCS 5/11A-3

Adsit v. Sanders, 157 Ill.App.3d 416, 510 N.E.2d 547, 109 Ill.Dec. 679, app. dismissed 117 Ill.2d 541, 517 N.E.2d 1083, 115 Ill.Dec. 397 (4th Dist. 1987)

**8:45   What happens to the debt of the previously exist-
ing school districts when a new unit school district is formed?**

The petition to create the new unit may provide that the
entire territory of the new unit school district assumes the bonded indebtedness of the previously existing district(s). In all other
cases the debt remains with the geographical territory of the
entity which incurred the debt.

105 ILCS 5/11A-3
105 ILCS 5/11A-12(b)

**8:50   Who may vote in an election to organize a
community unit school district?**

Only those residents in the territory described in the petition for organizing a community unit school district may vote in
such an election. The proposition must be approved by a majority of the votes cast in each of the affected school districts, not
merely by a majority of the votes cast in the total combined territory.

105 ILCS 5/11A-8

**8:60   What assistance does the State Board of
Education provide to a school district
considering consolidation?**

The State Board of Education Department of School District
Organization assists school districts in studying school district
organizational problems. It provides consultation to school districts considering consolidation.

105 ILCS 5/2-3.35

**8:70   How does school district reorganization affect
state aid?**

The State provides financial incentives to encourage school
district consolidation. For fixed specified periods of time after a
consolidation, the State may provide additional supplementary
state aid to newly consolidated districts. The supplementary

state aid wholly or partially offsets the costs incurred by a district in acquiring another district's deficits and differences in financial structure and partially offsets the costs associated with merging the teacher salary schedules of combining school districts. The schedule of payments takes into account the size of the resulting school district and provides larger incentives to newly created districts with the highest student average daily attendance.

> 105 ILCS 5/18-8.2
> 105 ILCS 5/18-8.3
> 105 ILCS 5/18-8.5

BOUNDARY CHANGES

8:80   How may school district boundaries be changed?

School district boundaries may be changed by detachment, annexation, division, dissolution, or any combination thereof. The regional board(s) of school trustees is authorized to change the boundaries when petitioned under certain circumstances: (1) by the boards of each of the districts affected; (2) by a majority of the registered voters in each district affected by the boundary change; (3) by two-thirds of the registered voters in any territory proposed to be detached from one or more districts; (4) by two-thirds of the registered voters in each of one or more districts proposed to be annexed to another district, or (5) if there are no legal voters residing in the territory to be detached, by all of the real estate owners of record.

The regional board of trustees must detach and annex any elementary or high school district territory constituting no more than five percent of the detaching district's equalized assessed property value and five percent or less of the territory of the district when petitioned to do so by two-thirds of the registered voters of the detaching territory and where granting the petition makes the boundaries of the annexing district coterminous with its dual district counterpart (elementary or high school). No district may lose more than five percent of its equalized assessed value or more than five percent of its territory through this type of detachment and annexation.

> 105 ILCS 5/7-1
> 105 ILCS 5/7-2
> 105 ILCS 5/7-2b

8:90   May a school district be entirely dissolved?

Yes. Upon petition by a majority of the legal voters residing in the district proposed to be dissolved, or by a petition filed by the board of education of the school district seeking dissolution, the regional board of school trustees may dissolve a school district and annex its territory to another district or districts.

105 ILCS 5/7-2a

8:100   What is detachment and annexation?

Detachment is the removal of a portion of the territory of a school district. Annexation is the addition of territory to a school district. Detachment and annexation, therefore, is the removal of territory from one school district and the addition of it to the territory of another school district.

105 ILCS 5/7-1 et seq.

8:105   Do provisions for dissolution, detachment and annexation apply to all school districts in Illinois?

Yes. However, statutory procedures for detachment and annexation involving a special charter district differ somewhat from the procedures applicable for other districts. Procedures that apply to special charter districts are addressed beginning with question 8:300.

NON-CHARTER DISTRICT DETACHMENT AND ANNEXATION

8:110   May territory be detached and annexed to a school district if the resulting district is not compact and contiguous?

School district boundaries resulting from detachment and annexation must be compact and contiguous, although a school district may have "highly irregular" boundaries and still be compact and contiguous if children residing therein can reasonably avail themselves of school. In general, corridors are compact and contiguous; islands are not.

People on rel. of Community Unit School District No. 1, Macon County v. Decatur School District No. 61, 45 Ill.App.2d 33, 194 N.E.2d 659 (3rd Dist. 1963)

Streator Township High School District No. 40 v. County Board of School Trustees of Livingston County, 14 Ill.App.2d 251, 144 N.E.2d 531 (2nd Dist. 1957)

People ex rel. Warren v. Drummet, 415 Ill. 411, 114 N.E.2d 364 (1953)

People ex rel. McLain v. Gardner, 408 Ill. 228, 96 N.E.2d 551 (1951)

People v. Deatherage, 401 Ill. 25, 81 N.E.2d 581 (1948)

People ex rel. Bartlett v. Vass, 325 Ill. 64 (1927)

8:120 What is the effective date of change for the change of boundaries of a school district?

In case a petition is filed for the creation of or the change in boundaries of or for an election to vote on the proposition of creating any school district after August 1, and the change is granted or the election carries and no appeal is taken, the change is effective after the time for appeal has run for the purpose of all elections; however, the change does not affect the administration of the schools until July 1 following the date the petition is granted or upon which the election is held, and the school boards of the districts as they existed prior to the change exercise the same power and authority over their own territory until that date; however, the new districts can organize and elect officers within the time prescribed by the general election law.

In the event that the granting of a petition has become final, the change in boundaries becomes effective immediately. However, if the granting of the petition becomes final between September 1 and June 30 of any year, the administration of and attendance at the schools is not affected until the following July 1, when the change in boundaries becomes effective for all purposes. After the granting of a petition has become final, the date when the change is effective for purposes of administration and attendance may be accelerated or postponed by stipulation of each of the school boards of each district affected and approved by the regional board of school trustees.

105 ILCS 5/7-9

8:130 When do school board members' terms of office expire after the annexation of the school district from which they were elected?

Upon the close of the current school year during which any school district is annexed to another school district, the terms of office of the school board members of the annexed school district are terminated and the school board of the annexing district performs all of the duties and has all of the powers of the school board of the annexed district.

105 ILCS 5/7-12

8:140   What happens to the assets and liabilities of an annexed district?

The annexing district as it is constituted on and after the time of annexation usually receives all the assets and assumes all the obligations and liabilities, including the bonded indebtedness, of the original annexing district and of the district annexed. In certain dissolutions and under certain conditions in the case of a detachment-annexation, the bonded indebtedness does not become the obligation of the annexing district but remains the obligation of the taxable property that was situated within the boundaries of the dissolved district at the time of the issuance of each bond issue. The territory of the dissolved district does not assume the bonded indebtedness of the annexing district unless the school board of the dissolved district votes before dissolution to assume the debt.

When two or more school districts receive territory from a dissolved school district, the regional board of school trustees has authority to divide the assets and liabilities of the dissolved school district. As a practical matter, however, the division of assets and liabilities of the dissolved district is generally resolved by intergovernmental agreement between the annexing districts. The intergovernmental agreement is usually ratified by the regional board of school trustees.

105 ILCS 5/7-11
105 ILCS 5/7-12
105 ILCS 5/7-14
Board of Education of Community Unit School District No. 325, Peoria County v. Board of Education of Special Charter School District No. 150, Peoria County, 2 Ill.App.3d 643, 276 N.E.2d 732 (3rd Dist. 1971)

8:143   What method is used to determine an annexing district's share of bonded debt which accompanies territory detached from another district?

The amount of bonded debt accompanying annexed territory is prorated based on the equalized assessed valuation (EAV) of the annexed territory as a percentage of the total EAV of the original detaching district.

105 ILCS 5/7-14
105 ILCS 5/19-29

8:145   Are state financial incentives provided to offset the cost to an annexing district of absorbing non-certificated personnel?

No state incentives are provided to offset the costs of absorbing non-certificated personnel. The lack of incentives can be an important deterrent when there are large differences between the salaries and benefits paid to non-certificated employees in the two districts affected.

105 ILCS 5/18-8.05

DETACHMENT AND ANNEXATION PETITIONS

8:150   How frequently may a petition for detachment be submitted?

Any territory involved in a boundary change proceeding that is not approved may not be involved in another boundary change proceeding for at least two years after final determination of the first proceeding unless during the two-year period a petition filed is substantially different than any other previously filed petition during the previous two years or if a school district involved is placed on the academic or financial watch list, or if the first petition was brought under 7-2b (a petition by voters to make the boundaries of an annexing elementary or high school district coterminous).

105 ILCS 5/7-8
Helmig v. Regional Board of School Trustees, 286 Ill.App.3d 220, 675 N.E.2d 966, 221 Ill.Dec. 542 (3rd Dist. 1997)
Board of Education of Community Unit School District No. 300, Kane, Cook, McHenry and Lake Counties v. County Board of School Trustees of Kane County, 60 Ill.App.3d 415, 376 N.E.2d 1054, 17 Ill.Dec. 725 (2nd Dist. 1978)
Hall Township High School District No. 502 Bureau County v. School Trustees of Bureau County, 80 Ill.App.2d 475, 225 N.E.2d 228 (3rd Dist. 1967)
Board of Education of Consolidated School District No. 138 of Winnebago County v. County Board of School Trustees of Winnebago County, 37 Ill.App.2d 166, 185 N.E.2d 374 (2nd Dist. 1962)

8:160   May a detachment petition be filed when a school district affected by the petition has a bond referendum pending?

No. When notice of a bond issue election has been published, no petition affecting the boundaries of the school district may be filed pending defeat of the bond issue proposal, issuance of the bonds, a board resolution abandoning its plan to issue bonds, or the elapse of 75 days following the election, whichever comes first. This prohibition applies only to the first such election called in any calendar year, and the period of the prohibition may be affected if the district is involved in a legal boundary dispute at the time the election notice is published.

105 ILCS 5/7-3

8:165   May a detachment and annexation petition be withdrawn after filing to allow students to be tuitioned to another school?

At any time prior to the granting of a petition for detachment and annexation of non-coterminous territory, the Committee of Ten which petitioned the annexation and detachment may amend the petition to withdraw the detachment and annexation proposal and substitute a proposal to require the school district from which the territory would have been detached to pay the per capita tuition costs for each pupil residing in the non-coterminous territory to attend the school in the school district to which the territory would have been annexed.

105 ILCS 5/7-2b

8:170   May a petitioner remove his name from an annexation or detachment petition?

A petitioner may have his name removed from a detachment or annexation petition at any time prior to final determination by the regional board of school trustees.

Konald v. Board of Education of Community Unit School District No. 220, 114 Ill.App.3d 512, 448 N.E.2d 555, 69 Ill.Dec. 837 (2nd Dist. 1983)

Board of Education of Avoca School District No. 37, Cook County, v. Regional Board of School Trustees of Cook County, 82 Ill.App.3d 1067, 403 N.E.2d 578, 38 Ill.Dec. 347 (1st Dist. 1980)

Board of Education of Metropolis Community High School District No. 20, Massac County v. County Board of School Trustees, Massac County, 34 Ill.App.3d 901, 341 N.E.2d 10 (5th Dist. 1976)

REGIONAL BOARD OF SCHOOL TRUSTEES

8:180   With what body is a detachment or annexation petition filed?

A detachment or annexation petition is filed with the appropriate regional board(s) of school trustees.

105 ILCS 5/7-1 et seq.
105 ILCS 5/7-2a

8:190   When a petition seeks to detach territory in two educational service regions, is approval of both regional boards of school trustees necessary?

Yes. A joint hearing is held, but approval of both regional boards is required.

105 ILCS 5/7-6 et seq.
Carver v. Bond / Fayette / Effingham Regional Board of School Trustees, 203 Ill.App.3d 799, 561 N.E.2d 135, 148 Ill.Dec. 829 (5th Dist. 1991) app. allowed 136 Ill.2d 542, 567 N.E.2d 329, 153 Ill.Dec. 375, aff'd. 146 Ill.2d 347, 586 N.E.2d 1273, 167 Ill.Dec. 1 (1992)

8:200   What happens following the filing of a detachment and annexation petition?

The secretary of the regional board of school trustees sends the petition to the school board of each school district involved. Notice is published in a local newspaper pursuant to statutory requirements, and a hearing before the regional board of school trustees is held between 10 and 15 days after the publication of the notice.

105 ILCS 5/7-6
Board of Education of Rockford School District No. 205 Winnebago and Boone Counties v. Hearing Board of Counties of Boone and Winnebago, 152 Ill.App.3d 936, 505 N.E.2d 32, 105 Ill.Dec. 906 (2nd Dist. 1987) app. den. 115 Ill.2d 535, 511 N.E.2d 425, 110 Ill.Dec 453
Phillips v. Special Hearing Board of Boone and Winnebago Counties, 154 Ill.App.3d 799, 504 N.E.2d 1251, 105 Ill.Dec. 733 (2nd Dist. 1986) app. den. 115 Ill.2d 550, 511 N.E.2d 436, 110 Ill.Dec. 464 (1987)
Board of Education of Niles Township High School District 219, Cook County v. Regional Board of School Trustees of Cook County, 127 Ill.App.3d 210, 468 N.E.2d 1247, 82 Ill.Dec. 467 (1st Dist. 1984)

8:210   Who bears the burden of proof in a detachment or annexation proceeding?

The petitioners bear the burden of proof in a detachment or annexation proceeding.

Rhinehart v. Board of Education of Bloomington School District No. 87, McLean County, 132 Ill.App.2d 1078, 271 N.E.2d 104 (4th Dist. 1971)

8:220   What factors must regional boards consider in ruling on detachment petitions?

The regional board of school trustees must consider the ability of the districts affected to meet statutory standards of recognition, and whether the detaching district will be able to remain financially healthy after annexation. It must also consider what is best for the pupils in the entire area, as well as for the school districts affected by the petition. The overall benefit to the annexing district and detachment area must clearly outweigh the detriment to the losing district and surrounding community as a whole. There must not be serious harm done to the financial or educational resources of either district.

105 ILCS 5/7-2.6

Carver v. Bond / Fayette / Effingham Regional Board of School Trustees, 203 Ill.App.3d 799, 561 N.E.2d 135, 148 Ill.Dec. 829 (5th Dist. 1991) app. allowed 136 Ill.2d 542, 567 N.E.2d 329, 153 Ill.Dec. 375, aff'd. 146 Ill.2d 347, 586 N.E.2d 1273, 167 Ill.Dec. 1 (1992)

Board of Education of Golf School District No. 67 v. Regional Board of School Trustees of Cook County, 89 Ill.2d 392, 433 N.E.2d 240, 60 Ill.Dec. 443 (1982)

Board of Education of Pearl City Community Unit School District No. 200 v. Regional Board of School Trustees of Stephenson County, 98 Ill.App.3d 599, 424 N.E.2d 808, 54 Ill.Dec. 58 (2nd Dist. 1981)

Board of Education of Jonesboro Community Consolidated School District v. Regional Board of School Trustees of Union County, 86 Ill.App.3d 230, 407 N.E.2d 1084, 41 Ill.Dec. 586 (5th Dist. 1980)

Richmond v. County Board of School Trustees of Whiteside County, 93 Ill.App.2d 142, 235 N.E.2d 657 (3rd Dist. 1968)

Sesser Community Unit District No. 196, Franklin County v. County Board of School Trustees of Franklin County, 74 Ill.App.2d 152, 219 N.E.2d 364 (5th Dist. 1966)

Board of Education of Community Unit School District No. 323, Winnebago and Stephenson Counties v. County Board of School Trustees of Winnebago and Stephenson Counties, 19 Ill.App.2d 196, 153 N.E.2d 378 (2nd Dist. 1958)

Oakdale Community Consolidated School District No. 1 v. County Board of School Trustees, 12 Ill.2d 190, 145 N.E. 736 (1957)

People v. Deatherage, 401 Ill. 25, 81 N.E.2d 581 (1948)

8:230 May a regional board of school trustees amend a detachment or annexation petition?

No. In ruling on a detachment or annexation petition, a regional board of school trustees may allow or deny a petition but cannot modify it.

Board of Education of Wellington Community Unit School District No. 7 of Iroquois County v. County Board of School Trustees of Vermilion County, 13 Ill.App.2d 561, 142 N.E.2d 742 (3rd Dist. 1957)

Trico Community Unit School District No. 176 v. County. Board of School Trustees, 8 Ill.App.2d 494, 131 N.E.2d 829 (5th Dist. 1956)

Oakdale Community Consolidated School District No. 1, v. County Board of School Trustees of Randolph County, 12 Ill.App.2d 260, 139 N.E.2d 795 (4th Dist. 1956)

8:240 May a detachment petition be granted solely based on expanded educational opportunities for a student?

When there are no countervailing factors, and when the best interests of the children involved are served by the detachment, the courts usually apply the "whole child" and "community of interest" tests.

The "whole child" test considers whether or not there will be increased participation in school activities by the students and their families and how the educational, social and extracurricular needs of the student can best be satisfied. The "community of interest" test considers whether the detachment area is identified with the school district and community to which annexation is sought.

Carver v. Bond / Fayette / Effingham Regional Board of School Trustees, 203 Ill.App.3d 799, 561 N.E.2d 135, 148 Ill.Dec. 829 (5th Dist. 1991) app. allowed 136 Ill.2d 542, 567 N.E.2d 329, 153 Ill.Dec. 375, aff'd. 146 Ill.2d 347, 586 N.E.2d 1273, 167 Ill.Dec. 1 (1992)

Fixmer v. Regional Board of School Trustees of Kane County, 146 Ill.App.3d 660, 497 N.E.2d 152, 100 Ill.Dec. 272 (2nd Dist. 1986)

City National Bank of Kankakee v. Schott, 113 Ill.App.3d 388, 447 N.E.2d 478, 69 Ill.Dec. 261 (3rd Dist. 1983)

Granfield v. Regional Board of School Trustees of Bureau County, 108 Ill.App.3d 703, 438 N.E.2d 497, 64 Ill.Dec. 246 (3rd Dist. 1982)

Board of Education of Golf School District No. 67 v. Regional Board of School Trustees of Cook County, 89 Ill.2d 392, 433 N.E.2d 240, 60 Ill.Dec. 443 (1982)

Board of Education of Community High School District No. 154, McHenry County v. Regional Board of School Trustees of McHenry County, 84 Ill.App.3d 501, 405 N.E.2d 495 (2nd Dist. 1980)

Burnidge v. County Board of School Trustees of Kane County, 25 Ill.App.2d 503, 167 N.E.2d 21 (3rd Dist. 1960)

8:250   What is the benefit-detriment analysis?

The benefit-detriment analysis is used to determine whether the benefit derived from the annexation of the affected territory will outweigh the detriment to the losing district, the territory, and the community as a whole.

Carver v. Bond/Fayette/Effingham Regional Board of School Trustees, 203 Ill.App.3d 799, 561 N.E.2d 135, 148 Ill.Dec. 829 (5th Dist. 1991) app. allowed 136 Ill.2d 542, 567 N.E.2d 329, 153 Ill.Dec. 375, aff'd. 146 Ill.2d 347, 586 N.E.2d 1273, 167 Ill.Dec. 1 (1992)

Burnidge v. County Board of School Trustees of Kane County, 25 Ill.App.2d 503, 167 N.E.2d 21 (3rd Dist. 1960)

People v. Deatherage, 401 Ill. 25, 81 N.E.2d 581 (1948)

8:260   May the regional board of school trustees consider parental preference and convenience in deciding a petition for detachment and annexation?

While they may be treated as one factor in ruling on the detachment petition, parental preference and convenience alone are usually insufficient to support a detachment and annexation petition.

Carver v. Bond/Fayette/Effingham Regional Board of School Trustees, 203 Ill.App.3d 799, 561 N.E.2d 135, 148 Ill.Dec. 829 (5th Dist. 1991) app. allowed 136 Ill.2d 542, 567 N.E.2d 329, 153 Ill.Dec. 375, aff'd. 146 Ill.2d 347, 586 N.E.2d 1273, 167 Ill.Dec. 1 (1992)

Eble v. Hamilton, 52 Ill.App.3d 550, 367 N.E.2d 788 (3rd Dist. 1977)

Ottawa Township High School District No. 140 of LaSalle County v. County Board of School Trustees, 106 Ill.App.2d 439, 246 N.E.2d 138 (3rd Dist. 1969)

Burgner v. County Board of School Trustees of Peoria County, 60 Ill.App.2d 267, 208 N.E.2d 54 (3rd Dist. 1965)

Trico Community Unit School District No. 176 v. County Board of School Trustees, 8 Ill.App.2d 494, 131 N.E.2d 829 (4th Dist. 1956)

8:270   What considerations apply to detachment and annexation petitions involving territory where no students reside?

In detachment and annexation hearings concerning property which is either uninhabited and/or in which no students reside, it is the duty of the regional board of school trustees to determine whether the annexation would be beneficial to the educational welfare of any pupils who might later reside in that area. Educational welfare is to be determined by considering whether or not the territory involved is part of an integral or main activity of the community served by the receiving school district, the residential potential of the tract of land involved, and the distance students would travel along and across any heavily traveled roads in order to attend school.

Pontiac Township High School District No. 90 v. Regional Board of School Trustees for Livingston County, 183 Ill.App.3d 885, 539 N.E.2d 885, 132 Ill.Dec. 322 (4th Dist. 1989)

City National Bank of Kankakee v. Schott, 113 Ill.App.3d 388, 447 N.E.2d 478, 69 Ill.Dec. 261 (3rd Dist. 1983)

Rhinehart v. Board of Education of Bloomington School District No. 87, McLean County, 132 Ill.App.2d 1078, 271 N.E.2d 104 (4th Dist. 1971)

Board of Education of Springfield School District No. 186 v. Scott, 105 Ill.App.2d 192, 244 N.E.2d 821 (4th Dist. 1969)

8:280 Who may appeal an annexation, detachment or dissolution decision of a regional board of school trustees?

Any resident who appears at the hearing or any petitioner may file a complaint for judicial review within 35 days of service of the decision by registered mail in detachment-annexation cases and within 10 days of service of the decision by registered mail in dissolution-annexation cases. A board of education of a district affected by an annexation or detachment may appeal, but a board of education lacks standing to appeal a dissolution.

105 ILCS 5/7-7
105 ILCS 5/7-11

8:290 What happens if an annexation, detachment or dissolution decision of a regional board of school trustees is appealed?

If a decision of a regional board of school trustees is appealed, the complaint for judicial review operates as a stay of enforcement, and there is no enforcement of the decision until there is final disposition of the review. This means the entire matter of the dissolution, detachment or annexation is in limbo until all appeals have been exhausted.

105 ILCS 5/7-7
105 ILCS 5/7-11

8:295   What happens if the regional board of school trustees fails to act on a detachment, annexation, division or dissolution petition?

If within nine months after a petition is submitted under Section 7-1 of the School Code the regional board of school trustees fails to approve or deny the petition, the school boards or registered voters of the districts affected that submitted the petition (or the committee of ten) may submit a copy of the petition directly to the State Superintendent of Education for approval or denial.

105 ILCS 5/7-6 (1)

CHARTER DISTRICT DETACHMENT AND ANNEXATION

8:300   How is a petition for annexation to or detachment of territory from a charter district filed?

A request for annexation or detachment of territory may be initiated by any district affected by the filing of a petition signed by the school board and by a petition signed by 25 percent or 1,000 of the legal voters of the district, whichever is less, or by a petition signed by 50 percent of the legal voters residing in any territory requesting to be annexed or detached, or if there are no legal voters residing within the territory proposed to be detached or annexed, the petition may be signed by 50 percent of the owners of real estate of record.

There is a provision which permits the attachment of land by petition only to a special charter school district located in a special charter city under very narrow conditions specified in the statute.

65 ILCS 5/1-1-1 et seq.
105 ILCS 5/7-2.3 et seq.
Schreiber v. County Board of School Trustees of Peoria County, 31 Ill.2d 121, 198 N.E.2d 848 (1964)
People ex rel. Community Unit School District No. 1, Macon and DeWitt Counties v. Decatur School District No. 61, 45 Ill.App.2d 33, 194 N.E.2d 659 (4th Dist. 1964)

8:310   With what body is a charter district detachment or annexation petition filed?

A detachment or annexation petition is filed with the governing body of the special charter district. A certified copy of the petition must be sent to each district affected and to the board of school trustees of the counties in which the territory to be detached is located.

65 ILCS 5/1-1-1 et seq.
105 ILCS 5/7-2.4

8:320   What happens following the filing of a charter district detachment and annexation petition?

If no objection is filed with the regional board of school trustees or the governing body of the special charter district within 30 days after notice of the petition has been given to affected districts, the detachment/annexation takes effect subject however to stay rules in the event of appeal and other statutory time lines. If an objection is filed, the regional board of school trustees and the school district must appoint a hearing board. The regional board of school trustees appoints two members and the school board appoints two members. These four members meet and appoint three more members who reside outside the area to be detached or annexed.

105 ILCS 5/7-2.5 et seq.
105 ILCS 5/7-9
Board of Education of Rockford School District No. 205 Winnebago and Boone Counties v. Hearing Board of Counties of Boone and Winnebago, 152 Ill.App.3d 936, 505 N.E.2d 32, 105 Ill.Dec. 906, app. den. 115 Ill.2d 535, 511 N.E.2d 425, 110 Ill.Dec 453 (2nd Dist. 1987)
Board of Education of Rockford School District No. 205 Winnebago and Boone Counties v Regional Board of School Trustees of Boone and Winnebago Counties, 135 Ill.App.3d 486, 481 N.E.2d 1266, 90 Ill.Dec. 355 (2nd Dist. 1985)
Board of Education of Niles Township High School District 219, Cook County v. Regional Board of School Trustees of Cook County, 127 Ill.App.3d 210, 468 N.E.2d 1247, 82 Ill.Dec. 467 (1st Dist. 1984)

8:330   What factors must the hearing board consider in ruling on petitions?

The hearing board must consider: (a) the school needs and conditions of the territory in the area within and adjacent to the area to be attached or detached and the ability of the districts affected to meet the standards of recognition as prescribed by the State Board of Education, (b) the division of funds and assets which will result from any change of boundaries, (c) the will of the people of the area affected, and (d) the best interests of the schools of the area and the educational welfare of the pupils.

105 ILCS 5/7-2.6
First National Bank of Elgin v. West Aurora School District 129, 200 Ill.App.3d 210, 558 N.E.2d 686, 146 Ill.Dec. 723 (2nd Dist. 1990)
Desmond v. Regional Board of School Trustees, Malta Community Unit School District No. 433, 183 Ill.App.3d 316, 538 N.E.2d 1350, 131 Ill.Dec. 794 (2nd Dist. 1989), app. den. 127 Ill.2d 614, 545 N.E.2d 108, 136 Ill.Dec. 584
Phillips v. Special Hearing Board of Boone and Winnebago Counties, 154 Ill.App.3d 799, 504 N.E.2d 1251, 105 Ill.Dec. 733 (2nd Dist. 1986) app. den. 115 Ill.2d 550, 511 N.E.2d 436, 110 Ill.Dec. 464 (1987)
City National Bank of Kankakee v. Schott, 113 Ill.App.3d 388, 447 N.E.2d 478, 69 Ill. Dec. 261 (4th Dist. 1983)
Wirth v. Green, 96 Ill.App.3d 89, 420 N.E.2d 1200, 51 Ill.Dec. 642 (3rd Dist. 1981)
Board of Education of Springfield School District No. 186, Sangamon County v. Scott, 105 Ill.App.2d 192, 244 N.E.2d 821 (4th Dist. 1969)
Board of Education of City of Bloomington, McLean County v. County Board of School Trustees of McLean County, 77 Ill.App.2d 368, 222 N.E.2d 343 (4th Dist. 1966)
Horth v. Board of Education of School District No. 205, Winnebago County, 42 Ill.App.2d 65, 191 N.E.2d 601 (2nd Dist. 1963)

8:340   What is the effective date of change for the creation or change of boundaries of a charter school district?

When a petition is filed for the change in boundaries of a charter school district, the commencement of any action for judicial review acts as a stay of enforcement, and no further proceedings may be had until final disposition of the review. A petition for rehearing operates as a stay until the hearing board enters its final order on the petition for rehearing.

In the event the granting if a petition becomes final, either through failure to seek administrative review or by final decision of a court on review, the change in boundaries becomes effective immediately. If, however, the granting of a petition becomes final between September 1 and June 30 of any year, there is no change in administration or attendance of the schools affected until the following July 1 unless all the affected school boards and the regional board of school trustees agree otherwise.

105 ILCS 5/7-2.6
105 ILCS 5/7-2.7
105 ILCS 5/7-9

9: CONTROL AND USE OF SCHOOL PROPERTY

ACQUISITION AND OWNERSHIP

9:10 What was the original source of school property in Illinois?

The Northwest Ordinance in 1787 set aside the sixteenth section (640 acres) in every congressional township for the maintenance of public schools. This land was used for school sites or, more often, for rental or sale with proceeds used to support the schools. Common school land today is defined as "the sixteenth section in every township and the sections and parts of sections granted in place of all or part of the sixteenth section."

1 U.S. Land Laws 852
105 ILCS 5/15-1

9:20 Who holds title to public school property?

Public school property is actually state property. Prior to 1993, title to most school property was held by boards of township school trustees in Class II counties (Cook) and by regional boards of school trustees in Class I counties (all other counties). School boards could hold title to certain property acquired by gift or legacy or property acquired for vocational training projects.

As a result of legislation enacted in 1993, school boards outside Cook County hold title to real property formerly held by the regional board of school trustees, as well as real or personal property acquired from a direct grant, gift, donation or legacy to the board. Also, in Cook County, certain school districts may, by resolution, withdraw from the jurisdiction of the trustees of schools and thereby acquire title to real property.

Title to public school property in Chicago is held by the city.

105 ILCS 5/5-1
105 ILCS 5/5-21
105 ILCS 5/7-28
105 ILCS 5/10-23.3
105 ILCS 5/16-1
105 ILCS 5/34-20

9:40   How may a school board acquire property?

A school board may acquire school property by purchase or lease; condemnation; grant, gift, donation, devise, or bequest, or by receipt of a beneficial interest from a trust.

50 ILCS 605/1 et seq.
65 ILCS 5/11-78-1 et seq.
105 ILCS 5/10-22.12
105 ILCS 5/10-22.35A
105 ILCS 5/10-23.6

9:44   May a school board purchase real property with a contract for deed?

A school board may purchase school sites or sites for office facilities by contracting for the deed. The contract may not exceed ten years in length and installment payments on the contract must be made from the operations and maintenance fund.

105 ILCS 5/10-22.35a
105 ILCS 5/17-7

9:46   May a school board enter into a lease-purchase agreement for school buildings or grounds?

A school board may lease school buildings and/or grounds for up to ten years, or may enter into a 99-year lease with a two-thirds vote of the full membership of the school board (five votes on a seven member board). A school board may levy a tax at a rate up to .05 (.10 with voter approval) to pay the rent on such a lease.

If the school board takes title to the property at the end of the lease period, however, the acquisition of title calls into question whether or not the payment contract which the parties called a lease actually was a lease, or rather was a contract for deed or some other financing arrangement.

105 ILCS 5/10-22.12
105 ILCS 5/17-2.2c

9:50   May a school board exercise power of eminent domain?

In appropriate circumstances, a school district may benefit from acquisition of private property by eminent domain. The Illinois Constitution provides in pertinent part:

"Private property shall not be taken or damaged for public use without just compensation as provided by law. Such compensation shall be determined by a jury as provided by law."

Ill. Const. art. I, sec. 15

Scheller v. Trustees of Schools, Township 41 North, 67 Ill.App.3d 857, 384 N.E.2d 971, 24 Ill.Dec. 104 (2nd Dist. 1978)

County Board of School Trustees of DuPage County v. Boram, 26 Ill.2d 167, 186 N.E.2d 275 (1962)

9:60 How is the price determined when property is acquired by eminent domain?

The courts establish the price to be paid when the governmental unit and the property owner cannot agree upon a price. Fair market value is the price standard applied. Fair market value is established by competent evidence.

105 ILCS 5/16-6

Chicago in Trust for Schools v. Albert J. Schorsch Realty Co., 6 Ill.App.3d 1074, 287 N.E.2d 93 (1st Dist. 1972)

Board of Junior College District 515 v. Wagner, 3 Ill.App.3d 1006, 279 N.E.2d 754 (1st Dist. 1971)

9:70 May a school board acquire property which is not contiguous to school grounds for use as a playground or athletic field?

Property acquired by a school board for use as playgrounds, recreational fields, or athletic fields need not be contiguous to any school grounds.

105 ILCS 5/16-7

9:80 May a school board purchase land located outside the boundaries of its school district?

Under certain conditions, a school district may have statutory authority to purchase land outside the boundaries of its school district. Such authority is frequently required to accommodate the school building requirements of joint agreements and cooperative education arrangements.

105 ILCS 5/10-22.31b
105 ILCS 5/10-23.6
105 ILCS 5/22-16

9:90   May a municipality transfer real estate to a school district?

A municipality may transfer real estate to a school district. The corporate authority of municipalities includes the power to transfer all of the rights, title, and interest held by it to a school district.

50 ILCS 605/2

9:100   May a school district require a land developer to set aside property for school purposes?

A school district has no direct means to require a developer to set aside land. A municipality may require a developer to set aside land and/or money for school purposes by passing an ordinance to that effect.

55 ILCS 5/5-1041.1
165 ILCS 5/11-12-5.1
Krughoff v. Naperville, 68 Ill.2d 352, 369 N.E.2d 892, 12 Ill.Dec. 185, (1977)
Board of Education School District No. 68 DuPage County v. Surety Developers, Inc., 24 Ill.App.3d 638, 321 N.E.2d 99 (2nd Dist. 1974)
Board of Education Community Consolidated School District No. 59, Cook County v. E.A. Herzog Construction Co., 29 Ill.App.2d 138, 172 N.E.2d 645 (1st Dist. 1961)

DISPOSING OF SCHOOL PROPERTY

9:110   Who has power to decide that a school site is unnecessary, unsuitable, or inconvenient for a school building?

A school board may decide when a site or building has become unnecessary, unsuitable, or inconvenient for use as a school. By resolution adopted by at least two-thirds of its membership, a school board may elect to sell, enter into a contract for deed or convey a site under a seller-will-finance agreement.

50 ILCS 605/0.01 et seq.
105 ILCS 5/5-22

**9:120   Under what conditions may a school board
            deactivate its high school and send its
            students to another school district?**

There is a statutory process whereby a school district may
deactivate its high school and pay tuition to send its high school
students to another school district. The process requires voter
approval and is subject to numerous statutory limitations and
conditions.

105 ILCS 5/10-22.2b

**9:130   May one school district sell school land to
            another school district?**

If a school board decides a schoolhouse site, with or without
a building, is of no further use to the district and agrees on a
price with the school board of another school district within or
next to the boundaries of the site, it may, after complying with
statutory procedures, transfer the use of the site to the purchasing district.

105 ILCS 5/16-3

**9:140   How may a school board offer real estate for
            public sale?**

School real estate may be sold by auction or sealed bid, with
or without a minimum selling price. If the school board specifies
a minimum selling price and the price is not met, or no bids are
received, a real estate broker may be employed pursuant to
statutory terms. If at any time the school board lowers the minimum selling price, a new auction or sealed bid procedure must
follow. The school board may increase the minimum selling
price without repeating the public sale procedures.

105 ILCS 5/5-22

**9:145   Must a school district selling property notify a
            buyer of hazardous materials in school buildings
            and on school grounds?**

In most cases, a school district selling real property must
disclose to the buyer the presence of hazardous materials on the

property. A disclosure statement is required by law to identify the existence of asbestos or certain underground storage tanks, for example.

42 U.S.C. 11022
53 U.S.C. 2641 et seq.
765 ILCS 90/1 et seq.
Bonnell v. Regional Board of School Trustees of Madison County, 258 Ill.App.3d 485, 630 N.E.2d 547, 196 Ill.Dec. 612, (5th Dist. 1994)

9:150   May the citizens of a school district initiate the sale of school land?

Citizens may petition a school board to sell school buildings and grounds to another school district or other municipality. The petition must be signed by at least 10 percent of the voters of the district. Upon receipt of the petition, the school board must adopt a resolution for the sale, fix the price, and order the school board secretary to certify the proposition to the election authorities for submission to the voters.

105 ILCS 5/5-24
105 ILCS 5/15-7

9:160   If a school board decides to close a school building and sell the property, may the land be sold separately from the building?

Title to any building erected on school grounds may be disposed of separately from the site upon which it is located.

Miner v. Yantis, 410 Ill. 401, 102 N.E.2d 524 (1952)

9:165   How may the school board take payment for real estate?

The school board may take cash, may enter into a contract for deed, mortgage, or may sell on the basis of another seller-financed basis as determined by the school board.

105 ILCS 5/5-22

9:170   May a school board exchange school property for other property?

By a two-thirds majority vote of its members, a school board may exchange a school site or a site with a building on it for another site. To do so, the school board must file a Certificate of Findings and Declarations with the Recorder of Deeds and comply with other statutory procedures.

105 ILCS 5/5-23

9:180   How may a school board use the proceeds from the sale of school property?

A school board must use the proceeds from the sale of school sites, buildings, or other real estate first to pay the principal and interest on any outstanding bonds on the property being sold. After all such bonds have been retired, the proceeds from the sale may be used for any authorized purpose and may be deposited into any district fund.

105 ILCS 5/5-22

9:190   May a school board lease school property to a third party?

A school board may lease school property to another school district, municipality, not-for-profit school organization, suitable lessee for educational purposes, another governmental body, or for any other purpose which serves the interests of the community. The permissible terms of the initial lease vary according to the type of lessee.

A referendum is required for leasing to a private not-for-profit school organization for use in the care of the trainable and educable mentally handicapped or for the education of the gifted.

A lease for a permissible term in excess of 10 years or the modification of a lease whose unexpired term is in excess of 10 years requires a vote of two-thirds of the full membership of the school board.

105 ILCS 5/10-22.11 et seq.

SCHOOL BUILDINGS

9:200   May a school board construct school buildings?

A school board is authorized to build or purchase schools or office facilities upon voter approval at a referendum. A board also may issue bonds to finance construction upon voter approval.

105 ILCS 5/10-22.36
105 ILCS 5/19-1 et seq.

9:210   May a school board accumulate operating funds for the purpose of constructing a school building?

A building intended for permanent use as school property may be constructed only after voter approval at a referendum. Voter approval is also required for the accumulation of funds in the operations and maintenance fund.

105 ILCS 5/10-22.36
105 ILCS 5/17-5.1

9:215   Must a school district make its facilities handicapped accessible?

New building construction and alterations which affect the usability of the facility or a part of it must be handicapped accessible if first occupancy is after January 26, 1993. There is no requirement that existing facilities be altered to be handicapped accessible unless a student's individualized education program, an accommodation for a handicapped employee, or some other specific accommodation so requires.

42 U.S.C. 12201 et seq.

9:220   Is a school board authorized to build an athletic stadium or arena for spectator sports?

A school board may issue revenue bonds to build an athletic stadium or arena and has wide authority to operate, control and manage it. Funds to retire the bonds are acquired through charges and fees for the use of the facility.

105 ILCS 5/19a-1 et seq.

STATE CONSTRUCTION AID

9:230   Does the State offer financial assistance to public school districts in the construction of school facilities?

For school districts which qualify and when monies are appropriated by the legislature for this purpose, the State offers assistance in the building of school facilities. The Capital Development Board distributes and administers assistance funds.

30 ILCS 390/1 et seq.
30 ILCS 420/3 et seq.
105 ILCS 5/35-1
105 ILCS 230/5-10

9:240   What is the Illinois Capital Development Board?

The Illinois Capital Development Board is a state agency which administers distribution of funds for school sites, buildings and equipment subject to statutory limitations. The State Board of Education establishes eligibility standards and priorities and notifies the Capital Development Board of approved construction projects.

20 ILCS 3105/13 et seq.
30 ILCS 390/1 et seq.

9:250   How does a school district get a Capital Development Board grant?

A school district may apply to the State Board of Education for a school construction project grant. A school district must establish eligibility for such a grant by submitting a District Facility Plan, subject to review and approval by the State Board of Education.

The facilities plan must include an assessment of present and future district facility needs as required by present and anticipated educational programming, the availability of local financial resources including current revenues, fund balances, and unused bonding capacity, a fiscal plan for meeting present and anticipated debt service obligations, and a maintenance plan and schedule that contain necessary assurances that new, renovated and existing facilities are being or will be properly maintained.

If a district that applies for a grant has no unused bonding capacity or if its unused bonding capacity is less than the cost of the project that the district would be required to finance with non-grant funds, the application and facility plan submitted by the district must provide an estimate of the project cost the district proposes to finance by the issuance of bonds.

20 ILCS 3105/13.4
105 ILCS 230/5-20

9:255   What is a construction debt service grant?

School districts that have issued approved construction bonds are eligible to apply for debt service grants. If awarded, a debt service grant is equal to 10 percent of the principal amount of approved school construction bonds issued by the district times the grant index for the district.

Debt service grants can be used by the district to retire principal of approved school construction bonds, restructure debt service on such bonds, or to abate the property taxes levied for the district's bond and interest fund by an amount identical to the amount of the debt service grant.

105 ILCS 230/5-45

9:260   How are the building needs of school districts prioritized?

Under a 1997 amendment to The School Code, the State Board of Education establishes eligibility standards for school construction project grants and debt service grants. The Capital Development Board establishes project standards for all school construction project grants.

The State Board of Education prioritizes projects as follows:

1) replacement or reconstruction of school buildings destroyed or damaged by flood, tornado, fire, earthquake or other disasters either man-made or produced by nature;

2) projects designed to alleviate a shortage of classrooms due to population growth or to replace aging school buildings;

3) projects resulting from interdistrict reorganization of

school districts contingent on local referenda;

4) replacement or reconstruction of school facilities determined to be severe and continuing health or life safety hazards;

5) alternations necessary to provide accessibility for qualified individuals with disabilities;

6) other unique solutions to facility needs.

The Capital Development Board considers the current average daily attendance in the district and its attendance areas and the probable average daily attendance for the succeeding five years in the light of the growth trend of the district, the effect of slum clearance and large-scale housing projects, the pattern of attendance between private and public schools and plans for the curtailment or additions to private school facilities in the area, and any other factors bearing upon the probable continuing building needs of the district. It also determines the number of available classrooms which meet the minimum requirements specified by the State Board of Education. It proceeds on the assumption that each district needs one classroom for every 32 pupils in average daily attendance in grades K-6, one classroom for each 28 students in average daily attendance in grades 7-9, and one classroom for every 25 students in average daily attendance in grades 10-12.

105 ILCS 5/35 6 et seq.
105 ILCS 230/5-25
105 ILCS 230/5-30

9:265   What is the meaning of school construction grant index?

The grant index is a figure for each school district equal to one minus the ratio of the district's equalized assessed valuation per pupil in average daily attendance to the equalized assessed valuation of the district in the 90th percentile for all districts of the same type. The grant index is no less than .35 and no greater than .75 for each district except that a district whose equalized assessed valuation per pupil in average daily attendance is at the 99th percentile and above for all districts of the same type receives a grant index of zero.

105 ILCS 230/5-5

9:266 What is a school construction project?

A school construction project in the context of school construction grants is the acquisition, development, construction, reconstruction, rehabilitation, improvement, architectural planning and installation of capital facilities consisting of buildings, structures, durable equipment and land for educational purposes.

105 ILCS 230/5-5

9:267 What is a school maintenance project?

A school maintenance project in the context of school construction grants is a project other than a school construction project intended to provide maintenance or upkeep of buildings or structures for educational purposes but does not include ongoing operational costs.

105 ILCS 230/5-5

9:268 What is a school project maintenance grant?

The State Board of Education can make grants paid to school districts from the School Infrastructure Fund for school maintenance projects. No one grant for one fiscal year can exceed $50,000, but a school district can receive grants for more than one project during one fiscal year. A school district must provide local matching funds in an amount equal to the amount of the grant. There is grant entitlement.

The State Board of Education will adopt rules to implement the grants. The rules specify: (1) the manner of applying for grants; (2) project eligibility requirements; (3) restrictions on the use of grant moneys; (4) the manner in which school districts must account for the use of grant moneys; and (5) any other provision that the State Board determines to be necessary or useful for the administration of this Section. The rules specify the methods and standards used by the State Board to prioritize applications.

School maintenance projects are prioritized in the following order: (i) emergency projects; (ii) health/life safety projects; (iii) State Program priority projects; (iv) permanent improvement projects; and (v) other projects.

105 ILCS 230/5-100

9:270 What qualifications must a school district meet in order to receive assistance from the Capital Development Board?

No school district is entitled to have a building acquired or constructed by the Capital Development Board (CDB) unless:

1) The CDB determines the district will require, in addition to its present classrooms and those for which funds have been provided by the district, classrooms for at least 110 pupils in average daily attendance in grades 9-12 and 200 pupils in average daily attendance in grades K-12 at the beginning of the ensuing fall school term and the need for such additional classrooms will continue through five ensuing school years.

2) The district has either reduced its bonding power to less than $5,000 or will have done so in complying with the provisions of this requirement.

3) The school board has been authorized to levy a special tax sufficient in amount to provide the rent for the facilities to be so provided, but the CDB may approve an application for the construction of a classroom in a district contingent upon compliance with this provision within 60 days after such approval.

105 ILCS 5/35-7

9:280 May the Capital Development Board lease facilities to school districts?

The Capital Development Board may lease facilities to school districts.

105 ILCS 5/22-17
105 ILCS 5/35-5(c)
105 ILCS 5/35-5(i)

9:290 If a school district is to build a facility with Capital Development Board assistance, who has control over site selection?

The Capital Development Board may reject any site selected by a school board if the site does not meet minimum engineering and construction standards.

20 ILCS 3105/10.16

BUILDING CONTRACTORS

9:300   Must a school district pay "prevailing wages" to workers on a construction contract?

Laborers, workers, and mechanics employed by or on behalf of a school district, its contractors, or subcontractors to perform construction work must be paid not less than the hourly wage generally prevailing for similar work in the area. A school district employer need not pay prevailing wages to its own employees.

The school district must ascertain the prevailing rate of wages on a per-hour basis or ask the Department of Labor to ascertain the rate. The school district must specify in its resolution and call for bids that the prevailing hourly rate will be paid for each worker, and must stipulate in the contract that all workers must be paid no less than such prevailing rate. The school district must require contractors to include in their bonds provisions to guarantee the payment of prevailing wage rates.

820 ILCS 130/1 et seq.
People ex rel. Bernardi Roofing Systems, Inc., 101 Ill.2d 424, 463 N.E.2d 123, 78 Ill.Dec. 945 (1984)
Beaver Glass and Mirror Co. v. Board of Education of Rockford School District No. 205, 59 Ill.App.3d 880, 36 N.E.2d 377, 17 Ill.Dec. 378 (2nd Dist. 1978)
City of Monmouth v. Payes, 39 Ill.App.2d 32, 188 N.E.2d 48 (2nd Dist. 1963)
Bradley v. Casey, 415 Ill. 576, 114 N.E.2d 681 (1953)

9:305   Must a school board require a building contractor or subcontractor to supply a performance bond to guarantee construction work?

A school district must require every contractor to supply and deliver a bond for work costing over $5,000. A bank letter of credit is not sufficient surety unless the funding which supports the project which the bond would otherwise insure does not include monies received from state or federal sources and the contract is under $100,000. The amount of the bond may be established by the school board and among other conditions must be conditioned upon the completion of the contract, the payment of material used in the work, and for all labor performed in the work whether by the contractor, subcontractor or otherwise.

30 ILCS 550/0.01 et seq.

9:310   Is school district property subject to a mechanic's lien?

School district real estate is not subject to a mechanic's lien. Subcontractors may acquire a mechanic's lien on the money, bonds, or warrants due or which may become due.

770 ILCS 60/23
Board of Education of School District No. 108, Tazewell Co. for Use of A.Y. McDonald Manufacturing Company v. Collum, 77 Ill.App.2d 479, 222 N.E.2d 804 (3rd Dist. 1966)
Spaulding Lumber Company v. Brown, 171 Ill. 487, 49 N.E. 725 (1898)

SAFETY

9:320   Is school district property subject to any laws regarding safety?

School building construction and maintenance are subject to State Board of Education regulations contained in the Illinois Life-Safety Code. Schools also are subject to the occupational safety standards of the Illinois Department of Labor. Other safety standards applicable to schools include various environmental requirements, such as asbestos abatement and safe drinking water, traffic safety, and the common law "duty of care" owed to students while on school premises.

9:330   What is the Life-Safety Code?

The Life-Safety Code is the common name used to identify State Board of Education regulations governing school building construction and safety specifications.

105 ILCS 5/2-3.12
23 Ill. Admin. Code 175.10 et seq.
23 Ill. Admin. Code 185.05 et seq.
Board of Education of City of Rockford v. Page, 33 Ill.2d 372, 211 N.E.2d 361 (1965)
Board of Education of School District No. 33, DuPage County v. City of West Chicago, 55 Ill.App.2d 401, 205 N.E.2d 63 (2nd Dist 1965)

9:335   What is the School Building Code?

The School Building Code is a document prepared by the State Board of Education with the advice of the Department of Public Health, the Capital Development Board, and the State

Fire Marshal to "conserve the health and safety and general welfare of the pupils," school personnel and others who use public school facilities.

105 ILCS 5/2-3.12

9:337   What is a Safety Survey Report?

School buildings must be surveyed by an architect or engineer who, upon completion of the survey, issues a Safety Survey Report to the local school board. The survey is generally required on a 10-year cycle. The report contains prioritized recommendations and, upon approval of the regional superintendent of schools and the State Superintendent of Education, may require a local school board to make corrections.

105 ILCS 5/2-3.12

9:340   Who is responsible for school inspections under the Life-Safety Code?

The regional superintendent of schools is charged with the responsibility to inspect the plans and specifications for the heating, ventilating, lighting, seating, water supply, toilets, and fire safety of all the public school rooms and buildings within his region to ensure compliance with the Life-Safety Code. If the regional superintendent of schools does not approve or deny plans submitted to him within 30 days, the school board may submit the plans or specifications directly to the state superintendent of schools for approval or denial.

105 ILCS 5/3-14.20 et seq.

9:345   What agencies have authority to inspect school cafeterias for health and safety?

The county health department has such authority. The regional superintendent does not have exclusive authority to conduct inspections for sanitation or health control.

Macon County v. Board of Education of Decatur School District No. 61, 165 Ill.App.3d 1, 518 N.E.2d 653, 116 Ill.Dec. 31 (4th Dist. 1987) app. den. 119 Ill.2d 558, 517 N.E.2d 1246, 119 Ill.Dec. 387

9:350 Can a regional superintendent of schools condemn a school building?

If a regional superintendent of schools believes a school building to be unsafe, he may request the Department of Public Health, the State Fire Marshal, or the supervising architect to inspect public school buildings and temporary school facilities which appear to him to be unsafe, unsanitary, or unfit for occupancy. These officials must inspect, and if, in their opinion, the buildings or temporary facilities are unsafe, unsanitary, or unfit for occupancy, they must state in writing in what particular they are deficient. When he receives the statement, the regional superintendent must condemn the building or temporary facility and notify the school board in writing stating the reasons for the condemnation.

105 ILCS 5/3-14.22

9:355 What happens if a school district doe not correct deficiencies identified in a life-safety report?

If a regional superintendent determines that a school board has failed in a timely manner to correct urgent items identified in a previous life-safety report or as otherwise previously ordered by the regional superintendent, the superintendent can order the school board to adopt and submit a plan for the immediate correction of the building violations. The plan must be adopted after the conduct of a public hearing by the school board. The hearing must be preceded by notice published at least seven days before the hearing in a newspaper of general circulation within the school district. If the deficiencies are not corrected by the next annual inspection, the State can withhold general state aid. State aid sufficient to correct the violations may be withheld and remitted to the regional superintendent who has the power to contract on behalf of the school board to cause repairs to be made which will correct the violations.

105 ILCS 5/3-14.21

9:360   Which standards control fire prevention and safety for public school buildings, those of the State Fire Marshal or the Illinois State Board of Education?

The State Board of Education Life-Safety Code applies. The State Fire Marshal's Grey Book does not apply.

Board of Education of Minooka Community High School District No. 111 Grundy, Kendall and Will Counties v. Carter, 119 Ill.App.3d 857, 458 N.E.2d 50, 75 Ill.Dec. 882, (3rd Dist. 1983)

9:361   Does the Life-Safety Code prevent fire inspections by agencies other than the State Board of Education or the Regional Superintendent of Schools?

No. Schools may be investigated pursuant to Section 9 of the Fire Investigation Act and by other agencies which may have jurisdiction. Such investigations must be coordinated with the regional superintendent of schools and the Life-Safety Code must be used as the standard for compliance.

105 ILCS 5/2-3.12
425 ILCS 25/9

9:365   Are sprinkler systems required in schools?

Sprinkler systems are required in all new public school buildings, building additions, and remodeling projects involving 50 percent or more of a school building. An addition of less than 7,200 square feet to an existing building may be equipped with an automatic fire detection system in lieu of a sprinkler system.

30 ILCS 805/8.15
105 ILCS 5/22-23

9:370   What is the Illinois Health and Safety Act?

The Health and Safety Act requires employers, including school districts, to provide employees with a safe workplace. It is administered by the Illinois Department of Labor (IDOL), which has enacted rules implementing the statute. Employers are required, among other things, to: (a) post notices of employee rights under the act, including the right to file complaints with the Department of Labor; (b) submit to IDOL inspections and provide access to requested information and records, and (c) keep records of injuries arising in the workplace.

820 ILCS 225/1 et seq.

9:375 May a school board designate smoking areas in its school buildings for its employees who smoke?

No. Federal law requires that a school district prohibit smoking in every indoor, enclosed school facility that is owned, leased or contracted for and utilized for the provision of routine and regular kindergarten, elementary and secondary education and library services to students. A school district which violates the law risks loss of federal funds.

The School Code requires schools to prohibit the use of tobacco on school property when the property is being used for any school purpose. The school board may not authorize or permit any exception or exemption from the prohibition at any place or at any time. The tobacco ban includes all events or activities or other use of school property that the school board or school officials authorize or permit on school property including interscholastic or extracurricular activities or other events sponsored by the school board in which students participate. The ban includes cigarettes, cigars or tobacco in any other form including loose, cut, shredded, ground, powdered, compressed or leaf tobacco that is intended to be placed in the mouth without being smoked.

20 U.S.C. 6082
105 ILCS 5/10-20.5b

9:380 Is a school board required to provide crossing guards for students walking to and from school?

A school board may employ persons to direct traffic on school grounds, or on or along streets and highways within a radius of one mile from school grounds. If a board elects to hire crossing guards, the cost may be shared with any unit of local government.

105 ILCS 5/10-22.28a

9:381   May a municipality that has shared the cost of providing crossing guards unilaterally decide to stop doing so?

Yes. While the School Code permits school districts to share the cost of crossing guards with other units of local government, there is no means by which a school district can compel a unit of local government to share in the cost.

9:390   May a school board establish a school safety patrol?

A school board may establish a school safety patrol. Student participation requires written parental consent.

105 ILCS 5/10-22.28

9:400   May a school district install traffic signals at crossings where students walk to and from school?

A school board may acquire, install, operate, and maintain traffic signals outside city, village or incorporated town limits and within a one-mile radius of school grounds, subject to certain statutory limitations.

105 ILCS 5/10-22.28a

9:410   What is the purpose of the Asbestos Abatement Act?

The purpose of the Illinois Asbestos Abatement Act is to provide for the identification, containment, or removal of those asbestos materials that constitute a significant health hazard to students, school personnel, parents, or visitors in the public elementary and secondary schools of the State of Illinois.

15 U.S.C. 2641 et seq.
105 ILCS 105/1 et seq.

USE OF SCHOOL FACILITIES

9:420 May a school district hold a child's parents financially responsible for damage the child does to school property?

A civil suit under common law may be instituted. Recovery is also possible pursuant to the Parental Responsibility Act, under which a school district may hold a minor's parents responsible for actual damages or for the willful or malicious acts of a minor, to a maximum of $1,000, for injury to persons or school property. A minor in this context is any unemancipated person who is over 11 but not yet 19 years of age and who lives with his parents or legal guardian. The Parental Responsibility Act permits the recovery of attorney fees for successful plaintiffs who are not governmental entities.

740 ILCS 115/3 et seq.

9:430 May a school board allow an outside organization to use school facilities during non-school hours?

A school board may permit use of school facilities by outside organizations during non-school hours. Statutory authority exists for use for religious meetings, Sunday schools, evening schools, literary societies, and for such other meetings as the school board deems proper.

105 ILCS 5/10-22.10
Resnick v. East Brunswick Township Board of Education, 77 N.J. 88, 389 A.2d 944 (1978)
Board of Education of the City of Chicago v. Crilly, 312 Ill.App. 177, 37 N.E.2d 873 (1941)

9:432 May a school district determine which groups are given access to school facilities?

If a school district allows use of its facilities generally, it may not discriminate among users on the basis of the content of the speech of a potential user. A school may have the ability to deny use to a student group only if recognition would "materially and substantially interfere with the school's over-arching mission to educate its students."

Hsu v. Roslyn Union Free School District No. 3, 85 F.3d 839 (2nd Cir. 1996)

Hurley v. Irish American Gay, Lesbian and Bisexual Group of Boston, 115 S.Ct. 2338, 515 U.S. 557, 132 L.Ed.2d 487 (1995)

Lamb's Chapel v. Center Moriches Union Free School District, 113 S.Ct. 2141, 508 U.S. 384, 124 L.Ed.2d 352 (1993)

9:440   May or must a school board charge fees to outside organizations for the use of school facilities?

A school board may establish fees for the use of school facilities, but is not required to do so. However, any fees not applied equally to all organizations must be structured by some reasonable classification, such as with lower fees or no fees for school-related groups (e.g., PTA, band boosters) or not-for-profit groups. Fees structured to discriminate against groups espousing unpopular views, for example, may be subject to challenge on constitutional grounds.

105 ILCS 5/10-22.10

10: THE EDUCATIONAL PROGRAM

CURRICULAR AUTHORITY

10:10 What authority does a school board have to establish curriculum?

The School Code mandates certain courses of study for all pupils in Illinois public schools. School boards may set requirements in excess of those mandated by the State.

105 ILCS 5/10-20.8
105 ILCS 5/27-1 et seq.
People ex rel. McKeever v. Board of Education of Drummer Township High School, 176 Ill.App. 491 (3rd Dist. 1913)

10:20 Who has authority to determine appropriate class size?

Except with respect to special education, and unless a collective bargaining agreement provides otherwise, the school board has authority to determine appropriate class size. Class size is, however, a mandatory subject of bargaining, and a school board decision affecting class size may trigger a demand to bargain from affected employee bargaining units.

Board of Education Decatur District No. 61 v. Illinois Educational Labor Relations Board, 180 Ill.App.3d 770, 536 N.E.2d 743, 129 Ill.Dec. 693 (4th Dist. 1989)

10:30 Who establishes requirements for high school graduation?

The school board has the authority to establish the requirements for high school graduation. However, by law, those requirements must include the following core curriculum:

1) three years of language arts (two units in a three-year high school);

2) two years of mathematics, one of which may be related to computer technology;

3) one year of science;

4) two years of social studies, at least one of which must be American history or a combination of history of the United States and American government, and;

5) one year chosen from music, art, foreign language, or vocational education.

State law also requires the student to acquire 16 units in grades 9-12 (for four-year high schools) and 12 units in grades 10-12 (for three-year high schools). Students also must receive instruction in the principles of representative government and other specified related subjects.

Students who seek admission to any Illinois public community college, college, or university beginning in 1993 must have completed four years of English; three years each of social studies, mathematics, and science; and two years of music, art, or a foreign language.

A school board may not require a student to meet occupational standards for graduation unless the student is voluntarily enrolled in a job training program.

105 ILCS 5/10-20.31
105 ILCS 5/27-1 et seq.
105 ILCS 5/27-22
105 ILCS 5/27-22.05
23 Ill. Admin. Code 1.440

10:34   May a school board establish a community service requirement for high school graduation?

A school board may establish a community service requirement for graduation provided the requirement has an educational objective and is not otherwise suspect by reason of constitutional infirmity.

A school board contemplating a service requirement should be careful that the requirement does not infringe on student right to free speech and free exercise of religion and that the service requirement is not onerous.

Herndon v. Chapel Hill-Carrboro City Board of Education, 89 F.3d 174 (4th Cir. 1996)

Immediato by Immediato v. Rye Neck School District, 73 F.3d 454 (2nd Cir. 1996) cert. den. 117 S.Ct. 60, 519 U.S. 813, 136 L.Ed.2d 22 (1996)

10:40   May a school board grant academic credit on the basis of a proficiency exam?

A school board may, by policy, determine to allow or prohibit proficiency credit. Note, however, the School Code requires students to "successfully complete" those courses required for high school graduation and probably does not contemplate exemption by proficiency examination except where expressly allowed.

105 ILCS 5/27-22
23 Ill. Admin. Code 1.460

10:50   May a student, by demonstrating proficiency, become exempt from state-required instructional programs?

Only the state's consumer education requirement permits exemption based on proficiency. The State Board of Education each year provides high schools a uniform Consumer Education Proficiency Test. The test is administered to students who elect to take it, and those that make a passing score are exempt from the consumer education course requirement. No student can take the test more than once in any school year.

105 ILCS 5/27-12.1

10:60   May a student be permitted to receive credit by demonstrating proficiency in behind-the-wheel driver education?

A school district may adopt a policy to permit proficiency examinations for the practice driving part of driver's education after three hours of behind the wheel instruction.

School districts are required by law to offer driver education to high school students but students are not required by law to take the course.

105 ILCS 5/27-23
105 ILCS 5/27-24.2
625 ILCS 5/6-408.5
Acorn Auto Driving School, Inc. v. Leyden High School District No. 212, 27 Ill.2d 93, 187 N.E.2d 722 (1963)

10:62   Must a school district provide driver education for parochial, private and home school students residing in the district?

A school district must provide classroom driver education for:

1) each public and non-public high school student resident of the school district who either received a passing grade in at least eight courses during the previous two semesters or has received a waiver from the local superintendent (public school student) or chief school administrator (non-public school student); and

2) each out-of-school resident of the district between the ages of 15 and 21 years who requests the classroom course.

A school district may provide classroom driver education for any resident of the district over age 55 who requests the classroom course, but only if space remains after all eligible public and non-public high school students and out-of-school residents between 15 and 21 who request the course have registered for it and only for the resident of the district who is over 55 and has not been a licensed driver previously in Illinois or any other state or country.

105 ILCS 5/27-23
105 ILCS 5/27-24.2
625 ILCS 5/6-408.5

10:64   May a dropout obtain driver education?

There are statutory obstacles which must be overcome for a dropout who is under 18 to obtain a certificate of completion of a driver training program. A dropout must have a waiver from the superintendent of schools or:

1) be enrolled in a GED program (high school equivalency); or

2) be enrolled in an alternative education program; or

3) have a GED certificate; or

4) prior to dropping out received a passing grade in at least eight courses during the two previous semesters last ending prior to requesting a certificate of completion; or

5) have the written consent from the dropout's parents or guardians and the regional superintendent of schools.

625 ILCS 5/6-408.5

10:70   May a school board award academic credit for foreign language proficiency?

A school board may award credit to high school students who have studied a foreign language in an approved ethnic school or may grant one year of high school foreign language credit to any student who has graduated from elementary school and who can demonstrate proficiency in a foreign language. Foreign language includes American Sign Language.

105 ILCS 5/2-3.44 et seq.
105 ILCS 5/10-22.43 et seq.

10:80   By whom are high school equivalency tests administered?

The regional superintendent of schools must make a high school equivalency testing program available to qualified individuals residing within the region.

105 ILCS 5/3-15.12

10:82   Who is eligible to take the high school equivalency test (GED)?

A person is eligible to apply to the regional superintendent for the region in which he resides if he is:

1) a person who is 18 years of age or older, has maintained a residence in the State of Illinois and is not a high school graduate, but whose high school class has graduated;

2) a member of the U.S. armed forces on active duty who is 17 years of age or older and who is stationed in Illinois or who is a legal resident of Illinois;

3) a ward of the Department of Corrections or an inmate confined in any branch of the Illinois State penitentiary or in a correctional facility who is 17 years of age or older;

4) a female who is 17 years of age or older who is unable to attend school because she is either pregnant or the mother of one or more children;

5) a male who is 17 years of age or older who is unable to attend school because he is the father or one or more children;

6) a person who is completing an alternative education program approved by the State Superintendent of Education;

7) a person enrolled in a youth education program sponsored by the Illinois National guard;

8) a person who is at least 17 years of age who has been a drop out for a period of at least one year;

9) a person who has successfully completed the statutory alternative education program.

105 ILCS 5/3-15.12

10:90   May a school board make sex education a required course offering?

A school board may not require a pupil to take or participate in a sex education class if the pupil's parent or guardian submits a written objection to the school district. A student may not be disciplined by reason of the parental objection.

105 ILCS 5/27-9.1 et seq.

Brown v. Hot, Sexy and Safer Productions, Inc. 68 F.3d 525 (1st Cir. 1995) cert. den., 116 S.Ct. 1044, 516 U.S. 1159, 134 L.Ed.2d 191 (1996)

Bergstrand v. Rock Island Board of Education, School District No. 41, 161 Ill.App.3d 180, 514 N.E.2d 256, 112 Ill.Dec. 790 (3rd Dist. 1987)

10:95   May a school district distribute condoms to students?

It is likely that a school distribution program would survive parental objections and court challenges. Parents have a liberty interest to be free from unnecessary governmental intrusion in the rearing of their children, but mere exposure to a program offered at school does not amount to unconstitutional interference without some compulsory aspect to the program. Plaintiffs have also failed to convince the courts that a voluntary distribution program violates parental or student rights to free exercise of religion.

Curtis v. School Committee of Falmouth, 652 N.E.2d 580 (Ma. 1995)

Carey v. Population Services International, 97 S.Ct. 2010, 431 U.S. 678, 52 L.Ed.2d 675 (1977)

10:100   May a school board require its students to receive instruction on disease?

A student is not required to take or participate in instruction on disease if the student's parent or guardian submits written objections on constitutional grounds. A student may not be disciplined by reason of the parental objection.

105 ILCS 5/27-11

10:105   Who is a gifted student?

Gifted and talented children means children whose mental development is accelerated beyond the average, or who have demonstrated a specific aptitude or talent and can profit from specially planned educational services to the extent they need them. The term includes children with exceptional ability in academic subjects, high level thought processes, divergent thinking, creativity, and the arts.

105 ILCS 5/14A-1 et seq

10:106   Must boards of education provide special programming for gifted or talented children similar to that of the individualized educational program provided for handicapped children?

A school district must make available a program for gifted and talented children. A school district may voluntarily create such a program or enter into joint agreements for the creation of specific programs. Such programs are under the supervision of the State Board of Education and may be administered by the local district, regional superintendent, community college, college or university and may include area service centers, experimental projects, institutes, special summer programs, and similar program offerings.

The laws governing the operation of gifted or talented programs do not require school districts to provide individualized educational programs for children enrolled in them.

105 ILCS 5/14A-1 et seq.
Board of Education of City of Peoria School District No. 150 v. Sanders, 150 Ill.App.3d 755, 502 N.E.2d 730, 104 Ill.Dec. 233 (3rd Dist. 1986) app. den. 115 Ill.2d 536, 508 N.E.2d 208, 108 Ill.Dec. 47, cert. den. 108 S.Ct. 290, 484 U.S. 926, 98 L.Ed.2d 250

10:120   Under what conditions may a child be excused from the daily physical education requirement?

A child may be excused from physical education when an appropriate excuse is submitted by a doctor, parent or guardian. A school board may excuse a pupil in grade 11 or 12 who requests to be excused if the student is an ongoing participant in interscholastic athletics.

A student in grades 9-12 may be excused upon request if the student is enrolled in a for-credit marching band program.

A student in grades 9-12 may be excused if the student is enrolled in a Reserve Officer's Training Corps (ROTC) program sponsored by the school district.

A student in grades 11 or 12 may be excused from physical education in order to enroll in a class which if not taken would prevent the student from graduating or result in the student's being denied admission to the institution of higher learning of the student's choice. Under conditions specified in the law, vocational or technical education courses may be substituted for physical education.

105 ILCS 5/27-6
105 ILCS 5/27-22.05

10:130   May a school district offer a summer school program?

A school board may operate a summer school program. Tuition may be charged in an amount not to exceed the per capita cost of the program. A school board may give regular school credit for satisfactory completion of summer school courses which are approved for credit by the State Board of Education. A statutory funding formula provides limited funds to support summer school programs.

The school board may require the attendance at summer school of academically at risk students. Written notice requiring attendance sent to the parent or guardian of the student not later than the close of the school term immediately preceding the summer term is required.

105 ILCS 5/10-22.33A
105 ILCS 5/10-22.33B
105 ILCS 5/18-4.3
105 ILCS 5/26-1

10:140   When is a school district required to provide transitional bilingual education?

Every school age child of limited English speaking ability must be provided a program in transitional bilingual education (or, under certain circumstances, a transitional instructional program in his own language) for a period of three years or until the child learns sufficient English language skills to allow him to perform successfully in classes taught in English, whichever occurs first.

105 ILCS 5/14B-1 et seq.
Teresa P. v. Berkeley Unified School District, 724 F.Supp. 698 (N.D. Cal. 1989)
Castenada v. Pickard, 648 F.2d 989 (5th Cir. 1981)

10:150   How are school district work experience programs limited by child labor laws?

Child labor laws regulate the work which may be performed by minors. Generally, minors below age 14 are subject to stringent regulation and are, in most cases, prohibited from employment. The employment of minors between the ages of 14 and 16 is permitted in limited circumstances. The child labor laws state at what age minors may be employed in specific occupations, how many hours a day they may work, and cover many other work related subjects.

820 ILCS 205/1

10:155   May a school district require a student to meet occupational standards?

A school board may not require a student to meet occupational standards for grade level promotion or graduation unless the student is voluntarily enrolled in a job training program.

105 ILCS 5/2-3.126

10:160   May a school board establish a full-day kindergarten?

A school board may provide a full-day or half-day kindergarten. However, if a full-day program is offered, a half-day program must also be offered as an alternative for parents.

105 ILCS 5/10-22.18
105 ILCS 5/10-22.19a
Morgan v. Board of Education of Trico Community Unit School District 176, 22 Ill.App.3d 241, 317 N.E.2d 393 (5th Dist. 1974)

10:170   May a school board establish a before or after school day care center?

There is statutory authorization for the establishment of before or after school programs for grades K-6. The school district may charge parents of participating students a fee not to exceed the cost of the program. The program may include time for homework, physical exercise, afternoon nutritional snacks, and educational offerings which are in addition to those offered during the regular school day.

The schedule of these programs may follow the work calendar of the local community rather than the regular school calendar. Programs must be coordinated by teachers or persons who meet the requirements for supervising day care centers.

105 ILCS 5/10-22.18b

10:180   If a school board chooses to establish a before or after school day care center, must it provide transportation for the students?

The parents or guardians of the participating students are responsible for the transportation of the students to and from a before or after school day care center operated by a school district.

105 ILCS 5/10-22.18b

10:190   May a school board offer adult education classes?

A school board may establish classes for the instruction of persons 21 years of age and over and of persons less than 21 and not otherwise in attendance in public school. A statutory funding formula provides limited funds to support such programs. If a school board establishes an adult education program, it must provide transportation and child care. A school board may establish a tuition charge for persons enrolled who are not subject to state reimbursement not to exceed the per capita cost of the classes.

105 ILCS 5/10-22.20

10:200   May a school district operate a nursery school?

School districts maintaining grades 1-8 or 1-12 may establish nursery schools for the instruction of children between the ages of two and six years if sufficient funds obtained from sources other than local district taxes are available to pay the costs of the nursery school.

105 ILCS 5/10-23.2

10:210   May school boards enter into joint agreements with other school districts or agencies to provide educational programs?

Two or more educational agencies, including school districts, may establish an educational joint agreement or cooperative by agreeing in writing to work together to provide some educational program. Common examples are vocational and special education cooperatives. In some cases, a new joint agreement school district results from the cooperative effort, and in some cases an existing school district becomes the administrative district for the resulting cooperative and, as a result, no new entity is formed. Some cooperative agreements require voter approval.

School districts with small high schools also may agree to jointly operate a cooperative attendance center.

105 ILCS 5/10-22.22c
105 ILCS 5/10-22.31 et seq.

10:220   May a school district and a park district operate a joint recreational program?

Park districts have authority to develop, operate, finance, and participate in joint recreational programs with school districts and to enter into joint agreements.

70 ILCS 1205/8-18
70 ILCS 1205/9.1-5 et seq.

THE SCHOOL YEAR AND DAY

10:230   What is the minimum number of days in a school year?

Each school board is required by law to annually prepare a calendar for the school term which specifies both the opening and closing dates of the term. The calendar must provide a minimum term of at least 185 days which generally includes five emergency days and four teacher institute days in order to ensure 176 days of actual pupil attendance. Any teachers' institute day not used for an institute or used as a parental institute increases the minimum term of 176 pupil attendance days by the number of unused teacher institute days.

The adoption of a school calendar may have collective bargaining implications with respect to recognized bargaining units.

105 ILCS 5/10-19
105 ILCS 5/10-22.18d
105 ILCS 5/24-1
Board of Education Arbor Park School District No. 145, Cook County v. Ballweber, 105 Ill.App.3d 412, 434 N.E.2d 448, 61 Ill.Dec. 295 (1st Dist. 1981) aff'd. 96 Ill.2d 520, 451 N.E.2d 858, 71 Ill.Dec. 704 (1982)
Miller v. School District No. 189 East St. Louis, 26 Ill.App.3d 172, 325 N.E.2d 43 (5th Dist. 1975)

10:240   What is an "institute day?"

An "institute day" is any educational gathering, demonstration of methods of instruction, or visitation of schools or other institutions or facilities held or approved by the regional superintendent. Teacher "institutes" may include inservice training workshops or equivalent professional education experiences. Under circumstances provided for in the law, a school district may have up to two parental institute days in any given year instead of teacher institute days.

105 ILCS 5/3-11
105 ILCS 5/10-22.18d
Miller v. School District No. 189, East St. Louis, 26 Ill.App.3d 172, 325 N.E.2d 43 (5th Dist. 1975)

10:245   What is a parental institute day?

A school district may use up to two teacher institute days to conduct parental institutes for the parents and guardians of students. Parental institute days require the consent of the district's in-service advisory committee or, if the district does not have an in-service advisory committee, parental institute days must be approved by the district's teachers.

Parental institute days may be held during that period of the day which is not part of the regular school day and may be held on Saturday. A school district may establish reasonable fees, not to exceed the cost of holding the parental institute, but must waive the fee for parents or guardians who cannot afford the fee.

105 ILCS 5/10-22.18d

10:250 When may institute days be used?

A regional superintendent of schools may arrange for or conduct district, regional or county institutes or equivalent professional educational experiences not more than four days annually. Of those four days, two days may be used as a teacher's workshop when approved by the regional superintendent, up to two days may be used for conducting parent-teacher conferences or up to two days may be used as parental institute days under conditions specified in the law. A school district may use one of its institute days on the last day of the school term. Institute days may be held on consecutive or separate days at the option of the regional superintendent of schools.

105 ILCS 5/3-11
105 ILCS 5/10-22.18d

10:270 What is the minimum school day?

A school day must consist of no less than five clock hours under the direct supervision of teachers in order to meet State Board of Education standards and to qualify as a full day of school in calculating state aid entitlements. Some exceptions are authorized.

105 ILCS 5/18-8.05

10:280 What are the exceptions to the minimum five clock hour school day?

There are six exceptions:

1) Two and one half hours may be counted as a half-day for students in grades 2 through 12.

2) Four clock hours may be counted as a day of attendance for first-graders and full day kindergartners.

3) Two clock hours may be counted as a half-day of attendance for first graders and full day kindergartners.

4) One clock hour may count as a half-day of attendance for handicapped children below the age of six who cannot attend a two-hour session because of handicap or immaturity.

5) Days of attendance may be less than five clock hours on the opening and closing days of the school term, and upon the second or third day of the school term if the first and second days are used as institutes or teachers' workshops. Four clock hours may be counted as a day of attendance upon certification by the regional superintendent and approval of the State Superintendent of Education.

6) A session of three or more clock hours up to a maximum of five half-days per school year may be counted as a full day of attendance when the remainder of the day is used for an in-service training program for teachers. Two full days may be used for parent-teacher conferences. Any full day used reduces the number of allowable half-days by two. In either instance, the programs must have the prior approval of the State Board of Education's Public School Approval Section.

105 ILCS 5/18-8.05 (F) (2) et seq.
23 Ill. Admin. Code 1.420

TESTING AND REPORTING

10:290   May a school district require minimum competency testing?

Minimum competency testing is standardized testing to measure the acquisition of skills at or beyond a certain defined minimum standard. The use of minimum competency testing is within the discretionary authority of a school board.

105 ILCS 5/2-3.42
105 ILCS 5/10-20.25
105 ILCS 5/14-6.01

10:300   What student performance assessments are required by law?

The State Board of Education (ISBE) establishes standards and assesses the performance of students. Until the end of the 1997-1998 school year, ISBE annually tested students in grades three, six, eight and ten in language arts and math, and students in grades four, seven and eleven in biological, physical and social sciences. Beginning in the 1998-1999 school year, ISBE will test pupils in the third, fifth, and eighth grades in reading, writing and math and all pupils in the fourth and seventh grades in the biological and physical sciences.

Every individualized educational program of a special education student must identify the components of the state test which are appropriate for the student and which are not. The State Board of Education prescribes alternate assessments for students for whom the state test is inappropriate.

Beginning with the 1998-1999 school year, the State assessment will identify pupils in the third or fifth grades who do not meet state standards. If, by performance of the State assessment or local assessments or by teacher judgment, a student's performance is determined to be two or more grades below current placement the student must be provided a remediation program developed by the district in consultation with the parents or guardians.

105 ILCS 5/2-3.64

10:302   What is the Prairie State Achievement Examination?

Beginning with the 1999-2000 school year, each high school will annually administer the state-developed and required examination to its twelfth grade students. The test is administered in January of each year and measures student performance in reading, writing, math, science and social studies. Recognition by the Illinois State Board of Education (ISBE) is given to students whose scores on the test are determined by ISBE to be excellent.

Each student, except a student whose individualized educational program identifies the examination as inappropriate for the student, is required to take the examination in grade 11. Score reports for each fundamental academic area indicate the score that qualifies as an excellent score on that portion of the examination. Any student who obtains a satisfactory composite score but who fails to earn a qualifying score in any one or more of the fundamental academic areas on the initial test or who wishes to improve is permitted to retake that portion(s) of the examination during grade 12.

105 ILCS 5/3.64

10:303   May a student be denied a high school diploma by reason of a poor score on the Prairie State Achievement test?

A student may not be denied a diploma if he completes all other applicable high school graduation requirements.

105 ILCS 5/3.64

10:304   May a special education student be required to take the Prairie State Achievement test?

The test may not be required by school officials unless the student's individualized education program (IEP) identifies the test as appropriate. But the law allows students whose IEPs do not require the test to take it if such students elect to do so.

105 ILCS 5/3.64

10:305   Must students enrolled in transitional bilingual education take the Prairie State Achievement test?

Any student who has been enrolled in a State approved bilingual education program less than three academic years may be exempted if the student's lack of English would keep the student from understanding the test. The school district must have an alternative assessment program in place for the student.

105 ILCS 5/2-3.64

10:310   What must a school board report publicly with respect to the performance of the district's schools and students?

Each school district must submit to parents, taxpayers of the district, the Governor, the General Assembly, and the State

Board of Education a school report card assessing the performance of its schools and students. The report card must describe the performance of students by school attendance center and must describe the district's use of financial resources. This report card must be presented at a regular school board meeting, must be made available to a newspaper of general circulation serving the district, and must be sent home to parents. The report card must include indicators of parental involvement in each attendance center.

The report card form is prepared by the State Board of Education and is disseminated prior to October 31 in each school year.

105 ILCS 5/10-17a

10:315   May a parent require that a child be excused from school testing for religious or moral reasons?

A federal law requires that no student be compelled to submit to a survey, analysis or evaluation that reveals information concerning:

1) political affiliations;

2) mental and psychological problems potentially embarrassing to the student or his family;

3) sex behavior and attitudes;

4) illegal, anti-social, self incriminating and demeaning behavior;

5) critical appraisals of other individuals with whom the respondents have close family relationships;

6) legally recognized privileged or analogous relationships, such as those of lawyers, physicians and ministers;

7) income (other than that required by law to determine eligibility for participation in a program or for receiving financial assistance under such program).

20 U.S.C. 1232(h)

10:317   Could state mandated achievement tests be required of students attending private schools?

If the legislature so determined, the tests could be required of all students, public and private.

Ohio Association of Independent Schools v. Goff, 92 F.3d 419 (6th Cir. 1996)

GRADES AND GRADING

10:320   Who has final authority to determine whether a student is promoted or retained at grade level?

Except in the case of a student who has been found to be in need of special education, a school board has general authority to determine retention and promotion.

A 1997 amendment to the School Code prohibits social promotion of students and prevents promotion based upon age or any other social reason not related to the academic performance of the student. Decisions to retain or promote must be based on successful completion of the curriculum, attendance, performance on the Illinois Goals and Assessment Program tests (IGAP), the Iowa Test of Basic Skills, other testing or other criteria established by the school board.

Students who do not qualify for promotion must be provided remedial assistance which may include, but is not limited to, a summer bridge program of not less than 90 hours, tutoring, increased or concentrated instructional time, modification of instructional materials and retention in grade. Each school district must have a promotion-retention policy in place by not later than September 1, 1998.

105 ILCS 5/10-20.9a
105 ILCS 5/10-20.9b
Morgan v. Board of Education of Trico Community Unit School District 176, 22 Ill.App.3d 241, 317 N.E.2d 393 (5th Dist. 1974)

10:330   May a school district adopt a policy permitting student grade reduction for disciplinary infractions?

This area of school law is unsettled. Some courts have allowed policies which tie grade reductions to disciplinary infractions, and some have not. Whether or not any such policy is permissible will depend upon the terms of the policy and the facts relating to its implementation. A student challenging a grade reduction probably cannot make a claim grounded in a substantive due process ("I violated the rule but the punishment was unfair"), but can make a viable claim if the student was not provided appropriate procedural due process.

Dunn and McCullough v. Fairfield Community High School District No. 225, 158 F.3d 962 (7th Cir. 1998)

Hamer v. Board of Education of Township High School District 113, 66 Ill.App.3d 7, 383 N.E.2d 231, 22 Ill.Dec. 755 (2nd Dist. 1978)

Knight v. Board of Education of Tri-Point Community Unit School District 6J, 38 Ill.App.3d 603, 348 N.E.2d 299 (4th Dist. 1976)

10:340 Can a non-custodial parent require a school district to report student progress?

In the absence of a court order to the contrary, upon the request of either parent of a pupil whose parents are divorced, a school board must mail all correspondence and reports which are furnished to one parent to the other parent.

105 ILCS 5/10-21.8

EDUCATIONAL MATERIALS

10:350 What statutory authority is given a school board with respect to the adoption of textbooks?

A school board has statutory authority to adopt such printed instructional materials as are needed in the schools. Publishers are required to meet certain state standards. A record of the adoption of texts and other print materials must be filed with the regional superintendent of schools.

105 ILCS 5/28-6
105 ILCS 5/28-21

10:360 Do citizens have a right to inspect instructional materials?

State law provides that any member of the public may inspect all text and instructional material used in the public schools. The term "instructional material" includes both printed and non-print materials that are used in the educational process.

Federal law requires that parents be permitted to inspect instructional materials including teacher's manuals, films, tapes, or other supplementary material which is to be used in connection with any "survey, analysis or evaluation." Neither law permits parental inspection of test questions.

20 U.S.C 1232h
105 ILCS 5/28-19.1 et seq.

10:370   May a school board charge a rental fee for textbooks?

A school board may purchase textbooks and rent them or resell them to students.

105 ILCS 5/10-22.25
105 ILCS 5/28-8
Hamer v. Board of Education, School District No. 109, Lake County, 9 Ill.App.3d 663, 292 N.E.2d 569 (2d Dist. 1977)

10:380   Under what circumstances must a school district provide free textbooks to all its students?

Whenever petitioned by five percent or more of the voters, a school board must submit to the voters at a general election the question of whether to furnish free school textbooks.

105 ILCS 5/28-14 et seq.

10:390   Must a school board provide textbooks at no charge to children whose parents are unable to pay for them?

A school board must provide at no charge textbooks for children whose parents are unable to afford them.

105 ILCS 5/10-20.13
105 ILCS 5/28-19.2
Latham v. Board of Education of City of Chicago, 31 Ill.2d 178, 201 N.E.2d 111 (1964)

**10:400   May a school board order the removal of books
from the school curriculum or the school
library, or may the school board block the
acquisition of books because school officials
determine the ideas contained in the books are
offensive?**

School boards have broad authority to manage the schools,
including the authority to select or remove textbooks from the
curriculum and to determine courses of study. The First
Amendment imposes limitations on the discretion of a school
board to remove library books from the schools or to otherwise
limit student access to ideas.

106 ILCS 5/10-20.8

Kreimer v. Bureau of Police for the Town of Morristown, 958 F.2d 1242
(3rd Cir. 1992)

*Board of Education of Island Trees Union Free School District No. 26 v.
Pico,* 102 S.Ct. 2799, 457 U.S. 853, 73 L.Ed.2d 435 (1982)

11: STUDENTS AND PARENTS

COMPULSORY ATTENDANCE

11:10 What are the ages of compulsory school attendance in Illinois?

A child must attend school from his seventh birthday until his 16th birthday.

105 ILCS 5/13-3
105 ILCS 5/26-1
Chicago Board of Education v. Terrile, 47 Ill.App.3d 75, 361 N.E.2d 778, 5 Ill.Dec. 455 (1st Dist. 1977)
Scoma v. Chicago Board of Education, 391 F.Supp. 452 (N.D. Ill. 1974)

11:20 What is the minimum age for kindergarten attendance?

Any child who will be five on or before September 1 of any school year may attend school at the beginning of the school term. Based on an assessment of a child's readiness, a school district may permit a child to enter at a younger age.

105 ILCS 5/10-20.12
Morrison by Morrison v. Chicago Board of Education, 188 Ill.App.3d 588, 544 N.E.2d 1099, 136 Ill.Dec. 324 (1st Dist. 1989)
Morgan v. Board of Education of Trico Community Unit School District No. 176, 22 Ill.App.3d 241, 317 N.E.2d 393 (5th Dist. 1974)

11:30 Do compulsory attendance laws require that children attend kindergarten?

Kindergarten attendance is optional. Compulsory attendance laws do not require children to attend kindergarten.

105 ILCS 5/26-1
Morgan v. Board of Education of Trico Community Unit School District No. 176, 22 Ill.App.3d 241, 317 N.E.2d 393 (5th Dist. 1974)

11:40 Under what circumstances is a child of compulsory school age exempt from compulsory attendance?

A child is exempt from public school attendance under the following circumstances:

1) if the child attends a private or parochial school where instruction is in the English language;

2) if the child is physically or mentally unable to attend school or is excused for temporary absence for cause by the principal or teacher of the school which the child attends;

3) if the child is necessarily and lawfully employed consistent with child labor laws, the child may be excused from school by the regional superintendent of schools or the superintendent of the public school which the child should be attending, and upon approval in either instance of the child's school board;

4) if the child is over 12 and under 14 years of age the child must be excused to attend confirmation classes;

5) a child must be excused if the tenets of his religion prohibit secular activity on a particular day or days or at a particular time of day.

105 ILCS 5/26-1

People v. Berger, 109 Ill.App.3d 1054, 441 N.E.2d 915, 65 Ill.Dec. 600 (2nd Dist. 1982)

Morton v. Board of Education of City of Chicago, 69 Ill.App.2d 38, 216 N.E.2d 305 (1st Dist. 1966)

People ex rel. Latimer v. Board of Education of City of Chicago, 394 Ill. 228, 68 N.E.2d 305 (1946)

11:41 Under what circumstances must a school district deny enrollment to a student who resides in the school district?

A school district must deny enrollment in its secondary schools to any child above the age of 16 years who has dropped out of school and who could not, because of age and lack of credits, attend classes during the normal school year and graduate before his twenty-first birthday.

To deny enrollment the school district must schedule a hearing "as required in cases of expulsion." If as a result of the hearing the child is denied enrollment, the school district must provide counseling to the child and direct him to alternative educational programs that lead to graduation or receipt of a GED.

No child may be denied re-enrollment in violation of the Individuals with Disabilities Education Act (IDEA) or the Americans with Disabilities Act (ADA)

20 U.S.C. 1400 et seq.
42 U.S.C. 12101 et seq.
105 ILCS 5/26-2

HOME SCHOOLING

11:42 May a school district or the State Board of Education adopt rules regulating home schools?

Courts in other states have upheld state regulation of home schooling, including certification requirements for home-school teachers and minimum curriculum requirements, finding that the state has a compelling interest in the education of children. In Illinois, however, the General Assembly has opted to not interfere with home schooling and has not enacted legislation.

Local school districts have the authority to regulate their own programs, which has the indirect effect of regulating certain aspects of home schooling to the extent home schooled students avail themselves of various aspects of the public school program.

State v. Schmidt, 505 N.E.2d 627 (Ohio 1987)
State v. Patzer, 382 N.W.2d 631 (North Dakota 1986)
State v. Rivinius, 328 N.W.2d 220 (North Dakota 1982)
People v. Levisen, 404 Ill. 574, 90 N.E.2d 213, (1950)

11:44 Must a school district accept a home-schooled student for enrollment in some, but not all, public school classes?

This is an unsettled area of the law. There is a School Code provision which governs part-time attendance and which permits a school board to limit enrollment to situations where space permits and to applications submitted before May 1 of any year. If a school district has a policy which limits the enrollment of part-time students, the policy must be uniformly applied and must serve a legitimate state interest. The policy must limit enrollment prohibitions to situations wherein the school district lacks space or other resources to properly educate the child. Until the courts resolve this issue, the safer approach is to admit home-schooled students on a part-time basis except when it can be shown the school district would suffer real hardship and has a policy prohibiting such enrollment.

105 ILCS 5/10-20.24
Swanson v. Guthrie Independent School District No. I-1, 942 F.Supp. 511, (W.D. Okla. 1996)

11:45 May a school district limit a home schooler's access to participation in extra-curricular activities?

It is not clear whether the School Code provision governing part-time attendance has application to extra-curricular activities. A school district can probably establish a policy which requires students to be in attendance before they are eligible to participate in extra curricular activities. The Illinois High School Association (IHSA) has proposed rules which will prevent home schoolers from participating in certain IHSA activities. At the time of this writing it seems likely the rules will be challenged in court and in the General Assembly. Before the most recent rules change, IHSA permitted a resident home schooler to participate if the public school could establish the student's academic eligibility.

105 ILCS 5/10-20.24
IHSA By-law 3.025
Swanson v. Guthrie Independent School District No. 1-1, 942 F.Supp. 511, (W.D. Okla. 1996)

11:46 May a school district discriminate against a parent or a student because the student is home schooled?

Many home schoolers have elected home schooling because of their underlying religious beliefs. School attempts to retaliate against home schoolers for the election of a non-public education implicate First Amendment issues.

Peterson v. Minidoka County School District No. 331, 118 F.3d 1351 (9th Cir. 1997)

TRUANCY

11:50 What is a truant?

A truant is a child subject to compulsory school attendance who is absent from school without valid cause for a school day or any portion of a school day.

105 ILCS 5/26-2a
705 ILCS 405/3-1
People v. R.G., 131 Ill.2d 328, 546 N.E.2d 533, 137 Ill.Dec. 588 (1989)
In Interest of Burr, 119 Ill.App.2d 134, 255 N.E.2d 57 (4th Dist. 1969)

11:60   What duty does a school district have to notify parents of a student absence?

If a child in grades K-8 is absent from school, and there is no record the absence is for a valid cause and there is no notification the absence has been authorized, the school must, within two hours after the first class in which the child is enrolled, make a reasonable effort to telephone and notify the parent, legal guardian, or other person having legal custody of the child of the child's absence from school.

105 ILCS 5/26-3b

11:70   What is the penalty for encouraging truancy?

Any person who has custody or control of a child subject to compulsory attendance who knowingly or willfully permits the child to persist in truancy, if convicted, is guilty of a Class C misdemeanor and may be subject to up to 30 days imprisonment and/or a fine of up to $1500. Any person who willfully induces or attempts to induce any child to be absent from school or who knowingly employs or harbors any child who is unlawfully absent from school for three consecutive school days, if convicted, is guilty of a Class C misdemeanor. Any person who prevents or interferes with a child's attendance at school by threat, menace or intimidation is guilty of a Class A misdemeanor. A Class A misdemeanor is punishable by imprisonment for a term up to a year and a fine not to exceed $2500.

In any such proceeding against parents or guardians the school district must demonstrate it has attempted to counsel the student and the person(s) having custody and control of the student and has provided support services, alternative programs and other school resources in an effort to correct the truant behavior.

105 ILCS 5/26-8 et seq.
730 ILCS 5/5-8-3
730 ILCS 5/5-9-1

11:80   Who has jurisdiction to act with respect to truant minors?

Under given circumstances a school district, the school district truant officer, the regional superintendent of schools, the state's attorney and/or the Illinois Department of Children and Family Services may have jurisdiction.

105 ILCS 5/26-2a et seq.
305 ILCS 5/1 et seq.
705 ILCS 405/3-1 et seq.

11:90   What is a chronic or habitual truant?

A chronic or habitual truant is a child subject to compulsory attendance laws who is absent without valid cause from school for 10 percent or more of the previous 180 regular attendance days.

105 ILCS 5/26-2a

11:100   What restrictions are placed on a school district in dealing with a chronic or habitual truant?

Compulsory attendance laws provide a school district may take no punitive action against a chronic or habitual truant for truancy until the district has made available to the student all support services and other school resources in order to correct the chronic or habitually truant behavior.

105 ILCS 5/26-12

11:110   How are truant officers appointed?

Truant officers are appointed in one of two ways. A school board may appoint a truant officer and fix and pay his salary from school district funds. The regional superintendent of schools is required to appoint a truant officer for those districts which fail to appoint. The person appointed receives such compensation as may be fixed by the county board, and is paid by the county. The county truant officer appointment must be approved by a circuit judge.

105 ILCS 5/3-13
105 ILCS 5/26-5
Burris v. Board of Education, 221 Ill.App. 397 (4th Dist. 1920)

RIGHT TO ATTEND SCHOOL

11:120   Who is authorized to establish school attendance boundaries?

A school district with two or more attendance centers at the same grade level may establish attendance boundaries for each attendance center. A school board may not cause students to be segregated between two or more elementary schools on the basis of such factors as race, color, creed, national origin, sex, religion or other constitutionally-impermissible factor. In the absence of such factors, the establishment of school attendance zones is a discretionary power of a school board and neither students nor their parents may require the school board to assign them to any particular attendance center.

105 ILCS 5/10-21.3
Tometz v. Board of Education Waukegan City School District No. 61, 39 Ill.2d 593, 237 N.E.2d 498 (1968)

11:150   What is title IX?

Title IX is a federal statute which prohibits discrimination on the basis of sex. Title IX provides in part:

"No person in the United States shall, on the basis of sex, be excluded from participation in, be denied the benefits of, or be subjected to discrimination under any education program or activity receiving Federal financial assistance."

20 U.S.C. 1681

11:160   May a student be excluded from school because she is pregnant?

A school board may not exclude a student because of pregnancy. A school district is required to provide home instruction, correspondence courses or other courses of instruction for students who are unable to attend school because of pregnancy and for up to three months following the birth of a child or miscarriage.

105 ILCS 5/10-22.6a
105 ILCS 5/26-1

11:170 May a school district discipline a student because she is pregnant out of wedlock?

No.

20 U.S.C. 1681

Wort v. Vierling, 778 F.2d 1233 (7th Cir. 1985)

STUDENT RESIDENCY AND TUITION

11:180 Is a child living in a school district necessarily entitled to tuition-free enrollment in the schools of the district where he lives?

A child is entitled to tuition-free enrollment in the school district wherein he resides. Residency, in this context, has a specific meaning in the law. A child is presumed to be a resident of the school district wherein the persons who have legal custody of him reside. After a divorce, a child is presumed to reside with the custodial parent. A school district has a duty to charge tuition to nonresident pupils.

105 ILCS 5/10-20.12a

105 ILCS 5/10-20.12b

105 ILCS 5/10-22.5

Martinez Morales v. Bynum, 103 S.Ct. 1838, 461 U.S. 321, 75 L.Ed.2d 879 (1983)

Kraut v. Rochford, 51 Ill.App.3d 200, 366 N.E.2d 497, 9 Ill.Dec. 240 (1st Dist. 1977)

Turner v. Board of Education North Chicago Community High School District 123, 54 Ill.2d 68, 294 N.E.2d 264 (1973)

11:185 For purposes of school attendance, what is residence?

Residence is physical presence with an intention to remain on a permanent basis.

Connelly v. Gibbs, 112 Ill.App.3d 257, 445 N.E.2d 477, 68 Ill.Dec. 29 (1st Dist. 1983)

11:190 For purposes of establishing a student's residency, what does "legal custody" mean?

Legal custody means one of the following:

1) Custody exercised by a natural or adoptive parent with whom the student resides;

2) Custody granted by order of a court of competent jurisdiction to a person with whom the pupil resides for reasons other than to have access to the educational programs of the school district;

3) Custody exercised under a statutory short-term guardianship, provided that within 60 days of the pupil's enrollment a court order is entered that establishes a permanent guardianship and grants custody to a person with whom the pupil resides for reasons other than to have access to the educational programs of the school district;

4) Custody exercised by an adult caretaker relative who is receiving aid under the Illinois Public Aid Code for the pupil who resides with the adult caretaker relative for purposes other than to have access to the educational programs of the school district;

5) Custody exercised by an adult who demonstrates that, in fact, he or she has assumed and exercises legal responsibility for the pupil and provides the pupil with a regular fixed night time abode for purposes other than to have access to the educational programs of the school district.

105 ILCS 5/10-20.12b

11:195   May a school district waive tuition for a nonresident student?

In most cases, a school district need not admit a nonresident pupil and may require the student to attend school in the school district in which he resides.

A school district may permit a student from an adjacent school district to attend its schools tuition free when requested for the student's health and safety by the student or parent and when both school districts involved determine that the student's health and safety will be served by the enrollment. Neither school district is required to alter its existing transportation services as a result of such an agreement.

In other circumstances, if the school district elects to admit a nonresident pupil, it has a duty to charge tuition and may not waive tuition charges except in circumstances authorized by statute.

105 ILCS 5/10-20.12a
105 ILCS 5/20-20.12b

105 ILCS 5/10-22.5
105 ILCS 5/10-22.5a
Cohen v. Wauconda Community Unit School District No. 118, 779 F.Supp.
88 (N.D. Ill. 1991)

11:200　What is the amount of tuition for a nonresident pupil?

A school board has a duty to charge nonresident pupils tuition in an amount not to exceed 110 percent of the per capita cost of maintaining the schools of the district for the preceding school year. Per capita costs are computed by dividing the total cost of conducting and maintaining the schools of the district by the average daily attendance, including tuition pupils.

105 ILCS 5/10-20.12a

11:205　If a school district finds that an enrolled student is a non-resident, how can the student be required to pay tuition or removed from school?

Once a child has been enrolled in the school district the child must be provided due process before he can be charged tuition or barred from attendance. To charge tuition, the school board must notify the person who enrolled the student by certified mail of the amount of tuition due. Within ten days of the receipt of the notice the person who enrolled the student may request a hearing before the school board to review the determination. Within ten days after the receipt of the request, the school board must notify by certified mail the person requesting the hearing of the time and place of the hearing which must be held not less than ten nor more than 20 days after the notice of hearing is given.

The board or a hearing officer designated by it must conduct the hearing. The board and the person who enrolled the pupil may be represented at the hearing by representatives of their choice. The person who enrolled the pupil has the burden of going forward with the evidence. If the hearing is conducted by a hearing officer, the hearing officer, within five days after the conclusion of the hearing shall send a written report of his findings by certified mail to the board and to the person who enrolled the pupil. The person who enrolled the pupil may, within five days after receiving the findings, file written objections to the findings with the school board by sending the objections by certified mail addressed to the district superintendent.

Whether the hearing is conducted by the school board or a hearing officer, the school board shall, within fifteen days after the conclusion of the hearing decide whether the pupil is a resident of the district and the amount of any tuition required to be charged as a result of the pupil's attendance in the schools of the district. The school board must send a copy of its decision to the person who enrolled the pupil, and its decision is final.

If a hearing is requested, the pupil may, at the request of the person who enrolled the pupil, continue attendance at the schools of the district pending a final decision of the school board following the hearing. However, attendance of the pupil in the schools of the district does not relieve any person who enrolled the pupil of the obligation to pay the tuition charged for attendance if the final decision of the school board is that the pupil is a non-resident of the district.

If a pupil is determined to be a non-resident of the district for whom tuition is required to be charged, the school board must refuse to permit the pupil to continue attending the schools of the district unless the required tuition is paid for the pupil.

105 ILCS 5/20.12b

11:210   What is the penalty for providing false information regarding the residency of a pupil?

A person who knowingly or willfully provides false information to a school district regarding the residency of a pupil for the purpose of enabling the pupil to attend any school in the district without the payment of a nonresident tuition charge commits a Class C misdemeanor (not more than 30 days in jail and/or a fine not to exceed $1500).

105 ILCS 5/20.12b
730 ILCS 5/5-9-1

11:215   If a child begins a school term enrolled in a school district, may the child complete the school term in that district even if the child moves out of the district during the school term?

If a student becomes nonresident during a school term, the child must be permitted to attend school in the school district in which the child was originally enrolled and cannot be charged tuition for the remainder of the school term in which the child became non-resident.

105 ILCS 5/10-20.12a

11:220 Can residence of a child for school purposes be established by the temporary transfer of custody of the child to a relative?

The facts surrounding any temporary transfer of custody will determine whether or not residency has been established. The mere creation of a guardianship, transfer of custody, or change of address is not sufficient to establish residence for school attendance purposes.

105 ILCS 5/20.12b

Israel S. By Owens v. Board of Education of Oak Park and River Forest High School District 200, Cook County, 235 Ill.App.3d 652, 601 N.E.2d 1264, 176 Ill.Dec. 566 (1st Dist. 1992)

Kraut v. Rachford, 51 Ill.App.3d 206, 366 N.E.2d 497, 9 Ill.Dec. 240 (1st Dist. 1977)

Turner v. Board of Education North Chicago Community High School District 123, 54 Ill.2d 68, 294 N.E.2d 264 (1973)

11:225 Which school district must pay for a child's educational costs if the child is in a residential program to correct alcohol or drug dependency?

Except in the case of special education students, and unless otherwise agreed by the parties involved and unless educational services are not otherwise provided for, if an Illinois student under the age of 21 is enrolled in a residential program designed to correct alcohol or other drug dependency, the child's education is provided by the school district in which the residential facility is located and paid for by the school district in which the child resides.

105 ILCS 5/10-20.12a

Carbondale Community High School District No. 165 v. Herrin Community Unit School District No. 4, 303 Ill.App.3d 656, 708 N.E.2d 844, 237 Ill.Dec. 41 (5th Dist. 1999)

HOMELESS CHILD

11:230   Must a school district enroll a homeless child regardless of the child's residency?

Homeless child is broadly defined in the law to include (but is not limited to):

1) a person who lacks a fixed regular and adequate nighttime place of abode;

2) a person who has a permanent nighttime abode that is a supervised publicly or privately operated shelter designed to provide temporary living accommodations or an institution that provides temporary residence for a person intended to be institutionalized or a public or private place not designed or ordinarily used as a regular sleeping accommodation for human beings.

The parents of a homeless child have the option of:

• continuing the child's education in the school of origin for as long as the child remains homeless or if the child becomes permanently housed until the end of the academic year during which the housing was acquired;

• or enrolling the child in any school that non-homeless students who live in the attendance area in which the child is actually living are eligible to attend.

105 ILCS 45/1-5
105 ILCS 45/1-10

11:235   Must a school district provide transportation for a homeless child?

If a child becomes homeless or if a homeless child changes temporary living arrangements and if the child's parents or guardians decide to continue the child's education in the school of origin, the parents or guardians must provide or attempt to provide or may authorize relatives, friends, or a shelter to provide the child with transportation. If transportation is not provided in this manner it must be provided:

1) If the homeless child continues to live in the school district in which the school of origin is located, the child's to and from the school of origin must be provided by the school district in which the school of origin is located.

2) If the homeless child's living arrangements in the school district of origin terminate and the child, though continuing his education in the school of origin, begins living in another school district, the responsibility and the cost of providing the child with transportation to and from the school of origin shall be apportioned between the two districts unless the districts cannot agree on the apportionment in which case the costs shall be shared equally.

105 ILCS 45/1-15

HEALTH EXAMINATION AND IMMUNIZATION

11:240   At what grade levels are students required to show proof of health examination and immunization?

Proof of health examination and proof of immunization against preventable communicable disease are required upon entry to kindergarten or the first grade level a school offers, prior to entrance into nursery school, upon entering fifth and ninth grades, and upon first entry into any school. Additional examinations, including dental and vision examinations, may be required when deemed necessary by school authorities.

Tuberculosis examinations are required by the Department of Health when the child involved resides in an area which has a high incidence of tuberculosis.

105 ILCS 5/27-8.10

11:250   May a school board exclude a student for failure to show proof of immunization?

If a child does not present proof of health examination and immunizations by October 15 of a year in which such proof is required, the school board is required to suspend the child from school. There are limited statutory medical and/or constitutional circumstances under which the October 15 deadline may be extended for a particular child.

105 ILCS 5/27-8.1

11:252   May a school board establish a date earlier than October 15 for proof of immunization?

Yes, provided the school district gives notice of the requirement at least 60 days prior to the established earlier date.

105 ILCS 5/27-8.1(5)

11:255   May a child be exempted from immunizations or health examinations for religious reasons?

Children whose parents or guardians object to health examinations or immunizations on religious grounds may be exempted from examinations or immunizations on presentation to the local school authority a signed statement of objection.

105 ILCS 5/27-8.1 (8)

STUDENT FEES

11:260   May a school district charge student fees?

No fees may be charged which would have the effect of abridging a student's right to a free appropriate public education. Reasonable fees may be charged for services and activities which are tangential to the educational program; however, a school board must waive fees for those unable to pay. Book and towel rental fees have been held permissible. Tuition fees are not permissible.

105 ILCS 5/10-20.13
105 ILCS 5/10-22.25
Hamer v. Board of Education, School District No. 109, Lake County, 9 Ill.App.3d 663, 292 N.E.2d 569 (2d Dist. 1977)
Polzin v. Rand, McNally & Co., 250 Ill. 561, 95 N.E. 623 (1911)

11:270   May a school district charge a fee for driver education?

A school district may charge up to $50 for district residents between the ages of 15 and 21 years who take part in the driver education course. However, the fee must be waived for any such resident who is unable to pay, regardless of whether the individual is in school or out of school.

When space permits, the district also may provide driver education for residents above age 55 who have never been licensed to drive and may charge a fee not to exceed actual costs.

105 ILCS 5/27-23

STUDENT INSURANCE

11:280   Must a school board provide health insurance for student athletes?

A school board may provide accident and health insurance on a group or individual basis, or through nonprofit hospital service corporations or medical service plan corporations, or both, for its pupils who are injured while participating in any athletic activity under the jurisdiction of or sponsored or controlled by the district. The cost of the insurance, when paid from the funds of the district, must, to the extent there is sufficient money to do so, be paid from money derived from athletic activities. To the extent that money derived from athletic activities is insufficient, the cost may be paid from the educational fund.

105 ILCS 5/22-15

Frederich v. Board of Education of Community Unit School District No. 304, 59 Ill.App.3d 49, 375 N.E.2d 141, 16 Ill.Dec. 510 (2nd Dist. 1978)

STATUS OF MINORS

11:290   What is an emancipated minor?

An emancipated minor is a person 16 to 18 years old who has demonstrated the ability and capacity to manage his own affairs and to live wholly or partially independent of his parents or guardians. Such an individual may petition a circuit court for a declaration of complete or partial emancipation. Marriage emancipates a minor for most purposes in the law.

750 ILCS 30/2 et seq.

Kowalski v. Liska, 78 Ill.App.3d 64, 397 N.E.2d 39, 33 Ill.Dec. 706 (1st Dist. 1979)

11:295   May an emancipated minor establish residence in a school district other than that in which his parents reside?

An emancipated minor may establish his own residence.

750 ILCS 30/2 et seq.

11:300   May minors buy tobacco products?

State law prohibits the purchase of tobacco or tobacco products in any form by minors under 18 years of age. The statute also prohibits persons who have reached majority from buying tobacco for minors. The law does not prohibit the possession of tobacco products by minors.

720 ILCS 675/1

CHILD ABUSE AND NEGLECT

11:310   What is an "abused" child?

An "abused child" is a child whose parent or immediate family member, or any person responsible for the child's welfare, or any individual residing in the same home as the child, or a paramour of the child's parent does any of the following:

1) inflicts, causes to be inflicted, or allows to be inflicted upon such child physical injury, by other than accidental means, which causes death, disfigurement, impairment of physical or emotional health, or loss or impairment of any bodily function;

2) creates substantial risk of physical injury to such child by other than accidental means which would be likely to cause death, disfigurement, impairment of physical or emotional health, or loss or impairment of any bodily function;

3) commits or allows to be committed any sex offense against such child, and extending the Criminal Code definitions of sex offenses to include children under 18 years of age;

4) commits or allows to be committed an act or acts or torture upon such child; or

5) inflicts excessive corporal punishment.

6) commits or allows to be committed the offense of female genital mutilation against the child.

325 ILCS 5/3

11:320   What is a "neglected" child?

A "neglected child" is any child who is not receiving the proper or necessary nourishment or medically indicated treatment, including food or care not provided solely on the basis of present or anticipated mental or physical impairment as determined by a physician acting alone or in consultation with other physicians or otherwise is not receiving the proper or necessary support, education as required by law, or medical or other remedial care recognized under state law as necessary for a child's well-being, or other care necessary for his well-being, including adequate food, clothing, and shelter; or who is abandoned by his parents or other person responsible for the child's welfare without a proper plan of care. A child is not neglected for the sole reason that the child's parent or other person responsible for the child's welfare has left the child with an adult relative for any period of time.

325 ILCS 5/3

11:330   Are school personnel responsible for reporting suspected cases of child abuse or neglect?

All school personnel are required to report any suspected child abuse or neglect directly to the Illinois Department of Children and Family Services (DCFS) by telephoning a toll-free number to a DCFS central register.

Any person required by law to report child abuse and neglect who willfully fails to report is guilty of a Class A misdemeanor.

325 ILCS 5/3
325 ILCS 5/4.02
325 ILCS 5/7

11:340   What information must be included in a report of child abuse or neglect?

All reports from educational employees required by law to report cases of child abuse or neglect must include, when known, the name and address of the child and his parents or other persons having his custody, the child's age, the nature of the child's condition including any evidence of previous injuries or disabilities, and any other information which the person reporting believes might be helpful in establishing the cause of such abuse or neglect and the identity of the person believed to have caused the abuse or neglect.

325 ILCS 5/7

**11:350   What action may be taken against a school
            employee who files a report of child abuse or
            neglect that turns out to be false?**

School personnel are granted broad immunities against civil
and criminal claims when they file a report of suspected child
abuse or neglect in good faith, even if the report proves ground-
less. Such immunities are not available, however, to the individual who knowingly files a false report.

325 ILCS 5/4
325 ILCS 5/9

STUDENT TRANSPORTATION

**11:360   For which students must a school board
            provide free transportation to and from school?**

Community consolidated, community unit, consolidated,
consolidated high school and combined school districts which
include a district which was previously required to provide free
transportation are required to provide free transportation for
students residing one and one-half miles or more from any
school to which they are assigned for attendance unless adequate public transportation is available. Charter districts, elementary school districts, community high school districts, township high school districts and certain unit districts are not
required to provide free transportation (although almost all do).

105 ILCS 5/29-3

**11:365   When a school district is obligated to provide
            transportation, must the district transport the
            student the full distance, door to door, from
            home to school and back?**

No. The school district may establish bus routes which pick
up students from and deliver students to specified pick up
points not more than 1.5 miles from the students' homes. A
school district must be careful to meet its duty to protect the
safety of the students in establishing bus stops and bus routes.

105 ILCS 5/29-3

Garrett v. Grant School District No. 124, 139 Ill.App.3d 569, 487 N.E.2d 699, 93 Ill.Dec. 874 (2nd Dist. 1985)

Posteher v. Pana Community Unit School District, 96 Ill.App.3d 709, 421 N.E.2d 1049, 52 Ill.Dec. 186 (4th Dist. 1981)

Katamay v. Chicago Transit Authority, 53 Ill.2d 27, 289 N.E.2d 623 (1972)

Sims v. Chicago Transit Authority, 351 Ill.App. 314, 115 N.E.2d 96 (1st Dist. 1953), rev. on other grounds 4 Ill.2d 60, 122 N.E.2d 221 (1954)

11:370 For purposes of requiring a school board to bus students to and from school, how is the one-and-one-half-mile minimum distance measured?

The one-and-one-half-mile minimum distance is measured from the exit of the property where the student resides to the point where pupils are normally unloaded at the school attended. The distance is measured by determining the shortest distance on normally traveled roads or streets.

105 ILCS 5/29-3

11:380 When must a school board provide free transportation for students living less than one and one-half miles from school?

A school board must provide free transportation for students living less than one and one-half miles from school when conditions are such that walking either to or from the school to which a pupil is assigned for attendance or to or from a pick-up point or bus stop constitutes a serious hazard to the safety of the pupil due to vehicular traffic. Transportation need not be provided if adequate public transportation is available.

There is a procedure whereby a parent may petition the school board to conduct a study and make findings regarding alleged safety hazards. The initial determination of what constitutes a serious hazard is made by the school board with review by the Illinois Department of Transportation (IDOT) in consultation with the State Superintendent of Education. IDOT's decision may be appealed to circuit court under the provisions of the Administrative Review Act.

105 ILCS 5/29-3
735 ILCS 5/3-101 et seq.

11:390 Is a school district required to provide transportation to and from summer school classes?

A school district is not required to provide summer school transportation except for special education students. If the school district chooses to provide transportation, it may charge participating students a transportation fee not to exceed cost.

105 ILCS 5/29-3.2a

11:394 Must a school district provide transportation to and from extra curricular activities?

The school district may elect to provide transportation, but is not required to do so. The school district may charge for the transportation in an amount not to exceed its cost (which can include a reasonable allowance for depreciation of the vehicles used). If the school board elects not to provide transportation it should carefully consider the practical aspects and risks associated with having students drive themselves and other students to and from such events and should weigh those risks against the value of the program offered and the cost of providing transportation.

105 ILCS 5/29-3.1

ACADEMIC CLUBS AND EXTRA-CURRICULAR ACTIVITIES

11:400 Do students have a right to fairness in the selection process for student clubs?

A student does not have a property interest in membership in a particular student club or activity. Therefore, a suit based solely on the fairness of the selection process for membership in the club or activity without the allegation of some other constitutional deprivation will fail.

Dangler v. Yorktown Central Schools, 771 F.Supp. 625 (S.D. N.Y. 1991)
Price v. Young, 580 F.Supp. 1 (E.D. Ark. 1983)
Karnstein v. Pewaukee School Board, 557 F.Supp. 565 (E.D. Wisc. 1983)
Dallam v. Cumberland Valley School District, 391 F.Supp. 358 (M.D. Pa. 1975)

11:403 May a school prevent a student from participating in extra curricular activities because of pregnancy or because the student has had a child out of wedlock?

Cases wherein the school officials have health or safety concerns about the student's participation should be distinguished from cases wherein the desire to exclude is based on moral or character considerations. When a student's health or safety might be endangered by participation, school officials may prevent the student's participation on the same grounds for which they would exclude any other student with any other medical condition. Generally, school officials should seek advice from a physician before making the exclusion decision.

Students may not be denied admission or otherwise excluded from activities (e.g., National Honor Society) because of character or moral concerns relating to pregnancy or giving birth out of wedlock, because to do so would likely violate both title IX and the Pregnancy Discrimination Act. Character or moral considerations generally have as their basis the school's disapproval of premarital sex, but such policies target pregnant students and female students who have given birth out of wedlock without affecting male students or female students who have had premarital sex without having become pregnant.

Chipman v. Grant County School District, 30 F.Supp.2d 975 (E.D. Ky. 1998)

11:405 What grade point average must a student maintain to be eligible for extra-curricular activities?

Beginning with the 1998-1999 school year, school districts which maintain a high school must have a "no-pass, no-play" policy. The relevant statute does not mandate a specific minimum average, but it does require the school board to "establish, implement and enforce a uniform and consistent policy" under which a student in grades 9-12 who fails to maintain a specified minimum grade point average or a specified minimum grade in each course in which the student is enrolled, or both, is suspended from further participation in any school sponsored or school supported athletic or extra-curricular activities for a specified period or until a specified minimum grade point average or minimum grade or both are earned by the student.

105 ILCS 5/10-20.30

SEXUAL HARASSMENT OF STUDENTS

11:410   May a student bring a suit under title IX for sexual harassment by a teacher?

Sexual harassment of a student by a teacher is prohibited by title IX and provisions of the Illinois Human Rights Act. There are two kinds of sexual harassment: sexual harassment which occurs when the teacher conditions the grant of a benefit on the receipt of a sexual favor (or punishes the student for rejecting the favor) and hostile environment harassment which occurs when there is a sexually intimidating, hostile or offensive environment. An individual's personal liability is broad. An educational employer's liability is relatively narrow.

34 C.F.R 106.31 et seq.

62 C.F.R. 12033

Doe By and Through Doe v. Petaluma City School District, 54 F.3d 1447 (9th Cir. 1996) reversing 830 F.Supp. 1560 (N.D. Cal. 1993)

Franklin v. Gwinnett County Public Schools, 112 S.Ct. 1028, 503 U.S. 60, 117 L.Ed.2d 208 (1992)

11:415   Under what circumstances may school district officials be held liable for the sexual abuse of a student by a school employee?

School officials may be held liable if they:

1) had notice of unconstitutional conduct;

2) demonstrated deliberate indifference or tacitly authorized the conduct;

3) failed to take remedial steps and

4) the failure resulted in damage to the child.

62 C.F.R. 12033

Gebser et al. v. Lago Vista Independent School District, 118 S.Ct.1989, 524 U.S. 274, 141 L.Ed.2d 277 (1998)

Canutillo Independent School District v. Leija, 101 F.3d 393 (5th Cir. 1997) reh. and sugg. for reh. den. 106 F.3d 399, cert. den. 117 S.Ct. 2434, 520 U.S. 1265, 138 L.Ed.2d 195

Smith v. Metropolitan School District, Perry Township, 128 F.3d 1014 (7th Cir. 1997)

Rosa H. v. San Elizario Independent School District, 106 F.3d. 648 (5th Cir. 1997)

Jojola v. Chavez, 55 F.3d 488 (10th Cir. 1995)
Doe v. Taylor Independent School District, 15 F.3d 443 (5th Cir. 1994)

11:416 Must a student harassment plaintiff prove that sexual advances from a school employee were unwelcome?

In a title IX suit for damages, the age of the student will be determinative of whether or not such a proof is necessary. A student under age 16 cannot consent to sexual advances. In other possible related causes of action (a teacher dismissal case, for example) age and consent may be irrelevant.

Mary M. v. North Lawrence Community School Corp., 951 F.Supp. 82 (S.D. Ind. 1997) rev. 91 F.3d 1220 (7th Cir. 1997) reh.den., cert.den. 118 S.Ct. 2369, __ U.S.__, 141 L.Ed.2d 737 (1998)

11:417 May a student who has been sexually harassed by a school employee sue for money damages?

Money damages are available under title IX of the Education Amendments of 1972. Under title IX, a plaintiff may not recover using principles of agency (the school is responsible for its employee's actions whether it knows about them or not) or constructive notice (the school was responsible because it should have known what its employee was doing), nor can a plaintiff recover alleging the school had a duty to protect the student from harm.

Gebser et al. v. Lago Vista Independent School District, 118 S.Ct.1989, 524 U.S. 274, 141 L.Ed.2d 277 (1998)
Gates v. Unified School District No. 449 of Leavenworth County, 996 F.2d 36 (10th Cir. 1993)
Franklin v. Gwinnett County Public Schools, 112 S.Ct. 1028, 503 U.S. 60, 117 L.Ed.2d 208 (1992)
Doe v. Taylor Independent School District, 975 F.2d 137 (5th Cir. 1992)

11:420 Must a school district take action to prevent student-to-student sexual harassment?

A school must take action to stop student-to-student sexual harassment that occurs when students are involved in school activities or otherwise under the supervision of school authorities and when such harassment is known to school officials. To prevail in a student-to-student case, the plaintiff must show:

1) the victim was subjected to unwelcome harassment based on gender;

2) the harassment was sufficiently severe or pervasive and objectively offensive that it can be said to deprive the victim of access to educational opportunities or benefits provided by the school (hostile environment);

3) the school knew of the harassment and failed to take appropriate remedial action.

School officials have title IX liability only when they are "deliberately indifferent" to acts of student-on-student sexual harassment and only when their response is "clearly unreasonable in light of the known circumstances."

62 C.F.R. 12033

Adusumilli v. Illinois Institute of Technology, 191 F.3d 455 (7th Cir. 1999)

Davis v. Monroe County Board of Education, 119 S.Ct.1661, 526 U.S.629, 143 L.Ed.2d 839 (1999)

Doe v. University of Illinois, 138 F.3d 653 (7th Cir. 1998)

Seamon v. Snow, 84 F.3d 1226 (10th Cir. 1996)

Doe By and Through Doe v. Petaluma City School District, 54 F.3d 1447 (9th Cir. 1996) reversing 830 F.Supp. 1560 (N.D. Cal. 1993)

D.R. v. Middle Bucks Area Vocational Technical School, 972 F.2d 1364 (3rd Cir. 1992) cert.den. 113 S.Ct. 1045, 506 U.S. 1079, 122 L.Ed.2d 354(1993)

Franklin v. Gwinnett County Public Schools, 112 S.Ct. 1028, 503 U.S. 60, 117 L.Ed.2d 208 (1992)

11:422   Which factors will the courts consider in determining whether there is a student-to-student hostile environment?

To determine whether an environment is hostile because of student-to-student sexual harassment, the court considers:

1) the frequency of the conduct;

2) the severity of the conduct;

3) whether the conduct is physically threatening or humiliating rather than merely offensive;

4) whether the conduct unreasonably interfered with the victim's performance.

62 C.F.R. 12033

Davis v. Monroe County Board of Education, 119 S.Ct.1661, 526 U.S.629, 143 L.Ed.2d 839 (1999)

11:428   Does a school district have a duty to protect a student from harassment based on the victim's homosexuality?

While sexual orientation is not explicitly protected by Illinois or federal law, the courts are issuing decisions which suggest the trend is to provide protection for homosexuals, often through title IX claims. A school district's duties and potential liabilities are no greater than those applicable in the instance of gender-based sexual harassment allegations which require actual notice to school officials and deliberate indifference or tacit endorsement of the harassment.

62 C.F.R. 12033
Doe v. Dallas Independent School District, 153 F.3d 211 (5th Cir. 1998)
Nabozny v. Podlesny, et al., 92 F.3d 446 (7th Cir. 1996)
Kinman v. Omaha Public School District, 94 F.3d 463 (8th Cir. 1996)

11:430   Does a school district have a constitutional duty to protect a student from harm?

Unless particular facts exist which establish that the school district has a custodial relationship with respect to the student, a school district has no affirmative duty to protect the student from harm. The state has a duty to protect when the student is in the involuntary custody of the state or when the state creates a dangerous situation or renders the student more vulnerable to danger. The student's mandatory attendance at school is not sufficient to create such a custodial relationship. To create constitutional duty, affirmative action by a state actor to harm a student or to subject the student to danger is necessary.

Stevens v. Umsted, 131 F.3d 697 (7th Cir. 1997)
Becerra v. Asher, 105 F.3d 1042 (5th Cir. 1997) supp. on den. of reh., reh. and sugg. for reh.den. 11 F.3d 894
Seamon v. Snow, 84 F.3d 1226 (10th Cir. 1996)
Wilson v. Webb, 869 F.Supp. 496 (W.D. Ky. 1994)
Doe v. Board of Education of Hononegah School District No. 207, 833 F.Supp. 1366 (N.D. Ill. 1993)
DeShaney v. Winnebago County Department of Social Services, 109 S.Ct. 998, 489 U.S. 189, 103 L.Ed.2d 249 (1989)

11:435   Must a school district defend an employee charged by a student or staff member with sexual misconduct?

A school board's duty to indemnify and defend employees against civil rights damages and claims is triggered when scope of employment allegations are made in the lawsuit. However, if other facts alleged in the complaint make it impossible to conclude that the employee's improper actions were within the scope of employment, the employer will be relieved of its duty to indemnify and defend. If the lawsuit alleges sexual misconduct and that misconduct, as alleged, serves no conceivable public purpose and advances completely personal objectives, the employer has no duty to indemnify and defend.

   105 ILCS 5/10-20.20
   Deloney v. Board of Education of Thornton Township School District No. 205, Cook County, Illinois, 281 Ill.App.3d 775, 666 N.E.2d 792, 217 Ill.Dec. 123 (1st Dist. 1996)

11:440   How long after the occurrence of an alleged incident of abuse may a student wait to bring a claim against a school or a school official before the claim is barred?

Statutes of limitations prevent the award of damages for certain stale claims. In cases in which the plaintiff was an adult at the time of the injury, the limitations period usually begins running at the moment of the injury. In the instance of claims involving under-age plaintiffs, the limitations period does not begin to run until the minor reaches majority—18 years of age in Illinois.

Generally, in repressed memory cases, the limitation period begins when the victim knew or reasonably should have known of the injury. In most cases, the limitations period for sexual abuse cases in Illinois is two years.

   M.H.D. v. Westminster School, 172 F.3d 797 (11th Cir. 1999)
   W.J.L v. Bugge, 573 N.W.2d 677 (Minn. Sup. Ct. 1998)
   Ernstes v. Warner, 860 F.Supp. 1338 (S.D. Ind. 1994)

11:450   Does the exposure of a student to sexually explicit curriculum material constitute sexual harassment?

Probably not. While opt-out opportunities should be offered to parents and students who may be offended by sexually explicit material, absent a showing of actions by school officials which would shock the conscience, no cause of action for exposure to such material would survive.

Brown v. Hot, Sexy and Safer Productions, Inc. 68 F3d 525 (1st Cir. 1995) cert.den., 116 S.Ct. 1044, 516 U.S. 1159, 134 L.Ed. 2d 191 (1996)

12: STUDENT DISCIPLINE

DISCIPLINARY AUTHORITY

12:10 Who is responsible for maintaining student discipline in the public schools?

Teachers, other certificated employees and any other person whether or not a certificated employee who provides a related service for or with respect to a student have a statutory duty to maintain discipline in school, on school grounds, at extra-curricular events, and with respect to all school programs. Each school board must establish a policy on student discipline.

105 ILCS 5/24-24

Prest by Prest v. Sparta Community Unit School District No. 140, 157 Ill.App.3d 569, 510 N.E.2d 595, 109 Ill.Dec. 727 (5th Dist. 1987)

12:20 What is "in loco parentis"?

"In loco parentis" means in place of parent. The phrase is used in education to describe the relationship of certificated school officials to students. While certain school officials have in loco parentis authority by statute, the power of school officials to exercise control over students is not so broad as that of a parent.

The doctrine of in loco parentis protects certain school district employees from liability for employment related acts of ordinary negligence. Such employees may create liability for the school district resulting from certain employment related acts which constitute willful and wanton misconduct.

105 ILCS 5/24-24

Ausmus by Ausmus v. Board of Education of City of Chicago, 155 Ill.App.3d 705, 508 N.E.2d 298, 108 Ill.Dec. 137 (1st Dist. 1987)

Montag v. Board of Education, School District No. 40, Rock Island County, 112 Ill.App.3d 1039, 446 N.E.2d 299, 68 Ill.Dec. 565 (3rd Dist. 1983)

People v. Davis, 88 Ill.App.3d 728, 410 N.E.2d 673, 43 Ill.Dec. 673 (2nd Dist. 1980)

Thomas v. Chicago Board of Education, 60 Ill.App.3d 729, 377 N.E.2d 355, rev. on other grounds 77 Ill.2d 178, 395 N.E.2d 538, 32 Ill.Dec. 308 (1978)

Kobylanski v. Chicago Board of Education, 63 Ill.2d 165, 347 N.E.2d 705 (1976)

12:30   May a school district extend its disciplinary control of students to instances of misbehavior which occur off school grounds?

A school district's authority to regulate student conduct on or off school grounds is limited to that conduct which relates to the administration of the school's educational process.

Klein v. Smith, 635 F.Supp. 1440 (Me. 1986)

Board of Education of Rogers, Arkansas v. McCluskey, 102 S.Ct. 3469, 458 U.S. 966, 73 L.Ed.2d 1273 (1982) on rem. 688 F.2d 596, reh. den. 103 S.Ct. 16 103 S.Ct. 16, __ U.S. __, 73 L.Ed.2d 1402 (1982)

McNaughton v. Circleville Board of Education, 46 Ohio Misc. 12, 345 N.E.2d 649 (1974)

12:35   May school officials adopt a student "no loitering" policy?

A "no loitering" policy will not present constitutional concerns with respect to speech or assembly so long as school officials can show a justifiable governmental reason for the policy, such as the avoidance of damage to property or the prevention of traffic hazards posed by students.

Wiemerslage v. Maine Township High School District 207, 29 F.3d 1147 (7th Cir. 1994)

12:40   May a school board establish rules of conduct governing spectators at extra-curricular activities?

A school board may make and enforce reasonable rules of conduct and sportsmanship for all athletic and extra-curricular school events. Any person who violates the rules, whether adult or student, may be denied admission to school events for not more than one year, provided a written 10-day notice of the violation is given and a hearing held on the violation by the school board.

The administration of any school may sign a complaint as agent of the school against any person committing any offense at a school event.

105 ILCS 5/24-24

12:45   May students be disciplined by assignment of Saturday detentions?

A school district may assign students to serve Saturday detentions. However, teachers may not be required to teach on Saturdays. Provided the school district has complied with its bargaining obligations, it may seek teacher volunteers to supervise a Saturday detention class.

105 ILCS 5/24-2

12:46   Must a school district provide transportation for students required to attend after-school detention?

If the student is required to attend the detention, the school district must provide advance notice to the parents and must provide transportation for those students for whom the district provides transportation to and from school (no transportation is required for walkers). The common method of avoiding the requirement is to offer a punishment alternative to the student and his parents.

105 ILCS 5/29-3
105 ILCS 5/29-3.1

12:60   What input on student discipline policies must a school board allow members of the public?

Every school board is required to establish a parent-teacher advisory committee on student discipline and school bus safety. The committee maintains a reciprocal reporting system between local law enforcement officials and the school district regarding criminal offenses committed by students. Schools are required to provide parents with a copy of the student discipline policy within 15 days of the start of school each year or within 15 days after a student who transfers into the district starts classes and must inform students of the contents of the student discipline policy.

105 ILCS 5/10-20.14
23 Ill. Admin. Code 1.280 c) et seq.

PARENT AND STUDENT PROTECTIONS

12:70   What is due process?

There are two types of due process, substantive and procedural. Both relate to the fairness of rules regulating conduct. Substantive due process requires rules be reasonably defined, fairly administered and related to a valid purpose. Procedural due process refers to the procedures employed to guarantee substantive due process.

To determine what process is constitutionally due, the courts balance three factors:

1) the private interest that will be affected by the official action;

2) the risk of an erroneous deprivation of the interest through the procedures used and the probable value, if any, of additional or substitute procedural safeguards; and

3) the government's interest.

Gilbert v. Homar, 117 S.Ct. 1807, 520 U.S. 924, 138 L.Ed.2d 120 (1997) on rem. 149 F.3d 1164

Cleveland Board of Education v. Loudermill, 105 S.Ct. 1487, 470 U.S. 532, 84 L.Ed.2d 494 (1985) on rem. 763 F.2d 202 (6th Cir. 1985)

Goss v. Lopez, 95 S.Ct. 729, 419 U.S. 565, 42 L.Ed.2d 725 (1975)

Wood v. Strickland, 95 S.Ct. 992, 420 U.S. 308, 43 L.Ed.2d 214 (1975), reh. den. 95 S.Ct. 1589, 42 U.S. 921, 43 L.Ed.2d 790 (1975)

12:80   In what instances is a student entitled to a hearing before discipline can be invoked by school authorities?

Some form of hearing is required in each instance when, as a result of the discipline, the student will be deprived of access to educational services.

105 ILCS 5/10-22.6

Goss v. Lopez, 95 S.Ct. 729, 419 U.S. 565, 42 L.Ed.2d 725 (1975)

Wood v. Strickland, 95 S.Ct. 992, 420 U.S. 308, 43 L.Ed.2d 214 (1975), reh. den. 95 S.Ct. 1589, 42 U.S. 921, 43 L.Ed.2d 790 (1975)

Linwood v. Board of Education of Peoria School District 150, 463 F.2d 763 (7th Cir. 1972)

12:100   Are communications between a student and an administrator or guidance counselor considered privileged?

There is no privilege with respect to communications between school officials and students. School officials, including guidance counselors, may be required to testify as to the content of conversations they have with students.

Cook County Federal Savings and Loan Association v. Griffin, 73 Ill.App.3d 210, 391 N.E.2d 473, 29 Ill.Dec. 210 (1st Dist. 1979)

12:110   May a parent bring a suit for damages against a drug dealer who sells drugs to the parent's child?

The Parental Right of Recovery Act provides any person who (1) sells or transfers an illegal drug to a minor, or (2) supplies to a seller or to any other person an illegal drug which is ultimately sold or transferred to a minor under circumstances where it is reasonably foreseeable the drug may eventually be sold or transferred to a minor is liable to the parent or legal guardian of the minor to whom such illegal drug is sold or transferred for any damages proximately caused by the sale or transfer.

The parent or legal guardian may recover actual damages suffered by the parent or legal guardian resulting from the sale or transfer of the illegal drug to the minor, including pain and suffering. A parent or legal guardian who is awarded damages under the Act may be entitled to punitive damages and/or attorney fees.

740 ILCS 120/3

STUDENT EXPRESSION AND DRESS

12:120   Does the First Amendment protect student political expression?

The First Amendment protects student speech. A school board may not regulate a student's individual political expression unless it can show the expression is obscene or that without regulation there would be material and substantial disorder or invasion of the rights of others. When the speech might reasonably be perceived to bear the imprimatur of the school, school officials are entitled to greater control over student expression. School officials have the discretion to disassociate the school from an entire range of speech, including speech that is ungrammatical, poorly written, inadequately researched, biased or prejudiced, vulgar or profane or unsuitable for immature audiences.

Denno v. School Board of Volusia County, Florida, 193 F.3d 1178 (11th Cir. 1999)

Chandler v. McMinnville School District, 978 F.2d 524 (9th Cir. 1992)

Tinker v. Des Moines Independent School District, 89 S.Ct. 733, 393 U.S. 503, 21 L.Ed.2d 731 (1969)

12:122   May a school district regulate personal student internet sites, messages or web pages?

Unless school officials can show that the message, page or site and its contents would materially interfere with or disrupt the educational process, or substantially interfere with school discipline, the message, page or site is protected by the First Amendment. Even if the messages posted are unpopular or critical of the school or school officials, school officials may not limit them, because to do so would be an impermissible attempt to regulate speech based solely on its content. Under appropriate circumstances school officials may regulate what material or data may be accessed, keyboarded, saved or loaded on school owned computers.

Urofsky v. Gilmore, 161 F.3d 191 (4th Cir 1999)

Beussink v. Woodland R-IV School District, 30 F.Supp.2d 1175 (E.D. Mo. 1998)

12:123   May a school district prohibit student political buttons?

A school district may not restrict student political speech absent a showing of substantial disruption or material interference with school activities. Therefore, absent such a showing, "scab buttons" during a teacher strike, candidate buttons during a political campaign, or other political speech which is neither offensive nor vulgar may not be regulated.

Chandler v. McMinnville School District, 978 F.2d 524 (9th Cir. 1992)

**12:125   May a school board or school administration
            establish a student dress code?**

Courts recognize a student's right to freedom of expression
with respect to manner of dress and length of hair. While there
is not absolute uniformity of judicial interpretation, caution is
advisable in the adoption of student dress codes or hair length
regulations. To safely regulate, a school board must demonstrate disruption of the orderly process of a school function or
endangerment to health or safety.

105 ILCS 5/10-22.25b
Phoenix Elementary School District No. 1 v Green, 943 P.2d 836 (1997)
Alabama and Coushatta Tribes of Texas v. Trustees of Big Sandy, 817
F.Supp. 1319 (E.D. Tex. 1993)
Olesen v. Board of Education of School District 228, 676 F.Supp. 820
(N.D. Ill. 1987)
Harper v. Edgewood Board of Education, 655 F.Supp. 1353 (S.D. Ohio
1987)
Copeland v. Hawkins, 352 F.Supp. 1022 (N.D. Ill. 1973)
Arnold v. Carpenter, 459 F.2d 939 (7th Cir. 1972).
Laine v. Dittman, 125 Ill.App.2d 136, 259 N.E.2d 824 (2nd Dist. 1970)
Breen v. Kahl, 419 F.2d 1034 (7th Cir. 1969)

**12:126   May a school board adopt a mandatory dress
            code which requires students to wear uniforms
            to school?**

Illinois statutes permit a school board to "adopt a school uniform or dress code policy that governs all or certain individual
attendance centers that is necessary to maintain the orderly
process of a school function or prevent the endangerment of student health or safety."

A school board contemplating a mandatory uniform or dress
code policy should carefully examine court decisions cited here
and elsewhere in this section to determine the legality of any
specific limitation contemplated. Mandatory uniform policies
are constitutionally suspect, as are many common dress code
limitations.

105 ILCS 5/10-22.25b
Phoenix Elementary School District No. 1 v. Green, 943 P.2d 836 (1997)

12:127   May a school board ban student tattoos or non-ear piercings?

The courts have given student tattoos and body piercings First Amendment protections when a school district has been unable to demonstrate health or safety concerns.

Stephenson v. Davenport Community School District, 110 F.3d. 1303 (8th Cir. 1997)

Olesen v. Board of Education of School District 228, 676 F.Supp. 820 (N.D. Ill. 1987)

12:128   May a school board ban student T-shirts which contain offensive sayings or which depict offensive or obscene material?

The courts are divided as to the breadth of school's authority to regulate student speech in this context. To safely regulate, the school should have a clear policy prohibiting the item to be banned and must show that the speech would undermine the authority of school administrators or disrupt school operations. Speculation as to the potential for subversion of authority or disruption will likely be insufficient to support regulation.

Many of the court cases in this area are fact-driven. The more excessive the conduct being regulated, the more likely the courts are to uphold the school's right to establish limitations.

105 ILCS 5/10-22.25b

Pyle v. Hadley School Committee, 861 F.Supp. 157 (D.Mass. 1994)

McIntire v. Bethel Independent School District No. 3, 804 F.Supp. 1415 (W.D. Okla. 1992)

Broussard v. School Board of the City of Norfolk, 801 F.Supp. 1526 (E.D. Va. 1992)

Poling v. Murphy, 872 F.2d 757 (6th Cir. 1989)

Gano v. School District 411, 674 F.Supp. 796 (D.C. Ida. 1987)

STUDENT PUBLICATIONS

12:130   May school officials regulate student publications?

School officials may regulate the contents of school sponsored student expression under certain limited circumstances. In instances when the expression is not in the context of a public forum and a valid educational purpose for regulation exists, reasonable regulation of school-sponsored speech is permissible.

These principles would most often apply to publications produced in class as part of the curriculum or to publications sponsored by the school for particular educational purposes.

Student personal expression is not subject to the same limitations and is broadly protected by the First Amendment. Thus, publications not sponsored by the school are not subject to regulation by the school, other than through reasonable rules regulating distribution on school premises.

Rosenberger v. Rector and Visitors of the University of Virginia, 115 S.Ct. 2510, 515 U.S. 819, 132 L.Ed.2d 700 (1995)

Hazelwood v. Kuhlmeier, 108 S.Ct. 562, 484 U.S. 260, 98 L.Ed.2d 592 (1988), on rem. 840 F.2d 596 (8th Cir. 1988)

Scoville v. Board of Education of Joliet Township High School District 204, 425 F.2d 10 (7th Cir. 1972)

Fujishama v. Board of Education, 460 F.2d 1355 (7th Cir. 1972)

12:133   What are a public forum, a limited public forum and a non-public forum?

A public forum is a forum that has, by tradition, been held open for free expression. In these places, the state must show a narrowly tailored compelling state interest to limit debate. The compelling state interest standard is very difficult to meet.

A non-public forum is one which has been traditionally restricted by the state so that expression has been limited to comport with the purpose of the property. To regulate debate in a non-public forum, the state need only avoid the suppression of speech based solely on its content and demonstrate a rational reason to regulate.

A limited public forum is an otherwise non-public forum which the state has intentionally opened for expressive use by the public. In a limited public forum, the state must show a compelling state interest to limit debate and the regulation must be narrowly tailored to meet that objective.

In forum analysis, the difficult determination is whether a forum has remained non-public or, because certain uses have been permitted, the forum has become a limited public forum.

Planned Parenthood of Southern Nevada v. Clark County School District, 941 F.2d 817 (9th Cir. 1991)

Perry Education Association v. Perry Local Educators' Association, 103 S.Ct. 948, 460 U.S. 37, 74 L.Ed.2d 794 (1983)

12:135 May school officials regulate the content of advertising in school publications?

In most circumstances, school publications are not public forums and schools have a right to impose reasonable restrictions on the advertisements which may appear in them. Schools may adopt reasonable policies for the acceptance and rejection of advertisements in school publications, such as the school yearbook, newspaper and athletic programs.

Yeo v. Town of Lexington, 131 F.3d 241 (1st Cir. 1997) cert. den. 118 S.Ct. 2060, __U.S.__, 141 L.Ed.2d 138 (1998)

Planned Parenthood of Southern Nevada v. Clark County School District, 941 F.2d 817 (9th Cir. 1991)

Hazelwood v. Kuhlmeier, 108 S.Ct. 562, 484 U.S. 260, 98 L.Ed.2d 592 (1988), on rem. 840 F.2d 596 (8th Cir. 1988)

12:140 May a school board adopt rules regulating the distribution of student publications?

A school board may establish reasonable regulations setting forth the time, manner, and place at which distribution of student written material may occur.

Fujishama v. Board of Education, 460 F.2d 1355 (7th Cir. 1972)

PROHIBITED BEHAVIORS

12:150 Are there criminal penalties for the unlawful use of weapons on school grounds?

There are criminal penalties ranging from Class A misdemeanor to Class X felony for unlawful use of weapons on school grounds. The statutory definition of what constitutes a weapon is broad.

720 ILCS 5/24-1

12:155 What is the penalty for a student who is found to have brought a weapon to school?

Illinois law provides that "a student who is determined to have brought a weapon to school, any school sponsored activity or event which bears a reasonable relationship to school shall be expelled for a period of not less than one year, except that the expulsion period may be modified by the superintendent and the superintendent's determination may be modified by the board on a case by case basis."

It is unclear how a school district should treat a special education student.

105 ILCS 5/10-22.6 (d)
Honig v. Doe, 108 S.Ct. 592, 484 U.S. 305, 98 L.Ed.2d 686 (1988)
United States v. Lopez, 115 S.Ct. 1624, 514 U.S. 549, 131 L.Ed.2d 626 (1995)

12:156   Must school officials report gun or drug incidents at school to law enforcement authorities?

Upon receipt of any written, electronic or verbal report from any school personnel regarding a verified incident involving a firearm or drugs at school or on any school owned or leased property (including vehicles), the superintendent or his designee must immediately report the incident to local law enforcement authorities and to the State Police in a form, manner and frequency prescribed by the State Police. For the purposes of this law, firearm has the meaning set forth in the Firearm Owners Identification Card Act, and drugs means cannabis as defined in the Cannabis Control Act or narcotic drug as defined in the Controlled Substances Act.

105 ILCS 5/10-27.1A
105 ILCS 5/10-27.1B
430 ILCS 65/1.1
720 ILCS 550/3
720 ILCS 570/102

12:157   What is a weapon for school disciplinary purposes?

The term weapon means possession, use, control or transfer of any gun, rifle, shotgun, a weapon as defined by Section 921 of Title 18 of United States Code, firearm as defined in Section 1.1 of the Firearm Owners Identification Act, or use of a weapon as defined in Section 24-1 of the Criminal Code or any other object if used or attempted to be used to cause bodily harm including but not limited to knives, brass knuckles, billy clubs, or look-alikes of any of any weapon as defined in this section. Such items as baseball bats, pipes, bottles, locks, sticks, pencils and pens may be considered weapons if used or attempted to be used to cause bodily harm.

105 ILCS 5/10-22.6(d)

12:160   What is the penalty for unlawful sale or delivery of firearms on school property?

Any person 18 years of age or older who sells, gives, or delivers any firearm to any person under 18 years of age in any school or on the real property comprising any school commits a Class 1 felony.

720 ILCS 5/24-3

12:165   May a student possess an electronic paging device or a cellular telephone in school?

Electronic paging devices and cellular telephones are prohibited in the schools unless the use or possession of such a device has first been expressly authorized by the building principal and the school board.

105 ILCS 5/10-20.28
105 ILCS 5/10-21.10

12:170   Are fraternities, sororities or secret organizations permitted in public schools?

A school board must suspend or expel any pupil who is a member or who becomes or promises to become a member, or who becomes pledged to become a member or who solicits any other person to promise to join or be pledged to become a member of any public school fraternity or sorority or secret society.

105 ILCS 5/31-3 et seq.

12:180   Are there criminal penalties for using threats to recruit students into street gangs?

A person who expressly or impliedly threatens to do bodily harm or does bodily harm to an individual or to that individual's family or uses any other criminally unlawful means to solicit or cause any person to join, or deter any person from leaving any organization or association, regardless of the nature of such organization or association, is guilty of a Class 3 felony.

The matter becomes a Class 2 felony when a person older than 18 years threatens a person younger than 18 years. A person convicted of violation of this statute cannot be sentenced to probation, conditional discharge or periodic imprisonment.

720 ILCS 5/12-6.1 et seq.
In Interest of V.W., 112 Ill.App.3d 587, 445 N.E.2d 445, 67 Ill.Dec. 965 (1st. Dist. 1983)

CORPORAL PUNISHMENT

12:190   Does state law authorize the use of corporal punishment in Illinois schools?

State law prohibits corporal punishment. The School Code requires each school district to adopt a policy which prohibits intentional infliction of bodily harm, slapping, paddling or prolonged maintenance of students in physically painful positions.

The School Code permits teachers, other certificated employees and any other person who provides a related service for or with respect to a student to use reasonable force "to maintain safety for the other students, school personnel or persons or for the purpose of self defense or for the defense of property...."

105 ILCS 5/24-24
Wallace v. The Batavia School District 101, 68 F.3d 1010 (7th Cir. 1995)
Thrasher v. General Casualty Co. of Wisconsin, 732 F.Supp. 966 (W.D. Wisc. 1990)
Metzger by and through Metzger v. Osbeck, 841 F.2d 518 (3rd Cir. 1988)
Wisconsin v. Pea Ridge School District, 855 F.2d 560 (8th Cir. 1988)
Hall v. Tawney, 621 F.2d 607 (4th Cir. 1980)
Carter v. State Board of Education, 90 Ill.App.3d 1042, 414 N.E.2d 153, 46 Ill.Dec. 431 (1st Dist. 1980)
Ingraham v. Wright, 97 S.Ct. 1401, 430 U.S. 651, 51 L.Ed.2d 711 (1977)
Baker v. Owen, 395 F.Supp. 294 (M.D.N.C. 1975), aff'd. 96 S.Ct. 210, 423 U.S. 907, 46 L.Ed.2d 137 (1975)
City of Macomb v. Gould, 104 Ill.App.2d 361, 244 N.E.2d 634 (3rd Dist. 1969)

12:195   May a student be punished by being physically restrained?

The State Board of Education has adopted rules governing use of "time out" and the physical restraint of students. The following forms of punishment are prohibited:

1) use of a locked room other than one with a locking mechanism that engages only when a key or handle is being held by a person;

2) use of a confining space such as a closet or box;

3) use of a room where the student cannot be continually observed;

4) or use of any other room or enclosure or time out procedure that is contrary to State Board of Education guidelines.

The use of physical restraints is prohibited except when (i) the student poses a physical risk to himself, herself, or others, (ii) there is no medical contraindication to its use, and (iii) the staff applying the restraint have been trained in its safe application.

"Restraint" does not include momentary periods of physical restriction by direct person-to-person contact, without the aid of material or mechanical devices, accomplished with limited force and that are designed (i) to prevent a student from completing an act that would result in potential physical harm to himself or another or damage to property or (ii) to remove a disruptive student who is unwilling to voluntarily leave the area.

The use of physical restraints that are consistent with the law may be included in a student's individualized education plan where deemed appropriate by the student's individualized education plan team. Whenever physical restraints are used, school personnel must fully document the incident, including the events leading up to the incident, the type of restraint used, the length of time the student is restrained, and the staff involved. The parents or guardian of a student must be informed whenever physical restraints are used.

105 ILCS 5/2-3.126
105 ILCS 5/10-20.31

STUDENT SEARCHES

12:230   What is permissible in conducting student searches?

The Fourth Amendment's prohibition of unreasonable searches and seizures applies to searches conducted by public school officials. The balance between a student's legitimate expectations of privacy and a school's legitimate need to maintain an appropriate environment for learning requires some easing of the restrictions to which searches by public authorities are ordinarily subject.

School officials need not obtain a warrant before searching a student. A search is justified at its inception when there are reasonable grounds for suspecting the search of a particular child will turn up evidence the student has violated or is violating either the law or the rules of the school.

A search is permissible in its scope when the measures adopted are reasonably related to the objectives of the search and not excessively intrusive in light of the age and sex of the student and the nature of the infraction.

105 ILCS 5/22.6(e)
Howlett by and through Howlett v. Rose, 110 S.Ct. 2430, 496 U.S. 356, 110 L.Ed.2d 332 (1990) on rem. 571 So.2d 29 (1990)
New Jersey v. T.L.O., 105 S.Ct. 733, 469 U.S. 325, 83 L.Ed.2d 720 (1985)

12:231   May school officials strip search a student?

The Fourth Amendment does not prohibit invasive searches, but rather, limits the circumstances under which such searches are constitutional. A school district should exercise extraordinary care that constitutional requirements are met before an invasive search is attempted.

105 ICLS 5/22.6(e)
Jenkins v. Talladega City Board of Education, 95 F.3d 1036 (11th Cir. 1996)
Cornfield By Lewis v. School District No. 230, 991 F.2d 1316 (7th Cir. 1993)

12:234   May school officials conduct random drug testing of student athletes?

The procedures used to conduct random drug testing of student athletes are searches within the meaning of the Fourth Amendment. However, under certain narrowly defined circumstances, random drug testing of student athletes is permissible.

In determining the reasonableness of a search, the courts examine whether the school has a legitimate governmental interest in testing which outweighs the athlete's Fourth Amendment right to be free from such a search.

School officials should be careful to document a legitimate

need for random drug testing before a program is initiated. The manner in which drug testing is performed is also critical; the privacy interests of the students from whom urine is to be collected must be protected. The urine tests must look for standard drugs only, not medical conditions, and the test results must be released to a limited number of school officials.

Todd, et al. v Rush County Schools, et al., 133 F.3d 984 (7th Cir. 1998) reh. and sugg. for reh.den. 139 F.3d 571, cert.den. 119 S.Ct. 68, __U.S.__, 142 L.Ed.2d 53

Vernonia School District 47J, v. Wayne Acton, et ux., etc., 115 S.Ct. 2386, 515 U.S. 646, 132 L.Ed.3d 564 (1995)

Moule v. Paradise Valley Unified School District No. 69, 863 F.Supp. 1098 (D.C. Ariz. 1994)

12:235 May school officials conduct random drug testing of students in other extra-curricular activities or as a condition precedent to the privilege of driving to school?

A school district may conduct such tests as a condition of participation in extra-curricular activities or as a condition of the privilege of driving to school provided the test results are not used for the discipline of a student testing positive. The student and his family must be given an opportunity to explain a positive test result and must be given an opportunity for re testing. The school's response to a positive test must be limited to removal from the activity.

Miller v. Wilkes, 172 F.3d 574 (8th Cir. 1999)

Todd, et al. v. Rush County Schools, et al., 133 F.3d 984 (7th Cir. 1998) reh. and sugg. for reh.den. 139 F.3d 571, cert.den. 119 S.Ct. 68, __U.S.__, 142 L.Ed.2d 53

Willis v. Anderson Community School Corporation, 158 F.3d 415 (7th Cir. 1998), cert.den. 119 S.Ct. 1254, __U.S.__, 143 L.Ed.2d 351 (1999)

12:238 What is "reasonable suspicion?"

There is reasonable suspicion to search when school officials reasonably infer from all the circumstances that the student is committing, is about to commit, or has committed an offense. School officials must identify specific articulated facts which, when taken with their natural inferences, make the intrusion reasonable.

The facts need not rise to the level of probable cause, but

they must be more than a hunch. A school official's search may be as thorough as required by the circumstances.

Bridgman v. New Trier High School District No. 203, 128 F.3d 1146 (7th Cir. 1997)
    People v. Taylor, 253 Ill.App.3d 768, 625 N.E.2d 785, 192 Ill.Dec. 630 (4th Dist. 1993)
    New Jersey v. T.L.O., 105 S.Ct. 733, 469 U.S. 325, 83 L.Ed.2d 720 (1985)
    Terry v. Ohio, 88 S.Ct. 1868, 392 U.S. 1, 20 L.Ed.2d 889 (1968)

12:240 May school officials search school lockers used by students?

School officials should inform students that school lockers are school district property made available to students for their convenience. Lockers may be searched randomly and without meeting any cause standard.

The nature of locker use and locker construction create evidentiary problems which make it difficult to discipline students solely on the basis of the fruits of a locker search.

105 ILCS 5/10-22.6 (e)
Chicago Firefighters Local 2 v. Chicago, 717 F.Supp. 134 (N.D. Ill. 1989)
O'Connor v. Ortega, 107 S.Ct. 1492, 480 U.S. 709, 94 L.Ed.2d 714 (1987)
New Jersey v. T.L.O., 105 S.Ct. 733, 469 U.S. 325, 83 L.Ed.2d 720 (1985)
Picha v. Wieglos, 410 F.Supp. 1214 (N.D. Ill. 1976)

12:242 May school officials search other places on school grounds?

An Illinois statute permits searches of "lockers, desks, parking lots and other school property owned or controlled by the school as well as personal effects left in those places and areas by students without notice or the consent of the student and without a search warrant." However, the statute does not restrict the Fourth Amendment rights of students, and school officials should be very cautious when conducting searches which infringe the privacy rights of students. The Illinois statute does not universally permit the warrantless search of student automobiles or student personal effects in which the student has an expectation of privacy.

If a search is conducted in a place where a student has no expectation of privacy, proving what is found in that place belongs to any particular student is problematic. Therefore, a student disciplinary case based on such evidence is often difficult.

105 ILCS 5/10-22.6(e)

12:250   Does the Fourth Amendment protect students from physical seizure by school officials?

Seizures of students by school officials are subject to constraints of the Fourth Amendment. However, the reasonableness of a Fourth Amendment seizure must be evaluated in the context of the school environment, where restricting the liberty of students is a necessary component of the educational process.

A teacher or administrator who seizes a student violates the Fourth Amendment only when the restriction of liberty is "unreasonable under the circumstances then existing and apparent." A person is seized within the meaning of the Fourth Amendment when, by a show of authority or use of physical force, his freedom of movement is restrained. If the person subject to questioning is free to disregard the questions and walk away there is no intrusion on the person's liberty or privacy such that the Fourth Amendment requires a particularized and objective justification.

People v. Parker, 284 Ill.App.3d 860, 672 N.E.2d 813, 219 Ill.Dec.960 (1st Dist. 1996)

Wallace v. The Batavia School District 101, 68 F.3d 1010 (7th Cir. 1995)

POLICE SEARCHES AND ARRESTS

12:300   What standard applies to student searches when law enforcement officers are involved?

When school officials involve police officers in searches of students conducted in schools, the search standard may increase from "reasonable suspicion" to "probable cause." What standard applies to any particular search depends upon whether the search is one in which:

1) school officials initiate the search and where police involvement is minimal, or

2) school police or liaison police officers are acting on their own authority, or

3) outside police officers initiate a search where the involvement of school officials is limited.

An increase in the search standard from reasonable suspicion to probable cause is significant, because if officials have not met the appropriate search standard at the initiation of the search, the fruits of the search may not be used to discipline the offender. This principle is known as the exclusionary rule.

There is at least one federal court of appeals which has held the exclusionary rule does not apply to school administrative searches. The exclusionary rule applies to administrative searches conducted in Illinois.

Generally, searches by school officials where police involvement is minimal or searches by school police or liaison officers are held to the reasonable suspicion standard, and school searches by outside officers acting on their own authority require probable cause. A search warrant may be required under certain circumstances when police officials are involved with school officials in the conduct of a search.

Thompson v. Carthage, 87 F.3d 979 (8th Cir. 1996)

People v. Dilworth, 169 Ill.2d 195, 661 N.E.2d 310,214 Ill.Dec. 456 (1996), cert. den. 116 S.Ct. 1692, 517 U.S. 1197, 134 L.Ed.2d 793 (1996)

In re S.F., 607 A.2d 793 (Pa.Super. 1992)

Skinner v. Railway Labor Executives' Association, 109 S.Ct. 1402, 489 U.S. 602, 103 L.Ed.2d 639 (1989)

Treasury Employees' Union v. Van Raab, 109 S.Ct. 1384, 489 U.S. 656, 103 L.Ed.2d 685 (1989)

New Jersey v. T.L.O., 105 S.Ct. 733, 469 U.S. 325, 83 L.Ed.2d 720 (1985)

Martens v. District No. 220 Board of Education, 620 F.Supp. 29 (N.D.Ill. 1985)

Picha v. Wieglos, 410 F.Supp. 1214 (N.D. Ill. 1976)

12:310 Are police dog searches of school grounds legal?

Police dogs may not be used to conduct generalized searches of students or places where students have a reasonable expectation of privacy. Police dogs may be used to conduct searches of public places on school grounds, including school parking lots (but not necessarily the automobiles located on the parking lots). Whether or not additional cause or a warrant may be necessary before a more intrusive search is conducted after a police dog alerts is a matter which depends on the facts surrounding the particular search.

The fruits of searches of public places are often useless to discipline student offenders because the discovered contraband cannot be certainly connected to any particular student.

105 ILCS 5/10-22.6(e)

Jennings v. Joshua Independent School District, 948 F.2d 194 (5th Cir. 1991) reh. den. 952 F.2d 402, cert. den. 112 S.Ct. 2303, 504 U.S. 956, 119 L.Ed.2d 226 (1992)

Horton v. Goose Creek, 690 F.2d 470, reh. den. 693 F.2d 524 (5th Cir. 1982) cert. den. 103 S.Ct. 3536, 363 U.S. 1207, 77 L.Ed.2d 1387 (1982)

Zamora v. Pomeroy, 639 F.2d 662 (10th Cir. 1981)

Doe v. Renfrow, 475 F.Supp. 1012, aff'd in part, rem. in part, 631 F.2d 582 (7th Cir. 1979) cert. den. 101 S.Ct. 3015, 451 U.S. 1022, 69 L.Ed.2d 395

Camara v. Municipal Court of City and County of San Francisco, 87 S.Ct. 1727, 387 U.S. 523, 18 L.Ed.2d 930 (1967)

12:315   May school officials use metal detectors to search students?

The use of a metal detector is a search within the meaning of the Fourth Amendment. Provided the search is justified at its inception by the reality of violence in the schools and the search as conducted is reasonably related in scope to the circumstances which justified the interference in the first place, a metal detector search will probably be legal. School officials should exercise caution to be sure any such search meets the guidelines required by the courts.

People v. Pruitt et al., 278 Ill.App.3d 194, 662 N.E.2d 540, 214 Ill.Dec. 974 (1st Dist. 1996)

United States v. Epperson, 454 F.2d 769 (4th Cir. 1972)

12:317   May school officials require that a student be searched by a metal detector?

A metal detector search is a warrantless search. In order for a warrantless search to be permissible under the Fourth Amendment, there must be reasonable grounds for suspecting that the search will turn up evidence the student has violated or is violating either the law or the rules of the school.

A school official contemplating a metal detector search should be aware that a distinction must be drawn between a student who voluntarily and without any coercion submits to a metal detector search and a student who is detained and required to submit to a search. The former search requires no cause, while the latter requires either reasonable suspicion or probable cause depending on the circumstances. A student may not be detained for a search against his will or required to submit to a search unless the appropriate search standard has been met.

People v. Parker, 284 Ill.App.3d 860, 672 N.E.2d 813, 219 Ill.Dec.960 (1st Dist. 1996)

12:320   If a police dog alerts on a student's locked car in the school parking lot, may school officials or the police open the car and search it?

If the student is 18 years of age or over and gives consent for the search, the car may be searched. If the student is under 18, the student's parents must give consent or a warrant must be obtained in order to conduct a completely safe search.

105 ICLS 5/10-22.6(e)

12:330   Under what circumstances may law enforcement authorities enter school buildings?

Law enforcement authorities may enter school buildings when they have reason to believe a crime has been committed, when they possess a warrant, or when they have been invited into the school by school officials. A school district may regulate by policy access to students by law enforcement authorities who do not possess warrants.

42 U.S.C. 1983
New Jersey v. T.L.O., 105 S.Ct. 733, 469 U.S. 325, 83 L.Ed.2d 720 (1985)
Doe v. Renfrow, 631 F.2d 91 (7th Cir. 1980)
Picha v. Wieglos, 410 F.Supp. 1214 (N.D. Ill. 1976)

12:340   Must a school district allow police officials to question or arrest students during the school day?

A police officer must be permitted to arrest a student on school property during the school day when the officer possesses a warrant or when the officer is in hot pursuit of a suspect. A school district may regulate by policy warrantless police interrogations.

Doe v. Renfrow, 631 F.2d 91 (7th Cir. 1980)
Picha v. Wieglos, 410 F.Supp. 1214 (N.D. Ill. 1976)

12:350   What notice does a school district receive if one of its students is involved in juvenile proceedings?

All courts and law enforcement agencies of the state and its political subdivisions must report to the principal of any public school whenever an enrolled child is detained for proceedings under the Juvenile Court Act or for any criminal offense or any violation of a municipal or county ordinance. The report must include the basis for detaining the child, the circumstances surrounding the events which led to the child's detention and the status of proceedings. The report must be updated as appropriate to notify the principal of developments and the disposition of the matter. The information derived from this report must be kept separate from and must not become a part of the official school record of the child and is not a public record. Such information must be used solely by the principal, counselors, and teachers of the school to aid in the rehabilitation of the child.

105 ILCS 5/10-20.14
105 ILCS 5/22-20
705 ILCS 405/1-1

12:360   Must law enforcement officials cooperate with school officials in the prosecution of juveniles charged with school-related criminal offenses?

The Juvenile Justice Reform Act of 1998 permits law enforcement agencies to disclose certain student juvenile criminal records to school officials. The provision of such information is limited to records transmitted to the appropriate school official by a local law enforcement agency under a reciprocal reporting system established and maintained between the school district and the local law enforcement agency concerning a minor enrolled in the school district who has been arrested for a felony or a Class A or B misdemeanor.

105 ILCS 5/22-20
705 ILCS 405/5-905

SUSPENSION AND EXPULSION

12:380   What is a student disciplinary suspension?

A student disciplinary suspension is a temporary removal from school or from riding a school bus for a maximum of 10 days per suspension. Except under some circumstances involving some students classified as in need of special education, a suspension is permitted for gross disobedience or misconduct. A suspension from riding a school bus may exceed 10 days for safety reasons.

105 ILCS 5/10-22.6(b)

Goss v. Lopez, 95 S.Ct. 729, 419 U.S. 565, 42 L.Ed.2d 725 (1975)

Linwood v. Board of Education of Peoria School District 150, 463 F.2d 763 (7th Cir. 1972)

12:390   Which school officials may suspend a student from school?

A school board may authorize the superintendent, principal, assistant principal, or dean of students to suspend a student for gross disobedience or misconduct if the student has been provided the requisite due process and proper notice has been given.

105 ILCS 5/10-22.6(b)

12:400   What procedures must be followed to notify a student's parents of his suspension from school?

Any suspension must be immediately reported to the parents or guardian of a student along with a full statement of the reasons for the suspension and a notice of right to a review, a copy of which must be given to the school board.

Upon request of the parents or guardian, the school board or a hearing officer appointed by it must review the action of the suspending school official. At the review, the parents or guardian of the student may appear and discuss the suspension with the school board or its hearing officer.

If a hearing officer is appointed by the board, he must report to the board a written summary of the evidence heard at the meeting. After its hearing, or upon receipt of the written report of its hearing officer, the board may take such action as it finds appropriate.

105 ILCS 5/10-22.6(b)

12:410   What due process is required with respect to a student suspension from school?

A student must be provided with the following due process in connection with any suspension from school:

1) oral or written notice of the charges and evidence supporting the charges;

2) if the charges are denied, a student must be given an opportunity to explain his version of the events to the suspending school official;

3) the suspension (except from riding a bus for safety reasons) may not exceed 10 days;

4) to have his parents or guardian immediately receive a report of the suspension along with a full statement of the reasons for it and a notice of right to review;

5) if a hearing is requested, the parents or guardian may appear and may discuss the suspension with the board or its hearing officer;

6) any decision rendered must be based upon the evidence; and

7) with respect to any suspension invoked, the student has a right to be informed of its beginning and ending dates.

The rules regulating the suspension of a student identified as in need of special education are different, and disposition will depend upon the facts presented in each case.

105 ILCS 5/10-22.6(b)

Sieck v. Oak Park-River Forest High School District No. 200, 807 F.Supp. 73 (N.D.Ill. 1992)

Carey v. Piphus, 97 S.Ct. 1642, 435 U.S. 247, 52 L.Ed.2d 355 (1978)

Goss v. Lopez, 95 S.Ct. 729, 419 U.S. 565, 42 L.Ed.2d 725 (1975)

12:440   What is a student disciplinary expulsion?

A student disciplinary expulsion is the removal of a student from school for gross disobedience or misconduct for a period of time ranging from in excess of 10 days to a definite period of time not to exceed two school years.

105 ILCS 5/10-22.6(a)

Robinson v. Oak Park and River Forest High School, Board of Education District 200, 213 Ill.App.3d 77, 571 N.E.2d 931, 156 Ill.Dec. 951 (1st Dist. 1991)

Betts v. Board of Education of City of Chicago, 466 F.2d 629 (7th Cir. 1972)

12:450   Which school officials have authority to expel a student from school?

Only a school board may expel a student. Its authority to expel may not be delegated. A school board may consider recommendations from the administration and may appoint a hearing officer to conduct an expulsion hearing, but must retain authority to render the final decision.

105 ILCS 5/10-22.6(a)

12:460   May a school board expel a student for an indefinite period?

A student, other than a student identified as in need of special education, may be expelled for a definite period of time not to exceed two school years.

105 ILCS 5/10-22.6(a)
105 ILCS 5/10-22.6(d)
Linwood v. Board of Education of Peoria School District 150, 463 F.2d 763 (7th Cir. 1972)

12:470   What procedures must a school board follow in expelling a student from school?

When a student is accused of gross disobedience or misconduct sufficiently severe to warrant expulsion, the expulsion may not take place until after the parents have been requested to appear at a meeting of the school board, or with a hearing officer appointed by it, to discuss the student's behavior. Notice of hearing must be made by registered or certified mail and must state the time, place, and purpose of the meeting. The school board or a hearing officer appointed by it must state the reasons for the expulsion and the date on which the expulsion is to become effective.

If a hearing officer is appointed by the board, he must report to the board a written summary of the evidence heard at the meeting and the board may take such action thereon as it finds appropriate.

If a student expulsion hearing is held in closed session, the school board must prepare and make available for public inspection a written decision setting forth its determinative reasoning.

The rules regulating the expulsion of students identified as in need of special education are different than the above.

5 ILCS 120/2

105 ILCS 5/10-22.6(a)

Robinson v. Oak Park and River Forest High School, Board of Education District 200, 213 Ill.App.3d 77, 571 N.E.2d 931, 156 Ill.Dec. 951 (1st Dist. 1991)

Linwood v. Board of Education of Peoria School District 150, 463 F.2d 763 (7th Cir. 1972)

Betts v. Board of Education of City of Chicago, 466 F.2d 629 (7th Cir. 1972)

Whitfield v. Simpson, 312 F.Supp. 889 (N.D. Ill. 1970)

12:475 What due process is required with respect to a student expulsion from school?

A student must be provided with the following due process with respect to any expulsion from school:

1) The expulsion shall take place only after a student's parents or guardian have been requested to appear at a meeting of the school board, or with a hearing officer appointed by it, to discuss the student's behavior. A student may be suspended from school pending this meeting but must be provided the due process required to support a suspension;

2) A notice of hearing must be sent to the parents or guardian by registered or certified mail stating the time place and purpose of the hearing;

3) The school board or its appointed hearing officer must provide a full statement of the reasons for the proposed expulsion at the hearing and must provide notice of the date on which the proposed expulsion is to become effective;

4) The student is entitled to consult with counsel at the student's expense (this right is to be distinguished from the right to be represented by counsel at the hearing);

5) Adequate time must be given to prepare a defense;

6) The student must be given an opportunity to call and examine witnesses, to cross-examine opposing witnesses, and to introduce evidence;

7) The decision to expel or not to expel must be made by the school board and must be based upon the evidence presented.

105 ILCS 5/10-22.6(a)

Colquitt v. Rich Township High School District No. 227, 298 Ill.App.3d 856, 699 N.E.2d 1109, 232 Ill.Dec. 924 (1st Dist., 1998)

Osteen v. Henley, 13 F.3d 221 (7th Cir. 1993)

Newsome v. Batavia Local School District, 842 F.2d 920 (6th Cir. 1988)
Carey v. Piphus, 97 S.Ct. 1642, 435 U.S. 247, 52 L.Ed.2d 355 (1978)
Wood v. Strickland, 95 S.Ct. 992, 420 U.S. 308, 43 L.Ed.2d 214 (1975),
reh. den. 95 S.Ct. 1589, 42 U.S. 921, 43 L.Ed.2d 790 (1975)
Linwood v. Board of Education of Peoria School District 150, 463 F.2d 763
(7th Cir. 1972)

12:477   May an expulsion hearing witness be protected by introducing a written statement rather than requiring that the witness appear?

A student accused of wrongdoing and facing expulsion has the constitutional right to confront and cross examine his accusers. The admission of statements rather than the production of the witness denies the accused his right to test the evidence against him. Courts will consider the substitution of written statements for live testimony only when there is a real and demonstrated threat of retaliation against the witness or when a written statement is available but the witness is unavailable.

A school district seeking to protect a child witness would be wise to have evidence that such protection is necessary to protect the welfare of the child witness or that the witness would be traumatized by the presence of the "defendant." The trauma must be significant and not just excitement, nervousness or reluctance to testify.

Colquitt v. Rich Township High School District No. 227, 298 Ill.App.3d
856, 699 N.E.2d 1109, 232 Ill.Dec. 924 (1st Dist., 1998)
Maryland v. Craig, 110 S.Ct. 3157, 497 U.S. 836, 111 L.Ed.2d 666 (1990)

12:478   Is a verbatim transcript required in an expulsion hearing?

The absence of a court reporter, in and of itself, is neither a denial of due process nor a denial of equal protection. There is no requirement to provide a stenographer's transcript in every case so long as there is some other means to allow for adequate and effective review.

Colquitt v. Rich Township High School District No. 227, 298 Ill.App.3d
856, 699 N.E.2d 1109, 232 Ill.Dec. 924 (1st Dist., 1998)

12:480   What factors will a court consider in reviewing a school board's decision to expel a student?

In reviewing a school board's decision to expel, the court will consider:

1) the egregiousness of the student's conduct;

2) the history or record of the student's past conduct;

3) the likelihood that such conduct will affect the delivery of educational services to other students;

4) the severity of the punishment; and

5) the interest of the child.

Robinson v. Oak Park and River Forest High School, Board of Education District 200, 213 Ill.App.3d 77, 571 N.E.2d 931, 156 Ill.Dec. 951 (1st Dist. 1991)

12:490   May a student who has been suspended or expelled from one school district enroll and attend classes in another school district during the term of the suspension or expulsion?

The School Code provides that if a student has been suspended or expelled for knowingly possessing in a school building or on school grounds a weapon as defined in the Gun Free Schools Act, for knowingly possessing, selling, or delivering in a school building or on school grounds a controlled substance or cannabis, or for battering a staff member of the school, and if the period of suspension or expulsion has not expired at the time the student attempts to transfer into another public school in the same or any other school district:

1) any school student records required to be transferred must include the date and duration of the period or suspension or expulsion; and

2) the student must not be permitted to attend class in the public school into which he is transferring until the student has served the entire period of the suspension or expulsion imposed by the school from which the student is transferring except that the school board may approve placement of the student in an alternative school.

No school district is required to admit a new student who is transferring from an out-of-state public school unless the parent or guardian of the student certified in writing that the student is not currently serving a suspension or expulsion.

A school district which anticipates denying a student enrollment by reason of this statute should carefully consider:

1) whether the school district which suspended or expelled the student complied with all School Code requirements and

procedural and substantive due process requirements in imposing the suspension or expulsion; and

2) whether or not the student is properly a resident of the school district in which he seeks to enroll.

105 ILCS 5/2-3.13a

12:495   What process is due a student whom the school district contemplates suspending or expelling from athletics or other extra-curricular activity?

Many athletic suspensions and expulsions and some extra-curricular exclusions have high community visibility and often result in media coverage. Disciplinary outcomes are often challenged by parents.

School officials should take great care to examine all the facets of a proposed suspension or expulsion before proceeding to any disciplinary conclusion. They should be certain there is sufficient connection between the events and school or educational interests so as to give the school district, rather than the student's parents or the criminal or juvenile justice system, authority to invoke discipline.

School districts or school officials may adopt team rules, athletic codes, student handbook provisions and/or policies governing athletic or extra curricular conduct and eligibility. Having done so, however, a school district will be required to follow its own policies and procedures to the letter. School officials should take care to insure that relevant provisions agree from source to source.

One Illinois appellate court case suggests no due process is necessary in the case of an athletic or extra-curricular exclusion unless a school's rules, regulations or policies entitle the student to due process. However, the case warns that "school officials cannot impose student punishment in a completely arbitrary and capricious manner." The case suggests that, "in order to establish a violation of a student's substantive, rather than procedural due process rights, the student must show arbitrary and capricious conduct on the part of school officials."

Jordan by Edwards v. O'Fallon Township High School District No. 203 Board of Education, 302 Ill.App.3d 1070, 706 N.E.2d 137, 235 Ill.Dec.877 (5th Dist. 1999)

Peterson v. Independent School District No, 811, 999 F.Supp. 665 (D. Minn. 1998)

Robinson v. Illinois High School Association, 45 Ill.App.2d 277, 195 N.E.2d 38 (2nd Dist. 1963) cert. den. 85 S.Ct. 647, 379 U.S. 960, 13 L.Ed.2d 555 (1965)

ALTERNATIVE SCHOOLS

12:500   What is an alternative school?

An alternative school created under the Safe Schools Law is a school intended to educate disruptive students who would otherwise be subject to suspension or expulsion. Such students may be administratively transferred to the alternative school.

105 ILCS 5/13A-4

12:510   How is an alternative school established under the Safe Schools Law?

The regional superintendent, after consultation with each local superintendent of schools in the regional superintendent's region and the regional board, determines the location and need of the alternative school within the region. The regional superintendent must consider:

1) the possible utilization of existing buildings, including but not limited to governmental buildings that are, or could reasonably be made, usable;

2) which option would be least costly;

3) distances that administratively transferred students would need to travel and the costs of that travel.

Upon the determination of the need for establishment of an alternative school, each school district located within the region shall provide the regional superintendent with a copy of the district's discipline policies and procedure for effecting suspension or expulsion. Thereafter, the regional superintendent in cooperation with a representative from each school district in the region shall establish an alternative school program and each school district in the region shall adopt policies and procedures for the identification and placement of students in the program.

105 ILCS 5/13A-3

12:520   May an educational service region have more than one alternative school?

Upon recommendation of the regional superintendent and with the approval of the State Board of Education, an educational service region may add one or more alternative schools to the region. In determining whether an additional school is necessary and appropriate, the State Board considers:

1) the geographic size of the educational service region and distances that students within that region must travel in order to attend the existing alternative school;

2) the student population of schools comprising the educational service region and the likely student population of all alternative school programs within that region if the petition is granted;

3) any other logistical considerations;

4) the cost necessitated by establishing an additional alternative school in that educational service region.

105 ILCS 13A-3(f)

12:530   Who is a "disruptive student" within the meaning of the Safe Schools Law?

A disruptive student includes students in grades 6 through 12 who have been found eligible for suspension or expulsion through the discipline process established by the school district. School officials may not administratively transfer a student to an alternative school without first providing the student with due process as provided in the law and by reason of the school district's discipline policies.

105 ILCS 5/13A-2.5

12:540   May a school district avoid special education implications by transferring a behavior disordered student to an alternative school?

No.

105 ILCS 5/13A-1 (k)
105 ILCS 5/13A-1 (l)

12:550   What is an alternative education plan?

At the earliest time following an administrative transfer to an alternative school, appropriate personnel from the sending school district and appropriate personnel of the alternative program shall meet to develop an alternative education plan for the student. The student's parent or guardian shall be invited to the meeting. The student may be invited. The alternative educational plan must include:

1) The duration of the plan, including a date after which the student may be returned to the regular educational program in the transferring district;

2) The specific academic and behavioral components of the plan;

3) The method and time frame for reviewing the student's progress.

105 ILCS 5/13A-4

12:560   What happens if the parents of a student placed in an alternative school object to the child's return to the regular school program?

If the parent or guardian of a student who is scheduled to be returned to the regular educational program in the public schools of the district files a written objection to the return with the principal of the alternative school, the matter shall be referred by the principal to the regional superintendent of the educational service region in which the alternative school is located for a hearing. Notice of the hearing shall be given by the regional superintendent to the student's parent or guardian. After the hearing, the regional superintendent may take such action as he or she finds appropriate and in the best interest of the student. The determination of the regional superintendent is final.

105 ILCS 5/13A-4

13: CHILDREN WITH DISABILITIES AND SPECIAL EDUCATION

Asserting that the 1997 reauthorization of the federal Individuals with Disabilities Education Act created a need for numerous revisions to its rules on the subject, the Illinois State Board of Education on September 3, 1999, proposed the repeal of its rules for special education. At the time this edition was being prepared (January 1, 2000) the repeal had not been perfected and no new rules had been adopted. The rules in effect (cites to Ill. Admin. Code) at the time of this printing are cited below. New rules are expected to become effective in the spring or early summer of 2000.

SPECIAL EDUCATION DEFINED

13:10 What is "special education?"

"Special education" is specially designed instruction provided at no cost to parents or guardians specifically designed to meet the unique needs of a child with certain educational disabilities a "free and appropriate public education." Special education may be conducted in the classroom, in the home, in hospitals or institutions and or in other settings and must, when appropriate, include the provision of non-educational services necessary to support education. Special education includes instruction in physical education.

20 U.S.C. 1401(2)
105 ILCS 5/14-8.02
Irving Independent School District v. Tatro, 104 S.Ct. 3371, 468 U.S. 883, 82 L.Ed.2d 664 (1984), on rem. 741 F.2d 82 (1984)

13:20 What are the elements of a "free and appropriate public education?"

A free and appropriate public education for children with disabilities includes special education and related services which (1) are provided at public expense, under public supervision and direction, and without charge; (2) meet the standards of the State Board of Education and federal rules and regulations; (3) include preschool, elementary, or secondary school education; and (4) are provided in conformity with the individualized education program as required by state and federal law.

20 U.S.C. 1401(8)
34 C.F.R. 300 et seq.

13:25 Is a school district required to maximize a student's educational benefit to meet the free and appropriate standard?

No. In meeting the free and appropriate standard a school district must provide the student with some educational benefit, but need not provide the optimum educational placement or deliver optimum educational services.

J.S.K. v. Hendry County School Board, 941 F.2d 1563 (11th Cir. 1991)
Board of Education of Hendrick Hudson Central School District, Board of Education Westchester County v. Rowley, 102 S.Ct. 3034, 458 U.S. 176, 73 L.Ed.2d 690 (1982)

13:30 Must school buildings and/or programs be accessible to handicapped persons?

The Rehabilitation Act requires program accessibility for handicapped persons. It mandates:

1) All new facilities must be constructed so as to be readily accessible and usable by handicapped persons.

2) Although every existing facility need not be totally physically accessible, programs must be accessible.

3) While flexibility is allowed in choosing methods which make programs in existing facilities accessible, structural changes in facilities must be undertaken if no other means of assuring program accessibility is available.

The Americans with Disabilities Act also contains requirements which apply to schools.

29 U.S.C. 701 et seq.
42 U.S.C. 12101 et seq.
45 C.F.R. 84.21 et seq.
71 Ill. Admin. Code 400.110 et seq.
71 Ill. Admin. Code 400.310

13:40   What is an individualized education program (IEP)?

The term individualized education program (IEP), means a written statement for each child with a disability that is developed, reviewed and revised in accordance with special education law. The IEP statement must include:

1) a statement of the present levels of educational performance of the child including how the child's disability affects the child's involvement and progress in the general curriculum or for preschool children, as appropriate, how the disability affects the child's involvement and progress in the general curriculum or for preschool children, as appropriate, how the disability affects the child's participation in appropriate activities.

2) a statement of measurable annual goals, including benchmarks or short-term objectives related to meeting the child's needs that result from the child's disability to enable the child to be involved in and progress in the general curriculum and meeting each of the child's other educational needs that result from the child's disability.

3) a statement of the special education and related services and supplementary aids and services to be provided to the child, or on behalf of the child and a statement of the program modifications or supports for school personnel that will be provide for the child to advance appropriately toward attaining the annual goals; to be involved and progress in the general curriculum and to participate in extracurricular and other nonacademic activities; to be educated and participate with other children with disabilities and non-disabled children; an explanation of the extent, if any, to which the child will not participate with non-disabled children in the regular class and other activities. The IEP must also include a statement of any individual modifications in the administration of the State or district-wide assessments of student achievement that are needed in order for the child to participate in such assessment. If the IEP team determines that the child will not participate in a particular State or district-wide assessment of student achievement or part of such test, the IEP must include a statement as to why the assessment is not appropriate for the child and how the child will be assessed.

4) the projected date for beginning of the services and modifications and the anticipated frequency, location, and duration of those services and modifications.

5) beginning at age 14, and updated annually, a statement of the transition service needs of the child under the applicable components of the child's IEP that focuses on the child's courses of study such as participation in advanced placement courses or vocational education program. Beginning at age 16 (or younger if determined appropriate by the IEP team), a statement of needed transition services for the child, including, when appropriate, a statement of the interagency responsibilities or any needed linkages. Beginning at least one year before the child reaches the age of majority under state law, a statement that the child has been informed of his or her rights under the special education law that will transfer to the child on reaching the age of majority.

6) a statement of how the child's progress toward the annual goals will be measured and how the child's parents will be regularly informed (by such means as periodic report cards), at least as often as parents are informed of their non-disabled children's progress, of their child's progress toward annual goals and the extent to which that progress is sufficient to enable the child to achieve the goals by the end of the year.

An IEP commits the school district to its terms.

20 U.S.C. 1401(11)
20 U.S.C. 1414(d) et seq.
105 ILCS 5/14-8.02
34 C.F.R. 300.340
23 Ill. Admin. Code 226.562

13:50   What is "mainstreaming?"

"Mainstreaming" is educational jargon for an application of the principle of "least restrictive environment." Mainstreaming is the placement of children with disabilities, to the maximum extent appropriate, with children who do not have disabilities. Placement in special classes, separate schools, or other removal of children with disabilities from the regular educational environment may occur only when the nature or the severity of the

disability is such that education in a regular class with the use
of supplementary aids and services cannot be achieved.

20 U.S.C. 1412(a)(5)
34 C.F.R.300.550 et seq.
105 ILCS 5/14-8.02
23 Ill. Admin. Code 226.5
23 Ill. Admin. Code 226.125
Board of Education of Sacramento City School District v. Holland, 786
F.Supp. 874 (E.D. Cal. 1992)
Evans v. District No. 17 of Douglas County, 841 F.2d 824 (8th Cir. 1988)
Martin v. School Board of Prince Georges County, 3 Va.App.197, 348
S.E.2d 857 (1986)
Community High School District No. 155 v. Denzby Veronico, 124
Ill.App.3d 129, 463 N.E.2d 998, 79 Ill.Dec. 444 (2nd Dist. 1984)

13:55 Under what conditions should a student with a disability be educated in a regular classroom?

A student with a disability must be educated in a regular
classroom if the child can receive a satisfactory education in the
class with the help of support services, even if the regular class
is not the best academic setting for the child. The education of
the child in a regular classroom is sometimes called "full inclusion." Four factors are considered in the placement analysis:
academic benefits to the child, nonacademic benefits to the
child, possible negative effects on other students and cost to the
school district.

Board of Education of Sacramento City School District v. Holland, 786
F.Supp. 874 (E.D. Cal. 1992)
Greer v. Rome City School District, 950 F.2d 688 (11th Cir. 1991)

ELIGIBILITY FOR SPECIAL EDUCATION

13:64 When does a school district's obligation to provide special education to a disabled child end?

The protections of "stay put" and all other special education
entitlements (except remedial orders for compensatory education) cease when a child reaches the age of 21.

*Board of Education of Oak Park and River Forest High School District v.
Illinois State Board of Education,* 79 F.3d 654 (7th Cir. 1996)

13:70   For which children must a public school district provide special education?

Every public school district must provide special education facilities and programs to all children between the ages of three and 21 who are residents of the school district who are found to require special education services and including students who have been suspended or expelled from school. Under most circumstances a school district is responsible for the delivery of special education to children residing in the district who are enrolled in nonpublic schools or are wards of the state, children who are living in orphanages, foster homes, children's homes, and state housing units located within the district

> 20 U.S.C. 1412(a)(1)(A)
> 34 C.F.R. 300.121(a)
> 105 ILCS 5/14-7.03
> *Nickerson v. Thompson*, 504 F.2d 813 (7th Cir. 1974)

13:71   How is the resident district determined when there is a question where the parents of the special education student reside?

The resident district is the one in which the parent or guardian, or both parent and guardian of the student reside when:

1) the parent has legal guardianship of the student and resides within Illinois; or

2) an individual guardian who resides in Illinois has been appointed by the courts; or

3) an Illinois public agency has legal guardianship and the student resides either in the home of the parent or within the same district as the parent; or

4) an Illinois court orders residential placement but the parents retain legal guardianship.

In cases of divorced or separated parents, when only one parent has legal guardianship or custody, the district in which the parent having legal guardianship or custody resides is the resident district. When both parents retain legal guardianship or custody, the resident district is the district of the parent who claims the child as a dependent on his or her federal income tax return.

When the parent or individual who has legal guardianship

lives outside Illinois, the parent, legal guardian or placing agent must make arrangements to provide reimbursement to the Illinois school district.

105 ILCS 5/14-1.11

13:72   When is the school district in which the student resides the resident district?

The resident district is the school district in which the student resides when:

1) the parent has legal guardianship but the location of the parent is unknown; or

2) an individual guardian has been appointed but the location of the guardian is unknown; or

3) the student is 18 years of age or older and no legal guardian has been appointed; or

4) the student is legally an emancipated minor; or

5) an Illinois public agency has legal guardianship and has placed the student residentially outside the school district in which the parent lives.

In cases where an Illinois public agency has legal guardianship and has placed the student residentially outside of Illinois, the last school district that provided at least 45 days of educational service to the student continues to be the district of residence until the student is no longer under guardianship of an Illinois public agency or until the student is returned to Illinois.

The residence of a homeless student is the Illinois district in which the student enrolls for educational services.

105 ILCS 5/14-1.11a

13:80   How is a child's eligibility for special education programs and services determined?

A free and appropriate public education must be available to all children with disabilities. Children are eligible for special education if a determination of eligibility results from a case study reviewed by professional personnel in a multidisciplinary staff conference and after recommendation of qualified specialists.

20 U.S.C. 1400 et seq.
105 ILCS 5/14-8.02
Max M. v. Illinois State Board of Education, 585 F.Supp. 317, on reconsideration 629 F.Supp. 1504 (N.D. Ill. 1984)
Max M. v. Thompson, 585 F.Supp. 317, on reconsideration 592 F.Supp. 1437 (N.D. Ill. 1984)

13:90   Who are "children with specific learning disabilities?"

"Children with specific learning disabilities" means children between the ages of 3 and 21 years who have a disorder in one or more of the basic psychological processes involved in understanding or in using language, spoken or written, which may manifest itself in imperfect ability to listen, think, speak, read, write, spell, or do mathematical calculations. Such disorders include conditions such as perceptual disabilities, brain injury, minimal brain dysfunction, dyslexia, and developmental aphasia.

The term does not include children who have learning problems that are primarily the result of visual, hearing or motor disabilities, of mental retardation, emotional disturbance or environmental disadvantage.

20 U.S.C 1401(26)
34 C.F.R. 300.7(b)
105 ILCS 5/14-1.03a
23 Ill. Admin. Code226 552

13:95   What is meant by "children with disabilities" as defined by The Individuals with Disabilities Education Act?

"Children with disabilities" is defined as children with mental retardation; hearing impairments (including deafness); speech or language impairments; visual impairments (including blindness); serious emotional disturbance; orthopedic impairments; autism; traumatic brain injury; other health impairments or specific learning disabilities and who by reason thereof need special education and related services.

20 U.S.C. 1401 (a)(1)(A)(i) et seq.
20 U.S.C. 1401(3)
34 C.F.R. 300.7
105 ILCS 5/14-1.02

13:96   What is meant by "children with disabilities" for children aged 3-9 as defined by The Individuals with Disabilities Education Act?

"Children with disabilities" for children aged 3-9 may include, at the discretion of the State and the local school district, children with developmental delays as defined by the State and as measured by appropriate diagnostic instruments and procedures in one or more of the following areas: physical development, cognitive development, communication development, social or emotional development, or adaptive development and who by reason thereof need special education and related services.

20 U.S.C. 1401 (3)(B)(i) et seq.
34 C.F.R. 300.7(a)(2)(b)

13:100   Do children with Acquired Immune Deficiency Syndrome (AIDS) qualify for special education?

The Individuals with Disabilities Education Act applies to AIDS victims only if their physical condition is such that it adversely affects their educational performance.

Robertson by Robertson v. Granite City Community Unit School District No. 9, 684 F.Supp. 1002 (S.D. Ill. 1988)
Doe by Doe v. Belleville Public School District No. 118, 672 F.Supp. 342 (S.D. Ill. 1987)

13:110   Are school districts required to provide special education services to eligible students who reside in the school district but who attend nonpublic schools?

The school district has the obligation to identify and provide services to all students who are in need of special education and related services whether such students attend private, parochial or home schools.

A school board is required to accept for part-time attendance eligible children with disabilities who reside in the school district but are enrolled in nonpublic schools. Transportation for students in part-time attendance must be provided only if required in the child's individualized educational program on the basis of the child's disabling condition or as the location of the special education program may require.

20 U.S.C. 1412(3)
20 U.S.C. 1412(10)
34 C.F.R. 300.125
105 ILCS 5/14-6.01
23 Ill. Admin. Code 226.20

13:114 May a school district provide special education services on site at a parochial school?

Yes. However, only public employees can deliver the services, assignment of public employees should be made without regard to the religious affiliation of the employee, all religious symbols should be removed from the private school classroom where services are to be delivered, consultations between the public school teacher and the private school teacher should be limited to mutual concerns regarding the students public education, and there should be monitoring of the program for separation of religious and secular purposes.

Agostini v. Felton, 117 S.Ct. 1997, 521 U.S. 203, 138 L.Ed.2d 391 (1997)

SPECIAL PROGRAMS AND SERVICES

13:120 What special education facilities and services must school districts provide for qualified students with disabilities?

Special educational facilities and services include special schools; special classes; special housing, including residential facilities; special instruction; special reader service; braillists and typists for visually disabled children; sign language interpreters; transportation; maintenance; instructional material; physical and or occupational therapy; professional consultant services; medical services only for diagnostic and evaluation purposes provided by a physician licensed to practice medicine in all its branches to determine a child's need for special education and related services; psychological services; school social worker services; special administrative services; salaries of all required special personnel; and other special educational services, including special equipment for use in the classroom required by the child because of his disability if such services or special equipment are approved by the State Superintendent of Education and the child is eligible under the regulations of the State Board of Education.

105 ILCS 5/14-1.08

13:140   What are "related services" in the context of special education?

"Related services" means transportation and such developmental, corrective, and other supportive services (including speech-language pathology and audiology services, psychological services, physical and occupational therapy, recreation, including therapeutic recreation, social work services, counseling services, including rehabilitation counseling, orientation and mobility services, and related medical services as may be required to assist a child with a disability to benefit from special education and includes the early identification and assessment of handicapping conditions in children. It is unsettled law, but it may be possible for a school district to argue undue burden in an attempt to avoid providing certain related medical services.

20 U.S.C. 1401(22)
34 C.F.R. 300.24(a)
23 Ill. Admin Code 226
Cedar Rapids Community School District v. Garret F ex rel. Charlene F, 119 S.Ct.992, 526 U.S. 66, 143 L.Ed.2d 154 (1999)
Morton Community Unit School District No. 709 v. J.M., 152 F.3d 583 (7th Cir. 1998) cert. den. 119 S.Ct. 1140, __U.S.__, 143 L.Ed.2d 208
Irving Independent School District v. Tatro, 104 S.Ct. 3371, 468 U.S. 883, 82 L.Ed.2d 664 (1984), on rem. 741 F.2d 82 (1984)

13:145   What are supplementary aids and services?

Supplementary aids and services are aids, services and other supports that are provided in regular education classes or other education related settings to enable children with disabilities to be educated with non-disabled children to the maximum extent appropriate under special education law.

20 U.S.C 1401(29)
34 C.F.R. 300.28

13:150   Under what circumstances must a school district provide a child with a disability with medical services?

A school district is not required to provide special education students with medical services except for purposes of diagnosis or evaluation. Medically related services which could be provided by a nurse or a trained lay person which are necessary to permit a student to benefit from special education must be provided.

105 ILCS 5/10-22.21b

Morton Community Unit School District No. 709 v. J.M., 152 F.3d 583 (7th Cir. 1998) cert. den. 119 S.Ct. 1140, __U.S.__, 143 L.Ed.2d 208

Cedar Rapids Community School District v. Garret F ex rel. Charlene F, 119 S.Ct.992, 526 U.S. 66, 143 L.Ed.2d 154 (1999)

Bevin H. by Michael H. v. Wright, 666 F.Supp. 71 (W.D. Pa. 1987)

Irving Independent School District v. Tatro, 104 S.Ct. 3371, 468 U.S. 883, 82 L.Ed.2d 664 (1984), on rem. 741 F.2d 82 (1984)

Max M. v. Illinois State Board of Education, 585 F.Supp. 317, on reconsideration 629 F.Supp. 1504 (N.D. Ill. 1984)

Max M. v. Thompson, 585 F.Supp. 317, on reconsideration 592 F.Supp. 1437 (N.D. Ill. 1984)

Darlene L. v. Illinois State Board of Education, 568 F.Supp. 1340 (N.D. Ill. 1983)

T.G. on Behalf of D.G. v. Board of Education of Piscataway, New Jersey, 576 F.Supp. 420 (D.C. N.J. 1983) aff'd. 738 F.2d 420, cert. den. 105 S.Ct. 592, 469 U.S. 1086, 83 L.Ed.2d 701 (1984)

13:160   Must a school district provide an interpreter for a deaf student?

If the child's individual educational plan (IEP) requires an interpreter, an interpreter must be provided at school district expense.

23 Ill. Admin. Code 226.250 4)

Zobrest v. Catalina Foothills School District, 113 S.Ct. 2462, 506 U.S. 813, 125 L.Ed.2d 1 (1993)

Board of Education of Hendrick Hudson Central School District, Board of Education Westchester County v. Rowley, 102 S.Ct. 3034, 458 U.S. 176, 73 L.Ed.2d 690 (1982)

13:161   Must a school district provide an on-site interpreter, teaching aide or consultant teacher on private school grounds?

No. Provided the school district provides an opportunity for the student to receive a free appropriate public education, it has met its obligation. A school district must expend an "amount equal to a proportionate amount of federal funds" to educate such students

20 U.S.C. 1412(a)(10)(A) et seq.
34 C.F.R. 300.452
105 ILCS 14-6.01
Celafu on Behalf of Celafu v. East Baton Rouge Parish School Board, 907 F.Supp. 966, vac. 103 F.3d 393, opinion withdrawn and superceded on reh. 117 F.3d 231, rev. 117 F.3d 231 (5th Cir. 1997)
Board of Education of Enlarged City School District of the City of Watervliet v. Russman, 117 S.Ct. 2502, 521 U.S. 111, 138 L.Ed.2d 1008 (1997)
Unifed School District No. 259 v. Fowler and Fowler v. Unified School District No. 259, 117 S.Ct. 2503, 521 U.S. 1115, 138 L.Ed.2d 1008 (1997)

13:165   What are transition services?

Transition services means a coordinated set of activities for a student with a disability that is designed within an outcome oriented process, which promotes movement from school to post school activities, including post secondary education, vocational training, integrated employment (including supported employment), continuing adult education, adult services, independent living, or community participation. Transition services must be based on individual student needs, taking into account the student's preferences and interests and includes instruction, related services, community experiences, the development of employment in other post school adult living objectives, and, when appropriate, acquisition of daily living skills and functional vocational evaluation.

20 U.S.C. 1401(30)
34 C.F.R. 300.29
105 ILCS 5/10-20.31
23 Ill. Admin. Code 226.5

13:170   What special training is required of persons employed to work in special education programs?

No person may be employed to teach any class or program in special education who does not hold a valid teaching certificate as provided by law and unless he has had special training as the State Board of Education may require. All other professional personnel employed in any class, service, or program authorized by law must hold the certificate and shall have received such training as the State Board of Education may require. A school board may employ necessary workers to assist properly certified teachers with the special education facilities, but such workers must have training prescribed by the State Board of Education.

105 ILCS 5/14-9.01

13:180   What are the special education class size limits?

The principle determinants of the number of students served in each special education instructional program is the age of the students, the nature and severity of their exceptional characteristics, and the degree of intervention necessary.

All exceptions to the program size limitations require the written approval of the State Board of Education prior to the implementation of the program. Specific limitations are as follows:

1) Early childhood instructional programs must have a maximum ratio of one qualified teacher to five students in attendance at any one time; total enrollment is limited according to the needs of the students for individualized programming.

2) Instructional programs which primarily serve children whose exceptional characteristics are either profound in degree or multiple in nature shall have a maximum enrollment of five students.

3) Instructional programs which primarily serve children whose principle exceptional characteristics are severe visual, auditory, physical, speech or language impairments, or behavioral disorders must have a maximum enrollment of 10 students.

4) Instructional programs which primarily serve children whose principle exceptional characteristics are learning disabilities or severe mental impairment; programs which are primarily diagnostic or developmental; or programs which serve children with differing exceptional characteristics shall have a maximum enrollment of 10 students.

5) Instructional programs which primarily serve children whose principal exceptional characteristics are moderate visual or auditory impairment shall have a maximum enrollment of 12 students.

6) Instructional programs which primarily serve children whose principal exceptional characteristics are educational disabilities or mild/moderate mental impairment shall have a maximum enrollment of 12 students at the primary level and 15 students at the intermediate, junior high, and secondary levels.

A school district may increase the enrollment in a special education instructional program by a maximum of two additional students to meet unique circumstances which occur during the school year. Such additions may be made only when the educational needs of all students who would be enrolled in the expanded program can be adequately and appropriately met, or the school district may increase the enrollment in a special education instructional program by a maximum of five additional students when the program is provided with a full-time, noncertified assistant.

There is a procedure allowing variance from class size limitations by application to the State Board of Education.

23 Ill. Admin. Code 226.225

EVALUATION AND PLACEMENT

13:190   What is the definition of "evaluation" in the context of special education?

Evaluation means procedures used in accordance with federal and state regulations to determine whether a child has a disability and the nature and extent of the special education and related services the child needs.

20 U.S.C. 1414 (a)(1) et seq.
34 C.F.R. 300.500 (b)(2)
105 ILCS 5/14-8.02(b)

13:200   Who may refer a child for a special education evaluation?

A child may be referred for a special education evaluation by school district personnel, the parents of the child, community service agencies, persons having primary care and custody of the child, other professional persons having knowledge of the child's problems, the child, or the State Board of Education.

23 Ill. Admin. Code 226.5
23 Ill. Admin. Code 226.515 b)

13:210   How often must a special education student be reevaluated?

Special education students must be reevaluated at least once every three years or more frequently if conditions warrant. Reevaluation must be considered upon parental request. The educational status and continued special education placement of each child must be reviewed at least annually in a conference attended by those professionals working with the student, the parents, the child when appropriate, the special education director or designee who is qualified to supervise the provision of special education, and others at the discretion of the parent or school district.

23 U.S.C. 1414(a)(2)
34 C.F.R. 300.536
23 Ill. Admin. Code 226.535
23 Ill. Admin. Code 226.578

13:215   Does a special education student's individualized education program (IEP) necessarily follow him from elementary school to high school?

When a special education student reaches 14 1/2 years old, the elementary district in which the student resides must notify the high school district in which the student resides of the student's special education eligibility, program and evaluation data. The high school district may accept the current placement or may elect to conduct its own evaluation and multidisciplinary conference and formulate its own IEP.

105 ILCS 5/14-6.01

13:216   What happens to a special education student's individualized education program (IEP) when the student and his family change their residence from one school district to another?

When a parent presents a copy of the student's then current IEP to the new school, the student must be placed in a special education program in accordance with that described in the student's IEP.

105 ILCS 10/8.1

13:220   When is a special education student eligible for placement in a residential facility?

When a residential placement for educational purposes is considered, the necessity for the placement must be individually based upon evidence the student's needs are so profound or unusual that his educational needs cannot be met in a less restrictive placement. The evidence from recent diagnostic assessments and other pertinent information must indicate that, while the student can benefit from instructional services, he is so severely disabled his educational needs cannot be met in a less restrictive environment.

If there is evidence of a condition which presents a danger to the physical well-being of the student or to other students, the evidence must be considered a factor in making a residential placement.

23 Ill. Admin. Code 226.420
Vander Malle v. Ambach, 667 F.Supp. 1015 (S.D. N.Y. 1987)
Cochran v. District of Columbia, 660 F.Supp. 314, (D.C. D.C. 1987)
Christopher T. by Brogna v. San Francisco Unified School District, 553 F.Supp. 1107 (N.D. Cal. 1982)

RIGHTS OF CHILDREN AND PARENTS

13:230   What notice must a school board publish concerning the education of children with disabilities residing in the district?

A school board must publish a public notice regarding the right of all children with disabilities to a free and appropriate public education. The notice must be published in a school district newsletter of general circulation or in the newsletter of another governmental entity of general circulation in the district or, if neither is available in the district, in a newspaper of general circulation in the district.

The notice must identify the location and phone number of the office or agent of the school district to whom inquiries should be directed regarding the identification, assessment, and placement of such children. A school board must provide, upon request, written materials and other information that indicates the specific policies, procedures, rules, and regulations regarding the identification, evaluation, or educational placement of children with disabilities. Such information shall include all rights and entitlements of such children and of the opportunity to present complaints with respect to any matter relating to educational placement of the student, or the provision of a free and appropriate public education, and to have an impartial due process hearing on the complaint. The notice must inform the parents or guardian in the parents' or guardian's native language, unless it is clearly not feasible to do so, of their rights and all procedures available. The notice shall also inform the parents or guardian of the availability upon request of a list of free or low-cost legal and other relevant services available locally to assist parents or guardians in exercising their entitlements under the School Code

105 ILCS 5/14-6.01

13:240   Must a school district obtain parental consent before conducting a special education evaluation of a student?

A school district must obtain written parental consent to evaluate a student for special education. If consent is not given by the parent or guardian, a school district may request a due process hearing to determine if the evaluation should be conducted.

23 U.S.C. 1414(C)
34 C.F.R. 300.500(b)(1)
34 C.F.R. 300.505 (a)(1)
105 ILCS 5/14-8.02
23 Ill. Admin. Code 226.525
23 Ill. Admin. Code 226.530

13:250   If the school district has obtained a proper parental consent for a special education evaluation, must the school district obtain another parental consent for any reevaluation?

Yes.

23 U.S.C. 1414(a)(1)(C)
34 C.F.R. 300.505(a)(1)(i)
105 ILCS 5/14-8.02(b)
23 Ill. Admin. Code 226.525

13:260   May parents challenge the conclusions and recommendations of a multi-disciplinary staff conference?

Yes. At the conclusion of the multidisciplinary staff conference, the parent or guardian of the child must be given a copy of the multidisciplinary conference summary report and recommendations, which includes options considered, and must be informed of their right to obtain an independent educational evaluation if they disagree with the findings. If the school district's evaluation is shown to be inappropriate, the school district must reimburse the parent for the cost of the independent evaluation.

The State Board of Education supplies school districts with a list of suggested independent evaluators and must make the list available to parents at their request. A school district must make the list available to parents at the time they are informed of their right to obtain an independent educational evaluation. However, a school district may initiate an impartial due process hearing within five days of any written parent or guardian request for an independent educational evaluation to show that its evaluation is appropriate. If the final decision is the evaluation is appropriate, the parent retains the right to an independent educational evaluation, but not at public expense.

An independent educational evaluation at public expense must be completed within 30 days of a parent or guardian's written request unless the school district initiates an impartial due process hearing or the parent or guardian or school district offers reasonable grounds to show that the 30-day time period should be extended. If the due process hearing decision indicates the parent or guardian is entitled to an independent educational evaluation, it must be completed within 30 days of the decision unless the parent or guardian or the school district offers reasonable grounds to show the 30 day period should be extended.

If a parent disagrees with the summary report or recommendations of the multidisciplinary conference or the findings of any educational evaluation which results therefrom, the school district cannot proceed with a placement based upon the evaluation and the child must remain in his regular classroom setting or other current placement.

> 23 U.S.C. 1415(b)
> 34 C.F.R. 502(a)(3)
> 105 ILCS 5/14-8.02
> 23 Ill. Admin. Code 226.544

13:270 What right of review exists if the parents and the school district fail to agree on an appropriate special education placement for a particular child?

If there is disagreement between the parent or guardian and the school about the appropriate placement of a student with a disability, either the parent or guardian or the school district may seek a due process hearing before an impartial hearing officer. The decision of the hearing officer may be appealed by either party.

> 23 U.S.C. 1414(f)
> 34 C.F.R. 300.507(a)
> 105 ILCS 5/14-8.02(h)
> 105 ILCS 5/14-8.02a

13:275 Is parental hostility to a school district's proposed educational placement an appropriate factor to consider when analyzing the placement's expected educational benefits?

Yes, although hostility is a fact question which may be rebutted with evidence to the contrary at hearing.

> *Board of Education of Community Consolidated School District 21 v. Brozer,* 938 F.2d 712 (7th Cir. 1991)

13:280   Is a school district required to permit parental involvement in formulating and implementing an individualized educational program (IEP)?

Parents must be given, on an ongoing basis, reasonable opportunity for comment on and input into their child's educational program.

23 Ill. Admin. Code 226.562
Muth v. Central Bucks School District, 839 F.2d 113 (3rd Cir. 1988) cert. den. 109 S.Ct. 103, cert. granted 109 S.Ct. 52, rev. sub nom. on other grounds *Dellmuth v. Muth,* 109 S.Ct. 2397, 491 U.S. 223, 105 L.Ed.2d 181 (1989) on rem. sub nom. *Muth v. Central Bucks School District,* 884 F.2d 1384 (3rd Cir. 1989)

13:290   Do the course requirements for receiving a high school diploma apply to special education or students with disabilities whose education is governed by an individualized education program?

No.

105 ILCS 5/27-22

13:300   May a student with a disability be retained in grade level or prevented from graduating for failure to pass a minimal competency test?

No student with a qualifying disability may be denied promotion, graduation or a general diploma on the basis of failing a minimal competency test when the failure can be directly related to the student's disability.

105 ILCS 5/3.64
105 ILCS 5/14-6.01

13:310   What special provisions exist for special education students affected by a teachers strike?

If a strike by educational employees results in the closing of schools, and the district is party to a joint agreement for special education, any resident students who are enrolled in special education programs of the joint agreement district must be permitted to attend special education programs in any other district which is a party to the same joint agreement and whose schools are not closed as a result of the strike.

105 ILCS 5/10-22.31

FINANCIAL OBLIGATIONS

13:320 If a school district accepts a properly placed non-resident child with a disability, which school district bears the cost of the child's education?

If a school district accepts a non-resident child with a disability for admission into any of its special education programs pursuant to the child's individualized educational plan (IEP), the school district in which the child resides bears the cost of educational services provided the child.

Doe v. Sanders, 189 Ill.App.3d 572, 545 N.E.2d 454, 136 Ill.Dec. 930 (1st Dist. 1989)

William C. v. Board of Education of the City of Chicago, 71 Ill.App.3d 793, 390 N.E.2d 479, 28 Ill.Dec. 312 (1st Dist. 1979)

13:325 Which school district must pay for a child's special education costs if the child is placed in an out-of-district residential facility?

A child in need of special education who is properly placed in a residential facility is presumed to be a resident of the school district in which his parents reside. Unless a contrary residence is proven (usually by showing that the parents no longer have custody and control of the child) the school district in which the parents reside is responsible for the costs of the residential placement.

William C. v. Board of Education, City of Chicago, 71 Ill.App.3d 793, 390 N.E.2d 479, 28 Ill.Dec. 312 (1st Dist. 1979)

School District No. 153, Cook County v. School District 154 1/2, Cook County, 54 Ill.App.3d 587, 370 N.E.2d 22, 12 Ill.Dec. 399 (1st Dist. 1977)

13:330   May a school district pass on to parents any portion of the tuition charge for a student with a disability who is appropriately placed in a nonpublic school?

The education of children with disabilities is the responsibility of the school district and no part of the tuition charged by a nonpublic facility may be passed on to the parents of the child with a disability if the child is appropriately placed in the nonpublic facility.

Elliot v. Board of Education of the City of Chicago, 64 Ill.App.3d 229, 380 N.E.2d 1137, 20 Ill.Dec. 928 (1st Dist. 1978)

13:340   What is the effect of unilateral residential placement of special education students by their parents?

If a child with a disability has available a free and appropriate public education, the school district has otherwise complied with special education laws and the parents choose to place the child in a private school or facility, the school board is not required to pay for the child's education at the private school or facility. Disagreements between a parent and a school regarding the availability of a program appropriate for the child and the question of financial responsibility are subject to due process procedures.

20 U.S.C. 1412(a)(10)(B)
20 U.S.C. 1415
34 C.F.R. 300.302
23 Ill. Admin. Code 226.430(b)
Florence County School District Four v. Carter, 112 S.Ct. 1932, 504 U.S. 906, 118 L.Ed.2d 540 (1993)
Burlington School Committee of the Town of Burlington, Massachusetts v. Department of Education of Massachusetts, 105 S.Ct 1996, 471 U.S. 359, 85 L.Ed.2d 385 (1985)

13:350   Are there circumstances under which a school district may be held liable for the costs associated with the parent of a child with a qualifying disability removing the child from a public school program and unilaterally placing the child in a private facility?

A school district may be liable for the costs of such a placement if the child's physical health would be endangered if an alternative placement were not made or if the school district has acted in bad faith by failing to comply with statutory provisions for resolving the dispute over the child's educational placement, or if the school district has not otherwise provided the child with an appropriate educational placement.

Florence County School District Four v. Carter, 112 S.Ct. 1932, 504 U.S. 906, 118 L.Ed.2d 540 (1993)
Anderson v. Thompson, 658 F.2d 1205 (7th Cir. 1981)

DISCIPLINE OF STUDENTS WITH DISABILITIES

13:360 May a school district suspend a special education student for disciplinary reasons?

A suspension in this context is defined as a removal from the child's current educational setting for not more than ten consecutive school days for each disciplinary event. A child may be suspended for disciplinary reasons for up to ten cumulative days (not necessarily consecutive) during a school year without the requirement that the school district provide services to the child. After ten cumulative days, the school district must provide services to the child during the term of the suspension or expulsion, whether or not the removal constitutes a change in placement. In-school suspensions which isolate the child or deny him access to mainstreaming or aspects of his individualized educational program count as suspension days in the above calculations. A school district may suspend a child for a cumulative number of days in a school year in excess of ten if the suspensions taken together do not constitute a change in placement.

To suspend a special education student for more than 10 days in a school year, the school district must have procedures in place which allow the members of the student's individualized education program (IEP) team to determine whether each suspension event constitutes a change in placement. The IEP team must consider such factors as the total amount of time the student is excluded from school, the proximity of the suspensions to one another and the length of each suspension.

While there appears to be legislative intent to permit broader use of disciplinary suspensions (in excess of ten cumulative days in a school term) in the reauthorized special education law, until there is clear judicial interpretation of certain conflicts in the statute and the rules, the safer approach for school officials is to limit cumulative suspensions to not more than ten days per school year.

20 U.S.C. 1415
34 C.F.R. 300.300
34 C.F.R. 300.520
105 ILCS 5/14-8.05
23 Ill. Admin. Code 226.40
23 Ill. Admin. Code 226.605
Parents of Student W v. Payallup School District No. 3, 31 F. 3d 1489 (9th Cir. 1994)
Honig v. Doe, 108 S.Ct. 592, 484 U.S. 305, 98 L.Ed.2d 686 (1988)
Board of Education City of Peoria v. Illinois State Board of Education, 531 F.Supp. 148 (C.D. Ill. 1982)

13:370 May a school district expel a special education student from school?

Unlike a short term disciplinary suspension, an expulsion is a change in placement. If the behavior giving rise to the expulsion is found to be related to the child's disability, expulsion may not be invoked. The law is unsettled as to whether a special education student may be expelled from school when the behavior giving rise to the discipline is not related to the child's disability. It is clear, however, that after "expulsion" the school district must continue to provide services to the child.

A formal special education staffing must be held prior to any disciplinary hearing to determine the relatedness of the student's alleged misbehavior to his disability. This hearing is commonly called "a manifestation hearing." A school district may seek injunctive relief to bar a dangerous student from school pending disposition of change in placement proceedings.

34 C.F.R. 300.300
105 ILCS 5/14-8.01
105 ILCS 5/14-8.05
23 Ill. Admin. Code 226.40
Doe v. Board of Education of Oak Park and River Forest High School District 200, 115 F.3d 1273 (7th Cir. 1997)
Commonwealth of Virginia v. Riley, 86 F.3d 1337 (4th Cir. 1996)
Metropolitan School District of Wayne Township, Marion County Indiana v. Davila, 969 F.2d 485 (7th Cir. 1992) cert. den. 113 S.Ct. 1360, 507 U.S. 949, 122 L.Ed.2d 740 (1993)
Honig v. Doe, 108 S.Ct. 592, 484 U.S. 305, 98 L.Ed.2d 686 (1988)
S-1 v. Turlington, 635 F.2d 1210 (4th Cir. 1985)

13:371   Under what circumstances may a special education child be placed in an alternative educational setting for disciplinary reasons?

A special education student may be removed from his current educational setting for more than 10 school days if his individualized education plan (IEP) is amended to allow for the change in placement. In other cases the student may be involuntarily removed to an alternative educational setting for offenses involving weapons or drugs. The placement in the alternative educational setting may not exceed 45 calendar days (without changing the child's IEP).

In this context, weapon is defined as "a device, instrument, material or substance that is used for, or is readily capable of, causing death or serious bodily injury," except that it does not include a pocket knife unless the blade is at least 2-1/2 inches long.

A special education student may be removed for up to 45 days by a hearing officer or a court for behavior which creates a threat of injury.

20 U.S.C. 1415(b)(5)
34 C.F.R. 300.520 et seq.
105 ILCS 5/14-8.02b(ii)

13:373   Under what circumstances may an expedited hearing occur?

An expedited hearing may be requested by a parent, guardian or by a student if the student is at least eighteen years of age or emancipated if there is a disagreement regarding a determination that the student's behavior was not a manifestation of the student's disability, or if there is a disagreement regarding a school district's decision to move the student to an interim alternative educational setting for a weapon and drug violation as defined by IDEA. An expedited hearing may be requested by a school district if school personnel maintain that it is dangerous for the student to be in the current placement during the pendency of a due process hearing.

23 U.S.C. 1415(k)
34 C.F.R. 300.520 et seq.
105 ILCS 5/14-8.02b

13:375   What factors must a school district consider in the discipline of a student with disabilities?

When behavioral interventions are used, they must take into consideration the pupil's physical freedom and social interaction, and must be administered in a manner that respects human dignity and personal privacy and that ensures a pupil's right to placement in the least restrictive environment. Behavioral management plans must be developed and used, to the extent possible, in a consistent manner when a local educational agency has placed a student in a day or residential setting for education purposes.

105 ILCS 5/14-8.05

SPECIAL EDUCATION FACILITIES

13:410   May a school board use its special education tax levy to construct buildings?

Yes. By proper resolution, the school board may accumulate funds in the special education fund for up to eight years for building purposes.

105 ILCS 5/17-2.2a

13:420   What may school districts do with special education facilities no longer needed for special education purposes?

If it is no longer feasible or economical to utilize classroom facilities constructed with revenues raised and accumulated by the tax for special education building purposes, the district may use such facilities for regular school purposes with the approval of the regional superintendent of schools and the State Superintendent of Education. The district must make comparable facilities available for special education purposes at another attendance center which is in a more practical location due to the proximity of the students served.

By unanimous consent of participating school districts, a cooperative special education district may exercise the same discretion.

105 ILCS 5/17-2.2a

SPECIAL EDUCATION JOINT AGREEMENTS

13:430   Must each school district maintain special education facilities?

Each school district must establish and maintain such special educational facilities as may be needed for children with disabilities who are residents of the school district. School districts need not provide special education facilities independently, however. School districts are empowered to enter into joint agreements as a means for providing such required facilities.

105 ILCS 5/14-4 01

13:440   What governs the formation of a special education school district?

The School Code permits school districts to enter into joint agreements to provide special education services and facilities for the education of students. A copy of any joint agreement or amendment to a joint agreement entered into on or after January 1, 1989 must be filed with the State Board of Education.

105 ILCS 5/10-22.31

13:450   How may a joint agreement be amended?

A joint agreement may be amended at any time as provided in the joint agreement, or if the joint agreement does not provide a procedure for amendment, it may be amended at any time by adoption of concurring resolutions by the school boards of all the member districts.

105 ILCS 5/10-22.31

13:460   Under what circumstances may a school district withdraw from a special education joint agreement?

A school district desiring to withdraw from a joint agreement may petition the regional board of school trustees of all counties having jurisdiction over one or more of the districts in the joint agreement. Upon receipt of a petition for withdrawal, the regional boards of school trustees having jurisdiction over the cooperating districts must publish notice and conduct a joint hearing on the issue. The notice and hearing procedures are conducted as provided in detachment cases. Approval of a withdrawal petition requires "a two-thirds vote of all trustees of those regional boards, at a joint meeting." A withdrawal takes effect as provided in Section 7-9 of the School Code.

105 ILCS 5/7-6 et seq.
105 ILCS 5/10-22.31

SPECIAL EDUCATION DUE PROCESS HEARINGS

13:500   Who may request a special education due process hearing?

A hearing may be requested by a parent or guardian, student of at least 18 years of age, an emancipated student or a school district.

20 U.S.C. 1415 et seq.
34 C.F.R. 300.507
105 ILCS 5/14-8.02a(f)

13:505   Under what circumstances may the parent or legal guardian of a child with a qualifying disability demand a due process hearing?

A hearing may be requested by the child, the parents, other persons having primary care and custody of the child, or the school district regarding, but not limited to, the following:

1) objection to signing consent for proposed case study evaluation or initial placement;

2) failure of the local school district to provide a case study evaluation that has been requested by the parents, other persons having primary care and custody of the child, the child, or the Illinois State Board of Education;

3) failure of a local school district to consider evaluations completed by qualified professional personnel outside the school district;

4) objection to a proposed special education placement, either an initial placement, a continuation of a previous placement, or a change in the placement;

5) termination of a special education placement;

6) failure of the local school district to provide a special edu-

cation placement consistent with the finding of the case study evaluation and the recommendations of the multidisciplinary conference;

7) failure of the local school district to provide the least restrictive special education placement appropriate to the child's needs;

8) provision of special education instructional or resource programs, or related services in an amount insufficient to meet the child's needs;

9) recommendation for the graduation of a student;

10) failure of the local school district to ensure compliance with the rules regarding expulsion of students;

11) failure of the local school district to comply with any of these rules and/or the School Code;

12) failure of the local school district to provide an exceptional child with a free and appropriate public education.

20 U.S.C. 1415 (f) et seq.
34 C.F.R. 300.507 et seq.
105 ILCS 5/14-8.02
23 Ill. Admin. Code 226.605

13:510   Under what circumstances may parents of a handicapped child bring suit in court to determine the child's appropriate placement before they have exhausted administrative remedies?

A suit in court may be brought before administrative remedies are exhausted in an emergency situation when exhaustion would cause the child to suffer serious and irreversible mental or physical damage.

Komninos v. Upper Saddle River Board of Education, 13 F.3d 775 (3rd Cir. 1994)

13:515   What change in placement is possible for a child with a qualifying disability from the time a local level due process hearing is requested until all appeals have been exhausted?

During the pendency of any special education proceeding, unless the school district and the parents or guardian otherwise agree, the student must remain in his then current educational placement, or if applying for initial admission to the school district, must, with the consent of the parents or guardian, be placed in the school district program until all such proceedings have been completed.

> 20 U.S.C. 1415(j)
> 34 C.F.R. 300.514
> 105 ILCS 5/14-8.02(k)
> *Florence County School District Four v. Carter,* 112 S.Ct. 1932, 504 U.S. 906, 118 L.Ed.2d 540 (1993)
>> *Honig v. Doe,* 108 S.Ct. 592, 484 U.S. 305, 98 L.Ed.2d 686 (1988)
>> *Walker v. Cronin,* 107 Ill.App.3d 1053, 438 N.E.2d 582, 63 Ill.Dec. 651 (1st Dist. 1982)

13:520   What is a child's current educational placement if a child has not yet acquired an individualized educational program (IEP)?

Stay put provisions of the Individuals with Disabilities Education Act require that a child's educational program not be changed during the pendency of a dispute over the placement. If a child does not yet have an IEP when a dispute over the child's appropriate placement arises, the child must remain in the last placement in which the child was receiving an education until the dispute is resolved or until the parents otherwise agree. If the dispute arises when the school district has expulsion proceedings pending, stay put provisions effectively block the expulsion if the school district knew or reasonably should have known of the student's disability.

> 23 U.S.C. 1415(j)
> 34 C.F.R. 300.514
> 105 ILCS 5/14-8.02a(j)
> *Rodiriecus L. By Betty H. v. Waukegan School District No. 60,* 90 F.3d 249 (7th Cir. 1996)
> *Thomas v. Cincinnati Board of Education,* 918 F.2d 618 (6th Cir. 1990)

13:525   What notice obligations does a school district have when a due process request has been made?

If a school district is requesting the hearing, the school district makes its request in writing to the State Board of Education and must thereafter promptly mail a copy of the request to the parents or guardian of the student at their last known address. A parent, guardian or student request is made in writing to the superintendent of schools who must forward the request to the State Board of Education within five days of receipt.

105 ILCS 5/14-8.02a(f)

13:530 Do parents of students with qualifying disabilities have a right to counsel at special education due process hearings?

Parents and guardians of students with qualifying disabilities have the right to be represented by counsel at their own expense. After certain findings, the school district may be required to reimburse the parents and guardians of such students for their attorney fees.

Doe v. Baltimore County, Maryland Board of Education, 165 F.3d 260 (4th Cir. 1999)

John T. v. Marion Independent School District, 173 F.3d 684 (9th Cir. 1999)

Warner v. Independent School District No. 625, 134 F.3d 1333 (8th Cir 1998), cert. den. 119 S.Ct. 67, __ U.S.__, 142 L.Ed.2d 53

Fenneman v. Town of Gorham, 802 F.Supp. 542 (D.C. Me. 1992)

McSomebodies v. Burlingame Elementary School, 897 F.2d 974 (9th Cir. 1989)

Moore v. District of Columbia, 886 F.2d 335 (D.C. Cir. 1989)

Mitten by and through Mitten v. Muscogee County School District, 877 F.2d 932 (11th Cir. 1989) cert. den. 110 S.Ct. 1117, 493 U.S. 1072, 107 L.Ed.2d 1024 (1990)

Duane M. v. Orleans Parish School Board, 861 F.2d 115 (5th Cir. 1988)

Eggers v. Bullit County School District, 854 F.2d 892 (6th Cir. 1988)

Daniel B. v. Wisconsin Dept. of Public Instruction, 581 F.Supp. 585 (D.C. Wisc.), 776 F.2d 1051 (7th Cir. 1984) cert. den. 106 S.Ct. 1462, 475 U.S. 1083, 89 L.Ed.2d 719 (1984)

New York Gaslight Club, Inc. v. Carey, 100 S.Ct. 204, 444 U.S. 897, 62 L.Ed.2d 132 (1980)

13:535 How are due process hearing officers selected?

Due process hearing officers are qualified by the State Board of Education and selected by the parties from lists of five names each provided by the State Board of Education using an alternate strike system. The State Board of Education provides panels by use of a rotating selection system.

105 ILCS 5/14-8.02a(b)
105 ILCS 5/14-8.02a(f)

13:538 Are special education due process hearings open or closed to the public?

A special education due process hearing is closed to the public unless the parents or guardian request that it be open to the public.

105 ILCS 5/14-8.02a(g)

13:540 When and where are due process hearings held?

The hearing must be held at a time and place which are reasonably convenient to the parties. At the request of a party the hearing officer must hold the hearing at a no-cost neutral site.

105 ILCS 5/14-8.02a(g)

13:543 What is a special education pre-hearing conference?

A hearing officer must convene a pre-hearing conference no later than fourteen days before the scheduled date for the due process hearing. The parties receive ten days advance notice of the pre-hearing conference which may be conducted in person or by telephone.

105 ILCS 5/14-8.02a(f)

13:545 What disclosures are required at a pre-hearing conference?

Each party must disclose:

1) whether it is represented by legal counsel or intends to retain legal counsel;

2) the matters it believes to be in dispute and the specific relief to be sought;

3) whether there are any additional evaluations for the student that it intends to introduce into the hearing record that have not been previously disclosed;

4) a list of all documents it intends to introduce into the hearing record;

5) the names of all witnesses it intends to call.

105 ILCS 5/14-8.02a(g)

13:547 What happens if a party fails to timely disclose evidence to the other party?

Any party to a due process hearing has the right to prohibit the introduction of evidence at the hearing which has not been disclosed to that party at least five business days before the hearing.

23 U.S.C. 1415(f)(2)
34 C.F.R. 300.509(b)
105 ILCS 5/14-8.02a(g)

13:550 What evidence must a school district present at a due process hearing?

The school district must present evidence that the special education needs of the child have been appropriately identified and that the special education program and related services proposed to meet the needs of the child are adequate, appropriate and available. If at issue, the school district must present evidence that it has properly identified and evaluated the nature and severity of the students suspected or identified disability and that, if the student has been or should have been determined eligible for special education and related services that it is providing or has offered a free appropriate public education to the student in the least restrictive environment, consistent with procedural safeguards and in accordance with the students individualized education program.

105 ILCS 5/14-8.02a(g)

13:552 What rights do the parties have at a due process hearing?

Any party has the right to:

1) be represented by counsel and be accompanied and advised by persons with special knowledge or training with respect to the problems of children with disabilities;

2) present evidence and confront and cross examine witnesses;

3) move for the exclusion of witnesses from hearing until they are called to testify except that this provision cannot be used to exclude a party's representative or someone providing the party assistance;

4) obtain a written or electronic verbatim record of the proceedings within 30 days of a written request from the parent or school district;

5) obtain a written decision including findings of fact and conclusions of law within ten days after the conclusion of the hearing.

23 U.S.C. 1415(h)
34 C.F.R. 300.509
105 ILCS 5/14-8.02a(g)
23 Ill. Admin. Code 226.636

13:555   Once a hearing has been requested, how quickly should the parties expect a decision?

A written decision, including findings of fact and law, must be issued within ten days of the conclusion of the hearing. Unless the hearing officer has granted specific extensions of time, the decision must be reached and mailed to the parties not later than 45 days after the initial request for hearing is received by the school district, public agency or State Board of Education, whichever is sooner.

23 U.S.C. 1415(h)
34 C.F.R. 300.511
105 ILCS 5/14-8.02a(h)
23 Ill. Admin. Code 226.675

13:557   What elements must a due process decision contain?

In addition to being in writing and containing findings of fact and conclusions of law, the decision must specify the educational and related services that must be provided the student in accordance with the students needs.

105 ILCS 5/14-8.02a(h)

13:560   May a party seek clarification of a hearing officer's decision?

A party may request clarification of a hearing officer's decision by submitting a request in writing to the hearing officer within five days of the party's receipt of the decision. The request for clarification must specify the portions of the decision for which clarification is sought and must be mailed to all the parties and to the State Board of Education. The hearing officer must issue a clarification of the specified portion of the decision or issue a partial or full denial of the request in writing within ten days of receipt of the request and mail copies to all parties to whom the decision was mailed. The parties may not request reconsideration of the decision itself.

> 105 ILCS 5/14-8.02a(h)
> 23 Ill. Admin. Code 226.675

13:562   How may a due process hearing result be appealed?

Any party aggrieved by the decision has the right to begin a civil action with respect to the issues presented in the impartial due process hearing. The action must be brought in a court of competent jurisdiction within 120 days after a copy of the decision of the hearing officer is mailed to the party. The limitations period for seeking review of the decision is tolled from the date a request for clarification is submitted until the date the hearing officer acts upon the request.

> 23 U.S.C. 1415(i)
> 34 C.F.R. 300.510
> 105 ILCS 5/14-8.02a(h)
> 105 ILCS 5/14-8.02a(i)

13:565   Can a successful special education parent recover his attorney fees?

Yes. A court can award reasonable attorney fees based on the prevailing rate for the kind and quality of services furnished in the community in which the action or proceeding arose. Under certain circumstances, an offer of settlement by the school district will serve to prevent the award of attorney fees.

> 23 U.S.C. 1415(i)(3)
> 34 C.F.R. 300.513
> *G.M. ex rel. R.F. v. New Britain Board of Education,* 173 F.3d 77 (2nd Cir. 1999)
> *McCartney C. By Sara S. v. Herrin Community Unit School District No. 4,* 21 F.3d 173 (7th Cir. 1994)

13:570 Can a successful special education plaintiff recover his expert witness fees after a civil trial?

The courts have not finally decided this issue. The costs of hiring an expert witness can be high, sometimes several tens of thousands of dollars. Therefore, whether or not a defendant school district has to pay its own expert as well as the plaintiff's expert is crucial. It is uncertain but possible that a successful parent plaintiff in a civil case brought after a special education due process hearing will recover the entire cost of his expert witness from the defendant school district.

20 U.S.C. 1415(i)(C) et seq.
Fed.R.Civ.P. 54(d)(1)
West Virginia Hospitals v. Casey, 111 S.Ct. 1138, 499 U.S. 83, 113 L.Ed.2d 68 (1991)
Cynthia K. v. Board of Education of Lincoln-Way High School District No. 210, 95 C 7172, 1996 WL 164381 (N.D. Ill. 1996)
Hunger v. Leininger, 15 F.3d 664 (7th Cir. 1994) cert. den. 115 S.Ct. 123, 513 U.S. 839, 130 L.Ed.2d 67
DAS v. McHenry School District No. 15, 41 F.3d 1510 (7th Cir. 1994)

14: RELIGION AND RACE AND THE PUBLIC SCHOOLS

A. Religious Issues

CONSTITUTIONAL PRINCIPLES

14:10 **What constitutional principle underlies all legal questions regarding separation of church and state?**

The First Amendment to the United States Constitution provides in part:

"Congress shall make no law respecting the establishment of religion, or prohibiting the free exercise thereof."

The first part is known as the "establishment" clause and the second part is known as the "free exercise" clause. It is balancing the establishment clause against the free exercise clause that makes the analysis of religious freedom questions difficult. Often a situation which seems clearly consistent with the establishment clause is not so clearly consistent with the free exercise clause, and vice versa.

14:20 **What test do the courts apply to determine whether a government action is constitutional under the establishment clause?**

The test, commonly called the "Lemon Test," requires that the government action must have a secular purpose, its primary effect must neither advance nor inhibit religion, and the action must not cause excessive government entanglement with religion.

The Lemon Test has been under attack in recent Supreme Court decisions. It has not been formally abandoned, however, and no new test has been developed to replace it. There is some sentiment on the court for the principle that religious expression cannot violate the establishment clause when it is purely private and occurs in a traditional or designated public forum that is publicly announced and open to all on equal terms.

Capitol Square Review and Advisory Board v. Pinette, 114 S.Ct. 626, 510 U.S. 1307, 126 L.Ed.2d 636 (1995)
Lemon v. Kurtzman, 91 S.Ct. 2105, 403 U.S. 602, 29 L.Ed.2d 745 (1971), reh. den. 92 S.Ct. 24, 404 U.S. 876, 30 L.Ed.2d 123, on rem. 348 F.Supp. 300, aff'd. 93 S.Ct. 1463, 411 U.S. 192, 36 L.Ed.2d 151 (1971)

14:25   What is the Religious Freedom Restoration Act?

In 1998, the State of Illinois enacted a Religious Freedom Restoration Act, which provides that the government may not "substantially burden a person's exercise of religion, even if the burden results from a rule of general applicability, unless it demonstrates that application of the burden to the person is in furtherance of a compelling government interest and is the least restrictive means of furthering that compelling governmental interest." The constitutionality of the Religious Freedom Restoration Act is uncertain.

775 ILCS 35/1 et seq.
City of Boerne v. P.F. Flores, 117 S.Ct.2157, 521U.S.507, 138 L.Ed.2d 624 (1997)

14:30   May the state compel students to attend public schools?

The free exercise clause of the First Amendment has been read by the courts to prevent the state from compelling public school attendance. The state may require all students, public and parochial, to receive a minimum number of hours of instruction from qualified teachers in a prescribed secular curriculum.

105 ILCS 5/26-1 et seq.
Wisconsin v. Yoder, 92 S.Ct. 1526, 406 U.S. 205, 32 L.Ed.2d 15 (1972)
Board of Education of Central School District No. 1 v. Allen, 88 S.Ct. 1923, 392 U.S. 236, 20 L.Ed.2d 1060 (1968)
Pierce v. Society of Sisters of the Holy Names of Jesus and Mary, 45 S.Ct. 571, 268 U.S. 510, 69 L.Ed 1070 (1925)
Meyer v. State of Nebraska, 43 S.Ct. 625, 262 U.S. 390, 67 L.Ed. 1042 (1923)

14:35   May a school district release students during the school day for religious instruction?

A school district must allow any child over 12 and under 14 years of age release time to attend confirmation classes. Whether release time is permissible for other kinds of religious instruction depends upon the underlying facts. The more the facts suggest public school endorsement of, or entanglement with, religion, the less likely the courts will approve any particular practice. Release time for religious classes held within the public schools or the expenditure of public funds for religious education are, in most cases, prohibited.

105 ILCS 5/26-1

Zorach v. Clauson, 92 S.Ct. 679, 343 U.S. 306, 96 L.Ed. 954 (1952)

Illinois ex rel. McCollum v. Board of Education of School District No. 71, Champaign County, Illinois, 68 S.Ct. 461, 333 U.S. 203, 92 L.Ed. 649 (1948)

People ex rel. Latimer v. Board of Education of the City of Chicago, 394 Ill. 228, 68 N.E.2d 305 (1946)

PRAYER

14:40   May students pray in school?

Yes. So long as the students respect school rules, regulations and policy regarding disruption of the educational process, students may pray in school. This means students may read their Bibles during study hall or other non-structured time, may say grace, and may discuss religion with their peers during non-directed free time, such as time spent on the playground, on a school bus, in the hallways or in the cafeteria.

Chandler v. James, 180 F.3d 1254 (11th Cir. 1999)

Bown v. Gwinnett County School District, 112 F.3d 1464 (11th Cir. 1997)

Clark v. Dallas Independent School District, 806 F.Supp. 116 (N.D. Tex. 1992)

Wallace v. Jaffree, 105 S.Ct. 2479, 472 U.S. 38, 86 L.Ed.2d 29 (1985)

14:50   Is a moment of silence for voluntary student prayer permissible?

The recitation of any state composed or endorsed prayer in school is constitutionally prohibited. This is true even if students are not required to participate in the prayer, and even if the prayer is facially neutral as to religious denomination. Moment of silence statutes which disclaim religious purposes are probably constitutional.

Illinois has a moment of silence statute, known as the Silent Reflection Act, but its constitutionality is not certain.

105 ILCS 20/1

Bown v. Gwinnet County School District, 112 F.3d 1464 (11th Cir. 1997)
Wallace v. Jaffree, 105 S.Ct. 2479, 472 U.S. 38, 86 L.Ed.2d 29 (1985)
School District of Abington Township v. Schempp, 83 S.Ct. 1560, 374 U.S.
203, 10 L.Ed.2d 844 (1963)
Engel v. Vitale, 82 S.Ct. 1261, 370 U.S. 421, 8 L.Ed.2d 601 (1962)

14:53 Does the recitation of the Pledge of Allegiance in school violate the First Amendment?

Ceremonial references to a deity are distinguished by the courts from prayer, benedictions or invocations. The Pledge of Allegiance in school is permissible so long as students who object are not compelled to participate.

105 ILCS 5/27-3
Sherman v. Community Consolidated School District No. 21 of Wheeling Township, 980 F.2d 437 (7th Cir. 1992) cert. den. 113 S.Ct. 2439, 508 U.S. 950, 124 L.Ed.2d 658 (1993)

14:55 May a school coach lead his players in voluntary prayer at an athletic contest?

No. Such a prayer would violate the establishment clause of the Constitution.

Doe v. Santa Fe Independent School District, 168 F.3d 806 (5th Cir. 1999) sugg. reh. den. 171 F.3d 1013, cert. granted 120 S.Ct. 494, __ U.S.__, __ L.Ed.2d __ (1999)
Doe v. Duncanville Independent School District, 986 F.2d 953 (5th Cir. 1993)

14:60 Is a non-sectarian graduation ceremony benediction, invoking the deity and delivered by a member of the clergy, permissible?

No. A non-sectarian benediction, invoking the deity and delivered by a member of the clergy, at a public school graduation ceremony violates the First Amendment's "establishment" clause. A school district may not avoid establishment clause implications by making the graduation ceremony or the prayer voluntary.

Lee v. Weisman, 112 S.Ct. 2649, 505 U.S. 577, 120 L.Ed.2d 467 (1992)
Stein v. Plainwell Community Schools, 610 F.Supp. 43, rev. 822 F.2d 1406 (6th Cir. 1987)
Marsh v. Chambers, 103 S.Ct. 3330, 463 U.S. 783, 77 L.Ed.2d 1019 (1983)

14:61 May a student volunteer write and deliver a nonsectarian invocation or benediction at graduation?

The answer to this question depends upon the facts surrounding the composition and delivery of the prayer. Prayers composed and delivered by students and which do not carry the endorsement of the school district or from which the school district disassociates itself are more likely to be constitutionally permissible than those which seem to carry the endorsement of the school district.

A democratically conducted student vote to pray does not render the prayer permissible, and delegation of the decision to pray to students is not in and of itself sufficient to disentangle the state from the impermissible aspects of prayer in the context of a graduation exercise otherwise controlled by school officials.

Adler v. Duval County, 851 F.Supp. 446, aff'd. 112 F.3d 1475 (11th Cir. 1999), reh and sugg. for reh. den. 120 F.3d 276

Doe v. Santa Fe Independent School District, 168 F.3d 806 (5th Cir. 1999) sugg. reh. den. 171 F.3d 1013, cert. granted 120 S.Ct. 494, __ U.S.__, __ L.Ed.2d __ (1999)

Ingebretsen on Behalf of Ingebretsen v. Jackson Public School District, 88 F.3d 274 (5th Cir. 1996), reh. and reh. den., cert.den. *Moore v. Ingebretsen* 117 S.Ct. 388, 519 U.S. 965, 136 L.Ed.2d 304 (1997)

Goluba v. School District of Ripon, 45 F.3d 1035 (7th Cir. 1995)

Harris v. Joint School District No. 241, 821 F.Supp. 638 (D.C. Ida. 1993) 41 F.3d 447 (9th Cir. 1994) vac. 115 S.Ct. 2604, 515 U.S.1104, 132 L.Ed.2d 849 (1995) on rem. 62 F.3d 1233, cert. granted, vacating *Citizen's Preserving America's Heritage, Inc. v. Harris,* 115 S.Ct. 2604, 515 U.S. 1104, 132 L.Ed.2d 849, op. vac. 62 F.3d 1233 (9th Cir. 1996)

American Civil Liberties Union of New Jersey v. Blackhorse-Pike Regional Board of Education, 84 F.3d 1431 (3rd Cir. 1996)

Lee v. Weisman, 112 S.Ct. 2649, 505 U.S. 577, 120 L.Ed.2d 467 (1992)

Jones v. Clear Creek Independent School District, 930 F.2d 416 (5th Cir. 1991) vac. and rem. 112 S.Ct 3020, 505 U.S. 1215, 120 L.Ed.2d 892 (1992) on rem. 977 F.2d 963 (5th Cir. 1993)

14:62 May a school district sponsor a baccalaureate ceremony?

Under the U.S. Supreme Court decision in *Lee v. Weisman,* a baccalaureate ceremony is unconstitutional if the school district or its agents sponsor, direct or participate. As is the case in the analysis of school prayer questions, whether or not the ceremony is voluntary for the students is not relevant to its constitutionality. Under circumstances wherein it may appear that the state is endorsing a privately organized baccalaureate ceremony it may be necessary for school officials to affirmatively disclaim official endorsement.

Lee v. Weisman, 112 S.Ct. 2649, 505 U.S. 577, 120 L.Ed.2d 467 (1992)
Lemon v. Kurtzman, 91 S.Ct. 2105, 403 U.S. 602, 29 L.Ed.2d 745 (1971), reh. den. 92 S.Ct. 24, 404 U.S. 876, 30 L.Ed.2d 123, on rem. 348 F.Supp. 300, aff'd. 93 S.Ct. 1463, 411 U.S. 192, 36 L.Ed.2d 151 (1971)

14:70   May a school board open its meetings with a prayer?

Probably not. At least one federal circuit court has determined that prayer at a school board meeting (which is open to the public and at which students are sometimes present) violates the establishment clause. The court considered and rejected the argument that the "deliberative body" exception should apply. That exception permits, for example, prayer at the beginning of sessions of the General Assembly.

Coles v. Cleveland Board of Education, 950 F.Supp. 1337, rev. 171 F.3d 369 (6th Cir. 1999)

PAROCHIAL SCHOOL SERVICES

14:80   Is it constitutionally permissible for a public school district to provide transportation for parochial school students?

A public school district must provide transportation for parochial school students under certain circumstances and subject to certain limitations. If a school district provides a school bus or other conveyance to transport students to and from school, it must transport, without charge, certain parochial school students who live along the public school district's regular bus routes.

105 ILCS 5/29-4 et seq.
People ex rel. Board of Education of School District 142, Cook County v. Illinois Board of Education, 62 Ill.2d 517, 344 N.E.2d 5 (1976)
Board of Education School District 142 v. Bakalis, 54 Ill.2d 448, 299 N.E.2d 737 (1973)
Everson v. Board of Education of Ewing Township, 67 S.Ct. 504, 330 U.S. 1, 91 L.Ed. 711 (1947) reh. den. 67 S.Ct. 962, 330 U.S. 855, 91 L.Ed. 1297 (1947)

14:90 May a public school board assign public school teachers to perform secular teaching duties in a parochial school?

A public school district may permit public school teachers (including Title I teachers), guidance counselors, psychologists, teacher aides, consulting teachers or social workers to teach secular subjects on site in parochial schools. A public school must assign a sign language interpreter for a child with a disability enrolled in a parochial school.

Agostini v. Felton, 117 S.Ct. 1997, 521 U.S. 203, 138 L.Ed.2d 391(1997)
Zobrest v. Catalina Foothills School District, 113 S.Ct. 2462, 506 U.S. 813, 125 L.Ed.2d 1 (1993)

14:95 May parochial school teachers instruct students on public school grounds during the public school day?

No. Public schools may not allow religious instruction by anyone during the school day.

Doe v. Shenandoah County School Board, 737 F.Supp. 913 (W.D. Va. 1990)
Doe v. Human, 725 F.Supp. 1499 (W.D. Ark. 1989) aff'd. without opinion 923 F.2d 857 (8th Cir. 1990) cert. den. 111 S.Ct. 1315, 499 U.S. 922, 113 L.Ed.2d 248 (1991)

14:100 May a school board provide free diagnostic services, such as speech, hearing, and psychological services, for nonpublic school students on public school property?

Yes.

Wolman v. Walter, 97 S.Ct. 2593, 433 U.S. 229, 53 L.Ed.2d 714 (1977)

SCHOOL FACILITIES

14:120 May a school board regulate or prohibit the distribution of religious literature on school grounds?

Students and members of the public are not agents of the state. However, the interplay between the school and persons seeking to use the school as a conduit to distribute a religious message may have the effect of having a religious purpose, advancing religion or entangling the state with religion, any of which violates the establishment clause of the U.S. Constitution. Whether any particular distribution of material violates the establishment clause or not is a fact question which requires an analysis of the time, place, means and circumstances of the distribution.

If a student seeks to distribute material in a nonpublic forum (e.g., a kindergarten through sixth grade building), prior restraint is constitutional if the prior restraint is reasonable.

While being cautious not to violate the establishment clause, a school district must also be mindful not to abridge the free speech rights of private persons, including students. A school district may adopt reasonable rules regarding the time, place and manner of distribution of religious materials by private persons.

20 U.S.C. 4071
Peck et al. v. Upshur County Board of Education, 155 F.3d 274 (4th Dist. 1998)
Muller v. Jefferson Lighthouse School, 98 F.3d 1530 (7th Cir. 1996)
Berger by Berger v. Rensselaer Central School Corporation, 982 F.2d 1160 (7th Cir. 1993) reh. den., cert. den. 113 S.Ct. 2344
Hedges by and through Hedges v. Wauconda Community Unit School District No. 118 et al., 807 F.Supp. 444, 9 F.3d 1295 (7th Cir. 1993)
Board of Education of Westside Community Schools v. Mergens, 110 S.Ct. 2356, 496 U.S. 226, 110 L.Ed.2d 191 (1990)
Garnett v. Benton School District, 865 F.2d 1211 (9th Cir. 1989)
Widmar v. Vincent, 102 S.Ct. 269, 454 U.S. 263, 70 L.Ed.2d 440 (1981)

14:123   May a school district erect a Christmas tree or display religious symbols?

Whether any particular religious symbol or display violates the establishment clause depends upon the underlying facts. If the court determines the display has the primary effect of advancing or inhibiting religion, it is found unconstitutional.

The same symbol may be found proper or improper depending upon the context in which it is displayed. A display accompanied by a religious message might, for example, make an otherwise permissible display unconstitutional. No recent decisions have addressed religious symbols or displays in schools.

Capitol Square Review and Advisory Board v. Pinette, 114 S.Ct. 626, 510 U.S. 1307, 126 L.Ed.2d 636 (1995)
Bloomingdale Public Schools v. Washgesic, 33 F.3d 689 (6th Cir. 1994)
Clever v. Cherry Hill Township Board of Education, 838 F. Supp. 929 (D.C. N.J. 1993)

Lee v. Weisman, 112 S.Ct. 2649, 505 U.S. 577, 120 L.Ed.2d 467 (1992)
*Allegheny County v. American Civil Liberties Union, Greater Pittsburgh
Chapter,* 109 S.Ct. 3086, 492 U.S. 573, 106 L.Ed.2d 472 (1989) on rem. 887
F.2d 260
Lemon v. Kurtzman, 91 S.Ct. 2105, 403 U.S. 602, 29 L.Ed.2d 745, reh.
den. 92 S.Ct. 24, 404 U.S. 876, 30 L.Ed.2d 123, on rem. 348 F.Supp. 300, aff'd.
93 S.Ct. 1463, 411 U.S. 192, 36 L.Ed.2d 151 (1971)

**14:124 May a school district post The Ten
Commandments in school board offices or in
classrooms?**

No. The posting of The Ten Commandments in a public
school violates the establishment clause.

Stone v. Graham, 101 S.Ct. 192, 449 U.S. 39, 66 L.Ed.2d 199 (1980) reh.
den. 101 S.Ct. 904, 449 U.S. 1104, 66 L.Ed.2d 832 on rem. 612 S.W.2d 133
(S.Ct. of Ky. 1981)

**14:130 May a school board deny an adult,
non-curriculum related religious
organization the use of school facilities?**

Requests by churches or other adult, non-curriculum related organizations for the after-hours use of school facilities must
be handled in a non-discriminatory manner. An organization
may not be denied access purely on the basis of its religious con-
victions. If the school district has allowed non-religious groups
open access to school facilities, it has probably created an open
public forum. The existence of a limited open forum may not prevent the school board from adopting a policy prohibiting the
holding of religious services or religious instruction on school
grounds.

The Bronx Household of Faith v. Community School District No. 10, 127
F.3d 127 (2nd Cir. 1997)
Fairfax Covenant Church v. Fairfax County School Board, 17 F.3d 703
(4th Cir. 1994)
Grace Bible Fellowship v. School Administration, District 5, 941 F.2d 45
(1st Cir. 1991)
Youth Opportunities Unlimited v. Board of Public Education, 769 F.Supp.
1346 (W.D. Pa. 1991)
Lemon v. Kurtzman, 91 S.Ct. 2105, 403 U.S. 602, 29 L.Ed.2d 745, reh.
den. 92 S.Ct. 24, 404 U.S. 876, 30 L.Ed.2d 123, on rem. 348 F.Supp. 300, aff'd.
93 S.Ct. 1463, 411 U.S. 192, 36 L.Ed.2d 151 (1971)

14:140   Must school boards permit student religious groups to use school property when not in use by the district for other school purposes?

The federal Equal Access Act provides that student religious organizations must be given the same access to high school facilities as any other student organization unless the school board limits access to those organizations that are curriculum related. The Act does not apply to elementary school facilities.

20 U.S.C. 4071

Pope v. East Brunswick Board of Education, 12 F.3d 1244 (3rd Cir. 1993)

Board of Education of Westside Community Schools v. Mergens, 110 S.Ct. 2365, 496 U.S. 226, 110 L.Ed.2d 191 (1990)

Garnett v. Benton School District, 865 F.2d 1211 (9th Cir. 1989)

Widmar v. Vincent, 102 S.Ct. 269, 454 U.S. 263, 70 L.Ed.2d 440 (1981)

14:145   Must a school district permit local clergy to use school facilities for a privately organized baccalaureate?

If the school permits use of its facilities by other non-school groups, it must make its facilities available on the same bases to the non-school organizers of a high school baccalaureate ceremony. If it appears by reason of the location of the services that the school is endorsing the baccalaureate, school officials should disclaim such endorsement.

Good News/Good Sports Club v. School District of City of LaDue, 859 F.Supp. 1239, (D.C. 1993) 28 F.3d 1501 (8th Cir. 1994) cert. den., reh. and sugg. for reh. den., 115 S.Ct. 2640, 515 U.S. 1173, 132 L.Ed.2d 878 (1995)

Lamb's Chapel v. Center Moriches Union Free School District, 113 S.Ct. 2141, 508 U.S. 384, 124 L.Ed.2d 352 (1993)

14:150   May teachers hold prayer meetings with students in school facilities before or after school?

No. Teachers are bound by the prohibitions of the First Amendment which bar a teacher from advancing religion when the teacher is acting in his official capacity.

May v. Evansville-Vanderburg School Corporation, 787 F.2d 1005 (7th Cir. 1986)

CURRICULAR ISSUES

14:200   May a school district include religious instruction in its curriculum?

A school district may include instruction in comparative religions, Bible history and may educate students about religion in general, but may not sponsor or advocate the teaching of a particular religion or group of religions (such as Christianity, Judaism, or Islam), religious practice, or religious belief.

> *Gibson v Lee County School Board,* 1 F.Supp.2d 1426 (M.D. Fla. 1998)
> *Edwards v. Aguillard,* 107 S.Ct. 2573, 482 U.S. 578, 96 L.Ed.2d 510 (1987)
> *Stone v. Graham,* 101 S.Ct. 192, 449 U.S. 39, 66 L.Ed.2d 199 (1980) reh. den. 101 S.Ct. 904, 449 U.S. 1104, 66 L.Ed.2d 832 on rem. 612 S.W.2d 133 (S.Ct. of Ky. 1981)
> *School District of Abington Township v. Schempp,* 83 S.Ct. 1560, 374 U.S. 203, 10 L.Ed.2d 844 (1963)

14:210   May parents object to curriculum content on the grounds that a student's participation violates the child's free exercise of religion?

Parental objections of this type are common. Usually a school can defend by allowing the objecting child to opt out of the objectionable portion of the curriculum (by curriculum substitution or removal to home or private school).

> *Mozert v. Hawkins County,* 827 F.2d 1058 (6th Cir. 1987)
> *Thomas v. Review Board,* 101 S.Ct. 1425, 450 U.S. 707, 67 L.Ed.2d 624 (1981)
> *Sherbert v. Verner,* 83 S.Ct. 1790, 374 U.S. 398, 10 L.Ed.2d 965 (1963)

14:220   May a teacher prevent a student from preparing a school paper on a religious theme?

A student's right to freedom of expression may be limited to achieve an educational goal. For example, free speech rights or the right to religious expression may be limited when either interferes with the educational process.

A teacher may prevent a student from writing a research paper on a religious theme if the topic interferes with the goals of the assignment, even if the topic otherwise would constitute exercise of religious freedom and otherwise would be permissible in an educational setting.

Settle v. Dickson County School Board, 53 F.3d 152 (6th Cir. 1995)

14:225 Does a school musical group performing religious songs violate the establishment clause?

Whether or not there is an establishment clause violation will depend upon the facts surrounding the performance. Most school Christmas programs or holiday time choir performances do not violate the establishment clause because they would not lead a reasonable observer to conclude the activity was promoting religion or advancing a particular religious belief.

Bauchman by and through Bauchman v. West High School, 900 F.Supp. 254 aff'd. *Bauchman for Bauchman v. West High School*, 132 F.3d 542 (10th Cir. 1997) cert. den. 118 S.Ct. 2370, __U.S.__, 141 L.Ed.2d 738

14:230 May a school district require a teacher to teach evolution if the teacher has religious objections to doing so?

Such a teacher may be required to teach evolution and should be directed not to discuss the Biblical view of the subject with his students.

Helland v. South Bend Community School Corporation, 93 F.3d 327 (7th Cir. 1996)

Peloza v. Capistrano Unified School District, 37 F.3d 517 (9th Cir. 1994)

14:231 May a school district curriculum include alternatives to evolution such as creation science or intelligent design?

Curriculum materials which attempt to inject the Biblical view of the origins of man or to attack the scientific underpinnings of evolution have been given many creative names. To the extent a curriculum attempts to offer the Biblical view of the origin of man or challenges a scientific theory with a Biblical theory it will not likely survive a challenge in court. Neither creation science nor intelligent design is likely to survive a First Amendment challenge.

Freiler v. Tangipahoa Parish Board of Education, 185 F.3d 337 (5th Cir. 1999)

B. Racial Issues

SCHOOL DESEGREGATION

14:400   What constitutional principle underlies school desegregation?

School segregation by race deprives minority students of equal protection, which is guaranteed by the Fourteenth Amendment to the Constitution of the United States.

Brown v. Board of Education of Topeka, Shawnee County, Kansas, 74 S.Ct. 686, 347 U.S. 483, 98 L.Ed. 873, 38 ALR2d 1180, supp. 75 S.Ct. 753, 349 U.S. 294, 99 L.Ed. 1083 (1954)

14:410   What is the role of the Illinois State Board of Education in preventing school segregation?

When the State Board of Education receives a complaint signed by at least 50 residents of a school district or 10 percent of the residents of a district, whichever is less, charging either students have been segregated on the basis of race, nationality, or religion, or school employees or applicants for employment have been discriminated against on the same basis, the State Board must notify the district of the complaint and, within 30 days, set a hearing on the charges. If, after hearing, it is determined the charges are valid, the State Board must send its findings to the Illinois Attorney General for prosecution.

105 ILCS 5/18-12
Aurora East School District No. 131 v. Cronin, 92 Ill.2d 305, 442 N.E.2d 511, 66 Ill.Dec. 85 (1982)

14:420   May a school admit students to school programs under a system intended to take into account the race of the students?

Racial or ethnic classifications of any sort are inherently suspect and call for strict judicial scrutiny. The goal of racial diversity will support the consideration of race in affirmative action programs intended to encourage minority participation. However, such programs may not preclude applicants solely on the basis of race.

Regents of the University of California v. Bakke, 98 S.Ct. 2733, 438 U.S. 265, 57 L.Ed.2d 750 (1978)

SEGREGATION REMEDIES

14:440   If a school system is found to be segregated, how quickly must the district act to rectify the problem?

A school district's obligation is to end segregation at once and to operate now and hereafter only integrated schools.

Alexander v. Holmes County Board of Education, 90 S.Ct. 21, 396 U.S. 19, 24 L.Ed.2d 19 (1969)

14:450   What must a school district do to comply with a desegregation order?

A school district subject to a desegregation order must remedy the racial imbalance which resulted in the constitutional violation. A school district may not be required to fully integrate its schools to accomplish this. Once racial imbalance due to the constitutional violation has been remedied, the school district is under no duty to remedy imbalance that is caused by demographic factors.

Freeman v. Pitts, 112 S.Ct. 1430, 503 U.S. 467, 118 L.Ed.2d 108 (1992)

14:460   Is the purpose of a plan significant in determining whether or not it advances desegregation objectives?

The purpose of a plan is significant in that it must comport with the requirements of the law. More important from the standpoint of judicial scrutiny is whether or not the effect of the plan ends segregation.

Wright v. Council of the City of Emporia, 92 S.Ct. 2196, 407 U.S. 451, 33 L.Ed.2d 51 (1972)

14:470   If a school system is found to be segregated, will an "open enrollment" plan suffice to desegregate it?

Open enrollment or free transfer plans are not sufficient to alone serve to desegregate a school system which has been found to be segregated. A school board must take affirmative steps to assure that racial discrimination is eliminated. Open enrollment plans are not inherently suspect, they simply may not be enough to achieve desegregation.

Green v. County School Board of New Kent County, 88 S.Ct. 1689, 391 U.S. 430, 20 L.Ed.2d 716 (1968)
Monroe v. Board of Commissioners of City of Jackson, Tennessee, 88 S.Ct. 1700, 391 U.S. 450, 20 L.Ed.2d 733 (1968)
Raney v. Board of Education of Gould School District, 88 S.Ct. 1697, 391 U.S. 443, 20 L.Ed.2d 727 (1968)

14:480   Is a law constitutional when it prohibits assignment of students to an attendance center on the basis of race but forbids bussing such students?

Laws which forbid bussing for purposes of integration are unconstitutional because they deprive school officials of a tool necessary to eliminate segregation.

20 U.S.C. 1701 et seq.
North Carolina State Board of Education v. Swann, 91 S.Ct. 1284, 402 U.S. 43, 28 L.Ed. 2d 586 (1971)

14:490   Does a court have the power to order a multi-district remedy when one school district produces a segregative effect in one or more other school districts?

The court has such power if it can be shown that the discriminatory acts of the state or one or more school districts have been a substantial cause of interdistrict segregation. An interdistrict desegregation order is, however, an extreme remedy which would be ordered only very reluctantly by a court. To justify an interdistrict remedy, it must be shown that the state or the outlying districts engaged in activity that had a cross district discriminatory effect.

20 U.S.C. 1715
Milliken v. Bradley, 94 S.Ct. 3112, 418 U.S. 717, 41 L.Ed.2d 1069, on rem. 402 F.Supp. 1096, on rem. 411 F.Supp. 943, aff'd. cause rem. 540 F.2d 229, aff'd. 97 S.Ct. 2749, 433 U.S. 267, 53 L.Ed.2d 745 (1977) on rem. 620 F.2d 1143, cert. den. 101 S.Ct. 2017, 449 U.S. 870, 66 L.Ed.2d 89

14:500   What criteria are considered when a court is petitioned for relief from a desegregation order?

The court considers:

1) compliance with the desegregation decree in areas where relief is sought;

2) the necessity or practicality of retaining judicial supervision in other areas; and

3) good faith efforts by the school district towards the students and parents in the disfavored race in complying with the desegregation decree.

Missouri v. Jenkins, 115 S.Ct. 2573, 515 U.S. 1139, 132 L.Ed.2d 824 (1995)

EMPLOYMENT

14:510   In determining whether an employer has discriminated, with what is the racial composition of employees compared?

In determining whether there is a pattern or practice of racial discrimination, a comparison is made between the percentage of minority employees and the percentage of minorities in the relevant labor pool. Once discrimination has been established by statistical work force disparities, the employer is given an opportunity to show that the claimed discriminatory pattern is a product of hiring which occurred before the enactment of title VII of the 1964 Civil Rights Act rather than unlawful post-Act discrimination.

Hazelwood School District v. U.S., 97 S.Ct. 2736, 433 U.S. 299, 53 L.Ed.2d 768 (1977)

International Brotherhood of Teamsters v. U.S., 97 S.Ct. 1843, 431 U.S. 324, 52 L.Ed.2d 396 (1977)

14:520   Is a testing program which has a racially disproportionate impact unconstitutional?

If the test is otherwise non-discriminatory and there is a rational relationship between the test and its constitutional purpose, the test is not unconstitutional simply because it has a racially disproportionate impact. However, an employer may not require a test where there is no showing the test criteria are significantly related to job performance and the test has a disparate impact on blacks.

National Education Association v. South Carolina, 98 S.Ct. 756, 434 U.S. 1026, 54 L.Ed.2d 775 (1978) affirming *U.S. v. State of South Carolina*, 445 F.Supp. 1094 (D.C. S.C. 1978)

Washington v. Davis, 96 S.Ct. 2040, 426 U.S. 229, 48 L.Ed.2d 597 (1976)

Griggs v. Duke Power Company, 91 S.Ct. 849, 401 U.S. 424, 28 L.Ed.2d 158 (1971)

14:530   May a school board adopt a plan to hire minorities in specified numbers in order to remedy past discrimination?

If the plan is justified by a compelling state interest in eliminating the discriminatory exclusion of minorities and is narrowly tailored to serve that purpose, an affirmative action plan is constitutional. Quota relief is a temporary remedy which is used to create as quickly as possible a climate in which neutral employment criteria can successfully operate to select public employees solely on the basis of job-related merit.

Messer v. Meno, 936 F.Supp. 1280 (W.D. Tex. 1996) aff'd. in part rev. in part 130 F.3d 130 (5th Cir. 1997)

United States v. Paradise, 107 S.Ct. 706, 480 U.S. 149, 102 L.Ed.2d 854 (1987)

Wygant v. Jackson Board of Education, 106 S.Ct. 1842, 476 U.S. 267 (1986) reh. den. 106 S.Ct. 3320, 478 U.S. 1014, 92 L.Ed.2d 728

Local 28 of the Sheet Metal Workers International Association v. Equal Employment Opportunities Commission, 106 S.Ct. 3019, 478 U.S. 421, 92 L.Ed.2d 344 (1986)

14:540   May a school board require that a certain percentage of bids be let to minority contractors?

To do so the school board must demonstrate a compelling state interest justifying the plan. The school board must have a proven history of discrimination which the plan is narrowly tailored to remedy.

To determine whether there is a history of discrimination, the appropriate test is to compare the percentage of minority business enterprises in the relevant market that are qualified to undertake the work to be let with the percentage of total relevant dollars that are awarded to minority business enterprises.

City of Richmond v. J.A. Croson Co., 109 S.Ct. 706, 488 U.S. 469, 102 L.Ed.2d 854 (1989)

Fullilove v. Klutznick, 100 S.Ct. 2758, 448 U.S. 448, 65 L.Ed.2d 902 (1980)

15: TERMS AND CONDITIONS OF TEACHER EMPLOYMENT

STATE CERTIFICATION

15:10 Who is a teacher?

A teacher, for most purposes under Illinois law, is any school district employee whose job requires teacher certification. The term "teacher" usually includes superintendents, principals, other certificated administrators, guidance counselors, deans, classroom teachers and may include other job titles.

> 105 ILCS 5/24-11
> 105 ILCS 5/10-23.8
> 105 ILCS 5/10-23.8a
> *Lester v. Board of Education of School District No. 119, Jo Daviess County,* 87 Ill.App.2d 269, 230 N.E.2d 893 (2nd Dist. 1967).

15:20 Must all teachers be certificated?

Most teachers must obtain either regular (initial, standard or master), substitute or provisional certification. There are a number of special exceptions to regular certification requirements in the areas of vocational education, career education and with respect to joint public school and community college cooperative agreements.

> 105 ILCS 5/10-22.20a
> 105 ILCS 5/21-1 et seq.
> *Frazier v. Garrison Independent School District,* 980 F.2d 1541 (5th Cir. 1993)

15:23 What is the difference between a valid and active teaching certificate and a valid and exempt teaching certificate?

A *valid and active* certificate is issued to persons employed and performing services in a certificated teaching position on a full or part time basis in an Illinois public or State operated elementary school, secondary school, cooperative or joint agreement with a governing body or board of control or who are employed in a charter school.

A *valid and exempt* certificate is issued to persons who have a standard teaching certificate but who are not employed in positions which require teacher certification in a public elementary, secondary school, joint agreement or cooperative or charter school. A valid and exempt certificate is issued, for example, to persons who hold teacher certification but are employed as aides, teachers in non-public schools, retired teachers, teachers without jobs and administrators.

105 ILCS 5/21-14(d)

15:25   What are initial, standard and master teacher certificates?

Beginning February 15, 2000, persons who have completed and are recommended by an approved teacher preparation program, have passed the State Board of Education's initial teaching certification examinations and have met all other criteria established by the State Board are issued an initial teaching certificate which is valid for four years of teaching.

Beginning February 15, 2000, persons who have completed four years of teaching in an Illinois public school with an initial certificate or an initial alternative certificate, have met all other criteria established by the State Board of Education; or who have completed four years of teaching on a valid equivalent certificate in another state or territory of the United States, or have completed four years of teaching in an nonpublic Illinois elementary or secondary school with an initial certificate or an initial alternative certificate and have met all other criteria established by the State Board of Education; or who were issued teaching certificates prior to February 15, 2000 and are renewing those certificates after February 15, 2000 are issued a standard certificate valid for five years and renewable thereafter every five years.

Beginning July 1, 2003, persons who have completed four years of teaching as described above and have successfully completed the Standard Teaching Certificate Examinations, and have met all other criteria established by the State Board of Education are issued standard certificates.

Beginning February 15, 2000, persons who have achieved National Board certification through the National Board for

Professional Teaching Standards are issued a master certificate valid for ten years and renewable thereafter every ten years. Master certificate holders are entitled to pay incentives including a one time payment of $3,000 for having earned master status.

105 ILCS 5/21-2
105 ILCS 5/21-14
105 ILCS 5/21-27

15:27 May a person who does not have conventional training in education acquire a teaching certificate?

There is an alternative route to teacher certification which results in the award of a one-year, non-renewable provisional alternative teaching certificate. The certificate is available to persons who have entered the alternative route to teacher certification course of study and who have successfully completed the curriculum and student teaching elements of the program, have a bachelor's degree from an accredited college or university, have been employed for at least five years in an area requiring application of the person's education and have passed the tests required for certification.

The required course of study includes an intensive curriculum in education theory, instructional methods and practice teaching and leads to assignment for one year with a teacher mentor advisor to a full time teaching position and is followed by comprehensive assessment of the person's teaching performance.

105 ILCS 5/21-5b
105 ILCS 5/21-5c

15:28 May a teacher employed under a provisional alternative certificate or an initial certificate receive less pay or benefits than a teacher working under a regular certificate?

No. Even if a collective bargaining agreement provides otherwise, a person possessing a provisional alternative certificate or an initial teaching certificate must be treated as a regularly certified teacher for purposes of compensation, benefits and other terms and conditions of employment.

105 ILCS 5/21-5c

15:30   Are there different certification requirements for teachers at different grade levels and for teaching different subject matters?

Yes.

105 ILCS 5/21-1 et seq.
23 Ill. Admin. Code 1.1610 et seq.

15:40   Does a teaching certificate indicate the subject areas the teacher may teach?

Teaching certificates issued after June 30, 1986, are endorsed by the State Board of Education for each subject the holder of the certificate is certified to teach. Certificates which were issued prior to July 1, 1986, may have been endorsed on the date of issue (depending on the date of issue) or may, on application to the State Board of Education, be endorsed for each subject the holder is certified to teach.

105 ILCS 5/21-1b
Zink v. Board of Education of Chrisman, 146 Ill.App.3d 1016, 497 N.E.2d 835, 100 Ill.Dec. 657 (4th Dist. 1986)

15:45   What are the certification requirements for school nurses?

A school board may employ a registered professional nurse and may define the duties of the nurse consistent with the rules established by the State Board of Education.

Nurses first employed on or after July 1, 1976 whose duties require teaching or the exercise of instructional judgment or educational evaluation of pupils must have a school service personnel certificate. To obtain a school service personnel certificate, the applicant must have a bachelor's degree.

A school district may employ a noncertificated registered nurse to perform nursing services.

105 ILCS 5/10-22.23
105 ILCS 5/21-25
23 Ill. Admin Code 1.760(h)

15:50   Must a school board help a teacher secure a teaching certificate?

It is the sole responsibility of a teacher to apply for and secure teaching certification.

Hagopian v. Board of Education of Tampico Community Unit School District No. 4 of Whiteside and Bureau Counties, 56 Ill.App.3d 940, 372 N.E.2d 990, 14 Ill.Dec. 711 (3rd Dist. 1978), app. after rem. 83 Ill.App.3d 1097, 404 N.E.2d 899, 39 Ill.Dec. 308, (3rd Dist. 1980), rev. on other grounds 84 Ill.2d 436, 420 N.E.2d 147, 50 Ill.Dec. 830 (1981)

Relph v. Board of Education of Depue Unit School District No. 103 of Bureau County, 84 Ill.2d 436, 420 N.E.2d 147, 50 Ill.Dec. 830 (1978)

15:60 Under what conditions may a teacher's certificate be suspended or revoked?

A teacher's certificate may be suspended for a period not to exceed one calendar year by either the regional superintendent or State Superintendent of Education upon evidence of immorality, a condition of health detrimental to the welfare of pupils, incompetency, unprofessional conduct, the neglect of any professional duty, willful failure to report an instance of suspected child abuse or neglect as required by the Abused and Neglected Child Reporting Act, or just cause.

Unprofessional conduct includes neglect or unnecessary delay in making of statistical and other reports required by school officers, refusal to attend or participate in institutes, teachers' meetings, professional readings, or to meet other reasonable requirements of the regional superintendent or State Superintendent of Education.

No certificate may be suspended until the teacher has an opportunity for a hearing at the educational service region. Appeal may be had to the State Teacher Certification Board.

Any certificate may be revoked by the State Superintendent of Education for the same reasons which must underlie a suspension. No certificate may be revoked until the teacher has an opportunity for a hearing before the State Teacher Certification Board.

When the holder of any teaching certificate has been convicted of certain sex or narcotics offenses, the regional superintendent or the State Superintendent of Education must suspend the certificate. If the conviction is reversed and the holder is acquitted of the offense in a new trial or the charges against him are dismissed, the suspending authority must terminate the suspension of the certificate. If the conviction becomes final, the State Superintendent of Education must revoke the certificate.

105 ILCS 5/2-3.9
105 ILCS 5/21-23
105 ILCS 5/21-23a

15:63　Must a school board make a report to the State Board of Education when one of it teachers is convicted of a felony?

Whenever the holder of any teaching certificate who is employed by a school district is convicted after trial or by a plea of guilty of any offense for which a sentence of death "or a term of imprisonment in a penitentiary for one year or more is provided," the school board must promptly notify the State Board of Education in writing of the name of the certificate holder and location of the court in which the conviction occurred.

105 ILCS 5/21-23b

15:65　What protection does a school district have that a teacher or other certificated employee will not lie about his qualifications on a job application?

An applicant for a teacher, principal, superintendent or other certificated position who willfully makes a false statement which is material to his qualifications for employment on his job application is guilty of a Class A misdemeanor. There also are penalties for failure to include important job application information.

105 ILCS 5/22-6.5

15:70　What recourse is available to a school board if a teacher signs an initial employment contract but refuses to perform?

There is no mechanism whereby a school board can compel a teacher to specifically perform teaching duties pursuant to contract. A school board might sue the teacher for breach of contract, but damages would likely be limited to the cost of finding a suitable replacement. A school board may petition the regional superintendent of schools to initiate teacher certificate suspension proceedings. Proceedings relative to certification involve a regional hearing, and the decision is appealable to the State Teacher Certification Board.

105 ILCS 5/21-23

CERTIFICATE RENEWAL

15:80 What is the procedure for renewal of a teaching certificate?

Prior to the enactment of legislation in 1999, a teaching certificate was renewed by filing a renewal form with the regional superintendent of schools. Beginning in 2000, certificate renewal requires the certificate holder to adopt a professional development plan and to have the plan approved by a local Professional Development Committee.

105 ILCS 5/21-14

15:84 What is a local professional development committee?

Each school district, charter school and cooperative or joint agreement with a governing body or board of control that employs certificated staff must establish and implement in conjunction with its exclusive bargaining representative, if any, one or more local professional development committees. The professional development committee:

1) reviews and approves certificate renewal plans and any changes made to those plans including transferred plans;

2) maintains a file of approved certificate renewal plans;

3) monitors certificate holders' progress in completing plans;

4) assists in the development of certificate renewal plans;

5) determines whether certificate holders have met the requirements of the their plans and notifies certificate holders of its determinations;

6) provides a certificate holder the opportunity to address the committee when the committee finds that the holder has not met the requirements of his plan;

7) issues and forwards recommendations for renewal or non-renewal of certificates to the regional superintendent of schools with 30 day advance notice (with return receipt in the case of a non-renewal recommendation) to the certificate holder as to whether or not the certificate holder has met the requirements of his approved renewal plan;

8) reconsiders its recommendation of certificate non-renewal on request of the certificate holder within 30 days of receipt of written notification that the local professional development committee will make a nonrenewal recommendation and forwards to the regional superintendent its recommendation within 30 days of receipt of the certificate holder's request.

105 ILCS 5/21-14(f)

15:85 Who are the members of a professional development committee?

A professional development committee consists of a least three classroom teachers chosen by a the exclusive bargaining representative or the teachers who come within the committee's authority if there is no representative; one superintendent or chief administrator of the school district or his designee; and one at-large member chosen by the school district who must be either a parent, a member of the business community, community member or administrator, with preference given to a person chosen from among a parent, member of the business community and a community member in order to secure representation of an interest not already represented on the committee.

If the school district and its exclusive bargaining representative agree, additional members may be added, provided that a majority of the members of the committee are classroom teachers. The terms of service for members of a professional development committee are determined locally by agreement of the school district and the teachers' exclusive bargaining representative, if any.

105 ILCS 5/21-14(f)

15:88 What must be included in a certificate renewal plan?

A certificate renewal plan must include at least three individual improvement goals developed by the certificate holder. The goals must reflect (1), (2) and (3) below and may reflect (4) of the following professional development purposes:

1) advance both the certificate holder's knowledge and skills as a teacher in the certificate holder's areas of certification, endorsement or teaching assignment;

2) develop the certificate holder's knowledge and skills in "State priorities" — critical areas as defined by the State Board of Education (ISBE). ISBE has adopted three areas for the first five-year certification renewal cycle: reading, integration of technology into teaching and learning, and standards/assessment/IGAP/ISAT;

3) address the knowledge, skills and goals of the certificate holder's local school improvement plan;

4) expand knowledge and skills in an additional teaching field or toward acquisition of another teaching certificate, endorsement or relevant education degree.

A certificate renewal plan must include a description of how the goals are to be achieved, an explanation of selected continuing professional development activities to be completed, and a timeline for completion.

105 ILCS 5/21-14(e)

15:92   What professional development activities are included in a certificate renewal plan?

Continuing professional development activities included in a certificate renewal plan may include, but are not limited to, the following activities:

(A) at least 8 semester hours of coursework in an approved education-related program, of which at least 2 semester hours relate to the certificate holder's knowledge and skills as a teacher in the certificate holder's areas of certification, endorsement or teaching assignment, except that a plan need not include any other continuing professional development activities nor reflect or contain activities related to the other continuing professional development purposes;

(B) continuing education units that satisfy the continuing professional development purposes, with each continuing education unit equal to 5 clock hours, provided that a plan that includes at least 24 continuing education units (or 120 clock/contact hours) need not include any other continuing professional development activities;

(C) completion of the National Board of Professional Teaching Standards (NBPTS) process, provided that a plan that includes completion of the NBPTS process need not include any other continuing professional development activities nor reflect or contain activities related to the continuing professional development purposes;

(D) completion of 120 continuing professional development units that satisfy the continuing professional development purposes and may include without limitation the activities identified in(E) through (I) below;

(E) collaboration and partnership activities related to improving the teacher's knowledge and skills as a teacher, including the following:

(i) participating on collaborative planning and professional improvement teams and committees;

(ii) peer review and coaching;

(iii) mentoring in a formal mentoring program, including service as a consulting teacher participating in a remediation process formulated under Section 24A-5 of the School Code;

(iv) participating in site-based management or decision making teams, relevant committees, boards, or task forces directly related to school improvement plans;

(v) coordinating community resources in schools, if the project is a specific goal of the school improvement plan;

(vi) facilitating parent education programs for a school, school district, or regional office of education directly related to student achievement or school improvement plans;

(vii) participating in business, school, or community partnerships directly related to student achievement or school improvement plans;

(viii) supervising a student teacher or teacher education candidate in clinical supervision, provided that the supervision may only be counted once during the course of 5 years;

(F) college or university coursework related to improving the teacher's knowledge and skills as a teacher as follows:

(i) completing undergraduate or graduate credit earned from a regionally accredited institution in coursework relevant to the certificate area being renewed, provided the coursework meets Illinois Professional Teaching Standards or Illinois Content Area Standards and supports the essential characteristics of quality professional development; or

(ii) teaching college or university courses in areas relevant to the certificate area being renewed, provided that the teaching may only be counted once during the course of 5 years;

(G) conferences, workshops, institutes, seminars, and symposiums related to improving the teacher's knowledge and skills as a teacher, including the following:

(i) completing non-university credit directly related to student achievement, school improvement plans, or State priorities;

(ii) participating in or presenting at workshops, seminars, conferences, institutes, and symposiums;

(iii) training as external reviewers for Quality Assurance;

(iv) training as reviewers of university teacher preparation programs;

(H) other educational experiences related to improving the teacher's knowledge and skills as a teacher, including the following:

(i) participating in action research and inquiry projects;

(ii) observing programs or teaching in schools, related businesses, or industry that is systematic, purposeful, and relevant to certificate renewal;

(iii) traveling related to ones teaching assignment, directly related to student achievement or school improvement plans and approved at least 30 days prior to the travel experience, provided that the traveling shall not include time spent commuting to destinations where the learning experience will occur;

(iv) participating in study groups related to student achievement or school improvement plans;

(v) serving on a statewide education-related committee, including but not limited to the State Teacher Certification Board, State Board of Education strategic agenda teams, or the State Advisory Council on Education of Children with Disabilities;

(vi) participating in work/learn programs or internships; or

(I) professional leadership experiences related to improving the teacher's knowledge and skills as a teacher, including the following:

(i) participating in curriculum development or assessment activities at the school, school district, regional office of education, State, or national level;

(ii) participating in team or department leadership in a school or school district;

(iii) participating on external or internal school or school district review teams;

(iv) publishing educational articles, columns, or books relevant to the certificate area being renewed; or

(v) participating in non-strike related professional association or labor organization service or activities related to professional development.

105 ILCS 5/21-14(e)

ADDITIONAL TEACHER QUALIFICATIONS

15:100   May a school board require a teacher to undergo a psychiatric examination to determine mental fitness to teach?

Yes. A psychiatric exam may be required in appropriate circumstances.

105 ILCS 5/24-5
Dusanek v. Hannon, 677 F.2d 538 (7th Cir. 1982)
   Tetmeir v. Board of Education of School District No. 149, Cook County, 5 Ill.App.3d 982, 284 N.E.2d 280 (1st Dist. 1972)

15:110   May a school board require teachers to demonstrate continued professional growth?

A school board may require teachers to demonstrate continued professional growth provided, however, that the requirements are not contrary to the teacher certification statutes.

Before the teacher registration and renewal law was amended in 1998 and 1999, some collective bargaining agreements and some school board policy manuals contained continuing education requirements. Most of these provisions are likely to be deleted or altered significantly because the professional development plans previously required by local policy or bargaining agreement are now required by statute.

105 ILCS 5/24-5
Heifner v. Board of Education of Morris Community Unit School District No. 101, Grundy County, 32 Ill.App.3d 83, 335 N.E.2d 600 (3rd Dist. 1975)

Last v. Board of Education of Community Unit School District No. 321, Winnebago and Stephenson Counties, 37 Ill.App.2d 159, 185 N.E.2d 282 (2nd Dist. 1962)

Richards v. Board of Education of Township High School District No. 201, 21 Ill.2d 104, 171 N.E.2d 37 (1960)

TEACHING ASSIGNMENTS AND WORKLOADS

15:160   May a school board assign or transfer teachers to and from positions for which they are qualified at will?

In the absence of a constitutional restriction (such as a civil rights implication), or a limitation contained in a collective bargaining agreement, a school board may assign, reassign, or transfer teachers to and from positions they are qualified to fill as the school board sees fit in order to meet the needs of the district. However, a school board may not use transfer to defeat the tenure rights of teachers.

105 ILCS 5/24-12

Stamper v. Board of Education of Elementary School District No. 143, 141 Ill.App.3d 884, 491 N.E.2d 36, 96 Ill.Dec. 222 (1st Dist. 1986)

Peters v. Board of Education of Rantoul Township High School District No. 193 of Champaign County, 97 Ill.2d 166, 454 N.E.2d 310, 73 Ill.Dec. 450 (1983)

15:170   Does a teacher's tenured status restrict the authority of a school board to assign the teacher?

Tenure does not limit the power of a school board to transfer or assign a teacher to a position for which the teacher is certified and qualified. The provisions of a collective bargaining agreement or duty to bargain obligations may limit the school board, however.

Stamper v. Board of Education of Elementary School District No. 143, 141 Ill.App.3d 884, 491 N.E.2d 36, 96 Ill.Dec. 222 (1st Dist. 1986)

15:180   Is there a statutory limit on the work load which may be assigned a school teacher?

There is no statutory provision or State Board of Education rule or regulation governing teacher work load. Work load is to be distinguished from "preparations." Work load is the number of class periods in a specified time period for which any teacher is responsible. Preparations is the number of different lesson plans for different subjects or grade levels which a teacher must prepare in a specified time period. A maximum work load may exist by reason of a provision in a collective bargaining agreement.

15:190   Is there a maximum number of preparations a high school teacher may be assigned?

The State Board of Education has adopted a rule which provides: "No (high school) teacher should have more than five different preparations." Whether this statement absolutely prevents the assignment of a high school teacher to more than five preparations is unclear. There are differences in the meanings of teaching load, preparations and class assignments.

23 Ill. Admin. Code 1.440 c)

15:200   Is a teacher entitled to a duty-free lunch?

Every teacher whose duties require attendance at school for four or more clock hours in any school day must be allowed a duty-free lunch period equal to the regular school lunch period but not less than 30 minutes during each school day.

105 ILCS 5/24-9
Board of Education of Community Unit School District No. 4, Champaign County v. Champaign Education Association, 15 Ill.App.3d 335, 304 N.E.2d 138 (4th Dist. 1973)

15:210   Do statutes fix the length of a teacher's work day?

The School Code does not fix the length of a teacher's work day. Statutes set forth the minimum number of pupil attendance hours required in order to receive state financial aid. Absent a recognized bargaining unit, a school board may unilaterally establish length of work day. In school districts with recognized bargaining units, work day must be bargained at prescribed times on demand.

15:220   May a school board require a teacher to teach on Saturday?

A school board may not require its teachers to teach on Saturdays or to work on legal school holidays. School boards are also prohibited from making any deduction from the time or compensation of a teacher on account of any legal or special holiday.

105 ILCS 5/24-2
District 300 Education Association v. Board of Education of Dundee Community Unit School District No. 300 of Kane et al. Counties, 31 Ill.App.3d 550, 334 N.E.2d 165 (2nd Dist. 1975)

15:230   May a school board assign its teachers to perform extracurricular duties?

A teacher may be assigned to extracurricular duties which are reasonably related to the educational program and which are not onerous, unreasonably time consuming, demeaning to the professional stature of the teacher or assigned in a discriminatory manner. The performance of extra duties and the salary therefor must be bargained at appropriate times on demand by a recognized bargaining representative.

Where a collective bargaining contract includes an extra duty salary schedule and no limitations on the assignment of extra duties, the union has effectively conceded that the school board has the authority to make extra duty assignments.

Lewis v. North Clay Community Unit School District No. 25, 181 Ill.App.3d 689, 537 N.E.2d 435, 130 Ill.Dec. 368 (5th Dist. 1989)
Board of Education of Berwyn School District No. 100 v. Metskas, 106 Ill.App.3d 943, 436 N.E.2d 587, 62 Ill.Dec. 561 (1st Dist. 1982)
Littrell v. Board of Education of Cave in Rock Community Unit School District No. 2, 45 Ill.App.3d 690, 360 N.E.2d 102, 4 Ill.Dec. 355 (5th Dist. 1977)
District 300 Education Association v. Board of Education of Dundee Community Unit School District No. 300 of Kane et al. Counties, 31 Ill.App.3d 550, 334 N.E.2d 165 (2nd Dist. 1975)
Simcox v. Board of Education of Lockport Township High School District No. 205, 443 F.2d 40 (7th Cir. 1970)

15:235   May a teacher use a "just cause" provision in a collective bargaining agreement to challenge his discipline or dismissal from an extra duty assignment?

A "just cause" provision is one which requires that an employee's discipline be "fair" or for "just cause." A "just cause" provision in a collective bargaining agreement is fully enforceable to the extent it is used to challenge the discipline or dismissal of a teacher from an extra duty assignment. Moreover, a teacher assigned to an extra duty job may have an expectation of continued employment by reason of the facts surrounding his employment and retention from year to year in the extra duty job.

Princeville Community Unit School District No. 326, 13 PERI 1017 (IELRB Opinion and Award, Dec. 6, 1996)

Board of Education of Rockford School District No. 205, v. The Illinois Educational Labor Relations Board, 165 Ill.2d 80, 649 N.E.2d 369, 208 Ill.Dec. 313 (1995)

PROBATIONARY EMPLOYMENT

15:250   What is the maximum length of time a school board may require a teacher to serve as a probationary employee?

For teachers employed in a school district on or before December 31, 1997 the probationary period is two years. A teacher in the middle of his probationary period on January 1, 1998 achieves tenure at the end of two years of consecutive full time service in the district that employed him provided the teacher was first employed by the district on or before December 31, 1997.

Initially, the 1998 changes in the tenure law allowed no possibility for the extension of the probationary term to a third year for a teacher subject to a two year probationary term. Before January 1, 1998, a third probationary year had been a statutory alternative available to school boards with respect to new teachers who had not yet achieved tenure. An amendment to Section 24-11 of the School Code restored the third probationary year option for a teacher "first employed prior to January 1, 1998 who has not had one school term of full time teaching experience before the beginning of a probationary period of two consecutive school terms." The employing board may extend the probationary period for one additional school term by giving the teacher written notice by certified mail, return receipt requested, at least 45 days before the end of the second school term of the period of two consecutive school terms. The notice must state the reasons for the extension and must outline the corrective actions that the teacher must take to satisfactorily complete probation.

For a teacher first employed by a school district as a full time teacher on or after January 1, 1998 and who has not already achieved tenure in that district, the probationary period is four years. For purposes of service credit computations for determining acquisition of tenure, initial employment before November 1 of the first probationary year is treated as a full year of employment, and initial employment after October 31 is not treated as time credited to the acquisition of tenure.

The phrase "first employed" is contained in the relevant law and its meaning is unclear. For example, it is uncertain whether a teacher who is employed by a school board before January 1, 1998 but not in the service of that board on January 1, 1998, and who is later (after January 1, 1998) re-employed by the same board achieves tenure in two or four years.

A part time teacher who has never had two consecutive years of full time service if employed before January 1, 1998 or four consecutive years of full time service if employed on or after January 1, 1998 may remain a probationary employee indefinitely.

105 ILCS 5/24-11

15:260   What is required to extend probationary employment to a third year?

Initially, the 1998 changes in the tenure law allowed no possibility for the extension of the probationary term to a third year for a teacher subject to a two year probationary term. Before January 1, 1998, a third probationary year had been a statutory alternative available to school boards with respect to new teachers who had not yet achieved tenure. An amendment to Section 24-11 of the School Code restored the third probationary year option for a teacher "first employed prior to January 1, 1998 who has not had one school term of full time teaching experience before the beginning of a probationary period of two consecutive school terms." The employing board may extend the probationary period for one additional school term by giving the teacher written notice by certified mail, return receipt requested, at least 45 days before the end of the second school term of the period of two consecutive school terms. The notice must state the reasons for the extension and must outline the corrective actions that the teacher must take to satisfactorily complete probation.

105 ILCS 5/24-11

SUBSTITUTE TEACHERS

15:300   Who may be employed as a substitute teacher?

A fully certificated teacher may be employed as a substitute teacher. A teacher not fully certified to teach the subject or grade level for which a substitute is sought may be employed, provided that the teacher holds a substitute teacher's certificate.

A substitute teacher's certificate may be issued upon request of the regional superintendent of schools in any region in which the teacher is to teach. To qualify, an applicant must either hold a valid teaching certificate, or hold a bachelor's degree, or have had two years of teaching experience and meet other State Board of Education rules and regulations. Substitute teacher certificates are not endorsed.

105 ILCS 5/21-9

15:310   How many days a year may an individual be employed as a substitute teacher?

A substitute teacher holding a substitute teaching certificate may teach for no more than 90 paid school days or 450 paid school hours in any one school district in any one school term. When such teaching is partly on a daily and partly on an hourly basis, a school day is considered to be five hours. A person holding a regular teaching certificate may serve as a substitute teacher without regard to the day or hour limitations.

105 ILCS 5/21-9
Woods v. East St. Louis School District No. 189, 147 Ill.App.3d 776, 498 N.E.2d 801, 101 Ill.Dec. 477 (5th Dist. 1986)

15:320 Do minimum salary laws apply to a substitute teacher?

There is no minimum or maximum salary law which applies to a teacher serving as a day-to-day substitute. However, if a substitute teacher is employed for an extended period in the same position, his status may be changed from substitute teacher to full time temporary teacher, in which case minimum salary laws or collectively bargained provisions applicable to full time certificated employees may apply.

105 ILCS 5/24-8
105 ILCS 5/21-9
Woods v. East St. Louis School District No. 189, 147 Ill.App.3d 776, 498 N.E.2d 801, 101 Ill.Dec. 477 (5th Dist. 1986)

EVALUATING TEACHERS

15:350 Are schools required to have a formal evaluation plan?

Each school district must establish, in cooperation with its teachers or, when applicable, with the official bargaining representative of its teachers, a plan for evaluating its tenured teachers. In the event any substantive change is made in the evalua tion plan, the new plan must be submitted to the State Board of Education for review and comment.

105 ILCS 5/24A-4
Board of Education of Leroy Community Unit School District No. 2 v. Illinois Educational Labor Relations Board, 199 Ill.App.3d 347, 556 N.E.2d 857, 145 Ill.Dec. 239 (4th Dist. 1990) 149 Ill.2d 496, 599 N.E.2d 892, 174 Ill.Dec. 808 (1992)

15:360 Whom must a school district evaluate?

A school district must evaluate each of its tenured teachers at least once in the course of any two years.

105 ILCS 5/24A-5

15:370 What must be included in an evaluation plan?

An evaluation plan must include a description of each teacher's duties and responsibilities and the standards to which that teacher is expected to conform. The plan may provide for evaluation of personnel whose positions require administrative certification by independent evaluators not employed by or affiliated with the school district. The results of the school district administrators' evaluations shall be reported to the employing school board, together with such recommendations for remediation as the evaluator or evaluators may deem appropriate.

Evaluation of teachers whose positions do not require administrative certification shall be conducted by a qualified administrator and shall include at least the following components:

1) personal observation of the teacher in the classroom by a district administrator qualified pursuant to statute to conduct evaluations unless the teacher has no classroom duties;

2) consideration of the teacher's attendance, planning, and instructional methods, classroom management, where relevant, and competency in the subject matter taught, where relevant;

3) rating of the teacher's performance as "excellent," "satisfactory," or "unsatisfactory;"

4) specification as to the teacher's strengths and weaknesses, with supporting reasons for the comments made; and

5) inclusion of a copy of the evaluation in the teacher's personnel file and provision of a copy to the teacher.

105 ILCS 5/24A-5

15:380   What procedures are required when a tenured teacher receives an unsatisfactory evaluation rating?

If a tenured teacher receives an unsatisfactory evaluation rating the following procedures are required:

1) Within 30 days after completion of an evaluation rating a teacher as "unsatisfactory," development and commencement by the district of a remediation plan designed to correct deficiencies cited, provided the deficiencies are deemed remediable.

2) Participating in the remediation plan by the teacher rated "unsatisfactory," a qualified district administrator and a consulting teacher selected by the participating administrator or by the principal of the teacher who was rated "unsatisfactory." The consulting teacher must be an educational employee as

defined in the Educational Labor Relations Act, have at least five years teaching experience, have a reasonable familiarity with the assignment of the teacher being evaluated, and must have received an "excellent" rating on his or her most recent evaluation. Where no teachers who meet these criteria are available within the district, the district must request and the State Board of Education supply, to participate in the remediation process, an individual who meets these criteria. In a district with an exclusive bargaining agent, the bargaining agent may, if it so chooses, supply a roster of qualified teachers from whom the consulting teacher is to be selected. That roster must, however, contain the names of at least five teachers, each of whom meets the criteria for consulting teacher with regard to the teacher being evaluated, or the names of all teachers so qualified if that number is less than five. In the event of a dispute as to qualification, the State Board shall determine qualification.

3) Evaluations and ratings once every 30 school days for the 90-school-day remediation period immediately following receipt of a remediation plan. These subsequent evaluations shall be conducted by the participating administrator. The consulting teacher must provide advice to the teacher rated "unsatisfactory" on how to improve teaching skills and to successfully complete the remediation plan. The consulting teacher must participate in developing the remediation plan, but the final decision as to the evaluation shall be done solely by the administrator, unless an applicable collective bargaining agreement provides to the contrary.

4) Reinstatement of a schedule of biennial evaluation for any teacher who completes the 90-school-day remediation plan with a "satisfactory" or better rating, unless the district's plan regularly requires more frequent evaluations.

5) Dismissal in accordance with the School Code of any teacher who fails to complete the remediation plan with a "satisfactory" or better rating.

This portion of the relevant statute was not amended by the reform legislation of 1997 and, as a result, the time limits contained in this part of Section 24A conflict with the time limits contained in other parts of the statute.

105 ILCS 5/24A-5

15:382   What period of time is required for remediation?

A school district must provide for 90 school days of remediation within the classroom.

105 ILCS 5/24A-5

15:383   What happens if the school district's collective bargaining agreement contains remediation provisions which are different from the statute?

The 1997 amendment to Article 10, Section 24A of the School Code provides that, in a district subject to a collective bargaining agreement in effect on January 1, 1998, changes made by the 1997 statute that are contrary to the express terms and provisions of the agreement go into effect only upon expiration of the agreement.

105 ILCS 5/24A-5

TEACHER COMPENSATION

15:400   Is there a statutory minimum teacher salary?

Yes. A school board must pay minimum annual salaries of $10,000 for a teacher holding a bachelor's degree and $11,000 for a teacher holding a master's degree. The following minimum increases must be paid:

- $750 after five years of experience for a teacher with less than a bachelor's degree;
- $1,000 after five years and $1,600 after eight years for a teacher with a bachelor's degree;
- $1,250 after five years and $2,000 after eight years for a teacher with a master's degree.

The minimum salary statute is ambiguous as to what constitutes "years of experience" both for purposes of prior experience credit and for purposes of salary schedule advancement after initial employment.

105 ILCS 5/24-8

Winters v. Board of Education of Piasa Community Unit School District No. 9 of Macoupin County, 66 Ill.App.3d 918, 384 N.E.2d 519, 23 Ill.Dec. 725 (4th Dist. 1978)

Hardway v. Board of Education of Lawrenceville Township High School District No. 71, 1 Ill.App.3d 298, 274 N.E.2d 213 (5th Dist. 1971)

15:410   Is there a minimum salary provision which applies to summer school employment?

No. Summer school salaries may be established by a school board subject only to minimum hourly wage provisions and collective bargaining requirements.

29 U.S.C. 201

15:420   Must a school board recognize all prior teaching experience of a new employee on its salary schedule?

Illinois appellate courts are divided on this issue. The safer approach is to recognize full prior experience credit. A school board that fully recognizes prior experience must be cautious that it does not commit age discrimination by screening out all older and more experienced job applicants in the hiring process.

105 ILCS 5/24-8

Equal Employment Opportunity Commission v. Francis W. Parker School, Memorandum Opinion 91 C 4674, 61 F.E.P. 967 (BNA) (N.D. Ill. 1993)

Winters v. Board of Education of Piasa Community Unit School District No. 9 of Macoupin County, 66 Ill.App.3d 918, 384 N.E.2d 519, 23 Ill.Dec. 725 (4th Dist. 1978)

Hardway v. Board of Education of Lawrenceville Township High School District No. 71, 1 Ill.App.3d 298, 274 N.E.2d 213 (5th Dist. 1971)

15:430   When must a teacher submit evidence of additional education in order to advance on the salary schedule?

Unless a collective bargaining agreement provides otherwise, a teacher who submits a certificate of completion to the school office prior to the first day of the school term must be considered to have the degree stated on the certificate.

105 ILCS 5/24-8

Board of Education of Valley View Community Unit School District No. 365U v. Schmidt, 64 Ill.App.3d 513, 381 N.E.2d 400, 21 Ill.Dec. 291 (1st Dist. 1978)

15:432   May a school board "freeze" teacher salaries?

A teacher salary "freeze" is a denial of teacher access to a salary schedule step increase and no increase in base salary. Increases in the base salary are generally within the control of the school board. Absent contract language to the contrary, or specific bargaining history, a school board may "freeze" base salary by simply refusing to offer an increase in the base.

"Freezing" teachers on step (denying a step increase) is more complicated. "Status quo" rules may require that the school board grant a step increase to teachers until a contrary result is bargained. Whether or not a school board must grant step increases for years of experience depends, in large measure, upon its previous bargaining history.

Vienna School District No. 55 v. Illinois Educational Labor Relations Board, 162 Ill.App.3d 503, 515 N.E.2d 476, 113 Ill.Dec. 667 (4th Dist. 1987)

15:440   Is a school board required to pay its teachers "vacation time?"

No statute requires a school board to pay teachers vacation pay.

15:450   If a teacher is honorably dismissed as a result of a reduction in force, when must the teacher be paid all accrued earnings?

Any teacher honorably dismissed as a result of a decrease in the total number of teachers or the discontinuance of some educational service must be paid all earned compensation on or before the third business day following the last day of pupil attendance in the regular school term.

105 ILCS 5/24-12

15:460   How may teachers be held to account for school property in their possession?

Each teacher has a statutory duty to protect school district property. No teacher may be paid unless the teacher has satisfactorily accounted for books, apparatus, and other property belonging to the school district.

105 ILCS 5/24-17

15:470   What options are available to a school district which is financially unable to pay its teachers?

A school district may choose either of two procedures when unable to pay teachers' wages for lack of funds. The school district may establish a voucher system of expenditures, or may require the district treasurer to pay funds of the school district upon an order of the school board signed by the president.

When an order issued for the wages of a teacher is presented to the treasurer and is not paid for want of funds, the treasurer is required to endorse over his signature "not paid for want of funds" with the date of presentation and shall keep a record of that endorsement. The order, thereafter, bears interest at a rate not exceeding the maximum rate authorized by the Bond Authorization Act until the maturity date established by the school board or, in the absence of such maturity date, until the treasurer notifies the clerk or secretary in writing that he has funds to pay the order.

When the treasurer obtains sufficient funds to pay any such order, he must set them aside for such purpose and shall not use them to pay any other order until the order previously presented and not paid is paid or otherwise discharged.

30 ILCS 305/0.01
105 ILCS 5/8-16

RETIREMENT SYSTEM CONTRIBUTIONS

15:500   Are teachers covered by Social Security?

No deduction or employer contribution is made from teacher pay for Social Security. Teachers may make Social Security payments by having non-teaching jobs for which such contributions are made.

Teachers are required to participate in the Teacher Retirement System. Teachers and other school employees hired after March 31, 1986, are subject to a 1.45 percent Medicare tax.

26 U.S.C. 3121(u)(2)(c)
40 ILCS 5/21-101 et seq.
40 ILCS 5/21-102.12 et seq.

15:510   What contribution to the Teacher Retirement System on behalf of each teacher is required?

A school board is required to contribute nine percent of each teacher's gross pay to the Teacher Retirement System (TRS). Gross pay includes sums paid the teacher for extra duties and certain fringe benefits provided under a cafeteria plan. TRS has gross income treatments which differ from Internal Revenue Service treatments, and a school board should be wary to examine both effects when considering any new fringe benefit program. Beginning July 1, 1998 school districts were required to pay an employer contribution to TRS on behalf of each teacher. The rate beginning July 1, 1999 is .58 per cent of each teacher's salary.

40 ILCS 5/16-152

15:520   What is the significance of the multiplier .098901 for Teacher Retirement System contribution purposes?

If a teacher's gross pay including Teacher Retirement System (TRS) contribution equals X, then the amount of the TRS contribution is calculated by multiplying X(.09). If the amount of X(.09) is subtracted from the teacher's gross pay, the result is the teacher's taxable pay. To get from the teacher's taxable pay to the teacher's gross pay, one must multiply taxable pay by 1.098901. To determine the amount of TRS contribution due knowing only the amount of a teacher's taxable pay, one must multiply taxable pay by .098901. The multiplier .098901 is unnecessary and burdensome if the teacher's gross pay is known.

40 ILCS 5/16-152 et seq.

15:530   What is the Teacher Health Insurance Security Fund?

On July 1, 1995, all active contributors to the Teacher Retirement System were required to begin making contributions toward the cost of annuitant and survivor health benefits. The rate of contribution is .5 percent of salary. While the employer may pay the contribution for the employee, there is no

Internal Revenue Service ruling upon which an employer may rely which permits the shelter of the payment from federal income taxation.

5 ILCS 375/6.6

LEAVES

15:540   May a school board allow sabbatical leave?

A school board may, by statutory authority, grant a sabbatical leave of absence to a teacher, principal, or superintendent performing contractual continued service, for a period of at least four school months but not in excess of one school term, for resident study, research, travel, or other purposes designed to improve the school system.

The statute which sets forth the conditions under which a sabbatical leave may be granted contains numerous and complicated procedural conditions for the leave. A school board may provide additional leave, provide leave for other classes of employees or add procedural requirements not contained in statute in a collectively bargained agreement or, absent a recognized bargaining representative, by the adoption of a policy.

105 ILCS 5/24-6.1

Thrash v. Board of Education School District No. 189, 106 Ill.App.3d 182, 435 N.E.2d 866, 62 Ill.Dec. 68 (5th Dist. 1982)

15:550   Is personal leave or professional leave required by law?

Personal leave is paid leave of absence, with or without procedural or use restrictions, and is commonly provided to teachers in amounts ranging from one to three days per year. Professional leave is paid or partially paid leave to attend meetings relating to the improvement of teaching. Neither leave is required by law. A school board may bargain either leave, or in the absence of a timely demand to bargain from a recognized bargaining representative, may regulate such leave by adoption of policy.

15:560   How much sick leave is provided a teacher by law?

Unless a collective bargaining agreement, or board policy in the absence of a recognized bargaining representative, provides more, each full time teacher is entitled by statute to a minimum of 10 sick leave days at full pay in each school year. Unused sick leave must be allowed to accumulate to a minimum available leave of 180 days at full pay, including the leave of the current year.

105 ILCS 5/24-6

15:570   Must a school board provide part time teachers sick leave benefits?

There is no statutory requirement that part time teachers be provided with sick leave benefits. Sick leave is a mandatory subject of bargaining. If part time teachers are included in a recognized bargaining unit, their sick leave benefits will be stated in a collective bargaining agreement. If part time teachers are not represented, a school board may unilaterally establish their sick leave benefits.

105 ILCS 5/24-6

15:580   May a teacher be disciplined for excessive use of sick leave?

A teacher may not be disciplined for appropriate use of accumulated sick leave. Once a teacher has exhausted accumulated sick leave, the teacher may not be discharged if the disability giving rise to the use of sick leave is caused by a temporary incapacity.

A school board may collectively bargain a provision in its contract or, in the absence of a recognized bargaining representative or in the absence of demand to bargain by a bargaining representative, adopt a policy defining permanent incapacity and listing it as cause for dismissal.

105 ILCS 5/10-22.4
105 ILCS 5/24-6
105 ILCS 5/24-13

Board of Education, School District No. 151, Cook County v. Illinois State Board of Education, 154 Ill.App.3d 175, 507 N.E.2d 134, 107 Ill.Dec. 470 (1st Dist. 1987)

   deOliveira v. State Board of Education, 158 Ill.App.3d 111, 511 N.E.2d 172, 110 Ill.Dec. 337 (2nd Dist. 1987)

   Elder v. Board of Education of School District No. 127 1/2, Cook County, 60 Ill.App.2d 56, 508 N.E.2d 423 (1st Dist. 1965)

15:590 Does a teacher lose accumulated sick leave by reason of school district combination?

If by reason of any change in the boundaries of a school district, or by reason of the creation of a new school district, the employment of a teacher is transferred to a new or different school board, the accumulated sick leave of the teacher is not lost but is transferred to the new or different school district.

   105 ILCS 5/24-6

TEACHER RESIGNATIONS

15:600 When may a tenured teacher resign without penalty?

A tenured teacher may resign at any time by agreement of the school board or by serving at least 30-days written notice upon the secretary of the board. However, no teacher may resign during the school year to accept another teaching assignment without the concurrence of the school board. A teacher who resigns on terms inconsistent with the above risks suspension of his teaching certificate for a period not to exceed one year.

   105 ILCS 5/21-23
   105 ILCS 5/24-14
   Braught v. Board of Education of Mount Prospect School District No. 57, 136 Ill.App.3d 486, 483 N.E.2d 623, 91 Ill.Dec. 277 (1st Dist. 1985)

15:610 When is a teacher's resignation effective?

In the sense that an unwilling teacher cannot be compelled to perform teaching duties, a teacher resignation is effective when the teacher determines to resign. Whether or not a school board can penalize the teacher for having resigned without the consent of the school board is determined by the facts of each resignation. When a particular resignation is perfected depends upon the timing of the intended resignation and the facts surrounding its delivery.

Braught v. Board of Education of Mount Prospect School District No. 57, 136 Ill.App.3d 486, 483 N.E.2d 623, 91 Ill.Dec. 277 (1st Dist. 1985)

Arduini v. Board of Education of Pontiac Township High School District 90, Livingston County, 92 Ill.2d 197, 441 N.E.2d 73, 65 Ill.Dec. 281 (1982)

Gras v. Clark, 46 Ill.App.3d 803, 361 N.E.2d 316, 5 Ill.Dec. 177 (2nd Dist. 1977)

16: TEACHER TENURE AND SENIORITY RIGHTS

TEACHER TENURE

16:10 Do all teachers enjoy the same employment rights under Illinois law?

Illinois teachers fall into three broad categories for purposes of statutory employment rights:

Probationary teachers who are not in their last year of probationary service have the fewest rights. All part time teachers who have not achieved and maintained tenured status have rights similar to such probationary teachers.

Probationary teachers in their final year of probationary service comprise the second category, and have slightly greater rights than other probationary teachers.

The third category is comprised of tenured teachers, who have dramatically more rights than either of the other two categories of teachers.

105 ILCS 5/24-11
105 ILCS 5/24-12

16:20 What is tenure?

Tenure is the common name for contractual continued service, which is the status conferred by law upon certificated employees who have satisfactorily completed a term of probationary employment. The employee in contractual continued service is:

1) deemed to be continuously employed from year to year unless given proper notice of honorable dismissal (lay off) or dismissal for cause;

2) entitled to seniority rights granted by law or collective bargaining agreement in the event a school board reduces its staff or discontinues a program; and

3) entitled to substantial rights of due process in the event of dismissal for cause.

105 ILCS 5/24-12

16:30   What is the difference between contractual continued service and tenure?

There is no difference between the terms. Tenure is the common name for contractual continued service.

105 ILCS 5/24-11
105 ILCS 5/24-12

16:40   What is the difference between a probationary teacher and a non-tenured teacher?

The terms have the same meaning, as does the phrase "teacher who has not entered into contractual continued service."

16:50   Must a tenured teacher be issued an annual employment contract?

Tenured teachers have a continuing employment relationship which does not require the issuance of an annual contract. Assuming there is no collectively bargained provision which prevents the issuance of an annual contract and no demand to bargain, a school board may issue individual teacher contracts. The terms of the contract must be consistent with the terms of applicable collectively bargained provisions. A tenured teacher cannot be compelled to sign such a contract, but may voluntarily enter into a contract providing for additional obligations in exchange for additional benefits.

Bond v. Board of Education of Mascoutah Community Unit School District No. 19, 81 Ill.2d 242, 408 N.E.2d 714, 42 Ill.Dec. 136 (1980)

Bagley v. Board of Education of Seneca Community Consolidated School District No. 170, LaSalle County, 83 Ill.App.3d 247, 403 N.E.2d 1285, 38 Ill.Dec. 681, aff'd. 84 Ill.2d 477 (1980)

Littrell v. Board of Education of Cave in Rock Community Unit School District No. 2, 45 Ill.App.3d 690, 360 N.E.2d 102, 4 Ill.Dec. 355 (5th Dist. 1977)

Davis v. Board of Education of Aurora Public School District No. 131 of Kane County, 19 Ill.App.3d 644, 312 N.E.2d 335 (2nd Dist. 1974)

16:55   Does tenure protect a teacher's right to a particular job assignment?

The safeguards of tenure do not assure employment in a particular job assignment, grade level, or attendance center, but rather protect the individual's job as a teacher.

Caviness v. Board of Education of Ludlow Community Consolidated School District No. 142 of Champaign County, 59 Ill.App.3d 28, 375 N.E.2d 157, 16 Ill.Dec. 526 (4th Dist. 1978)

Danno v. Peterson, 421 F.Supp. 950 (N.D. Ill. 1976)

Van Dyke v. Board of Education of School District No. 57, Cook County, 115 Ill.App.2d 10, 254 N.E.2d 76 (1st Dist. 1969)

ACQUISITION OF TENURE

16:60   Which employees may acquire tenure?

A teacher may acquire tenure. The term "teacher" in this context includes all school district employees whose jobs require teacher certification. Superintendents, principals, other administrators, deans, department heads, and counselors may acquire teacher tenure if such employees meet statutory requirements.

Tenure does not attach to a particular job, but rather to teaching employment in the school district generally. For example, a principal cannot earn tenure as a principal, but earns tenure as a teaching employee.

105 ILCS 5/10-23.8 et seq.

105 ILCS 5/24-12

Davis v. Board of Education of Farmer City-Mansfield Community Unit School District No. 17, 63 Ill.App.3d 495, 380 N.E.2d 58, 20 Ill.Dec. 381 (4th Dist. 1978)

Lester v. Board of Education of School District No. 119, Jo Daviess County, 87 Ill.App.2d 269, 230 N.E.2d 893 (2nd Dist. 1967)

16:70   When does a teacher acquire tenure?

For a teacher employed in a particular school district before January 1, 1998, tenure was or will be achieved after service of a probationary period of two full-time consecutive school terms unless the teacher is given written notice of dismissal by the school board. The notice must state the specific reason for the dismissal, and must be delivered by certified mail, return receipt requested, at least 45 days before the end of the school term. The school board may, by following the requisite procedures, extend probation to a third year if the probationary teacher has not previously had one term of full time teaching experience.

For a teacher first employed by a school district on or after January 1, 1998 and who has not before that date already achieved tenure in that district, the probationary period is four consecutive school terms. The relevant statute does not provide guidance as to the meaning of the term "first employed." A collective bargaining agreement may require notice in excess of 45 days.

For the purpose of determining contractual continued service, the first probationary year is any full-time employment from a date before November 1 through the end of the school year.

A school board may not award tenure sooner than the statute allows.

105 ILCS 5/24-11
Dunlop v. Colgan, 687 F.Supp. 406 (N.D. Ill. 1988)
Williams v. Board of Education of Hardin County Community Unit School District No. 1, 166 Ill.App.3d 765, 520 N.E.2d 954, 117 Ill.Dec. 603 (5th Dist. 1988) app. den. 121 Ill.2d 587, 526 N.E.2d 841, 122 Ill.Dec. 448 (1988)
Bessler v. Board of Education of Charter School District No. 150 of Peoria County, 43 Ill.App.3d 322, 356 N.E.2d 1253, 1 Ill.Dec. 920 (3rd Dist. 1977), aff'd. in part, rev. in part 69 Ill.2d 191, 370 N.E.2d 1050, 13 Ill.Dec. 23 (1978)

16:80 Does a teacher hired to replace a teacher on an approved leave of absence acquire tenure?

Tenure is not acquired by a person while employed to replace a teacher who is in the military service of the United States, one who is serving in the General Assembly, or one who by agreement of a school board is on leave to teach in a Department of Defense dependents' school. In any other circumstance, whether or not a teacher replacing a teacher on an approved leave of absence acquires tenure or not is a fact-specific question.

105 ILCS 5/24-13
105 ILCS 5/24-13.1
Fisher v. Board of Education of West Washington County Community Unit District No. 10, Washington County, 181 Ill.App.3d 653, 537 N.E.2d 354, 130 Ill.Dec. 287 (5th Dist. 1989)

16:90 If a certified teacher is employed in a special education district or cooperative, in which school district or districts does such a teacher acquire tenure?

A teacher employed after July 1, 1987 as a full time teacher in a program of special education joint agreement, whether the program is operated by the joint agreement or a member district on behalf of the joint agreement, achieves tenure in all of the programs conducted by the joint agreement which the teacher is qualified to hold. In the event of dissolution of the joint agreement, such a teacher has bumping rights in a member district of the joint agreement.

A teacher employed full time in a special education cooperative before September 23, 1987 and who achieved tenure in the cooperative acquired tenure in all participating districts in the cooperative. In the event the program is terminated, the teacher must be assigned to any comparable position in a member district for which he is qualified and which is currently held by a non-tenured teacher or one with shorter length of service.

Tenure in all participating school districts is commonly called super-tenure. Teachers employed in a special education cooperative after September 23, 1987 cannot acquire super-tenure but do have bumping rights into member districts on the occasion of the dissolution of the special education district.

105 ILCS 5/14-9.01
105 ILCS 5/24-11
Seim v. Board of Education of Community Unit School District No. 87 of McLean County, 21 Ill.App.3d 386, 315 N.E.2d 282 (4th Dist. 1974)

16:100   Do teachers employed in a joint agreement vocational area center have super-tenure?

No.

Aken v. Board of Control of Lake County Area Vocational Center, 237 Ill.App.3d 97, 604 N.E.2d 524, 178 Ill.Dec. 268 (2nd Dist 1992)
Koppi v. Board of Control of Whiteside Area Vocational Center, 133 Ill.App.3d 591, 479 N.E.2d 36, 88 Ill.Dec. 701 (3rd Dist. 1985)

16:110   Does service as a teacher's aide or a paraprofessional count toward earning tenure if the person so employed has teacher certification?

No.

Strejcek v. Board of Education of Berwyn School District No. 100, 78 Ill.App.3d 400, 397 N.E.2d 448, 33 Ill.Dec. 942 (1st Dist. 1979)

16:120   Is a teacher employed in a program which is wholly federally funded accruing time toward the acquisition of tenure?

Probably not. Courts have found teachers employed in programs which are wholly federally funded are not "full time teachers" within the meaning of teacher tenure laws.

Kuykendall v. Board of Education of Evanston Township High School District No. 202, 111 Ill.App.3d 809, 444 N.E.2d 766, 67 Ill.Dec. 530 (1st Dist. 1982)

16:130   Can a teacher earn tenure in an extra duty assignment?

No. Tenure is not acquired in-position, but as a generic teaching employee of the school district. A coach cannot acquire tenure as a coach. A collective bargaining agreement may, however, extend contractual rights to such employees.

Smith v. Board of Education of Urbana School District No. 116, 708 F.2d 258 (7th Cir. 1983)

Brunstrom v. Board of Education of Riverdale Community Unit School District 100 of Rock Island County, 52 Ill.App.3d 653, 367 N.E.2d 1065, 10 Ill.Dec. 456 (3rd Dist. 1977)

16:150   If two or more school districts combine, do the tenured teachers from the predecessor school districts lose tenure?

No. If by reason of any change in the boundaries of school districts, or by reason of the creation of a new school district, the position held by any teacher having tenured status is transferred from one school board to the control of a new or different board, the tenure of the teacher is not lost. The new or different school board is subject to the tenure laws with respect to the teacher in the same manner as if the teacher were its employee and had been its employee during the time the teacher was actually employed by the board from whose control the position was transferred.

105 ILCS 5/24-12

PART TIME TEACHERS

16:160   Can a part time teacher acquire tenure?

No. To acquire tenure, an employee must complete the statutory period of full time service. However, a part time teacher can have tenure if the tenure was acquired while the teacher was in full time service (and the teacher was later reduced to part time status).

105 ILCS 5/24-11
Kuykendall v. Board of Education of Evanston Township High School District No. 202, 111 Ill.App.3d 809, 444 N.E.2d 766, 67 Ill.Dec. 530 (1st Dist. 1982).
Johnson v. Board of Education of Decatur School District No. 61 of Macon County, 87 Ill.App.3d 441, 409 N.E.2d 139, 42 Ill.Dec 644 (4th Dist. 1980) aff'd. 85 Ill.2d 338, 423 N.E.2d 903, 53 Ill.Dec. 234 (1981)

16:170   May a school board confer tenure on a part time teacher or on a teacher who has served less than the requisite probationary period?

No. Tenure attaches by operation of law, not by any action taken by a school board. A school board cannot "confer" tenure. The requisite probationary period must be served. However, a school board that makes a promise to a teacher may be held to its bargain if the promise has the requisite elements to elevate it to a contract. The promise of tenure may confer upon a teacher rights other than tenure.

Faculty Association of District 205, IEA-NEA v. Illinois Educational Labor Relations Board, 175 Ill.App.3d 880, 530 N.E.2d 548 (4th Dist. 1988) app. den. 124 Ill.2d 554 (1989)
Evans v. Benjamin School District No. 25, 134 Ill.App.3d 875, 480 N.E.2d 1380, 89 Ill.Dec. 637 (2nd Dist. 1985)
Kuykendall v. Board of Education of Evanston Township High School District No. 202, 111 Ill.App.3d 809, 444 N.E.2d 766, 67 Ill.Dec. 530 (1st Dist. 1982)

SENIORITY AND REDUCTION IN FORCE

16:190   Do probationary or part time teachers accrue seniority rights?

Probationary and part time teachers do not accrue seniority rights as a result of any statutory requirement. Sometimes such employees acquire seniority rights by reason of a provision in a collective bargaining agreement. In the absence of a demand to bargain or if the affected teachers are not members of a recognized bargaining unit, a school board may unilaterally establish seniority rules for such teachers.

105 ILCS 5/24-12

16:200   What is RIF?

RIF is an acronym for "reduction in force," which is the decision of a school board to decrease the number of teachers employed or to discontinue some particular type of teaching service.

105 ILCS 5/24-12

16:210   What is the difference between the terms "layoff" and "reduction in force?"

An employee is laid off when an employer conducts a reduction in force.

16:220   What seniority rights may tenured teachers assert against less senior teachers in the event of a reduction in force?

A school board contemplating a reduction in teaching force must first remove or dismiss all non-tenured teachers in a particular position before removing or dismissing any tenured teacher who is legally qualified to hold the position.

As between tenured teachers, the teacher or teachers with the shorter length of continuing service to the district must be dismissed first unless an alternate method of determining the sequence of dismissal is established in a collective bargaining agreement.

A school board must comply with all procedures required by its collective bargaining agreement in conducting a reduction in force.

105 ILCS 5/24-12
Schaefer v. Board of Education of Arlington Heights School District No. 25, 157 Ill.App.3d 884, 510 N.E.2d 1186, 110 Ill.Dec. 155 (1st Dist. 1987) app. den. 116 Ill.2d 576, 515 N.E.2d 126, 113 Ill.Dec. 317 (1987)

Catron v. Board of Education of Kansas Community Unit School District No. 3 of Edgar County, 126 Ill.App.3d 693, 467 N.E.2d 621, 81 Ill.Dec. 750 (4th Dist. 1984)

Birk v. Board of Education of Flora Community Unit School District No. 35, Clay County, 104 Ill.2d 252, 472 N.E.2d 407, 84 Ill.Dec. 447 (1984)

Wilson v. Board of Education Limestone Walters School District No. 316, 127 Ill.App.3d 433, 468 N.E.2d 995, 82 Ill.Dec. 341 (3rd Dist. 1984)

Caviness v. Board of Education of Ludlow Community Consolidated School District No. 142 of Champaign County, 59 Ill.App.3d 28, 375 N.E.2d 157, 16 Ill.Dec. 526 (4th Dist. 1978)

16:230 Is the reduction of a tenured teacher from ten-month employment to nine-month employment a reduction in force?

The reduction of a tenured teacher's employment from a ten-month extended contract to a nine-month regular contract is a reduction in force. Absent agreement from the teacher, the reduction of a tenured teacher from full time to part time may only be accomplished at the beginning of a new school term following legally sufficient notice to the teacher at least 60 days before the end of the preceding school term.

The notification procedure is the same as that required for notice of dismissal or layoff. The seniority rights of tenured teachers must be respected in any such reduction and all collectively bargained procedures must be followed.

105 ILCS 5/24-12

Duncan v. Board of Education of United Township High School District No. 30, 177 Ill.App.3d 806, 532 N.E.2d 927, 127 Ill.Dec. 98 (3rd Dist. 1988)

Pennell v. Board of Education of Equality Community Unit School District 4, Gallatin County, 137 Ill.App.3d 139, 484 N.E.2d 445, 91 Ill.Dec. 886 (5th Dist. 1986)

Birk v. Board of Education of Flora Community Unit School District No. 35, Clay County, 104 Ill.2d 252, 472 N.E.2d 407, 84 Ill.Dec. 447 (1984)

Wilson v. Board of Education Limestone Walters School District No. 316, 127 Ill.App.3d 433, 468 N.E.2d 995, 82 Ill.Dec. 341 (3rd Dist. 1984)

16:235 Can a tenured teacher who accepts a part time position and later requests return to full time teaching assert bumping rights against a new non-tenured teacher?

Under most circumstances, bumping rights can be asserted only when a reduction in force triggers the bumps. When, however, a tenured teacher has retained tenure after a reduction to part time status, the tenured teacher may later return to full time status by asserting bumping rights against a new non-tenured teacher who has been hired to teach in a position which the tenured teacher is qualified to fill.

Deem v. Board of Education of Triad Community Unit School District No. 2, Madison County, 200 Ill.App.3d 903, 558 N.E.2d 291, 146 Ill.Dec. 328 (5th Dist. 1990)

16:240   What is required to reduce a tenured teacher from full time to part time employment?

Without the agreement of the teacher, the reduction of a tenured teacher from full time to part time may only be accomplished at the beginning of a new school term following legally sufficient notice to the teacher at least 60 days before the end of the preceding school term. The notification procedure is the same as that required for notice of dismissal or layoff. The seniority rights of tenured teachers must be respected in any such reduction and all collectively bargained procedures must be followed.

105 ILCS 5/24-12

Pennell v. Board of Education of Equality Community Unit School District 4, Gallatin County, 137 Ill.App.3d 139, 484 N.E.2d 445, 91 Ill.Dec. 886 (5th Dist. 1986)

Board of Education of Bremen Community High School District No. 228, Cook County v. Bremen District No. 228 Joint Faculty Association, 114 Ill.App.3d 1051, 449 N.E.2d 960, 70 Ill.Dec. 613 (1st Dist. 1983) aff'd. in part, rev. in part on other grounds 101 Ill.2d 115, 461 N.E.2d 406, 77 Ill.Dec. 783 (1983)

Hagopian v. Board of Education of Tampico Community Unit School District No. 4 of Whiteside and Bureau Counties, 56 Ill.App.3d 940, 372 N.E.2d 990, 14 Ill.Dec. 711 (3rd Dist. 1978) app. after rem. 83 Ill.App.3d 1097, 404 N.E.2d 899, 39 Ill.Dec. 308 (3rd Dist 1980), rev. on other grounds 84 Ill.2d 436, 420 N.E.2d 147, 50 Ill.Dec. 830 (1981)

16:250   If a teacher has earned tenure and later is reduced to part time without a break in service, does the teacher lose tenure?

No.

Wilson v. Board of Education Limestone Walters School District No. 316, 127 Ill.App.3d 433, 468 N.E.2d 995, 82 Ill.Dec. 341 (3rd Dist. 1984)

Caviness v. Board of Education of Ludlow Community Consolidated School District No. 142 of Champaign County, 59 Ill.App.3d 28, 375 N.E.2d 157, 16 Ill.Dec. 526 (4th Dist. 1978)

Brown v. Board of Education Gallatin Community Unit School District
No. 1, 38 Ill.App.3d 403, 347 N.E.2d 791, app. after rem. People ex rel. Brown
v. Board of Education Gallatin Community Unit School District No. 1, 66
Ill.App.3d 167, 383 N.E.2d 711 (5th Dist. 1976)

16:260 In a reduction in force, must all non-tenured teachers be dismissed before the first tenured teacher is dismissed?

No. A non-tenured teacher must be reduced first only if he
holds a position which is to be reduced or if he is bumped by a
teacher with greater seniority.

105 ILCS 5/24-12
Piquard v. Board of Education of Pekin Community High School District
No. 303, 242 Ill.App.3d 477, 610 N.E.2d 757, 182 Ill.Dec. 888 (3rd Dist. 1993)

16:270 In what manner must a school board notify a teacher of honorable dismissal by reason of reduction in teaching force or discontinuance of teaching service?

If a teacher on tenure is removed or dismissed as a result of
the decision of the school board to decrease the number of teachers employed by the board or to discontinue some particular
type of teaching service, a written notice must be mailed to the
teacher and also given the teacher either by certified mail,
return receipt requested, or personal delivery with receipt at
least 60 days before the end of the school term, together with a
statement of honorable dismissal and the reason therefor.

Probationary teachers, except those in their final probationary year, need not be provided reasons for their terminations.
The relevant statute requires that these employees be properly
notified of termination not later than 45 days before the end of
the school term. However, in the case of a reduction in force, the
exercise of bumping rights by tenured teachers over
non-tenured teachers may create issues unless the reduction in
force decisions are made by the employing school board in
advance of the notice requirements for tenured teachers and the
termination notices are sent at essentially the same time to both
tenured and non-tenured teachers who are being bumped and
such notices are received by the tenured teachers at least 60
days before the end of the school term.

The notice requirements of the relevant statutes were
amended in 1998. A school district contemplating the

non-renewal or lay off of an employee should make sure its local policies, evaluation plans and contracts do not require notification timelines which are different from those required by statute.

105 ILCS 5/24-12
23 Ill. Admin. Code 51.30
Koerner v. Joppa Community High School District No. 21, 143 Ill.App.3d 162, 492 N.E.2d 1017, 97 Ill.Dec. 358 (5th Dist. 1986)

16:280   When must a school board hold a public hearing before conducting a reduction in force?

Whenever the number of honorable dismissal notices based upon economic necessity exceeds five or 150 percent of the average number of teachers honorably dismissed in the preceding three years, whichever is greater, then the school board must hold a hearing on the question of the dismissals. Following the hearing and board review, the action to approve any such reduction in staff requires a majority vote of the school board.

105 ILCS 5/24-12
23 Ill. Admin. Code 51.20
Wheatley v. Board of Education of Township High School District No. 205, Cook County, 113 Ill.App.3d 129, 446 N.E.2d 1257, 68 Ill.Dec. 860 (1st Dist. 1983)

SENIORITY AND BUMPING

16:290   At what date are teacher qualifications fixed for purposes of a school board decision to reduce force?

A school board must base its decision to reduce force on the qualifications held by a teacher no later than 60 days before the end of the school term in which the notice of reduction in force is to be sent.

105 ILCS 5/24-12
Hagopian v. Board of Education of Tampico Community Unit School District No. 4 of Whiteside and Bureau Counties, 56 Ill.App.3d 940, 372 N.E.2d 990, 14 Ill.Dec. 711 (3rd Dist. 1978) app. after rem. 83 Ill.App.3d 1097, 404 N.E.2d 899, 39 Ill.Dec. 308 (3rd Dist 1980), rev. on other grounds 84 Ill.2d 436, 420 N.E.2d 147, 50 Ill.Dec. 830 (1981)

16:300 Are the terms "legally qualified" and "certified" synonymous?

No. Certified refers to State Board of Education teacher certification. Legally qualified has a wider meaning. A teacher may be certified to hold a position, but not legally qualified to hold it.

Zink v. Board of Education of Chrisman, 146 Ill.App.3d 1016, 497 N.E.2d 835, 100 Ill.Dec. 657 (4th Dist. 1986)

Lenard v. Board of Education of Fairfield School District No. 112 of Wayne County, 57 Ill.App.3d 853, 373 N.E.2d 477, 15 Ill.Dec. 131 (5th Dist. 1978), app. after rem. 74 Ill.2d 260, 384 N.E.2d 1321, 24 Ill.Dec. 163 (1978)

16:310 Must a school board develop a teacher seniority list?

Each year, each school board must, in consultation with any exclusive bargaining representatives, establish a list categorized by positions, showing the length of continuing service of each teacher in the district who is qualified to hold any position. Copies of this list must be distributed to the exclusive bargaining representative on or before February 1 of each year.

105 ILCS 5/24-12

16:315 Is the definition of seniority a mandatory subject of bargaining?

Yes. If questions arise which have not been fully bargained with respect to computation of seniority affecting a recognized bargaining unit, the school board may unilaterally define seniority only after notice to the union and in the absence of a union demand to bargain thereafter.

115 ILCS 5/10

16:320 What are bumping rights?

When a more senior teacher "bumps" a less senior teacher from his job in the event of a reduction in force, he exercises "bumping rights." Bumping rights derive from statutory seniority, and therefore apply only to tenured teachers unless a collective bargaining agreement extends such rights to other classes of teachers.

105 ILCS 5/24-12
Caviness v. Board of Education of Ludlow Community Consolidated School District No. 142 of Champaign County, 59 Ill.App.3d 28, 375 N.E.2d 157, 16 Ill.Dec. 526 (4th Dist. 1978)

16:330   Is a school board required to realign teaching assignments in a reduction in force to protect the jobs of senior tenured teachers?

A school board is not required to combine parts of existing teaching assignments in a reduction in force to protect the jobs of senior tenured teachers. Absent a collectively bargained provision to the contrary, bumping rights may be exercised by tenured teachers to claim "whole positions." A school board may not realign teaching assignments in a reduction in force to defeat the tenure rights of a senior teacher.

105 ILCS 5/24-12
Peters v. Board of Education of Rantoul High School District No. 193 of Champaign County, 97 Ill.2d 166, 454 N.E.2d 310, 73 Ill.Dec. 450 (1983)

16:340   For how long after layoff does a teacher have recall rights?

Unless a collective bargaining agreement provides otherwise, only tenured teachers have recall rights. Recall rights extend for one calendar year from the beginning of the school term following the layoff, unless the original layoff exceeded 15 percent of the number of full time equivalent positions filled by certified employees (excluding principals and administrative personnel) during the preceding school year, in which case the recall rights extend for two calendar years from the beginning of the school term following the layoff.

105 ILCS 5/24-12
Walter v. Board of Education of Quincy School District No. 172, 93 Ill.2d 101, 442 N.E.2d 870, 66 Ill.Dec. 309 (1982)
Huetteman v. Board of Education of Community Unit School District 3A, 56 Ill.App.3d 933, 372, N.E.2d 716, 14 Ill.Dec. 520 (4th Dist. 1978)

16:350 Do probationary employees have recall rights after layoff?

Not unless they are granted recall rights in a collective bargaining agreement. Statutory preferential right of recall applies to tenured teachers and support staff only.

105 ILCS 5/10-23.5
105 ILCS 5/24-11
105 ILCS 5/24-12

17: SCHOOL EMPLOYMENT IN GENERAL

EMPLOYMENT STANDARDS

17:10 May a school board require employees to show evidence of freedom from communicable diseases?

A school board must require a new employee to present evidence of physical fitness to perform the duties assigned and freedom from communicable disease, including tuberculosis. Evidence must consist of a physical examination and a tuberculin skin test and, if appropriate, an X-ray made by a physician licensed in Illinois or any other state to practice medicine and surgery in all its branches not more than 90 days preceding the time of presentation to the school board. The cost of the examination is paid by the employee.

A school board may from time to time require an examination of any employee by a physician licensed in Illinois to practice medicine and surgery in all of its branches and must pay the expenses of this examination from school funds.

105 ILCS 5/24-5

17:20 Must a school board conduct criminal background checks on applicants for employment?

A school board may not knowingly employ a person for whom a criminal background investigation has not been begun. Applicants for employment with a school district are required as a condition of employment to authorize an investigation to determine if they have been convicted of any of a specified list of criminal and drug offenses. A school board may not knowingly employ a person who has been convicted of any of a list of offenses specified.

105 ILCS 5/10-21.9

17:30 Are criminal background checks required for employees of an independent contractor doing business with a school district?

If the employees of the independent contractor have direct, daily contact with students, a criminal background check is required.

105 ILCS 5/10-21.9

17:33 May an employer be liable for failing to investigate an employee's background at the time of hiring?

Yes; mere reliance on a criminal background check is not sufficient to protect the employer from the potential for liability. If the employer fails to adequately investigate the background of the employee before the employee is hired and the employee later harms a third party, the employer may be liable for negligently hiring or retaining the employee if the employer knew or should have known the employee was unfit for the job to which he was assigned.

How much diligence an employer must exercise to investigate the background of a job candidate is proportionate to the nature of the job to which the employee will be assigned.

Geise v. Phoenix Company of Chicago, Inc., 159 Ill.2d 507, 639 N.E.2d 1273, 203 Ill.Dec. 454 (1994)
Fallon v. Indian Trail School, 148 Ill.App.3d 931, 500 N.E.2d 101, 102 Ill Dec. 479 (2nd Dist. 1986)
Bates v. Doria, 150 Ill.App.3d 1025, 502 N.E.2d 454, 104 Ill. Dec. 191 (2nd Dist. 1986)

17:35 May an employer be liable for obscuring a work history of criminal misconduct of a former employee?

A school district which attempts to obscure the criminal misconduct of a former employee risks liability if the employee commits a subsequent similar criminal act during employment by a later employer. A school district should notify all relevant state agencies of criminal misconduct committed by its employees.

Doe v. Methacton School District, 880 F.Supp. 380 (E.D.Pa. 1995)

**17:40   May a school district give employment
          preference to veterans?**

If all bargaining obligations are met, a school district may
give preferential treatment in employment to veterans of any
branch of United States military service.

775 ILCS 5/2-104(2)

**17:44   May a school board require its employees to be
          residents of the school district?**

Residency may not be used as a factor in filling any teaching or support staff position or in the determination of compensation, retention, promotion, assignment or transfer. A superintendent of schools may be required to reside in the school district.

105 ILCS 5/10-23.5
105 ILCS 5/24-4.1

**17:47   May a school district have an anti-nepotism rule
          which forbids or restricts the employment of
          spouses of school board members or staff super-
          visors?**

Yes, anti-nepotism rules are legally permissible generally.
Although Illinois law prevents discrimination by reason of marital status, the term "marital status" means a person's state of
being married, single, separated, divorced or widowed. The definition does not include the identity of a person's spouse.

105 ILCS 5/10-22.4
775 ILCS 5/1-103-J et seq.
Boaden v. State Department of Law Enforcement, 171 Ill.2d 230, 664
N.E.2d 61, 215 Ill.Dec. 664 (1996)
*River Bend Community Unit School District No. 2 v. Illinois Human
Rights Commission et al.,* 232 Ill.App.3d 838, 597 N.E.2d 842, 173 Ill.Dec. 868
(3rd Dist. 1992) app. den. 147 Ill.2d 637, 606 N.E.2d 1235, 180 Ill.Dec. 158
(1993)
Kraft, Inc. v. State of Minnesota, 284 N.W.2d 386 (Minn.Sup.Ct. 1979)
Hollister v. North, 50 Ill.App.3d 56, 365 N.E.2d 258, 8 Ill.Dec. 20 (4th
Dist. 1977)

17:50 If a school board elects not to hire a qualified job applicant, must it give reasons for the rejection?

Provided there is no policy or contract provision to the contrary and provided there are no constitutional implications to the rejection, a school board may decide not to hire any job applicant without giving reasons, notwithstanding the applicant is qualified to meet the needs of the school district as specified in the job announcement.

Halfacre v. Board of Education of School District No. 167, 331 Ill.App. 404, 73 N.E.2d 124 (1947)

COMPENSATION

17:60 Does the Federal Fair Labor Standards Act apply to public schools?

Yes. A public school board is subject to the requirements of the Act, including its minimum wage and overtime provisions. Teachers are not subject to the provisions of the Act; support staff are.

29 U.S.C. 201 et seq.

Garcia v. San Antonio Metropolitan Transit Authority, 105 S.Ct. 1005, 469 U.S. 528, 83 L.Ed.2d 1016 (1985)

17:70 What is the federal Equal Pay Act?

The federal Equal Pay Act is a non-discrimination law. It provides in part:

"No employer . . . shall discriminate, within any establishment in which such employees are employed, between employees on the basis of sex by paying wages to employees in such establishment at a rate less than the rate at which he pays wages to employees of the opposite sex in such establishment for equal work on jobs the performance of which requires equal skill, effort, and responsibility, and which are performed under similar working conditions, except where such payment is made pursuant to (i) a seniority system; (ii) a merit system; (iii) a system which measures earnings by quantity or quality of production; or (iv) a differential based on any other factor other than sex."

19 U.S.C. 206(d)(1)

SALARY DEDUCTIONS

17:100   Is a school board required to withhold union dues from salary?

A school board must, upon the written request of an employee, withhold from the compensation of that employee any dues, payments, or contributions payable by such employee to any employee labor organization as defined in the Illinois Educational Labor Relations Act. Under such arrangement, an amount must be withheld from each regular payroll period which is equal to the pro rata share of the annual dues plus any payments or contributions. The school board must transmit such withholdings to the specified labor organization within 10 working days from the time of the withholding. Dues deduction procedures are usually contained in collective bargaining agreements.

105 ILCS 5/24-21.1
115 ILCS 5/1 et seq.

17:110   What is "fair share?"

If included in a collective bargaining agreement, a fair share clause requires a school board to deduct from each employee's salary a sum equal to the union's cost of representing the employee in the bargaining process and for grievance representation. Usually the fair share fee is a percentage of union dues in excess of 75 percent and often approaching 100 percent. The specific percentage is established by a union showing of the actual cost of representation. A fair share provision is a common union bargaining demand. A school board may, but need not, agree to fair share.

115 ILCS 5/11
Abood v. Detroit Board of Education, 97 S.Ct. 1782, 431 U.S. 209, 52 L.Ed. 261, reh. den. 97 S.Ct. 2989, 433 U.S. 915, 53 L.Ed.2d 1102 (1977)
Chicago Teachers Union Local 1, AFT, AFL-CIO v. Hudson, 106 S.Ct. 1066, 475 U.S. 292, 89 L.Ed.2d 232 (1986)

17:120   Must a school board withhold delinquent child or family service payments from an employee's salary?

A school district may receive a certified Order for Support and an Income Withholding Notice directing the district to deduct child or family support payments from the salary of an employee. In addition to the required support payment, a school district may deduct a five dollar fee per month from the income of the employee in order to meet the requirements of this law.

750 ILCS 22/605 et seq.
305 ILCS 5/10-16.2

HOLIDAYS AND LEAVES

17:140 Which holidays are school holidays?

A teacher can not be required to teach on Saturdays nor on legal school holidays, which are January 1, New Year's Day; the third Monday in January, the birthday of Dr. Martin Luther King, Jr.; February 12, the birthday of President Abraham Lincoln; the first Monday in March, Casimir Pulaski's birthday; Good Friday; the day designated as Memorial Day by federal law; July 4, Independence Day; the first Monday in September, Labor Day; the second Monday in October, Columbus Day; November 11, Veteran's Day; the Thursday in November commonly called Thanksgiving Day; and December 25, Christmas Day.

Other school employees cannot be required to work on legal school holidays, other than those noncertificated school employees whose presence is necessary because of an emergency or for the continued operation of school facilities or property.

A school board may grant a special holiday whenever in its judgment it is advisable except that no special holiday may be declared on an election day when members of the Illinois General Assembly are elected. No deduction may be made from the time or compensation of a school employee on account of any legal or special holiday.

Treatment of holidays may have collective bargaining implications with respect to recognized bargaining units.

105 ILCS 5/24-2
District 300 Education Association v. Board of Education of Dundee Community Unit School District No. 300 of Kane County et al, 31 Ill.App.3d 550, 334 N.E.2d 165 (2nd Dist. 1975)

17:142 Must hourly employees be paid for hours not worked on legal school holidays?

There is no law which requires that employees be paid for work not done on a holiday if the holiday falls on a day when they were not scheduled to work. For example, a 10-month employee (August-June) need not be paid for July 4th. On the other hand, an hourly employee must be paid for a holiday that occurs during his regular work schedule. Collective bargaining agreements and employer policy manuals usually define holiday pay.

105 ILCS 5/24-2

17:150   What is sick leave?

Unless the definition is expanded by a collective bargaining agreement or board policy, sick leave is time away from work for personal illness, quarantine at home, or serious illness or death in the immediate family or household. Immediate family is parents, spouse, brothers, sisters, children, grandparents, grandchildren, parents-in-law, brothers-in-law, sisters-in-law, and legal guardians.

105 ILCS 5/24-6

17:160   When may a school board require an employee to provide a physician's certificate documenting the employee's illness?

Unless a collective bargaining agreement or board policy provides otherwise, a school board may require a physician's certificate as a basis for pay during sick leave after an absence of three days for personal illness or as it may deem necessary in other cases. If the treatment is by prayer or spiritual means, a certificate may be required from a spiritual advisor or practitioner of the employee's faith.

If a school board requires a physician's certificate, or a certificate from a spiritual healer, as a basis for pay during leave for sick purposes of less than three days, the school board must pay the expenses incurred by the employee in obtaining the physician's certificate.

105 ILCS 5/24-5

Deizman v. Board of Education District 201, Cook County, 53 Ill.App.3d 1050, 369 N.E.2d 257 (1st Dist. 1977)

Lippincott v. Board of Education of Community Unit School District No. 5 of Coles County, 342 Ill.App. 642, 97 N.E.2d 566 (3rd Dist. 1951)

17;170 Must a pregnant employee be permitted to use sick leave for pregnancy?

A school board must allow use of sick leave for employees who are disabled because of pregnancy. However, unless a collective bargaining agreement so provides, a school board need not permit the use of sick leave for pregnancy without disability.

Where no bargaining agreement provides to the contrary, a school board may require a doctor's certificate to establish a pregnant woman's inability to work. When a pregnant employee uses accumulated sick leave for pregnancy based disability, she must return to work when her disabling condition no longer exists.

42 U.S.C. 2000e
105 ILCS 5/24-6
Maganuco v. Leyden Community High School District No. 212, 867 F.2d 974 (7th Cir. 1989)
Scherr v. Woodland Consolidated School District No. 50, 867 F.2d 974 (7th Cir. 1989)
Winks v. Board of Education of Normal Community Unit School District No. 5 of McLean County, 78 Ill.2d 128, 398 N.E.2d 823, 34 Ill.Dec. 832 (1979)

17:180 Is a school board required by law to grant maternity leave?

Maternity, paternity and parental leave are permissive under the law, but no such leave is required. However, a school board may not discriminate against pregnant employees with respect to the grant or denial of unpaid leaves of absence. A school board may bargain leaves, or in the absence of a recognized bargaining representative or if a bargaining representative fails to make timely demand to bargain, may regulate leaves by adoption of policy.

42 U.S.C. 2000e
Schafer v. Board of Public Education of School District of Pittsburgh, 732 F.Supp. 565 (W.D. Pa. 1990)
Winks v. Board of Education of Normal Community Unit School District No. 5 of McLean County, 78 Ill.2d 128, 398 N.E.2d 823, 34 Ill.Dec. 832 (1979)

17:190   May a school board require an employee to take a maternity leave?

A school board may not require an employee to take maternity leave if the employee is physically able to work.

42 U.S.C. 2000e
Cleveland Board of Education v. LaFleur, 94 S.Ct. 791, 414 U.S. 632, 39 L.Ed.2d 52 (1974)

17:200   May a collective bargaining agreement require a pregnant employee to choose between paid disability leave or unpaid leave of absence so as to prevent the employee from combining the two leaves?

Yes, provided employees who are not pregnant are also prohibited from combining a disability leave with unpaid leave of absence.

Equal Employment Opportunity Commission v. Elgin Teachers Association, 780 F.Supp. 1195 (N.D. Ill. 1991)
Maganuco v. Leyden Community High School District 212, 939 F.2d 440 (7th Cir. 1991)

17:210   What procedures may an employer use to determine whether a pregnant employee is able to work?

An employer may not single out pregnancy-related conditions for special procedures for determining an employee's ability to work. An employer may use any procedure used to determine the ability of any other employee to work and apply that procedure to pregnancy-related conditions.

If an employer requires employees to submit a doctor's statement before granting leave or paying sick leave benefits, the employer may require employees affected by pregnancy related conditions to submit such statements.

42 U.S.C. 2000e
Cleveland Board of Education v. LaFleur, 94 S.Ct. 791, 414 U.S. 632, 39 L.Ed.2d 52 (1974)

17:220   Must a school district include maternity coverage in a health insurance program which it provides for its employees?

An employer must include maternity coverage in any health insurance program which the employer provides for its employees.

42 U.S.C. 2000e(k)
29 C.F.R. 1604

17:230   Must a school board pay an employee who is called to active military service?

The answer depends upon the circumstances under which the employee will be absent from work for military service. If the employee is mobilized to active military duty as a result of an order of the President of the United States, the employer is obligated to continue the "same regular compensation" and health insurance or other benefits the employee was receiving at the time of the call-up minus the amount of the employee's base pay for military service for the duration of the active military service.

There is no statutory obligation to pay employees who are called to active service under other circumstances. Such employees may avail themselves of paid or unpaid leave provisions in a relevant collective bargaining agreement or policy. Wages and leave provisions applicable to persons called to active service are mandatory subjects of bargaining.

105 ILCS 5/10-20.7b

WORKERS' COMPENSATION

17:240   Do the Workers' Compensation Act and the Occupational Disease Act apply to school employees?

The Workers' Compensation Act and the Occupational Disease Act provide benefits, on a no-fault basis, to which school employees may be entitled in the event of job-related injury, illness or death. An employee may qualify for medical expense reimbursement, compensation for lost earnings, and/or permanent disability payments for work-related injury, illness or death.

820 ILCS 305/1(a)1 et seq.
820 ILCS 310/1 et seq.

17:250   Are worker compensation benefits available to workers paid by outside organizations, such as the PTA?

A school district may be treated as an employer for worker compensation purposes whether or not the school district pays direct compensation to a worker if the work performed by the worker is primarily for the benefit of the school district and a school district supervisor controls the employee and supervises his work.

Board of Education of the City of Chicago v. Industrial Commission, 57 Ill.2d 330, 312 N.E.2d 244 (1974)

17:260   Are volunteer workers eligible for worker compensation benefits?

No.

Board of Education of the City of Chicago v. Industrial Commission, 53 Ill.2d 167, 290 N.E.2d 247 (1972)

17:270   May an employee recover both sick leave and worker compensation benefits at the same time?

Absent a collectively bargained agreement to the contrary, an employee is entitled to an election of benefits—either sick leave at full pay (to the extent the employee has such benefits available) or worker compensation benefits (to the extent of eligibility).

Chicago Board of Education v. Chicago Teachers Union, 86 Ill.2d 469, 427 N.E.2d 1199, 56 Ill.Dec. 653 (1981)

UNEMPLOYMENT INSURANCE

17:280 Are school employees eligible for unemployment compensation benefits?

School employees may be eligible for unemployment compensation if the conditions of the former employee's severance are qualifying. Employees discharged for cause or who leave work voluntarily are usually ineligible for unemployment compensation. Persons otherwise eligible for unemployment compensation may be disqualified if they are not able, available for, and actively seeking work.

820 ILCS 405/100 et seq.

17:290 Is an employee eligible for unemployment compensation benefits after resignation?

An employee may be eligible for unemployment compensation after a voluntary resignation if the resignation was for "good cause."

Davis v. Board of Review of the Department of Labor, 125 Ill.App.3d 67, 465 N.E.2d 576, 80 Ill.Dec. 464 (1st Dist. 1984)

17:300 Are school employees eligible for unemployment compensation between school terms?

A person is ineligible for benefits, on the basis of wages for service in employment in an instructional, research, or principal administrative capacity performed for an educational institution, during a period between two successive academic years, or during a period of paid sabbatical leave provided for in the person's contract, if the person performed such service in the first of such academic years [or terms] and if there is a contract or a reasonable assurance the person will perform service in any capacity for any educational institution in the second of such academic years [or terms].

820 ILCS 405/612
Doran v. Department of Labor, 116 Ill.App.3d 471, 452 N.E.2d 118, 72 Ill.Dec. 186 (1st Dist. 1983)

17:310 May an employee receiving worker compensation benefits be concurrently eligible for unemployment compensation?

No.

820 ILCS 405/606

AMERICANS WITH DISABILITIES ACT

17:350 What is the Americans with Disabilities Act?

The Americans with Disabilities Act (ADA) is a federal law which prohibits discrimination against persons with disabilities. The ADA requires that the employer make reasonable accommodation for a qualified individual with a disability unless accommodation would cause an undue hardship.

42 U.S.C. 121111 et seq.

17:355 What is the meaning of "disability" under the ADA?

A disability is a physical or mental impairment that substantially limits one or more of the major life activities of an individual. The Act requires that there be a record of the impairment and requires that the individual be regarded as having such an impairment. The term "substantially limits" means significantly restricted in the ability to perform either a class of jobs or a broad range of jobs in various classes as compared to the average person having comparable training, skills and abilities. The inability to perform a single, particular job does not constitute a substantial limitation in the major life activity of working.

42 U.S.C. 12102(2)
29 C.F.R. 1630.2(j)(3)(i)
Bragdon v. Abbott, 118 S.Ct. 2196, 524 U.S.624, 141 L.Ed.2d 540 (1998)
Swain v. Hillsborough County School Board, 146 F.3d 855 (11th Cir. 1998)
Olson v. Dubuque Community School District, 137 F.3d 609 (8th Cir. 1998)

17:360 Who is a qualified individual with a disability under the ADA?

A qualified individual with a disability is an individual who, with or without reasonable accommodation, can perform the essential functions of the job. An employer who denies reasonable accommodation to a qualified person with a disability who, with reasonable accommodation, could perform the essential functions of the job has committed a discriminatory act under the ADA.

42 U.S.C. 12112(b)(5)

Harton v. City of Chicago Department of Public Works and Department of Transportation, 301 Ill.App.3d 378, 703 N.E.2d 493, 234 Ill.Dec. 632 (1st Dist. 1998) app.den. 182 Ill.2d 549, 707 N.E.2d 239, 236 Ill.Dec. 669

Nowak v. St. Rita High School, 142 F.3d 999 (7th Cir. 1998)

Brickers v. Cleveland Board of Education, 145 F.3d 846 (6th Cir. 1998)

17:362   Is a medical condition which can be treated (a mental disorder, for example) a disability within the meaning of the ADA?

The determination as to whether a particular condition constitutes a disability within the meaning of the Americans With Disabilities Act is based on the employee's unmedicated or untreated state.

Taylor v. Phoenixville School District, 174 F.3d 142 (3rd Cir. 1999)

17:370   What is "undue hardship" under the ADA?

The employer need not provide a reasonable accommodation if to do so would create significant difficulty or expense or if to do so would create a direct threat to health and safety.

42 U.S.C. 12111(3)
42 U.S.C. 12111(10)

Vande Zande v. Wisconsin Department of Administration, 44 F.3d 538 (7th Cir. 1995)

17:380   Is an employer required to reassign an employee to reasonably accommodate him?

In most cases, the employer is not required to reassign an employee to reasonably accommodate him. The employer's obligation is limited to the duty to find reasonable accommodation to allow the employee to perform the essential functions of the job in his current assignment.

Willis v. Conopco, Inc. 108 F.3d. 282 (11th Cir. 1997)

Hartlein v. Illinois Power Co., 151 Ill.2d 142, 601 N.E.2d 720, 176 Ill.Dec. 22 (1992)

Illinois Bell Telephone Company v. Human Rights Commission, 190 Ill.App.3d 1036, 547 N.E.2d 499, 138 Ill.Dec. 332 (1st Dist. 1989) app. den. 129 Ill.2d 563, 550 N.E.2d 556, 140 Ill.Dec. 671 (1990)

17:384 Does an employer assume liability if it tries to accommodate an employee and the employee is subsequently injured in the process of performing his accommodated job?

Probably not. The employer does not assume a duty of care to the employee by trying to accommodate the employee's disability. When an employee continues to work and does not follow his doctor's orders, the employer will not have Americans with Disabilities Act exposure if the employee is injured on the job. One Illinois appellate court has reasoned that to hold that an employer has a duty would deter employers from attempting to accommodate employees with temporary work restrictions.

Brown v. Walker Nursing Home, Inc. 307 Ill.App.3d 721, 718 N.E.2d 373, 240 L.Ed.2d 892 (4th Dist. 1999)

17:390 Must an employee provide the employer with information about his disability so that the employer can make reasonable accommodation decisions?

To trigger the employer duty to reasonably accommodate, the employer must have knowledge of the disability or the employee must inform the employer of the disability. Thereafter, the employer must make a reasonable effort to determine a reasonable accommodation. The employee and the employer are then required to work together to determine a reasonable accommodation.

42 U.S.C. 12112(b)(5)
56 Ill.Admin.Code 2500.408
Beck v. University of Wisconsin Board of Regents, 75 F.3d 1130 (7th Cir. 1996)

17:400 What is the effect of a rejection by an employee of an employer's offer of reasonable accommodation?

If an employee rejects an offer by his employer of a reasonable accommodation necessary to perform the essential functions of his position, the employee loses his protection under the ADA because he is no longer a qualified individual with a disability.

Kerno v. Sandoz Pharmaceuticals Corp., 93 C 20012 (N.D. Ill. 1994)

17:410 May a school board dismiss or otherwise discipline an employee who cannot perform his job because he has a disability?

An employee with a disability may be dismissed or disciplined if he cannot do the work his job requires and the employee cannot be otherwise accommodated by the employer. A plaintiff claiming discrimination must show that he is: an individual with a disability within the meaning of the law; is otherwise qualified for the job; has been excluded from programs solely because of the disability; and the school receives federal funds.

Byrne v. Board of Education, School of West Allis-West Milwaukee, 979 F.2d 560 (7th Cir. 1992)

School Board of Nassau County v. Arline, 107 S.Ct. 1123, 480 U.S. 273, 94 L.Ed.2d 307 (1987)

EMPLOYEE SPEECH

17:450 May an employee be dismissed for publicly criticizing school board decisions?

The First Amendment right to freedom of speech applies to employees. Employees may speak out publicly on issues of public concern without fear of reprisal.

Freedom of speech is not absolute, however. There are circumstances under which an employee may be disciplined by reason of something he has said. Only speech on matters of public concern is protected. Courts have tended to interpret public concern to mean broad social or policy issues.

Teachers who speak on issues which are self-serving risk discipline. The three steps the courts apply when deciding these cases are as follows:

1) Would the employee's speech be protected by the First Amendment were it spoken by someone who was not a public employee?

2) Is the speech a matter of public concern or a personal grievance?

3) Does the employer have a convincing reason to forbid the speech?

In mixed issue cases (when the speech contains some matters of public concern but is also self-serving), the courts will frequently balance the importance of the speech against the employer's interest in maintaining order and its interest in effective operation.

Colleen M. Wales v. Board of Education of Community Unit School District 300, et al., 120 F.3d 82 (7th Cir. 1997)

Khuans v. School District 110, 123 F.3d 1010 (7th Cir. 1997)

Dishnow v. School District of Rib Lake, 77 F.3d 194 (7th Cir. 1996)

Waters v. Churchill, 114 S.Ct. 1878, 511 U.S. 661, 128 L.Ed.2d 686 (1994)

Sanguigni v. Pittsburgh Board of Public Education, 968 F.2d 393 (3rd Cir. 1992)

Stroman v. Colleton County School District, 981 F.2d 152 (4th Cir. 1992)

Vukadinovich v. Board of School Trustees of the Michigan City Area Schools, 978 F.2d 403 (7th Cir. 1992)

Rankin v. McPherson, 107 S.Ct. 2891, 483 U.S. 378, 97 L.Ed.2d 315 (1987)

Knapp v. Whitaker, 757 F.2d 827 (7th Cir. 1985)

Connick v. Myers, 103 S.Ct. 1684, 461 U.S. 138, 75 L.Ed.2d 708 (1983)

Mt. Healthy City School District Board of Education v. Doyle, 97 S.Ct. 568, 429 U.S. 274, 50 L.Ed.2d 471 (1977) app. after rem. 670 F.2d 59 (6th Cir. 1982) (1977)

Brubaker v. Board of Education of School District No. 149, Cook County, 502 F.2d 973 (7th Cir. 1974)

Pickering v. Board of Education of Township High School District No. 205, Will County, Illinois, 88 S.Ct. 1731, 391 U.S. 563, 20 L.Ed.2d 811 (1968)

17:455   May a school board adopt an employee dress code?

Yes, although there are a number hazards in the drafting of a policy which a school board should be careful to avoid. First, the implementation of a dress code is a mandatory subject of bargaining and requires the school board to meet its bargaining obligations in the event of a demand to bargain by an employee bargaining agent.

Second, the drafting of a dress code which passes constitutional muster is tricky. The code cannot infringe on the rights of employees which are otherwise protected (sex, religion or speech discrimination, for example) without the demonstration of a compelling government interest (which is a very high standard and difficult to meet). A dress code must be reasonably related to the school's educational mission and must employ the least restrictive means to obtain the desired end. The purpose for the dress code should be clearly stated in the policy.

Mississippi Employment Security Commission v. McGlothin, 556 So.2d 324 (Miss. 1990)

East Hartford Education Association v. Board of Education, 562 F.2d 83 (Conn. 1977)

   Ball v. Kerrville Independent School District, 529 S.W.2d 792 (Tex. 1975)

   Blanchet v. Vermillion Parish School Board, 220 So.2d 534 (La. 1969)

17:460   May a school district discriminate against employees on the basis of political preference?

No. A school district may not discriminate as to promotion, recall, transfer or hiring based on party affiliation.

   Rutan v. Republican Party of Illinois, 110 S.Ct. 2729, 497 U.S. 62, 111 L.Ed.2d 52, reh. den. 111 S.Ct. 13, 111 L.Ed.2d 828 (1990)

   Branti v. Finkel, 100 S.Ct. 1287, 445 U.S. 507, 63 L.Ed.2d 574 (1980)

   Elrod v. Burns, 96 S.Ct. 2673, 427 U.S. 347, 49 L.Ed.2d 547 (1976)

17:470   May employees engage in political campaigning or other political activities?

Employees may engage in political campaigning or other political activities. The Local Governmental Employees Political Rights Act prevents school districts from inhibiting employees in the exercise of their political rights or "engaging in political activities while at work or on duty." Political rights are defined by the Act to include the right to petition, make public speeches, to campaign for or against political candidates, to speak out on questions of public policy, to distribute political literature, to make campaign contributions and to seek public office. The right to engage in political activities extends not only to conventional political causes, but also to political organizations which hold unpopular or controversial views.

A school board may regulate the espousal of political views in the classroom by establishment of curriculum.

   50 ILCS 135/1

   Castle v. Colonial School District, 933 F.Supp. 458 (E.D. Pa. 1996)

   McLaughlin v. Tilendis, 398 F.2d 287 (7th Cir. 1968)

17:475   May a school district limit what employees may keystroke, access or download into school owned computers?

This is a developing area of the law. It appears school districts may place reasonable limits on what employees may do with school owned computers and networks. Where collective bargaining agreements cover employees affected by a school district computer use policy, school districts should take care that all bargaining obligations are considered and met.

Urofsky v. Gilmore, 167 F.3d 191 (4th Cir 1999)

17:480   May a school board discipline a teacher for inappropriate classroom speech?

The First Amendment rights of teachers to free speech are limited while they are in the classroom because the classroom is not a public forum and public school employers may limit classroom speech to promote educational goals. A school board may make reasonable rules regarding appropriate speech in the classroom and may discipline those who break those rules.

Teachers have a right to notice as to what speech is prohibited, but the school need not expressly prohibit every imaginable inappropriate conduct by teachers. The relevant inquiry is whether, given school policies, rules and regulations and other communication from the school to the teacher, it was reasonable to expect the teacher would know the conduct was prohibited.

Lacks v. Ferguson-Florissant Reorganized School District, R-2, 147 F.3d 718 (8th Cir. 1998) sugg. for reh. den. 154 F.3d 904, cert. den. 119 S.Ct. 1158, __ U.S.__, 143 L.Ed.2d 233

Ward v. Hickey, 996 F.2d 448 (1st Cir. 1993)

Miles v. Denver Public Schools, 944 F.2d 773 (10th Cir. 1991)

Krizek v. Board of Education, 713 F.Supp. 1131 (N.D. Ill. 1989)

Hazelwood v. Kuhlmeier, 108 S.Ct. 562, 484 U.S. 260, 98 L.Ed.2d 592 (1988), on rem. 840 F.2d 596 (8th Cir. 1988)

Zykan v. Warsaw Community School Corporation, 631 F.2d 1300 (7th Cir. 1980)

17:482   May a school board discipline a teacher for the teacher's selection of controversial instructional material?

A school board may discipline a teacher for the teacher's failure to follow clear and established curriculum. In this context a school board could, for example, ban classroom profanity of any kind or limit the exposure of students to graphic sex or violence in movies shown in class. A school board should be careful in considering discipline that the speech rights of the teacher have been considered and that the school district has legitimate pedagogical concerns.

> *Boring v. Buncombe County Board of Education,* 98 F.3d 1474 (4th Cir. 1998)
> *Lacks v. Ferguson-Florissant Reorganized School District,* R-2, 147 F.3d 718 (8th Cir. 1998) sugg. for reh. den. 154 F.3d 904, cert. den. 119 S.Ct. 1158, _ U.S._, 143 L.Ed.2d 233

SEXUAL HARASSMENT

17:500   What is sexual harassment?

Sexual harassment is any unwelcome sexual advances or requests for sexual favors or any conduct of a sexual nature when (1) submission to such conduct is made either explicitly or implicitly a term or condition of an individual's employment, (2) submission to or rejection of such conduct by an individual is used as the basis for employment decisions affecting such individual, or (3) such conduct has the purpose or effect of substantially interfering with an individual's work performance or creating an intimidating, hostile or offensive working environment.

> 42 U.S.C. 2000e et seq.
> 29 C.F.R. 1604.11
> 775 ILCS 5/1-101 et seq.
> *Henson v. City of Dundee,* 682 F.2d 897 (11th Cir. 1982)
> *Bundy v. Jackson,* 641 F.2d 934 (D.C. Cir. 1981)
> *Tomkins v. Public Service Electric and Gas Company,* 568 F.2d 1044 (3rd Cir. 1977)

17:504   May a plaintiff recover under title VII alleging agency principles?

Unlike title IX, which governs employee-student harassment, title VII, which governs employer-employee cases, permits causes of action premised on principles of agency (the school is responsible for its employee's actions) or constructive notice (the school was responsible because it knew or should have known what its employee was doing and failed to stop it). A school is liable for the actions of its employees when the employer was negligent or reckless, or when the employee purported to speak or act on behalf of the employer and there was reliance on the authority, or when the employee was aided in accomplishing the act by the existence of his agency relationship with the employer.

42 U.S.C. 2000e(b)
Burlington Industries, Inc. v. Kimberly B. Ellerth, 118 S.Ct. 2257, 524 U.S. 742, 141 L.Ed.2d 633 (1998)
 Faragher v. City of Boca Raton, 118 S.Ct. 2275, 524 U.S. 775, 141 L.Ed.2d 662 (1998) on rem. 166 F.3d 1152
 Gebser et al. v. Lago Vista Independent School District, 118 S.Ct.1989, 524 U.S. 274, 141 L.Ed.2d 277 (1998)
 Meritor Savings Bank v. Vinson, 106 S.Ct. 2399, 477 U.S. 57, 91 L.Ed.2d 49 (1986) on rem. *Vinson v. Taylor* 801 F.2d 1436 (D.C. Cir. 1986)

17:505   What defense does an employer have to a charge of agency-based sexual harassment?

To assert a defense, the employer must be able to demonstrate that it exercised reasonable care to prevent and correct promptly any sexually harassing behavior and that the employee unreasonably failed to take advantage of any preventive or corrective opportunities provided by the employer or to avoid harm otherwise. The defense is not available when a supervisor's harassment culminates in a tangible employment action such as discharge, demotion, or undesirable reassignment.

Faragher v. City of Boca Raton, 118 S.Ct. 2275, 524 U.S. 775, 141 L.Ed.2d 662 (1998) on rem. 166 F.3d 1152

17:510   What is a hostile environment for purposes of establishing sexual harassment?

A hostile environment exists when the workplace is permeated with discriminatory behavior that is sufficiently severe or pervasive to create an environment a reasonable person would find hostile or abusive. The courts may also consider the victim's subjective perception of abusiveness. Whether an environment is abusive is determined by examination of all the circumstances which includes the frequency of the conduct, its severity, whether it is physically threatening or humiliating, and whether it unreasonably interferes with work performance.

Butler v. Ysleta Independent School District, 161 F.3d 263 (5th Cir. 1998
Harris v. Forklift Systems, Inc., 114 S.Ct. 367, 510 U.S. 17, 126 L.Ed.2d 295 (1993)
Meritor Savings Bank v. Vinson, 106 S.Ct. 2399, 477 U.S. 57, 91 L.Ed.2d 49 (1986) on rem. *Vinson v. Taylor* 801 F.2d 1436 (D.C. Cir. 1986)

17:520 Must a person prove injury to prove sexual harassment?

To prove hostile environment, the offensive conduct need not seriously affect the person psychologically, nor need the conduct lead to injury.

Harris v. Forklift Systems, Inc., 114 S.Ct. 367, 510 U.S. 17, 126 L.Ed.2d 295 (1993)

17:530 May a sexual harassment victim bring a tort claim against an employer in court?

Tort remedies (bringing a lawsuit for damages) are probably not available unless the victim first exhausts remedies available under the Illinois Human Rights Act.

Geise v. Phoenix Co. of Chicago, 159 Ill 2d 507, 039 N.E.2d 1273, 203 Ill.Dec. 454 (1994)

17:570 May an employer discipline or dismiss an employee because of the employee's sexual orientation?

Title VII of the Civil Rights Act of 1964 prohibits an employer from discriminating against an individual because of the person's sex with respect to his compensation, terms conditions or privileges of employment. Nothing in title VII bars a claim of discrimination because of sex merely because the plaintiff and defendant are of the same sex. The successful title VII plaintiff must show that members of one sex are exposed to disadvantageous terms or conditions of employment to which members of the other sex are not exposed and that the conduct at issue was not merely tinged with offensive sexual connotations, but actually constituted discrimination because of sex. The behavior complained of must be so objectively offensive as to alter the conditions of the victim's employment. The objective severity of the harassment is judged from the perspective of a reasonable person in plaintiff's position considering all the circumstances.

42 U.S.C. 200e-2(a)(1)

Oncale v. Sundowner Offshore Services, Incorporated, et al., 83 F.3d 118 (5th Cir. 1995) reh. and sugg. for reh. den. 95 F.3d 56, cert. granted 117 S.Ct. 2430, 520 U.S. 1263, 138 L.Ed.2d 192, rev. 118 S.Ct. 998, 523 U.S.75, 140 L.Ed.2d 201, on rem. 140 F.3d 595 (1998)

Romer v. Evans, 116 S.Ct.1620, 517 U.S. 620, 134 L.Ed.2d 855 (1996)

17:571   May a school district restrict a teacher's assignment because of the teacher's sexual orientation?

No. To remove a teacher or refuse to assign a teacher to a duty because the teacher is gay or lesbian violates the teacher's right to equal protection. Moreover, a school district may not limit the speech of gay or lesbian teachers (even with respect to their sexual orientation) absent a showing of a compelling state interest and then only when the restriction is narrowly tailored to meet the desired end.

Weaver v. Nebo School District, 29 F.Supp. 1279 (D. Utah 1998)

EMPLOYMENT RIGHTS AND EMPLOYEE DISCIPLINE

17:600   May a school board policy give employees a right to continuing employment or create employee enforceable property rights?

A school board policy can give rise to constitutionally protected property rights. If, for example, the school board adopts a clearly worded "just cause" dismissal policy which contains a promise, and if the school board disseminates that policy to employees, and if the employees implicitly accept the policy, the policy is enforceable by the employee against the school district as if the policy were a contract between the employee and employer.

Hohmeier v. Leyden Community High Schools District 212, 954 F.2d 461 (7th Cir. 1992)

Mitchell v. Jewel Food Stores, 142 Ill.2d 152, 568 N.E.2d 827, 136 Ill.Dec. 813 (1990)

Fumarolo v. Chicago Board of Education, 142 Ill.2d 54, 566 N.E.2d 1283, 153 Ill.Dec. 177 (1990)

Duldulao v. St. Mary of Nazareth Hospital Center, 115 Ill.2d 482, 505 N.E.2d 314, 106 Ill.Dec. 8 (1986)

17:610   Can a school board's policies create contracts which may be relied upon by employees and enforced against the school board?

A school board's rules, regulations or policies when reasonably relied upon by employees may bind the school board. To rise to the level of a contract, the policy, rule or regulation must contain a promise which is clear enough for an employee to believe it is an offer. The offer must be disseminated to the employee so the employee is aware of its contents and believes it is an offer. And the employee must accept the offer by beginning or continuing to work after learning of the offer.

Doyle v. Holy Cross Hospital, 186 Ill.2d 104, 708 N.E.2d 1140, 237 Ill.Dec. 100 (1999)

Condon v. American Telephone and Telegraph Company, Inc., 210 Ill.App.3d 701, 569 N.E.2d 518, 155 Ill.Dec. 337 (2nd Dist 1991) app. den. 141 Ill.2d 537, 580 N.E.2d 110, 162 Ill.Dec. 484 (1992)

Duldulao v. Saint Mary of Nazareth Hospital Center, 115 Ill.2d 482, 505 N.E.2d 314, 106 Ill.Dec. 8 (1987)

17:620 May a school district use age as a qualification for employment or promotion?

Federal law prohibits age-related discrimination in the hiring, promotion, and other conditions of employment for employees age 40 and over. A school board may attach age requirements to a job if it can show age is a bona fide occupational qualification.

29 U.S.C. 621 et seq.
29 C.F.R. 1625 et seq.
775 ILCS 5/1-101 et seq.

17:630 May a school board adopt a mandatory employee retirement policy for employees who reach a specified age?

No. A mandatory retirement policy for any class of employees without demonstration of bona fide occupational qualification violates the federal Age Discrimination Act.

29 U.S.C. 623(f)(2)
29 C.F.R. 1625 et seq.
775 ILCS 5/1-101 et seq.

17:635 What is required to obtain a release to prevent an age discrimination claim?

If an employer attempts to resolve an age discrimination claim in return for a release from liability, the Older Workers Benefit Protection Act requires the employer give the employee

a reasonable amount of time in which to consider his options
and seven days after the signing of a release to reconsider.

29 U.S.C. 626 (f)(1)
Oubre v. Entergy Operations, Inc. 118 S.Ct. 838, 522 U.S. 422, 139
L.Ed.2d 849 (1998) on rm. 136 F.3d 1342

17:640   What control may a school board exercise with respect to employee "moonlighting?"

Unless a school board can demonstrate the employee's second job is negatively affecting his performance at school, the
school board may not regulate or restrict the employee's outside
activities.

*Cook County College Teachers Union Local 1600 IFT, AFT, AFL-CIO v.
Board of Trustees Community College District No. 505, Cook County,* 134
Ill.App.3d 489, 481 N.E.2d 40, 89 Ill.Dec. 688 (1st Dist. 1985)
Kaufmann v. Board of Trustees Community Consolidated District 508, 522
F.Supp. 90 (N.D. Ill. 1981)
Meredith v. Board of Education of Community Unit School District No. 7,
7 Ill.App.2d 477, 130 N.E.2d 5 (3rd Dist. 1955)
Yuhas v. Libbey-Owens-Ford Company, 562 F.2d 496 (7th Cir. 1976) cert.
den. 98 S.Ct. 1510, 435 U.S. 934, 55 L.Ed.2d 531 (1978)

17:650   Can an employer discharge, refuse to hire, or otherwise discriminate against a woman because she has had or is contemplating having an abortion?

No.

42 U.S.C. 2000e et seq.

17:660   Do statutes require report of attacks on school personnel?

Upon receipt of a written complaint from any school personnel, a superintendent must report any incident of battery committed against a teacher, teacher personnel, or administrative
personnel to local law enforcement authorities immediately
after the occurrence of the attack and to the Department of
State Police's Illinois Uniform Crime Reporting Program no
later than three days after the occurrence of the attack.

105 ILCS 5/10-21.7

17:670   May a school district require its employees to administer medication to students?

Neither teachers nor other non-administrative school employees, except certified school nurses, can be required to administer medication to students. This prohibition includes uncertified school nurses. Volunteers may be sought—and certified school nurses may be required—to administer medication, but potential bargaining obligations should be considered in each case.

105 ILCS 5/10-22.21b

17:672   May a nurse refuse to administer prescribed medication if he believes the medication would be harmful to the child?

If the school district has a policy which allows the nurse to refuse to administer medication in excess of *Physician's Desk Reference* (PDR) recommendations, the nurse may refuse to administer medication which violates the terms of the policy.

Davis v. Francis Howell School District, 104 F.3d 204 (8th Cir. 1998)

17:680   May a school board dismiss an employee who has been charged with a felony?

Persons charged with crimes are presumed to be innocent until proven guilty. Investigation, arrest, and/or indictment do not establish guilt. In order to dismiss a contractual employee for commission of a crime, the employer must provide the employee with requisite procedural and substantive due process. The employer has the burden of proving the crime was committed and must show that the crime had a connection to the employee's employment sufficient to warrant dismissal.

McBroom v. Board of Education District No. 205, 144 Ill.App.3d 463, 494 N.E.2d 1191, 98 Ill.Dec. 864 (2nd Dist. 1986)

17:685   Must an employee charged with a felony be provided a pre-suspension hearing before he is suspended without pay?

When a school board must act quickly or when it is impractical to provide pre-deprivation due process, post-deprivation due process is sufficient. If an important government interest is present and that interest is accompanied by a substantial assurance that the deprivation is not baseless or unwarranted, in limited cases demanding prompt action there is justification for postponing the opportunity to be heard until after the initial deprivation.

Gilbert v. Homar, 117 S.Ct. 1807, 520 U.S. 924, 138 L.Ed.2d 120 (1997) on rem. 149 F.3d 1164

17:690   May a school board dismiss an employee who has been convicted of a crime?

The employer must demonstrate the crime had a connection to the employee's employment and was sufficiently serious to warrant dismissal. The employer must provide the employee with requisite substantive and procedural due process prior to dismissal.

Reinhardt v. Board of Education of Alton Community Unit School District No. 11, Madison and Jersey Counties, 19 Ill.App.3d 481, 311N.E.2d 710 (5th Dist. 1974) vac. on other grounds 61 Ill.2d 101, 329 N.E.2d 218

17:700   May a school district discipline or dismiss an employee for actions for which the employee was criminally charged but acquitted?

The same set of facts may support both a criminal acquittal and defensible school discipline. The charges underlying a criminal case and those inherent in a disciplinary case, the elements of each case, and the burdens of proof for each are generally different.

Hall v. Board of Education of the City of Chicago, 227 Ill.App.3d 560, 592 N.E.2d 245, 169 Ill.Dec. 758 (1st Dist. 1992)

17:710   Are "last chance agreements" permissible?

In a last chance agreement, the employer agrees to withdraw the threat of discipline in exchange for the employee's agreement to refrain from future infractions and to give up the right to review in the event of future discipline, including the right to arbitration under a collectively bargained grievance procedure.

The presumption in favor of arbitrability is overcome only if the last chance agreement expressly excludes a particular grievance from arbitration. The last chance agreement must expressly exclude grievances based on the employee's guilt or innocence of the subsequent infraction and must expressly exclude grievances on the nature of the discipline to be effective to bar last chance grievances.

United Steelworkers of America v. Lukens Steel Co., 969 F.2d 1468 (3rd Cir. 1992)

17:720 May an employee be discharged for insubordination?

Insubordination can be grounds for dismissal of an employee. Insubordination is a willful or intentional disregard of the lawful and reasonable rules or instructions of the employer. To determine whether a rule is reasonable, the courts will consider the rule's relationship to workplace efficiency, safety or discipline, its clarity or precision and the extent to which it infringes upon an employee's legally protected behavior. There must be some connection between the rule and employment, and a rule is not reasonable unless it provides guidelines that are or should be known by the employee.

Warnings or disciplinary measures contemplated for violations of the rule must be both explicit and specific to the conduct for which an employee would be reprimanded.

Board of Education of Round Lake Area Schools, Community Unit School District No. 116 v. The State Board of Education, John F. Rozner and Barbara Cohn, 292 Ill.App.3d 101, 685 N.E.2d 412, 226 Ill.Dec.309 (2nd Dist. 1997)

Caterpillar, Inc. v. Fehrenbacher, 286 Ill.App.3d 614, 676 N.E.2d 710, 221 Ill.Dec. 907 (2nd Dist. 1997)

17:730 May schools conduct suspicionless searches of school employees?

The Fourth Amendment to the Constitution prohibits unreasonable searches and seizures.

The Sixth Circuit federal court of appeals has found that the need to assure drug-free teachers outweighs the teachers' privacy expectations because teachers serve in safety sensitive positions. The court permitted urinalysis drug testing for certain employees who were candidates for and attempting to transfer to a select group of positions. Random testing was not involved. The court's decision was narrow and any school district contemplating such searches should limit the tests to safety sensitive positions. Such positions might include administrators, teachers, aides, secretaries and bus drivers.

The Fifth Circuit has approved a policy requiring suspicionless random testing of custodial personnel.

A school district contemplating an employee search policy should consider bargaining implications and the possibility that while another federal appeals court may have approved such searches, the Seventh Circuit (which has jurisdiction over Illinois school districts) has not offered an opinion on the matter and may have a contrary view.

Knox County Education Association v. Knox County Board of Education, 158 F.3d 361 (6th Cir. 1998), cert. den. 120 S.Ct. 46, __ U.S.__, __ L.Ed.2d__ (1999)

Aubrey v. School Board of Lafayette Parish, 92 F.3d 316 (5th Cir. 1998) app. after rem. 148 F.3d 559

17:740   Is an employee entitled to union representation of his choosing during an employer interview when the employer is considering disciplining the employee or investigating an incident which might reasonably lead to discipline of the employee?

An employee is entitled to knowledgeable representation, not necessarily the representation of his choosing. A representative with basic factual familiarity with the matter under investigation will suffice; the employer need not delay proceedings to wait for a union representative with training or prior experience representing employees in disciplinary matters. Unless a collective bargaining agreement provides otherwise, the employee must request representation. An employee is not entitled to Miranda-like warnings. Generally, it is in the best interest of the employer to provide representation for the employee, whether or not the employee asks for it.

Hubbard v. Illinois State Labor Relations Board and Village of Streamwood, 293 Ill.App.3d 1122, 78 N.E.2d 1083, 241 Ill.Dec. 229 (1st Dist. 1997)

17:750   Are school employees subject to the State Gift Ban Act?

Yes.   All school employees, both certificated and non-certificated, are subject to the Gift Ban Act.

5 ILCS 425/1 et seq.

18: TEACHER DISMISSAL FOR CAUSE

DISMISSAL OF THE PROBATIONARY TEACHER

18:10   What steps must be taken when a school district intends not to renew the contract of a first, second or third year probationary teacher?

To dismiss a teacher first employed by the school district on or after January 1, 1998 at the end of the first, second or third year of probationary employment, the school district must (a) fully comply with its evaluation plan and collectively bargained evaluation procedure, if applicable, and (b) give written notice of dismissal by certified mail, return receipt requested. The notice must be received by the teacher at least 45 days before the end of the school term. If a school board fails to give such notice, the teacher is re-employed for the following school term.

Often collective bargaining agreements, policies and/or evaluation plans have different notice requirements from that provided in the statute. The employer should be careful to meet all relevant notice requirements.

105 ILCS 5/24-11

18:20   What steps must be taken when a school district intends not to renew the contract of a fourth year probationary teacher?

To dismiss a fourth year probationary teacher at the end of a school term, the school district must have fully complied with its evaluation plan and collectively bargained evaluation procedure, if applicable.

No later than 45 days before the end of the final probationary school term, the fourth year probationary teacher must receive written notice of dismissal from the school board. Often collective bargaining agreements, policies and/or evaluation plans have different notice requirements from that provided in the statute. The employer should be careful to meet all relevant notice requirements. The notice must state the specific reason for the dismissal, and it must be delivered by certified mail, return receipt requested. If a school board fails to give such notice, the teacher is re-employed for the following school term.

105 ILCS 5/24-11

People ex rel. Head v. Board of Education of Thornton Fractional South High School District No. 215, 95 Ill.App.3d 78, 419 N.E.2d 505, 50 Ill.Dec. 397 (1st Dist. 1981)

Wade v. Granite City Community Unit School District No. 9, Madison County, 71 Ill.App.2d 34, 218 N.E.2d 19 (5th Dist. 1966)

18:25   May a non-tenured teacher file a grievance alleging violation of a "just cause" provision in the collective bargaining agreement to challenge his dismissal?

A "just cause" provision is one which requires that an employee's discipline be "fair" or for "just cause." When a provision of a collective bargaining agreement is in violation of, inconsistent with or in conflict with an Illinois statute it may not be "implemented in an arbitration award." A just cause provision in a collective bargaining agreement is inconsistent with and conflicts with the Illinois statutes which govern the dismissal of tenured and non-tenured teachers.

105 ILCS 5/10-22.4
105 ILCS 5/24-11
115 ILCS 5/10(b)

Board of Education of Rockford School District No. 205, v. The Illinois Educational Labor Relations Board, 165 Ill.2d 80, 649 N.E.2d 369, 208 Ill.Dec. 313 (1995)

Midwest Central Education Association v. Illinois Educational Labor Relations Board, et al., 277 Ill.App.3d 440, 660 N.E.2d 151, 213 Ill.Dec. 984 (1st Dist. 1995)

18:30   Must a notice to remedy deficiencies be issued or a remediation plan be instituted before a probationary employee is dismissed?

The remediation plan requirements of Section 24A of the School Code apply to tenured employees only. If a school board seeks to dismiss a probationary employee at the end of a school term, no notice to remedy is necessary unless otherwise required by school board policy or as collectively bargained.

A notice to remedy may be necessary under certain circumstances if dismissal is sought during a school term.

105 ILCS 5/24-11
105 ILCS 5/24A-1 et seq.

18:40 May a school board dismiss a non-tenured (probationary) teacher during a school term?

A school board may dismiss a non-tenured teacher during the school year. However, such teachers are contractual employees of the school district and have a "property right" to employment for the term of their contracts. To dismiss such an employee the school board has the burden to prove breach of contract and must accord the employee substantive and procedural due process.

Board of Regents of State Colleges v Roth, 92 S.Ct. 2701, 408 U.S. 564, 33 L.Ed.2d 548 (1972)

18:50 Is a probationary teacher entitled to a hearing on the reasons for his dismissal if his contract is not being renewed for the following year?

The School Code does not require a hearing for a probationary teacher to examine the reasons for dismissal. When a school board has fully complied with statutory and local contract requirements, rules and regulations, no hearing is required unless the reasons for the dismissal raise constitutional issues with respect to the teacher's dismissal.

Howard v. Board of Education of Freeport School District No. 145, 160 Ill.App.3d 309, 513 N.E.2d 545, 112 Ill.Dec. 131 (2nd Dist. 1987)

Newborn v. Morrison, 440 F.Supp. 623 (N.D. Ill. 1977)

Mt. Healthy City School District Board of Education v. Doyle, 97 S.Ct. 568, 429 U.S. 274, 50 L.Ed.2d 471 (1977) app. after rem. 670 F.2d 59 (6th Cir. 1982)

Bishop v. Wood, 96 S.Ct. 2074, 426 U.S. 341, 48 L.Ed.2d 864 (1976)

Board of Regents of State Colleges v. Roth, 92 S.Ct. 2701, 408 U.S. 564, 33 L.Ed.2d 548 (1972)

18:60   Under what circumstances does a school board infringe on a teacher's constitutionally protected liberty interests so as to give rise to due process?

A teacher's constitutionally protected liberty interests may be infringed when (a) the cause for dismissal does serious damage to the person's standing and associations in the community, or (b) the cause for dismissal creates a stigma or inability to take advantage of future employment opportunities.

If a school board infringes on a teacher's constitutionally protected liberty interests in dismissal proceedings, the teacher will be entitled to certain due process guarantees including, upon demand by the teacher, a name-clearing hearing.

Strasburger v. Board of Education Hardin County Community Unit School District No. 1, et al., 143 F.3d 351 (7th Cir. 1998)

Austin v. Board of Education of Georgetown Community Unit School District No. 3 of Vermilion County, Illinois, 562 F.2d 446 (7th Cir. 1977)

Bishop v. Wood, 96 S.Ct. 2074, 426 U.S. 341, 48 L.Ed.2d 864 (1976)

Miller v. School District No. 167, Cook County, Illinois, 354 F.Supp. 922 (N.D. Ill. 1973), aff'd. on other grounds 495 F.2d 658, reh. den. 500 F.2d 711 (7th Cir. 1974)

Hostrop v. Board of Junior College District 515, Cook and Will Counties and State of Illinois, 471 F.2d 488 (7th Cir. 1972) cert. den. 93 S.Ct. 2150, 411 U.S. 967, 36 L.Ed.2d 688 (1973) on rem. 399 F.Supp. 609, aff'd. in part, rev. in part 523 F.2d 569, cert. den. 96 S.Ct. 1748, 425 U.S. 963, 48 L.Ed.2d 208 (1974)

Board of Regents of State Colleges v. Roth, 92 S.Ct. 2701, 408 U.S. 564, 33 L.Ed.2d 548 (1972)

Perry v. Sindermann, 92 S.Ct. 2694, 408 U.S. 593, 33 L.Ed.2d 570 (1972)

DISMISSAL OF THE TENURED TEACHER

18:70   May a tenured teacher be fired?

A tenured teacher may be dismissed for commission of a dismissible offense as defined by statute, provided however the school board first must comply with the procedural requirements of its collective bargaining agreement and must provide the requisite statutory substantive and procedural due process.

105 ILCS 5/10-22.4
105 ILCS 5/24-12

Board of Trustees of Community College District No. 508 v. Cook County College Teachers Union Local 1600, AFT, IFT, AFL-CIO, 167 Ill.App.3d 998, 522 N.E.2d 93, 118 Ill.Dec. 638 (1st Dist. 1987)

Chicago Board of Education v. Payne, 102 Ill.App.3d 741, 430 N.E.2d 310, 58 Ill.Dec. 368 (1st Dist. 1981)

Lowe v. Board of Education of City of Chicago, 76 Ill.App.3d 348, 395 N.E.2d 59, 32 Ill.Dec. 122 (1st Dist. 1979)

Fender v. School District No. 25, Arlington Heights, Cook County, 37 Ill.App.3d 736, 347 N.E.2d 270 (1st Dist. 1976)

Gould v. Board of Education of Ashley Community Consolidated School District No. 15 of Washington County, 32 Ill.App.3d 808, 336 N.E.2d 69 (5th Dist. 1975)

18:72   What is the likelihood of the repeal of the tenure law?

In addition to being politically improbable, a repeal of the tenure law would probably affect only teachers who had not yet acquired tenure and would not serve to remove tenure protections from teachers who already have them. The practical effect would be that unions would attempt to bargain the equivalent of tenure contract by contract.

Indiana ex rel. Anderson v. Brant, 58 S.Ct. 443, 303 U.S. 95, 82 L.Ed. 685 (1938)

18:80   How many school board votes are required to dismiss a tenured teacher?

A motion to dismiss a tenured teacher for cause requires a majority vote of all the members of the school board to carry.

105 ILCS 5/24-12

18:90   To what kind of notice of causes for dismissal is a tenured teacher entitled?

A tenured teacher is entitled to a dismissal notice, or bill of particulars, which states both the cause or causes for the dismissal and the charge or charges supporting the dismissal action. The notice must be sufficiently precise in order that the teacher is fully informed of the causes and charges and is able to prepare a defense.

105 ILCS 5/10-22.4
105 ILCS 5/24-12

Carrao v. Board of Education, City of Chicago, 46 Ill.App.3d 33, 360 N.E.2d 536, 4 Ill.Dec. 600 (1st Dist. 1977)

Reinhardt v. Board of Education of Alton Community Unit School District No. 11, 61 Ill.2d 101, 329 N.E.2d 218 (1975)

Wade v. Granite City Community Unit School District No. 9, Madison County, 71 Ill.App.2d 34, 218 N.E.2d 19 (5th Dist. 1966)

Donahoo v. Board of Education of School District No. 303 Moultrie County, 346 Ill.App. 241, 104 N.E.2d 833 (3rd Dist. 1952), rev. 413 Ill. 422, 109 N.E.2d 787 (1952)

CAUSES FOR DISMISSAL

18:100   What causes will support the dismissal of a tenured teacher?

A school board may dismiss a tenured teacher for incompetency, cruelty, negligence, immorality, or other sufficient cause. A teacher may also be dismissed for failure to complete a remediation plan with a "satisfactory" or better rating, and may be dismissed whenever, in the school board's opinion, he is not qualified to teach or whenever the interests of the schools require it.

Temporary mental or physical incapacity to perform teaching duties, as found by a medical examination, is not a cause for dismissal.

To support a tenured teacher dismissal, a school board must prove a serious infraction or series of infractions; must comply with all of its own internal rules, regulations and policies regarding dismissal, including relevant contract provisions and its evaluation plan; must comply with all relevant statutory requirements; and must provide the teacher with requisite substantive and procedural due process.

105 ILCS 5/10-22.4
105 ILCS 5/24-12
Wells v. Board of Education of Community Consolidated School District No. 64, Cook County, 85 Ill.App.2d 312, 230 N.E.2d 6 (1st Dist. 1967)

18:110   What is required to dismiss a tenured teacher for incompetency?

Incompetency is a remediable offense. A school board is required to attempt to cure incompetency by evaluation and the adoption of a remediation plan prior to dismissal.

105 ILCS 5/10-22.4
105 ILCS 5/24-12
105 ILCS 5/24A-1 et seq.

18:120   What is cruelty?

Cruelty is the intentional or malicious infliction of physical or mental suffering upon other persons. Cruelty as a cause of tenured teacher dismissal may be either remediable or irremediable depending upon its seriousness.

Lowe v. Board of Education, City of Chicago, 76 Ill.App.3d 148, 395 N.E.2d 59, 32 Ill.Dec. 112 (1st Dist. 1979).

Welch v. Board of Education of Bement Community Unit School District No. 5 of Piatt County, 45 Ill.App.3d 35, 358 N.E.2d 354, 3 Ill.Dec. 679 (4th Dist. 1977)

Rolando v. School Directors of District No. 125, 44 Ill.App.3d 658, 358 N.E.2d 945, 3 Ill.Dec. 402 (3rd Dist. 1976)

18:130   What is negligence?

Negligence is failing to do something a reasonable person would ordinarily do under a particular set of circumstances or doing something that a reasonable and prudent person would ordinarily not do under a given set of circumstances and conditions. Negligence as a cause for dismissal of a tenured teacher may be either remediable or irremediable depending on the circumstances and degree of negligence.

105 ILCS 5/10-22.4
105 ILCS 5/24-12
Board of Education of Niles Township High School District No. 219 Cook County v. Epstein, 72 Ill.App.3d 723, 391 N.E.2d 114, 28 Ill.Dec. 915 (1st Dist. 1979)

18:140   What is immorality?

Immorality is behavior which is inimical to the public welfare according to the standards of society. A dismissal for immorality will not be sustained unless the school board can prove the conduct of the teacher has had some serious negative impact on the teacher's relationship with students, effectiveness in the classroom, relationship with teacher's superiors, or the operation of a school district. Dismissals for immorality often raise constitutional questions.

105 ILCS 5/10-22.4
105 ILCS 5/24-12
Board of Education of Tonica Community Unit School District No. 360, LaSalle County v. Sickley, 133 Ill.App.3d 921, 479 N.E.2d 1142, 89 Ill.Dec. 136 (3rd Dist. 1985)
Reinhardt v. Board of Education of Alton Community Unit School District No. 11, 61 Ill.2d 101, 329 N.E.2d 218 (1975)
Lombardo v. Board of Education School District No. 27, Cook County, 100 Ill.App.2d 108, 241 N.E.2d 495 (1st Dist. 1968)

18:150   What is insubordination?

Insubordination is willful disregard of implied or specific legitimate directives or an attitude so defiant as to be equivalent. Insubordination is usually a remediable offense and requires legally sufficient warning prior to dismissal.

Christopherson v. Spring Valley Elementary School District, 90 Ill.App.3d 460, 413 N.E.2d 199, 45 Ill.Dec. 866 (3rd Dist. 1980)

Allione v. Board of Education, South Fork Community High School District No. 310, Christian County, 29 Ill.App.2d 261, 173 N.E.2d 13 (3rd Dist. 1961)

Beilan v. Board of Public Education of Philadelphia, 78 S.Ct. 1317, 357 U.S. 399, 2 L.Ed.2d 1414 (1958)

18:160   May a tenured teacher be dismissed for conduct which occurs away from school and during non-school hours?

To dismiss a tenured teacher for behavior which occurs away from school and during non-school hours, the school board must be able to demonstrate that the conduct had a sufficiently serious negative impact on a legitimate school related objective to warrant dismissal of the teacher.

A teacher has constitutional rights which protect the teacher from school board interference in private non-school related conduct. The private deportment of a teacher is properly of concern to a school board only when the behavior of the teacher interferes with the effectiveness of the teacher as a teacher in the school district or with the overall operation of the school district.

Carrao v. Board of Education, City of Chicago, 46 Ill.App.3d 33, 360 N.E.2d 536, 4 Ill.Dec. 600 (1st Dist. 1977)

Reinhardt v. Board of Education of Alton Community Unit School District No. 11, 61 Ill.2d 101, 329 N.E.2d 218 (1975)

18:170   May a school board dismiss a tenured teacher for conduct which occurred during the teacher's supervision of extracurricular activities?

The teacher may be dismissed if the conduct is sufficiently serious to support dismissal and is either irremediable or repeated after legally sufficient warning. Dismissal requires full procedural compliance with applicable statutes and collectively bargained provisions.

105 ILCS 5/10-22.4

18:175 May a tenured teacher be dismissed for conduct which prevents him from functioning as a role model to students?

A teacher's actions are subject to much greater scrutiny than those of the average person. A tenured teacher may be dismissed without a prior warning when it can be shown that the teacher's conduct:

1) has significantly harmed his reputation and credibility, and

2) has sufficiently damaged the respect and esteem in which the teacher is held by his co-workers and other members of the school community, and

3) when the teacher can no longer serve as a credible role model for students, and

4) when the conduct giving rise to the dismissal could not have been corrected had the teacher been warned.

McCullough v. Illinois State Board of Education, 204 Ill.App.3d 1082, 562 N.E.2d 1233, 150 Ill.Dec. 430 (5th Dist. 1990)

McBroom v. Board of Education District No. 205, 144 Ill.App.3d 463, 494 N.E.2d 1191, 98 Ill.Dec. 864 (2nd Dist. 1986)

Chicago Board of Education v. Payne, 102 Ill.App.3d 741, 430 N.E.2d 310, 58 Ill.Dec. 368 (1st Dist. 1981)

Scott v. Board of Education, 20 Ill.App.2d 292, 156 N.E.2d 1 (4th Dist. 1959)

REMEDIABILITY

18:180 What is irremediable conduct?

Conduct is irremediable when the damage which has been done to students, faculty, or the school is irreparable.

Consideration is also given to whether or not the conduct could have been corrected had the employee been warned.

Board of Education of City of Chicago v. Harris, 218 Ill.App.3d 1017, 578 N.E.2d 1244, 161 Ill.Dec. 598 (1st Dist. 1991)

McCutcheon v. Board of Education, City of Chicago, 94 Ill.App.3d 993, 419 N.E.2d 451, 50 Ill.Dec. 343 (1st Dist. 1981)

Board of Education of School District No. 131 v. Illinois State Board of Education, 82 Ill.App.3d 820, 403 N.E.2d 277, 38 Ill.Dec. 189 (2nd Dist. 1980)

Waller v. Board of Education Century School District No. 100, 13 Ill.App.3d 1056, 302 N.E.2d 190 (5th Dist. 1973)

18:190   Who determines whether a conduct giving rise to discipline is remediable or irremediable?

A school board is empowered to make an initial determination of the remediability or irremediability of conduct. The school board's decision is subject to review by a hearing officer in a dismissal case and in some cases reviewable in other tribunals with respect to other forms of discipline.

The determination of the remediability of any particular conduct is important in deciding whether the employee requires legally sufficient warning before dismissal. If conduct is determined to be irremediable, no such warning is necessary before dismissal.

105 ILCS 5/24-12

105 ILCS 5/24A-1 et seq.

Gilliland v. Board of Education of Pleasant View Consolidated School District No. 622 of Tazewell County, 67 Ill.2d 143, 365 N.E.2d 322, 8 Ill.Dec. 84 (1977)

Welch v. Board of Education of Bement Community Unit School District No. 5 of Piatt County, 45 Ill.App.3d 35, 358 N.E.2d 354, 3 Ill.Dec. 679 (4th Dist. 1977)

Fender v. School District No. 25, Arlington Heights, 37 Ill.App.3d 736 (1st Dist. 1976)

Everett v. Board of Education of District 201, Cook County, 22 Ill.App.3d 594, 317 N.E.2d 753 (1st Dist. 1974)

Waller v. Board of Education Century School District No. 100, 13 Ill.App.3d 1056, 302 N.E.2d 190 (5th Dist. 1973)

Miller v. Board of Education, School District No. 132, Cook County, 51 Ill.App.2d 20, 240 N.E.2d 471 (1st Dist. 1964)

18:200   Which party has the burden of proving irremediability?

The school board has the burden of proving that conduct leading to dismissal is not remediable.

Gilliland v. Board of Education of Pleasant View Consolidated School District No. 622 of Tazewell County, 67 Ill.2d 143, 365 N.E.2d 322, 8 Ill.Dec. 84 (1977)

18:210   If a tenured teacher's conduct is properly determined to be irremediable, must a school board issue a warning (notice to remedy) before dismissal?

No. A notice to remedy is essential only where the teacher's conduct is determined to be remediable.

Lowe v. Board of Education, City of Chicago, 76 Ill.App.3d 348, 395 N.E.2d 59, 32 Ill.Dec. 112 (1st Dist. 1979)

Welch v. Board of Education of Bement Community Unit School District No. 5 of Piatt County, 45 Ill.App.3d 35, 358 N.E.2d 354, 3 Ill.Dec. 679 (4th Dist. 1977)

Wells v. Board of Education of Community Consolidated School District No. 64, Cook County, 85 Ill.App.2d 312, 230 N.E.2d 6 (1st Dist. 1967)

18:220   If a school board determines a teacher's behavior is improper and remediable but not related to classroom competence, what warning is required prior to dismissal?

If a school board has determined a tenured teacher's improper but remediable behavior is related to classroom competence, the remediation requirements of Section 24A of the School Code apply. If the behavior is not related to classroom competence, or is related to the classroom competence of a non-tenured teacher whom the school board is seeking to dismiss before the end of the school term, the school board must invoke the following procedures prior to dismissal:

1) the teacher must be provided with a notice to remedy the behavior in question;

2) the notice must specifically identify the objectionable behavior and state that if not remedied the teacher may be subject to dismissal;

3) the notice must provide the teacher with reasonably specific corrective action the school board requires the teacher to undertake if appropriate; and

4) the notice must identify a reasonable period of time in which the school board expects the corrective action to be successfully completed if appropriate.

105 ILCS 5/24-12

Grissom v. Board of Education of Buckley Loda Community School District No. 8, 75 Ill.App.2d 314, 388 N.E.2d 398, 26 Ill.Dec. 683 (4th Dist. 1979)

Gilliland v. Board of Education of Pleasant View Consolidated School District No. 622 of Tazewell County, 67 Ill.2d 143, 365 N.E.2d 322, 8 Ill.Dec. 84 (1977)

Paprocki v. Board of Education of McHenry Community High School District No. 156, 31 Ill.App.3d 112, 334 N.E.2d 841 (2nd Dist. 1975)

Everett v. Board of Education of District 201, Cook County, 22 Ill.App.3d 594, 317 N.E.2d 753 (1st Dist. 1974)

Waller v. Board of Education Century School District No. 100, 13 Ill.App.3d 1056, 302 N.E.2d 190 (5th Dist. 1973)

Wells v. Board of Education of Community Consolidated School District No. 64, Cook County, 85 Ill.App.2d 312, 230 N.E.2d 6 (1st Dist. 1967)

Werner v. Community Unit School District No. 4, Marshall County, 40 Ill.App. 491, 190 N.E.2d 184 (2nd Dist. 1963)

18:230   What is a notice to remedy?

A notice to remedy is a legally sufficient written warning issued by a school board and properly delivered to an employee which warns the employee of improper conduct and the consequences thereof.

105 ILCS 5/24-12

Paprocki v. Board of Education of McHenry Community High School District No. 156, 31 Ill.App.3d 112, 334 N.E.2d 841 (2nd Dist. 1975)

18:235   May a teacher file a grievance challenging a notice to remedy?

When a provision of a collective bargaining agreement is in violation of, inconsistent with or in conflict with an Illinois statute it may not be "implemented in an arbitration award." The procedural requirements in the law for dismissal of a teacher incorporate the school board's duty to make the initial determination of whether a teacher's conduct is remediable. Therefore, a teacher may not challenge the employer's determination to issue a notice to remedy by use of the grievance procedure.

105 ILCS 5/10-22.4
105 ILCS 5/24-12
115 ILCS 5/10(b)
Board of Education of Rockford School District No. 205, v. The Illinois Educational Labor Relations Board, 165 Ill.2d 80, 649 N.E.2d 369, 208 Ill.Dec. 313 (1995)

18:240   How much time must teachers be given to correct remediable deficiencies?

A school board must give a teacher a reasonable amount of time to remedy. The amount of time which is necessary depends upon the deficiencies to be remedied.

105 ILCS 5/24-12
Board of Education of School District No. 131 v. Illinois State Board of Education, 82 Ill.App.3d 820, 403 N.E.2d 277, 38 Ill.Dec. 189 (2nd Dist. 1980)
  Litin v. Board of Education of City of Chicago, 72 Ill.App.3d 889, 391 N.E.2d 62, 28 Ill.Dec. 863 (1st Dist. 1979)
  Aulwurm v. Board of Education of Murphysboro Community Unit School District of Jackson County, 67 Ill.2d 434, 317 N.E.2d 1337 (1977)

DUE PROCESS AND TEACHER DISMISSAL

18:250   What pre-hearing procedures apply to the dismissal of a tenured teacher?

A "Loudermill-type" pre-termination hearing may be required before the school board votes on the dismissal of a teacher. Under limited circumstances which are fact-driven, post-deprivation due process may be sufficient. The school board must approve a motion containing specific charges by a majority vote of all its members. Written notice of the charges must be served on the teacher within five days of the adoption of the motion.

The notice must contain a bill of particulars. No hearing on the charges is required unless the teacher, within 10 days of receiving the notice, requests in writing of the school board a hearing be scheduled, in which case the school board must schedule a hearing on the charges before a disinterested hearing officer pursuant to statutory requirements.

105 ILCS 5/24-12

Gilbert v. Homar, 117 S.Ct. 1807, 520 U.S. 924, 138 L.Ed.2d 120 (1997) on rem. 149 F.3d 1164

Massie v. East St. Louis School District No. 189, 203 Ill.App.3d 965, 561 N.E.2d 246, 148 Ill.Dec. 940 (5th Dist. 1990)

Cleveland Board of Education v. Loudermill, 105 S.Ct. 1487, 470 U.S. 532, 84 L.Ed.2d 494 (1985) on rem. 763 F.2d 202 (6th Cir. 1985)

Morelli v. Board of Education of District 303, Tazewell County, 42 Ill.App.3d 722, 356 N.E.2d 438, 1 Ill.Dec. 312 (3rd Dist. 1976)

18:260   Is prehearing discovery permitted in a tenured teacher dismissal?

A party to a tenured teacher dismissal is entitled to:

1) discovery of the names and addresses of persons who may be called as expert witnesses at the hearing (failure to reveal the name and address of a witness precludes that person from testifying at the hearing in the absence of a showing of good cause and the express permission of the hearing officer);

2) a list of persons and their addresses who may have knowledge of facts related to the charges or the defenses thereto. This is not to be construed as a list of witnesses, but no person whose name is not so disclosed may testify except upon good cause shown and by permission of the hearing officer;

3) bills of particulars upon order of the hearing officer for good cause shown;

4) written interrogatories upon order of the hearing officer for good cause shown;

5) production of relevant documents upon order of the hearing officer for good cause shown.

105 ILCS 5/24-12

23 Ill. Admin. Code 51.55

18:270   How is a tenured teacher dismissal hearing conducted?

The order of proceedings is as follows:

1) The hearing is opened by the recording of the place, time, and date of the hearing, the presence of the hearing officer and

the parties and counsel, if any, and any stipulations as to facts. Pre-hearing motions are heard at this time.

2) Upon the opening of the hearing, the hearing officer allows the parties to make opening statements.

3) The school board proceeds first to present its evidence sustaining the dismissal.

4) Either party may confront the witnesses, offer evidence, and present a defense.

5) All testimony is taken under oath administered by the hearing officer.

6) The hearing officer may issue subpoenas requiring the attendance of witnesses or production of documents and, at the request of either of the parties, shall issue such subpoenas but may limit the number of witnesses to be subpoenaed in behalf of either party to not more than ten.

7) The hearing officer causes a record of the proceedings to be kept and must employ a competent reporter to take stenotype notes of all the testimony. The State Board of Education pays for the attendance and services of the court reporter.

8) Exhibits, when offered by either party, may be received in evidence by the hearing officer. The names and addresses of all witnesses and exhibits in order received shall be made a part of this record. The hearing officer makes rulings on the admissibility of exhibits.

9) The hearing officer for good cause shown may continue the hearing upon the request of the teacher or the board or upon his own initiative, and adjourns when the teacher and the board agree thereto.

10) The hearing may proceed in the absence of either party, who, after due notice, fails to be present or fails to obtain a continuance.

11) The hearing officer is required to consider and give weight to all the teacher's evaluations.

12) The hearing officer may, in his discretion, vary the normal procedure under which the board first presents its claim, but in any case shall afford full and equal opportunity to all parties for presentation of relevant proofs.

13) Upon the close of the hearing, each party may make a

closing statement (orally and/or written at the discretion of the hearing officer) incorporating arguments of fact and law.

14) The hearing is not considered closed until all evidence has been submitted and briefs, if allowed, have been received by the hearing officer.

105 ILCS 5/24-12
23 Ill. Admin. Code 51.60(c)

18:280 Who may serve as a hearing officer for a tenured teacher dismissal?

The hearing officer in a tenured teacher dismissal case must be selected through a statutory procedure from a list supplied by the State Board of Education. Hearing officers must possess the following minimum qualifications:

1) accreditation by a national arbitration association and have had a minimum of five years of experience directly related to labor and employment relations matters between educational employers and educational employees or their collective bargaining representatives;

2) not a resident of the school district seeking the dismissal;

3) disinterested and impartial; and

4) no financial or personal interest in the result of the hearing.

105 ILCS 5/24-12
23 Ill. Admin. Code 51.20

18:290 Is a tenured teacher dismissal hearing open to the public?

Dismissal hearings are routinely closed by the hearing officer. The decision to open or close the hearing is at the discretion of the hearing officer.

105 ILCS 5/24-12
23 Ill. Admin. Code 51.40(a)

18:300 Who pays the hearing officer in a tenured teacher dismissal case?

The per diem allowance for the hearing officer is paid by the State Board of Education.

105 ILCS 5/24-12

18:305   How is the hearing officer in a tenured teacher dismissal case selected?

Within five days after receiving a notice of hearing, the State Board of Education must provide the parties with a list of five prospective impartial hearing officers. Within three days of receipt of the list, the parties have the right to reject all the hearing officers named on the first list and the State Board of Education is required to provide a second list of five prospective impartial hearing officers none of whom were named on the first list.

An alternate strike system is used to select the hearing officer. The teacher has the option to strike first.

The parties may mutually agree to select an impartial hearing officer who is not on a list received from the State Board of Education either by direct appointment by the parties or by using procedures for the appointment of an arbitrator established by the Federal Mediation and Conciliation Service or the American Arbitration Association. The parties must notify the State Board of Education of their intent to select a hearing officer using an alternative procedure within three days of receipt of a list of prospective hearing officers from the State Board of Education.

Hearing officers selected under the alternative procedure must have the same qualifications and authority as a hearing officer selected from a list provided by the State Board of Education.

105 ILCS 5/24-12

18:310   What procedures are followed in appointing a hearing officer to a tenured teacher dismissal case?

Notice of the appointment of the hearing officer is mailed to the hearing officer by the State Board of Education, and the signed acceptance of the hearing officer must be filed with the State Board within five days of receipt of notice of appointment.

Upon notice of appointment as a hearing officer, the prospective hearing officer must disclose any circumstances which he believes might disqualify him. Upon receipt of such information, the State Board must immediately disclose it to the parties. The parties may waive the presumptive disqualification. But if either party declines to waive the presumptive disqualification, the State Board must declare a vacancy.

If a hearing officer resigns, dies, withdraws, refuses, is unable or disqualified to perform his duties, the State Board must, on proof satisfactory to it, declare the position vacant. Vacancies are filled in the same manner as the making of the original appointment. If a vacancy occurs during the course of a hearing, the entire matter must be reheard by the new hearing officer. All communication from the parties to the hearing officer must be in writing and copies must be sent at the same time to the opposing party and the State Board of Education.

105 ILCS 5/24-12
23 Ill. Admin. Code 51.40

18:320   How does a hearing officer render a decision in a tenured teacher dismissal case?

A hearing officer in a tenured teacher dismissal case must abide by the following procedures:

1) The hearing officer must, with reasonable dispatch, make a decision in writing as to whether or not the teacher is to be dismissed. The decision must include findings of fact.

2) The decision should be rendered no later than 30 days from the date of closing the hearing.

3) A copy of the decision must be given to the State Board of Education to be forwarded to both the teacher and the school board.

4) The decision of the hearing officer is final unless reviewed under the Administrative Review Act.

5) If neither party appeals the decision, then either party desiring a transcript of the hearing must pay for the cost thereof.

6) In the event review is instituted, any costs of preparing and filing the record of proceedings is paid by the State Board of Education.

7) The record of the hearing must include all pleadings and exhibits; a statement of matters officially noticed; a transcript of the hearing; and the decision of the hearing officer.

105 ILCS 5/24-12
23 Ill. Admin. Code 51.60 et seq.

18:330   What rules of evidence apply to tenured teacher dismissal hearings?

Formal rules of evidence do not apply to tenured teacher dismissal hearings, but the following guidelines apply:

1) The parties may offer such evidence as they desire and shall produce such additional evidence as the hearing officer may deem necessary to an understanding and determination of the dispute.

2) The hearing officer is the judge of the relevancy and materiality of the evidence offered and strict conformity to legal rules of evidence is not necessary.

3) Objections to evidentiary offers may be made and are noted in the record. The hearing officer has the power to make rulings and the power to exclude evidence. Offers of proof are permitted.

4) Any hostile witness may be examined as if under cross examination.

5) All documents not filed with the hearing officer at the hearing but which are arranged at the hearing or subsequently by agreement of the parties to be submitted, must be filed with the State Board of Education for transmission to the hearing officer and other parties.

105 ILCS 5/24-12
23 Ill. Admin. Code 51.60(d)

18:340   What burden of proof does a school board have in a teacher dismissal case?

A school board must prove its case by a preponderance of the evidence.

Board of Education of Minooka Community Consolidated School District No. 201 v. Ingels, 75 Ill.App.3d 334, 394 N.E.2d 69, 31 Ill.Dec. 153 (3rd Dist. 1979)

18:350   May a school board raise charges not included in the bill of particulars for the first time at a dismissal hearing?

New charges or proofs unrelated to the bill of particulars are not permitted.

105 ILCS 5/24-12
Aulwurm v. Board of Education of Murphysboro Community Unit School District of Jackson County, 67 Ill.2d 434, 317 N.E.2d 1337 (1977)

18:360   What is the time limit for appealing a hearing officer's decision in a teacher dismissal case?

Appeal must be perfected within 35 days of the date the hearing officer's decision was served on the party affected by the decision.

735 ILCS 5/3-103
Board of Education of St. Charles Community Unit School District No. 303 v. Adelman, 137 Ill.App.3d 965, 485 N.E.2d 584, 92 Ill.Dec. 773 (2nd Dist. 1985)

TEACHER SUSPENSION

18:370   May a school board suspend a tenured teacher without pay pending the outcome of a dismissal hearing?

If, in the opinion of a school board, the interests of the school require it, the board may suspend a teacher without pay pending a dismissal hearing. However, if reinstated, the teacher must have lost salary restored.

105 ILCS 5/24-12
Gilbert v. Homar, 117 S.Ct. 1807, 520 U.S. 924, 138 L.Ed.2d 120 (1997) on rem. 149 F.3d 1164
Spinelli v. Immanuel Lutheran Evangelical Congregation, Inc., 118 Ill.2d 389, 515 N.E.2d 1222, 113 Ill.Dec. 915 (1987)
Yuen v. Board of Education of Community Unit School District No. 46, Kane County, 77 Ill.App.2d 353, 222 N.E.2d 570 (3rd Dist. 1966)
Pearson v. Board of Education of Community Unit School District No. 5 of Macoupin County, 27 Ill.App.2d 12, 169 N.E.2d 7 (3rd Dist. 1960)

18:380   Must a school board provide a teacher a hearing on a suspension without pay pending dismissal?

It is likely that no hearing beyond that required to review the dismissal need be provided because the relevant statute specifies all necessary procedures. However, there is some case law which suggests a separate hearing must be held before the suspension without pay is invoked.

105 ILCS 5/24-12
Massie v. East St. Louis School District No. 189, 203 Ill.App.3d 965, 561 N.E.2d 246, 148 Ill.Dec. 940 (5th Dist. 1990)
Spinelli v. Immanuel Lutheran Evangelical Congregation, Inc., 118 Ill.2d 389, 515 N.E.2d 1222, 113 Ill.Dec. 915 (1987)

Cleveland Board of Education v. Loudermill, 105 S.Ct. 1487, 470 U.S. 532, 84 L.Ed.2d 494 (1985) on rem. 763 F.2d 202 (6th Cir. 1985)

Barszcz v. Board of Trustees of Community College District No. 504, Cook County, 400 F.Supp. 675 (N.D. Ill. 1975)

18:390 May a school board suspend a teacher without pay for disciplinary reasons without a dismissal pending?

A school board may invoke a disciplinary suspension without pay provided it has an underlying collectively bargained contract provision allowing such a suspension or, in the absence of a demand to bargain it by a recognized bargaining unit, a policy allowing such a suspension.

Spinelli v. Immanuel Lutheran Evangelical Congregation, Inc., 118 Ill.2d 389, 515 N.E.2d 1222, 113 Ill.Dec. 915 (1987)

18:400 May a teacher challenge a temporary disciplinary suspension through the collective bargaining agreement grievance procedure?

Yes, provided there is a clause in the agreement supporting the challenge and provided the suspension is not in conjunction with pending dismissal proceedings. The arbitration of a grievance arising from the temporary disciplinary suspension of a teacher is not inconsistent with or in conflict with the implied power of the district to suspend nor is it in violation of, inconsistent with or in conflict with any statute.

115 ILCS 5/10b

Granite City Community Unit School District No. 9 v. Illinois Educational Labor Relations Board, 279 Ill.App.3d 439, 664 N.E.2d 1060, 216 Ill.Dec. 132 (4th Dist. 1996)

Spinelli v. Immanuel Lutheran Evangelical Congregation, Inc., 118 Ill.2d 389, 515 N.E.2d 1222, 113 Ill.Dec. 915 (1987)

19: SCHOOL ADMINISTRATORS

DUTIES OF ADMINISTRATORS

19:10   What are the duties of a superintendent?

A superintendent has charge of the administration of the schools under the direction of the school board. In addition to his administrative duties, a superintendent is required to make recommendations to the board concerning the budget, building plans, the locations of sites, the selection, retention, and dismissal of teachers and all other employees, the selection of textbooks, instructional material, and courses of study.

The superintendent has reporting responsibilities under the Abused and Neglected Child Reporting Act. The superintendent must keep or cause to be kept the records and accounts as directed and required by the board, aid in making reports required by the board, and perform such other duties as the board may delegate to him.

105 ILCS 5/10-21.4

19:20   What are the duties of a principal?

A principal must hold a valid supervisory or administrative certificate. He supervises the operation of one or more attendance centers. The principal administers his duties under the supervision of the superintendent, and in accordance with reasonable rules and regulations of the school board, for the planning, operation, and evaluation of the educational program of the attendance area to which he is assigned.

A principal's job description must specify his primary responsibility is the improvement of instruction. A majority of the principal's time must be spent on curriculum and staff development through both formal and informal activities, establishing clear lines of communication regarding school goals, accomplishments, practices, and policies with parents and teachers.

A principal is required to submit recommendations to the superintendent concerning the appointment, retention, promotion, and assignment of all personnel assigned to the attendance center.

105 ILCS 5/10-21.4a

19:25 May an administrator issue a teacher a notice to remedy?

A notice to remedy is an official warning to a teacher that the teacher's behavior, if not remedied, may lead to dismissal. Only a school board may issue a notice to remedy. Therefore no disciplinary letter signed by a superintendent or principal is a notice to remedy and such a letter from an administrator has a less serious disciplinary effect.

105 ILCS 5/24-12
Board of Education of School District No. 131 v. Illinois State Board of Education, 82 Ill. App.3d 820, 404 N.E.2d 277, 38 Ill.Dec. 189 (2nd Dist. 1980)

19:30 May a school district employ one administrator as both superintendent and principal?

Yes, provided the full-time equivalency of the combination results in a maximum of one full-time position.

23 Ill. Admin. Code 1.310 f) 1)

19:40 May a school board assign one principal to supervise more than one attendance center?

Yes.

23 Ill. Admin. Code 1.310
Kenney v. Interim General Superintendent of Schools, 112 Ill.App.3d 342, 445 N.E.2d 356, 67 Ill.Dec. 876 (1983)
Dolnick v. General Superintendent of Schools of Chicago, 67 Ill.App.3d 8, 384 N.E.2d 408, 23 Ill.Dec. 614 (1st Dist. 1978)

19:50 Who may serve as principal in the absence of the principal?

If a principal is absent due to extended illness or leave of absence, an assistant principal may be assigned as acting principal for a period not to exceed 60 school days.

105 ILCS 5/10-21.4a
23 Ill. Admin. Code 1.310 b)

ADMINISTRATOR QUALIFICATIONS

19:60   What is required to be a superintendent of schools?

A superintendent of schools must have a master's degree and hold a state certificate with a superintendent endorsement. An endorsement requires the successful completion of at least 30 semester hours of graduate credit beyond the master's degree in a program for the preparation of superintendents of schools, including 16 semester hours of graduate credit in professional education.

Endorsement also requires at least two years experience as an administrator or supervisor in public schools, the State Board of Education, educational service regions, or in certain approved non-public schools, or two years of experience as a supervisor or administrator while holding an all-grade supervisory certificate or a certificate comparable in validity and educational and experience requirements.

105 ILCS 5/21-7.1

19:65   What is required to be a principal?

A principal, assistant principal, assistant superintendent and related or similar positions as determined by the State Superintendent of Education must have a general administrative endorsement. The endorsement requires at least 20 semester hours of graduate credit in educational administration and supervision.

Endorsement also requires at least two years of full-time teaching experience or school service personnel experience in public schools, schools under the supervision of the department of corrections, schools under the administration of Vocational Rehabilitation, in certain non-public schools approved by the State Superintendent of Education, or comparable out of state recognition standards as approved by the State Superintendent of Education.

105 ILCS 5/21-7.1

19:70   Are there continuing education requirements for administrators who evaluate certified personnel?

Administrators who evaluate certified personnel must participate in a State Board of Education training program on evaluation of certified personnel at least once every two years.

105 ILCS 5/24A-3

19:75   Are department chairpersons required to have administrative or supervisory teaching certificates?

Department chairpersons are required to have administrative or supervisory endorsements if first assigned to their jobs after September 1, 1978 and if their jobs require supervision or evaluation of teachers.

105 ILCS 5/21-7.1
23 Ill. Admin. Code 1.310 e)

19:80   Is there an alternative route to administrator certification?

The alternative route to administrator certification is available for a standard administrative certificate with a general administrative, chief school business official or superintendent endorsement. It is not available for persons wishing to serve as principals or assistant principals.

To qualify for alternative certification, the applicant must complete a program comprised of three phases: an intensive course of study in education management, governance, organization and planning; assignment to a full-time position for one school year as an administrator; and comprehensive assessment of performance.

A provisional alternative administrative certificate is valid for one year and is not renewable. To qualify for the alternative certificate, the applicant must have a master's degree from an accredited college or university or a bachelor's degree and the life experience equivalent of a master's degree in a management field as determined by the State Board of Education, must have been employed for a period of at least five years in a management level position, must have successfully completed the phase one curriculum, and must have passed any examination required by the State Board of Education.

A person who successfully completes all phases of the program may obtain a standard administrative certificate.

105 ILCS 5/21-5d

EMPLOYMENT CONTRACTS

19:90   May a school board issue multi-year employment contracts to its administrators?

For new contracts issued after December 31, 1997 and after the expiration of contracts in effect on January 1, 1998, school districts may only employ administrators under a one-year or a performance-based multi-year contract for a period not exceeding five years.

Before January 1, 1998, superintendents or principals could be issued multi-year contracts without performance provisions, and rollover clauses were permissible. Multi-year contracts which were in effect on January 1, 1998 are valid until they expire.

105 ILCS 5/10-23.8
105 ILCS 5/10-23.8a

19:91   What is a performance-based contract?

The School Code requires that multi-year administrator contracts be linked to student performance and academic improvement within the district. Performance-based contracts must include goals and indicators of student performance and academic improvement as determined by the local school board to measure the performance and effectiveness of the administrator and such other information as the local school board may determine.

105 ILCS 5/10-23.8
105 ILCS 5/10-23.8a

19:92 Which administrators may be issued performance contracts?

Before January 1, 1998, the School Code explicitly authorized multi-year contracts only for superintendents and principals. After December 31, 1997, the statute explicitly requires that if any class of administrator is issued a multi-year contract, it must be a performance-based contract.

105 ILCS 5/10-23.8
105 ILCS 5/10-23.8a

19:93 For what term may administrator contracts be issued?

For contracts in effect on January 1, 1998, the contract is effective for its stated term. Before January 1, 1998, the School Code permitted a one-year contract for any class of administrator, a two-year contract for a first time superintendent or principal, or a three-year contract for an experienced superintendent or principal.

For administrator contracts of all types executed after December 31, 1997, the School Code authorizes either a contract for a period not to exceed one year or a performance-based contract for a period not exceeding five years.

105 ILCS 5/10-23.8
105 ILCS 5/10-23.8a

19:94 May an administrator rely on an oral multi-year agreement?

A multi-year agreement which lacks all the elements necessary to form a contract violates the Illinois statute of frauds. The statute of frauds requires that multi-year contracts be reduced to writing to be enforceable. Oral multi-year extensions of written contracts also violate the statute of frauds.

For multiple documents to satisfy the statute of frauds, all essential terms of the contract must be in writing, there must be a connection between the documents, physical or otherwise, so as to demonstrate that they relate to the same contract.

The statute of frauds may be overcome by misrepresentation by word or conduct about material facts or concealment of material facts. The statute of frauds does not bar enforcement of an oral contract if there has been part performance by one party in reliance on the promise of the other party.

740 ILCS 80/1
McInerney v. Charter Golf, Inc., 176 Ill.2d 482, 680 N.E.2d 1347, 223 Ill.Dec. 911 (1997)
Dickens v. Quincy College Corporation, 245 Ill.App.3d 1055, 615 N.E.2d 381, 185 Ill.Dec. 822 (4th Dist. 1993)
Johnson v. George J. Ball, Inc., 248 Ill.App.3d 859, 617 N.E.2d 1355, 187 Ill.Dec. 634 (2nd Dist. 1993)

### 19:96	May a school board write residency requirements into a principal or superintendent's contract?

Residency requirements may be included and are enforceable in a superintendent's contract. Unless residency was made an express condition of the principal's employment or continued employment as a principal at the time of the person's initial employment as a principal, residency within the school district may not at any time thereafter be made a condition of that person's employment or continued employment as a principal.

The residency within a school district of a principal may not be considered in determining the compensation, assignment or transfer of a principal to an attendance center.

105 ILCS 5/10-21.4a
105 ILCS 5/24-4.1

### 19:100	What is a rollover provision in an administrator's employment contract?

Before January 1, 1998, the School Code permitted the extension of a principal's or superintendent's multi-year contract for an additional three years at the end of any year. Some principal and superintendent contracts written before January 1, 1998 automatically extended for an additional three years at the end of each year if the school board did not give notice of non-renewal. The contract clause which provides for automatic contract extension is commonly called a "rollover" or "evergreen" clause. Rollover clauses may not be included in administrator contracts executed after December 31, 1997.

105 ILCS 5/10-23.8
105 ILCS 5/10-23.8a

19:102   When does a contract expire if it was executed before January 1, 1998 and it contains a rollover clause?

The answer will be driven by the provisions of the contract and the facts surrounding its execution. In most cases, the contract will be effective for at least three years (until the end of the 2000-2001 school term). If the employer fails to give the notice required to terminate the contract, it is possible for the contract to survive for a longer period.

105 ILCS 5/10-23.8
105 ILCS 5/10-23.8a

19:105   Does an administrator's multi-year contract survive the dissolution or consolidation of the school district which employs him?

The liabilities of dissolved school districts, including the remaining obligations under any multi-year administrator contracts, become the responsibility of the annexing or newly-consolidated district.

105 ILCS 5/7-12
105 ILCS 5/7A-11
105 ILCS 5/11C-1 et seq.

TENURE

19:110   May an administrator acquire tenure?

Any administrator who has teacher certification, and if first employed by his employer before January 1, 1998, acquires tenure after employment for two full-time consecutive school terms unless the administrator is employed under the terms of a multi-year contract.

Any administrator who has teacher certification and who was employed after December 31, 1997 acquires tenure after employment for four full-time consecutive school terms unless the administrator is employed under the terms of a multi-year contract.

However, the tenured administrator is not necessarily entitled to any particular position. Rather, tenure entitles the administrator to continued employment in the district so long as there is a position available for which he is qualified.

105 ILCS 5/10-23.8
105 ILCS 5/10-23.8a
105 ILCS 5/24-11 et seq.
Davis v. Board of Education of Farmer City-Mansfield Community Unit School District, 63 Ill.App.3d 495, 380 N.E.2d 58, 20 Ill.Dec. 381 (4th Dist. 1978)
Lane v. Board of Education of Fairbury Cropsey Community Unit School District No. 3, 38 Ill.App.3d 742, 348 N.E.2d 470 (4th Dist. 1976)
Danno v. Peterson, 421 F.Supp. 950 (N.D. Ill. 1976)
Lester v. Board of Education of School District No. 119 of Jo Daviess County, 87 Ill.App.2d 269, 230 N.E.2d 893 (2nd Dist. 1967)
McNely v. Board of Education of Community Unit School District No. 7, 9 Ill.2d 143, 137 N.E.2d 63 (1956)

19:120   If an administrator has acquired tenure and is subsequently removed from his administrative position, does he have "bumping rights?"

Yes.

105 ILCS 5/24-12
Brubaker v. Community Unit School District No. 16, Sangamon and Morgan Counties, 46 Ill.App.3d 588, 360 N.E.2d 1228, 4 Ill.Dec. 853 (4th Dist. 1977).

19:130   Does an administrative employee waive any rights by accepting a multi-year employment contract?

By accepting the terms of a multi-year contract, a administrator waives all rights otherwise granted him under Sections 24-11 through 24-16 of the School Code, which includes tenure rights, for the duration of the contract. Upon acceptance of a multi-year contract the administrator does not lose previously acquired tenure rights.

105 ILCS 5/10-23.8
105 ILCS 5/10-23.8a

RECLASSIFICATION OF PRINCIPALS

19:140   What rights are due principals on demotion or reclassification to a lower paying position?

No principal who has completed two or more years of administrative service in a school district may be reclassified by demotion or reduction in rank from one position in a school district to another for which a lower salary is paid without written notice from the board of the proposed reclassification by April 1 of the year in which the principal's contract expires. Within 10 days of the principal's receipt of this notice, the school board must provide the principal with a written statement of facts regarding the reclassification, and the principal must be granted, upon request, a private hearing with the board to discuss the reclassification.

If the principal is not satisfied with the results of the private hearing, he may within five days thereafter request a public hearing on the reclassification. The principal may be represented by counsel at either hearing.

If the school board decides to proceed with the reclassification, it shall give the principal written notice of its decision within 15 days of the private hearing, or 15 days of the public hearing, whichever is later. The decision of the school board thereupon becomes final. Nothing in the law prohibits a school board from ordering lateral transfers of principals to positions of similar rank and equal salary.

105 ILCS 5/10-23.8b

Meadows v. School District U-46, 141 Ill.App.3d 335, 490 N.E.2d 140, 95 Ill.Dec. 667 (2nd Dist. 1986)

Swanson v. Board of Education of Foreman Community Unit School District No. 124, Mason County, 135 Ill.App.3d 466, 481 N.E.2d 1248, 90 Ill.Dec. 337 (4th Dist. 1985)

Lyznicki v. Board of Education, School District No. 167, Cook County, 707 F.2d 949 (7th Cir. 1983)

19:150 Is an administrator entitled to hearing officer review of a school board decision to reclassify, demote or reassign?

No. However, under certain circumstances and when the administrator had been employed under a one-year contract, a reclassification, demotion or reassignment may be a reduction-in-force within the meaning of Sections 24-11 or 24-12 of the School Code.

105 ILCS 5/10-23.8b

DISMISSAL RIGHTS

19:160   May a school board dismiss an administrator during the term of his contract?

A school board may not dismiss an administrator during the term of his contract without providing both substantive and procedural due process. The type of due process necessary varies according to the kind of contract the administrator has. Under certain circumstances the due process protections of the teacher tenure laws apply.

A school board seeking to dismiss an administrator during the term of his contract must be able to prove substantial breach of contract by the administrator.

> 105 ILCS 5/24-12
> *Bakalis v. Golembeski*, 35 F.3d 318 (7th Cir. 1994)

19:170   What rights are due an administrator on dismissal?

A school board seeking to dismiss an administrator at the end of his contract must abide by the express terms of the contract and comply with School Code Sections 24-11 or 24-12 if the administrator has achieved tenure in the school district and is not serving under a multi-year contract.

An administrator first employed by his board after December 31, 1997 who serves a school district full time without a break in service under the terms of four successive one year contracts and begins his fifth year of such service, or who renders service without written contract during the same period of time, acquires teaching tenure in the school district. A school board may not dismiss such an administrator from employment in the school district without respecting the dismissal causes and procedures set forth in the School Code.

An administrator with teaching tenure may be relieved of his administrative duties, but is entitled to bump into a teaching job for which he is qualified. For administrators first employed by their school boards before January 1, 1998, tenure is or was achieved after two consecutive full-time years of service.

> 105 ILCS 5/10-21.4
> 105 ILCS 5/10-23.8
> 105 ILCS 5/10-23.8b
> 105 ILCS 5/24-12

20: NONCERTIFICATED EMPLOYEES

DUTIES OF NONCERTIFICATED EMPLOYEES

20:10 Who are the noncertificated employees of a school district?

Noncertificated employees, referred to in the School Code as "educational support personnel," include all employees whose positions do not require state teacher certification. Both terms encompass secretarial and clerical employees, maintenance and janitorial staff, bookkeepers, bus drivers, security staff, and food service employees, among others.

20:20 May a school board employ educational support personnel (noncertificated) to assist in academically-related activities?

A school board may employ noncertificated personnel or use volunteer personnel for (a) non teaching duties that do not require instructional judgment or evaluation of pupils, (b) supervising study halls and long distance teaching reception areas used incident to instructional programs transmitted by electronic media such as computers, video and audio, and (c) supervising detention and discipline areas and school-sponsored extracurricular activities.

A school board also may use such employees or volunteers to assist in the instruction of pupils under the immediate supervision of a certificated teacher. The teacher must be continuously aware of the noncertificated person's activities and must be able to control or modify them.

Teacher aides require an approval form issued by the State Teacher Certification Board. Approval requires completion of 30 semester hours of college training or completion of an approved teacher aide program.

105 ILCS 5/10-22.34 et seq.
23 Ill. Admin. Code 1.630
23 Ill. Admin. Code 25.10 et seq.

**20:30   What certification requirements apply to
           playground supervisors, cafeteria supervisors,
           or study hall monitors?**

Playground and cafeteria supervisors do not require certification. Neither position involves instruction or instructional
judgment. A 1993 amendment to the School Code allows noncertificated personnel to supervise study halls. A school district
should be aware there are bargaining implications involved in
assigning such duties to either certificated or noncertificated
staff.

105 ILCS 5/10-22.34 et seq.
23 Ill. Admin. Code 1.630

**20:40   May a school board assign a teacher aide to
           substitute teach when the aide's supervising
           teacher is absent?**

A teacher aide cannot legally substitute teach unless he
holds certification as a teacher or substitute teacher.

105 ILCS 5/10-22.34
105 ILCS 5/21-1 et seq.
23 Ill. Admin. Code 1.630

**20:50   May a school board hire extra-duty supervisors
           or chaperons?**

A school board may designate noncertificated persons of
good character to serve as supervisors, chaperons or sponsors,
either on a voluntary or on a compensated basis, for school activities not connected with the academic programs of the schools.

105 ILCS 5/10-22.34a

**20:60   Do noncertificated employees enjoy the same
           defenses against tort liability that are accorded
           teachers under the principles of "in loco
           parentis?"**

No. Illinois law accords certificated employees special protections against liability for student injuries. Whereas the negligence standard which applies to teachers in the supervision of

students is "willful and wanton misconduct," the standard for a noncertificated employee is ordinary negligence.

In the area of liability for student injuries, the protections of "in loco parentis" represent an important distinction between certificated and noncertificated staff.

People v. Davis, 88 Ill.App.3d 728, 410 N.E.2d 673, 43 Ill.Dec. 473 (2nd Dist. 1980)

Edmunson v. Chicago Board of Education, 62 Ill.App.3d 211, 379 N.E.2d 27, 19 Ill.Dec. 512 (1st Dist. 1978)

Possekel v. O'Donnell, 51 Ill.App.3d 313, 366 N.E.2d 589, 9 Ill.Dec. 332 (1st Dist. 1977)

WAGES AND HOURS

20:70   What are the maximum hour limits of the Fair Labor Standards Act?

A school board is required to abide by the provisions of the federal Fair Labor Standards Act (FLSA). The FLSA requires that employees be paid overtime at the rate of not less than 1.5 times the regular hourly rate for time worked over 40 hours in any work week.

School administrators and teachers are usually exempt from the provisions of the FLSA. The FLSA wage and hour limits almost always apply to noncertificated personnel. The FLSA contains many technical provisions which define inclusions and exclusions.

29 U.S.C. 200 et seq.
29 U.S.C. 207
29 U.S.C. 213

20:80   Can the overtime provisions of the Fair Labor Standards Act be avoided by providing employees with compensatory time off?

In most cases, the obligation to pay overtime cannot be satisfied by giving the employee compensatory time off unless the compensatory time off is given in the week in which the overtime occurred. There are very limited exceptions to this rule.

29 U.S.C. 200 et seq.

20:90   Can an employer avoid the hour and overtime provisions of the Fair Labor Standards Act by employing the same employee in two different jobs?

The overtime pay provisions of the Fair Labor Standards Act apply to employees who are employed by a single employer in two different jobs. In most cases, a school district must pay overtime to an employee who exceeds 40 hours in a work week even if the excess results from the employee working more than one job for the same employer.

29 U.S.C. 207 f)

20:100   Is an employer obligated to pay overtime to an employee who voluntarily works overtime?

The employer may be required to pay overtime for such work if the work is known to, and tacitly approved by, the employee's supervisors.

29 U.S.C. 207

20:102   Do paid leaves count as hours for purposes of computing overtime?

The Fair Labor Standards Act requires that an employer pay overtime at the rate of 1.5 times straight time salary after an employee has worked 40 hours in a work week. Payments which are made for occasional periods when the employee is not at work due to vacation, holiday, illness, failure of the employer to provide sufficient work or other similar cause are not treated as hours worked for purposes of computing overtime. Neither are such hours credited towards overtime.

An employer policy, rule, regulation or collectively bargained agreement to the contrary may produce a different result.

29 C.F.R. 778.218 et seq.

20:110 Can the wage and hour provisions of the Fair Labor Standards Act be avoided by bargaining a contrary result?

Compliance with the Fair Labor Standards Act cannot normally be avoided by collectively bargaining a contrary lesser result. There are very limited exceptions which involve guaranteed hour agreements.

29 U.S.C. 200 et seq.

BENEFIT PROGRAMS

20:120 What state retirement program serves noncertificated school employees and how are employee contributions to the program treated?

Noncertificated employees of the school district are covered by the Illinois Municipal Retirement Fund. Each school district must pay employee contributions to the IMRF for all compensation earned. Such contributions are treated as employer contributions in determining tax treatment under the Internal Revenue Code and are thereby treated as non-taxable income for IRS purposes.

40 ILCS 5/7-132
40 ILCS 5/7-171

20:130 Are noncertificated employees entitled to minimum sick leave by law?

If a noncertificated employee is eligible to participate in the Illinois Municipal Retirement Fund under the 600-hour standard or under any other eligibility participation standard allowed by Section 7-198 of the Illinois Pension Code, the employee is entitled to a minimum statutory grant of 10 sick leave days per year cumulative to a minimum of 180 days. The minimums set forth above may be increased by contract when a bargaining unit is involved or by school board policy in other instances.

105 ILCS 5/24-6

DISMISSAL

**20:140   Is a noncertificated educational support
employee entitled to due process prior to
dismissal for cause?**

Assuming a collective bargaining agreement does not provide additional contractual rights, educational support personnel are entitled to 30 days notice prior to dismissal.
Such employees frequently have an expectation of employment beyond mere notice, because of the actions of their
employers. An employer guarantee to an employee of re-employ-
ment to avoid the employee's summer unemployment compensation claim would, for example, create a property right in continued employment and require the employer to provide substantive and procedural due process before the employee can be
dismissed.
Likewise, the existence of a "just cause" provision or a procedural due process clause in a collective bargaining agreement
might provide the employee with rights beyond those contained
in the law.
The statute governing the notice which must be given
non-certified employees before termination was amended in
1997. Employers should be certain their policies conform with
the changes before implementing the presumably less stringent
notice requirements of the amended statute.
To dismiss a noncertificated employee for cause during the
term of his employment expectation requires a pre-termination
hearing which allows the employee a fair opportunity to refute
the alleged causes for dismissal. In cases of disciplinary suspension based on criminal charges, a pre-disciplinary hearing may
not be required if due process is promptly provided.

105 ILCS 5/10-23.5
Gilbert v. Homar, 117 S.Ct. 1807, 520 U.S. 924, 138 L.Ed.2d 120 (1997) on
rem. 149 F.3d 1164
Cleveland Board of Education v. Loudermill, 105 S.Ct. 1487, 470 U.S.
532, 84 L.Ed.2d 494 (1985) on rem. 763 F.2d 202 (6th Cir. 1985)

**20:142   May a school board create an at-will
employment relationship with its
noncertificated employees?**

Whether or not an at-will relationship exists is a fact question which requires an examination of the employment relation-

ship between the employer and employee. Employer policies, rules and regulations, employment documents and other evidence of the relationship between the parties will define whether noncertified employees are at-will or contractual and whether or not any particular employee has an expectation of continued employment.

An employer wanting to rely on an at-will relationship should be certain its policy manual and employee handbook do not contain just cause dismissal language or promises of continuing employment. It is unlikely that a non-certificated employee in a recognized bargaining unit is an at-will employee. The safer approach for most employers is to assume its non-certificated employees are year-to-year contractual employees.

Doyle v. Holy Cross Hospital, 186 Ill.2d 104, 708 N.E.2d 1140, 237 Ill.Dec. 100 (1999)

Spear v. North Shore School District No. 112, 291 Ill.App.3d 117, 683 N.E.2d 218, 225 Ill.Dec. 274 (2nd Dist. 1997) app. den. 175 Ill.2d 555, 689 N.E.2d 147, 228 Ill.Dec. 726

Rojicek v. Community Consolidated School District No. 15, 888 F.Supp. 878 (N.D. Ill. 1995)

20:143   May a noncertificated educational support employee use a "just cause" provision in a collective bargaining agreement to challenge his discipline or dismissal?

A "just cause" provision is one which requires that an employee's discipline be "fair" or for "just cause." A "just cause" provision in a collective bargaining agreement covering noncertificated employees is probably enforceable.

105 ILCS 5/10-23.5

Board of Education of Rockford School District No. 205, v. The Illinois Educational Labor Relations Board, 165 Ill.2d 80, 649 N.E.2d 369, 208 Ill.Dec. 313 (1995)

Midwest Central Education Association v. Illinois Educational Labor Relations Board, et al., 277 Ill.App.3d 440, 660 N.E.2d 151, 213 Ill.Dec. 894 (1st Dist. 1995)

20:150   Do educational support personnel have seniority rights?

Unless a collective bargaining agreement provides otherwise, educational support personnel acquire seniority within the respective category of position in which they are employed from the first day of continuous service to the school district.

105 ILCS 5/10-23.5

20:160   Are part time educational support personnel entitled to seniority rights?

Yes. Unlike teachers, both full and part time educational support personnel are entitled to seniority by law.

105 ILCS 5/10-23.5

20:170   Do educational support personnel serve a probationary period before earning seniority rights?

No. Again unlike teachers, seniority accrues to educational support personnel employees from their first day of employment, rather than after a probationary period.

105 ILCS 5/10-23.5

20:180   What is the procedure for reducing the number of educational support staff employed by the district?

When the school board decides to decrease the number of educational support staff employed or to discontinue some particular type of educational support service, written notice must be mailed to the employee and also given to the employee either by certified mail, return receipt requested or personal delivery with receipt, at least 30 days before the employee is removed or dismissed, together with a statement of honorable dismissal and the reason therefor.

The employee(s) with the shorter length of continuing service with the district, within the respective category of position, must be dismissed first unless an alternative method of determining the sequence of dismissal is lawfully established in a collective bargaining agreement.

A collectively bargained alternative provision for determining the sequence of dismissal must not impair the operation of any affirmative action program in the district, regardless of whether it exists by operation of law or is conducted on a voluntary basis by the board.

105 ILCS 5/10-23.5
*Buckellew v. Board of Education of Georgetown-Ridge Farm Community
Unit School District No. 4*, 214 Ill.App.3d 506, 575 N.E.2d 556, 159 Ill.Dec. 58
(4th Dist. 1991)

20:182 Is a reduction in support staff work hours a reduction in force within the meaning of law?

The statute which governs the procedures for reduction in force of support staff probably applies only to the removal or dismissal of support employees and not to the reduction of their hours.

Georgetown-Ridge Farm Community Unit School District No. 4, 10 PERI 1044 (IELRB Opinion and Order, March 1, 1994)
*Buckellew v. Board of Education of Georgetown-Ridge Farm Community
Unit School District No. 4*, 214 Ill.App.3d 506, 575 N.E.2d 556, 159 Ill.Dec. 58
(4th Dist. 1991)

20:183 Must a school district follow the notice provisions of the reduction-in-force laws with respect to the reduction of temporary or substitute support employees?

No.

*Buckellew v. Board of Education of Georgetown-Ridge Farm Community
Unit School District No. 4*, 214 Ill.App.3d 506, 575 N.E.2d 556, 159 Ill.Dec. 58
(4th Dist. 1991)

20:190 Do educational support personnel have recall rights after layoff?

Yes. After a layoff, any vacancies occurring for the following school term or within one year from the beginning of that school term must be tendered to the employees removed from that specific category of position if they are qualified to hold such positions.

105 ILCS 5/10-23.5

20:200 Must a school board recall educational support personnel from a layoff pool in seniority order?

Employees need not be recalled from the recall pool in seniority order unless a collective bargaining agreement requires it.

105 ILCS 5/10-23.5

SCHOOL BUS DRIVERS

20:210   What are the qualifications for employment as a school bus driver?

A school bus driver must hold a valid school bus driver permit. To obtain a permit, an applicant must submit the results of a medical examination showing physical fitness to operate a school bus, submit to and pass a fingerprint-based criminal background check, have a safe driving record pursuant to statutory definition, demonstrate he has never been convicted of any of a list of specified criminal offenses, be at least 21 years of age, have not within the last five years been adjudged to be afflicted with or suffering from any mental disability or disease, and hold a valid and properly classified driver's license that has not been revoked, suspended or canceled during the previous three years or has not has his commercial motor vehicle driving privileges disqualified during the previous three years. There are numerous other requirements contained in the relevant statute.

49 CFR 382.301
625 ILCS 5/6-106.1

20:214   What must an employer do before he can employ a school bus driver?

The employer is responsible for conducting pre-employment interviews, distributing school bus driver applications and medical forms to be completed by the applicant, and submitting the applicant's fingerprint cards to the State Police. The employer must certify in writing to the Secretary of State that all pre-employment conditions have been met including completion of the criminal background check.

625 ILCS 5/6-106.1

20:220   May a school board suspend or revoke an employee's school bus driver permit?

No. The Secretary of State may suspend or revoke a school bus driver permit for specific causes provided in Illinois motor vehicle laws. A school board does not have this authority.

625 ILCS 5/6-106.1 (g)

20.230   What happens if a school bus driver fails the drug and alcohol test required by statute?

If an applicant fails to obtain a negative result on the mandatory drug and alcohol test necessary to obtain a school bus driver permit, the Secretary of State must refuse the applicant a permit for a period of three years.

625 ILCS 5/6-106.1 (g)

20:240   May a school bus driver who has an accident while driving a school bus refuse a drug or alcohol test?

No. The driver is subject to the implied consent requirements for commercial motor vehicle drivers.

49 CFR 382.211
49 CFR 382.303
625 ILCS 5/6-516(c)
625 ILCS 5/11-501.2

21: COLLECTIVE BARGAINING

ILLINOIS EDUCATIONAL LABOR RELATIONS ACT

21:10 What is the Illinois Educational Labor Relations Act?

The Illinois Educational Labor Relations Act is a state law which regulates the recognition of exclusive bargaining representatives and the collective bargaining relationships and procedures for all public school employers and all public school employees in the state.

Under terms of the Act, covered employees may organize, form, join, or assist in employee organizations, or engage in lawful concerted activities for the purpose of collective bargaining or other mutual aid and protection, or bargain collectively through representatives of their own free choice. Except as limited by the Act, employees also have the right to refrain from any or all such activities.

115 ILCS 5/1 et seq.
115 ILCS 5/3

21:20 Does the National Labor Relations Board have any jurisdiction with respect to Illinois educational labor relations?

No.

21:30 How is the Illinois Educational Labor Relations Act implemented and enforced?

The Illinois Educational Labor Relations Board (IELRB) promulgates and enforces rules necessary to carry out the purposes of the Act.

115 ILCS 5/1 et seq.

21:40 What is the Illinois Educational Labor Relations Board?

The Illinois Educational Labor Relations Board (IELRB) is a five-member board appointed by the Governor with the advice and consent of the Senate. No more than three IELRB members may be from the same political party. Members must have a minimum of five years experience directly related to labor and employment relations in representing educational employers or educational employees in collective bargaining matters.

Members of the IELRB generally serve six-year terms of office. However, the number of members making up the Board was increased in 1998 and during the transition, one member will serve a four-year term. Members of the IELRB may be removed only by the Governor upon notice and only for neglect of duty or malfeasance in office and for no other cause.

115 ILCS 5/5
Board of Education of Mundelein Elementary School District No. 75 v Illinois Educational Labor Relations Board, 179 Ill.App.3d 696, 534 N.E.2d 1022, 128 Ill.Dec. 577 (4th Dist. 1989)

21:50 Do rulings of the Illinois Educational Labor Relations Board have the effect of law?

Yes. But any party aggrieved by a final order of the Illinois Educational Labor Relations Board may appeal to either the First or Fourth District Appellate Courts at the option of the appellant.

115 ILCS 5/16

21:60 Does the Open Meetings Act apply to collective bargaining negotiations and grievance arbitrations?

No. Bargaining meetings at which collective bargaining will occur and arbitration hearings are not subject to the Open Meetings Act. The notice requirements and the closed meeting exceptions of the Open Meetings Act are not applicable.

School board meetings held solely to develop strategy, at which no bargaining actually occurs, and board meetings to plan arbitration strategy are subject to the Open Meetings Act.

115 ILCS 5/18

COVERED EMPLOYERS AND EMPLOYEES

21:70   What employers are covered by the Illinois Educational Labor Relations Act?

Employers covered by the Act are the governing bodies of any public school district, combination of public school districts (including the governing bodies of joint agreements of any type formed by two or more school districts), and any state agency whose major function is providing educational services.

115 ILCS 5/2

21:74   May the employees of an alternative school created under the Safe Schools Law petition for collective bargaining rights?

Yes.

105 ILCS 5/13A-1(m)

21:75   Who is the employer of alternative school employees?

The employer of alternative school employees is the regional board of school trustees where the alternative school is located.

105 ILCS 5/13A-5

21:80   Which school employees are covered by the Illinois Educational Labor Relations Act?

The Act covers any school district employee except supervisory, managerial, confidential, short-term, or student employees.

115 ILCS 5/2(b)

21:90   What is a supervisory employee?

A supervisor is any individual having authority in the interests of the employer to hire, transfer, suspend, lay off, recall, promote, discharge, reward, or discipline other employees within the appropriate bargaining unit and adjust their grievances, or to effectively recommend such action if the exercise of such authority is not of a merely routine or clerical nature, but requires the use of independent judgment. The term supervisor includes only those individuals who devote a preponderance of their employment time to exercising such authority.

115 ILCS 5/2(g)
Illinois Department of Management Services, 5 PERI 2012 (IELRB Decision and Order, April 28, 1989)
Virden Community Unit School District No. 4, 4 PERI 1060 (IELRB Hearing Officer, March 31, 1988)

21:100   What is a managerial employee?

A managerial employee is an individual who is engaged predominantly in executive and management functions and is charged with the responsibility of directing the effectuation of management policies and practices.

115 ILCS 5/2(o)
Lincoln Way Community High School District No. 210, 5 PERI 1025 (Executive Director's Recommended Decision and Order, January 11, 1989)

21:110   What is a confidential employee?

A confidential employee is an employee who (1) in the regular course of his duties, assists and acts in a confidential capacity to persons who formulate, determine, and effectuate management policies with regard to labor relations, or (2) in the regular course of his duties has access to information relating to the effectuation or review of the employer's collective bargaining policies.

115 ILCS 5/2(n)
Danville Community Consolidated School District No. 118, 5 PERI 1084 (IELRB Opinion and Order, April 12, 1989)
Board of Education of Plainfield Community Consolidated School District No. 202, Will and Kendall Counties v. Illinois Educational Labor Relations Board, et al., 143 Ill.App.3d 898, 493 N.E.2d 1130, 98 Ill.Dec. 109 (4th Dist. 1986)

21:115   What is a short-term employee?

A short-term employee is one who is employed for less than two consecutive calendar quarters during a calendar year and who does not have reasonable assurance that he or she will be rehired by the same employer for the same service in a subsequent calendar year.

115 ILCS 5/2(q)

21:120   May noncertificated employees seek union recognition and bargaining rights under the Educational Labor Relations Act?

Noncertificated school employees may seek recognition and bargaining rights under the Act provided they are school board employees and not the employees of an independent contractor. The employees of independent contractors (such as independent bus companies or janitorial service companies) are not covered under the Act.

115 ILCS 5/2(b)
Decatur School District No. 61, 3 PERI 1022 (IELRB Opinion and Order, February 10, 1987)
Alpha School Bus Company, 2 PERI 1008 (Executive Director's Recommended Decision and Order, November 7, 1985)

STATUTORY OBLIGATIONS OF EMPLOYERS

21:130   Does the Illinois Educational Labor Relations Act require school boards and their employees to bargain collectively?

The Act requires educational employers to collectively bargain with representatives of duly recognized employee bargaining units. If an appropriate bargaining unit gains voluntary recognition or recognition by election, the employer must bargain with it.

115 ILCS 5/10

21:140   What matters are educational employers obligated to bargain with their employees?

Covered employers are required to bargain collectively with regard to policy matters directly affecting wages, hours, and terms and conditions of employment, as well as the impact thereon, upon request by an employee representative. However, employers are not required to bargain over matters of inherent managerial policy.

115 ILCS 5/3
115 ILCS 5/4
Central City Education Association, IEA-NEA v. Illinois Educational Labor Relations Board and Central City Community Consolidated School District No. 133, 149 Ill.2d 496, 599 N.E.2d 892, 174 Ill.Dec. 808 (1992)
Board of Education Decatur District No. 61 v. Illinois Educational Labor Relations Board, 180 Ill.App.3d 770, 536 N.E.2d 743, 129 Ill.Dec. 693 (4th Dist. 1989)

21:145 May an employer avoid bargaining obligations by assigning a subject of bargaining to a non-bargaining committee for study or resolution?

When an employer assigns a mandatory subject of bargaining to a committee for resolution, the subject is not removed from the realm of collective bargaining—nor is the employer relieved of any bargaining obligations—even though the union agrees to the committee assignment. If both labor and management are represented on the committee to which the subject is assigned, agreements reached by the committee may be contractual unless there is an express waiver by the union to the contrary.

These assignments to committee most frequently occur when difficult and complicated issues (such as health insurance specifications) are being bargained and the issue is deemed too time consuming or complicated for resolution at the bargaining table.

Board of Education of DuPage High School District No. 88 v. Illinois Educational Labor Relations Board, 246 Ill.App.3d 967, 617 N.E.2d 790, 187 Ill.Dec. 333 (1st Dist. 1993)
Alton Community Unit School District No. 11 v. Illinois Educational Labor Relations Board, 209 Ill.App.3d 16, 567 N.E.2d 671, 153 Ill.Dec. 713 (4th Dist. 1991)

21:150 What are the inherent managerial policies which employers are not required to bargain?

Matters of inherent managerial policy include such areas of discretion or policy as the functions of the employer, standards of services, the overall budget, the organizational structure, and selection of new employees and direction of employees.

A balancing test is used to determine whether a particular subject is more nearly a "wage, hour or term and condition of employment" which must be bargained, or a management right which need not be bargained.

115 ILCS 5/4
115 ILCS 5/10
Central City Education Association, IEA-NEA v. Illinois Educational Labor Relations Board and Central City Community Consolidated School District No. 133, 149 Ill.2d 496, 599 N.E.2d 892, 174 Ill.Dec. 808 (1992)
Board of Education Leroy Community Unit School District No. 2 v. Illinois Educational Labor Relations Board, 199 Ill.App.3d 347, 556 N.E.2d 857, 145 Ill.Dec. 239 (4th Dist. 1990) 149 Ill.2d 496, 599 N.E.2d 892, 174 Ill.Dec. 808 (1992)
Board of Education Decatur District No. 61 v. Illinois Educational Labor Relations Board, 180 Ill.App.3d 770, 536 N.E.2d 743, 129 Ill.Dec. 693 (4th Dist. 1989)

21:160 Is the school board free to make unilateral decisions on matters of inherent managerial policy?

Yes, a school board may make decisions on matters of inherent managerial policy. However, when any such decision affects the wages, hours, and terms and conditions of employment of any employee, the school board may be required to bargain the decision and/or the impact of any decision upon timely request of a recognized bargaining agent. Whether or not the employer has an obligation to bargain in any given circumstance may be governed by a subjective balancing test. This obligation regarding the impact of managerial policy decisions is called "impact bargaining."

Central City Education Association, IEA-NEA v. Illinois Educational Labor Relations Board and Central City Community Consolidated School District No. 133, 149 Ill.2d 496, 599 N.E.2d 892, 174 Ill.Dec. 808 (1992)

21:166 May a school board unilaterally create a new extra duty or job assignment?

Yes. However, the wages to be paid for the new extra duty or new job assignment and the duties attendant to it must be bargained on demand by the exclusive representative.

Discussions between the employer and individual employee about wages or duties will likely result in unfair labor practice charges; extra duty bargaining must involve the employer and the union.

Board of Education of Sesser-Valier Community Unit School District No. 196 v. Illinois Educational Labor Relations Board and Sesser-Valier Education Association, IEA-NEA, 250 Ill.App.3d 878, 620 N.E.2d 418, 189 Ill.Dec. 450 (4th Dist. 1993)

21:170 How does bargaining the impact of a decision differ from bargaining the decision itself?

Decisional bargaining requires the employer to bargain with the exclusive bargaining agent over a decision to do something before the decision is made or implemented. Impact bargaining means that the employer is free to make an unfettered decision but is obligated to bargain, on demand, the effects of the decision on wages, hours and terms or conditions of employment.

Central City Education Association, IEA-NEA v. Illinois Educational Labor Relations Board and Central City Community Consolidated School District No. 133, 149 Ill.2d 496, 599 N.E.2d 892, 174 Ill.Dec. 808 (1992)

Berkeley School District No. 87, 2 PERI 1066 (IELRB Opinion and Order, May 30, 1986)

21:180 May an employer subcontract work performed by bargaining unit members to outside persons or firms?

With respect to non-instructional services, a 1997 amendment to the School Code makes uncertain what must be done before the work is sub-contracted. The statute provides:

"Notwithstanding any other law of this State, nothing in this Code [The School Code] prevents a board of education from entering into a contract with a third party for non-instructional services currently performed by any bargaining unit member. . ."

It is uncertain how bargaining obligations are affected by the new law since the relevant collective bargaining provisions are not contained in The School Code. Teacher bargaining unit work may not be sub-contracted until the employer has first met its obligation to bargain.

105 ILCS 5/10-22.34c

Buckellew v. Board of Education of Georgetown-Ridge Farm Community Unit School District No. 4, 214 Ill.App.3d 506, 575 N.E.2d 556, 159 Ill.Dec. 58 (4th Dist. 1991)

Service Employees International Local Union No. 316 v. Illinois Educational Labor Relations Board and Carbondale Community High School District No. 165, 153 Ill.App.3d 744, 505 N.E.2d 418, 106 Ill.Dec. 112 (4th Dist. 1987)

21:190 In addition to bargaining a union contract, may a school board be required to bargain during the term of that contract?

During the term of a collective bargaining agreement—absent a broad zipper clause—the school board must, on demand by the exclusive bargaining representative, bargain over wages, hours and terms and conditions of employment which were not fully bargained during the bargaining of the collective bargaining agreement. This is called "interim bargaining" or "midterm bargaining."

West Chicago School District 33 v. Illinois Educational Labor Relations Board, 218 Ill.App.3d 304, 578 N.E.2d 232, 161 Ill.Dec. 105 (1st Dist. 1991)

Waverly Community Unit School District No. 6, 5 PERI 1002 (IELRB Opinion and Order, November 23, 1988)

21:200 What is a zipper clause?

There are two kinds of zipper clauses—a broad zipper clause and narrow zipper clause. A zipper clause is a negotiated contract clause under which a union waives its right to engage in mid-term bargaining over mandatory subjects of bargaining.

A narrow zipper clause waives the right to bargain over issues actually negotiated by the parties. A broad zipper clause forecloses bargaining on any issue not included in the contract even if the issue was unknown or not within the contemplation of the parties at the time the contract was signed. A zipper clause is a form of waiver of a union right to bargain.

Mt. Vernon Education Association, IEA-NEA v. The Illinois Educational Labor Relations Board, 278 Ill.App.3d 814, 664 N.E.2d 1067, 215 Ill.Dec. 553 (4th Dist. 1996)

Board of Regents of the Regency University System (Northern Illinois University), 7 PERI 1113 (IELRB Opinion and Order, October 24, 1991)

East Richland Education Association v. IELRB, 173 Ill.App.3d 878, 528 N.E.2d 751, 124 Ill.Dec. 63 (4th Dist. 1988)
Rock Falls Elementary School District No. 13, 2 PERI 1150 (IELRB Opinion and Order, May 14, 1987) aff'd. sub nom.

21:202   Is a waiver or zipper clause a mandatory subject of bargaining?

An employer proposal for a broad zipper clause is a permissive subject of bargaining. The employer may not insist to impasse on a broad zipper clause without committing an unfair labor practice.

An employer proposal for a narrow zipper clause is a mandatory subject of bargaining. An employer may insist to impasse over a narrow zipper clause without committing an unfair labor practice.

A union may voluntarily agree to a broad waiver, but the employer should be cautious because the waiver may be withdrawn unilaterally by the union during an appropriate bargaining period. If the waiver was bargained to neutralize or as a trade for some otherwise consequential language in the collective bargaining agreement, the effect of the removal of the waiver would be to leave the offending language in the contract but without the neutralizing waiver.

Waivers frequently take the form of attempts to exclude contract language from the grievance procedure, side agreements, zipper clauses and other attempts to avoid bargaining obligations.

Mt. Vernon Education Association, IEA-NEA v. The Illinois Educational Labor Relations Board, 278 Ill.App.3d 814, 664 N.E.2d 1067, 215 Ill.Dec. 553 (4th Dist. 1996)
Board of Regents of the Regency University System (Northern Illinois University), 7 PERI 1113 (IELRB Opinion and Order, October 24, 1991)

21:206   May a collective bargaining agreement contain an "election of remedies" clause?

Any clause which limits the rights of employees to file claims should be carefully considered before adoption or inclusion in a collective bargaining agreement. While some "election of remedies" clauses are undoubtedly permissible, others are not. The law is unsettled as to which forms are okay and which are not.

Equal Employment Opportunities Commission v. Board of Governors of State Colleges, 957 F.2d 424 (7th Cir. 1992)

BARGAINING UNITS

21:210   What is a bargaining unit?

A bargaining unit is a group of employees who have gained recognition, determined an exclusive representative and have bargaining rights under the terms of the Educational Labor Relations Act.

115 ILCS 5/2(m)

21:220   What is a wall-to-wall bargaining unit?

A wall-to-wall bargaining unit is a bargaining unit composed of both professional and noncertificated employees. To form a wall-to-wall bargaining unit, both the professional and the non-certificated employees must vote to approve the combined bargaining unit.

115 ILCS 5/7
Riverside-Brookfield Township District No. 208, 5 PERI 1136 (IELRB Decision and Order, July 25, 1989)

21:230   On what basis is a bargaining unit determined to be appropriate?

In determining the appropriateness of a unit, the Educational Labor Relations Board must decide in each case, in order to ensure employees the fullest freedom in exercising the rights guaranteed by the Illinois Educational Labor Relations Act, the unit appropriate for the purpose of collective bargaining based upon, but not limited to, such factors as historical pattern of recognition; community of interest, including employee skills and functions; degree of functional integration; interchangeability and contact among employees; common supervision, wages, hours and other working conditions of the employees involved; and the desires of the employees.

115 ILCS 5/7(a)

EXCLUSIVE BARGAINING REPRESENTATIVE

21:240   What is an exclusive representative?

An exclusive representative is the labor organization which has been designated by the Illinois Educational Labor Relations Board as the representative of the majority of educational employees in an appropriate unit, or one that has historically been recognized as the representative of an appropriate unit, or one that is voluntarily recognized by an employer upon evidence that the organization has been designated as the exclusive representative by a majority of the employees in an appropriate unit.

115 ILCS 5/2(d)

21:250   How may an exclusive representative gain recognition by election?

A labor organization may gain recognition as the exclusive representative of an employee unit by an election of the employees in the unit. Petitions requesting an election are filed with the Illinois Educational Labor Relations Board (IELRB). The IELRB investigates the petition and if it has reasonable cause to suspect a question of representation exists, it gives notice and conducts a hearing. If it finds upon the record of the hearing a question of representation exists, it must direct that an election be held no later than 90 days after the date the petition was filed. In many cases the parties waive hearing, enter into a consent agreement, and an election is held pursuant to the consent agreement.

115 ILCS 5/7
80 Ill. Admin. Code 1110.50 et seq.

21:260   What ballot choices are required in the election of an exclusive bargaining representative?

An incumbent bargaining representative is automatically placed on any ballot. An intervening labor organization may be placed on the ballot if the intervenor can demonstrate a 15 percent showing of interest. Any other bargaining representative seeking recognition requires a 30 percent showing of interest. In any election the voters must be given the choice of "no representative."

115 ILCS 5/7
115 ILCS 5/8

21:270   How are representation elections conducted?

Representation elections are conducted by secret ballot in accordance with rules and regulations established by the Illinois Educational Labor Relations Board (IELRB). Usually, notice of election announcing the election, noticing election dates, times and places and describing the proposition to be voted on is posted in prominent places in the school district for 30 days before the election. Absentee ballots are permitted when an individual would otherwise be unable to cast a ballot.

If none of the choices on the ballot receives a majority, a run-off is conducted between the two choices receiving the largest number of valid votes cast in the election. The IELRB must certify the results of the election within five working days after the final tally of votes unless a charge is filed by a party alleging improper conduct occurred which affected the outcome of the election.

115 ILCS 5/8
80 Ill. Admin. Code 1110.10 et seq.

21:274   What happens if an employer fails to include all the appropriate names on a representation election voter eligibility list?

The employer is responsible for the submission of a voter eligibility list to the Illinois Educational Labor Relations Board (IELRB) and all interested parties prior to a representation election. If the list the employer submits is incomplete and if the election tally is close, the election results may be set aside by the IELRB.

College of Lake County and College of Lake County Staff Council, Lake County Federation of Teachers, Local 504, IFT-AFT / AFL-CIO, 14 PERI 1095 (IELRB Decision and Order, October 8, 1998)

21:280 What is decertification?

A decertification results when an incumbent representative no longer represents the majority of the employees in the bargaining unit. A decertification petition requires an allegation and showing of interest by at least 30 percent of the employees in the appropriate bargaining unit. An employer cannot instigate or lend support to a decertification petition.

115 ILCS 5/7(c)
80 Ill. Admin. Code 1100.60 et seq.

21:282 How may an employer respond to a decertification question from a bargaining unit member?

An employer may not interfere, restrain or coerce employees who exercise rights guaranteed by the Illinois Educational Labor Relations Act. The employer should not respond to decertification questions by an employee except to give the employee the phone number of the Illinois Educational Labor Relations Board.

115 ILCS 5/14(a)(1)
District 114 Support Staff IEA-NEA and Fox Lake Elementary School District, 10 PERI 1097 (IELRB Administrative Law Judge, June 14, 1994)

21:290 When may employee representation be challenged?

A petition seeking a representation election may only be filed during certain specified time periods. There is a waiting period after a previous election in a particular bargaining unit before another petition may be filed, and petitions may only be filed during a specified window period during the life of a collective bargaining agreement.

115 ILCS 5/7
80 Ill. Admin. Code 1110.70

21:300 How are election objections filed?

A charge alleging improper election conduct which affected the outcome of an election may be filed with the Illinois Educational Labor Relations Board (IELRB) within five days of the final tally of votes. The IELRB must investigate the allegations, and if it finds probable cause that improper conduct occurred and could have affected the outcome of the election, it must set a hearing on the matter on a date falling within two weeks of when it received the charge.

If the IELRB determines, after the hearing, that the outcome of the election was affected by improper conduct, it must order a new election and must order corrective action which it considers necessary to ensure the fairness of the new election. If it determines upon investigation or after hearing the alleged improper conduct did not take place or it did not affect the results of the election, it must immediately certify the election results.

> 115 ILCS 5/8
> 80 Ill. Admin. Code 1110.150
> *Decatur Federation of Teachers IFT-AFT, AFL-CIO v. Educational Labor Relations Board,* 199 Ill.App.3d 190, 556 N.E.2d 780, 145 Ill.Dec. 162 (4th Dist. 1990)
> *Champaign Community Unit School District No. 4,* 5 PERI 1124 (Executive Director's Recommended Decision and Order, June 15, 1989)
> *Centralia School District No. 135,* 4 PERI 1044 (IELRB Opinion and Order, February 25, 1988)

NONUNION EMPLOYEES

21:310   May a contract provision require employees to join a union as a condition of employment?

No. A school board may enter into a collectively bargained agreement which requires all employees covered by the agreement to pay a "fair share" fee, but may not make union membership a condition of employment.

> 115 ILCS 5/11
> *Abood v. Detroit Board of Education,* 97 S.Ct. 1782, 431 U.S. 209, 52 L.Ed. 261, reh. den. 97 S.Ct. 2989, 433 U.S. 915, 53 L.Ed.2d 1102 (1977)
> *Chicago Teachers Union Local 1, AFT, AFL-CIO v. Hudson,* 106 S.Ct. 1066, 475 U.S. 292, 89 L.Ed.2d 232 (1986)

21:320   Must an exclusive bargaining representative represent non-union employees?

An exclusive bargaining representative has "a duty of fair representation" which extends to all members of the bargaining unit, whether the bargaining unit member is a union member or nut. If the exclusive bargaining representative fails to provide fair representation for any bargaining unit member, the member has a cause of action against the union.

115 ILCS 5/3
NEA, IEA Classroom Teachers Council of District 15 (Kostka), 5 PERI 1067 (Executive Director's Recommended Decision and Order, March 13, 1989)

21:330 What is the difference between fair share, agency shop and union shop?

Fair share and agency shop are synonymous terms and are permissible under the Educational Labor Relations Act. They are contract provisions which require non-union teachers to pay a representation fee to the union as a condition of employment.

The fair share agreement between a school board and a teachers union may require the non-union member to pay an amount to defray the cost of collective bargaining, contract administration, and union grievance representation. A union may not collect money from non-union members to be used in support of ideological causes which are not germane to its duties as collective bargaining agent. Thus, political action assessments may not be included in fair share fees.

Union shop is a contract provision which makes union membership a condition of employment. A union shop provision is illegal.

115 ILCS 5/11
80 Ill. Admin. Code 1125.10 et seq.
Lehnert v. Ferris Faculty Association, 111 S.Ct. 1950, 500 U.S. 507, 114 L.Ed.2d 572 (1991) reh. den. 111 S.Ct. 2878, 115 L.Ed.2d 1044, on rem. 937 F.2d 608
Abood v. Detroit Board of Education, 97 S.Ct. 1782, 431 U.S. 209, 52 L.Ed. 261, reh. den. 97 S.Ct. 2989, 433 U.S. 915, 53 L.Ed.2d 1102 (1977)
Chicago Teachers Union Local 1, AFT, AFL-CIO v. Hudson, 106 S.Ct. 1066, 475 U.S. 292, 89 L.Ed.2d 232 (1986)

21:340 May an employer exclude a union representative from a grievance adjustment meeting if the grievant is a non-union teacher and so requests?

No. Any individual employee or group of employees may at any time present grievances to the employer and have them adjusted without the intervention of the bargaining representative, provided that the adjustment is not inconsistent with the terms of a collective bargaining agreement then in effect. However, the bargaining representative must be given an opportunity to be present at such adjustment.

115 ILCS 5/3

UNFAIR LABOR PRACTICES

21:350   What is "bargaining in good faith?"

Parties subject to bargaining obligations must meet at reasonable times and confer in good faith with respect to wages, hours, and other terms and conditions of employment, and execute a written contract incorporating any agreements reached. Bargaining in good faith does not require a party to agree to a proposal or to make a concession. The totality of bargaining conduct is examined to determine whether or not any particular bargaining was conducted in good faith.

115 ILCS 5/10
Kewanee Community Unit School District No. 229, 4 PERI 1136 (IELRB Opinion and Order, September 15, 1988)

21:360   What is the remedy for failure to bargain in good faith?

Either the employee representative or the employer may file an unfair labor practice charge with the Illinois Educational Labor Relations Board alleging failure to bargain in good faith.

115 ILCS 5/10
115 ILCS 5/14
Thornton Township High School District No. 205, 5 PERI 1134 (Executive Director's Recommended Decision and Order, July 10, 1989)

21:370   What is an unfair labor practice charge?

An unfair labor practice charge is an allegation of conduct which is prohibited in 115 ILCS 5/14.

115 ILCS 5/14
80 Ill. Admin. Code 1120.10 et seq.

21:380   Who may file an unfair labor practice charge?

An unfair labor practice charge may be filed by an employer, an individual employee or a labor organization.

115 ILCS 5/14
80 Ill. Admin. Code 1120.20 a)

21:390   What are union unfair labor practices?

Employee organizations, their agents or representatives, or educational employees are prohibited from:

1) Restraining or coercing employees in the exercise of the rights guaranteed under the Educational Labor Relations Act.

2) Restraining or coercing an educational employer in the selection of his representative for the purposes of collective bargaining or the adjustment of grievances

3) Refusing to bargain collectively in good faith with an educational employer.

4) Violating any of the rules and regulations promulgated by the Educational Labor Relations Board regulating the conduct of representation elections.

5) Refusing to reduce a collective bargaining agreement to writing and signing such agreement.

6) Refusing to comply with the provisions of a binding arbitration award.

115 ILCS 5/14 a)

21:400   What are employer unfair labor practices?

Educational employers, their agents or representatives are prohibited from:

1) Interfering, restraining, or coercing employees in the exercise of the rights guaranteed under the Illinois Educational Labor Relations Act.

2) Dominating or interfering with the formation, existence, or administration of any employee organization.

3) Discriminating in regard to hiring or tenure of employment or any term or condition of employment to encourage or discourage membership in any employee organization.

4) Discharging or otherwise discriminating against an employee because he or she has signed or filed an affidavit,

authorization card, petition or complaint, or given any information or testimony under the Educational Labor Relations Act.

5) Refusing to bargain collectively in good faith with an employee representative which is the exclusive representative of employees in an appropriate unit, including, but not limited to, the discussing of grievances with the exclusive representative; provided, however, that if an alleged unfair labor practice involves interpretation or application of the terms of a collective bargaining agreement, and said agreement contains a grievance and arbitration procedure, the Educational Labor Relations Board may defer the resolution of such dispute to the grievance and arbitration procedure contained in said agreement.

6) Refusing to reduce a collective bargaining agreement to writing and signing such agreement.

7) Violating any of the rules and regulations promulgated by the Educational Labor Relations Board regulating the conduct of representation elections.

8) Refusing to comply with the provisions of a binding arbitration award.

115 ILCS 5/14 b)

21:410   How is an unfair labor practice charge filed?

An unfair labor practice charge may be filed with the Educational Labor Relations Board (IELRB) on forms provided by the IELRB. A charge must be signed and must contain the name address and affiliation of both the charging party and respondent. It also must contain a complete statement of facts supporting the alleged unfair labor practice, including dates, times and places of occurrence of each act alleged and the sections of the Act alleged to have been violated. It must also include a statement of relief sought.

Upon receipt of a charge, the IELRB investigates. If the IELRB determines the charge states an issue of law or fact sufficient to warrant a hearing, it issues a complaint. Thereafter, a hearing is held on the charges and a decision rendered. The parties have the right to various appeals.

115 ILCS 5/15
23 Ill. Admin. Code 1120.20 et seq.
Lake Zurich School District No. 45, 1 PERI 1031 (IELRB Opinion and Order, November 30, 1984)

21:420   Is there a limitations period for unfair labor practice charges?

No order may be issued on an unfair labor practice occurring more than six months before the filing of the charge alleging the unfair labor practice.

115 ILCS 5/15
80 Ill. Admin. Code 1100.30
80 Ill. Admin. Code 1120.20 d)
Charleston Community Unit School District No. 1 v. Illinois Educational Labor Relations Board and Charleston Education Association, IEA-NEA, 203 Ill.App.3d 619, 561 N.E.2d 331, 149 Ill.Dec. 53 (4th Dist. 1990)
Wapella Education Association, IEA-NEA v. Illinois Educational Labor Relations Board, 177 Ill.App.3d 153, 531 N.E.2d 1371, 126 Ill.Dec. 532 (4th Dist. 1988)

21:430   Must a school board permit union representatives to enter the schools during the school day to meet with school employees?

The agents of an exclusive bargaining representative must be allowed to meet with school employees in school buildings during employee duty-free times.

105 ILCS 5/24-25

IMPASSES AND STRIKES

21:440   What is impasse?

Impasse exists if, in view of all the circumstances of bargaining, further discussions would be futile. Impasse does not exist if there is a ray of hope with a real potentiality for agreement if explored in good faith bargaining sessions. In examining whether or not impasse has been reached the following factors are examined:

1) bargaining history;
2) the good faith of the parties in negotiations;
3) the length of the negotiations;
4) the importance of the issue(s) as to which there is disagreement; and

5) the contemporaneous understanding of the parties as to the state of negotiations.

115 ILCS 5/12
80 Ill. Admin. Code 1130.10 et seq.
Kewanee Community School District No. 229, 4 PERI 1136 (IELRB Opinion and Order, September 15, 1988)

21:450 What is the difference between a mediator, a fact-finder and an arbitrator?

All three terms refer to third parties brought into a dispute in an effort to assist in its resolution. A mediator can suggest a resolution to the parties, usually does not make his recommendation public, and has no authority to enforce any recommended solution.

A fact finder also suggests resolutions but usually makes his recommendations public. Like a mediator, a fact finder has no power of enforcement.

An arbitrator makes a formal ruling, makes the ruling public, and has power to enforce the ruling.

Mediation of contract formation disputes is mandatory at the request of either party under the Educational Labor Relations Act; fact finding and interest arbitration are permissive under the Act.

115 ILCS 5/12
80 Ill. Admin. Code 1130.30 et seq.
80 Ill. Admin. Code 1130.50

21:460 Must a contract bargaining dispute be submitted to binding arbitration?

No. Interest arbitration—the process whereby an arbitrator is employed to resolve differences which arise between the parties in reaching contract agreement—is permissible under the Illinois Educational Labor Relations Act (the parties may agree to it). But it is not required.

Grievance arbitration is a process whereby an arbitrator is employed to resolve differences which arise between the parties in interpreting the meaning of contract language. Grievance arbitration is mandatory under the Illinois Educational Labor Relations Act.

115 ILCS 5/12

21:470 What options are there in the selection of a mediator?

Unless an applicable collective bargaining agreement provides otherwise, the parties to a bargaining dispute have several options in the selection of a mediator. The parties may mutually agree to engage:

1) any qualified, impartial individual who is mutually acceptable to the parties under terms established by the parties.

2) an individual assigned or selected under the auspices of a private service, such as the American Arbitration Association. Filing fees are often charged, and the mediators selected or assigned charge the parties a per diem fee.

3) a federal mediator assigned by the Federal Mediation and Conciliation Service (FMCS). FMCS does not charge for its services. If either party requests the use of mediation services from the FMCS, the other party must either join in the request or bear the additional cost of mediation services from another source.

The IELRB may invoke mediation at the request of either party or on its own motion after a reasonable period of negotiation and absent agreement by the parties on a mediator. Mediators provided by the IELRB charge the parties a per diem fee.

115 ILCS 5/12
80 Ill. Admin. Code 1130.30
80 Ill. Admin. Code 1130.80

21:480 What is a no-strike clause?

A no-strike clause is a contract provision which prohibits strikes during the term of a contract agreement. A no-strike clause does not prohibit a strike after an agreement expires. The Educational Labor Relations Act requires each collective bargaining agreement to contain a no-strike clause. A no-strike clause may explicitly define the meaning of the term "strike" to prohibit work slow-downs and other job actions during the term of a contract.

115 ILCS 5/10(c)
80 Ill. Admin. Code 1130.70 a)

21:490   When are strikes permitted?

Educational employees are prohibited from participation in a strike except under the following conditions:

1) they are represented by an exclusive bargaining representative;

2) mediation has been used without success;

3) at least ten days have elapsed after a notice of intent to strike has been given by the exclusive bargaining representative to the educational employer, the regional superintendent, and the Illinois Educational Labor Relations Board;

4) the collective bargaining agreement between the educational employer and educational employees, if any, has expired; and

5) the employer and the exclusive bargaining representative have not mutually agreed to submit the unresolved issues to arbitration.

115 ILCS 5/13
80 Ill. Admin. Code 1130.40

21:495   Must a school make up the school days lost to a teacher strike?

There is no statutory requirement that school days lost to a teacher strike be made up during vacation periods or after the school term would, but for the strike, have ended. Whether school days are made up or lost after a strike is a mandatory subject of bargaining.

The resolution of the issue is generally defined in the agreement that ends the strike. If a school district does not make up strike days, it routinely loses state aid for each day during the strike that school was not in session and for which an educational program was not provided.

21:500   May striking school board employees picket the home of a school board member or administrator?

It is unlawful to picket before or about the residence or dwelling of any person, except when the residence or dwelling is used as a place of business. Peaceful picketing is not prohibited if it is at a place of a meeting or assembly or is on premises commonly used to discuss subjects of general public interest.

720 ILCS 5/21.1-2

GRIEVANCE RESOLUTION

21:510   What is a grievance?

What constitutes a grievance is usually defined in a collective bargaining agreement. Commonly, the definition provides that a grievance is an allegation by an employee, group of employees or exclusive bargaining representative that there has been a violation of a specific provision of the contract.

Staunton Community Unit School District No. 6 v. Illinois Educational Labor Relations Board, 200 Ill.App.3d 370, 158 N.E.2d 751, 146 Ill.Dec. 788 (4th Dist. 1990)

Moraine Valley Community College, 5 PERI 1102 (IELRB Opinion and Order, May 12, 1989)

21:520   Must a collective bargaining agreement allow grievance arbitration?

The collective bargaining agreement negotiated between representatives of the educational employees and the educational employer must contain a grievance resolution procedure which must apply to all employees in the unit and must provide for binding arbitration of disputes concerning the administration or interpretation of the agreement.

115 ILCS 5/10(c)
80 Ill. Admin. Code 1130.70 a)
River Grove School District No. 85 1/2, 3 PERI 1019 (IELRB Opinion and Order, January 30, 1987)

21:530   What is the difference between interest arbitration and grievance arbitration?

Interest arbitration is a process whereby an arbitrator is employed to resolve differences which arise between the parties in reaching contract agreement. Under the Illinois Educational Labor Relations Act, interest arbitration is permissible (the parties may agree to it).

Grievance arbitration is a process whereby an arbitrator is employed to resolve differences which arise between the parties in interpreting the meaning of contract language. Grievance arbitration is mandatory under the Illinois Educational Labor Relations Act.

115 ILCS 5/10(c)
115 ILCS 5/12

21:540   Which body has jurisdiction to vacate or modify an arbitration award?

The Illinois Educational Labor Relations Board has sole and exclusive jurisdiction to vacate or modify arbitration awards. A school board seeking to appeal a decision of an arbitrator must refuse to comply with the provisions of the arbitrator's award and await an unfair labor practice charge. Circuit courts lack jurisdiction to vacate or modify arbitration awards.

115 ILCS 5/14
115 ILCS 5/16
Board of Education Warren Township High School District No. 121 v. Warren Township High School Federation of Teachers Local 504, IFT/AFL-CIO, 128 Ill.2d 155, 538 N.E.2d 524, 131 Ill.Dec. 149 (1989)
Board of Education of Community Unit School District No. 1 v. Compton, 123 Ill.2d 216, 526 N.E.2d 149, 122 Ill.Dec. 9 (1988)

21:542   What is the likelihood an arbitration award will be overturned on appeal?

The review standard applied by the Illinois Educational Labor Relations Board and the courts is extremely limited. When considering whether a school board has committed an unfair labor practice by refusing to comply with a binding arbitration award, the inquiry is limited to whether the award was binding, the content of the award, and whether or not the school board has complied with the award.

Board of Education of DuPage High School District No. 88 v. Illinois Educational Labor Relations Board, 246 Ill.App.3d 967, 617 N.E.2d 790, 187 Ill.Dec. 333 (1st Dist. 1993)

CONTRACTUAL PROVISIONS

21:550   What is the maximum term of a collective bargaining agreement?

A collective bargaining agreement may be negotiated for a period not exceeding three years. Collective bargaining agreements in excess of three years may or may not be permissible depending upon their express provisions. A bargaining agreement of less than three years may be extended up to three years if the extension is agreed to in writing before the filing of an election petition.

115 ILCS 5/7

21:560   May a collective bargaining agreement give teachers or other employees more rights than are provided by law?

The parties to the collective bargaining process may implement a provision in a collective bargaining agreement if that provision has the effect of supplementing any provision in any state statute pertaining to wages, hours, or other conditions of employment.

However, the parties may not implement any contract provision that contradicts any such state statute. Whether a contract provision granting employees more rights than are provided by law is legal, therefore, depends upon whether it is construed as supplementary or contradictory to state statutes.

115 ILCS 5/10(b)

21:565   What is a "just cause" provision?

A "just cause" provision in a collective bargaining agreement is a contract clause which limits the employer to the discipline or dismissal of employees only when there is "just cause" to do so. Some "just cause" clauses use synonymous phrases such as: "for good cause shown" or "only for good reasons." A "just cause" provision is enforceable to the extent it is not in violation of, inconsistent with or in conflict with Illinois law.

115 ILCS 5/10(b)
Board of Education of Rockford School District No. 205, v. The Illinois Educational Labor Relations Board, 165 Ill.2d 80, 649 N.E.2d 369, 208 Ill.Dec. 313 (1995)
Midwest Central Education Association v. Illinois Educational Labor Relations Board, et al., 277 Ill.App.3d 440, 660 N.E.2d 151, 213 Ill.Dec. 894 (1st Dist. 1995)

21:570   May an employee group agree in a collective bargaining agreement to give up some statutory rights in exchange for other rights or money? For example, could a teacher bargaining unit trade tenure for a large salary increase?

No. The parties to a collective bargaining agreement may not effect or implement a provision in a collective bargaining agreement if the implementation of that provision would be inconsistent or in conflict with any statute enacted by the General Assembly.

No provision in a collective bargaining agreement may be effected or implemented if such provision has the effect of negating, abrogating, replacing, reducing, diminishing, or limiting in any way any employee rights, guarantees, or privileges pertaining to wages, hours, or other conditions of employment provided in statute. Any such provision in a collective bargaining agreement is void and unenforceable, but does not affect the validity, enforceability, and implementation of other permissible provisions of the collective bargaining agreement.

115 ILCS 5/10(b)

21:580   May a collective bargaining agreement include a cost of living adjustment (COLA) clause or any other clause which ties salary increases to outside factors?

Yes.

Libertyville Education Association IEA-NEA v. Board of Education, 56 Ill.App.3d 503, 371 N.E.2d 676, 13 Ill.Dec. 741 (2nd Dist. 1977)

21:590   What benefits must be provided employees after expiration of a collective bargaining agreement and before a successor agreement is reached?

The school board must maintain the status quo. An employer's unilateral alteration of prevailing terms and conditions of employment under negotiation during the course of bargaining is an unfair labor practice.

Vienna School District No. 55 v. Illinois Educational Labor Relations Board, 162 Ill.App.3d 503, 515 N.E.2d 476, 113 Ill.Dec. 667 (4th Dist. 1987)

22: SCHOOL DISTRICTS AND LIABILITY FOR INJURIES

TORT IMMUNITY CONCEPTS

22:10   What is a tort?

A tort is a private or civil wrong or injury, other than a breach of contract, for which the law provides a remedy in an action for damages. The elements of every tort require a duty flowing from the defendant to the plaintiff, a breach of that duty and damages which proximately result.

22:12   What are punitive damages?

Punitive damages are those given in addition to compensation for a loss sustained in order to punish and make an example of the wrongdoer.

25 C.J.S. Damages 2

22:14   What is willful and wanton misconduct?

Willful and wanton misconduct is an intentional act or an act committed under circumstances exhibiting a reckless disregard for the safety of others, such as a failure, after knowledge of impending danger, to exercise ordinary care to prevent it or a failure to discover the danger through recklessness, or carelessness when it could have been discovered by ordinary care. The Tort Immunity Act defines willful and wanton misconduct as "a course of action which shows actual or deliberate intention to cause harm or which, if not intentional, shows an utter indifference to or conscious disregard for the safety of others or their property."

745 ILCS 10/1-210
Burke v. 12 Rothschild's Liquor Mart, Inc., 209 Ill.App.3d 192, 568 N.E.2d 80, 154 Ill.Dec. 80, app.den. 139 Ill. 2d 594, 575 N.E.2d 912, 159 Ill.Dec. 105, order vac. on reconsideration ___ Ill.2d ___, 575 N.E.2d 1234, 159 Ill.Dec. 174,

app. allowed 141 Ill.2d 536, 580 N.E. 2d 109, 162 Ill. Dec. 483, aff'd. 148 Ill.2d
429, 593 N.E.2d 522, 170 Ill. Dec. 633 (1992)
    *Braun v. Board of Education of Red Bud Community Unit School District
No. 132*, 151 Ill.App.3d 787, 502 N.E.2d 1076, 104 Ill.Dec. 416 (5th Dist. 1986)
app. den. 115 Ill.2d 538, 511 N.E.2d 426, 110 Ill.Dec. 454 (1987)
    Gammon v. Edwardsville Community Unit School District No. 7, 82
Ill.App.3d 586, 403 N.E.2d 43, 38 Ill.Dec. 28 (5th Dist. 1980)

22:15   What is the difference between negligence and willful and wanton misconduct?

Ordinary negligence is a failure to exercise that degree of care which the ordinary prudent person would exercise under similar conditions. Willful and wanton misconduct requires an intentional act or an act committed under circumstances exhibiting a reckless disregard for the safety of others.

Ramos v. Waukegan Community Unit School District No. 60, 188
Ill.App.3d 1031, 544 N.E.2d 1302, 136 Ill.Dec. 527 (2nd Dist. 1989)
    *Lynch v. Board of Education of Collinsville Community Unit School
District No. 10*, 82 Ill.2d 415, 412 N.E.2d 447, 45 Ill.Dec. 96 (1980)
    Thomas v. Chicago Board of Education, 77 Ill.2d 165, 395 N.E.2d 538, 32
Ill.Dec. 308 (1979)
    Gerrity v. Beatty, 71 Ill.2d 47, 373 N.E.2d 1323, 15 Ill.Dec. 639 (1978)
    McCauley v. Chicago Board of Education, 66 Ill.App.3d 676, 384 N.E.2d
100, 23 Ill.Dec. 464 (1st Dist. 1978)
    Kobylanski v. Chicago Board of Education, 63 Ill.2d 165, 347 N.E.2d 705
(1976)
    Clay v. Chicago Board of Education, 22 Ill.App.3d 437, 318 N.E.2d 153
(1st Dist. 1974)
    Mancha v. Field Museum of Natural History, 5 Ill.App.3d 699, 283 N.E.2d
899 (1st Dist. 1972)
    *Woodman v. Litchfield Community Unit School District No. 12,
Montgomery County*, 102 Ill.App.2d 330, 242 N.E.2d 780 (5th Dist. 1968)
    Fustin v. Board of Education of Community Unit School District No. 2,
101 Ill.App.2d 113, 242 N.E.2d 308 (5th Dist. 1968)

22:18   What is the intentional infliction of emotional distress?

To establish a cause of action for intentional infliction of emotional distress, a plaintiff must prove: 1) the defendant's conduct was extreme and outrageous, 2) the defendant either intended that his conduct should inflict severe emotional distress or knew there was a high probability that his conduct would cause severe emotional distress, and 3) the conduct in fact caused severe emotional distress.

Strasburger v. Board of Education Hardin County Community Unit School District No. 1, et al., 143 F.3d 351 (7th Cir. 1998)
    Public Finance Corporation v. Davis, 66 Ill.2d 85, 360 N.E.2d 765, 4 Ill.Dec. 652 (5th Dist. 1976)

TORT IMMUNITIES

22:20   Are there tort liability immunities which apply to school boards?

Neither a school board nor its employees or agents may be held liable for injuries caused under certain conditions specified in the tort immunity section of the statutes.

745 ILCS 10/1-101 et seq.
    Henrich by Henrich v. Libertyville High School et al., 186 Ill.2d 381, 712 N.E2d 298, 238 Ill.Dec. 596 (1999)

22:22   May a school district be liable for negligent supervision of an activity?

The Tort Immunity Act provides that "neither a local public entity nor a public employee who undertakes to supervise an activity on or the use of any public property is liable for an injury unless the local public entity or public employee is guilty of willful and wanton conduct in its supervision proximately causing such injury." Failure to supervise includes improper supervision. The same statute provides: "Except as otherwise provided (in the Act) neither a local public entity nor a public employee is liable for an injury caused by a failure to supervise an activity on or the use of any public property unless the employee or the local public entity has a duty to provide supervision imposed by common law, statute, ordinance code or regulation and the local or public employee is guilty of willful and wanton conduct in its failure to provide supervision proximately causing such injury." When properly raised in failure to

supervise cases, the immunity provided by The Tort Immunity
Act controls over the protections of Section 24-24 of the School
Code.

745 ILCS 10/3-108
Henrich by Henrich v. Libertyville High School et al., 186 Ill.2d 381, 712
N.E2d 298, 238 Ill.Dec. 596 (1999)
*Grandalski ex rel. Grandalski v. Lyons Township High School District
204*, 305 Ill.App.3d 1, 711 N.E.2d 372, 238 Ill.Dec. 269 (1st Dist. 1999)

22:30   May a school district be held liable for civil rights violations?

A school district may be held liable for civil rights violations.
An employee or agent of a school district has available a qualified good faith immunity defense. This defense is not available
to a school district.

Owen v. City of Independence, 100 S.Ct. 1398, 445 U.S. 622, 63 L.Ed.2d
673, on rem. 623 F.2d 550, reh. den. 100 S.Ct. 2979, 446 U.S. 993, 64 L.Ed.2d
850 (1980)

22:35   Is a school district liable for civil rights violations committed by school district employees?

A school district is potentially liable when it sanctions or
orders the action which results in the violation. Violations may
be explicitly or implicitly sanctioned by the policy or past practice of a school district.

105 ILCS 5/10-20.20
Spann for Spann v. Tyler Independent School District, 876 F.2d 437 (5th
Cir. 1989)
Pembaur v. Cincinnati, 106 S.Ct. 1292, 475 U.S. 469, 89 L.Ed.2d 452
(1986)

22:50   May a school district be liable for punitive damages?

No, but its school board members and employees may be
held liable.

745 ILCS 10/2-102
Collins v. School District No. 189, St. Clair County, 115 Ill.App.3d 100,
450 N.E.2d 387, 70 Ill.Dec. 914 (5th Dist. 1983)

LIABILITY OF INDIVIDUALS

22:60   Can a school employee, volunteer, or school board member be held personally liable for an act or failure to act which was done or not done for the benefit of the school?

The school district must indemnify and protect school board members, employees, volunteers and student teachers against civil rights damage claims and suits, constitutional rights damage claims and suits and death and bodily injury and property damage claims and suits, including the costs of defense, when damages are sought for negligent or wrongful acts alleged to have been committed in the scope of employment or under the direction of the school board.

105 ILCS 5/10-20.20
745 ILCS 10/1 101 et seq.
Bridewell v. Board of Education of Shawnee Community Unit School District No. 84 of Union, et al. Counties, 2 Ill.App.3d 684, 276 N.E.2d 745 (5th Dist. 1971)

22:64   Under what circumstances do school employees or school board members have qualified immunity from liability for civil rights violations?

Governmental officials performing discretionary functions are usually shielded from liability for civil damages insofar as their conduct does not violate clearly established statutory or constitutional rights of which a reasonable person would have known. The contours of the right must be sufficiently clear that a reasonable official would understand that what he is doing is wrong.

Harlow v. Fitzgerald, 102 S.Ct 2727, 457 U.S. 800, 73 L.Ed.2d 396 (1982)
Anderson v. Creighton, 107 S.Ct. 3034, 483 U.S. 635, 97 L.Ed.2d 523 (1987)

22:70   May a school employee, volunteer or school board member be personally liable for punitive damages?

Punitive damages are intended to punish the party on whom they are assessed. Indemnity and immunity protections insulate public officials from liability for punitive damages in any action

arising out of an act or omission made by the public official
while serving in an official executive, legislative, quasi-legisla-
tive or quasi-judicial capacity.

In all other circumstances, school-connected individuals
may be liable for punitive damages. Punitive damage awards
are rare, however, and are imposed only in instances of extraordinary wrongdoing.

105 ILCS 5/10-20.20
745 ILCS 10/2-102

22:75   What are the risks when a school board member exceeds his authority?

A school board member who acts outside the scope of his
authority may be personally liable for his wrongdoing.

INJURIES TO EMPLOYEES

22:80   May a school employee sue the school district for a work-related injury?

School employees are subject to worker compensation
statutes and may recover only under the provisions of those
laws. However, it is sometimes possible to bring related causes
of action under the Illinois Human Rights Act or under the
grievance procedure contained in a collective bargaining agreement.

820 ILCS 305/1 et seq.

22:90   Does the Occupational Safety and Health Act (OSHA) apply to public school districts?

No. The federal Occupational Safety and Health Act
excludes school districts. The Illinois Department of Labor, however, often adopts and enforces OSHA standards.

29 U.S.C. 652 (5)

INJURIES TO STUDENTS

22:100 Under what circumstances may a school employee be held liable for injuries to students while in school?

If an "in loco parentis" relationship is found to exist between an injured student and a defendant school employee, the employee cannot be liable for ordinary negligence. The student can recover only if he can prove willful and wanton misconduct. If an in loco parentis relationship does not exist, the employee would be liable for injuries arising out of ordinary negligence, and the school board would be responsible to defend and indemnify the employee for his negligent or wrongful acts if they were committed within the scope of employment or under the direction of the school board.

105 ILCS 5/10-20.20
105 ILCS 5/24-24
Sidwell v. Griggsville Community Unit School District No. 4, 146 Ill.2d 467, 588 N.E.2d 1185, 167 Ill. Dec. 1055 (1992)
Plesnicar v. Kovach, 102 Ill.App.3d 867, 430 N.E.2d 648, 58 Ill.Dec. 616 (1st Dist. 1981)
O'Brien v. Township High School District No. 214, 83 Ill.2d 462, 415 N.E.2d 1015, 47 Ill.Dec. 702 (1980)
Thomas v. Chicago Board of Education, 60 Ill.App.3d 729, 377 N.E.2d 55, 17 Ill.Dec. 865, rev. on other grounds 77 Ill.App.2d 165, 395 N.E.2d 538, 32 Ill.Dec. 308 (1st Dist. 1978)
Kobylanski v. Chicago Board of Education, 63 Ill.2d 165, 347 N.E.2d 705 (1976)
Clay v. Chicago Board of Education, 22 Ill.App.3d 437, 318 N.E.2d 153 (1st Dist. 1974)

22:110 Which employees enjoy the protections of "in loco parentis?"

Teachers and other certificated employees stand in place of parents for students under their supervision and, therefore, cannot be held liable for ordinary negligence. Noncertificated employees do not enjoy this defense against ordinary negligence claims.

105 ILCS 5/24-24

22:112　Can a school district assert "in loco parentis" immunity?

Limited immunity under Section 24-24 of the School Code is available only to teachers and other certificated educational employees, not school districts. A school district vicariously benefits when a cause of action predicated on negligence is brought against an educational employee, however.

Sidwell v. Griggsville Community Unit School District No. 4, 146 Ill.2d 467, 588 N.E.2d 1185, 167 Ill.Dec. 1055 (1992)

22:140　Does the "in loco parentis" status of teachers extend to activities outside school?

The in loco parentis status of teachers is restricted to those activities which are connected to the total school program. It extends to extracurricular activities, but may not extend to other activities which have a more tenuous connection to the total school program.

Stiff v. Eastern Illinois Area of Special Education, 251 Ill.App.3d 859, 621 N.E.2d 218, 190 Ill.Dec. 349 (4th Dist. 1993)

Montag v. Board of Education of School District No. 40, Rock Island County, 112 Ill.App.3d 1039, 446 N.E.2d 299, 68 Ill.Dec. 565 (3rd Dist. 1983)

Weiss v. Collinsville Community Unit School District No. 10, Madison County, 119 Ill.App.3d 68, 456 N.E.2d 614, 74 Ill.Dec. 893 (5th Dist. 1983)

Plesnicar v. Kovach, 102 Ill.App.3d 867, 430 N.E.2d 648, 58 Ill.Dec. 616 (1st Dist. 1981)

Lynch v. Board of Education of Collinsville Community Unit School District No. 10, 82 Ill.2d 415, 412 N.E.2d 447, 45 Ill.Dec. 96 (1980)

Woodman v. Litchfield Community Unit School District No. 12, Montgomery County, 102 Ill.App.2d 330, 242 N.E.2d 780 (5th Dist. 1968)

Fustin v. Board of Education of Community Unit School District No. 2, 101 Ill.App.2d 113, 242 N.E.2d 308 (1968)

22:145　What duty does a school district have to a student riding or leaving a school bus?

A school district has a very high duty of care to students while they are riding a school bus. The duty becomes a duty of reasonable care with respect to the students once they have left the bus and are on their way home. This latter duty means the school district cannot expose the students to unreasonable risks by reason of the school district's selection of bus routes, drop off points or procedures.

Garrett v. Grant School District No. 124, 139 Ill.App.3d 569, 487 N.E.2d 699, 93 Ill.Dec. 874 (2nd Dist. 1985)

Posteher v. Pana Community Unit School District, 96 Ill.App.3d 709, 421 N.E.2d 1049, 52 Ill.Dec. 186 (4th Dist. 1981)

Katamay v. Chicago Transit Authority, 53 Ill.2d 27, 289 N.E.2d 623 (1972)

Sims v. Chicago Transit Authority, 351 Ill.App. 314, 115 N.E.2d 96 (1st Dist. 1953), rev. on other grounds 4 Ill.2d 60, 122 N.E.2d 221 (1954)

22:150 What responsibilities and liabilities do school districts incur when providing medical treatment to students?

When a medical emergency occurs and trained medical personnel are unavailable, teachers standing in loco parentis may render necessary emergency treatment to pupils. Teachers are not expected to possess expert medical knowledge but, rather, to act reasonably and prudently.

745 ILCS 10/6-104 et seq.

22:160 If an Illinois public school student is injured on an out-of-state field trip, which state's immunity laws control?

Immunity defenses to tort claims are governed by the laws of the state in which the lawsuit is properly brought.

Nevada v. Hall, 99 S.Ct. 1182, 440 U.S. 410, 59 L.Ed.2d 416, reh. den. 99 S.Ct. 2018, 441 U.S. 917, 60 L.Ed.2d 389 (1979)

22:164 If a parent provides a permission slip for his child to participate in a school activity, will the school be protected from liability if an accident occurs?

A parent's waiver of liability will not prevent the minor child from bringing suit. While such waivers do not violate public policy in Illinois, they are not favored by the courts and are strictly construed against the benefiting party. A minor does not have capacity to waive liability.

Meyer by Meyer v. Naperville Manor, Inc., 262 Ill.App.3d 141, 634 N.E.2d 411, 199 Ill.Dec. 572 (2nd Dist. 1994)

Masciola v. Chicago Metropolitan Ski Council, 257 Ill.App.3d 313, 628 N.E.2d 1067, 195 Ill.Dec. 603 (1st Dist. 1993)

22:167 Does tort immunity protect a school district from liability when an injury occurs on a school playground?

Neither a school district nor its employees can be held liable for an "...injury where the liability is based on the existence of a condition of any public property intended or permitted to be used for recreational purposes..." unless the school district or employee has caused the injury by willful and wanton misconduct. Whether or not the property is used for recreational purpose depends upon the character of the property, not the activity performed on it at any given time.

745 ILCS 10/3-106
Bubb v. Springfield School District No. 186, et al., 167 Ill.2d 372, 657 N.E.2d 887, 194 Ill.Dec. 518 (1995)

22:170 Is there a cause of action for educational malpractice?

Educational malpractice lawsuits have, for the most part, been unsuccessful. There is no recognized duty to educate, the breach of which would create a cause of action.

Donohue v. Copiague Union Free School District, 418 N.Y.S.2d 375, 47 N.Y.2d 440 (1979)

SAFETY REQUIREMENTS

22:180 What safety requirements are contained in the School Code to protect persons on school property from injury?

Every student, teacher, and visitor must wear an industrial quality eye protective device when participating in or observing any of the following courses in public schools:

1) vocational or industrial arts shops or laboratories involving experience with the following: hot molten metals; milling, sawing, turning, shaping, cutting, grinding, or stamping of any solid materials; heat treatment, tempering, or kiln firing of any metal or other materials; gas or electric arc welding; repair or servicing of any vehicle; caustic or explosive materials;

2) chemical or combined chemical-physical laboratories involving caustic or explosive chemicals or hot liquids or solids.

105 ILCS 115/1

22:190 What other statutory safety requirements are imposed on school boards to protect persons from injury while on school property?

School building construction and maintenance are subject to stringent State Board of Education regulations in the Illinois Life-Safety Code. Schools also are subject to the occupational safety standards contained in the Illinois Health and Safety Act and enforced by the Illinois Department of Labor. Other safety standards applicable to schools include various environmental requirements, such as asbestos abatement and safe drinking water, traffic safety, and the common law "duty of care" owed to students while on school premises.

15 U.S.C. 2641 et seq.
105 ILCS 5/2-3.12
820 ILCS 225/1
23 Ill. Admin. Code 175
23 Ill. Admin. Code 185
Jastram v. Lake Villa School District No. 41, 192 Ill.App.3d 599, 549 N.E.2d 9, 139 Ill.Dec. 29 (2nd Dist. 1989)

22:193 What safety standards apply to the construction and operation of school buses?

There are both federal and state rules and regulations which govern school bus construction and safety standards for school vehicles.

49 C.F.R. 571.100 et seq.
92 Ill.Admin.Code 440 et seq.
92 Ill.Admin. Code 442 et seq.
92 Ill.Admin.Code 444 et seq.

22:196 May a school district purchase a 12- or 15-passenger van for use as a school bus?

Under federal law, a school bus is a passenger motor vehicle designed to carry 11 or more persons. Any such vehicle must meet federal bus safety standards. A school district should not purchase, lease or use a van which is designed to carry 11 or more passengers unless the vehicle meets federal standards, even if state law suggests otherwise. To ignore the federal law will potentially increase the school board's exposure in the event of an accident.

49 U.S.C. 30101 et seq.

22:200   What immunities and/or defenses against tort liability would be available to a school board for injuries arising out of violations of statutory safety requirements?

School boards owe a "duty of care" to students, employees and visitors where the safety of buildings, grounds and equipment are concerned. The protections of "in loco parentis" are available only where an injury arises from the supervisory duties of a certificated employee, and would not protect the school district where the injury arises, for example, from faulty equipment or unsafe building conditions.

Whether any of the immunities specified in the tort immunity statute would apply to unsafe building conditions would depend upon the facts in each situation.

745 ILCS 10/1-101 et seq.

22:210   What standard of care does a school district owe invitees on school property?

A school district must exercise reasonable care with respect to invitees on school property. Invitees include spectators at athletic contests and parents attending a conference day.

Borushek v. Kincaid, 78 Ill.App.3d 295, 397 N.E.2d 172, 33 Ill.Dec. 839 (1st Dist. 1979)

Tanari v. School Directors of District No. 502, County of Bureau, 69 Ill.2d 63, 373 N.E.2d 5, 14 Ill.Dec. 874 (1977)

JUDGMENTS

22:230   What manner of payment may a school board elect in paying a settlement or judgment?

If a school board does not pay a tort judgment during the fiscal year in which it becomes final and if, in the opinion of the school board, the payment of the judgment creates an unreasonable financial hardship for the school district, it shall pay the balance of the judgment with interest in installments subject to conditions set forth in statute.

745 ILCS 10/9-104
Evans v. City of Chicago, 689 F.2d 1286 (7th Cir. 1982)

22:240   Is a school district which loses a civil rights suit responsible to pay the attorney fees and expert witness fees of the plaintiff?

The school district defendant would be liable to pay the attorney fees of the plaintiff, but not the plaintiff's expert witness fees.

West Virginia University Hospital v. Casey, 111 S.Ct. 1138, 499 U.S. 83, 113 L.Ed.2d 68 (1991)

22:250   With what resources does a school board pay settlements and related legal costs?

A school board is authorized to maintain a Tort Immunity Fund and to levy taxes and/or to issue bonds in an amount necessary to pay judgments and related expenses specified by statute.

105 ILCS 5/17-2.5
745 ILCS 10/9-102 et seq.

23: PROPERTY TAX INCOME

AUTHORITY TO LEVY TAXES

23:10   On what property may a school board levy taxes?

A school district may levy on all taxable property within school district boundaries, including property which at the time of the levy was part of the school district but which at a later date in the same tax year was detached.

People ex rel. Nordstom v. Barry, 11 Ill.2d 259, 142 N.E.2d 26 (1957)
People ex rel. Davis v. Spence, 3 Ill.2d 244, 120 N.E.2d 565 (1954)

23:20   May vocational education or special education cooperatives levy taxes?

No. However, a special education joint agreement district, composed of one member of the school board of each cooperating district, has the authority to borrow by issuance of bonds or notes. Each member district has an obligation to repay but that obligation does not affect the debt limitation of the member district.

105 ILCS 5/10-22.31

23:30   May a school district levy a personal property tax?

No.

Ill. Const. art. IX, sec. 5(c)
Cherry Bowl, Inc. v. Property Tax Appeal Board, 100 Ill.App.3d 326, 426 N.E.2d 618, 55 Ill.Dec. 472 (2nd Dist. 1981)
Central Illinois Light Co. v. Johnson, 84 Ill.2d 275, 418 N.E.2d 275, 49 Ill.Dec. 676 (1981)

PROPERTY ASSESSMENTS

23:40   How is property assessed?

The county assessor appraises all real property. Railroad property used for transportation, private car lines, pollution control equipment, and capital stock are assessed by the State Department of Revenue, which certifies these valuations to the county clerk. In some counties, township assessors do the assessments.

The appraisals are subject to appeal by the taxpayer to the county board of appeals. The assessor's appraisals are equalized by the Illinois Department of Revenue. The purpose of equalization is to develop a common level of assessments among counties. (Equalization of assessments is essential to provide an equitable basis for distributing state aid to schools.) The Department equalizes assessments by means of multipliers assigned to each county.

The multiplier is applied to all assessments in a county to adjust assessments by a given percentage in order to bring the county level to a specified percentage of fair market value. In all Illinois counties except Cook, the statutory standard for equalization of property assessments is 33 1/3 percent of fair market value. In Cook County, property assessment standards vary with the classification or type of property, ranging from 16 percent of fair market value for residential property up to 38 percent for some commercial property.

35 ILCS 200/9-145 et seq

23:50   How does a school district secure information on the taxable property located within its boundaries?

The county clerk must furnish the school board of any school district, upon request, a certificate showing the last ascertained full, fair cash value of the taxable property of the district. When a school district lies partly in two or more counties, the county clerk of each county in which any part of the district lies must furnish the school board, upon request, a certificate showing the last ascertained full, fair cash value of the taxable property in that part of the district lying in each county.

105 ILCS 5/17-10
Board of Education of Beach Park Community Consolidated School District No. 3, Lake County v. Hess, 140 Ill.App.3d 653, 488 N.E.2d 1358, 95 Ill.Dec. 15 (2nd Dist. 1986)

23:60   What happens to the value of taxable property in an area that is included in a tax increment financing district?

The equalized assessed valuation of property within a tax increment financing district is frozen at its current valuation insofar as its impact on school district property tax revenue is concerned. Revenue generated by the school district tax levy on any future increase in assessed valuation is paid over to a special tax increment district re-development fund controlled by the municipality that created it.

Under provisions of the Real Property Tax Increment Allocation Development Act, revenue derived from future increases in assessed value may be lost to the school district for up to 23 years, depending upon provisions of the municipal ordinance creating the tax increment financing district.

65 ILCS 5/11-74.4-1 et seq.
105 ILCS 5/18-8.05
People ex rel. City of Canton v. Crouch, 79 Ill.2d 356, 403 N.E.2d 242 (1980)

23:61   What notice does a school district get prior to the creation of a redevelopment area?

If a municipality or a commission adopts an ordinance or resolution providing for a feasibility study on the designation of an area as a redevelopment project area, a copy of the ordinance must be sent to the school district. The ordinance must contain notice of the boundaries of the area; the purpose of the project; a general description of the tax increment allocation financing; and the name, phone number, and address of the municipal officer who can be contacted for additional information. A public hearing is required before a municipality can designate an area for redevelopment.

65 ILCS 5/11-74.4-4.1
65 ILCS 5/11-74.4-4.5

23:65   May a school district acquire information about the financial condition of a tax increment financing district?

If a majority of the taxing districts represented on the review board in which the redevelopment project area is located request it, the municipality must provide detailed financial information within 180 days after the close of each fiscal year to the taxing bodies as required by statute.

65 ILCS 5/11-74.4-5(d)

23:68   What happens if land in a tax increment financing district is not developed as anticipated?

If a redevelopment project has not been initiated in a redevelopment project area within seven years after the area was designated by ordinance, the municipality must adopt an ordinance repealing the area's designation as a redevelopment project area. The definition of a development project is the existence of a signed redevelopment agreement or expenditures on eligible redevelopment project costs associated with a redevelopment project.

65 ILCS 5/11-74.4-4(r)

23:70   May a school board intervene if it believes that certain taxable property is under-assessed?

Yes, a school board may challenge any property assessment by filing a complaint with the county board of review within a time frame specified by statute. Decisions of the county board of review may be appealed to the State Tax Appeals Board and then to the courts, or in some cases directly to the courts on Administrative Review.

35 ILCS 205/16-55 et seq.
35 ILCS 205/16-160 et seq.

TAX LEVIES

23:80   What is a certificate of tax levy?

A certificate of tax levy is a document authorized by formal action of the school board, signed by the president and clerk or secretary of the board, and issued to the county clerk. The document certifies the amount of money necessary in each fund to be levied against the equalized assessed valuation of the taxable property of the school district for a given fiscal year.

105 ILCS 5/17-11

23:90   When is a certificate of tax levy filed?

The certificate of tax levy must be filed with each county clerk on or before the last Tuesday in December annually.

105 ILCS 5/17-11
Board of Education of Community Unit School District No. 16 v. Barrett, 67 Ill.2d 11, 364 N.E.2d 89, 7 Ill.Dec. 102 (1977)

23:100   When are property taxes levied and when are they collected?

Taxes which are levied on the current year's budget and filed in December with the county clerk are extended in the spring and usually received by a school treasurer in June and September, after the current school year has ended.

35 ILCS 200/20-50 et seq.
35 ILCS 200/20-130 et seq.

23:110   May a county clerk refuse to extend a school district's taxes if the district does not file required documents within the required time?

The governing authority of each taxing district must file with the county clerk within 30 days of their adoption a certified copy of its appropriation and budget resolutions, as well as an estimate, certified by its chief fiscal officer, of revenues, by source, anticipated to be received by the school district in the following fiscal year. Failure to file the required documents (after timely notice) authorizes the county clerk to refuse to extend the tax levy imposed by the governing authority until the documents are filed.

35 ILCS 200/18-50

23:115   When may a newly combined school district levy taxes?

If the election of the board of education of a newly created district does not occur in the same calendar year that the proposition to create the new district is approved, the districts from which the new district is formed may—by joint agreement and with approval of the regional superintendent—levy in the same calendar year in which the creation of the new districts is approved at the rates specified in the petition. The county clerk(s) is required to extend taxes even though no budget has been adopted.

105 ILCS 5/7A-7
105 ILCS 5/11B-8
105 ILCS 5/11D-13

23:120   If a school district is located in two or more counties, must the school district file a certificate of levy with the county clerk in each county?

When a school district lies partly in two or more counties, the school board, after ascertaining as nearly as practical the amount to be raised by special taxes through levy, is required to prepare a certificate of tax levy for each county in which the district lies and deliver one such certificate to each of the county clerks of the counties which are a part of the district.

105 ILCS 5/17-12

23:130   May a school board amend its tax levy?

Under certain circumstances, a school board may amend its certificate of tax levy to the amount necessary to raise its operating tax rate to the level necessary to qualify for the maximum amount of state aid. However, the general state aid program introduced for 1998-1999 and thereafter does not require a school board to levy a minimum qualifying tax rate to obtain its maximum state aid. Therefore, this statutory provision provides no basis for the school board to amend its tax levy.

105 ILCS 5/17-11.1
105 ILCS 5/18-8.05
In re County Collector of McHenry County, 181 Ill.App.3d 345, 536 N.E.2d 1288, 130 Ill.Dec. 77 (2nd Dist. 1989)

23:134   May a school board file an additional tax levy following voter approval of a tax rate increase?

The school board may make an additional tax levy whenever the voters approve a tax rate increase in the educational and/or operations and maintenance fund after the levy has been filed. To do so, the board must approve an additional or supplemental budget by a majority vote of its full membership and file an additional levy for that fiscal year. Because the tax rate is increased with voter approval, adoption of the additional budget and levy probably complies with the Truth in Taxation Act.

35 ILCS 200/18-55 et seq.
105 ILCS 5/17-3.2
In re County Collector of McHenry County, 181 Ill.App.3d 345, 536 N.E.2d 1288 (2nd Dist. 1989)

23:136   What is the latest date by which a school board may file an amended or additional tax levy?

Assuming that a school board has received voter approval for an increased tax rate or otherwise meets the criteria necessary for an amended levy, the amended certificate of levy must be filed with the county clerk in time to be incorporated in the tax bills without materially impeding the county's ability to extend and collect taxes.

105 ILCS 5/17-3.2
105 ILCS 5/17-11.1
In re County Collector of McHenry County, 181 Ill.App.3d 345, 536 N.E.2d 1288 (2nd Dist. 1989)

LEVY HEARINGS

23:140   When must a school board hold a public hearing on a proposed tax levy?

A school district outside of Cook County proposing to increase its aggregate levy more than 105 percent of its prior year's extension including any amount abated by the taxing district prior to any extension but exclusive of the cost of an election, must publish notice of hearing and thereafter hold a hearing as required by law.

Until January 1, 2003, an annual truth in taxation hearing is required for all Cook County school districts on the first

Wednesday in December for all high school districts and the first Tuesday in December for all other school districts.

35 ILCS 200/18-55 et seq.
35 ILCS 200/18-101.1 et seq.

23:150   When must a school board estimate its annual aggregate tax levy?

Not less than 20 days prior to adoption of its aggregate tax levy in school districts outside Cook County and not less than 30 days prior to adoption of its aggregate tax levy in school districts inside Cook County, a school board must determine the amount of money, exclusive of any portion of that levy attributable to election costs, estimated to be necessary to be raised by taxation for that year on the taxable property within its district.

35 ILCS 200/18-60
35 ILCS 200/18-101.15

23:160   What is included in a school board's aggregate levy?

The "aggregate levy" includes the entirety of a board's annual levy except any portion of a tax levy attributable to paying the cost of conducting an election which is required under the general election laws and taxes levied to pay the principal and interest on bonds, notes, and other obligations which were secured by property tax levies and amounts due under a public building commission lease.

35 ILCS 200/18-60
Board of Education of Township High School District 211, Cook County, v. Kusper, 92 Ill.2d 333, 422 N.E.2d 179, 65 Ill.Dec. 868 (1982)

PROPERTY TAX RATES

23:170   What amounts may a school board levy in the educational fund, operations and maintenance fund and transportation fund?

A school district may levy amounts for these funds within the tax rate limits established by law. Tax rate limits for each of these funds, which differ according to type of district, may be increased by referendum.

Further, a cap on property taxes may limit school district levies in these funds in the counties of Cook, DuPage, Kane, Lake, McHenry, Will and certain other counties which have voted to impose tax caps. The county clerks in these counties may not extend taxes in the aggregate for any taxing district in excess of 105 percent of the previous year's extension or the percentage increase in the consumer price index for the prior levy year (whichever is less). Although some portions of the tax levy are exempted from the cap, the cap can limit the amount of the extension to less than what the authorized tax rate would otherwise produce.

35 ILCS 200/18-185 et seq.
105 ILCS 5/17-2 et seq.
105 ILCS 5/17-4
105 ILCS 5/17-5 et seq.

23:175   What is a tax rate and how is it calculated?

A tax rate in Illinois reflects the dollars levied per $100 of equalized assessed valuation of real property. A tax rate is calculated by dividing the dollar amount of the tax levy by the total equalized assessed valuation (EAV) of the taxing district and multiplying the product by 100. Thus, a levy of $200,000 divided by a tax base of $20 million EAV would produce a tax rate of $1.00 per $100 EAV.

23:180   What are the school district types that distinguish among different tax rates authorized by law?

A "unit school district" provides education in grades kindergarten through twelve. "Dual district" is a term describing either an elementary school district or a high school district. An elementary school district provides education in grades kindergarten through eight and a high school district provides education in grades nine through 12. Each is called a dual district because both are required in a given geographical area to provide the same range of education as is provided by a unit district.

23:190 What are the maximum allowable tax rates without referendum?

A school board may annually levy a tax not to exceed the maximum rates and for the specified purposes upon all the taxable property of the district at the value, as equalized or assessed by the Department of Revenue, as follows:

1) Districts maintaining only grades 1 through 8 may levy up to .92 percent for educational purposes and .25 percent for operations and maintenance purposes.

2) Districts maintaining only grades 9 through 12 may levy up to .92 percent for educational purposes and .25 percent for operations and maintenance purposes.

3) Districts maintaining grades 1 through 12 may levy up to 1.84 percent for educational purposes and .375 for operations and maintenance purposes. (The school board may raise the permissive rate for operations and maintenance, subject to back door referendum, to .465 percent for the 1991-92 school year and .50 percent thereafter.)

4) All districts may levy up to .075 percent for capital improvement purposes if approved by the voters.

5) Districts maintaining only grades 1 through 8 may levy up to .12 percent for transportation purposes, except that under certain specified conditions a rate of up to .20 percent is permissible; districts maintaining only grades 9 through 12 may levy up to .12 percent for transportation purposes; and districts maintaining grades 1 through 12 may levy up to .20 percent for transportation purposes.

6) Districts providing summer classes may levy up to .15 percent for educational purposes if approved by the voters.

In addition, some school districts are subject to the Property Tax Extension Limitation Law. The Law effectively imposes a limit on the aggregate tax rate when the current year's tax extension reaches 105 percent of the prior year's extension or the percentage increase in the Consumer Price Index, whichever is less.

35 ILCS 200/18-190 et seq.
105 ILCS 5/17-2

23:195   At what rate may a school board levy taxes to pay the principal and interest on bonded debt?

Bonds represent general obligations of a school district. The county clerk levies a separate tax to pay the principal and interest of the bonds of the district without limitation as to rate or amount. Although there is no statutory limit on the tax rate for debt service, school district indebtedness is limited to an aggregate amount for all forms of debt expressed as a percentage of the total value of taxable property in the district.

105 ILCS 5/17-9
105 ILCS 5/19-1

23:200   May a school district levy a tax for special education?

A school board may, by resolution, levy a tax for special education. Dual districts (those maintaining only elementary or only secondary programs) may levy .02 percent. Unit districts (those maintaining programs in grades kindergarten through 12) may levy .04 percent. The rates may be increased to .40 and to .80 percent respectively with voter approval.

105 ILCS 5/17-2.2a

23:205   May a school district levy property taxes for gifted or talented education?

No. A school district may receive state aid as reimbursement for these programs, but may not levy a tax in support of them.

105 ILCS 5/14A-1 et seq.

23:207   May a school district levy a tax for computer technology?

A school district may use the lease tax to purchase computer technology, lease educational facilities or both. The lease tax rate may not exceed .05 percent, or .10 percent upon approval of the voters. The proceeds of the tax may be used to secure the payment of a lease, lease purchase or installment agreement.

105 ILCS 5/17-2.2c

23:210   How may a school board levy to support summer school?

A school board may, by proper resolution, cause a proposition to authorize an annual tax for summer school education purposes to be submitted to the voters of the district at a regularly scheduled election. If a majority of the votes cast on this proposition is in favor, the board may thereafter levy the tax as authorized in the referendum to a maximum of .15 percent.

105 ILCS 5/17-2.1

23:220   How much and for what purposes may a school district levy taxes in its tort immunity fund?

A school district may levy whatever amount is required to pay:

1) settlements or judgments as defined in the Tort Immunity Act;

2) insurance, individual or joint self-insurance (including reserves) including all operating and administrative costs and expenses directly attributable to loss prevention and loss reduction, legal services directly attributable to the insurance and educational, inspection and supervisory services directly related to loss prevention and reduction, participation in a reciprocal insurer including all costs directly attributable to being a member of an insurance pool;

3) the costs, principal and interest on certain tort immunity bonds;

4) the cost of certain risk care management programs.

105 ILCS 5/17-2.5
745 ILCS 10/9-102 et seq.

23:221   May a school district pay the portion of administrative salaries and expenses attributable to loss prevention from the tort fund?

Before 1999, some school districts were paying a portion of their administrative expenses from the tort fund. These payments were justified as "risk management" or "loss prevention." In 1999 the General Assembly amended the statute which allegedly justified the practice as follows:

"... the purpose of this Section is to provide an extraordinary tax for funding expenses relating to tort liability, insurance, and risk management programs. Thus, the tax has been excluded from various limitations otherwise applicable to tax levies. Notwithstanding the extraordinary nature of the tax authorized by this Section, however, it has become apparent that some units of local government are using the tax revenue to fund expenses more properly paid from general operating funds. These uses of the revenue are inconsistent with the limited purpose of the tax authorization. Therefore, the General Assembly declares, as a matter of policy, that (i) the use of the tax revenue authorized by this Section for purposes not expressly authorized under this Act is improper and (ii) the provisions of this Section shall be strictly construed consistent with this declaration and the Act's express purposes."

Expenditures from the tort immunity fund must be separately identified in the annual report or audit.

745 ILCS 10/9-107

23:222 May a school board transfer surplus funds from the Tort Immunity Fund to other school district funds?

No.

105 ILCS 5/10-22.33

REFERENDUM TO INCREASE TAX RATES

23:230 May a school board levy taxes at rates exceeding the maximums authorized by statute?

A school board may levy taxes at rates exceeding statutory maximums only where (a) the statute permits increases by referendum and (b) voters approve such an increase at a referendum. Statutes permit school boards to seek voter approval to increase maximum tax rates in the education fund, operations and maintenance fund, and transportation fund.

In addition, unit districts may, by school board resolution, raise their authorized rates in the operations and maintenance fund, subject to back door referendum.

105 ILCS 5/17-3 et seq.
105 ILCS 5/17-4
105 ILCS 5/17-5 et seq.

23:232 May a proposition be put to the voters authorizing, if passed, a temporary tax increase in the education fund?

A referendum to increase the tax rate in the education fund may provide for a permanent tax increase or a tax increase for a limited period of not less than three nor more than 10 years.

105 ILCS 5/17 3

23:235 May property tax limitations be raised by referendum?

Yes. In a school district subject to the Property Tax Extension Limitation Law, a voter-approved tax rate increase raises the aggregate extension base on which the district's property tax limitation is calculated.

Also, voters may approve a cap on property tax extensions that is higher than the cap specified by law—105 percent of the prior year's extension or the percentage increase in the Consumer Price Index, whichever is less. The voter-approved cap is not permanent, however; it allows the extension to rise for that year only.

35 ILCS 200/18-205 et seq.

23:240 What is a back door referendum?

A back door referendum is the submission of a public question to the voters of a political subdivision, initiated by a petition of voters or residents of the political subdivision, to determine whether an action by the governing body of the subdivision should be adopted or rejected.

10 ILCS 5/28-2
105 ILCS 5/17-2
105 ILCS 5/17-2.2
105 ILCS 5/20-7

23:250   Which school district tax levies are subject to back door referendum?

School district tax levies which are subject to back door referenda are the educational fund; operations and maintenance fund; funding bonds to pay orders for teachers' wages or other claims; non-high school tuition; and working cash fund bonds.

105 ILCS 5/12-13
105 ILCS 5/17-2
105 ILCS 5/17-5
105 ILCS 5/19-9

TAX ABATEMENTS

23:270   May a school district participate in a tax abatement program?

Yes. School districts are among the local governments authorized by law to abate property taxes to help spur commercial or industrial growth. A school board may agree to forgive all or a portion of the taxes on the assessed valuation of new or expanded commercial/industrial property for up to 10 years.

35 ILCS 20/18-45

24: STATE AID AND OTHER SCHOOL INCOME

SOURCES OF INCOME

24:10   In addition to property taxes, what other sources of income are used to support public schools in Illinois?

An Illinois school district derives income from any or all of the following: state aid, both general and special-purpose categorical aid; grants of various types; corporate personal property replacement tax; federal aid in various forms; investment income; fees and charges; insurance proceeds, and gifts.

Other than real estate taxes, state aid represents the most significant source of revenue for Illinois schools, providing a statewide average of more than 30 percent of school district income.

24:20   Where lies the primary responsibility for financing Illinois public schools?

The state constitution imposes upon the state the primary responsibility for financing the public schools. To carry out this responsibility, the state provides various forms of direct financial support and authorizes school boards to levy taxes on property, borrow money, invest idle funds, accept gifts, charge certain fees, and purchase insurance to protect school district assets. The constitutional mandate does not mean that more than 50 percent of the funds needed to finance public education must be derived from state aid.

State law also imposes upon school boards the duty "to provide for the revenue necessary to maintain schools in their districts."

Ill. Const. art. X, sec. 1
105 ILCS 5/10-20.3

24:30   What determines school district income?

A school district's income is affected by each of the following factors:

1) Property Values — The total property value in a school district determines how much revenue the district is capable of raising from property taxes. Property values are set by the marketplace and the assessor.

2) Tax Rates — Tax rates reflect the dollars levied per $100 of equalized assessed valuation of real property. The rate at which a community taxes itself also reflects its level of effort to support its schools. State law establishes maximum tax rates that may be levied by various types of school districts. Some rates may be raised with voter approval at a referendum. The aggregate tax rate of a school district may be limited if the district is located in a county that is governed by The Property Tax Extension Limitation Law.

3) State Guarantees — Each year, the state establishes a per pupil revenue guarantee called the "foundation level." State aid makes up the difference between the foundation level and a school district's "available local resources."

4) Pupil Enrollment — School district revenue from state aid increases and decreases in response to changes in student enrollment, as reflected in average daily attendance, because state aid is based in part on the number of students served.

35 ILCS 200/1-1 et seq.
105 ILCS 5/18-9
105 ILCS 5/18-10

STATE MANDATES

24:40   What is a state mandate?

A state mandate is any state-initiated statutory or executive action which requires a local government to establish, expand or modify its activities in such a way so as to necessitate additional expenditures from local revenues. As a result of the Mandates Act, the state is required to fully or partially fund certain program requirements which are statutorily imposed on units of local government.

30 ILCS 805/1 et seq.

24:50 Are there funding exemptions to the State Mandates Act?

The state is not obligated to pay for a mandate if it:

1) is imposed to accommodate a request from local government;

2) imposes additional duties of a nature which can be carried out by existing staff and procedures at no appreciable net cost increase;

3) creates additional costs but also provides offsetting savings resulting in no aggregate increase in net costs;

4) imposes a cost that is wholly or largely recovered from federal, state, or other external financial aid;

5) imposes additional annual net costs of less than $1,000 for each of the several local governments affected or less than $50,000 in the aggregate for all local governments affected;

6) results from legislation enacted by the General Assembly to comply with a federal mandate; or

7) is specifically exempted from compliance with the Mandates Act by reason of the express terms of the legislation.

Failure on the part of the General Assembly to make necessary appropriations relieves the local government of the obligation to implement a mandate unless an exemption is explicitly stated in the act establishing the mandate.

30 ILCS 805/1 et seq.
30 ILCS 805/8
Board of Education of Maine Township High School District No. 207 v. State Board of Education, 139 Ill.App.3d 460, 487 N.E.2d 1053, 94 Ill.Dec. 176 (1st Dist. 1985)

24:60 Is the state obligated to pay a percentage of school operating costs?

While the state has the primary responsibility to finance free public schools, the General Assembly is not obligated to fund schools at any particular level.

Committee for Educational Rights, et al., v. Edgar, 174 Ill.2d 1, 672 N.E.2d 1178, 220 Ill.Dec. 166 (1996)

San Antonio Independent School District v. Rodriguez, 93 S.Ct. 1278, 411 U.S. 1, 36 L.Ed.2d 16, reh. den. 93 S.Ct. 1919, 411 U.S. 959, 36 L.Ed.2d 418 (1973)

Blase v. Illinois, 55 Ill.2d 94, 302 N.E.2d 46 (1973)

McInnis v. Shapiro, 293 F.Supp. 327 (N.D. Ill. 1968), aff'd. *McInnis v. Ogilvie,* 89 S.Ct. 1197, 394 U.S. 322, 22 L.Ed.2d 308 (1969)

24:62   Is education a fundamental right for purposes of equal protection analysis?

Disparities in educational funding between school districts based on relative property wealth does not offend the efficiency requirement of the education provision of the Illinois Constitution, and the mere mention of educational equality by the framers of the Constitution does not give rise to a constitutional guarantee of fairness and parity in educational funding. The state constitutional right to education is not a fundamental right for purposes of equal protection analysis.

Committee for Educational Rights, et al., v. Edgar, 174 Ill.2d 1, 672 N.E.2d 1178, 220 Ill.Dec. 166 (1996)

San Antonio Independent School District v. Rodriguez, 93 S.Ct. 1278, 411 U.S. 1, 36 L.Ed.2d 16, reh. den. 93 S.Ct. 1919, 411 U.S. 959, 36 L.Ed.2d 418 (1973)

STATE AID

24:70   What is state aid?

State aid is money provided by the General Assembly to assist in supporting public education. State aid may be categorical or general. Also, some supplemental aid is appropriated to protect school districts against loss of revenue (hold harmless) and, beginning July 1, 1998, to assist districts with high concentrations of poverty-level students. (In prior years, poverty assistance was built into the general state aid formula.)

105 ILCS 5/18-1 et seq.

24:80   What are the differences between general state aid and categorical state aid?

Categorical state aid is earmarked for a particular purpose and may be used for that purpose only. Categorical and special program grants support special education, transportation, vocational education, school lunches and breakfasts, bilingual education, adult education, textbooks, and programs for both gifted students and students needing remedial help, as well as various school improvement programs for at-risk students.

General state aid, which combines with "available local resources" to provide a minimum foundation level of income per pupil, may be used at the discretion of the school district for any legal school purpose. The computation bases for aid distribution differ for categorical and general state aid.

105 ILCS 5/10-22.20
105 ILCS 5/14A-5
105 ILCS 5/14B-8;
105 ILCS 5/14C-12
105 ILCS 5/18-1 et seq.
105 ILCS 405/3-1

24:90 What is the source of state aid funds?

General state aid and some categorical aids come from the Common School Fund. This fund consists of moneys appropriated by the General Assembly for the support of common schools. It includes moneys set aside for education from the Retailers' Occupation and Use Tax (sales tax), the Illinois State Lottery, and other sources.

School districts also receive monies from such sources as the Education Assistance Fund, the General Revenue Fund and the Driver Education Fund.

20 ILCS 1605/2
35 ILCS 120/1 et seq.

STATE AID COMPUTATIONS

24:100 How is a school district's general state aid computed?

Beginning with the fiscal year that starts July 1, 1998, general state aid will be computed by multiplying equalized assessed valuation by a calculation tax rate (3.00 percent for unit districts, 2.30 percent for elementary districts and 1.05 percent for high school districts). The product is added to revenue from the Corporate Personal Property Replacement Tax and the total is divided by the best three months average daily pupil attendance to produce "available local resources per pupil." General state aid makes up the difference for each pupil between available local resources and the foundation level — $4,225 per pupil in FY 1999, $4,325 in 2000, and $4,425 in 2001.

The formula makes up the entire difference for any district with available local resources of less than 93 percent of the foundation level. Where local resources represent 93 to 175 percent of the foundation amount, state aid is reduced on a sliding scale.

A district with local resources representing 175 percent or more of the foundation level receives a flat $219 per pupil.

Prior to legislation enacted in the waning days of 1997, general state aid computations also included grade level weightings (i.e., 1.25 for high school students and 1.05 for seventh and eighth graders), as well as a different formula for calculating the local share of the foundation level.

Other factors important in determining a school district's state aid include:

1) any applicable reductions in a district's equalized assessed valuation (i.e., resulting from the Farmland Assessment Act);

2) the number of special needs students in a district;

3) whether or not the district participates in a tax abatement or tax increment allocation program under the Real Property Tax Increment Allocation Redevelopment Act;

4) the amount of money a district receives as a replacement for taxes previously received from the corporate personal property tax;

5) the number of days the schools of the district are operating with students in attendance;

6) whether or not kindergarten students attend school for full day or one-half day sessions; and

7) whether the schools in the district are recognized by the State Board of Education as meeting state-required standards for recognition.

105 ILCS 5/18-8.05
105 ILCS 5/18-9

24:105   May a school district's state aid claim be recomputed and reduced after it has been paid?

The State Board of Education has authority to recompute within three years from the final date for filing of a claim any claim for reimbursement to any school district if the claim has been found to be incorrect. The State Board may adjust subsequent claims accordingly and may recompute and adjust any such claims within six years from the final date for filing when there has been an adverse court or administrative agency decision on the merits affecting the tax revenues of the school district. No adjustment is made regarding equalized assessed valuation (EAV) unless the district's EAV is changed by the greater of $250,000 or two percent.

105 ILCS 5/2-3.33

24:110   What is the state aid grade level weighting formula?

Prior to fiscal year 1999, pupils in grades pre-kindergarten through grade six were weighted 1.00; pupils in grades seven and eight were weighted 1.05; and pupils in grades 9-12 were weighted 1.25. A school district's pupil count also included weightings for federally-defined low-income pupils. All pupil weightings were abolished for FY 1999 and after.

105 ILCS 5/18-8.05

24:120   What school district state aid is provided for children in first grade and below who attend school for less than a full day?

State aid for children in the first grade and below may be claimed as follows:

1) A session of at least four clock hours may be counted as a day of attendance for first-grade pupils and pupils in full-day kindergartens, and a session of two or more hours may be counted as one-half day of attendance by pupils in half-day kindergartens.

2) For children with disabilities below the age of six years who cannot attend two or more clock hours because of disability or immaturity, a session of not less than one clock-hour may be counted as one-half day of attendance; however, for such children whose educational needs so require, a session of four or more clock hours may be counted as a full day of attendance.

105 ILCS 5/18-8.05(F)(2) et seq.

STATE AID PENALTIES

24:140   What is the penalty for failure to have school the minimum number of pupil attendance days?

If any school district fails to provide the minimum number of pupil attendance days, the school district's state aid is proportionally reduced. The school district may also suffer recognition penalties.

105 ILCS 5/18-12
Cronin v. Lindberg, 66 Ill.2d 47, 360 N.E.2d 360, 4 Ill.Dec. 424 (1976)

24:150   What is an "act of God" day?

Under certain circumstances, a school district may receive full state aid even though it has not provided the minimum school term. The State Superintendent of Education may determine that a failure to provide the minimum school term was occasioned by an act of God—or by conditions beyond the control of the school district—which posed a hazardous threat to the health and safety of pupils.

105 ILCS 5/18-12

STATE AID DISTRIBUTION SYSTEM

24:160   How are funds from the Common School Fund delivered to school districts?

In every instance possible, except by written agreement of the local school districts in an educational service region, funds due local school districts are dispersed by electronic transfer from the state school fund.

105 ILCS 5/3-9

24:170   How is state aid distributed when funds appropriated by the General Assembly are not adequate to cover all school district entitlements?

The legislature each year appropriates a specific sum of money to each of numerous programs. If the money appropriated for a particular program—such as pupil transportation or special education—is less than the money required to fully fund the entitlements of all the school districts in the state, the amount of money available is apportioned so that each school district has its aid for that program proportionately reduced.

Historically, the prorating of claims has not been generally applicable to general state aid, because school district entitlements have been based on the amount appropriated. However, effective July 1, 1998, the legislature has created a per pupil entitlement to general state aid by enacting specified "foundation levels" through Fiscal Year 2001. Failure of the legislature to make annual appropriations adequate to fund those statutory levels will require either the prorating of school district entitlements or supplemental appropriations.

105 ILCS 5/18-8.05
People ex rel. Carruthers v. Cooper, 404 Ill. 395, 89 N.E.2d 40 (1950)

24:175 What is a "delayed state aid payment?"

The term describes legislation enacted in 1991 to shift a general state aid payment from the last month of one fiscal year (June) to the first month of the following fiscal year (July). Although action by the Governor has advanced a state aid payment from time to time since then, the 1991 legislation has never been reversed to put payments back on the pre-1991 schedule. The delayed payment amounted to a reduction in general state aid for the 1991-1992 fiscal year.

105 ILCS 5/18-11

INVESTMENT INCOME

24:180 How is a depositary for school funds selected?

Trustees of schools in Class II county (Cook) school units, school boards in Class I county (all other counties) school units, and school boards in those Class II county school units that have elected or appointed their own school treasurer shall designate one or more banks or savings and loan associations, situated in the State of Illinois, in which school funds and moneys in the custody of the township treasurer or school treasurer shall be kept.

105 ILCS 5/8-7

24:182   Is a school district required to have an investment policy?

By not later than January 1, 2000 school districts are required to have a written investment policy. The policy must address safety of principal, liquidity of funds and return on investment. The policy must address:

1) a listing of authorized investments;

2) a rule such as "the prudent person rule" establishing the standard of care that must be maintained by the persons investing the public funds;

3) investment guidelines that are appropriate to the nature of the funds, the purpose for the funds and the amount of the public funds within the investment portfolio;

4) the policy regarding diversification of the investment portfolio that is appropriate to the nature of the funds, purpose of the funds, and the amount of the public funds within the investment portfolio;

5) guidelines regarding collateral requirements if any, for the deposit of public finds in a financial institution made pursuant tot he Act, and, if applicable, guidelines for contractual arrangements for the custody and safekeeping of that collateral;

6) a policy regarding the establishment of a system of internal controls and written operational procedures designed to prevent losses of funds that might arise from fraud, employee error, misrepresentation by third parties or imprudent action by school employees;

7) the identification of the chief investment officer who is responsible for establishing the internal controls and written procedures for the operation of the investment program;

8) performance measures that are appropriate to the nature of the funds, the purpose for the funds, and the amount of the public funds within the investment portfolio;

9) a policy regarding appropriate periodic review of the investment portfolio, its effectiveness in meeting the school district's need for safety, liquidity, rate of return, and diversification, and its general performance;

10) a policy establishing at least quarterly written reports of investment activities by the school district's chief financial officer for submission to the school board and superintendent. The

report must include information regarding securities in the portfolio by class or type, book value, income earned, and market value as of the report date;

11) a policy regarding the selection of investment advisors, money managers, and financial institutions; and

12) a policy regarding ethics and conflicts of interest.

30 ILCS 235/2.5

24:184   What kinds of investments are lawful for school moneys?

The investment of all public funds is regulated by law. Financial institutions must meet specified standards and obligations. Certificates of deposit, government securities, the commercial paper of private corporations, and interest bearing bank deposits are among the investment vehicles that are permissible for school funds if they meet specified standards.

In addition, school districts may combine their funds for investment purposes. Township and school treasurers are authorized to enter into agreements of any defined or undefined term regarding the deposit, investment, reinvestment or withdrawal of school funds, including, without limitation, agreements with other township and school treasurers, agreements with community college districts authorized by the Community College Act and agreements with educational service regions.

30 ILCS 235/2 et seq.
105 ILCS 5/3-9.1
105 ILCS 5/8-7

24:186   How may earnings from invested school funds be used?

Although moneys from various fund accounts may be combined for investment purposes, the amount of money belonging to each account must be reflected in the records of the treasurer. Interest earned on invested school funds must be credited to the same fund account as the principal and may be used for any lawful purpose for which the principal may be used.

105 ILCS 5/8-7

24:188   May school boards invest borrowed funds, such as the proceeds of a bond issue or sale of tax anticipation warrants?

Yes. However, such investments are subject to federal restrictions on arbitrage. The interest earned by an investor on school district debt instruments is treated as tax exempt under federal and state tax codes, which often enables school districts to borrow at lower rates of interest than the rates they earn when they reinvest those funds. In order to retain tax exempt status, the proceeds of district borrowing must meet certain requirements of the Internal Revenue Code that limit investment earnings for the district.

26 U.S.C. 1233

GIFTS

24:190   May a school district accept a gift, grant or bequest?

A school district or attendance center may accept a gift, grant or bequest. If the donor expresses an intention that the property be used for a particular purpose, the school board must effectuate the donor's intention until the school board in its discretion determines it is no longer practical to do so.

105 ILCS 5/16-1
Wauconda Community Unit School District No. 118, Lake County v. LaSalle National Bank, 143 Ill.App.3d 52, 492 N.E.2d 995, 97 Ill.Dec. 336 (2nd Dist 1986)
Community Unit School District No. 4 v. Booth, 1 Ill.2d 545, 116 N.E.2d 161 (1954)

24:200   May a tax exempt foundation be created to help raise funds for school purposes?

Yes. Although a school district is an eligible recipient of tax deductible charitable gifts, school officials and/or interested citizens also may make a school or school district the beneficiary of support from a tax exempt foundation qualified to accept gifts, donations, bequests and other contributions.

105 ILCS 5/2-3.74

24:210   What laws govern the creation and operation of a tax exempt educational foundation?

In order to acquire tax exempt status eligible to accept tax deductible contributions, an educational foundation must be organized as a not-for-profit corporation or as a charitable trust and make application to the federal Internal Revenue Service. In addition, any charitable corporation that solicits contributions in Illinois must register with the Attorney General and file informational returns with the Internal Revenue Service and the Attorney General. A foundation organized as a not-for-profit corporation also must file an annual report with the Illinois Secretary of State.

26 U.S.C. 501(c)3
760 ILCS 55/7
805 ILCS 105/101.01 et seq.

OTHER SOURCES OF INCOME

24:300   How may a school board dispose of school equipment that is no longer needed?

A school board is authorized to sell at public or private sale any personal property either no longer needed by the school district Aor available through an arrangement under which the personal property may be leased by the district from the purchaser." The school board may adopt a resolution declaring the property surplus and no longer needed for school purposes and may direct the superintendent to sell it. The board may establish a minimum selling price and may specify a public or private sale.

105 ILCS 5/10-22.8

25: BUDGETING AND MANAGING SCHOOL FUNDS

THE BUDGET

25:10   What is a school district budget?

Each school board must budget its income and expenses each year and make the budget available for public inspection. A public hearing must be held prior to the adoption of the budget. The budget is the school district's plan for receipt and expenditure of moneys. It is the basis for a school district's tax levy.

The board must file with the county clerk within 30 days of their adoption a certified copy of its appropriation and budget resolutions, as well as an estimate, certified by its chief fiscal officer, of revenues, by source, anticipated to be received by the school district in the following fiscal year. Failure to file the required documents (after timely notice) authorizes the county clerk to refuse to extend the tax levy imposed by the governing authority until the documents are filed.

35 ILCS 200/18-50
105 ILCS 5/2-3.27 et seq.
105 ILCS 5/17-1
People ex rel. Stanfield v. Pennsylvania Railroad, 3 Ill.2d 524, 121 N.E.2d 548 (1954)
People ex rel. Schlaeger v. Belmont Radio Corporation, 388 Ill. 11, 57 N.E.2d 479 (1944)
People ex rel. Toman v. Siebel, 388 Ill. 98, 57 N.E.2d 378 (1944)

25:20   What must be included in a budget?

Within or before the first quarter of each fiscal year, a school board must adopt an annual budget which it deems necessary to defray all necessary expenses and liabilities of the district, and which must specify the objects and purposes of each item and amount needed for each object or purpose. The budget is entered on a form provided by the State Board of Education and contains a statement of the cash on hand at the beginning of the fiscal year, an estimate of the cash expected to be received during such fiscal year from all sources, an estimate of the expenditures contemplated for the year, and a statement of the estimated cash expected to be on hand at the end of the year.

The estimate of taxes to be received may be based upon the amount of actual cash receipts which may reasonably be expected by the district during the fiscal year, estimated from the experience of the district in prior years and with due regard for other circumstances which may substantially affect receipts.

105 ILCS 5/17-1

25:25   Is there a limitation on the growth of administrative expenditures by a school district?

For the 1998-1999 school year and each year thereafter, school districts are required to undertake budgetary and expenditure control actions so that the increase in administrative expenditures for that school year over the prior school year do not exceed 5 percent. School districts with administrative expenditures per pupil in the 25th percentile and below for all districts of the same type as defined by the State Board of Education may waive the limitation for any year following a public hearing and by a vote of at least two-thirds of the members of the school board. Other districts may request a waiver if the district's failure to stay within the expenditure limit is beyond the control of the district and the district has "exhausted all available and reasonable remedies to comply with the limitation."

105 ILCS 5/17-1.5

25:27   What happens if a school district does not limit the growth of administrative expenditures as required by law?

If the State Superintendent finds that a school district has failed to comply with the administrative expenditure limitation, the district is notified of the violation and directed to take corrective action to bring the district's budget into compliance. The district has 60 days to provide assurance to the State that appropriate corrective actions have been or will be taken. If the district fails to provide adequate assurance or fails to undertake the necessary corrective action, the State Superintendent may impose progressive sanctions against the district that may include withholding all subsequent payments of general state aid due the district until the assurance is provided or the corrective action is taken.

105 ILCS 5/17-1.5

25:30   May a school board amend its budget?

A school board may from time to time amend its budget by the same procedure utilized to establish the original budget.

105 ILCS 5/17-1

25:35   What happens if a school district fails to timely adopt a budget?

The failure of a school board to adopt a budget or to comply with School Code Section 17-1 regarding the adoption of a budget does not affect the validity of any tax levy of the district which is otherwise in compliance with the law. Except as otherwise provided by law, a school board's adoption of an annual budget is not a prerequisite to the adoption of a valid tax levy and is not a limit on the amount of the levy.

105 ILCS 5/17-1

25:40   How does a school board amend its budget after a tax rate increase has been approved at a referendum for the educational fund or operations and maintenance fund?

Whenever the voters of a school district have voted in favor of an increase in the annual tax rate for educational or operations and maintenance purposes or both at an election held after the adoption of the annual school budget for any fiscal year, a school board may adopt or pass during that fiscal year an additional or supplemental budget under the sole authority of Section 17-3.2 of the School Code by a vote of a majority of the full membership of the board, any other provision of the School Code notwithstanding, in and by which such additional or supplemental budget the board shall appropriate such additional sums of money as it may find necessary to defray expenses and liabilities of the district to be incurred for educational or operations and maintenance purposes or both of the district during that fiscal year, but not in excess of the additional funds estimated to be available by virtue of such voted increase in the annual tax rate for educational or operations and maintenance purposes or both.

105 ILCS 5/17-3.2
In re County Collector of McHenry County, 181 Ill.App.3d 345, 536 N.E.2d 1288, 130 Ill.Dec. 77 (2nd Dist. 1989)

ACCOUNTING PROCEDURES

25:50 What accounting system can a school district use?

A school district may use either a cash basis or accrual system of accounting; however, any board electing to use the accrual system may not change to a cash basis without the permission of the State Board of Education.

105 ILCS 5/2 3.27
105 ILCS 5/10-17

25:60 What is a school district fund?

A fund is an independent fiscal accounting entity requiring its own set of books. A fund is governed by statutes, regulations, and restrictions that limit its use to a specific activity or certain objective. Each fund must be accounted for so the identity of its resources and obligations and its revenue and expenditures is continually maintained.

23 Ill. Admin. Code 110.110 et seq.

25:70 May a school board deposit general state aid in any fund it chooses?

A school district may deposit general state aid in any fund except the working cash fund.

105 ILCS 5/18-8.05 A 4

FUND ACCOUNTS

25:80   What is the educational fund?

The educational fund is used for all transactions not designated to another fund. The educational fund must be used to pay the direct costs of instruction, health, attendance and lunch programs and all costs of administration. Certain revenues must be credited to this fund, including educational tax levies, textbook rentals, athletics and lunch programs.

The salaries of janitors, and maintenance employees and the costs of fuel, lights, gas, water, telephone service, and custodial supplies and equipment must be charged to this fund unless a school board, by resolution, determines to pay such costs from the operations and maintenance fund.

105 ILCS 5/17-2
23 Ill. Admin. Code 110.Tab.A

25:90   What is the operations and maintenance fund?

The costs of maintaining, improving or repairing school building and property, renting buildings and property for school purposes, and the payment of insurance premiums on school buildings are charged to the operations and maintenance fund. Certain costs which otherwise would be charged to the educational fund may be paid out of the operations and maintenance fund if the school board passes a resolution authorizing the charge.

105 ILCS 5/17-2
23 Ill. Admin. Code 110.Tab.A

25:100   What options does a school board have in paying costs out of the district's operations and maintenance fund?

Any sum expended or obligations incurred for the improvement, maintenance, repair, or benefit of school buildings and property, including the cost of interior decorating and the installation, improvement, repair, replacement, and maintenance of building fixtures, for the rental of buildings and property for school purposes, or for the payment of all premiums for insurance upon school buildings and school building fixtures or for the purchase of equipment to be used in the school lunch program must be paid from the tax levied for operations and maintenance purposes and the purchase of school grounds.

The board may provide by resolution the payment of all salaries of janitors, engineers, or other custodial employees and all costs of fuel, lights, gas, water, telephone service, and custodial supplies and equipment or the cost of a professional survey of the conditions of school buildings, or any one or more of the preceding items shall be paid from the tax levied for operations and maintenance purposes and the purchase of school grounds in which event such salaries or specified costs, or both, must be so paid until the next fiscal year after the repeal of such resolution. Expenditures for all similar purposes not specified for this fund are made from the educational fund.

105 ILCS 5/17-7
23 Ill. Admin. Code 110.Tab.A

25:110   What is the transportation fund?

Any transportation operating costs incurred for transporting pupils to and from school and school-sponsored activities and the costs of acquiring equipment must be paid from a transportation fund. The transportation fund consists of moneys received from any tax levy for such purpose, state reimbursement for transportation, all funds received from other districts for transporting pupils, and any charges for transportation services rendered to individuals or auxiliary enterprises of the school. For the purpose of this fund, "transportation operating cost" includes all costs of transportation except interest and rental of building facilities.

105 ILCS 5/17-8
23 Ill. Admin. Code 110.Tab.A

25:120   What is the bond and interest fund?

Monies deposited in a bond and interest fund are the proceeds of taxes levied to pay the principal and interest on outstanding bonds and refunding bond proceeds. A school district may deposit corporate personal property replacement taxes and/or general state aid revenue in the bond and interest fund and abate a like amount of property tax.

23 Ill. Admin. Code 110.Tab.A

25:130 What is the municipal retirement/social security fund?

A municipal retirement/social security fund is created when a school district levies taxes to pay social security or retirement contributions for non-certificated employees.

40 ILCS 5/7-171
40 ILCS 5/21-101
40 ILCS 5/22-403
23 Ill. Admin. Code 110.Tab.A

25:135 What is the fire prevention, safety, environmental, and energy fund?

Under certain conditions specified in statute, a school district may levy for fire prevention, safety, the protection of the environment, energy conservation, handicapped accessibility or for school security purposes.

105 ILCS 5/17-2.11 et seq.

25:140 What is the site and construction fund?

New buildings and additions are generally constructed after an election authorizing special financing. The proceeds of each bond issue are placed in a site and construction fund to separate these moneys from operating moneys. The special moneys may be spent for purposes specified in the bond issue and on the ballot.

Often the cost of furniture and other equipment needed to open a new building is included in the amount of the bond issue. Expenditures which would ordinarily be charged to the educational fund, but which may be charged to the site and construction fund (unless paid before the site and construction fund is created) include election expenses, fidelity insurance, architect fees, legal fees for title searches, bond legal opinions and other administrative costs directly related to the construction project.

Expenditures which would ordinarily be charged to the operations and maintenance fund, but which may be charged to the site and construction fund (unless paid before the site and construction fund is created) include actual construction costs, builder's risk insurance, land purchase and other site costs, landscaping, parking lots, sidewalks, utility connections and other items directly related to the construction project.

105 ILCS 5/19-2 et seq.
23 Ill. Admin. Code 110.Tab.A

25:150 What is a rent fund?

When a tax is levied to provide revenue for paying rent to the Capital Development Board for a state-owned school building, the receipt of taxes and the payment of rent are recorded in the rent fund.

105 ILCS 5/35-23
23 Ill. Admin. Code 110.Tab.A

25:160 What is a capital improvement fund?

With voter approval at a referendum, a school board may create a capital improvement fund, levy an annual tax of up to .075 percent, and accumulate moneys in the fund to be spent only in accordance with purposes set forth in the resolution calling for the referendum and on the referendum ballot.

105 ILCS 5/17-2(4)
105 ILCS 5/17-2.3
23 Ill. Admin. Code 110.Tab.A

OTHER FUNDS

25:170 May a school board create revolving funds?

A school board may, by resolution, establish revolving funds for school cafeterias, lunch rooms, athletics, petty cash or similar purposes, provided such funds are in the custody of a bonded employee who shall be responsible to the board and to the treasurer, subject to regular annual audit by licensed public accountants and other such examinations as the school board shall deem advisable and kept in accordance with regulations prescribed by the State Board of Education.

A monthly report and an annual summary of all receipts and expenditures of the fund shall be submitted to the school board and the treasurer. All funds advanced by the treasurer to operate such revolving funds must be carried on the treasurer's books as cash obligations due to the district and all receipts of such revolving funds shall be deposited daily in a bank or savings and loan association to be approved by the treasurer unless there is no bank or savings and loan association in the community, in which event receipts shall be deposited intact not less than once each week in the bank or savings and loan association approved by the treasurer.

All reimbursements to any such revolving funds from the district funds shall be completely itemized as to whom paid, for what purpose, and against what budgetary item the expenditure is chargeable.

105 ILCS 5/10-20.19(2)
23 Ill. Admin. Code 110.125
23 Ill. Admin. Code 125.10

25:175 What is the difference between student activity accounts and convenience accounts?

Student activity accounts are those funds which are owned, operated and managed by organizations, clubs or groups within the student body under the guidance and direction of one or more faculty or staff members for educational, recreational or cultural purposes. Examples of student activity accounts include: homeroom monies, yearbook collections, class year accounts, choral and band accounts, class projects, student clubs, student council and student bookstore monies.

Convenience accounts are those funds maintained by the local education agency at the request of and for the convenience of faculty, staff, faculty-parent organizations or similar non-student groups. Examples of convenience accounts include: scholarship funds, faculty-parent organization accounts, faculty funds and employee coffee funds.

Different fund management requirements apply to each type of account.

The following funds are sometimes mistaken as activity funds, but are budgeted district accounts: lunch program, athletic programs, building trades program, restricted grants-in-aid from state or federal sources, towel-locker and book rentals, student insurance, and sales of district supplies and services.

23 Ill. Admin. Code 125.10

25:180   What control must a school board exercise over funds raised by student organizations?

A school board must:

1) establish rules and regulations governing conditions under which school classes, clubs, and associations may collect or acquire funds in the name of any school, and

2) provide for the safeguarding of such funds for the educational, recreational, or cultural purposes they are designed to serve.

105 ILCS 5/10-20.19(2)
23 Ill. Admin. Code 125.10

FINANCIAL REPORTS AND AUDITS

25:190   What financial reports are required of Illinois school districts?

Prior to December 1 of each year, each school district is required to compile and publish in a newspaper of general circulation published in the school district a statement of financial affairs showing the district's revenue, expenditures and financial condition in a form prescribed by the State Board of Education.

The report also must be filed with the regional superintendent of schools by December 15. Any resident of the district may obtain a copy of the report by paying a reasonable fee to defray the cost of copying.

105 ILCS 5/10-17

25:200   When are school district accounts audited?

Each school district is required to cause an annual audit of its accounts to be made by a person who is lawfully qualified to practice public accounting in Illinois. A copy of the audit must be provided the regional superintendent on or before October 15 of each year, or by a time extended by the regional superintendent not to exceed 60 days.

105 ILCS 5/3-7

25:205   What is a school district's fiscal year?

A school district may establish its fiscal year. July 1 to June 30 is commonly selected.

105 ILCS 5/17-1

PURCHASING AND BIDDING REQUIREMENTS

25:210   What steps are required to release payment for school district purchases?

When the school board provides the treasurer with evidence that it has formally approved payment, the treasurer releases funds. The school board may provide the treasurer with a certified copy of the minutes of its meeting, reflecting the approval of specific bills approved and the budget items to be debited, or the board may adopt a voucher system or other procedure that meets standards of the State Board of Education.

105 ILCS 5/8-16
105 ILCS 5/10-20.19(1)

25:220   When do bidding requirements apply?

A school board is required to let all contracts for supplies, materials, or work or contracts with private carriers for transportation of pupils involving an expenditure in excess of $10,000 to the lowest responsible bidder considering conformity with specifications, terms of delivery, quality and serviceability after due advertisement.

However, certain contracts are exempted from competitive bidding requirements, including:

1) contracts for the services of individuals possessing a high degree of professional skill where the ability or fitness of the individual plays an important part;

2) contracts for the printing of finance committee reports and departmental reports;

3) contracts for the printing or engraving of bonds, tax warrants, and other evidences of indebtedness;

4) contracts for the purchase of perishable food and perishable beverages;

5) contracts for materials and work which have been awarded to the lowest responsible bidder after due advertisement, but

due to unforeseen revisions not the fault of the contractor for materials and work must be revised, causing expenditures not in excess of 10 percent of the contract price;

6) contracts for the maintenance or servicing of, or provision of repair parts for, equipment which are made with the manufacturer or authorized service agent of that equipment where the provision of parts, maintenance, or servicing can best be performed by the manufacturer or authorized service agent;

7) purchases and contracts for the use, purchase, delivery, movement, or installation of data processing equipment, software, or services and telecommunications and interconnect equipment, software, and services;

8) contracts for duplicating machines and supplies;

9) contracts for the purchase of natural gas when the cost is less than that offered by a public utility;

10) purchases of equipment previously owned by some entity other than the district itself;

11) contracts for repair, maintenance, remodeling, renovation, or construction, or a single project involving an expenditure not to exceed $20,000 and not involving a change or increase in the size, type, or extent of an existing facility;

12) contracts for goods or services procured from another governmental agency;

13) contracts for goods or services which are economically procurable from only one source, such as for the purchase of magazines, books, periodicals, pamphlets, and reports and for utility services such as water, light, heat, telephone or telegraph;

14) where funds are expended in an emergency and such emergency expenditure is approved by three-fourths of the members of the board.

All competitive bids for contracts involving an expenditure in excess of $10,000 must be sealed by the bidder and must be opened by a member or employee of the school board at a public bid opening at which the contents of the bids must be announced. Each bidder must receive at least three days' notice of the time and place of bid opening. At least one public notice must be given in a newspaper published in the district at least 10 days before the bid date.

105 ILCS 5/10-20.21

25:222   Under what circumstances can a school district negotiate with more than one bidder after bids have been opened but before a contract has been let?

The desire to negotiate with more than one bidder usually occurs when the school district cannot clearly distinguish the low bid from bids received or seeks to avoid awarding a contract to the low bidder.

When a low bid cannot be distinguished, fault can be found in the way the bid specifications were written. Negotiating with more than one bidder comes dangerously close under any circumstance to a violation of bidding statutes. The safest practice is to reject all bids, rewrite the bid specifications and rebid.

A school district seeking to avoid awarding a contract to the low bidder must find the bidder irresponsible within the meaning of the statute or award him the bid.

105 ILCS 5/10-20.21

Acme Bus Corp. v. Board of Education of the Roosevelt Union Free School District, 89 N.Y.2d 816, 681 N.E.2d 1304, 659 N.Y.S.2d 857 (1997)

25:223   Is the letting of insurance contracts subject to competitive bidding?

A school board is required to comply with the competitive bidding provisions of the School Code when awarding insurance contracts. The length of the contract and the facts surrounding its award will determine how soon after the original award the contract must be re-bid. Insurance contracts do not involve the type of professional skills which would except them from bidding requirements.

Self insurance plans and pools are not subject to bidding requirements.

Compass Health Care Plans v. Board of Education of the City of Chicago and Ted D. Kimbrough, 246 Ill.App.3d 746, 617 N.E.2d 6, 186 Ill.Dec. 767 (1st Dist. 1992)

25:225   Must a school board award contracts for architectural or engineering services to the lowest bidder?

No. Professional services are exempted from bidding requirements. When a school board needs architectural, engineering or land surveying services, the contract must be awarded on the basis of demonstrated competence and qualifications. Unless it already has a satisfactory relationship with one or more firms, the school board must advertise for (a) statements of interest in a particular project and (b) statements of qualifications and performance data. The school board must evaluate firms submitting these statements and select the top three based on qualifications, ability of professional personnel, past record and experience, performance data on file, willingness to meet time and budget requirements, location, workload and other applicable factors. The top three firms must be ranked in order of preference.

The school board must attempt to negotiate a satisfactory contract first with the top ranked firm and, if that fails, with the second and third firms, in the order ranked. Another list of three firms may be developed if the board is unable to negotiate a satisfactory contract with one of the first three firms.

50 ILCS 510/1 et seq.
105 ILCS 5/10-20.21

25:230   What may a school board consider to determine whether a bidder is responsible?

A school board may consider any of the following factors to determine if a bidder is responsible:

1) the quality of the work performed on other similar jobs;

2) the financial status of the bidder to assure a financial solvency sufficient to complete the contract;

3) the bidder's quantity and quality of experience on similar jobs;

4) the bidder's reputation;

5) the ability of the bidder to provide a satisfactory performance bond;

6) the bidder's reliability in completing similar contracts under the terms and conditions of those contracts; and

7) the board's past experience with the bidder.

105 ILCS 5/10-20.21
Compass Health Care Plans v. Board of Education of the City of Chicago and Ted D. Kimbrough, 246 Ill.App.3d 746, 617 N.E.2d 6, 186 Ill.Dec. 767 (1st Dist. 1992)
Carlson v. Moline Board of Education School District No. 40, 124 Ill.3d 967, 464 N.E.2d 1269, 80 Ill.Dec. 256 (3rd Dist. 1984)

Cardinal Glass v. Board of Education of Mendota Community Consolidated School District 289, 113 Ill.App.3d 442, 447 N.E.2d 546, 69 Ill.Dec. 329 (3rd Dist. 1983)

> *Beaver Glass and Mirror Company, Inc. v. Board of Education of Rockford School District No. 205, Winnebago County,* 59 Ill.App.3d 880, 376 N.E.2d 377, 17 Ill.Dec. 378 (2nd Dist. 1978)

25:240   What recourse is available to an unsuccessful low bidder?

A low bidder who is not awarded the contract may bring suit challenging the award of the contract. In appropriate circumstances, the low bidder may be awarded the contract or may recover money damages or both.

> *Court Street Steak House v. Tazewell County,* 249 Ill.App.3d 918, 619 N.E.2d 759, 189 Ill.Dec. 58 (3rd Dist. 1993)
>
> *L.E. Zannini & Co. v. Board of Education, Hawthorn School District 73,* 138 Ill.App.3d 467, 486 N.E.2d 426, 93 Ill.Dec. 323 (2nd Dist. 1985)
>
> *Cardinal Glass v. Board of Education of Mendota Community Consolidated School District 289,* 113 Ill.App.3d 442, 447 N.E.2d 546, 69 Ill.Dec. 329 (3rd Dist. 1983)

25:250   May a school board reject all bids?

Yes.

> *Premier Electric Construction Co. v. Board of Education of City of Chicago,* 70 Ill.App.3d 866, 388 N.E.2d 1088, 27 Ill.Dec. 125 (1st Dist. 1979)

25:260   May a school district give preference to local bidders when letting contracts?

If the contract requires competitive bidding, the school board may not give preference to a local bidder.

> *Doyle Plumbing and Heating Co. v. Board of Education, Quincy Public School District No. 172,* 291 Ill.App.3d 221, 683 N.E.2d 530, 225 Ill.Dec. 362 (4th Dist. 1997)
>
> *Cardinal Glass v. Board of Education of Mendota Community Consolidated School District 289,* 113 Ill.App.3d 442, 447 N.E.2d 546, 69 Ill.Dec. 329 (3rd Dist. 1983)

25:261   What is the meaning of the term "serviceability" in the bidding statutes?

Serviceability means "durability or usefulness and fitness of the supplies, materials or work on which bids are solicited."

Serviceability does not refer to the service call response time of a bidder.

Doyle Plumbing and Heating Co. v. Board of Education, Quincy Public School District No. 172, 291 Ill.App. 221, 683 N.E.2d 530, 225 Ill.Dec. 362 (4th Dist. 1997)

25:270   Are there any penalties for improperly influencing the outcome of school district bidding or purchasing procedures in order to favor a local bidder or other favored bidder?

Yes. Any action by a governmental body or employee to knowingly favor or assist any bidder over other bidders may be in violation of laws prohibiting the rigging or rotating of contracts or otherwise interfering with the letting of public contracts. Prohibited actions include the providing of information or criteria to one bidder that is not available to all bidders and the specification of particular subcontractors.

Most violations of the public contracts law are Class 3 or Class 4 felonies carrying fines up to $10,000 and imprisonment ranging from three to 10 years.

720 ILCS 5/33E-1 et seq.

INSTALLMENT PURCHASES AND CONTRACTS

25:280   May a school district borrow money to purchase a school bus?

A school district is not authorized to incur debt except when law specifically permits. The School Code allows contracts for the purchase of a school bus to be paid for over such period of time as does not exceed the vehicle's depreciable life. This provision has been widely interpreted to permit seller-financed agreements. It probably does not permit other forms of borrowing for the same purpose.

A school board is authorized to enter into a school bus lease agreement with a term not more than five years. The vote to enter into the lease requires an affirmative vote of two-thirds of the school board.

105 ILCS 5/10-23.4
105 ILCS 5/10-23.4a

25:285   May a school district enter into a multi-year transportation contract with a private carrier?

A school district may enter into a contract for up to three years for transportation of pupils to and from school. The contract may be extended for up to two more years by mutual agreement of the parties and, after that, may be extended on a year-to-year basis. No contract may be extended on a year-to-year basis if the school board receives a timely request from another interested contractor that a contract be let for bid.

105 ILCS 5/29-6.1
625 ILCS 5/6-106.11

25:290   May a school district acquire personal property under an installment contract?

A school district may obtain personal property by lease with or without an option to purchase or under an installment contract. These contracts are sometimes called "lease-purchase agreements." The term of the lease or contract may not exceed five years. The authorizing statute specifies the maximum interest rate. To enter into such a lease requires a two-thirds vote of the school board.

105 ILCS 5/10-22.25a

25:295   May a school district borrow money to purchase computer equipment?

The State Board of Education administers a loan program which allows school districts to borrow money for computer hardware, technology networks, and related wiring. The program does not finance the purchase of software. Loans are available on a three-year rotating basis: grades K-4 in year one of the program and each third year thereafter, grades 5-8 in year two and each third year thereafter and grades 9-12 in year three and each third year thereafter. The repayment period for the loans is three years or less.

105 ILCS 5/2-3.117a
105 ILCS 5/2-3.121

25:300   May a school district purchase energy saving systems by installment contract?

A school district or school districts in combination may enter into installment contracts or lease purchase agreements for the purchase and installation of energy conservation measures. There are detailed statutory provisions which govern how such a contract or agreement may be awarded.

Energy conservation means any improvement, repair, alteration or betterment of any building or facility owned or operated by a school district or any equipment, fixture or furnishing to be added to or used in a building or facility that is designed to reduce energy consumption or operating costs.

105 ILCS 5/19b-1 et seq.

26: SCHOOL BOARD BORROWING AND DEBT

INTERFUND TRANSFERS AND LOANS

26:10   May a school board loan or transfer money among the various funds established by law (e.g. educational fund, operations and maintenance fund)?

In the absence of statutory authority to make a particular interfund transfer or loan, a school board may not transfer or loan funds from one fund to another fund.

105 ILCS 5/10-22.14
105 ILCS 5/10-22.44
105 ILCS 5/17-2B
105 ILCS 5/20-5
People ex rel. Redfern v. Pennsylvania Central Company, 47 Ill.2d 412, 266 N.E.2d 334 (1971)

26:20   May a school board permanently transfer money among the educational fund, operations and maintenance fund, and/or the transportation fund?

A school board may transfer funds as listed below provided that:

• a proper resolution is adopted following a public hearing;

• the public hearing is preceded by at least one published notice occurring at least seven days prior to the hearing in a newspaper of general circulation within the school district setting forth the time, date, place and subject matter of the hearing.

Permissible transfers following these procedures are:

1) from the educational fund to the operations and maintenance fund, or

2) from the operations and maintenance fund to the educational fund, or

3) from the transportation fund to the educational or opera-

tions and maintenance fund.

The amount of money transferred from a fund may not exceed 20 percent of the tax actually received in the fund for the year previous to the transfer. Such a transfer may be made solely for the purpose of meeting one-time, non-recurring expenses.

105 ILCS 5/17-2A

26:24   May a school board transfer interest income earned in one fund to another fund?

In certain instances specified in the law, interest income may be transferred from the fund in which the interest was earned to another fund.

Interest earned on the proceeds of the life-safety levy may be transferred to the operations and maintenance (O and M) fund, but the O and M tax levy must be reduced by the amount of interest transferred.

Interest income from the debt service levy to pay building, tort immunity, working cash fund or life-safety bonds may be transferred to any fund. The working cash fund need not be repaid when bond income is transferred.

Interest earned on funds deposited in an insurance reserve fund, or earned on deposits resulting from the tort immunity levy if declared surplus, may be transferred to any fund.

Interest earned on funds deposited in the working cash fund which resulted from the working cash fund levy may be transferred to any fund without repaying the working cash fund.

105 ILCS 5/10-22.44
105 ILCS 5/17-2.11
105 ILCS 5/20-5
745 ILCS 10/9-107

26:25   Are there instances when interest income may not be transferred from the fund in which it was earned?

Yes. Interest earned on deposits resulting from the capital improvements tax levy and interest earned from deposits resulting from the Illinois Municipal Retirement Fund levy must be retained in the fund in which the original deposits were made.

105 ILCS 5/10-22.44
105 ILCS 5/17-2.3

26:30   May a school board transfer money among line items within a fund?

A school board may make transfers between the various items in any fund not exceeding in the aggregate 10 percent of the total of the fund as set forth in the budget.

105 ILCS 5/17-1

26:40   Which interfund loans are permissible?

The following interfund loans are permissible:

1) Operations and maintenance fund moneys may be loaned to the educational fund or transportation fund;

2) Educational fund moneys may be loaned to the operations and maintenance fund or transportation fund;

3) Transportation fund moneys may be loaned to the educational fund or operations and maintenance fund;

4) Working cash fund moneys may be loaned to another fund.

Moneys must be repaid to the loaning fund within three years, except working cash fund loans which must be repaid upon the collection of anticipated taxes. Exceptions to the payment of working cash fund loans exist when tax anticipation notes are outstanding.

105 ILCS 5/10-22.33
105 ILCS 5/20-5

WORKING CASH FUND

26:50   What is a working cash fund?

A school district may create a working cash fund by levying up to five cents per one hundred dollars of equalized assessed valuation. No working cash fund levy is permitted if bonds in the amount of 85 percent of the prior tax extensions for educational purposes have been issued for the working cash fund or if the amount of taxes to be extended will increase the working fund to an amount exceeding 85 percent (125 percent for a financially distressed district) of the taxes last extended for educational purposes.

105 ILCS 5/20-1 et seq.
Application of Walgenbach, 166 Ill.App.3d 629, 520 N.E.2d 78, 117 Ill.Dec. 88 (2nd Dist. 1988)
Application of Walgenbach, 104 Ill.2d 121, 470 N.E.2d 1015, 117 Ill.Dec. 88 (2nd Dist. 1984)

26:60   What is the purpose of the working cash fund?

The purpose of the working cash fund is to enable the school district "to have in its treasury at all times sufficient money to meet demands for ordinary and necessary expenses." Because school revenue is not always received according to schedule, the working cash fund provides a school board with a source of internal borrowing to meet short-term needs and reduce the need to borrow from outside sources that bear interest costs.

105 ILCS 5/20-1

26:70   May a school board abolish a working cash fund after such a fund has been created?

Any school board may abolish its working cash fund, upon the adoption of a resolution so providing, and direct the transfer of any balance in such fund to the educational fund at the close of the then current school year. Any outstanding loans to the transportation or operations and maintenance fund must be paid to the educational fund at the close of the then current school year. Thereafter, all outstanding working cash taxes of such school district must be collected and paid into the educational fund.

105 ILCS 5/20-8 et seq.
Bell v. School District No. 84, 47 Ill. 406, 95 N.E.2d 496 (1950)

26:80   May a school board that has abolished its working cash fund re-create the fund?

Yes.

105 ILCS 5/20-9

AUTHORITY TO BORROW

26:90   Are school boards authorized to borrow money?

School boards may borrow money and issue bonds for various purposes and in various ways specified by law.

105 ILCS 5/10-22.14

26:100   Is there any limit to the amount of money that a school board may borrow?

The maximum debt limitation for a unit district is 13.8 percent of the value of the taxable property located in the school district as determined by the last assessment before the indebtedness is to be incurred. The maximum debt limitation for an elementary district or high school district is 6.9 percent of the value of the taxable property located in the school district.

These debt limits, which apply to the aggregate of all forms of debt, may be increased by referendum or in certain emergency situations. If a school district is certified by the State Board of Education as financially distressed and if the school district meets certain other statutory requirements, it may incur debt beyond the debt limits. Under certain circumstances a school district may incur debt beyond its limits to finance school construction bonds issued in conjunction with a school construction project approved under the School Construction Law.

In addition to the limits on aggregate debt, there are limits to the amounts that may be borrowed against anticipated taxes and state aid.

105 ILCS 5/19-1
105 ILCS 5/19-1.5
People ex rel. Lindheimer v. Hamilton, 373 Ill. 124, 25 N.E.2d 517 (1940)

SHORT TERM BORROWING

26:110   What forms of short term debt may a school board incur in order to meet current operating expenses?

School boards are authorized to issue warrants or notes against anticipated property tax income; issue notes against anticipated state aid and corporate personal property replacement taxes; and to issue general obligation orders in the payment of teachers salaries.

30 ILCS 305/2
105 ILCS 5/8-16
105 ILCS 5/17-16
105 ILCS 5/18-18
105 ILCS 5/32-4.14

26:120   What are tax anticipation warrants?

Tax anticipation warrants are issued in expectation of the collection of taxes and may be issued to the extent of 85 percent of the total amount of the tax levied. The warrants must be repaid upon receipt of tax moneys by the district and bear interest at a statutory rate.

30 ILCS 305/2
105 ILCS 5/17-16
105 ILCS 5/18-8.05

26:130   When may a school board issue tax anticipation warrants?

When there is no money in the treasury of the school district to pay necessary expenses of the district, including amounts necessary to pay maturing principal and interest of bonds, a school board may issue warrants or may provide a fund to meet the expenses by issuing and disposing of warrants, drawn against and in anticipation of any taxes levied for the payment of the necessary expenses of the district, either for transportation, educational or for all operations and maintenance purposes, or for payments to the Illinois Municipal Retirement Fund, or for the payment of maturing principal and interest of bonds, as the case may be, to the extent of 85 percent of the total amount of the tax so levied. The warrants must show upon their face they are payable in the numerical order of their issuance solely from such taxes when collected and such taxes are to be set aside and held for their payment.

105 ILCS 5/17-16
105 ILCS 5/18-18
Hamer v. Board of Education of School District No. 113, Lake County, 132 Ill.App.2d 46, 267 N.E.2d 1 (2nd Dist. 1971)

26:140   How are tax anticipation warrants retired?

Tax anticipation warrants are payable solely from the taxes collected from the levy against which the warrants were issued.

Schreiner v. City of Chicago, 406 Ill. 75, 92 N.E.2d 133 (1950)

Leviton v. Board of Education of the City of Chicago, 374 Ill. 594, 30 N.E.2d 497 (1943)

Berman v. Board of Education of the City of Chicago, 360 Ill. 535, 196 N.E. 464 (1935)

People ex rel. Mathews v. Board of Education of the City of Chicago, 349 Ill. 390, 182 N.E. 455 (1932)

26:150   When may a school board issue tax anticipation notes?

A school board is authorized to issue full faith and credit tax anticipation notes as a means of securing operating funds. The issuance of such notes provides an alternative to the issuance of tax anticipation warrants. Tax anticipation notes are direct general obligations of the school district and the full faith and credit of the school district is pledged for the punctual payment of the principal and interest on the notes. Such notes may be issued in excess of any statutory debt limitation and do not reduce the debt incurring power of the district. The notes have a fixed maturity date, within two years from their date of issue, and the resolution authorizing their issuance must be filed with the county clerk of each county in which the district is located before the end of the calendar year during which the taxes being anticipated were levied.

No notes can be issued during any fiscal year in which there are tax anticipation warrants outstanding against the tax levied for such fiscal year. Tax anticipation notes may not be issued in an amount exceeding 85 percent of the taxes levied for a specific purpose for the year during which the notes are issued.

30 ILCS 305/2 et seq.
50 ILCS 420/1 et seq.

26:160   For what purposes may monies received from tax anticipation be used?

Monies from tax anticipation warrants are in place of the taxes in anticipation of which the warrants were issued. The money may be used only for the purpose for which the taxes were levied.

People ex rel. Mathews v. Board of Education of the City of Chicago, 349 Ill. 390, 182 N.E. 455 (1932)

26:170   What are corporate personal property replacement tax notes?

Corporate personal property replacement tax notes provide a means for a school district to finance anticipated cash flow deficits by issuing notes to anticipate replacement tax revenues. The replacement tax was intended to offset the revenue lost as a result of the abolition of the ad valorem personal property taxes which were abolished by the 1970 Constitution.

Personal property replacement tax notes may not be issued in an amount exceeding 75 percent of the entitlement of replacement taxes for the years anticipated. The entitlement amount must be certified by the director of the Department of Revenue. Personal property replacement tax notes may be issued for the current and next two succeeding calendar years from the time of the issuance of the notes. Notes must have a specific due date not more than 24 months after the date of issuance.

50 ILCS 420/4 et seq.

26:175   What are state aid anticipation certificates?

The school board of any district, by resolution, may borrow against its general state aid entitlement by issuing state aid anticipation certificates. The board may borrow up to 75 percent of its state aid allocation as certified by the State Superintendent of Education, less any funds available for transfer from the district's working cash fund. However, the total amount of state aid anticipation certificates, general obligation notes and tax anticipation warrants outstanding for any fiscal year may not exceed 85 percent of the taxes levied by the district for that year. State aid anticipation certificates may be outstanding for no more than 13 months and must be repaid by assigning state aid payments directly to the lender or to a trustee from the regional superintendent.

Proceeds from state aid anticipation certificates may be used only for the purposes set forth in the school board resolution authorizing their issuance.

To deal with the lost June state aid payment, any district

that has reached its maximum short term indebtedness may borrow up to 100 percent of the state aid payment to be received in July. The certificates must be redeemed no later than August 1 from July state aid payments.

105 ILCS 5/18-8.05

26:180   What are teachers' orders?

Teachers' orders are teachers' payroll warrants issued by a school district which may be cashed at a bank. By agreement between the school district and the bank, the district will redeem the orders at a future date when tax receipts are received and pay the bank a stipulated rate of interest.

105 ILCS 5/8-16

BOND ISSUES

26:190   What forms of long term debt is a school board authorized to incur through the issuance of bonds?

A school board may issue bonds as follows:

1) Building and School Site Bonds, with voter approval, for the purchase of a school site, construction of new facilities, equipping the facility, and repairing, remodeling or adding to an existing facility. School districts participating in vocational education or special education joint agreements may also issue such bonds.

2) Fire Prevention, Safety, Environmental and Energy Conservation Bonds, without voter approval, for the purpose of meeting fire prevention; life safety; environmental reasons; to reduce the consumption of energy; for repair of school sidewalks, playgrounds, parking lots, or school bus turnarounds under specified conditions; handicapped accessibility; and/or for school security purposes.

3) Funding Bonds, with voter approval if voters petition for an election (back door referendum), to pay for the salaries of teachers or claims against the district when they cannot be paid out of current revenues.

4) Refunding Bonds which are used to pay off outstanding bonds and interest due when funds are not available for pay-

ment, or when restructuring of such outstanding bond issues is advantageous to the district.

5) Working Cash Bonds, with voter approval if voters petition for an election (back door referendum), for the purpose of creating or increasing the Working Cash Fund. A district may not issue working cash bonds totaling more than 85 percent of the educational levy, plus 85 percent of the last known Corporate Personal Property Replacement Tax entitlement.

6) Bonds issued without voter approval by a district certified by the State Board of Education as financially distressed.

The amount of a public school district's debt is limited by statute.

30 ILCS 210/2
105 ILCS 5/17-2.11
105 ILCS 5/19-1 et seq.
105 ILCS 5/20-1 et seq.

26:200   What is a bond?

A bond is a written certificate or evidence of a debt signed by the president and clerk of the school board to pay a specific sum of money, frequently called the face value, at a fixed time in the future, frequently called the date of maturity, and at a fixed rate of interest.

A bond represents a general obligation of the district. Taxes in an amount necessary to pay principal and interest due each year are extended by the county clerk without regard to the tax rate or amount.

30 ILCS 305/1 et seq.
30 ILCS 345/1 et seq.
105 ILCS 5/17-9
105 ILCS 5/19-2

26:210   What powers do school boards have to borrow money by issuing bonds to pay for real property or improvements?

The powers of school directors and boards of education differ with respect to borrowing money by the issuance of bonds. For the purpose of building or repairing schoolhouses or purchasing or improving school sites, the directors of any school district, when authorized by a majority of the votes cast on such proposition conducted in accordance with the general election law, may borrow money and, as evidence of such indebtedness, may issue bonds, signed by the president and clerk of the board, in denominations of not less than $100 and bearing interest at a rate set by statutory formula.

Any school district governed by a board of education having less than 500,000 inhabitants and not governed by a special Act may borrow money for the purpose of building, equipping, altering, or repairing school buildings or purchasing or improving school sites, acquiring and equipping playgrounds, recreation grounds, athletic fields, and other buildings or land used or useful for school purposes, or for the purpose of purchasing a site, with or without a building or buildings thereon, or for the building of a house or houses on such site, or for the building of a house or houses on the school site of the school district, for residential purposes of the superintendent, principal, or teachers of the school district, and issue its negotiable coupon bonds therefor signed by the president and secretary of the board, in denominations of not less than $100 nor more than $5,000, payable at such place and at such time or times, not exceeding 20 years from the date of issuance, as the board of education may prescribe, and bearing interest at a rate set by statutory formula, payable annually, semiannually, or quarterly, but no such bonds shall be issued unless the proposition to issue them is submitted to the voters of the district at a referendum held at a regularly scheduled election after the board has certified the proposition to the proper election authorities in accordance with the general election law.

30 ILCS 305/2
105 ILCS 5/19-2
105 ILCS 5/19-3
Wilcoxen v. Board of Education of Canton Union School District No. 66, 116 Ill.App.3d 380, 452 N.E.2d 132, 72 Ill.Dec. 200 (3rd Dist. 1980)
Carstens v. East Alton-Wood River Community Unit School District, 27 Ill.2d 88, 187 N.E.2d 682 (1963)

26:220   What is the maximum bond interest rate a school board may pay?

The maximum bond interest rate allowable may not exceed the greater of 9 percent per annum or 125 percent of the rate specified in a statutorily designated bond index rate.

30 ILCS 305/2
Bates v. Board of Education, Allendale Community Consolidated School District No. 17, 136 Ill.2d 260, 555 N.E.2d 1 (1990)

26:230   What is the maximum maturity for a school bond issue?

A school bond issue must have a maturity date not exceeding 20 years from date of issue.

105 ILCS 5/19-3
105 ILCS 5/20-2

26:240   Must a school district abolish its working cash fund to issue working cash fund bonds?

No. A school district may issue working cash fund bonds pursuant to statute in an amount not exceeding in the aggregate 85 percent of the taxes permitted to be levied for educational purposes for the current year plus 85 percent of the school district's personal property replacement tax entitlement. Working cash fund bonds are subject to back door referendum.

105 ILCS 5/20-2 et seq.
In re Walgenbach, 104 Ill.2d 121, 470 N.E.2d 1015, 83 Ill.Dec. 595 (1984)

26:250   What are tort judgment bonds?

Tort judgment bonds may be used by all types of school districts and the taxes which may be levied for these bonds are not subject to any minimum or maximum rate requirements. Tort judgment bond revenues are used by school districts for the payment of liabilities created by a settlement or a tort judgment, defense costs, to pay liabilities under the Unemployment Insurance Act, Workers' Compensation Act, Occupational Diseases Act, or a risk care management program.

745 ILCS 10/9-105

26:260   May a school board issue bonds to pay teachers' orders when the bond issue would exceed the debt limitations established by law?

Bonds issued to pay teachers' orders may, when added to other indebtedness of the school district, exceed any statutory debt limit.

105 ILCS 5/19-8

DEBT AND FINANCIAL DIFFICULTY

26:270   What happens when a school board reaches its debt limit?

A school board that has reached its debt limit may continue to incur new debt by issuing orders to pay teachers salaries. Those orders will have first claim on any revenue that becomes available. If funds are not available to cover other types of expenditures, a school board can only take steps to curtail expenditures or increase revenue. The school district cannot close its doors.

Long before a school board's financial situation reaches this point, however, the State Board of Education will intervene and require the local board to adopt a spending plan that is fiscally sound and designed to rid the district of its indebtedness.

105 ILCS 5/1A-8

26:280   When does the State Board of Education determine a school district has financial difficulties?

The State Board of Education, after proper investigation of a school district's financial condition, may certify a district is in financial difficulty when any of the following conditions occur:

1) The district has issued school orders for wages or the district has issued funding bonds to retire teacher orders in three of the last five years;

2) The district has issued tax anticipation warrants or tax anticipation notes in anticipation of a second year's taxes when warrants or notes in anticipation of current year taxes are still outstanding;

3) The district has for two consecutive years shown an excess of expenditures and other financing uses over revenues and other financing sources and beginning fund balances on its annual financial report for the aggregate totals of the Educational, Operations and Maintenance, Transportation, and Working Cash Funds.

No school district is deemed to be in financial difficulty by reason of any of the above circumstances arising as a result of the failure of the county to make any distribution of property tax money due the district at the time such distribution is due; or if the district clearly demonstrates to the satisfaction of the State Board of Education at the time of its determination that such condition no longer exists.

The State Board of Education is empowered to require school districts in financial difficulty to develop, adopt and submit a financial plan within 45 days after certification of financial difficulty. The financial plan must be developed according to guidelines presented to the district by the State Board of Education within 14 days of certification. The guidelines address the specific nature of each district's financial difficulties. Any proposed budget of the district must be consistent with the financial plan approved by the State Board.

A district certified to be in financial difficulty must report to the State Board of Education at such times and in such manner as the State Board may direct concerning the district's compliance with each financial plan. The State Board may review the district's operations, obtain budgetary data and financial statements, require the district to produce reports, and have access to any other information in the possession of the district that it deems relevant. The State Board may issue recommendations or directives within its powers to the district to assure compliance with the financial plan. The district must produce such budgetary data, financial statements, reports, and other information and comply with such directives.

105 ILCS 5/1A-8

26:290   How does a school district become financially distressed?

A school district that levies its taxes for education and operations and maintenance at the maximum rates at which the district is authorized by statute with referendum to levy or that meets all of the following criteria may petition the State Board of Education to be certified as financially distressed:

1) The petition is filed with the State Board of Education pursuant to resolution of the school board.

2) The voters of the school district at the most recent general, general primary, consolidated, consolidated primary, or non-partisan election failed to approve a proposition submitted

to the voters at the election to increase the annual rate of tax levied by the school district for educational purposes.

3) The total aggregate indebtedness of the school district, including but not limited to working cash fund, funding, and tort liability bonds, at the time the petition is filed equals or exceeds the debt limitation applicable to the district.

4) The amount of general state aid distributed to the school district under Section 18-8 for the school year immediately preceding the year in which the petition is filed is at least 20 percent less than the amount of general state aid distributed to the district under Section 18-8 for the school year four years prior to the year in which the petition is filed.

5) The school board of the school district levied its taxes for educational purposes, for operation s and maintenance purposes, and for transportation purposes for each of the prior five school years at the maximum rate at which the district was authorized by statute or referendum to levy those taxes for those school years.

105 ILCS 5/19-1.5(a)

26:300   How long does a school district remain financially distressed after it has been certified financially distressed?

A school district remains financially distressed until it completes a fiscal year with a balanced budget under accounting and other principles established by the State Board of Education.

105 ILCS 5/19-1.5(c)

27: ILLINOIS HIGH SCHOOL ASSOCIATION

27:10   What is the IHSA?

IHSA is the Illinois High School Association, a voluntary association of Illinois public and private high schools. Unlike the National Collegiate Athletic Association (NCAA), the IHSA operates under color of state law and is a state actor for purposes of civil rights suits.

Libby by Libby v. South Interconference Association, 728 F.Supp. 504 (N.D. Ill. 1990)

NCAA v. Tarkanian, 109 S.Ct. 454, 488 U.S. 197, 102 L.Ed.2d 469 (1988)

Griffin v. Illinois High School Association, 822 F.2d 671 (7th Cir. 1987)

Menora v. Illinois High School Association, 683 F.2d 1030 (7th Cir. 1982) cert. den. 103 S.Ct. 801, 459 U.S. 1156, 74 L.Ed.2d 1003 (1983)

Bucha v. Illinois High School Association, 351 F.Supp. 69 (N.D. Ill. 1972)

Robinson v. Illinois High School Association, 45 Ill.App.2d 277, 195 N.E.2d 38 (2nd Dist. 1963) cert. den. 85 S.Ct. 647, 379 U.S. 960, 13 L.Ed.2d 555 (1965)

Sanders v. Louisiana High School Athletic Association, 242 So.2d 19 (La. App. 1970)

27:20   How is IHSA organized?

The IHSA is governed by a board of seven directors who are elected to office by the principals of the secondary schools which belong to the IHSA. The state is divided into seven geographical regions and one director from among the high school principals in each region is elected from each region.

IHSA Const. art. 1.320 et seq.

27:30   Can the IHSA regulate high school athletic eligibility by the adoption of rules regulating amateur status, extra-curricular participation, attendance, transfer and receipt of benefit?

Yes.

Gaines v. National Collegiate Athletic Association, 746 F.Supp. 738 (M.D. Tenn. 1990)

Banks v. National Collegiate Athletic Association, 746 F.Supp. 850 (N.D. Ind. 1990)

Shelton v. National Collegiate Athletic Association, 539 F.2d 1196 (9th Cir. 1976)

**27:35   May a school or student be punished by IHSA if
a court order sought by the student or school
against IHSA is vacated?**

If a student, or a member school otherwise in non-compli-
ance with IHSA rules, participates in an interscholastic contest
in accordance with a restraining order, injunction or other court
order against IHSA or a member school and the order or injunction expires without final determination or is vacated, stayed,
reversed, modified or found to have been entered in error, the
contests in which the student participated are subject to forfeit
and the school and student are subject to IHSA sanctions.

IHSA By-law 6.022
IHSA By-law 6.023

STANDARDS FOR SCHOOLS

**27:40   How is a school's size determined for purposes
of its placement in the IHSA Class A or Class AA
classification system?**

A school's class placement is determined by its student
enrollment as reported on September 30 of the preceding school
year to the State Board of Education in its Fall Housing Report.
For two-year high schools the total student enrollment figure is
doubled. For three-year high schools, one-third of the total student enrollment figure is added to the figure reported. For
schools which enroll boys or girls only, the number is doubled.

All Chicago Public League high schools are Class AA. The 65
percent of schools excluding Chicago high schools having the
smallest enrollment are annually classified Class A, and the 35
percent of schools excluding Chicago high schools having the
largest enrollment are annually classified Class AA.

A school may request a classification variance by submitting
a request for any given year to the executive director no later
than April 1. Variances may be granted for verifiable decreases
in enrollment equaling 20 percent or more or when a high school
houses out-of-district special education students.

IHSA Administrative Policies 20

27:50   May private or parochial schools become IHSA members?

Private or parochial high schools may be admitted to membership in IHSA provided a report of the systems of financial assistance to students available in the school is placed on file with the IHSA and the school complies with all other applicable membership rules. The membership and financial assistance report of a private or parochial school must be approved by the IHSA Board of Directors annually.

IHSA Const. art. 1.210
IHSA Const. art. 1.250

27:60   Under what conditions may high schools field cooperative athletic teams or activity programs?

Two or more public high schools may form cooperative athletic teams or activity programs upon approval of the IHSA Board of Directors, provided:

1) The schools are located in the same geographical area, and

2) All schools participating in the cooperative are IIISA Class A schools or, in the event one or more of the schools is a Class AA school, the cooperative team is for a sport other than boys football or boys or girls basketball, and

3) The cooperative agreement is established for a period of two consecutive years, is approved by the governing boards of all the participating schools, and a joint application is submitted to IHSA.

The combined enrollment of all the schools involved in the cooperative determines the IHSA classification of the cooperative team.

IHSA By-law 2.030

27:70   Under what circumstances may cooperative agreements be extended?

After completion of two years of approved operation, continuation of the cooperative agreement requires timely notice to IHSA which will permit the cooperative team to participate without further documentation for a period of another two years provided the cooperative team continues in its original format. Changes in the original cooperative agreement require complete reapplication to IHSA.

IHSA By-law 2.030

27:80   Under what circumstances are teams eligible to compete in IHSA tournaments?

To be eligible to compete in IHSA meets or tournaments, an established school team must have engaged in at least six inter-scholastic contests in the sport during the current season (or during the preceding IHSA season in the case of boys baseball, boys golf, boys tennis, girls softball, girls golf, and girls tennis).

Girls participating on a boys team will not satisfy the requirement for entry of a girls team in the state meet, but a girls team competing against boys teams will count toward the six-contest requirement.

IHSA By-law 3.054
Rules Application 86

27:90   If an IHSA member school participates in an event with a school from another state, or a school not governed by IHSA rules, which rules apply to the event?

IHSA members must abide by IHSA rules in all athletic and non-athletic contests and activities whether with members or non-members of IHSA. Waiver of eligibility rules is possible only by the IHSA Board of Directors.

IHSA By-law 2.010

27:100   May a school team practice or compete during a teacher strike at the school?

A school which does not have 51 percent of its students in attendance during a strike and which cannot offer a minimum program pursuant to State Board of Education rules and regulations may not engage in interscholastic activities. The school may host an activity in which the school on strike does not engage.

Practice sessions may be held if they are: approved by the

local board of education; conducted by personnel meeting IHSA supervision rules; and are conducted in a manner which assures the health and safety of participants. Students from a school on strike may not participate with a team from a school which is not on strike.

The 51 percent rule is applicable to strike situations only and does not prevent interscholastic activities on the same day a school is closed because of holiday, vacation or emergency day provided school is in full operation on the preceding school day.

IHSA By-law 2.130
IHSA Administrative Procedures, Guidelines and Policies, Number 7
Proulx by Proulx v. Illinois High School Association, 125 Ill.App.3d 781, 466 N.E.2d 620, 81 Ill.Dec. 34 (4th Dist. 1984)

SPORTSMANSHIP

27:110   Are there IHSA rules governing sportsmanship?

Yes. Persons found to be in gross violation of the ethics of competition or the principles of good sportsmanship may be barred by the Board of Directors from athletic contests or interscholastic activities.

IHSA By-law 3.150
IHSA By-law 4.060

27:120   May the IHSA penalize a school for unsportsmanlike conduct?

The IHSA executive director has authority to penalize an individual or a school for unsportsmanlike conduct.

IHSA By-law 2.041
IHSA By-law 6.00 et seq.
Rules Application 11

27:122   What penalty does IHSA impose if a player is ejected from a game?

If a player is ejected for unsportsmanlike conduct, he is ineligible for the next interscholastic contest at that level of competition and all other contests at any level in the interim in addition to any other penalties his school or the IHSA may impose.

IHSA By-law 6.011

27:124   What penalty does IHSA impose if a coach is ejected from a game?

If a coach is ejected for unsportsmanlike conduct, he is ineligible for the next interscholastic contest at that level of competition and all other contests at any level in the interim in addition to any other penalties his school or the IHSA may impose.

IHSA By-law 6.012

STUDENT ELIGIBILITY

27:130   Does a student have a constitutional right to participate in public school interscholastic activities?

There is no recognized constitutional right to participate in athletics. A student may, however, raise legitimate constitutional issues in the context of a claim addressing a ruling on eligibility by implicating, for example, a constitutionally protected property right, or alleging that a particular rule disadvantages a suspect class.

Jordan by Edwards v. O'Fallon Township High School District No. 203 Board of Education, 302 Ill.App.3d 1070, 706 N.E.2d 137, 235 Ill.Dec.877 (5th Dist. 1999)

Kulovitz v. Illinois High School Association, 462 F.Supp. 875 (N.D. Ill. 1978)

Board of Curators v. Horowitz, 98 S.Ct. 948, 435 U.S. 78, 55 L.Ed.2d 725 (1975)

Colorado Seminary (University of Denver) v. NCAA, 570 F.2d 320 (10th Cir. 1978)

Bucha v. Illinois High School Association, 351 F.Supp. 69 (N.D. Ill. 1972)

Mitchell v. Louisiana High School Association, 430 F.2d 1155 (5th Cir. 1970)

27:140   Does an athlete have a cause of action against IHSA if his school is penalized for rules violations and as a result the athlete is unable to compete?

Athletes have attempted to bring lawsuits against the National Collegiate Athletic Association (NCAA) on the premise that a penalty against their school for violation of an NCAA rule has denied them some benefit to which they were otherwise entitled. Usually, the lawsuit alleges violation of a property right, such as loss of opportunity to obtain a professional contract, or an equal protection argument alleging the penalties disproportionately affect some suspect classification of persons. The courts have held that such claims brought by athletes do not rise to the level of a constitutional right invoking due process requirements in connection with an athletic association's imposition of sanctions against a school.

Hawkins v. National Collegiate Athletic Association, 652 F.Supp. 602 (C.D. Ill. 1987)

Justice v. National Collegiate Athletic Association, 577 F.Supp. 356 (N.D. Ariz. 1983)

Colorado Seminary (University of Denver) v. National Collegiate Athletic Association, 570 F.2d 320 (10th Cir. 1978)

Parish v. National Collegiate Athletic Association, 506 F.2d 1028 (5th Cir. 1975)

27:150 May graduates or other unattached athletes compete in high school athletic contests?

No.

IHSA By-law 3.023
IHSA By-law 3.050 et seq.
Rules Application 118

27:160 May a student participate and be eligible in more than one sport at the same time?

Yes.

IHSA By-law 3.050
Rules Application 84

27:170 When are physical examinations required for participation in athletics?

Students in their first seven semesters of attendance must have filed with their high school principal a certificate of physical fitness issued by a licensed physician not more than one year preceding practice or participation in any interscholastic athletic contest or activity. Students in their eighth semester of attendance must have a certificate issued not more than 15 months preceding practice or participation on file.

IHSA By-law 3.071

27:180   Is a student physical examination by a chiropractor or by spiritual means sufficient for athletic eligibility?

Not unless the spiritual advisor or chiropractor is licensed in Illinois to practice medicine in all its branches.

IHSA By-law 3.070
Rules Application 91

27:190   What attendance requirements affect a student's IHSA athletic eligibility?

Except under very limited circumstances involving schools for the deaf and blind and the eligibility of ninth grade middle school students on high school teams, a student may only represent in competition the school he or she attends. To be eligible, a student must have been enrolled and in attendance not later than the beginning of the eleventh school day of the semester. Exceptions may be allowed by the IHSA under limited specific procedures and circumstances upon written application to the executive director.

Including a student's name on school attendance records for a period of 10 or more school days during any semester beginning with the student's first physical attendance and ending with the date of the student's withdrawal from school constitutes a semester of attendance for the student. If a student does not attend school for 10 days in a semester but participates in any interscholastic athletic activity, the student is considered to have completed a semester of attendance unless the withdrawal from school occurs prior to the 10 days attendance and is necessitated by disabling illness or injury which is certified by a physician.

A student may not have a lapse of school connection of greater than 10 consecutive school days during a semester. If there is a lapse of greater than 10 school days, the student is ineligible for the remainder of the semester. Exceptions may be considered only upon written verification that the lapse in school connection was caused by illness of the student or in the student's immediate family or under other circumstances acceptable to the IHSA Board of Directors. The request for exception must be submitted to the executive director for presentation to the Board of Directors.

IHSA By-law 3.010 et seq.
Rules Application 47 et seq.
Spath v. National Collegiate Athletic Association, 728 F.2d 25 (1st Cir. 1984)

27:200   How do attendance requirements differ for IHSA programs involving activities other than athletics?

The only differences are for music programs. IHSA allows grade school or junior high school students to participate with high school musical organizations or ensembles in interscholastic music activities. Joint music curricular programs involving two or more schools are also permitted.

IHSA By-law 4.017 et seq.

27:210   May a student who is absent from school because of illness on the day of an IHSA event participate in the event?

Provided there is no local school rule preventing participation, the student may compete. There is no IHSA rule or by-law requiring that a student attend school on the day he competes in an IHSA event.

IHSA By-law 10
Rules Application 47

27:220   In order to retain IHSA eligibility, what academic requirements must a student meet?

To retain IHSA eligibility, a student must be doing passing work in at least 20 credit hours of high school work per week. Except in the case of a student entering high school for the first time, a student must have received credit for 20 hours of high school work for the previous semester. The work must have been completed in the semester for which credit is granted or in a recognized summer school program which has been approved by the local board of education and for which graduation credit is received.

Passing work is defined as work of a grade that if on any given date the student would transfer to another school, passing grades for the course would be certified on the student's transcript to the school to which the student transfers.

Work taken in a junior college, college, university or by correspondence may be accepted for meeting eligibility requirements provided the work is recognized as credit toward graduation from high school by the local board of education.

To retain eligibility, the student must not have graduated from any four-year high school or its equivalent.

IHSA By-law 3.020 et seq.
IHSA By-law 4.021 et seq.
Rules Application 51 et seq.
Texas Education Agency v. Stamos, 817 S.W.2d 378 (Tex.Ct. App. 1991)
Associated Students, Inc. of California State University-Sacramento, et al. v. National Collegiate Athletic Association, 493 F.2d 1251 (9th Cir. 1974)
Howard University v. National Collegiate Athletic Association, 367 F.Supp. 926 (D.C. D.C. 1973)

27:230   When is eligibility regained after a student has been academically ineligible for a semester?

A student who has been academically ineligible for a semester does not regain eligibility (after satisfactory academic performance) until the first day of the next semester.

Rules Application 51

27:240   What residence requirements affect IHSA athletic eligibility for public school students?

A student is eligible if the student resides full time with his parents, custodial parent or guardian appointed by a judge of a court having jurisdiction, or he currently and for the last two years prior to the student's enrolling in high school has lived with another family member or relative who has provided full support and adult supervision for the student as though the family member or relative was the guardian, and the student and the family member or relative live within the school district in which the high school he attends is located; or the student resides or has attended a minimum of the seventh and eighth grades as a tuition paying non-resident student in the district in which the high school he attends is located. In all other cases, the student cannot participate without a ruling by the executive director.

IHSA By-law 3.031 et seq.
IHSA Administrative Procedures, Guidelines and Policies, Number 1

Rules Application 61 et seq.
Howard University v. National Collegiate Athletic Association, 367
F.Supp. 926 (D.C. D.C. 1973)

27:242   What residence requirements affect IHSA athletic eligibility for private school students?

A private school student is eligible at the high school in which he enrolls provided he resides full time with his parents, custodial parent or guardian appointed by a judge of a court having jurisdiction or he currently and for the last two years prior to the student's enrolling in high school has lived with another family member or relative who has provided full support and adult supervision for the student as though the family member or relative was the guardian, and the student and the family member or relative live within the school district in which the high school he attends is located; and

1) within the boundaries of the public school district in which the private high school he attends is located; or

2) he has attended private schools on a continuous basis for the last two consecutive school years before entering high school or for a total of not less than four school years from kindergarten through eighth grade; or

3) he attends the private member school attended by one or both of his parents or the current spouse of one of his parents; or

4) he attends a private member school within a 30 mile radius of his residence as defined above.

All other residency cases involving students who properly reside full time with a parent or guardian require an eligibility ruling by the executive director.

IHSA By-law 3.032 et seq.

27:244   What residence requirements affect IHSA athletic eligibility for students who attend public schools without boundaries?

A student attending a public member school which does not have a geographical boundary is eligible at the school in which he enrolls provided he resides full time with his parents, custodial parent or guardian appointed by a judge of a court having jurisdiction or he currently and for the last two years prior to the student's enrolling in high school has lived with another family member or relative who has provided full support and adult supervision for the student as though the family member or relative was the guardian, and the student and the family member or relative live within the school district in which the high school he attends is located; and

1) within the boundaries of the public high school district in which the non-boundaried public high school he attends is located; or

2) he has attended non-boundaried public schools or private schools on a continuous basis for the last two consecutive school years before entering high school or for a total of not less than four school years from kindergarten through eighth grade; or

3) he attends the non-boundaried public school attended by one or both of his parents or the current spouse of one of his parents; or

4) he attends a non-boundaried public member school within a 30 mile radius of his residence as defined above.

All other residency cases involving students who properly reside full time with a parent or guardian require an eligibility ruling by the executive director.

IHSA By-law 3.033 et seq.

27:246   Under what conditions are foreign exchange students eligible?

Foreign exchange students enrolled in IHSA-approved student exchange programs and attending school in Illinois are eligible for a maximum period of one calendar year beginning with the date of their enrollment and initial attendance at an IHSA school. To be considered for approval, a foreign exchange program must assign students to schools by a method which insures that no student, school, or other interested party may influence the assignment for athletic or other purposes.

IHSA By-law 3.034.3

27:247   Is a student ineligible if his parents move during his senior year?

A student who has attended the same school for his entire high school career, and whose parents move from the district following the student's completion of eleventh grade, may remain in the school and retain eligibility for the twelfth grade provided the student obtains the approval of the school's governing body and there is no evidence of undue influence to retain the attendance of the student.

IHSA By-law 3.034.2

27:248 What eligibility rules apply to special or vocational education students?

A student taking part of his work at a special or vocational education center and taking the remaining portion of his work at his home high school is eligible at the home high school only. A student who takes all of his work at a special center may make an eligibility election. Once the election of eligibility at the special center or the home school is made, however, the election may not be changed without loss of eligibility not to exceed one calendar year.

IHSA By-law 3.034.4 et seq.

27:250 What transfer rules affect a student's IHSA athletic eligibility?

Both the principal of the school from which and to which the student transfers must approve the transfer. A student is not eligible to participate in an interscholastic contest until a transfer form, fully executed by both principals, is on file in the offices of the school to which the student transfers.

Once classes begin in a school for the current school year, if a student changes attendance from that high school to another high school, the student is ineligible for the remainder of the school year in any sport in which he/she participated or was participating in a practice or interscholastic contest in the current school year at the school from which the transfer occurs; or

Once classes begin in a school for the current school year, if a student changes attendance from that high school to another high school, the student is ineligible for a period of 30 days, beginning on the first day of attendance at the new high school in any sport in which he/she was not participating or had not participated during the current school year at the school from which the student transferred.

A student who transfers attendance from one high school to

another high school is ineligible unless:

1) The student's transfer is in conjunction with a change in residence by both the student and his parents, custodial parent or guardian from one public high school district to a different public high school district; or

2) The student's transfer is from one public high school in a school district which supports two (2) or more public high schools to another public high school in that school district and the transfer is in conjunction with a change in residence by both the student and his parents, custodial parent or guardian to a residence within the boundaries established by the governing board of the school district for the high school to which the student transfers;

3) The student changes attendance from a private school or a public school with no boundaries to a public high school located in the school district in which the student resides full time with his parents, custodial parent or guardian; the student is enrolling for the first time in a public member high school with boundaries; and the principals of both of the high schools involved accept the transfer, concurring that there is no evidence of any violation or avoidance of any IHSA rules, nor any recruiting in connection with the transfer which violates any IHSA rules; or

4) The student changes attendance from one private school to a different private school which is located within a 30 mile radius of his residence, the student is changing high school attendance for the first time; and the principals of both private high schools involved accept the transfer, concurring that there is no evidence of any violation or avoidance of any IHSA rules nor any recruiting in connection with the transfer which violates any IHSA rules; or

5) The student, who is a child of divorced or legally separated parents, changes attendance from one high school to another in conjunction with a modification or other change in legal custody between the parents by action of a judge of a court of proper jurisdiction, and a copy of the petition for and the court order so changing custody is on file with the principal of the high school into which the student transfers; or

6) The student, who (a) is an orphan; (b) has one deceased parent; (c) is a child of divorced or legally separated parents without an accompanying modification or other change in legal custody by action of a judge of a court of proper jurisdiction; (d)

is a ward of the state or of a court; or (e) is a child whose legal guardianship has been changed by a judge of a court of proper jurisdiction, changes attendance from one high school to another. A ruling by the executive director is required to determine the student's eligibility. The student may practice but cannot participate in an interscholastic athletic contest until a ruling on the student's eligibility is made by the executive director.

If a transfer is caused by any of the reasons above those reason(s) shall be only a factor for the executive director's consideration and is not be an automatic basis for granting eligibility.

IHSA By-law 3.040 et seq.
IHSA Administrative Procedures, Guidelines and Policies, Number 1
Beck v. Missouri State High School Activities Association, 837 F.Supp. 998 (E.D. Mo. 1993)
Crane by Crane v. Indiana High School Athletic Association, 975 F.2d 1315 (7th Cir. 1992)
Griffin High School v. Illinois High School Association, 822 F.Supp. 875 (C.D. Ill. 1987)
Kulovitz v. Illinois High School Association, 462 F.Supp. 875 (N.D. Ill. 1978)

27:252 When is a student eligible if there is a court ordered change in custody?

If a student's transfer is based upon his being emancipated, an orphan, a child from a broken home, a child of a single parent home, a ward of the state or of a court, or a child whose legal guardianship has been changed by order of a court, a ruling by the executive director must be obtained before any such student is eligible. A copy of the custody order must accompany the principal's verification.

IHSA By-law 3.043

27:260 What is the age limitation for athletic eligibility?

A is eligible through age nineteen except that if the student will turn twenty during a sport season, his eligibility terminates on the first day of the sport season in which he will become twenty.

IHSA By-law 3.061
Butts v. NCAA, LaSalle University, 751 F.2d 609 (3rd Cir. 1984)
Robinson v. Illinois High School Association, 45 Ill.App.2d 277, 195 N.E.2d 38 (2nd Dist. 1963) cert. den. 85 S.Ct. 647, 379 U.S. 960, 13 L.Ed.2d 555 (1965)

27:262 Does the eligibility age limit discriminate against disabled athletes by denying them eligibility?

The age limit requirement probably does not violate either Section 504 of the Rehabilitation Act or the Americans with Disabilities Act. The IHSA age limit is an essential eligibility requirement which has a legitimate purpose in an interscholastic program. Reasonable accommodation does not require an institution to "lower or to effect substantial modification of standards to accommodate a handicapped person."

Pottgen v. Missouri State High School Activities Association, 40 F.3d 926 (8th Cir. 1994)

27:270 How does the age limit differ for interscholastic activities other than athletics?

A student may participate in non-athletic activities through age nineteen.

IHSA By-law 4.041
Robinson v. Illinois High School Association, 45 Ill.App.2d 277, 195 N.E.2d 38 (2nd Dist. 1963) cert. den. 85 S.Ct. 647, 379 U.S. 960, 13 L.Ed.2d 555 (1965)

27:280 How many semesters of athletic eligibility may a student have?

After a student enrolls in the ninth grade, the student is eligible for no more than eight semesters and no more than four school years of competition in any sport. The last two semesters of eligibility must be consecutive; other semesters of eligibility need not be consecutive.

IHSA By-law 3.050 et seq.
Spath v. National Collegiate Athletic Association, 728 F.2d 25 (1st Cir. 1984)

27:290 How do the semesters of eligibility rules differ for students enrolled in activities other than athletics?

Students participating in interscholastic activities other than athletics need not use their last two semesters of eligibility consecutively, nor do the six-contest rules applicable to team sports apply.

IHSA By-law 4.030 et seq.

BOYS AND GIRLS TEAMS

27:300   Are gender-based rule classifications subject to strict scrutiny?

A classification based on sex is a suspect classification under Illinois law, which, to be held valid, must withstand strict judicial scrutiny. This means that the state must show a compelling state interest to meet the strict scrutiny standard. Gender based classifications are not a suspect classification under federal constitutional law, and to meet the federal standard such classifications need only serve important governmental objectives and must be substantially related to achievement of those objectives.

Ill. Const. art. I, sec. 18
Craig v. Boren, 97 S.Ct. 451, 429 U.S. 190, 50 L.Ed.2d 397 (1976)
People v. Ellis, 57 Ill.2d 127, 311 N.E.2d 98 (1974)
In re Griffiths, 93 S.Ct. 2851, 413 U.S. 717, 37 L.Ed.2d 397 (1973)

27:305   May a school eliminate a sport in order to make its total athletic program comply with sex equity rules?

In order to prevail in a suit challenging the elimination of a sport from an educational institution's menu of sports, the plaintiff must show that exclusion from participation in or denial of access to benefits of the athletic program were based on gender, rather than some other legitimate purpose.

Gonyo v. Drake University, 837 F.Supp. 989 (S.D. Ia. 1993)

27:307   What test is used to determine if a school has given boys and girls equal opportunities to participate in athletics?

The U.S. Department of Education uses a three part test:

1) Does the school offer girls and boys opportunities to participate in athletic programs that are substantially proportionate to their respective enrollments?

2) Can the school demonstrate a history of program expansion for the under represented sex?

3) Can the school demonstrate that despite continuing low participation by one sex its interests have been fully and effectively met by the present program?

34 CFR 106.412(c)
Cohen v. Brown University, 879 F.Supp. 185 (D.C. R.I. 1995)

27:310   May a girl compete in a state tournament on a boys athletic team?

Yes, if all the following conditions are met:

1) the member school is in compliance with Illinois Sex Equity Rules;

2) the only team in the sport at the school is a boys team; and the girl participates on the boys team in that sport during the regular season.

Ill. Const. art. I, sec. 18
105 ILCS 5/27-1
IHSA Affirmative Action Policy for Girls on Boys State Series Teams

27:320   May a boy compete in a state tournament on a girls athletic team?

No.

IHSA Affirmative Action Policy for Girls on Boys State Series Teams
Petrie v. Illinois High School Association, et al., 75 Ill.App.3d 980, 394 N.E.2d 855, 31 Ill.Dec. 653 (4th Dist. 1979)
Massachusetts Interscholastic Athletic Association and Gomes v. Rhode Island Interscholastic League, 469 F.Supp. 659 (D.C. R.I. 1979)

27:330   Does IHSA regulate regular season participation of girls on boys teams or boys on girls teams?

No. IHSA rules address only eligibility for the state tournament series.

IHSA Affirmative Action Policy for Girls on Boys State Series Teams

27:340   May a girl be excluded from a boys team because the sport she wishes to participate in involves contact?

No. The case law and applicable statutes require that if there is no comparable girls team offered by a school, a girl seeking to play on a boys team must be given the opportunity to play even if the sport is a contact sport such as wrestling or football.

Leffel v. Wisconsin Interscholastic Athletic Association, 444 F.Supp. 1117, (E.D. Wis. 1978)

Darrin v. Gould, 85 Wash.2d 859, 540 P.2d 882 (1975)

Commonwealth of Pennsylvania by Israel Packel, Attorney General v. Pennsylvania Interscholastic Athletic Association, 18 Pa.Cmwlth. 45, 334 A.2d 839 (1975)

Brenden v. Independent School District 742, 477 F.2d 1292 (8th Cir. 1973)

Morris v. Michigan State Board of Education, 472 F.2d 1207 (6th Cir. 1973)

Gilpin v. Kansas State High School Activities Association, Inc., 377 F.Supp. 1233 (D.C. Kan. 1973)

Bucha v. Illinois High School Association, 351 F.Supp. 69 (N.D. Ill. 1972)

Reed v. Nebraska School Activities Association, 341 F.Supp. 258 (D.C. Neb. 1972)

Haas v. South Bend Community School Corporation, 259 Ind. 515, 289 N.E.2d 495 (1972)

COACHING AND PRACTICING

27:350   Who may be employed as a head coach?

Athletic head coaches in IHSA member schools must be certified to teach in Illinois and be:

1) teaching or supervising classroom activity at least two periods daily in the member school; or

2) employed full-time in any elementary or junior high school in the attendance area of the member high school; or

3) an assistant teacher, resource aide, lay supervisor or other paraprofessional who is employed at least half-time per day in the member school; or

4) a full-time teacher in any elementary district, any territory of which is part of the member high school's district;

5) teaching full-time in a member high school or vocational or special education cooperative in which the member school participates; or

6) a retired teacher from the member high school.

If a member school is unable to fill a coaching position with personnel acceptable to its board of education under the terms of the above, it may employ to serve as coach a regularly certified teacher who is not otherwise employed in the member school; and if it is unable to fill the position with any person acceptable to the school board and qualified as defined above it may employ a person with a bachelor's degree who has satisfactorily completed a coach training program approved by the IHSA Board of Directors.

IHSA By-law 2.070 et seq.

27:360   Who may be employed as an assistant coach?

If a member school is unable to fill an assistant coaching position with a person who is both acceptable to its board of education and qualified to be a head coach under IHSA rules, it may fill the position with a person who is a certified teacher who is not otherwise employed in the school district.

If the school is still unable to fill the position, it may, with the permission of the IHSA executive director, employ a person who possesses a substitute teacher's certificate. If the member school is still unable to fill the coaching position with personnel acceptable to its board of education under the terms of the above, it may employ to serve as coach a person who holds a minimum of a bachelor's degree, provided the person has satisfactorily completed a coach training program approved by the IHSA Board of Directors.

If the member school is still unable to fill the coaching position with personnel acceptable to its board of education under the terms of the above, it may employ to serve as coach a person who has satisfactorily completed a coach training program approved by the IHSA Board of Directors and subsequently is approved by the IHSA executive director.

IHSA By-law 2.070 et seq.
Rules Application 19 et seq.

27:370   May a student attend an athletic sports camp or coaching school without affecting his athletic eligibility?

During the school year a student may not participate in any coaching school for any interscholastic sport. A coaching school is any sponsored program which provides instruction in sports theory and skills to groups of persons. Attendance is permitted between the close of the school year and the opening of school in the fall, except that no student may attend a coaching school or participate in a physical education class for any fall sport after July 31.

Lessons in which no more than two students from the same school participate, school physical conditioning programs, recreational programs and non-school competitive programs are not coaching schools.

IHSA By-law 3.120 et seq.

27:380   May a school have an open gym policy without violating IHSA rules?

Yes, provided that:

1) the gym is open to all students, not just athletes; and

2) a variety of activities is available to students on any given date; and

3) there is no coaching or instruction in the skills and techniques of any sport; and

4) participation is voluntary and is not required directly or indirectly for membership on a high school squad; and

5) comparable opportunities are afforded boys and girls; and

6) school administration assumes responsibility for making certain there is adherence to these guidelines.

IHSA Administrative Policies 9

27:390   May a student take private lessons in his sport outside the school season from his high school coach?

If the lesson program is limited to students from the instructor's school, the lesson program is a form of organizing and practicing the school team and is in violation of the By-laws. If the lesson program also contains students from outside the coach's home school population, the program is permissible, but no lesson group may contain more than two students from the same school.

IHSA By-law 2.090
IHSA By-law 3.124
Rules Application 33

27:400   May a student tryout for a non-school team during his school team's season?

Yes, provided the tryout does not include any instruction, coaching practice, workout, or anything else beyond testing or screening for ability.

IHSA By-law 3.110 et seq.
Rules Application 149

27:410   May a booster group pay to send students to summer sports camps or clinics?

Yes, provided the club maintains its own funds separate from those of the school, and provided the funds provided to the students do not exceed the actual out-of-pocket costs incurred.

IHSA By-law 3.110 et seq.
Rules Application 162

27:420   May a coach be a staff member at a summer camp?

Yes, provided none of the coach's assignments at the camp involve exclusively students from the coach's school.

IHSA By-law 3.110 et seq.
Rules Application 165

27:430   May a student who is declared ineligible by IHSA practice with his school team?

Provided there are no local rules to the contrary, the student may practice. IHSA rules prohibit only participation in or dressing for interscholastic competition. An ineligible student may also sit on the bench or perform as a team manager so long as he does not dress for the game.

IHSA By-law 3.140
Rules Application 172 et seq.

RECRUITMENT

27:440 What is a special recruiting inducement?

It is a violation of IHSA rules to offer a student athlete any special inducement which is not made available to all applicants who enroll in or apply to a school. A special recruiting inducement includes but is not limited to the offer or acceptance of:

1) money or other valuable consideration by anyone connected with the school; or

2) room, board, or clothing or financial allotment for clothing; or

3) pay for work that is in excess of the amount regularly paid for the work; or

4) free transportation by a school connected person; or

5) residence with any school connected person; or

6) any privilege not afforded non-athletes; or

7) reduced rent for parents; or

8) payment of moving expenses for parents or assistance with the moving of parents; or

9) employment of parents in order to entice the family to move to a certain community if someone connected with the school makes the offer; or

10) help in securing a college scholarship.

IHSA By-law 3.082

27:450 Can a school recruit athletes if it provides them no special inducements?

Recruitment or attempted recruitment of athletes is prohibited by IHSA rules. Even when there are no inducements offered, the attempt to encourage any prospective student to attend any member school for the purpose of participating in athletics is a violation of IHSA rules.

IHSA By-law 3.081
IHSA By-law 3.083

27:460   What penalties may be invoked for recruiting violations?

A person found guilty of exercising undue influence to secure or retain the attendance of a student at a member school is ineligible to coach at a member school for one year. Sanctions are also imposed against the school. Persons and or schools may be penalized in the form of written warning, reprimand, and may be required to take affirmative corrective action. IHSA has authority to suspend or expel a person or school from participation in IHSA activities.

IHSA By-law 6.010
Kulovitz v. Illinois High School Association, 462 F.Supp. 875 (N.D. Ill. 1978)

27:470   May a private school recruit students without violating IHSA rules?

Academic recruitment programs are permitted, as are recruitment programs which are designed to attract students because of a school's overall academic and extra-curricular program. There are very specific IHSA rules governing what may and may not be done by a school in a multi-school district or by a private or parochial school in the recruitment of its general school population.

IHSA By-law 3.083

27:480   May a coach initiate contact with a prospective student-athlete?

No. School administrators or other school personnel who are not coaches may, however, initiate contact, provided that the contact is in the context of the enrollment of the student as a prospective student, not a prospective athlete.

IHSA By-law 3.080
Rules Application 97

27:490   May a coach attend and observe a grade school or unsanctioned athletic contest?

Yes, but the coach may not make improper contact with an athlete at the event.

IHSA By-law 3.080
Rules Application 113

27:500   May an alumnus or booster group provide financial assistance to needy students?

No direct financial assistance may be provided. Donations may, however, be provided to a school and distributed by the school to students who qualify for financial assistance. Student athletes may not receive any special consideration in the distribution of financial assistance.

IHSA By-law 3.080
Rules Application 105 et seq.

27:510   May a school employee, booster, alumnus or other individual connected with a school make a home visit to a prospective athlete for recruiting purposes?

No.

IHSA By-law 3.080
Rules Application 95

NON-SCHOOL EVENTS

27:520   May a student athlete compete on a non-school amateur team at the same time he is competing on a school team in the same sport?

During the school sport season, in a school which maintains a school team in that sport, a student may not participate on any non-school team, nor may the student compete as an individual unattached in school competition in that sport. An exception may be made by the Board of Directors for a student trying out for or competing as a representative of the United States or in recognized national or international events.

A school sport season begins with the team's first contest (not with the team's organizational meeting or first practice) and ends with the team's last contest as a team in that sport. The inclusion of a student's name on a valid eligibility certificate establishes membership on a team.

The effect of this rule, for example, prohibits a member of the track team from entering meets unattached during the track season or a member of the volleyball team from participating in a church league during the school season. A violation of this rule results in ineligibility of the athlete for a period not to exceed one semester.

IHSA By-law 3.110 et seq.
Rules Application 144

27:530   Does participation in an all-star game affect a student's athletic eligibility?

A student may not participate in an all-star game in basketball, football, soccer or volleyball during the student's high school career. After completion of a student's athletic eligibility, the student may compete in one IHSA-approved all-star game in that sport.

IHSA By-law 3.130

27:540   Are student-alumni games permitted under IHSA rules?

No. Alumni are not "school groups" within the meaning of the IHSA By-laws. A faculty-student game is permissible and such a game does not count against the number of contests to which a school team is limited.

IHSA By-law 2.050
Rules Application 13 et seq.

27:550   How many students may participate on a non-school team without violating length-of-season rules?

The limitations are as follows:

Basketball (five-player), 2 players may participate; soccer (eleven-player), 5; football (eleven-player), 5; football (seven-player passing), 3; volleyball (six-player), 2; swimming, 13; track, 17; gymnastics, 9; golf, 2; cross country, 3; wrestling, 5; badminton, 2; bowling, 2; tennis, 2.

IHSA By-law 2.090
Rules Application 34

27:560   May a student athlete compete on the same team with a professional athlete?

Yes, provided the student does not receive cash in any amount for winning or placing in competition or merchandise prizes which exceed 20 dollars in fair market value.

IHSA By-law 3.090
Rules Application 134

STUDENT AWARDS

27:570   May a student athlete accept a trophy for athletic accomplishment without violation of IHSA rules?

For winning or placing in athletic competition, a student may accept a medal, cup, trophy or plaque from the sponsoring agent regardless of cost. A student may accept any other award which does not exceed 20 dollars in fair market value for participation in an athletic contest or for athletic honors or recognition.

A student may receive and retain items of wearing apparel which are worn for non-school athletic competition as part of a team uniform provided for and worn by the student during competition. A student may accept a school letter regardless of cost.

IHSA By-law 3.090 et seq.
Wiley v. National Collegiate Athletic Association, 612 F.2d 473 (10th Cir. 1979)

27:580   May a student receive cash or an elaborate trophy for shooting a hole in one in a country club golf tournament without affecting his IHSA eligibility?

No. Cash, checks, money orders or transferable gift certificates are impermissible as prizes under any circumstance. A student may accept a trophy valued at more than 20 dollars only if it is for winning or placing in a competition or for sportsmanship. Otherwise, an award received must be merchandise with a fair market value of no more than 20 dollars.

IHSA By-law 3.090
Rules Application 128 et seq.

TABLE OF CASES

Listed here are all of the court decisions cited in the text of *Illinois School Law Survey*. Cases are arranged in alphabetical order by name of plaintiff.

Each case listed carries a full legal citation followed by the question number(s) in **bold face** where the case may be found cited in the text.

Abood v. Detroit Board of Education, 97 S.Ct. 1782, 431 U.S. 209, 52 L.Ed. 261, reh. den. 97 S.Ct. 2989, 433 U.S. 915, 53 L.Ed.2d 1102 (1977) **17:110, 21:310, 21:320**

Acme Bus Corp. v. Board of Education of the Roosevelt Union Free School District, 89 N.Y.2d 816, 681 N.E.2d 1304, 659 N.Y.S.2d 857 (1997) **25:222**

Acorn Auto Driving School, Inc. v. Leyden High School District No. 212, 27 Ill.2d 93, 187 N.E.2d 722 (1963) **10:60**

Adler v. Duval County, 851 F.Supp. 446, aff'd. 112 F.3d 1475 (11th Cir. 1999), reh and sugg. for reh. den. 120 F.3d 276 **14:61**

Adsit v. Sanders, 157 Ill.App.3d 416, 510 N.E.2d 547, 109 Ill.Dec. 679, app. dismissed 117 Ill.2d 541, 517 N.E.2d 1083, 115 Ill.Dec. 397 (4th Dist. 1987) **8:40**

Agostini v. Felton, 117 S.Ct. 1997, 521 U.S. 203, 138 L.Ed.2d 391 (1997) **13:114, 14:90**

Aken v. Board of Control of Lake County Area Vocational Center, 237 Ill.App.3d 97, 604 N.E.2d 524 , 178 Ill.Dec. 268 (2nd Dist. 1992) **16:100**

Alabama and Coushatta Tribes of Texas v. Trustees of Big Sandy, 817 F.Supp. 1319 (E.D. Tex. 1993) **12:125**

Alexander v. Holmes County Board of Education, 90 S.Ct. 21, 396 U.S. 19, 24 L.Ed.2d 19 (1969) **14:440**

Allegheny County v. American Civil Liberties Union, Greater Pittsburgh Chapter, 109 S.Ct. 3086, 492 U.S. 573, 106 L.Ed.2d 472 (1989) on rem. 887 F.2d 260 **14:123**

Allen v. Love, 112 Ill.App.3d 338, 445 N.E.2d 514, 68 Ill. Dec. 66 (1st Dist. 1983) **3:100, 3:110**

Allen v. Powell, 42 Ill.2d 66, 244 N.E.2d 596 (1969) **3:180, 3:185**

Allione v. Board of Education, South Fork Community High School District No. 310, Christian County, 29 Ill.App.2d 261, 173 N.E.2d 13 (3rd Dist. 1961) **18:150**

Alpha School Bus Company, 2 PERI 1008 (Executive Director's Recommended Decision and Order, November 7, 1985) **21:120**

Alton Community Unit School District No. 11 v. Illinois Educational Labor Relations Board, 209 Ill.App.3d 16, 567 N.E.2d 671, 153 Ill.Dec. 713 (4th Dist. 1991) **21:145**

American Civil Liberties Union of New Jersey v. Blackhorse-Pike Regional Board of Education, 84 F.3d 1431 (3rd Cir. 1996 **14:61**

Anderson v. Creighton, 107 S.Ct. 3034, 483 U.S. 635, 97 L.Ed.2d 523 (1987) **22:64**

Anderson v. Thompson, 658 F.2d 1205 (7th Cir. 1981) **13:350**

Application of Walgenbach, 104 Ill.2d 121, 470 N.E.2d 1015, 117 Ill.Dec. 88 (2nd Dist. 1984) **26:50**

Application of Walgenbach, 166 Ill.App.3d 629, 520 N.E.2d 78, 117 Ill.Dec. 88 (2nd Dist. 1988) **26:50**

Arduini v. Board of Education of Pontiac Township High School District 90 Livingston County, 92 Ill.2d 197, 441 N.E.2d 73, 65 Ill.Dec. 281 (1982) **15:610**

Argo High School Council of Local 571, I.F.T., A.F.T., A.F.L.-C.I.O. v. Argo Community High School District 217, 163 Ill.App.3d 78, 516 N.E.2d 834, 114 Ill.Dec. 679 (1st Dist. 1987) **6:100, 6:110, 6:120**

Arnold v. Carpenter, 459 F.2d 939 (7th Cir. 1972) **12:125**

Associated Students, Inc. of California State University-Sacramento, et al. v. National Collegiate Athletic Association, 493 F.2d 1251 (9th Cir. 1974) **27:220**

Aubrey v. School Board of Lafayette Parish, 92 F.3d 316 (5th Cir. 1998) app. after rem. 148 F.3d 559 **17:730**

Aulwurm v. Board of Education of Murphysboro Community Unit School District of Jackson County, 67 Ill.2d 434, 317 N.E.2d 1337 (1977) **18:240, 18:350**

Aurora East School District No. 131 v. Cronin, 92 Ill.2d 305, 442 N.E.2d 511, 66 Ill.Dec.85 (1982) **14:410**

Ausmus by Ausmus v. Board of Education of City of Chicago, 155 Ill.App.3d 705, 508 N.E.2d 298, 108 Ill.Dec. 137 (1st Dist. 1987) **12:20**

Austin v. Board of Education of Georgetown Community Unit School District No. 3 of Vermilion County, Illinois, 562 F.2d 446 (7th Cir. 1977) **18:60**

Ayers v. Martin, 233 Ill.App.3d 397, 584 N.E.2d 1028, 165 Ill Dec. 594 (4th Dist. 1991) **4:310**

Bagley v. Board of Education of Seneca Community Consolidated School District No. 170, LaSalle County, 83 Ill.App.3d 247, 403 N.E.2d 1285, 38 Ill.Dec. 681, aff'd. 84 Ill.2d 477 (1980) **16:50**

Bakalis v. Golembeski, 35 F.3d 318 (7th Cir. 1994) **19:160**

Baker v. Owen, 395 F.Supp. 294 (M.D.N.C. 1975), aff'd. 96 S.Ct. 210, 423 U.S. 907, 46 L.Ed.2d 137 (1975) **12:190**

Ball v. Kerrville Independent School District, 529 S.W.2d 792 (Tex. 1975) **17:455**

Banks v. National Collegiate Athletic Association, 746 F.Supp. 850 (N.D. Ind. 1990) **27:30**

Barszcz v. Board of Trustees of Community College District No. 504, Cook County, 400 F.Supp. 675 (N.D. Ill. 1975) **18:380**

Bates v. Board of Education, Allendale Community Consolidated School District No. 17, 136 Ill.2d 260, 555 N.E.2d 1 (1990) **26:220**

Bates v. Doria, 150 Ill.App.3d 1025, 502 N.E.2d 454, 104 Ill. Dec. 191 (2nd Dist. 1986) **17:33**

Bauchman by and through Bauchman v. West High School, 900 F.Supp. 254 aff'd. *Bauchman for Bauchman v. West High School,* 132 F.3d 542 (10th Cir. 1997) cert. den. 118 S.Ct. 2370, __U.S.__, 141 L.Ed.2d 738 (1998) **14:225**

Beaver Glass and Mirror Company, Inc. v. Board of Education of Rockford School District No. 205, Winnebago County, 59 Ill.App.3d 880, 376 N.E.2d 377, 17 Ill.Dec. 378 (2nd Dist. 1978) **9:300, 25:230**

Becerra v. Asher, 105 F.3d 1042 (5th Cir. 1997) supp. on den. of reh., reh. and sugg. for reh. den. 111 F.3d 894 **11:430**

Beck v. Board of Education of Harlem Consolidated School District No. 122, 27 Ill.App.3d 4, 325 N.E.2d 640 (2nd Dist. 1975) aff'd. 63 Ill.2d 10, 344 N.E.2d 440 **2:130**

Beck v. Missouri State High School Activities Association, 837 F.Supp. 998 (E.D. MO 1993) **27:250**

Beck v. University of Wisconsin Board of Regents, 75 F.3d 1130 (7th Cir. 1996) **17:390**

Beilan v. Board of Public Education of Philadelphia, 78 S.Ct. 1317, 357 U.S. 399, 2 L.Ed.2d 1414 (1958) **18:150**

Bell v. School District No. 84, 47 Ill. 406, 95 N.E.2d 496 (1950) **26:70**

Berger by Berger v. Rensselaer Central School Corporation, 982 F.2d 1160 (7th Cir. 1993) reh. den., cert. den. 113 S.Ct. 2344 **14:120**

Bergstrand v. Rock Island Board of Education, School District No. 41, 161 Ill.App.3d 180, 514 N.E.2d 256, 112 Ill.Dec. 790 (3rd Dist. 1987) **10:90**

Berkeley School District No. 87, 2 PERI 1066 (IELRB Opinion and Order, May 30, 1986) **21:170**

Berman v. Board of Education of the City of Chicago, 360 Ill. 535, 196 N.E. 464 (1935) **26:140**

Bessler v. Board of Education of Charter School District No. 150 of Peoria County, 43 Ill.App.3d 322, 356 N.E.2d 1253, 1 Ill.Dec. 920, (3rd Dist. 1977) aff'd. in part, rev. in part 69 Ill.2d 191, 370 N.E.2d 1050, 13 Ill.Dec. 23 (1978) **16:70**

Betts v. Board of Education of City of Chicago, 466 F.2d 629 (7th Cir. 1972) **12:440, 12:470**

Beussink v. Woodland R-IV School District, 30 F.Supp.2d 1175 (E.D. Mo. 1998) **12:122**

Bevin H. by Michael H. v. Wright, 666 F.Supp. 71 (W.D. Pa. 1987) **13:150**

Birk v. Board of Education of Flora Community Unit School District No. 35, Clay County, 104 Ill.2d 252, 472 N.E.2d 407, 84 Ill.Dec. 447 (1984) **16:220, 16:230**

Bishop v. Wood, 96 S.Ct. 2074, 426 U.S. 341, 48 L.Ed.2d 864 (1976) **6:226, 18:50, 18:60**

Blanchet v. Vermillion Parish School Board, 220 So.2d 534 (La. 1969) **17:455**

Blase v. Illinois, 55 Ill.2d 94, 302 N.E.2d 46 (1973) **24:60**

Bloomingdale Public Schools v. Washgesic, 33 F.3d 689 (6th Cir. 1994) **14:123**

Boaden v. State Department of Law Enforcement, 171 Ill.2d 230, 664 N.E.2d 61, 215 Ill.Dec. 664 (1996) **17:47**

Board of Curators v. Horowitz, 98 S.Ct. 948, 435 U.S. 78, 55 L.Ed.2d 725 (1975) **27:130**

Board of Education Arbor Park School District No. 145, Cook County v. Ballweber, 105 Ill.App.3d 412, 434 N.E.2d 448, 61 Ill.Dec. 295 (1st Dist. 1981) aff'd. 96 Ill.2d 520, 451 N.E.2d 858, 71 Ill.Dec. 704 (1982) **10:230**

Board of Education City of Peoria v. Illinois State Board of Education, 531 F.Supp. 148 (C.D. Ill. 1982) **13:360**

Board of Education Community Consolidated School District No. 59, Cook County v. E.A. Herzog Construction Co., 29 Ill.App.2d 138, 172 N.E.2d 645 (1st Dist. 1961) **9:100**

Board of Education Decatur District No. 61 v. Illinois Educational Labor Relations Board, 180 Ill.App.3d 770, 536 N.E.2d 743, 129 Ill.Dec. 693 (4th Dist. 1989) **10:20, 21:140, 21:150**

Board of Education Leroy Community Unit School District No. 2 v. Illinois Educational Labor Relations Board, 199 Ill.App.3d 347, 556 N.E.2d 857, 145 Ill.Dec. 239 (4th Dist. 1990) 149 Ill.2d 496, 599 N.E.2d 892, 174 Ill.Dec. 808 (1992) **15:350, 21:150**

Board of Education of Avoca School District No. 37, Cook County, v. Regional Board of School Trustees of Cook County, 82 Ill.App.3d 1067, 403 N.E.2d 578, 38 Ill.Dec. 347 (1st Dist. 1980) **8:170**

Board of Education of Beach Park Community Consolidated School District No. 3, Lake County, v. Hess, 140 Ill.App.3d 653, 488 N.E.2d 1358, 95 Ill.Dec. 15 (2nd Dist. 1986) **23:50**

Board of Education of Berwyn School District No. 100 v. Metskas, 106 Ill.App.3d 943, 436 N.E.2d 587, 62 Ill.Dec. 561 (1st Dist. 1982) **15:230**

Board of Education of Bremen Community High School District No. 228, Cook County v. Bremen District No. 228 Joint Faculty Association, 114 Ill.App.3d 1051, 449 N.E.2d 960, 70 Ill.Dec. 613 (1st Dist. 1983) aff'd. in part, rev. in part on other grounds 101 Ill.2d 115, 461 N.E.2d 406, 77 Ill.Dec. 783 (1983) **16:240**

Board of Education of Central School District No. 1 v. Allen, 88 S.Ct. 1923, 392 U.S. 236, 20 L.Ed.2d 1060 (1968) **14:30**

Board of Education of City of Bloomington, McLean County v. County Board of School Trustees of McLean County, 77 Ill.App.2d 368, 222 N.E.2d 343 (4th Dist. 1966) **8:330**

Board of Education of City of Chicago v. Chicago Teachers' Union, Local 1, 89 Ill.App.3d 861, 412 N.E.2d 587, 45 Ill.Dec. 236 (1st Dist. 1980) rev. on other grounds 88 Ill.2d 63, 430 N.E.2d 1111, 58 Ill.Dec. 860 (1981) **2:130**

Board of Education of City of Chicago v. Crilly, 312 Ill.App. 177, 37 N.E.2d 873 (1941) **9:430**

Board of Education of City of Chicago v. Harris, 218 Ill.App.3d 1017, 578 N.E.2d 1244, 161 Ill.Dec. 598 (1st Dist. 1991) **18:180**

Board of Education of City of Chicago v. Industrial Commission, 53 Ill.2d 167, 290 N.E.2d 247 (1972) **17:260**

Board of Education of City of Chicago v. Industrial Commission, 57 Ill.2d 330, 312 N.E.2d 244 (1974) **17:250**

Board of Education of City of Peoria School District No. 150 v. Sanders, 150 Ill.App.3d 755, 502 N.E.2d 730, 104 Ill.Dec. 233 (3rd Dist. 1986) app. den. 115 Ill.2d 536, 508 N.E.2d 208, 108 Ill.Dec. 47, cert. den. 108 S.Ct. 290, 484 U.S. 986, 98 L.Ed.2d 250 **10:106**

Board of Education of City of Rockford v. Page, 33 Ill.2d 372, 211 N.E.2d 361 (1965) **1:260, 9:330**

Board of Education of Community Consolidated School District 21 v. Brozer, 938 F.2d 712 (7th Cir. 1991) **13:275**

Board of Education of Community Consolidated School District 606, Tazewell County v. Board of Education of Community Unit District 124 of Mason and Tazewell Counties, 11 Ill.App.2d 408, 137 N.E.2d 721 (3rd Dist. 1956) **1:30**

Board of Education of Community High School District No. 154, McHenry County v. Regional Board of School Trustees of McHenry County, 84 Ill.App.3d 501, 405 N.E.2d 495 (2nd Dist. 1980) **8:240**

Board of Education of Community Unit School District No. 325, Peoria County v. Board of Education of Special Charter School District No. 150, Peoria County, 2 Ill.App.3d 643, 276 N.E.2d 732 (3rd Dist. 1971) **8:140**

Board of Education of Community Unit School District No. 300, Kane, Cook, McHenry and Lake Counties v. County Board of School Trustees of Kane County, 60 Ill.App.3d 415, 376 N.E.2d 1054, 17 Ill.Dec. 725 (2nd Dist. 1978) **8:150**

Board of Education of Community Unit School District No. 323, Winnebago and Stephenson Counties v. County Board of School Trustees of Winnebago and Stephenson Counties, 19 Ill.App.2d 196, 153 N.E.2d 378 (2nd Dist. 1958) **8:220**

Board of Education of Community Unit School District No. 1 v. Compton, 123 Ill.2d 216, 526 N.E.2d 149, 122 Ill.Dec. 9 (1988) **21:540**

Board of Education of Community Unit School District No. 16 v. Barrett, 67 Ill.2d 11, 364 N.E.2d 89, 7 Ill.Dec. 102 (1977) **23:90**

Board of Education of Community Unit School District No. 4, Champaign County v. Champaign Education Association, 15 Ill.App.3d 335, 304 N.E.2d 138 (4th Dist. 1973) **15:200**

Board of Education of Consolidated School District No. 138 of Winnebago County v. County Board of School Trustees of Winnebago County, 37 Ill.App.2d 166, 185 N.E.2d 374 (2nd Dist. 1962) **8:150**

Board of Education of DuPage High School District No. 88 v. Illinois Educational Labor Relations Board, 246 Ill.App.3d 967, 617 N.E.2d 790, 187 Ill.Dec. 333 (1st Dist. 1993) **21:145, 21:542**

Board of Education of Enlarged City School District of the City of Watervliet v. Russman, 117 S.Ct. 2502, 521 U.S. 111, 138 L.Ed.2d 1008 (1997) **13:161**

Board of Education of Golf School District No. 67 v. Regional Board of School Trustees of Cook County, 89 Ill.2d 392, 433 N.E.2d 240, 60 Ill.Dec. 443 (1982) **8:220, 8:240**

Board of Education of Hamilton County Community Unit School District No. 10, Hamilton County v. Regional Board of School Trustees of Jefferson and Hamilton Counties, 121 Ill.App.3d 848, 460 N.E.2d 100, 77 Ill.Dec. 241 (5th Dist. 1984) **8:20**

Board of Education of Hendrick Hudson Central School District, Board of Education Westchester County v. Rowley, 102 S.Ct. 3034, 458 U.S. 176, 73 L.Ed.2d 690 (1982) **13:25, 13:160**

Board of Education of Island Trees Union Free School District No. 26 v. Pico, 102 S.Ct. 2799, 457 U.S. 853, 73 L.Ed.2d 435 (1982) **10:400**

Board of Education of Jonesboro Community Consolidated School District v. Regional Board of School Trustees of Union County, 86 Ill.App.3d 230, 407 N.E.2d 1084, 41 Ill.Dec. 586 (5th Dist. 1980) **8:220**

Board of Education of Maine Township High School District No. 207 v. State Board of Education, 139 Ill.App.3d 460, 487 N.E.2d 1053, 94 Ill.Dec. 176 (1st Dist. 1985) **24:50**

Board of Education of Metropolis Community High School District No. 20, Massac County v. County Board of School Trustees, Massac County, 34 Ill.App.3d 901, 341 N.E.2d 10 (5th Dist. 1976) **8:170**

Board of Education of Minooka Community Consolidated School District No. 201 v. Ingels, 75 Ill.App.3d 334, 394 N.E.2d 69, 31 Ill.Dec. 153 (3rd Dist. 1979) **18:340**

Board of Education of Minooka Community High School District No. 111 Grundy, Kendall and Will Counties v. Carter, 119 Ill.App.3d 857, 458 N.E.2d 50, 75 Ill.Dec. 882, (3rd Dist. 1983) **1:260, 9:360**

Board of Education of Mundelein Elementary School District No. 75 v. Illinois Educational Labor Relations Board, 179 Ill.App.3d 696, 534 N.E.2d 1022, 128 Ill.Dec. 577 (4th Dist. 1989) **21:40**

Board of Education of Niles Township High School District 219, Cook County v. Regional Board of School Trustees of Cook County, 127 Ill.App.3d 210, 468 N.E.2d 1247, 82 Ill.Dec. 467 (1st Dist. 1984) **8:200, 8:320**

Board of Education of Niles Township High School District No. 219 Cook County v. Epstein, 72 Ill.App.3d 723, 391 N.E.2d 114, 28 Ill.Dec. 915 (1st Dist. 1979) **18:130**

Board of Education of Oak Park and River Forest High School District v. Illinois State Board of Education, 79 F.3d 654 (7th Cir. 1996) **13:64**

Board of Education of Pearl City Community Unit School District No. 200 v. Regional Board of School Trustees of Stephenson County, 98 Ill.App.3d 599, 424 N.E.2d 808, 54 Ill.Dec. 58 (2nd Dist. 1981) **8:220**

Board of Education of Plainfield Community Considated School District No. 202, Will and Kendall Counties v. Illinois Educational Labor Relations Board, et al., 143 Ill.App.3d 898, 493 N.E.2d 1130, 98 Ill.Dec. 109 (4th Dist. 1986) **21:110**

Board of Education of Rockford School District No. 205, v. The Illinois Educational Labor Relations Board, 165 Ill.2d 80, 649 N.E.2d 369, 208 Ill.Dec. 313 (1995) **15:235, 18:25, 18:235, 20:143, 21:565**

Board of Education of Rockford School District No. 205 Winnebago and Boone Counties v Hearing Board of Counties of Boone and Winnebago, 152 Ill.App.3d 936, 505 N.E.2d 32, 105 Ill.Dec. 906, (2nd Dist. 1987) app. den. 115 Ill.2d 535, 511 N.E.2d 425, 110 Ill.Dec 453 **8:200, 8:320**

Board of Education of Rockford School District No.205 Winnebago and Boone Counties v. Regional Board of School Trustees of Boone and Winnebago Counties, 135 Ill.App.3d 486, 481 N.E.2d 1266, 90 Ill.Dec. 355 (2nd Dist. 1985) **8:320**

Board of Education of Rogers, Arkansas v. McCluskey, 102 S.Ct. 3469, 458 U.S. 966, 73 L.Ed.2d 1273 (1982) on rem. 688 F.2d 596, reh. den. 103 S.Ct. 16, 458 U.S. 1132, 73 L.Ed.2d 1402(1982) **12:30**

Board of Education of Round Lake Area Schools, Community Unit School District No. 116 v. The State Board of Education, John F. Rozner and Barbara Cohn, 292 Ill.App.3d 101, 685 N.E.2d 412, 226 Ill.Dec.309 (2nd Dist. 1997) **17:720**

Board of Education of Sacramento City School District v. Holland, 786 F.Supp. 874 (E.D. Cal. 1992) **13:50, 13:55**

Board of Education of School District 33 v. City of West Chicago, 55 Ill.App.2d 401, 205 N.E.2d 63 (2nd Dist. 1965) **1:260**

Board of Education of School District No. 108, Tazewell Co. for Use of A.Y. McDonald Manufacturing Company v. Collum, 77 Ill.App.2d 479, 222 N.E.2d 804 (3rd Dist. 1966) **9:310**

Board of Education of School District No. 131 v. Illinois State Board of Education, 82 Ill.App.3d 820, 403 N.E.2d 277, 38 Ill.Dec. 189 (2nd Dist. 1980) **18:180, 18:240, 19:25**

Board of Education of School District No. 150 v. City of Peoria, 76 Ill.2d 469, 394 N.E.2d 399, 31 Ill.Dec. 197 (1979) **1:260**

Board of Education of School District No. 33, DuPage County v. City of West Chicago, 55 Ill.App.2d 401, 205 N.E.2d 63 (2nd Dist. 1965) **9:330**

Board of Education of Sesser-Valier Community Unit SChool District No. 196 v. Illinois Educational Labor Relations Board and Sesser-Valier Education Association, IEA-NEA, 250 Ill.App.3d 878, 620 N.E.2d 418, 189 Ill.Dec. 450 (4th Dist. 1993) **21:166**

Board of Education of Springfield School District No. 186 v. Scott, 105 Ill.App.2d 192, 244 N.E.2d 821 (4th Dist. 1969) **8:270, 8:330**

Board of Education of St. Charles Community Unit School District No. 303 v. Adelman, 137 Ill.App.3d 965, 485 N.E.2d 584, 92 Ill.Dec. 773 (2nd Dist. 1985) **18:360**

Board of Education of Tonica Community Unit School District No. 360, LaSalle County v. Sickley, 133 Ill.App.3d 921, 479 N.E.2d 1142, 89 Ill.Dec. 136 (3rd Dist. 1985) **18:140**

Board of Education of Township High School District 211, Cook County, v. Kusper, 92 Ill.2d 333, 422 N.E.2d 179, 65 Ill.Dec. 868 (1982) **23:160**

Board of Education of Valley View Community Unit School District No. 365U v. Schmidt, 64 Ill.App.3d 513, 381 N.E.2d 400, 21 Ill.Dec. 291 (1st Dist. 1978) **17:470**

Board of Education of Wellington Community Unit School District No. 7 of Iroquois County v. County Board of School Trustees of Vermilion County, 13 Ill.App.2d 561, 142 N.E.2d 742 (3rd Dist. 1957) **8:230**

Board of Education of Westside Community Schools v. Mergens, 110 S.Ct. 2365, 496 U.S. 226, 110 L.Ed.2d 191 (1990) **14:120, 14:140**

Board of Education School District 142 v. Bakalis, 54 Ill.2d 448, 299 N.E.2d 737 (1973) **14:80**

Board of Education School District No. 68 DuPage County v. Surety Developers, Inc., 24 Ill.App.3d 638, 321 N.E.2d 99 (2nd Dist. 1974) **9:100**

Board of Education Warren Township High School District No. 121 v. Warren Township High School Federation of Teachers Local 504, IFT/AFL-CIO, 128 Ill.2d 155, 538 N.E.2d 524, 131 Ill.Dec. 149 (1989) **21:540**

Board of Education, School District No. 151, Cook County v. Illinois State Board of Education, 154 Ill.App.3d 175, 507 N.E.2d 134, 107 Ill.Dec. 470 (1st Dist. 1987) **17:580**

Board of Junior College District 515 v. Wagner, 3 Ill.App.3d 1006, 279 N.E.2d 754 (1st Dist. 1971) **9:60**

Board of Regents of the Regency University System (Northern Illinois University) 7 PERI 1113 (IELRB Opinion and Order, October 24, 1991) **21:200, 21:220**

Board of Regents of the Regency University System v. Reynard, et al., 292 Ill.App.3d 968, 686 N.E.2d 122, 227 Ill.Dec. 66 (4th Dist. 1997) **6:10, 6:30, 6:35**

Board of Regents of State Colleges v. Roth, 92 S.Ct. 2701, 408 U.S. 564, 33 L.Ed.2d 548 (1972) **6:226, 18:40, 18:50, 18:60**

Board of Trustees of Community College District No. 508 v. Cook County College Teachers Union Local 1600, AFT, IFT, AFL-CIO, 167 Ill.App.3d 998, 522 N.E.2d 93, 118 Ill.Dec. 638 (1st Dist. 1987) **18:70**

Bobkoski v. Board of Education of Cary Consolidated School District 26, 141 F.R.D. 88 (N.D. Ill. 1992) **6:330**

Bond v. Board of Education of Mascoutah Community Unit School District No. 19, 81 Ill.2d 242, 408 N.E.2d 714, 42 Ill.Dec. 136 (1980) **16:50**

Bonnell v. Regional Board of School Trustees of Madison County, 258 Ill.App.3d 485, 630 N.E.2d 547, 196 Ill.Dec. 612, (5th Dist. 1994) **9:145**

Boring v. Buncombe County Board of Education, 98 F.3d 1474 (4th Cir. 1998) **17:482**

Borushek v. Kincaid, 78 Ill.App.3d 295, 397 N.E.2d 172, 33 Ill.Dec. 839 (1st Dist. 1979) **22:210**

Bowie v. Evanston Community Consolidated School District No. 65, 165 Ill.App.3d 101, 522 N.E.2d 669, 119 Ill.Dec. 7 (1st Dist. 1988) app. allowed 122 Ill.2d 570, 530 N.E.2d 239, 125 Ill.Dec. 211 7:320, aff'd. 128 Ill.2d 373, 538 N.E.2d 557, 131 Ill.Dec. 182 (1989) **7:320, 7:450**

Bown v. Gwinnett County School District, 112 F.3d 1464 (11th Cir. 1997) **14:40, 14:50**

Brady v. Board of Education of Palatine Community Consolidated School District No. 15, 284 Ill.App.3d 803, 672 N.E.2d 810, 219 Ill.Dec. 957 (1st Dist. 1996) **15:25**

Bradley v. Casey, 415 Ill. 576, 114 N.E.2d 681 (1953) **9:300**

Bragdon v. Abbott, 118 S.Ct. 2196, 524 U.S.624, 141 L.Ed.2d 540 (1998) **17:355**

Brandt v. Board of Co-op Educational Services, Third Supervisory District, Suffolk County, New York, 820 F.2d 41, app. after rem. 845 F.2d 416 (2nd Cir. 1988) **6:226**

Branti v. Finkel, 100 S.Ct. 1287, 445 U.S. 507, 63 L.Ed.2d 574 (1980) **17:460**

Braught v. Board of Education of Mount Prospect School District No. 57, 136 Ill.App.3d 486, 483 N.E.2d 623, 91 Ill.Dec. 277 (1st Dist. 1985) **15:600, 15:610**

Braun v. Board of Education of Red Bud Community Unit School District No. 132, 151 Ill.App.3d 787, 502 N.E.2d 1076, 104 Ill.Dec. 416 (5th Dist. 1986) app. den. 115 Ill.2d 538, 511 N.E.2d 426, 110 Ill.Dec. 454 (1987) **22:130**

Breen v. Kahl, 419 F.2d 1034 (7th Cir. 1969) **12:125**

Brenden v. Independent School District 742, 477 F.2d 1292 (8th Cir. 1973) **27:340**

Brickers v. Cleveland Board of Education, 145 F.3d 846 (6th Cir. 1998) **17:360**

Bridewell v. Board of Education of Shawnee Community Unit School District No. 84 of Union, et al. Counties, 2 Ill.App.3d 684, 276 N.E.2d 745 (5th Dist. 1971) **22:60**

Bridgman v. New Trier High School District No. 203, 128 F.3d 1146 (7th Cir. 1997) **12:238**

Bromberek School District No. 65 v. Sanders, 174 Ill.App.3d 301, 528 N.E.2d 1336, 124 Ill.Dec. 228 (1st Dist. 1988) app. den. 124 Ill.2d 553, 535 N.E.2d 912, 129 Ill.Dec. 147 (1989) **6:60**

The Bronx Household of Faith v. Community School District No. 10, 127 F.3d 207 (2nd Cir. 1997) **14:130**

Broussard v. School Board of the City of Norfolk, 801 F.Supp. 1526 (E.D. Va. 1992) **12:128**

Brown v. Board of Education Gallatin Community Unit School District No. 1, 38 Ill.App.3d 403, 347 N.E.2d 791, app. after rem. *People ex rel. Brown v. Board of Education Gallatin Community Unit School District No. 1,* 66 Ill.App.3d 167, 383 N.E.2d 711 (5th Dist. 1976) **16:250**

Brown v. Board of Education of Topeka, Shawnee County, Kansas, 74 S.Ct. 686, 347 U.S. 483, 98 L.Ed. 873, 38 ALR2d 1180, supp. 75 S.Ct. 753, 349 U.S. 294, 99 L.Ed. 1083 (1954) **14:400**

Brown v. Hot, Sexy and Safer Productions, Inc. 68 F.3d 525 (1st Cir. 1995) cert. den., 116 S.Ct. 1044, 516 U.S. 1159, 134 L.Ed.2d 191 (1996) **10:90, 11:450**

Brown v. Kirk, 33 Ill.App.3d 477, 342 N.E.2d 137 (5th Dist. 1975), rev. on other grounds 64 Ill.2d 144, 355 N.E.2d 12 (1975) **3:130**

Brown v. Walker Nursing Home, Inc. 307 Ill.App.3d 721, 718 N.E.2d 373, 240 L.Ed.2d 892 (4th Dist. 1999) **17:384**

Brubaker v. Board of Education of School District No. 149, Cook County, 502 F.2d 973 (7th Cir. 1974) **17:450**

Brubaker v. Community Unit School District No. 16, Sangamon and Morgan Counties, 46 Ill.App.3d 588, 360 N.E.2d 1228, 4 Ill.Dec. 853 (4th Dist. 1977) **19:120**

Brunstrom v. Board of Education of Riverdale Community Unit School District 100 of Rock Island County, 52 Ill.App.3d 653, 367 N.E.2d 1065, 10 Ill.Dec. 456 (3rd Dist. 1977), **16:130**

Bubb v. Springfeld School District No. 186, et al., 167 Ill.2d 372, 657 N.E.2d 887, 194 Ill.Dec. 518 (1995) **22:167**

Bucha v. Illinois High School Association, 351 F.Supp. 69 (N.D. Ill. 1972) **27:10, 27:130, 27:340**

Buckellew v. Board of Education of Georgetown-Ridge Farm Community Unit School District No. 4, 214 Ill.App.3d 506, 575 N.E.2d 556, 159 Ill.Dec. 58 (4th Dist. 1991) **20:180, 20:182, 20:183, 21:180**

Bundy v. Jackson, 641 F.2d 934 (D.C. Cir. 1981) **17:500**

Bunsen v. County Board of School Trustees of Lake County, 48 Ill.App.2d 291, 198 N.E.2d 735 (2nd Dist. 1964) **2:140**

Burgner v. County Board of School Trustees of Peoria County, 60 Ill.App.2d 267, 208 N.E.2d 54 (3rd Dist. 1965) **8:260**

Burke v. 12 Rothschild's Liquor Mart, Inc., 209 Ill.App.3d 192, 568 N.E.2d 80, 154 Ill.Dec. 80, app.den. 139 Ill. 2d 594, 575 N.E.2d 912, 159 Ill.Dec. 105, order vac. on reconsideration __ Ill.2d __, 575 N.E.2d 1234, 159 Ill.Dec. 174, app. allowed 141 Ill.2d 536, 580 N.E. 2d 109, 162 Ill. Dec.483, aff'd. 148 Ill.2d 429, 593 N.E.2d 522, 170 Ill. Dec. 633 (1992) **22:120**

Burlington Industries, Inc. v. Kimberly B. Ellerth, 118 S.Ct. 2257, 524 U.S. 742, 141 L.Ed.2d 633 (1998) **17:504**

Burlington School Committee of the Town of Burlington, Massachusetts v. Department of Education of Massachusetts, 105 S.Ct 1996, 471 U.S. 359, 85 L.Ed.2d 385 (1985) **13:340**

Burnidge v. County Board of School Trustees of Kane County, 25 Ill.App.2d 503, 167 N.E.2d 21 (3rd Dist. 1960) **8:240, 8:250**

Burris v. Board of Education, 221 Ill.App. 397 (4th Dist. 1920) **11:110**

Butler v. Ysleta Independent School District, 161 F.3d 263 (5th Cir. 1998) **17:510**

Butts v. NCAA, LaSalle University, 751 F.2d 609 (3rd Cir. 1984) **27:260**

Byrne v. Board of Education, School of West Allis-West Milwaukee, 979 F.2d 560 (7th Cir. 1992) **17:410**

Camara v. Municipal Court of City and County of San Francisco, 87 S.Ct. 1727, 387 U.S. 523, 18 L.Ed.2d 930 (1967) **12:310**

Canutillo Independent School District v. Leija, 101 F.3d 393 (5th Cir. 1997) reh. and sugg. for reh. den. 106 F.3d 399, cert. den. 117 S.Ct. 2434, 520 U.S. 1265, 138 L.Ed.2d 195 **11:415**

Capitol Square Review and Advisory Board v. Pinette, 114 S.Ct. 626, 510 U.S. 1307, 126 L.Ed.2d 636 (1995) **14:20**; **14:123**

Carbondale Community High School District No. 165 v. Herrin Community Unit School District No. 4, 303 Ill.App.3d 656, 708 N.E.2d 844, 237 Ill.Dec. 41 (5th Dist. 1999) **11:225**

Cardinal Glass v. Board of Education of Mendota Community Consolidated School District 289, 113 Ill.App.3d 442, 447 N.E.2d 546, 69 Ill.Dec. 329 (3rd Dist. 1983) **25:230, 25:240, 25:260**

Carey v. Piphus, 97 S.Ct. 1642, 435 U.S. 247, 52 L.Ed.2d 355 (1978) **12:410, 12:475**

Carey v. Population Services International, 97 S.Ct. 2010, 431 U.S. 678, 52 L.Ed.2d 675 (1977) **10:95**

Carlson v. Moline Board of Education School District No. 40, 124 Ill.3d 967, 464 N.E.2d 1269, 80 Ill.Dec. 256 (3rd Dist. 1984) **25:230**

Carrao v. Board of Education, City of Chicago, 46 Ill.App.3d 33, 360 N.E.2d 536, 4 Ill.Dec. 600 (1st Dist. 1977) **18:90, 18:160**

Carstens v. East Alton-Wood River Community Unit School District, 27 Ill.2d 88, 187 N.E.2d 682 (1963) **26:210**

Carter v. State Board of Education, 90 Ill.App.3d 1042, 414 N.E.2d 153, 46 Ill.Dec. 431 (1st Dist. 1980) **12:190**

Carver v. Bond / Fayette / Effingham Regional Board of School Trustees, 203 Ill.App.3d 799, 561 N.E.2d 135, 148 Ill.Dec. 829, (5th Dist. 1991) app. allowed 136 Ill.2d 542, 567 N.E.2d 329, 153 Ill.Dec. 375, aff'd. 146 Ill.2d 347, 586 N.E.2d 1273, 167 Ill.Dec. 1 (1992) **8:190, 8:220, 8:240, 8:260**

Castenada v. Pickard, 648 F.2d 989 (5th Cir. 1981) **10:140**

Castle v. Colonial School District, 933 F.Supp. 458 (E.D. Pa. 1996) **17:470**

Caterpillar, Inc. v. Fehrenbacher, 286 Ill.App.3d 614, 676 N.E.2d 710, 221 Ill.Dec. 907 (2nd Dist. 1997) **17:720**

Catron v. Board of Education of Kansas Community Unit School District No. 3 of Edgar County, 126 Ill.App.3d 693, 467 N.E.2d 621, 81 Ill.Dec. 750 (4th Dist. 1984) **16:220**

Caviness v. Board of Education of Ludlow Community Consolidated School District No. 142 of Champaign County, 59 Ill.App.3d 28, 375 N.E.2d 157, 16 Ill.Dec. 526 (4th Dist. 1978) **16:55, 16:220, 16:250, 16:300**

Cedar Rapids Community School District v. Garret F ex rel. Charlene F, 119 S.Ct.992, 526 U.S. 66, 143 L.Ed.2d 154 (1999) **13:140, 13:150**

Celafu on Behalf of Celafu v. East Baton Rouge Parish School Board, 907 F.Supp. 966, vac. 103 F.3d 393, opinion withdrawn and superceded on reh. 117 F.3d 231, rev. 117 F.3d 231 (5th Cir. 1997) **13:161**

Central City Education Association, IEA-NEA v. Illinois Educational Labor Relations Board and Central City Community Consolidated School District No. 133, 149 Ill.2d 496, 59 N.E.2d 892, 174 Ill.Dec. 808 (1992) **21:140, 21:150, 21:160, 21:170**

Central Illinois Light Co. v. Johnson, 84 Ill.2d 275, 418 N.E.2d 275, 49 Ill.Dec. 676 (1981) **23:30**

Centralia School District No. 135, 4 PERI 1044 (IELRB Opinion and Order, February 25, 1988) **21:300**

Champaign Community Unit School District No. 4, 5 PERI 1124 (Executive Director's Recommended Decision and Order, June 15, 1989) **21:300**

Chandler v. James, 180 F.3d 1254 (11th Cir. 1999) **14:40**

Chandler v. McMinnville School District, 978 F.2d 524 (9th Cir. 1992) **12:120; 12:123**

Charleston Community Unit School District No. 1 v. Illinois Educational Labor Relations Board and Charleston Education Association, IEA-NEA, 203 Ill.App.3d 619, 561 N.E.2d 331, 149 Ill.Dec. 53 (4th Dist. 1990) **21:420**

Cherry Bowl, Inc. v. Property Tax Appeal Board, 100 Ill.App.3d 326, 426 N.E.2d 618, 55 Ill.Dec. 472 (2nd Dist. 1981) **23:30**

Chicago Board of Education v. Chicago Teachers Union, 86 Ill.2d 469, 427 N.E.2d 1199, 56 Ill.Dec. 653 (1981) **17:270**

Chicago Board of Education v. Payne, 102 Ill.App.3d 741, 430 N.E.2d 310, 58 Ill.Dec. 368 (1st Dist. 1981) **18:70; 18:175**

Chicago Board of Education v. Terrile, 47 Ill.App.3d 75, 361 N.E.2d 778, 5 Ill.Dec. 455 (1st Dist. 1977) **11:10**

Chicago Firefighters Local 2 v. Chicago, 717 F.Supp. 134 (N.D. Ill. 1989) **12:240**

Chicago in Trust for Schools v. Albert J. Schorsch Realty Co., 6 Ill.App.3d 1074, 287 N.E.2d 93 (1st Dist. 1972) **9:60**

Chicago Teachers Union Local 1, AFT, AFL-CIO v. Hudson, 106 S.Ct. 1066, 475 U.S. 292, 89 L.Ed.2d 232 (1986) **17:110, 21:310, 21:320**

Chipman v. Grant County School District, 30 F.Supp.2d 975 (E.D. Ky. 1998) **11:403**

Christopher T. by Brogna v. San Francisco Unified School District, 553 F.Supp. 1107 (N.D. Cal. 1982) **13:220**

Christopherson v. Spring Valley Elementary School District, 90 Ill.App.3d 460, 413 N.E.2d 199, 45 Ill.Dec. 866 (3rd Dist. 1980) **18:150**

Citizens to Protect Public Funds v. Board of Education of Parsippany-Troy Hills, 13 N.J. 172 (1953) **4:340, 4:350, 4:360**

City National Bank of Kankakee v. Schott, 113 Ill.App.3d 388, 447 N.E.2d 478, 69 Ill.Dec. 261 (3rd Dist. 1983) **8:240, 8:270**

City of Boerne v. P.F. Flores, 117 S.Ct.2157, 521U.S.507, 138 L.Ed.2d 624 (1997) **14:25**

City of Kankakee v. Small, 317 Ill. 55, 147 N.E. 404 (1925) **2:170, 2:180**

City of Monmouth v. Payes, 39 Ill.App.2d 32, 188 N.E.2d 48 (2nd Dist. 1963) **9:300**

City of Richmond v. J.A. Croson Co., 109 S.Ct. 706, 488 U.S. 469, 102 L.Ed.2d 854 (1989) **14:540**

Clark v. Dallas Independent School District, 806 F.Supp. 116 (N.D. Tex. 1992) **14:40**

Clay v. Chicago Board of Education, 22 Ill.App.3d 437, 318 N.E.2d 153 (1st Dist. 1974) **22:100, 22:130**

Cleveland Board of Education v. LaFleur, 94 S.Ct. 791, 414 U.S. 632, 39 L.Ed.2d 52 (1974) **17:190, 17:210**

Cleveland Board of Education v. Loudermill, 105 S.Ct. 1487, 470 U.S. 532, 84 L.Ed.2d 494 (1985) on rem. 763 F.2d 202 (6th Cir. 1985) **12:70, 18:250, 18:380, 20:140**

Clever v. Cherry Hill Township Board of Education, 838 F. Supp. 929 (D.C. N.J. 1993) **14:123**

Cochran v. District of Columbia, 660 F.Supp. 314, (D.C. D.C. 1987) **13:220**

Cohen v. Brown University, 879 F.Supp. 185 (D.R.I. 1995) **27:307**

Cohen v. Wauconda Community Unit School District No. 118, 779 F.Supp. 88 (N.D. Ill. 1991) **11:195**

Cole v. McGillicuddy, 21 Ill.App.3d 645, 316 N.E.2d 109 (1st Dist. 1974) **3:180, 3:185**

Coles v. Cleveland Board of Education, 950 F.Supp. 1337, rev. 171 F.3d 369 (6th Cir. 1999) **14:70**

Colleen M. Wales v. Board of Education of Community Unit School District 300, et al., 120 F.3d 82 (7th Cir. 1997) **17:450**

College of Lake County and College of Lake County Staff Council, Lake County Federation of Teachers, Local 504, IFT-AFT/AFL-CIO, 14 PERI 1095 (IELRB Decision and Order, October 8, 1998) **21:274**

Collins v. School District No. 189, St. Clair County, 115 Ill.App.3d 100, 450 N.E.2d 387, 70 Ill.Dec. 914 (5th Dist. 1983) **22:50**

Colquitt v. Rich Township High School District No. 227, 298 Ill.App.3d 856, 699 N.E.2d 1109, 232 Ill.Dec. 924 (1st Dist., 1998) **12:475, 12:477, 12:478**

Colorado Seminary (University of Denver) v. National Collegiate Athletic Association, 570 F.2d 320 (10th Cir. 1978) **27:130, 27:140**

Committee for Educational Rights, et al. v. Edgar, 174 Ill.2d 1, 672 N.E.2d 1178, 220 Ill.Dec. 166 (1996) **24:60, 24:62**

Commonwealth of Pennsylvania by Israel Packel, Attorney General v. Pennsylvania Interscholastic Athletic Association, 18 Pa.Cmwlth. 45, 334 A.2d 839 (1975) **27:340**

Commonwealth of Virginia v. Riley, 86 F.3d 1337 (4th Cir. 1996) **13:370**

Communist Party of Illinois v. Ogilvie, 357 F.Supp. 105 (N.D. Ill. 1972) **4:180**

Community High School District No. 155 v. Denzby Veronico, 124 Ill.App.3d 129, 463 N.E.2d 998, 79 Ill.Dec. 444 (2nd Dist. 1984) **13:50**

Community Unit School District No. 4 v. Booth, 1 Ill.2d 545, 116 N.E.2d 161 (1954) **24:190**

Compass Health Care Plans v. Board of Education of the City of Chicago and Ted D. Kimbrough, 246 Ill.App.3d 746, 617 N.E.2d 6, 186 Ill.Dec. 767 (1st Dist. 1992) **25:223, 25:230**

Condon v. American Telephone and Telegraph Company, Inc., 210 Ill.App.3d 701, 569 N.E.2d 518, 155 Ill.Dec. 337 (2nd Dist 1991) app. den. 141 Ill.2d 537, 580 N.E.2d 110, 162 Ill.Dec. 484 (1992) **17:610**

Connelly v. Gibbs, 112 Ill.App.3d 257, 445 N.E.2d 477, 68 Ill.Dec. 29 (1st Dist. 1983) **11:185**

Connick v. Myers, 103 S.Ct. 1684, 461 U.S. 138, 75 L.Ed.2d 708 (1983) **17:450**

Cook County College Teachers Union Local 1600 IFT, AFT, AFL-CIO v. Board of Trustees Community College District No. 505, Cook County, 134 Ill.App.3d 489, 481 N.E.2d 40, 89 Ill.Dec. 688 (1st Dist. 1985) **17:640**

Cook County Federal Savings and Loan Association v. Griffin, 73 Ill.App.3d 210, 391 N.E.2d 473, 29 Ill.Dec.210 (1st Dist. 1979) **12:100**

Copeland v. Hawkins, 352 F.Supp. 1022 (N.D. Ill. 1973) **12:125**

Cornfield By Lewis v. School District No. 230, 991 F.2d 1316 (7th Cir. 1993) **12:231**

County Board of School Trustees of DuPage County v. Boram, 26 Ill.2d 167, 186 N.E.2d 275 (1962) **9:50**

Court Street Steak House v. Tazewell County, 249 Ill.App.3d 918, 619 N.E.2d 759, 189 Ill.Dec. 58 (3rd Dist. 1993) **25:240**

Craig v. Boren, 97 S.Ct. 451, 429 U.S. 190, 50 L.Ed.2d 397 (1976) **27:300**

Crane by Crane v. Indiana High School Athletic Association, 975 F.2d 1315 (7th Cir. 1992) **27:250**

Cronin v. Lindberg, 66 Ill.2d 47, 360 N.E.2d 360, 4 Ill.Dec. 424 (1976) **24:140**

Curtis v. School Committee of Falmouth, 652 N.E.2d 580 (Ma. 1995) **10:95**

Cynthia K. v. Board of Education of Lincoln-Way High School District No. 210, 95 C 7172, 1996 WL 164381 (N.D. Ill. 1996) **13:570**

Dallam v. Cumberland Valley School District, 391 F.Supp. 358 (M.D. Pa. 1975) **12:400**

Dangler v. Yorktown Central Schools, 771 F.Supp. 625 (S.D. N.Y. 1991) **12:400**

Daniel B. v. Wisconsin Dept. of Public Instruction, 581 F.Supp. 585 (D.C. Wis.) 776 F.2d 1051 (7th Cir. 1984) cert. den. 106 S.Ct. 1462, 475 U.S. 1083, 89 L.Ed.2d 719 (1984) **13:530**

Danno v. Peterson, 421 F.Supp. 950 (N.D. Ill. 1976) **16:55, 19:110**

Danville Community Consolidated School District No. 118, 5 PERI 1084 (IELRB Opinion and Order, April 12, 1989) **21:110**

Darlene L. v. Illinois State Board of Education, 568 F.Supp. 1340 (N.D. Ill. 1983) **13:150**

Darrin v. Gould, 85 Wash.2d 859, 540 P.2d 882 (1975) **27:340**

DAS v. McHenry School District No. 15, 41 F.3d 1510 (7th Cir. 1994) **13:404**

Davis v. Board of Education of Aurora Public School District No. 131 of Kane County, 19 Ill.App.3d 644, 312 N.E.2d 335 (2nd Dist. 1974) **16:50**

Davis v. Board of Education of Farmer City-Mansfield Community Unit School District No. 17, 63 Ill.App.3d 495, 380 N.E.2d 58, 20 Ill.Dec. 381 (4th Dist. 1978) **16:60, 19:110**

Davis v. Board of Review of the Department of Labor, 125 Ill.App.3d 67, 465 N.E.2d 576, 80 Ill.Dec. 464 (1st Dist. 1984) **17:290**

Davis v. Francis Howell School District, 104 F.3d 204 (8th Cir. 1998) **17:672**

Davis v. Monroe County Board of Education, 119 S.Ct.1661, 526 U.S.629, 143 L.Ed.2d 839 (1999) **11:420, 11:422**

Davis-El v. O'Leary, 626 F.Supp. 1037 (N.D. Ill. 1986) **6:300**

Decatur Federation of Teachers IFT-AFT, AFL-CIO v. Educational Labor Relations Board, 199 Ill.App.3d 190, 556 N.E.2d 780, 145 Ill.Dec. 162 (4th Dist. 1990) **21:300**

Decatur School District No. 61, 3 PERI 1022 (IELRB Opinion and Order, February 10, 1987) **21:120**

Deem v. Board of Education of Triad Community Unit School District No. 2, Madison County, 200 Ill.App.3d 903, 558 N.E.2d 291, 146 Ill.Dec. 328 (5th Dist. 1990) **16:235**

Deizman v. Board of Education District 201, Cook County, 53 Ill.App.3d 1050, 369 N.E.2d 257 (1st Dist. 1977) **17:160**

Deloney v. Board of Education of Thornton Township School District No. 205, Cook County, Illinois, 281 Ill.App.3d 775, 666 N.E.2d 792, 217 Ill.Dec. 123 (1st Dist. 1996) **11:435**

Denno v. School Board of Volusia County, Florida, 193 F.3d 1178 (11th Cir. 1999) **12:120**

deOliveira v. State Board of Education, 158 Ill.App.3d 111, 511 N.E.2d 172, 110 Ill.Dec. 337 (2nd Dist. 1987) **17:580**

DeShaney v. Winnebago County Department of Social Services, 109 S.Ct. 998, 489 U.S. 189, 103 L.Ed.2d 249 (1989) **11:430**

Desmond v. Regional Board of School Trustees, Malta Community Unit School District No. 433, 183 Ill.App.3d 316, 538 N.E.2d 1350, 131 Ill.Dec. 794 (2nd Dist. 1989), app. den. 127 Ill.2d 614, 545 N.E.2d 108, 136 Ill.Dec. 584 **8:330**

Dickens v. Quincy College Corporation, 245 Ill.App.3d 1055, 615 N.E.2d 381, 185 Ill.Dec. 822 (4th Dist. 1993) **19:94**

Dishnow v. School District of Rib Lake, 77 F.3d 194 (7th Cir. 1996) **17:450**

District 114 Support Staff IEA-NEA and Fox Lake Elementary School District, 10 PERI 1097 (IELRB administrative law judge, June 14, 1994) **21:282**

District 300 Education Association v. Board of Education of Dundee Community Unit School District No. 300 of Kane County et al., 31 Ill.App.3d 550, 334 N.E.2d 105 (2nd Dist. 1975) **15:220, 15:330, 17:140**

Doe by Doe v. Belleville Public School District No. 118, 672 F.Supp. 342 (S.D. Ill. 1987) **13:100**

Doe v. Baltimore County, Maryland Board of Education, 165 F.3d 260 (4th Cir. 1999) **13:530**

Doe v. Board of Education of Hononegah School District No. 207, 833 F.Supp. 1366 (N.D. Ill. 1993) **11:430**

Doe v. Board of Education of Oak Park and River Forest High School District 200, 115 F.3d 1273 (7th Cir. 1997) **13:370**

Doe v. Dallas Independent School District, 153 F.3d 211 (5th Cir. 1998) **11:428**

Doe v. Duncanville Independent School District, 986 F.2d 953 (5th Cir. 1993) **14:55**

Doe v. Human, 725 F.Supp. 1499 (W.D. Ark. 1989) aff'd. without opinion 923 F.2d 857 (8th Cir. 1990) cert. den. 111 S.Ct. 1315, 499 U.S. 922, 113 L.Ed.2d 248 (1991) **14:95**

Doe v. Maher, 793 F.2d 1470 (9th Cir. 1986) **13:370**

Doe v. Methucton School District, 880 F.Supp. 380 (E.D.Pa. 1995) **17:35**

Doe By and Through Doe v. Petaluma City School District, 54 F.3d 1447 (9th Cir. 1996) reversing 830 F.Supp. 1560 (N.D. Cal. 1993) **11:410, 11:420**

Doe v. Renfrow, 475 F.Supp. 1012, aff'd in part, rem. in part, 631 F.2d 582 (7th Cir. 1979) cert. den. 101 S.Ct. 3015, 451 U.S. 1022, 69 L.Ed.2d 395 **12:310, 12:330, 12:340**

Doe v. Sanders, 189 Ill.App.3d 572, 545 N.E.2d 454, 136 Ill.Dec. 930 (1st Dist. 1989) **13:320**

Doe v. Santa Fe Independent School District, 168 F.3d 806 (5th Cir. 1999) sugg. reh. den. 171 F.3d 1013, cert. granted 120 S.Ct. 494, __ U.S.__, __ L.Ed.2d __ (1999) **14:55, 14:61**

Doe v. Shenandoah County School Board, 737 F.Supp. 913 (W.D. Va. 1990) **14:95**

Doe v. Taylor Independent School District, 975 F.2d 137 (5th Cir. 1992) **11:417**

Doe v. Taylor Independent School District, 15 F.3d 443 (5th Cir. 1994) **11:415**

Doe v. University of Illinois, 138 F.3d 653 (7th Cir. 1998) **11:420**

Dolnick v. General Superintendent of Schools of Chicago, 67 Ill.App.3d 8, 384 N.E.2d 408, 23 Ill.Dec. 614 (1st Dist. 1978) **19:40**

Donahoo v. Board of Education of School District No. 303 Moultrie County, 346 Ill.App. 241, 104 N.E.2d 833 (3rd Dist. 1952), rev. 413 Ill. 422, 109 N.E.2d 787 (1952) **18:90**

Donato v. Plainview-Old Bethpage Central School District, 96 F.3d 623 (2nd Cir. 1996) cert. den. 117 S.Ct. 1083, 519 U.S. 1150, 137 L.Ed.2d 218 **6:226**

Donohue v. Copiague Union Free School District, 418 N.Y.S.2d 375, 47 N.Y.2d 440 (1979) **22:170**

Doran v. Department of Labor, 116 Ill.App.3d 471, 452 N.E.2d 118, 72 Ill.Dec. 186 (1st Dist. 1983) **17:300**

Doyle v. Holy Cross Hospital, 186 Ill.2d 104, 708 N.E.2d 1140, 237 Ill.Dec. 100 (1999) **17:610, 20:142**

Doyle Plumbing and Heating Co. v. Board of Education, Quincy Public School District No. 172, 291 Ill.App.3d 221, 683 N.E.2d 530, 225 Ill.Dec. 362 (4th Dist. 1997) **25:260, 25:261**

D.R. v. Middle Bucks Area Vocational Technical School, 972 F.2d 1364 (3rd Cir. 1992) cert. den. 113 S.Ct. 1045, 506 U.S. 1079, 122 L.Ed.2d 354 (1993) **11:420**

Duane M. v. Orleans Parish School Board, 861 F.2d 115 (5th Cir. 1988) **13:530**

Duldulao v. St. Mary of Nazareth Hospital Center, 115 Ill.2d 482, 505 N.E.2d 314, 106 Ill.Dec. 8 (1986) **17:600, 17:610**

Duncan v. Board of Education of United Township High School District No. 30, 177 Ill.App.3d 806, 532 N.E.2d 927, 127 Ill.Dec. 98 (3rd Dist. 1988) **16:230**

Dunlop v. Colgan, 687 F.Supp. 406 (N.D. Ill. 1988) **16:70**

Dunn and McCullough v. Fairfield Community High School District No. 225, 158 F.3d 962 (7th Cir. 1998) **10:330**

Dusanek v. Hannon, 677 F.2d 538 (7th Cir. 1982) **15:100**

East Hartford Education Association v. Board of Education, 562 F.2d 83 (Conn. 1977) **17:455**

East Richland Education Association v. IELRB, 173 Ill.App.3d 878, 528 N.E.2d 751, 124 Ill.Dec. 63 (4th Dist. 1988) **21:200**

East St. Louis Federation of Teachers Local 1220, American Federation of Teachers, AFL-CIO v. East St. Louis District Financial Oversight Panel, 178 Ill.2d 399, 687 N.E.2d 1050, 227 Ill.Dec.568 (1997) **3:190**

Eble v. Hamilton, 52 Ill.App.3d 550, 367 N.E.2d 788 (3rd Dist. 1977) **8:260**

Edmunson v. Chicago Board of Education, 62 Ill.App.3d 211, 379 N.E.2d 27, 19 Ill.Dec. 512 (1st Dist. 1978) **20:60**

Edwards v. Aguillard, 107 S.Ct. 2573, 482 U.S. 578, 96 L.Ed.2d 510 (1987) **14:200**

Eggers v. Bullit County School District, 854 F.2d 892 (6th Cir. 1988) **13:530**

Elder v. Board of Education of School District 127 1/2 of Cook County, 60 Ill.App.2d 56, 208 N.E.2d 423 (1st Dist. 1965) **2:210, 17:580**

Elliot v. Board of Education of the City of Chicago, 64 Ill.App.3d 229, 380 N.E.2d 1137, 20 Ill.Dec. 928 (1st Dist. 1978) **13:330**

Elrod v. Burns, 96 S.Ct. 2673, 427 U.S. 347, 49 L.Ed.2d 547 (1976) **17:460**

Elsenau v. City of Chicago, 334 Ill. 78, 165 N.E. 129 (1929) **4:340, 4:350, 4:360**

Engel v. Vitale, 82 S.Ct. 1261, 370 U.S. 421, 8 L.Ed.2d 601 (1962) **14:50**

Equal Employment Opportunities Commission v. Board of Governors of State Colleges, 957 F.2d 424 (7th Cir. 1992) **21:206**

Equal Employment Opportunity Commission v. Elgin Teachers Association, 780 F.Supp. 1195 (N.D. Ill. 1991) **17:200**

Equal Employment Opportunity Commission v. Francis W. Parker School, Memorandum Opinion 91 C 4674, 61 F.E.P. 967 (BNA) (N.D. Ill. 1993) **15:420**

Ernstes v. Warner, 860 F.Supp. 1338 (S.D. Ind. 1994) **11:440**

Evans v. Benjamin School District No. 25, 134 Ill.App.3d 875, 480 N.E.2d 1380, 89 Ill.Dec. 637 (2nd Dist. 1985) **16:180**

Evans v. City of Chicago, 689 F.2d 1286 (7th Cir. 1982) **22:230**

Evans v. District No. 17 of Douglas County, 841 F.2d 824 (8th Cir. 1988) **13:50**

Everett v. Board of Education of District 201, Cook County, 22 Ill.App.3d 594, 317 N.E.2d 753 (1st Dist. 1974) **18:190, 18:220**

Everson v. Board of Education of Ewing Township, 67 S.Ct. 504, 330 U.S. 1, 91 L.Ed. 711 (1947) reh. den. 67 S.Ct. 962, 330 U.S. 855, 91 L.Ed. 1297 (1947) **14:80**

Faculty Association of District 205, IEA-NEA v. Illinois Educational Labor Relations Board, 175 Ill.App 3d 880, 530 N.E.2d 548, 125 Ill.Dec. 390 (4th Dist. 1988) app. den. 124 Ill.2d 554. 535 N.E.2d 913, 129 Ill.Dec. 148 (1989) **16:180**

Fairfax Covenant Church v. Fairfax County School Board, 17 F.3d 703 (4th Cir. 1994) **14:130**

Fallon v. Indian Trail School, 148 Ill.App.3d 931, 500 N.E.2d 101, 102 Ill.Dec. 479 (2nd Dist. 1986) **17:33**

Fender v. School District No. 25, Arlington Heights, 37 Ill.App.3d 736 (1st Dist. 1976) **18:70, 18:190**

Fenneman v. Town of Gorham, 802 F.Supp. 542 (D.C. Me. 1992) **13:530**

Faragher v. City of Boca Raton, 118 S Ct. 2275, 524 U.S. 775, 141 L.Ed.2d 662 (1998) on rem. 166 F.3d 1152 **17:504, 17:505**

First National Bank of Elgin v. West Aurora School District 129, 200 Ill.App.3d 210, 558 N.E.2d 686, 146 Ill.Dec. 723 (2nd Dist. 1990) **8:330**

Fisher v. Board of Education of West Washington County Community Unit District No. 10, Washington County, 181 Ill.App.3d 653, 537 N.E.2d 354, 130 Ill.Dec. 287 (5th Dist. 1989) **16:80**

Fixmer v. Regional Board of School Trustees of Kane County, 146 Ill.App.3d 660, 497 N.E.2d 152, 100 Ill.Dec. 272 (2nd Dist. 1986) **8:240**

Florence County School District Four v. Carter, 112 S.Ct. 1932, 504 U.S. 906, 118 L.Ed.2d 540 (1993) **13:340, 13:350, 13:515**

Franklin v. Gwinnett County Public Schools, 112 S.Ct. 1028, 503 U.S. 60, 117 L.Ed.2d 208 (1992) **11:410, 11:417, 11:420**

Frazier v. Garrison Independent School District, 980 F.2d 1541 (5th Cir. 1993) **15:20**

Freedom Oil Company v. Illinois Pollution Control Board, 275 Ill.App.3d 508, 655 N.E.2d 1184, 211 Ill.Dec. 801 (4th Dist. 1995) **6:297, 6:298**

Freeman v. Pitts, 112 S.Ct. 1430, 503 U.S.467, 118 L.Ed.2d 108 (1992) **14:450**

Frederich v. Board of Education of Community Unit School District No. 304, 59 Ill.App.3d 49, 375 N.E.2d 141, 16 Ill.Dec. 510 (2nd Dist. 1978) **11:280**

Freiler v. Tangipahoa Parish Board of Education, 185 F.3d 337 (5th Cir. 1999) **14:231**

Fujishama v. Board of Education, 460 F.2d 1355 (7th Cir. 1972) **12:130, 12:140**

Fullilove v. Klutznick, 100 S.Ct. 2758, 448 U.S. 448, 65 L.Ed.2d 902 (1980) **14:540**

Fumarolo v. Chicago Board of Education, 142 Ill.2d 54, 566 N.E.2d 1283, 153 Ill.Dec. 177 (1990) **17:600**

Fustin v. Board of Education of Community Unit School District No. 2, 101 Ill.App.2d 113, 242 N.E.2d 308 (5th Dist. 1968) **22:130, 22:140**

Gaines v. National Collegiate Athletic Association, 746 F.Supp. 738 (M.D. Tenn. 1990) **27:30**

Gammon v. Edwardsville Community Unit School District No. 7, 82 Ill.App.3d 586, 403 N.E.2d 43, 38 Ill.Dec. 28 (5th Dist. 1980) **22:120**

Gann v. Harrisburg Community Unit School District, 73 Ill.App.2d 103, 218 N.E.2d 833 (5th Dist. 1966) **4:420**

Gano v. School District 411, 674 F.Supp. 796 (D.C. Ida. 1987) **12:128**

Garcia v. San Antonio Metropolitan Transit Authority, 105 S.Ct. 1005, 469 U.S. 528, 83 L.Ed.2d 1016 (1985) **17:60**

Garnett v. Benton School District, 865 F.2d 1211 (9th Cir. 1989) **14:120, 14:140**

Garrett v. Grant School District No. 124, 139 Ill.App.3d 569, 487 N.E.2d 699, 93 Ill.Dec. 874 (2nd Dist. 1985) **11:365, 22:145**

Gates v. Unified School District No. 449 of Leavenworth County, 996 F.2d 1035 (10th Cir. 1993) **11:417**

Gebser et al. v. Lago Vista Independent School District, 118 S.Ct.1989, 524 U.S. 274, 141 L.Ed.2d 277 (1998) **11:415, 11:417, 17:504**

Geise v. Phoenix Company of Chicago, Inc., 159 Ill.2d 507, 639 N.E.2d 1273, 203 Ill.Dec. 454 (1994) **17:33, 17:530**

Georgetown-Ridge Farm Community Unit School District No. 4, 10 PERI 1044 (IELRB Opinion and Order, March 1, 1994) **20:182**

Gerrity v. Beatty, 71 Ill.2d 47, 373 N.E.2d 1323, 15 Ill.Dec. 639 (1978) **22:130**

Gibson v. Kankakee School District No. 111, 34 Ill.App.3d 948, 341 N.E.2d 447 (3rd Dist. 1975) **4:420**

Gibson v Lee County School Board, 1 F.Supp.2d 1426 (M.D. Fla. 1998) **14:200**

Gilbert v. Homar, 117 S.Ct. 1807, 520 U.S. 924, 138 L.Ed.2d 120 (1997) on rem. 149 F.3d 1164 **12:70, 17:685, 18:250, 18:370, 20:140**

Gilbert v. Municipal Officers' Electoral Board of Deerfield, 97 Ill.App.3d 847, 423 N.E.2d 952, 53 Ill.Dec. 283 (2nd Dist. 1981) **4:240**

Gilliland v. Board of Education of Pleasant View Consolidated School District No. 622 of Tazewell County, 67 Ill.2d 143, 365 N.E.2d 322, 8 Ill.Dec. 84 (1977) **18:190, 18:200, 18:220**

Gilpin v. Kansas State High School Activities Association, Inc., 377 F.Supp. 1233 (D.C. Kan. 1973) **27:340**

G.M. ex rel. R.F. v. New Britain Board of Education, 173 F.3d 77 (2nd Cir. 1999) **13:565**

Goble v. Board of Education of Iuka Community Consolidated School District No. 7, Marion County, 83 Ill.App.3d 284, 404 N.E.2d 343, 38 Ill.Dec. 919 (5th Dist. 1980) **4:420**

Goedde v. Community Unit School District No. 7, Macoupin County, 21 Ill.App.2d 79, 157 N.E.2d 266 (3rd Dist. 1959) **1:100**

Goluba v. School District of Ripon, 45 F.3d 1035 (7th Cir. 1995) **14:61**

Gonyo v. Drake University, 837 F.Supp. 989 (S.D. Ia. 1993) **27:305**

Good News/Good Sports Club v. School District of City of LaDue, 859 F.Supp. 1239, (D.C. 1993) 28 F.3d 1501 (8th Cir. 1994) cert. den., reh. and sugg. for reh. den., 115 S.Ct. 2640, 515 U.S. 1173, 132 L.Ed.2d 878 (1995) **14:145**

Goss v. Lopez, 95 S.Ct. 729, 419 U.S. 565, 42 L.Ed.2d 725 (1975) **12:70, 12:80, 12:380, 12:410**

Gould v. Board of Education of Ashley Community Consolidated School District No. 15 of Washington County, 32 Ill.App.3d 808, 336 N.E.2d 69 (5th Dist. 1975) **18:70**

Grace Bible Fellowship v. School Administration, District 5, 941 F.2d 45 (1st Cir. 1991) **14:130**

Grandalski ex rel. Grandalski v. Lyons Township High School District 204, 305 Ill.App.3d 1, 711 N.E.2d 372, 238 Ill.Dec. 269 (1st Dist. 1999) **22:22**

Granfield v. Regional Board of School Trustees of Bureau County, 108 Ill.App.3d 703, 438 N.E.2d 497, 64 Ill.Dec. 246 (3rd Dist. 1982) **8:240**

Granite City Community Unit School District No. 9 v. Illinois Educational Labor Relations Board, 279 Ill.App.3d 439, 664 N.E.2d 1060, 216 Ill.Dec. 132 (4th Dist. 1996) **18:400**

Gras v. Clark, 46 Ill.App.3d 803, 361 N.E.2d 316, 5 Ill.Dec. 177 (2nd Dist. 1977) **15:610**

Green v. County School Board of New Kent County, 88 S.Ct. 1689, 391 U.S. 430, 20 L.Ed.2d 716 (1968) **14:470**

Greer v. Rome City School District, 950 F.2d 688 (11th Cir. 1991) **13:55**

Griffin v. Illinois High School Association, 822 F.2d 671 (7th Cir. 1987) **27:10**

Griffin High School v. Illinois High School Association, 822 F.Supp. 875 (C.D. Ill. 1987) **27:250**

Griggs v. Duke Power Company, 91 S.Ct. 849, 401 U.S. 424, 28 L.Ed.2d 158 (1971) **14:520**

Grissom v. Board of Education of Buckley Loda Community School District No. 8, 75 Ill.App.2d 314, 388 N.E.2d 398, 26 Ill.Dec. 683 (4th Dist. 1979) **18:220**

Hagopian v. Board of Education of Tampico Community Unit School District No. 4 of Whiteside and Bureau Counties, 56 Ill.App.3d 940, 372 N.E.2d 990, 14 Ill.Dec. 711 (3rd Dist. 1978) app. after rem. 83 Ill.App.3d 1097, 404 N.E.2d 899, 39 Ill.Dec. 308 (3rd Dist 1980), rev. on other grounds 84 Ill.2d 436, 420 N.E.2d 147, 50 Ill.Dec. 830 (1981) **15:50 16:240, 16:290**

Haas v. South Bend Community School Corporation, 259 Ind. 515, 289 N.E.2d 495 (1972) **27:340**

Halfacre v. Board of Education of School District No. 167, 331 Ill.App. 404, 73 N.E.2d 124 (1947) **17:50**

Hall v. Board of Education of the City of Chicago, 227 Ill.App.3d 560, 592 N.E.2d 245, 169 Ill.Dec. 758 (1st Dist, 1992) **17:700**

Hall Township High School District No. 502 Bureau County v. School Trustees of Bureau County, 80 Ill.App.2d 475, 225 N.E.2d 228 (3rd Dist. 1967) **8:150**

Hall v. Tawney, 621 F.2d 607 (4th Cir. 1980) **12:190**

Hamer v. Board of Education of School District No. 109, Lake County, 132 Ill.App.2d 46, 267 N.E.2d 1 (2nd Dist. 1971) **26:130**

Hamer v. Board of Education, School District No. 109, Lake County, 9 Ill.App.3d 663, 292 N.E.2d 569 (2d Dist. 1977) **10:370, 11:260**

Hamer v. Board of Education of Township High School District 113, 66 Ill.App.3d 7, 383 N.E.2d 231, 22 Ill.Dec. 755 (2nd Dist. 1978) **10:330**

Hamer v. Lentz, 132 Ill.2d 49, 547 N.E.2d 191, 138 Ill.Dec. 222 (1989) **7:460**

Hardway v. Board of Education of Lawrenceville Township High School District No. 71, 1 Ill.App.3d 298, 274 N.E.2d 213 (5th Dist. 1971) **17:47, 17:460**

Harlow v. Fitzgerald, 102 S.Ct 2727, 457 U.S. 800, 73 L.Ed.2d 396 (1982) **22:64**

Harper v. Edgewood Board of Education, 655 F.Supp. 1353 (S.D. Ohio 1987) **12:125**

Harris v. Forklift Systems, Inc., 114 S.Ct. 367, 510 U.S. 17, 126 L.Ed.2d 295 (1993) **17:510, 17:520**

Harris v. Joint School District No. 241, 821 F.Supp. 638 (D.C. Ida. 1993) 41 F.3d 447 (9th Cir. 1994) vac. 115 S.Ct. 2604, 515 U.S.1104, 132 L.Ed.2d 849 (1995) on rem. 62 F.3d 1233, cert. granted, vacating *Citizen's Preserving America's Heritage, Inc. v. Harris*, 115 S.Ct. 2604, 515 U.S. 1104, 132 L.Ed.2d 849, op. vac. 62 F.3d 1233 (9th Cir. 1996) **14:61**

Hartlein v. Illinois Power Co., 151 Ill.2d 142, 601 N.E.2d 720, 176 Ill.Dec. 122 (1992) **17:380**

Harton v. City of Chicago Department of Public Works and Department of Transportation, 301 Ill.App.3d 378, 703 N.E.2d 493, 234 Ill.Dec. 632 (1st Dist. 1998) app. den. 182 Ill.2d 549, 707 N.E.2d 239, 236 Ill.Dec. 669 **17:360**

Havens v. Miller, 102 Ill.App.3d 558, 429 N.E.2d 1292, 57 Ill.Dec. 929 (1st. Dist. 1981) **3:90, 4:420**

Hawkins v. National Collegiate Athletic Association, 652 F.Supp. 602 (C.D. Ill. 1987) **27:140**

Hayes v. Phoenix Talent School District, 893 F.2d 235 (9th Cir. 1990) **6:226**

Hazelwood v. Kuhlmeier, 108 S.Ct. 562, 484 U.S. 260, 98 L.Ed.2d 592 (1988) on rem. 840 F.2d 596 (8th Cir. 1988) **12:130, 12:135, 17:480**

Hazelwood School District v. U.S., 97 S.Ct. 2736, 433 U.S. 299, 53 L.Ed.2d 768 (1977) **14:510**

Hedges by and through Hedges v. Wauconda Community Unit School District No. 118 et al., 807 F.Supp. 444, 9 F.3d 1295 (7th Cir. 1993) **14:120**

Heifner v. Board of Education of Morris Community Unit School District No. 101, Grundy County, 32 Ill.App.3d 83, 335 N.E.2d 600 (3rd Dist. 1975) **15:110**

Henrich by Henrich v. Libertyville High School et al., 186 Ill.2d 381, 712 N.E2d 298, 238 Ill.Dec. 596 (1999) **22:20, 22:22**

Helland v. South Bend Community School Corporation, 93 F.3d 327 (7th Cir. 1996) **14:230**

Helmig v. Regional Board of School Trustees, 286 Ill.App.3d 220, 675 N.E. 2d 966, 221 Ill. Dec. 542 (3rd Dist. 1997) **8:150**

Henson v. City of Dundee, 682 F.2d 897 (11th Cir. 1982) **17:500**

Herndon v. Chapel Hill-Carrboro City Board of Education, 89 F.3d 174 (4th Cir. 1996) **10:34**

Hertel v. Boismenue, 229 Ill. 474, 82 N.E. 298 (1907) **5:140**

Hohmeier v. Leyden Community High Schools District 212, 954 F.2d 461 (7th Cir. 1992) **17:600**

Hollister v. North, 50 Ill.App.3d 56, 365 N.E.2d 258, 8 Ill.Dec. 20 (4th Dist. 1977) **3:160, 17:47**

Honig v. Doe, 108 S.Ct. 592, 484 U.S. 305, 98 L.Ed.2d 686 (1988) **12:155, 13:360, 13:370, 13:515**

Horth v. Board of Education of School District No. 205, Winnebago County, 42 Ill.App.2d 65, 191 N.E.2d 601 (2nd Dist. 1963) **8:330**

Horton v. Goose Creek, 690 F.2d 470, reh. den. 693 F.2d 524 (5th Cir. 1982) cert. den. 103 S.Ct. 3536, 363 U.S. 1207, 77 L.Ed.2d 1387 (1982) **12:310**

Hoskins v. Walker, 57 Ill.2d 503, 315 N.E.2d 25 (1974) **1:150**

Hostrop v. Board of Junior College District 515, Cook and Will Counties and State of Illinois, 471 F.2d 488 (7th Cir. 1972) cert. den. 93 S.Ct. 2150, 411 U.S. 967, 36 L.Ed.2d 688 (1973) on rem. 399 F.Supp. 609, aff'd. in part, rev. in part 523 F.2d 569, cert. den. 96 S.Ct. 1748, 425 U.S. 963, 48 L.Ed.2d 208 (1974) **18:60**

Howard v. Board of Education of Freeport School District No. 145, 160 Ill.App.3d 309, 513 N.E.2d 545, 112 Ill.Dec. 131 (2nd Dist. 1987) **18:50**

Howard University v. National Collegiate Athletic Association, 367 F.Supp. 926 (D.C. D.C. 1973) **27:220, 27:240**

Howlett by and through Howlett v. Rose, 110 S.Ct. 2430, 496 U.S. 356, 110 L.Ed.2d 332 (1990) on rem. 571 So.2d 29 (1990) **12:230**

Hsu v. Roslyn Union Free School District No. 3, 85 F.3d 839 (2nd Cir. 1996) **9:432**

Hubbard v. Illinois State Labor Relations Board and Village of Streamwood, 293 Ill.App.3d 1122, 78 N.E.2d 1083, 241 Ill.Dec. 229 (1st Dist. 1997) **17:740**

Huetteman v. Board of Education of Community Unit School District 3A, 56 Ill.App.3d 933, 372, N.E.2d 716, 14 Ill.Dec. 520 (4th Dist. 1978) **16:340**

Human Rights Authority of the State of Illinois Guardianship and Advocacy Commission by Aune v. Miller, 124 Ill.App.3d 701, 464 N.E.2d 833, 79 Ill.Dec. 929 (3rd Dist. 1984) **7:180**

Hunger v. Leininger, 15 F.3d 664 (7th Cir. 1994) cert. den. 115 S.Ct. 123, 513 U.S. 839, 130 L.Ed.2d 67 **13:404**

Hurley v. Irish American Gay, Lesbian and Bisexual Group of Boston, 115 S.Ct. 2338, 515 U.S. 557, 132 L.Ed.2d 487 (1995) **9:432**

Illinois Bell Telephone Company v. Human Rights Commission, 190 Ill.App.3d 1036, 547 N.E.2d 499, 138 Ill.Dec. 322 (1st Dis. 1989) app. den. 129 Ill.2d 563, 550 N.E.2d 556, 140 Ill.Dec. 671 (1990) **17:380**

Illinois Department of Management Services, 5 PERI 2012 (IELRB Decision and Order, April 28, 1989) **21:90**

Illinois Educational Labor Relations Board v Homer Community Consolidated School District No. 208, 160 Ill.App.3d 730, 514 N.E.2d 465, 112 Ill.Dec. 802 (4th Dist. 1987) aff'd. 132 Ill.2d 29, 547 N.E.2d 182, 138 Ill.Dec. 213 (1989) **6:330, 7:450**

Illinois ex rel. McCollum v. Board of Education of School District No. 71, Champaign County, Illinois, 68 S.Ct. 461, 333 U.S. 203, 92 L.Ed. 649 (1948) **14:35**

Illinois News Broadcasters Association v. City of Springfield, 22 Ill.App.3d 226, 317 N.E.2d 288 (4th Dist. 1974) **6:30**

Immediato by Immediato v. Rye Neck School District, 73 F.3d 454 (2nd Cir. 1996) cert. den. 117 S.Ct. 60, 519 U.S. 813, 136 L.Ed.2d 22 (1996) **10:34**

Indiana ex rel. Anderson v. Brant, 58 S.Ct. 443, 303 U.S. 95 82 L.Ed. 685 (1938) **18:72**

Ingebretsen on Behalf of Ingebretsen v. Jackson Public School District, 88
    F.3d 274 (5th Cir. 1996), reh. and reh. den., cert den. *Moore v.
    Ingebretsen* 117 S.Ct. 388, 519 U.S. 965, 136 L.Ed.2d 304 (1997) **14:61**
In Interest of Burr, 119 Ill.App.2d 134, 255 N.E.2d 57 (4th Dist. 1969) **11:50**
In Interest of V.W., 112 Ill.App.3d 587, 445 N.E.2d 445, 67 Ill.Dec. 965 (1st.
    Dist. 1983) **12:180**
In re County Collector of McHenry County, 181 Ill.App.3d 345, 536 N.E.2d
    1288, 130 Ill. Dec. 77 (2nd Dist. 1989) **23:130, 25:40**
In re Griffiths, 93 S.Ct. 2851, 413 U.S. 717, 37 L.Ed.2d 397 (1973) **27:300**
In re S.F., 607 A.2d 793 (Pa.Super. 1992) **12:300**
In re Walgenbach, 104 Ill.2d 121, 470 N.E.2d 1015, 83 Ill.Dec. 595 (1984)
    26:240
Ingraham v. Wright, 97 S.Ct. 1401, 430 U.S. 651, 51 L.Ed.2d 711 (1977)
    12:190
International Brotherhood of Teamsters v. U.S., 97 S.Ct. 1843, 431 U.S. 324,
    52 L.Ed.2d 396 (1977) **14:510**
Irving Independent School District v. Tatro, 104 S.Ct. 3371, 468 U.S. 883,
    82 L.Ed.2d 664 (1984) on rem. 741 F.2d 82 (1984) **13:10, 13:140, 13:150**
*Israel S. By Owens v. Board of Education of Oak Park and River Forest
    High School District 200, Cook County*, 235 Ill.App.3d 652, 601 N.E.2d
    1264, 176 Ill.Dec. 566 (1st Dist. 1992) **11:220**
J.S.K. v. Hendry County School Board, 941 F.2d 1563 (11th Cir. 1991)
    13:25
Jojola v. Chavez, 55 F.3d 488 (10th Cir. 1995) **11:415**
Jastram v. Lake Villa School District No. 41, 192 Ill.App.3d 599, 549 N.E.2d
    9, 139 Ill.Dec. 29 (2nd Dist. 1989) **22:190**
Jenkins v. Talladega City Board of Education, 95 F.3d 1036 (11th Cir.
    1996) **12:231**
Jennings v. Joshua Independent School District, 948 F.2d 194 (5th Cir.
    1991) reh. den. 952 F.2d 402, cert. den. 112 S.Ct.2303, 504 U.S. 956, 119
    L.Ed.2d 226 (1992) **12:310**
Jewell v. Board of Education DuQuoin Community Unit Schools, 19
    Ill.App.3d 1091, 312 N.E.2d 659 (5th Dist. 1974) **6:190**
John K v. Board of Education for School District No. 65, Cook County, 152
    Ill.App.3d 543, 504 N.E.2d 797, 105 Ill.Dec. 512 (1st Dist. 1987) app.
    den. 115 Ill.2d 542, 511 N.E.2d 429, 110 Ill.Dec. 457 (1987) **7:230, 7:270,
    7:340, 7:390**
John T. v. Marion Independent School District, 173 F.3d 684 (9th Cir. 1999)
    13:530
*Johnson v. Board of Education of Decatur School District No. 61 of Macon
    County*, 87 Ill.App.3d 441, 409 N.E.2d 139, 42 Ill.Dec. 644 (4th Dist.
    1980) aff'd. 85 Ill.2d 338, 423 N.E.2d 903, 53 Ill.Dec. 234 (1981) **16:160**
Johnson v. George J. Ball, Inc. 248 Ill.App.3d 859, 617 N.E.2d 1355, 187
    Ill.Dec. 634 (2nd Dist. 1993) **19:94**
Jones v. Clear Creek Independent School District, 930 F.2d 416 (5th Cir.
    1991) vac. and rem. 112 S.Ct 3020, 505 U.S. 1215, 120 L.Ed.2d 892
    (1992) on rem. 977 F.2d 963 (5th Cir. 1993) **14:61**
Jones v. Municipal Officers Electoral Board, 122 Ill.App.3d 926, 446 N.E.2d
    173, 61 Ill.Dec. 684 (1st Dist. 1983) **4:420**
*Jordan by Edwards v. O'Fallon Township High School District No. 203
    Board of Education*, 302 Ill.App.3d 1070, 706 N.E.2d 137, 235 Ill.Dec.
    877 (5th Dist. 1999) **12:495, 27:130**

Justice v. National Collegiate Athletic Association, 577 F.Supp. 356 (N.D. Ariz. 1983) **27:140**

Karnstein v. Pewaukee School Board, 557 F.Supp. 565 (E.D. Wisc. 1983) **12:400**

Katamay v. Chicago Transit Authority, 53 Ill.2d 27, 289 N.E.2d 623 (1972) **11:365, 20:205**

Kaufmann v. Board of Trustees Community Consolidated District 508, 522 F.Supp. 90 (N.D. Ill. 1981) **17:640**

Kenney v. Interim General Superintendent of Schools, 112 Ill.App.3d 342, 445 N.E.2d 356, 67 Ill.Dec. 876 (1983) **19:40**

Kerno v. Sandoz Pharmaceuticals Corp., 93 C 20012 (N.D. Ill. 1994) **17:400**

Kenyon v. Garrels, 184 Ill.App.3d 28, 540 N.E.2d 11, 132 Ill.Dec. 595 (4th Dist. 1989) **7:400**

*Kewanee Community School District No. 229, 4 PERI 1136 (IELRB Opinion and Order, September 15, 1988) **21:350, 21:440**

Khuans v. School District 110, 123 F.3d 1010 (7th Cir. 1997) **17:450**

Kinman v. Omaha Public School District, 94 F.3d 463 (8th Cir. 1996) **11:428**

Klein v. Smith, 635 F.Supp. 1440 (Me. 1986) **12:30**

Klingelmueller v. Haas, 111 Ill.App.3d 88, 443 N.E.2d 782, 66 Ill.Dec. 856 (3rd Dist. 1982) **4:150**

Knapp v. Whitaker, 757 F.2d 827 (7th Cir. 1985) **17:450**

Knight v. Board of Education of Tri-Point Community Unit School District 6J, 38 Ill.App.3d 603, 348 N.E.2d 299 (4th Dist. 1976) **10:330**

Knox County Education Association v. Knox County Board of Education, 158 F.3d 361 (6th Cir. 1998), cert. den. 120 S.Ct. 46, __ U.S.__, __ L.Ed.2d__ (1999) **17:730**

Kobylanski v. Chicago Board of Education, 63 Ill.2d 165, 347 N.E.2d 705 (1976) **12:20, 22:100, 22:130**

Koerner v. Joppa Community High School District No. 21, 143 Ill.App.3d 162, 492 N.E.2d 1017, 97 Ill.Dec. 358 (5th Dist. 1986) **16:270**

Komninos v. Upper Saddle River Board of Education, 13 F.3d 775 (3rd Cir. 1994) **13:510**

Konald v. Board of Education of Community Unit School District No. 220, 114 Ill.App.3d 512, 448 N.E.2d 555, 69 Ill.Dec. 837 (2nd Dist. 1983) **8:170**

Koppi v. Board of Control of Whiteside Area Vocational Center, 133 Ill.App.3d 591, 479 N.E.2d 36, 88 Ill.Dec. 701 (3rd Dist. 1985) **16:100**

Kowalski v. Liska, 78 Ill.App.3d 64, 397 N.E.2d 39, 33 Ill.Dec. 706 (1st Dist. 1979) **11:290**

Kraft, Inc. v. State of Minnesota, 284 N.W.2d 386 (Minn.Sup.Ct. 1979) **17:47**

Kraut v. Rachford, 51 Ill.App.3d 206, 366 N.E.2d 497, 9 Ill.Dec. 240 (1st Dist. 1977) **11:180, 11:220**

Kreimer v. Bureau of Police for the Town of Morristown, 958 F.2d 1242 (3rd Cir. 1992) **10:400**

Krizek v. Board of Education, 713 F.Supp. 1131 (N.D. Ill. 1989) **17:480**

Krughoff v. Naperville, 68 Ill.2d 352, 369 N.E.2d 892, 12 Ill.Dec. 185, (1977) **9:100**

Kulovitz v. Illinois High School Association, 462 F.Supp. 875 (N.D. Ill. 1978) **27:130, 27:250, 27:460**

Kuykendall v. Board of Education of Evanston Township High School District No. 202, 111 Ill.App.3d 809, 444 N.E.2d 766, 67 Ill.Dec. 530 (1st Dist. 1982) **16:120, 16:160, 16:180**

L.E. Zannini & Co. v. Board of Education, Hawthorn School District 73, 138 Ill.App.3d 467 486 N.E.2d 426, 93 Ill.Dec. 323 (2nd Dist. 1985) **25:240**

Lacks v. Ferguson-Florissant Reorganized School District, R-2, 147 F.3d 718 (8th Cir. 1998) sugg. for reh. den. 154 F.3d 904, cert. den. 119 S.Ct. 1158, __ U.S.__, 143 L.Ed.2d 233 **17:480, 17:482**

Laine v. Dittman, 125 Ill.App.2d 136, 259 N.E.2d 824 (2nd Dist. 1970) **12:125**

Lake County Forest Preserve District v. Northern Trust Bank, 207 Ill. App.3d 290, 565 N.E.2d 715, 152 Ill.Dec. 182 (2nd Dist. 1990) **6:290**

Lake Zurich School District No. 45, 1 PERI 1031 (IELRB Opinion and Order, November 30, 1984) **21:410**

Lamb's Chapel v. Center Moriches Union Free School District, 113 S.Ct. 2141, 508 U.S. 384, 124 L.Ed.2d 352 (1993) **9:432, 14:145**

Lane v. Board of Education of Fairbury Cropsey Community Unit School District No. 3, 38 Ill.App.3d 742, 348 N.E.2d 470 (4th Dist. 1976) **19:110**

Last v. Board of Education of Community Unit School District No. 321, Winnebago and Stephenson Counties, 37 Ill.App.2d 159, 185 N.E.2d 282 (2nd Dist. 1962) **15:110**

Latham v. Board of Education of Chicago, 31 Ill.2d 178, 201 N.E.2d 111 (1964) **2:20, 10:390**

Lee v. Weisman, 112 S.Ct. 2649, 505 U.S. 577, 120 L.Ed.2d 467 (1992) **14:60, 14:61, 14:62, 14:123**

Leffel v. Wisconsin Interscholastic Athletic Association, 444 F.Supp. 1117, (E.D. Wis. 1978) **27:340**

Lehnert v. Ferris Faculty Association, 111 S.Ct. 1950, 500 U.S. 507, 114 L.Ed.2d 572 (1991) reh. den. 111 S.Ct. 2878, 115 L.Ed.2d 1044, on rem. 937 F.2d 608 **21:330**

Lemon v. Kurtzman, 91 S.Ct. 2105, 403 U.S. 602, 29 L.Ed.2d 745 (1971) reh. den. 92 S.Ct. 24, 404 U.S. 876, 30 L.Ed.2d 123, on rem. 348 F.Supp. 300, aff'd. 93 S.Ct. 1463, 411 U.S. 192, 36 L.Ed.2d 151 (1971) **14:20, 14:123**

Lenard v. Board of Education of Fairfield School District No. 112 of Wayne County, 57 Ill.App.3d 853, 373 N.E.2d 477, 15 Ill.Dec. 131 (5th Dist. 1978) app. after rem. 74 Ill.2d 260, 384 N.E.2d 1321, 24 Ill.Dec. 163 (1978) **16:300**

Lester v. Board of Education of School District No. 119, Jo Daviess County, 87 Ill.App.2d 269, 230 N.E.2d 893 (2nd Dist. 1967) **15:10, 16:60, 19:110**

Leviton v. Board of Education of the City of Chicago, 374 Ill. 594, 30 N.E.2d 497 (1943) **26:140**

Lewis v. North Clay Community Unit School District No. 25, 181 Ill.App.3d 689, 537 N.E.2d 435, 130 Ill.Dec. 368 (5th Dist. 1989) **15:230**

Libby by Libby v. South Interconference Association, 728 F.Supp. 504 (N.D. Ill. 1990) **27:10**

Libertyville Education Association IEA-NEA v. Board of Education, 56 Ill.App.3d 503, 371 N.E.2d 676, 13 Ill.Dec. 741 (2nd Dist. 1977) **21:580**

Lincoln Way Community High School District No. 210, 5 PERI 1025 (Executive Director's Recommended Decision and Order, January 11, 1989) **21:100**

Lindblad v. Board of Education of Normal School District, 221 Ill. 261, 77 N.E. 450 (1906) **2:210**

Linwood v. Board of Education of Peoria School District 150, 463 F.2d 763 (7th Cir. 1972) **12:80, 12:330, 12:460, 12:470, 12:475**

Lippincott v. Board of Education of Community Unit School District No. 5 of Coles County, 342 Ill.App. 642, 97 N.E.2d 566 (3rd Dist. 1951) **17:160**

Litin v. Board of Education of City of Chicago, 72 Ill.App.3d 889, 391 N.E.2d 62, 28 Ill.Dec. 863 (1st Dist. 1979) **18:240**

Littrell v. Board of Education of Cave in Rock Community Unit School District No. 2, 45 Ill.App.3d 690, 360 N.E.2d 102, 4 Ill.Dec. 355 (5th Dist. 1977) **15:230, 16:50**

Local 28 of the Sheet Metal Workers International Association v. Equal Employment Opportunities Commission, 106 S.Ct. 3019, 478 U.S. 421, 92 L.Ed.2d 344 (1986) **14:530**

Lombardo v. Board of Education School District No. 27, Cook County, 100 Ill.App.2d 108, 241 N.E.2d 495 (1st Dist. 1968) **18:140**

Lowe v. Board of Education of City of Chicago, 76 Ill.App.3d 348, 395 N.E.2d 59, 32 Ill.Dec. 122 (1st Dist. 1979) **18:70, 18:120, 18:210**

Lynch v. Board of Education of Collinsville Community Unit School District No. 10, 82 Ill.2d 415, 412 N.E.2d 447, 45 Ill.Dec. 9G (1980) **22:130, 22:140**

Lyznicki v. Board of Education, School District No. 167, Cook County, 707 F.2d 949 (7th Cir. 1983) **19:140**

Madden v. Schumann, 105 Ill.App.3d 900, 435 N.E.2d 173, 61 Ill.Dec. 684 (1st Dist. 1982) **4:420**

Maganuco v. Leyden Community High School District No. 212, 867 F.2d 974 (7th Cir. 1989) **17:170**

Maganuco v. Leyden Community Hich School District 212, 939 F.2d 440 (7th Cir. 1991) **17:200**

Mancha v. Field Museum of Natural History, 5 Ill.App.3d 699, 283 N.E.2d 899 (1st Dist. 1972) **22:130**

Marsh v. Chambers, 103 S.Ct. 3330, 463 U.S. 783, 77 L.Ed.2d 1019 (1983) **14:60**

Martens v. District No. 220 Board of Education, 620 F.Supp. 29 (N.D.Ill. 1985) **12:300**

Martin v. School Board of Prince Georges County, 3 Va.App. 197, 348 S.E.2d 857 (1986) **13:50**

Martinez Morales v. Bynum, 103 S.Ct. 1838, 461 U.S. 321, 75 L.Ed.2d 879 (1983) **11:180**

Mary M. v. North Lawrence Community School Corp., 951 F.Supp. 82 (S.D. Ind. 1997) rev. 31 F.3d 1220 (7th Cir. 1997) reh. den., cert. den. 118 S.Ct. 2369, __ U.S. __, 141 L.Ed.2d 737 (1998) **11:416**

Maryland v. Craig, 110 S.Ct. 3157, 497 U.S. 836, 111 L.Ed.2d 666 (1990) **12:477**

Masciola v. Chicago Metropolitan Ski Council, 257 Ill.App.3d 313, 628 N.E.2d 1067, 195 Ill.Dec. 603 (1st Dist. 1993) **22:164**

Massachusetts Interscholastic Athletic Association and Gomes v. Rhode Island Interscholastic League, 469 F.Supp. 659 (D.C. R.I. 1979) **27:320**

Massie v. East St. Louis School District No. 189, 203 Ill.App.3d 965, 561 N.E.2d 246, 148 Ill.Dec. 940 (5th Dist. 1990) **18:250, 18:380**

Max M. v. Illinois State Board of Education, 585 F.Supp. 317, on reconsideration 629 F.Supp. 1504 (N.D. Ill. 1984) **13:80, 13:150**

May v. Evansville-Vanderburg School Corporation, 787 F.2d 1005 (7th Cir. 1986) **14:150**

McBroom v. Board of Education District No. 205, 144 Ill.App.3d 463, 494 N.E.2d 1191, 98 Ill.Dec. 864 (2nd Dist. 1986) **17:680, 18:175**

McCartney C. By Sara S. v. Herrin Community Unit School District No. 4, 21 F.3d 173 (7th Cir. 1994) **13:565**

McCauley v. Chicago Board of Education, 66 Ill.App.3d 676, 384 N.E.2d 100, 23 Ill.Dec. 464 (1st Dist. 1978) **22:130**

McCullough v. Illinois State Board of Education, 204 Ill.App.3d 1082, 562 N.E.2d 1233, 150 Ill.Dec. 430 (5th Dist. 1990) **18:175**

McCutcheon v. Board of Education, City of Chicago, 94 Ill.App.3d 993, 419 N.E.2d 451, 50 Ill.Dec. 343 (1st Dist. 1981) **18:180**

McInerney v. Charter Golf, Inc., 176 Ill.2d 482, 680 N.E.2d 1347, 223 Ill.Dec. 911 (1997) **19:94**

McInnis v. Shapiro, 293 F.Supp. 327 (N.D. Ill. 1968) aff'd. *McInnis v. Ogilvie,* 89 S.Ct. 1197, 394 U.S. 322, 22 L.Ed.2d 308 (1969) **24:60**

McIntire v. Bethel Independent School District No. 3, 804 F.Supp. 1415 (W.D. Okla. 1992) **12:128**

McLaughlin v. Tilendis, 398 F.2d 287 (7th Cir. 1968) **17:470**

McNaughton v. Circleville Board of Education, 46 Ohio Misc. 12, 345 N.E.2d 649 (1974) **12:30**

McNely v. Board of Education of Community Unit School District No. 7, 9 Ill.2d 143, 137 N.E.2d 63 (1956) **19:110**

McSomebodies v. Burlingame Elementary School, 897 F.2d 974 (9th Cir. 1989) **13:530**

Meadows v. School District U-46, 141 Ill.App.3d 335, 490 N.E.2d 140, 95 Ill.Dec. 667 (2nd Dist. 1986) **19:140**

Menora v. Illinois High School Association, 683 F.2d 1030 (7th Cir. 1982) cert. den. 103 S.Ct. 801, 459 U.S. 1156, 74 L.Ed.2d 1003 (1983) **27:10**

Menssen v. Eureka Unit District No. 140, 70 Ill.App.3d 9, 388 N.E.2d 273, 26 Ill.Dec. 649 (4th Dist. 1979) **4:420, 6:310**

Meridith v. Board of Education of Community Unit School District No. 7, 7 Ill.App.2d 477, 130 N.E.2d 5 (3rd Dist. 1955) **17:640**

Meritor Savings Bank v. Vinson, 106 S.Ct. 2399, 477 U.S. 57, 91 L.Ed.2d49 (1986) on rem. *Vinson v. Taylor,* 801 F.2d 1436 (D.C. Cir. 1986) **17:504, 17:510**

Messer v. Meno, 936 F.Supp. 1280 (W.D. Tex. 1996) aff. in part rev. in part 130 F.3d 130 (5th Cir. 1997) **14:530**

Metropolitan School District of Wayne Township, Marion County Indiana v. Davila, 969 F.2d 485 (7th Cir. 1992) cert. den. 113 S.Ct. 1360, 507 U.S. 949, 122 L.Ed.2d 740 (1993) **13:370**

Metzger by and through Metzger v. Osbeck, 841 F.2d 518 (3rd Cir. 1988) **12:190**

Meyer v. McKeown, 266 Ill.App.3d 324, 641 N.E.2d 1212, 204 Ill.Dec.593, (3rd Dist. 1994) **2:144**

Meyer by Meyer v. Naperville Manor, Inc. 262 Ill. App.3d 141, 634 N.E.2d 411, 199 Ill.Dec. 572 (2nd Dist. 1994) **22:164**

Meyer v. State of Nebraska, 43 S.Ct. 625, 262 U.S. 390, 67 L.Ed. 1042 (1923) **14:30**

M.H.D. v. Westminster School, 172 F.3d 797 (11th Cir. 1999) **11:440**

*Miceli v. Lavelle,*114 Ill.App.3d 311, 448 N.E.2d 989 (1st. Dist. 1983) **3:100, 3:110**

Midwest Central Education Association v. Illinois Educational Labor Relations Board, et al., 277 Ill.App.3d 440, 660 N.E.2d 151, 213 Ill.Dec. 894 (1st Dist. 1995) **18:25, 20:143, 21:565**

Miles v. Denver Public Schools, 944 F.2d 773 (10th Cir. 1991) **17:480**

Miller v. Board of Education, School District No. 132, Cook County, 51 Ill.App.2d 20, 240 N.E.2d 471 (1st Dist. 1964) **18:190**

Miller v. School District No. 167, Cook County, Illinois, 354 F.Supp. 922 (N.D. Ill. 1973) aff'd. on other grounds 495 F.2d 658, reh. den. 500 F.2d 711 (7th Cir. 1974) **18:60**

Miller v. School District No. 189 East St. Louis, 26 Ill.App.3d 172, 325 N.E.2d 43 (5th Dist. 1975) **10:230, 10:240**

Miller v. Wilkes, 172 F.3d 574 (8th Cir. 1999) **12:235**

Milliken v. Bradley, 94 S.Ct. 3112, 418 U.S. 717, 41 L.Ed.2d 1069, on rem. 402 F.Supp. 1096, on rem. 411 F.Supp. 943, aff'd. cause rem. 540 F.2d 229, aff'd. 97 S.Ct. 2749, 433 U.S. 267, 53 L.Ed.2d 745 (1977) on rem. 620 F.2d 1143, cert. den. 101 S.Ct. 2017, 449 U.S. 870, 66 L.Ed.2d 89 **14:490**

Miner v. Yantis, 410 Ill. 401, 102 N.E.2d 524 (1952) **9:160**

Mississippi Employment Security Commission v. McGlothin, 556 So.2d 324 (Miss. 1990) **17:455**

Missouri v. Jenkins, 115 S.Ct. 2573, 515 U.S. 1139, 132 L.Ed.2d 824 (1995) **14:500**

Mitchell v. Jewel Food Stores, 142 Ill.2d 152, 568 N.E.2d 827, 136 Ill.Dec. 813 (1990) **17:600**

Mitchell v. Louisiana High School Association, 430 F.2d 1155 (5th Cir. 1970) **27:130**

Mitten by and through Mitten v. Muscogee County School District, 877 F.2d 932 (11th Cir. 1989) cert. den. 110 S.Ct. 1117, 493 U.S. 1072, 107 L.Ed.2d 1024 (1990) **13:530**

Monroe v. Board of Commissioners of City of Jackson, Tennessee, 88 S.Ct. 1700, 391 U.S. 450, 20 L.Ed.2d 733 (1968) **14:470**

Montag v. Board of Education of School District No. 40, Rock Island County, 112 Ill.App.3d 1039, 446 N.E.2d 299, 68 Ill.Dec. 565 (3rd Dist. 1983) **12:20, 22:140**

Moore v. District of Columbia, 886 F.2d 335 (D.C. Cir. 1989) **13:530**

Moraine Valley Community College, 5 PERI 1102 (IELRB Opinion and Order, May 12, 1989) **21:510**

Morelli v. Board of Education of District 303, Tazewell County, 42 Ill.App.3d 722, 356 N.E.2d 438, 1 Ill.Dec. 312 (3rd Dist. 1976) **18:250**

Morgan v. Board of Education of Trico Community Unit School District No. 176, 22 Ill.App.3d 241, 317 N.E.2d 393 (5th Dist. 1974) **10:160, 10:320, 11:20, 11:30**

Morris v. Michigan State Board of Education, 472 F.2d 1207 (6th Cir. 1973) **27:340**

Morrison by Morrison v. Chicago Board of Education, 188 Ill.App.3d 588, 544 N.E.2d 1099, 136 Ill.Dec. 324 (1st Dist. 1989) **11:20**

Morton v. Board of Education of City of Chicago, 69 Ill.App.2d 38, 216 N.E.2d 305 (1st Dist. 1966) **11:40**

Morton Community Unit School District No. 709 v. J.M., 152 F.3d 583 (7th Cir. 1998) cert. den. 119 S.Ct. 1140, _U.S._, 143 L.Ed.2d 208 **13:140, 13:150**

Moule v. Paradise Valley Unified School District No. 69, 863 F.Supp. 1098 (D.C. Ariz. 1994) **12:234**

Mt. Vernon Education Association, IEA-NEA v. The Illinois Educational Labor Relations Board, 278 Ill.App.3d 814, 664 N.E.2d 1067, 215 Ill.Dec. 553 (4th Dist. 1996) **21:200, 21:202**

Mt. Healthy City School District Board of Education v. Doyle, 97 S.Ct. 568, 429 U.S. 274, 50 L.Ed.2d 471 (1977) app. after rem. 670 F.2d 59 (6th Cir. 1982) **17:450, 18:50**

Mozert v. Hawkins County, 827 F.2d 1058 (6th Cir. 1987) **14:210**

Muth v. Central Bucks School District, 839 F.2d 113 (3rd Cir. 1988) cert. den. 109 S.Ct. 103, cert. granted 109 S.Ct. 52, rev. sub nom. on other grounds *Dellmuth v. Muth*, 109 S.Ct. 2397, 491 U.S. 223, 105 L.Ed.2d 181 (1989) on rem. *Muth v. Central Bucks School District*, 884 F.2d 1384 (3rd Cir. 1989)**13:280**

Nabhani v. Coglianese, 552 F.Supp. 657 (N.D. Ill. 1983) **6:10**

Nabozny v. Podlesny, et. al., 92 F.3d 446 (7th Cir. 1996) **11:428**

National Education Association v. South Carolina, 98 S.Ct. 756, 434 U.S. 1026, 54 L.Ed.2d 775 (1978) affirming *U.S. v. State of South Carolina*, 445 F.Supp. 1094 (D.C. S.C. 1978) **14:520**

NCAA v. Tarkanian, 109 S.Ct. 454, 488 U.S. 197, 102 L.Ed.2d 469 (1988) **27:10**

NEA, IEA Classroom Teachers Council of District 15 (Kostka), 5 PERI 1067 (Executive Director's Recommended Decision and Order, March 13, 1989) **21:320**

Nevada v. Hall, 99 S.Ct. 1182, 440 U.S. 410, 59 L.Ed.2d 416, reh. den. 99 S.Ct. 2018, 441 U.S. 917, 60 L.Ed.2d 389 (1979) **22:160**

New Jersey v. T.L.O., 105 S.Ct. 733, 469 U.S. 325, 83 L.Ed.2d 720 (1985) **12:230, 12:238, 12:240, 12:300, 12:330**

New York Gaslight Club, Inc. v. Carey, 100 S.Ct. 204, 444 U.S. 897, 62 L.Ed.2d 132 (1980) **13:530**

Newborn v. Morrison, 440 F.Supp. 623 (N.D. Ill. 1977) **18:50**

Newsome v. Batavia Local School District, 842 F.2d 920 (6th Cir. 1988) **12:475**

Nickerson v. Thompson, 504 F.2d 813 (7th Cir. 1974) **13:70**

North Carolina State Board of Education v. Swann, 91 S.Ct. 1284, 402 U.S. 43, 28 L.Ed. 2d 586 (1971) **14:480**

Nowak v. St. Rita High School, 142 F.3d 999 (7th Cir. 1998) **17:360**

O'Brien v. Township High School District No. 214, 83 Ill.2d 462, 415 N.E.2d 1015, 47 Ill.Dec. 702 (1980) **22:100**

O'Connor v. Board of Education of School District No. 23, 645 F.2d 578 (7th Cir. 1981) cert. den. 102 S.Ct. 641, 454 U.S. 1084, 70 L.Ed.2d 619 (1981), on rem. 545 F.Supp. 376 **1:30**

O'Connor v. Ortega, 107 S.Ct. 1492, 480 U.S. 709, 94 L.Ed.2d 714 (1987) **12:240**

Oakdale Community Consolidated School District No. 1, v. County Board of School Trustees of Randolph County, 12 Ill.App.2d 260, 139 N.E.2d 795 (4th Dist. 1956) **8:220, 8:230**

Ohio Association of Independent Schools v. Goff, 92 F.3d 419 (6th Cir. 1996) **10:317**

Olesen v. Board of Education of School District 228, 676 F.Supp. 820 (N.D. Ill. 1987) **12:125, 12:127**

Olson v. Dubuque Community School District, 137 F.3d 609 (8th Cir. 1998) **17:355**

Oncale v Sundowner Offshore Services, Incorporated, et al., 83 F.3d 118 (5th Cir. 1995) reh and sugg. for reh. den. 95 F.3d 56, cert. granted 117 S.Ct. 2430, 520 U.S. 1263, 138 L.Ed.2d 192, rev. 118 S.Ct. 998, 523 U.S.75, 140 L.Ed.2d 201, on rem. 140 F.3d 595 (1998) **17:570**

Osteen v. Henley, 13 F.3d 221 (7th Cir. 1993) **12:475**

Ottawa Township High School District No. 140 of LaSalle County v. County Board of School Trustees, 106 Ill.App.2d 439, 246 N.E.2d 138 (3rd Dist. 1969) **8:260**

Oubre v. Entergy Operations, Inc. 118 S.Ct. 838, 522 U.S. 422, 139 L.Ed.2d 849 (1998) on rm. 136 F.3d 1342 **17:635**

Owen v. City of Independence, 100 S.Ct. 1398, 445 U.S. 622, 63 L.Ed.2d 673, on rem. 623 F.2d 550, reh. den.100 S.Ct. 2979, 446 U.S. 993, 64 L.Ed.2d 850 (1980) **22:30**

Paprocki v. Board of Education of McHenry Community High School District No. 156, 31 Ill.App.3d 112, 334 N.E.2d 841 (2nd Dist. 1975) **18:220, 18:230**

Parents of Student W v. Payallup School District No. 3, 31 F. 3d 1489 (9th Cir. 1994) **13:360**

Parish v. National Collegiate Athletic Association, 506 F.2d 1028 (5th Cir. 1975) **27:140**

Pearson v. Board of Education of Community Unit School District No. 5 of Macoupin County, 27 Ill.App.2d 12, 169 N.E.2d 7 (3rd Dist. 1960) **18:370**

Peck et al. v Upshur County Board of Education, 155 F.3d 274 (4th Dist. 1998) **14:120**

Peloza v. Capistrano Unified School District, 37 F.3d 517 (9th Cir. 1994) **14:230**

Pembaur v. Cincinnati, 106 S.Ct. 1292, 475 U.S. 469, 89 L.Ed.2d 452 (1986) **22:35**

Pennell v. Board of Education of Equality Community Unit School District 4, Gallatin County, 137 Ill.App.3d 139, 484 N.E.2d 445, 91 Ill.Dec. 886 (5th Dist. 1986) **16:230, 16:240**

People ex rel. Bartlett v. Vass, 325 Ill. 64 (1927) **8:110**

People ex rel. Bernardi Roofing Systems, Inc., 101 Ill.2d 424, 463 N.E.2d 123, 78 Ill.Dec. 945 (1984) **9:300**

People ex rel. Black v. Dukes, 108 Ill.App.3d 965, 439 N.E.2d 1305, 64 Ill.Dec. 497 (3rd Dist. 1982) vac. 96 Ill.2d 273, 449 N.E.2d 856, 70 Ill.Dec. 509 (1983) **3:30, 3:40**

People ex rel. Board of Education of School District 142, Cook County v. Illinois Board of Education, 62 Ill.2d 517, 344 N.E.2d 5 (1976) **14:80**

People ex rel. Carruthers v. Cooper, 404 Ill. 395, 89 N.E.2d 40 (1950) **24:170**

People ex rel. City of Canton v. Crouch, 79 Ill.2d 356, 403 N.E.2d 242 (1980) **23:60**

People ex rel. Cooper v. Carlson, 28 Ill.App.3d 569, 328 N.E.2d 675 (2nd Dist. 1975) **6:10, 6:40**

People ex rel. Davis v. Spence, 3 Ill.2d 244, 120 N.E.2d 565 (1954) **23:10**

People ex rel. Difanis v. Barr, 83 Ill.2d 191, 414 N.E.2d 731, 46 Ill.Dec. 678 (1980) **2:220, 6:10**

People ex rel. Head v. Board of Education of Thornton Fractional South High School District No. 215, 95 Ill.App.3d 78, 419 N.E.2d 505, 50 Ill.Dec. 397 (1st Dist. 1981) **18:20**

People ex rel. Hopf v. Barger, 30 Ill.App.3d 525, 332 N.E.2d 649 (2nd Dist. 1975) **5:20**

People ex rel. Howard v. Harris, 164 Ill.App. 136 (3rd Dist. 1911) **3:190**

People ex rel. Kolker v. Blair, 8 Ill.App.3d 197, 289 N.E.2d 688 (5th Dist. 1972) **3:190**

People ex rel. Latimer v. Board of Education of City of Chicago, 394 Ill. 228, 68 N.E.2d 305 (1946) **11:40, 14:35**

People ex rel. Lindheimer v. Hamilton, 373 Ill. 124, 25 N.E.2d 517 (1940) **26:100**

People ex rel. MacMahon v. Davis, 209 Ill.App. 117 (1st Dist. 1918) rev. 284 Ill. 439, 120 N.E. 326 **2:170, 2:180**

People ex rel. Mathews v. Board of Education of the City of Chicago, 349 Ill. 390, 182 N.E. 455 (1932) **26:140, 26:160**

People ex rel. Keenan v. McGuane, 13 Ill.2d 520, 150 N.E.2d 168(1958) **2:74**

People ex rel. McKeever v. Board of Education of Drummer Township High School, 176 Ill.App. 491 (3rd Dist. 1913) **10:10**

People ex rel. McLain v. Gardner, 408 Ill. 228, 96 N.E.2d 551 (1951) **8:110**

People ex rel. Myers v. Haas, 145 Ill.App. 283 (1st Dist. 1908) **3:30, 3:40**

People ex rel. Nordstom v. Barry, 11 Ill.2d 259, 142 N.E.2d 26 (1957) **23:10**

People ex rel. Recktenwald v. Janura, 59 Ill.App.3d 143, 376 N.E.2d 22, 17 Ill.Dec. 129 (1st Dist. 1978) **7:470**

People ex rel. Redfern v. Pennsylvania Central Company, 47 Ill.2d 412, 266 N.E.2d 334 (1971) **26:10**

People ex rel. Ryan v. Villa Park, 212 Ill.App.3d 187, 570 N.E.2d 882, 156 Ill.Dec. 406 (2nd Dist. 1991) **6:170**

People ex rel. Schlaeger v. Belmont Radio Corporation, 388 Ill. 11, 57 N.E.2d 479 (1944) **25:10**

People ex rel. Stanfield v. Pennsylvania Railroad, 3 Ill.2d 524, 121 N.E.2d 548 (1954) **25:10**

People ex rel. Talerico v. Lata, 96 Ill.App.2d 34, 238 N.E.2d 217 (1st Dist. 1968) **4:240**

People ex rel. Toman v. Siebel, 388 Ill. 98, 57 N.E.2d 378 (1944) **25:10**

People ex rel. Warren v. Drummet, 415 Ill. 411, 114 N.E.2d 364 (1953) **8:110**

People on rel. of Community Unit School District No. 1, Macon County v. Decatur School District No. 61, 45 Ill.App.2d 33, 194 N.E.2d 659 (3rd Dist. 1963) **8:110**

People v. Berger, 109 Ill.App.3d 1054, 441 N.E.2d 915, 65 Ill.Dec. 600 (2nd Dist. 1982) **11:40**

People v. Board of Education of District 170 of Lee and Ogle Counties, 40 Ill.App.3d 819, 353 N.E.2d 147 (2nd Dist. 1976) **6:220**

People v. Davis, 88 Ill.App.3d 728, 410 N.E.2d 673, 43 Ill.Dec. 473 (2nd Dist. 1980) **12:20, 20:60**

People v. Deatherage, 401 Ill. 25, 81 N.E.2d 581 (1948) **8:110, 8:220, 8:250**

People v. Dilworth, 169 Ill.2d 195, 661 N.E.2d 310,214 Ill.Dec. 456 (1996), cert. den. 116 S.Ct. 1692, 517 U.S. 1197, 134 L.Ed.2d 793 (1996) **12:300**

People v. Ellis, 57 Ill.2d 127, 311 N.E.2d 98 (1974) **27:300**

People v. Levisen, 404 Ill. 574, 90 N.E.2d 213, (1950) **11:42**

People v. Parker, 284 Ill.App.3d 860, 672 N.E.2d 813, 219 Ill.Dec.960 (1st Dist. 1996) **12:250, 12:317**

People v. Pruitt et al., 278 Ill.App.3d 194, 662 N.E.2d 540, 214 Ill.Dec. 974 (1st Dist. 1996) **12:315**

People v. R.G., 131 Ill.2d 328, 546 N.E.2d 533, 137 Ill.Dec. 588 (1989) **11:50**

People v. Taylor, 253 Ill.App.3d 768, 625 N.E.2d 785, 192 Ill.Dec. 630 (4th Dist. 1993) **12:238**

People v. Trustees of Schools, 42 Ill.App. 60 (2nd Dist. 1891) **2:170**

People v. White, 116 Ill.2d 171, 506 N.E.2d 1284, 107 Ill.Dec. 229 (1987) **4:380, 4:385**

Perry v. Sindermann, 92 S.Ct. 2694, 408 U.S. 593, 33 L.Ed.2d 570 (1972) **18:60**

Peters v. Board of Education of Rantoul High School District No. 193 of Champaign County, 97 Ill.2d 166, 454 N.E.2d 310, 73 Ill.Dec. 450 (1983) **15:160, 16:330**

Peterson v. Independent School District No, 811, 999 F.Supp. 665 (D. Minn. 1998) **12:495**

Peterson v. Minidoka County School District No. 331, 118 F.3d 1351 (9th Cir. 1997) **11:46**

Petrie v. Illinois High School Association, et al., 75 Ill.App.3d 980, 394 N.E.2d 855, 31 Ill.Dec. 653 (4th Dist. 1979) **27:320**

Phoenix Elementary School District No. 1 v Green, 943 P.2d 836 (1997) **12:125, 12:127**

Phillips v. Special Hearing Board of Boone and Winnebago Counties, 154 Ill.App.3d 799, 504 N.E.2d 1251, 105 Ill.Dec. 733 (2nd Dist. 1986) app. den. 115 Ill.2d 550, 511 N.E.2d 436, 110 Ill.Dec. 464 (1987) **8:200, 8:330**

Picha v. Wielgos, 410 F.Supp. 1214 (N.D. Ill. 1976) **12:240, 12:300, 12:330, 12:340**

Pickering v. Board of Education of Township High School District No. 205, Will County, Illinois, 88 S.Ct. 1731, 391 U.S. 563, 20 L.Ed.2d 811 (1968) **17:450**

Pierce v. Society of Sisters of the Holy Names of Jesus and Mary, 45 S.Ct. 571, 268 U.S. 510, 69 L.Ed 1070 (1925) **14:30**

Piquard v. Board of Education of Pekin Community High School District No. 303, 242 Ill.App.3d 477, 610 N.E.2d 757, 182 Ill.Dec. 888 (3rd Dist. 1993) **16:260**

Planned Parenthood of Southern Nevada v. Clark County School District, 941 F.2d 817 (9th Cir. 1991) **12:133; 12:135**

Plesnicar v. Kovach, 102 Ill.App.3d 867, 430 N.E.2d 648, 58 Ill.Dec. 616 (1st Dist. 1981) **22:100, 22:140**

Poling v. Murphy, 872 F.2d 757 (6th Cir. 1989) **12:128**

Polzin v. Rand, McNally & Co., 250 Ill. 561, 95 N.E. 623 (1911) **11:260**

Pontiac Township High School District No. 90 v. Regional Board of School Trustees for Livingston County, 183 Ill.App.3d 885, 539 N.E.2d 885, 132 Ill.Dec. 322 (4th Dist. 1989) **8:270**

Pope v. East Brunswick Board of Education, 12 F.3d 1244 (3rd Cir. 1993) **14:140**

Pope v. Parkinson, 48 Ill.App.3d 797, 363 N.E.2d 438, 6 Ill.Dec. 756 (4th Dist. 1977) **2:220**

Possekel v. O'Donnell, 51 Ill.App.3d 313, 366 N.E.2d 589, 9 Ill.Dec. 332 (1st Dist. 1977) **20:60**

Posteher v. Pana Community Unit School District, 96 Ill.App.3d 709, 421 N.E.2d 1049, 52 Ill.Dec. 186 (4th Dist. 1981) **11:365, 22:145**

Pottgen v. Missouri State High School Activities Association, 40 F.3d 926 (8th Cir. 1994) **27:262**

Premier Electric Construction Co. v. Board of Education of City of Chicago,
70 Ill.App.3d 866, 388 N.E.2d 1088, 27 Ill.Dec. 125 (1st Dist. 1979)
25:250

Prest by Prest v. Sparta Community Unit School District No. 140, 157
Ill.App.3d 569, 510 N.E.2d 595, 109 Ill.Dec. 727 (5th Dist. 1987) **12:10**

Price v. Young, 580 F.Supp. 1 (E.D. Ark. 1983) **12:400**

Princeville Community Unit School District No. 326, 13 PERI 1017 (IELRB
Opinion and Award, Dec. 6, 1996) **15:235**

Prosser v. Village of Fox Lake, 91 Ill.2d 389, 438 N.E.2d 134, 63 Ill.Dec. 396
(1982) **6:290**

Proulx by Proulx v. Illinois High School Association, 125 Ill.App.3d 781, 466
N.E.2d 620, 81 Ill.Dec. 34 (4th Dist. 1984) **27:100**

Pyle v. Hadley School Committee, 861 F.Supp. 157 (D.Mass. 1994) **12:128**

Quinn v. Stone, 211 Ill.App.3d 809, 570 N.E.2d 676, 156 Ill.Dec. 200 (1st
Dist. 1991) app. den. 141 Ill.2d 559, 580 N.E.2d 133, 162 Ill.Dec. 507
(1991) **7:415**

Ramos v. Waukegan Community Unit School District No. 60, 188 Ill.App.3d
1031, 544 N.E.2d 1302, 136 Ill.Dec. 527 (2nd Dist. 1989) **22:130**

Raney v. Board of Education of Gould School District, 88 S.Ct. 1697, 391
U.S. 443, 20 L.Ed.2d 727 (1968) **14:470**

Rankin v, McPherson, 107 S.Ct. 2891, 483 U.S. 378, 97 L.Ed.2d 315 (1987)
17:450

Reed v. Nebraska School Activities Association, 341 F.Supp. 258 (D.C. Neb.
1972) **27:340**

Regents of the University of California v. Bakke, 98 S.Ct. 2733, 438 U.S.
265, 57 L.Ed.2d 750 (1978) **14:420**

*Reinhardt v. Board of Education of Alton Community Unit School District
No. 11,* 61 Ill.2d 101, 329 N.E.2d 218 (1975) **18:90, 18:140, 18:160**

*Reinhardt v. Board of Education of Alton Community Unit School District
No. 11, Madison and Jersey Counties,* 19 Ill.App.3d 481, 311 N.E.2d 710
(5th Dist. 1974) vac. on other grounds 61 Ill.2d 101, 329 N.E.2d 218,
17:690

*Relph v. Board of Education of Depue Unit School District No. 103 of
Bureau County,* 84 Ill.2d 436, 420 N.E.2d 147, 50 Ill.Dec. 830 (1978)
15:50

Resnick v. East Brunswick Township Board of Education, 77 N.J. 88, 389
A.2d 944 (1978) **9:430**

*Rhinehart v. Board of Education of Bloomington School District No. 87,
McLean County,* 132 Ill.App.2d 1078, 271 N.E.2d 104 (4th Dist. 1971)
8:210, 8:270

Richards v. Board of Education of Township High School District No. 201,
21 Ill.2d 104, 171 N.E.2d 37 (1960) **15:110**

Richmond v. County Board of School Trustees of Whiteside County, 93
Ill.App.2d 142, 235 N.E.2d 657 (3rd Dist. 1968) **8:220**

*River Bend Community Unit School District No. 2 v. Illinois Human Rights
Commission et al.,* 232 Ill.App.3d 838, 597 N.E.2d 842, 173 Ill.Dec. 868
(3rd Dist. 1992) app. den. 147 Ill.2d 637, 606 N.E.2d 1235, 180 Ill.Dec.
158 (1993) **17:47**

River Grove School District No. 85 1/2, 3 PERI 1019 (IELRB Opinion and
Order, January 30, 1987) **21:520**

Riverside-Brookfield Township District No. 208, 5 PERI 1136 (IELRB
Decision and Order, July 25, 1989) **21:220**

Robertson by Robertson v. Granite City Community Unit School District No. 9, 684 F.Supp. 1002 (S.D. Ill. 1988) **13:100**

Robinson v. Illinois High School Association, 45 Ill.App.2d 277, 195 N.E.2d 38 (2nd Dist. 1963) cert. den. 85 S.Ct. 647, 379 U.S. 960, 13 L.Ed.2d 555 (1965) **12:495, 27:10, 27:260, 27:270**

Robinson v. Oak Park and River Forest High School, Board of Education District 200, 213 Ill.App.3d 77, 571 N.E.2d 931, 156 Ill.Dec. 951 (1st Dist. 1991) **12:440, 12:470, 12:480**

Rock Falls Elementary School District No. 13, 2 PERI 1150 (IELRB Opinion and Order, May 14, 1987) aff'd. sub nom. **21:200**

Rockford Newspapers, Inc. v. Northern Illinois Council on Alcoholism and Drug Dependence, 64 Ill.App.3d 94, 380 N.E.2d 1192, 21 Ill.Dec. 16 (2nd Dist. 1978) **2:220**

Rodiriecus L. By Betty H v. Waukegan School District No. 60, 90 F.3d 249 (7th Cir. 1996) **13:520**

Rojicek v. Community Consolidated School District No. 15, 888 F.Supp. 878 (N.D. Ill. 1995) **20:142**

Rolando v. School Directors of District No. 125, 44 Ill.App.3d 658, 358 N.E.2d 945, 3 Ill.Dec. 402 (3rd Dist. 1976) **18:120**

Romer v. Evans, 116 S.Ct. 1620, 517 U.S. 620, 134 L.Ed.2d 855 (1996) **17:570**

Rosa H. v. San Elizario Independent School District, 106 F.3d. 648 (5th Cir. 1997) **11:415**

Rosenberger v. Rector and Visitors of the University of Virginia, 115 S.Ct. 2510, 515 U.S. 819, 132 L.Ed.2d 700 (1995) **12:130**

Rutan v. Republican Party of Illinois, 110 S.Ct. 2729, 497 U.S. 62, 111 L.Ed.2d 52, reh. den. 111 S.Ct. 13, 111 L.Ed.2d 828 (1990) **17:460**

S-1 v. Turlington, 635 F.2d 1210 (4th Cir. 1985) **13:370**

San Antonio Independent School District v. Rodriguez, 93 S.Ct. 1278, 411 U.S. 1, 36 L.Ed.2d 16, reh. den. 93 S.Ct. 1919, 411 U.S. 959, 36 L.Ed.2d 418 (1973) **24:60, 24:62**

Sanders v. Louisiana High School Athletic Association, 242 So.2d 19 (La. App. 1970) **27:10**

Sanguigni v. Pittsburgh Board of Public Education, 968 F.2d 393 (3rd Cir. 1992) **17:450**

Schaefer v. Board of Education of Arlington Heights School District No. 25, 157 Ill.App.3d 884, 510 N.E.2d 1186, 110 Ill.Dec. 155 (1st Dist. 1987) app. den. 116 Ill.2d 576, 515 N.E.2d 126, 113 Ill.Dec. 317 (1987) **16:220**

Schafer v. Board of Public Education of School District of Pittsburgh, 732 F.Supp. 565 (W.D. Pa. 1990) **17:180**

Scheller v. Trustees of Schools, Township 41 North, 67 Ill.App.3d 857, 384 N.E.2d 971, 24 Ill.Dec. 104 (2nd Dist. 1978) **9:50**

Scherr v. Woodland Consolidated School District No. 50, 867 F.2d 974 (7th Cir. 1989) **17:170**

School Board of Nasau County v. Arline, 107 S.Ct. 1123, 480 U.S. 273, 94 L.Ed.2d 307 (1987) **17:410**

School District No. 153, Cook County v. School District 154 1/2, Cook County, 54 Ill.App.3d 587, 370 N.E.2d 22, 12 Ill.Dec. 399 (1st Dist. 1977) **13:325**

School District of Abington Township v. Schempp, 83 S.Ct. 1560, 374 U.S. 203, 10 L.Ed.2d 844 (1963) **14:50, 14:200**

Schreiner v. City of Chicago, 406 Ill. 75, 92 N.E.2d 133 (1950) **26:140**

Schumann v. Kumarich, 102 Ill.App.3d 454, 430 N.E.2d 99, 58 Ill.Dec. 157 (1st Dist. 1981) **4:240, 4:420**

Scoma v. Chicago Board of Education, 391 F.Supp. 452 (N.D. Ill. 1974) **11:10**

Scott v. Board of Education, 20 Ill.App.2d 292, 156 N.E.2d 1 (4th Dist. 1959) **18:175**

Scoville v. Board of Education of Joliet Township High School District 204, 425 F.2d 10 (7th Cir. 1972) **12:130**

Seamon v. Snow, 84 F.3d 1226 (10th Cir. 1996) **11:420, 11:430**

Seim v. Board of Education of Community Unit School District No. 87 of McLean County, 21 Ill.App.3d 386, 315 N.E.2d 282 (4th Dist. 1974) **16:90**

Service Employees International Local Union No. 316 v. Illinois Educational Labor Relations Board and Carbondale Community High School District No. 165, 153 Ill.App.3d 744, 505 N.E.2d 418, 106 Ill.Dec. 112 (4th Dist. 1987) **21:180**

Sesser Community Unit District No. 196, Franklin County v. County Board of School Trustees of Franklin County, 74 Ill.App.2d 152, 219 N.E.2d 364 (5th Dist. 1966) **8:220**

Settle v. Dickson County School Board, 53 F.3d 152 (6th Cir. 1995) **14:220**

Shelton v. National Collegiate Athletic Association, 539 F.2d 1196 (9th Cir. 1976) **27:30**

Sherbert v. Verner, 83 S.Ct. 1790, 374 U.S. 398, 10 L.Ed.2d 965 (1963) **14:210**

Sherman v. Community Consolidated School District No. 21 of Wheeling Township, 980 F.2d 437 (7th Cir. 1992) cert. den. 113 S.Ct. 2439, 508 U.S. 950, 124 L.Ed.2d 658 (1993) **14:53**

Shoresman v. Burgess, 412 F.Supp. 831 (N.D. Ill. 1976) **3:160**

Sidwell v. Griggsville Community Unit School District No. 4, 146 Ill.2d 467, 588 N.E.2d 1185, 167 Ill.Dec. 1055 (1992) **22:100, 22:112**

Sieck v. Oak Park-River Forest High School District No. 200, 807 F.Supp. 73 (N.D. Ill. 1992) **7:170; 12:410**

Simcox v. Board of Education of Lockport Township High School District No. 205, 443 F.2d 40 (7th Cir. 1970) **15:230**

Sims v. Chicago Transit Authority, 351 Ill.App. 314, 115 N.E.2d 96 (1st Dist. 1953) rev. on other grounds 4 Ill.2d 60, 122 N.E.2d 221 (1954) **11:365, 20:205**

Skinner v. Railway Labor Executives' Association, 109 S.Ct. 1402, 489 U.S. 602, 103 L.Ed.2d 639 (1989) **12:300**

Smith v. Board of Education of Urbana School District No. 116, 708 F.2d 258 (7th Cir. 1983) **16:130**

Smith v. Metropolitan School District, Perry Township, 128 F.3d 1014 (7th Cir. 1997) **11:415**

Spann for Spann v. Tyler Independent School District, 876 F.2d 437 (5th Cir. 1989) **22:35**

Spath v. National Collegiate Athletic Association, 728 F.2d 25 (1st Cir. 1984) **27:190, 27:280**

Spaulding Lumber Company v. Brown, 171 Ill. 487, 49 N.E. 725 (1898) **9:310**

Spear v. North Shore School District No. 112, 291 Ill.App.3d 117, 683 N.E.2d 218, 225 Ill.Dec. 274 (2nd Dist. 1997) app. den. 175 Ill.2d 555, 689 N.E.2d 147, 228 Ill.Dec. 726 **20:142**

Spinelli v. Immanuel Evangelical Lutheran Congregation, Inc., 144
Ill.App.3d 325, 494 N.E.2d 196, 98 Ill.Dec. 269 (2nd Dist. 1986) aff'd. in
part, rev. in part 118 Ill.2d 389, 515 N.E.2d 1222, 113 Ill.Dec. 915 **7:10,
7:40, 18:370, 18:380, 18:390, 18:400**

Stachura v. Truszkowski, 763 F.2d 211 (6th Cir. 1985) **6:225**

Stamper v. Board of Education of Elementary School District No. 143, 141
Ill.App.3d 884, 491 N.E.2d 36, 96 Ill.Dec. 222 (1st Dist. 1986) **15:160,
15:170**

State v. Patzer, 382 N.W.2d 631 (North Dakota 1986) **11:42**

State v. Rivinius, 328 N.W.2d 220 (North Dakota 1982) **11:42**

State v. Schmidt, 505 N.E.2d 627 (Ohio 1987) **11:42**

*Staunton Community Unit School District No. 6 v. Illinois Educational
Labor Relations Board,* 200 Ill.App.3d 370, 158 N.E.2d 751, 146 Ill.Dec.
788 (4th Dist. 1990) **21:510**

Stein v. County Board of School Trustees of DuPage County, 40 Ill.2d 477,
240 N.E.2d 668 (1968) **3:20**

Stein v. Howlett, 52 Ill.2d 570, 289 N.E.2d 409 (1972) **7:470**

Stein v. Plainwell Community Schools, 610 F.Supp. 43, rev. 822 F.2d 1406
(6th Cir. 1987) **14:60**

Stephenson v. Davenport Community School District, 110 F.3d. 1303 (8th
Cir. 1997), **12:127**

Stevens v. Umsted, 131 F.3d 697 (7th Cir. 1997) **11:430**

Stiff v. Eastern Illinois Area of Special Education, 251 Ill.App.3d 859, 621
N.E.2d 218, 190 Ill.Dec. 349 (4th Dist. 1993) **22:140**

Stone v. Graham, 101 S.Ct. 192, 449 U.S. 39, 66 L.Ed.2d 199 (1980) reh.
den. 101 S.Ct. 904, 449 U.S. 1104, 66 L.Ed.2d 832 on rem. 612 S.W.2d
133 (S.Ct.of Ky. 1981) **14:124, 14:200**

*Strasburger v. Board of Education Hardin County Coummunity Unit
School District No. 1 et al.,* 143 F.3d 351 (7th Cir. 1998) **18:60**

*Streator Township High School District No. 40 v. County Board of School
Trustees of Livingston County,* 14 Ill.App.2d 251, 144 N.E.2d 531 (2nd
Dist. 1957) **8:110**

Strejcek v. Board of Education of Berwyn School District No. 100, 78
Ill.App.3d 400, 397 N.E.2d 448, 33 Ill.Dec. 942 (1st Dist. 1979) **16:110**

Stroman v. Colleton County School District, 981 F.2d 152 (4th Cir. 1992)
17:450

Swain v. Hillsborough County School Board, 146 F.3d 855 (11th Cir. 1998)
17:355

*Swanson v. Board of Education of Foreman Community Unit School
District No. 124, Mason County,* 135 Ill.App.3d 466, 481 N.E.2d 1248, 90
Ill.Dec. 337 (4th Dist. 1985) **19:140**

Swanson v. Board of Police Commissioners, 197 Ill.App.3d 592, 555 N.E.2d
35 144 Ill. Dec. 138 (1990), cert. den., 133 Ill.2d 874 (1990) **6:227**

Swanson v. Guthrie Independent School District No. I-1, 942 F. Supp. 511,
(W.D. Okla. 1996) **11:44, 11:45**

T.G. on Behalf of D.G. v. Board of Education of Piscataway, New Jersey, 576
F.Supp. 420 (D.C. N.J. 1983) aff'd. 738 F.2d 420, cert. den. 105 S.Ct. 592,
469 U.S. 1086, 83 L.Ed.2d 701 (1984)**13:150**

Tanari v. School Directors of District No. 502, County of Bureau, 69 Ill.2d
63, 373 N.E.2d 5, 14 Ill.Dec. 874 (1977) **22:210**

Taylor v. Phoenixville School District, 174 F.3d 142 (3rd Cir. 1999) **17:362**

Teresa P. v. Berkeley Unified School District, 724 F.Supp. 698 (N.D. Cal. 1989) **10:140**

Terry v. Ohio, 88 S.Ct. 1868, 392 U.S. 1, 20 L.Ed.2d 889 (1968) **12:238**

Tetmeir v. Board of Education of School District No. 149, Cook County, 5 Ill.App.3d 982, 284 N.E.2d 280 (1st Dist. 1972) **15:100**

Texas v. United States, 118 S.Ct. 1257, 523 U.S. 296, 140 L.Ed2d 406 (1998) **1:350, 1:370, 3:190**

Texas Education Agency v. Stamos, 817 S.W.2d 378 (Tex. Ct. App. 1991) **27:220**

Thomas v. Board of Education of Community Unit School District of Pope County, 117 Ill.App.3d 374, 453 N.E.2d 150, 721 Ill.Dec. 845 (5th Dist. 1983) **2:210**

Thomas v. Chicago Board of Education, 60 Ill.App.3d 729, 377 N.E.2d 55, 17 Ill.Dec. 865, rev. on other grounds 77 Ill.App.2d 165, 395 N.E.2d 538, 32 Ill.Dec. 308 (1st Dist. 1978) **12:20, 22:100, 22:130**

Thomas v. Cincinnati Board of Education, 918 F.2d 618 (6th Cir. 1990) **13:520**

Thomas v. Review Board, 101 S.Ct. 1425, 450 U.S. 707, 67 L.Ed.2d 624 (1981) **14:210**

Thornton Township High School District No. 205, 5 PERI 1134 (Executive Director's Recommended Decision and Order, July 10, 1989) **21:360**

Thrash v. Board of Education School District No. 189, 106 Ill.App.3d 182, 435 N.E.2d 866, 62 Ill.Dec. 68 (5th Dist. 1982) **17:540**

Thrasher v. General Casualty Co. of Wisconsin, 732 F.Supp. 966 (W.D. Wis. 1990) **12:190**

Tinker v. Des Moines Independent School District, 89 S.Ct. 733, 393 U.S. 503, 21 L.Ed.2d 731 (1969) **12:120**

Todd, et al. v Rush County Schools, et al., 133 F.3d 984 (7th Cir. 1998) reh. and sugg. for reh. den. 139 F.3d 571, cert. den. 119 S.Ct. 68, __U.S.__, 142 L.Ed.2d 53 **12:234, 12:235**

Tometz v. Board of Education Waukegan City School District No. 61, 39 Ill.2d 593, 237 N.E.2d 498 (1968) **11:120**

Tomkins v. Public Service Electric and Gas Company, 568 F.2d 1044 (3rd Cir. 1977) **17:500**

Treasury Employees' Union v. Van Raab, 109 S.Ct. 1384, 489 U.S. 656, 103 L.Ed.2d 685 (1989) **12:300**

Trico Community Unit School District No. 176 v. County. Board of School Trustees, 8 Ill.App.2d 494, 131 N.E.2d 829 (5th Dist. 1956) **8:230, 8:260**

Turner v. Board of Education North Chicago Community High School District 123, 54 Ill.2d 68, 294 N.E.2d 264 (1973) **11:180, 11:220**

Unifed School District No. 259 v. Fowler and Fowler v. Unified School District No. 259, 117 S.Ct. 2503, 521 U.S. 1115, 138 L.Ed.2d 1008 (1997) **13:161**

United States v. Epperson, 454 F.2d 769 (4th Cir. 1972) **12:315**

United States v. Lopez, 115 S.Ct. 1624, 514 U.S. 549, 131 L.Ed.2d 626 (1995) **12:155**

United States v. Paradise, 107 S.Ct. 706, 480 U.S. 149, 102 L.Ed.2d 854 (1987) **14:530**

United Steelworkers of America v. Lukens Steel Co., 969 F.2d 1468 (3rd Cir. 1992) **17:710**

Urofsky v. Gilmore, 167 F.3d 191 (4th Cir 1999) **12:122, 17:475**

Van Dyke v. Board of Education of School District No. 57, Cook County, 115 Ill.App.2d 10, 254 N.E.2d 76 (1st Dist. 1969) **16:55**

Vander Malle v. Ambach, 667 F.Supp. 1015 (S.D. N.Y. 1987) **13:220**

Vande Zande v. Wisconsin Department of Administration, 44 F.3d 538 (7th Cir. 1995) **17:370**

Vernonia School District 47J, v. Wayne Acton, et ux., etc., 115 S.Ct. 2386, 515 U.S. 646, 132 L.Ed.3d 564 (1995) **12:234**

Vienna School District No. 55 v. Illinois Educational Labor Relations Board, 162 Ill.App.3d 503, 515 N.E.2d 476, 113 Ill.Dec. 667 (4th Dist. 1987) **15:432, 21:590**

Village of Elmwood Park v. Forest Preserve District of Cook County, 21 Ill.App.3d 597, 316 N.E.2d 140 (1st Dist. 1974) **1:270**

Virden Community Unit School District No. 4, 4 PERI 1060 (IELRB Hearing Officer, March 31, 1988) **21:90**

Vukadinovich v. Board of School Trustees of the Michigan City Area Schools, 978 F.2d 403 (7th Cir. 1992) **17:450**

Wade v. Granite City Community Unit School District No. 9, Madison County, 71 Ill.App.2d 34, 218 N.E.2d 19 (5th Dist. 1966) **18:20, 18:90**

Walker v. Cronin, 107 Ill.App.3d 1053, 438 N.E.2d 582, 63 Ill.Dec. 651 (1st Dist. 1982) **13:515**

Wallace v. The Batavia School District 101, 68 F.3d 1010 (7th Cir. 1995) **12:250**

Wallace v. Jaffree, 105 S.Ct. 2479, 472 U.S. 38, 86 L.Ed.2d 29 (1985) **14:40, 14:50**

Waller v. Board of Education Century School District No. 100, 13 Ill.App.3d 1056, 302 N.E.2d 190 (5th Dist. 1973) **18:180, 18:190, 18:220**

Walter v. Board of Education of Quincy School District No. 172, 93 Ill.2d 101, 442 N.E.2d 870, 66 Ill.Dec. 309 (1982) **16:340**

Wapella Education Association, IEA-NEA v. Illinois Educational Labor Relations Board, 177 Ill.App.3d 153, 531 N.E.2d 1371, 126 Ill.Dec. 532 (4th Dist. 1988) **21:420**

Ward v. Hickey, 996 F.2d 448 (1st Cir. 1993) **17:480**

Warner v. Independent School District No. 625, 134 F.3d 1333 (8th Cir 1998), cert. den. 119 S.Ct. 67, __ U.S.__, 142 L.Ed.2d 53 **13:530**

Washington v. Davis, 96 S.Ct. 2040, 426 U.S. 229, 48 L.Ed.2d 597 (1976) **14:520**

Waters v. Churchill, 114 S.Ct. 1878, 511 U.S. 661, 128 L.Ed.2d 686 (1994) **17:450**

Wauconda Community Unit School District No. 118, Lake County v. LaSalle National Bank, 143 Ill.App.3d 52, 492 N.E.2d 995, 97 Ill.Dec. 336 (2nd Dist 1986) **24:190**

Waverly Community Unit School District No. 6, 5 PERI 1002 (IELRB Opinion and Order, November 23, 1988) **21:190**

Weaver v. Nebo School District, 29 F.Supp. 1279 (D. Utah 1998) **17:571**

Weiss v. Collinsville Community Unit School District No. 10, Madison County, 119 Ill.App.3d 68, 456 N.E.2d 614, 74 Ill.Dec. 893 (5th Dist. 1983) **22:140**

Welch v. Board of Education of Bement Community Unit School District No. 5 of Piatt County, 45 Ill.App.3d 35, 358 N.E.2d 354, 3 Ill.Dec. 679 (4th Dist. 1977) **18:120, 18:190, 18:210**

Wells v. Board of Education of Community Consolidated School District No. 64, Cook County, 85 Ill.App.2d 312, 230 N.E.2d 6 (1st Dist. 1967) **18:100, 18:210, 18:220**

Werner v. Community Unit School District No. 4, Marshall County, 40 Ill.App. 491, 190 N.E.2d 184 (2nd Dist. 1963) **18:220**

West Chicago School District 33 v. Illinois Educational Labor Relations Board, 218 Ill.App.3d 304, 578 N.E.2d 232, 161 Ill.Dec. 105 (1st Dist. 1991) **21:190**

West Virginia University Hospital v. Casey, 111 S.Ct. 1138, 499 U.S. 83, 113 L.Ed.2d 68 (1991) **13:570, 22:240**

Wheatley v. Board of Education of Township High School District No. 205, Cook County, 113 Ill.App.3d 129, 446 N.E.2d 1257, 68 Ill.Dec. 860 (1st Dist. 1983) **16:280**

Whitfield v. Simpson, 312 F.Supp. 889 (N.D. Ill. 1970) **12:470**

Widmar v. Vincent, 102 S.Ct. 269, 454 U.S. 263, 70 L.Ed.2d 440 (1981) **14:120, 14:140**

Wiemerslage v. Maine Township High School District 207, 29 F.3d 1147 (7th Cir. 1994) **12:35**

Wilcoxen v. Board of Education of Canton Union School District No. 66, 116 Ill.App.3d 380, 452 N.E.2d 132, 72 Ill.Dec. 200 (3rd Dist. 1980) **26:210**

Wiley v. National Collegiate Athletic Association, 612 F.2d 473 (10th Cir. 1979) **27:570**

William C. v. Board of Education of the City of Chicago, 71 Ill.App.3d 793, 390 N.E.2d 479, 28 Ill.Dec. 312 (1st Dist. 1979) **13:320, 13:325**

Williams v. Board of Education of Hardin County Community Unit School District No. 1, 166 Ill.App.3d 765, 520 N.E.2d 954, 117 Ill.Dec. 603 (5th Dist. 1988) app. den. 121 Ill.2d 587, 526 N.E.2d 841, 122 Ill.Dec. 448 (1988) **16:70**

Willis v. Anderson Community School Corporation, 158 F.3d 415 (7th Cir. 1998), cert. den. 119 S.Ct. 1254, __U.S.__, 143 L.Ed.2d 351 (1999) **12:235**

Willis v. Conopco, Inc. 108 F.3d. 282 (11th Cir. 1997) **17:380**

Wilson v. Board of Education Limestone Walters School District No. 316, 127 Ill.App.3d 433, 468 N.E.2d 995, 82 Ill.Dec. 341 (3rd Dist. 1984) **16:220, 16:230, 16:250**

Wilson v. Webb, 869 F.Supp. 496 (W.D. Ky. 1994) **11:430**

Winks v. Board of Education of Normal Community Unit School District No. 5 of McLean County, 78 Ill.2d 128, 398 N.E.2d 823, 34 Ill.Dec. 832 (1979) **17:170, 17:180**

Winters v. Board of Education of Piasa Community Unit School District No. 9 of Macoupin County, 66 Ill.App.3d 918, 384 N.E.2d 519, 23 Ill.Dec. 725 (4th Dist. 1978) **17:47, 17:460**

Wirth v. Green, 96 Ill.App.3d 89, 420 N.E.2d 1200, 51 Ill.Dec. 642 (3rd Dist. 1981) **8:330**

Wisconsin v. Pea Ridge School District, 855 F.2d 560 (8th Cir. 1988) **12:190**

Wisconsin v. Yoder, 92 S.Ct. 1526, 406 U.S. 205, 32 L.Ed.2d 15 (1972) **14:30**

W.J.L v. Bugge, 573 N.W.2d 677 (Minn. Sup. Ct. 1998) **11:440**

Wolman v. Walter, 97 S.Ct. 2593, 433 U.S. 229, 53 L.Ed.2d 714 (1977) **14:100**

Wood v. Strickland, 95 S.Ct. 992, 420 U.S. 308, 43 L.Ed.2d 214 (1975) reh. den. 95 S.Ct. 1589, 42 U.S. 921, 43 L.Ed.2d 790 (1975) **12:70, 12:80, 12:475**

Woodman v. Litchfield Community Unit School District No. 12, Montgomery County, 102 Ill.App.2d 330, 242 N.E.2d 780 (5th Dist. 1968) **22:130, 22:140**

Woods v. East St. Louis School District No. 189, 147 Ill.App.3d 776, 498 N.E.2d 801, 101 Ill.Dec. 477 (5th Dist. 1986) **15:310, 15:320**

Wort v. Vierling, 778 F.2d 1233 (7th Cir. 1985) **11:170**

Wright v. Council of the City of Emporia, 92 S.Ct. 2196, 407 U.S. 451, 33 L.Ed.2d 51 (1972) **14:460**

Wygant v. Jackson Board of Education, 106 S.Ct. 1842, 476 U.S. 267 (1986) reh. den. 106 S.Ct. 3320, 478 U.S. 1014, 92 L.Ed.2d 728 **14:530**

Yeo v. Town of Lexington, 131 F.3d 241 (1st Cir. 1997) cert. den. 118 S.Ct. 2060, __U.S.__, 141 L.Ed.2d 138 (1998) **12:135**

Youth Opportunities Unlimited v. Board of Public Education, 769 F.Supp. 1346 (W.D. Pa. 1991) **14:130**

Yuen v. Board of Education of Community Unit School District No. 46, Kane County, 77 Ill.App.2d 353, 222 N.E.2d 570 (3rd Dist. 1966) **18:370**

Yuhas v. Libbey-Owens-Ford Company, 562 F.2d 496 (7th Cir. 1976) cert. den. 98 S.Ct. 1510, 435 U.S 934, 55 L.Ed.2d 531 (1978) **17:47**

Zamora v. Pomeroy, 639 F.2d 662 (10th Cir. 1981) **12:310, 12:330**

Zink v. Board of Education of Chrisman, 146 Ill.App.3d 1016, 497 N.E.2d 835, 100 Ill.Dec. 657 (4th Dist. 1986) **15:40, 16:300**

Zobrest v. Catalina Foothills School District, 113 S.Ct. 2462, 506 U.S. 813, 125 L.Ed.2d 1 (1993) **13:160, 14:00**

Zorach v. Clauson, 92 S.Ct. 679, 343 U.S. 306, 96 L.Ed. 954 (1952) **14:35**

Zykan v. Warsaw Community School Corporation, 631 F.2d 1300 (7th Cir. 1980) **17:480**

QUICK REFERENCE INDEX

This Quick Reference Index refers to question numbers rather than to page numbers. The reader is cautioned that, where a topic is discussed in a series of questions, only the first question is listed here. The reader often will find additional information under questions immediately following those listed.

The author has tried to make the entries in this Quick Reference Index reasonably narrow and detailed. The user who is trying to locate a narrow question of law, therefore, is advised to first look for that specific topic. If that proves unfruitful, look for a broader topic that may lead to a productive area of the text.

- A -

AAA, *see American Arbitration Association*
Abatement, asbestos, *see Asbestos*
Abatement, tax, 23:270
　　state aid calculations, 24:100
　　debt service grant, 9:255
Absence, leaves of, *see Leaves*
Absence, student, 11:40, 11:60
Absence, principal, 19:50
Absence, teacher, 20:40
Absent from meetings, 5:40, 5:70
　　minutes, 6:300
Abstain from voting,
　　conflict of interest, 3:150
　　counting votes, 6:290
　　recording the vote, 6:270
Abused child, *see Child abuse*
Academic penalties, 10:330
Academic credit, 10:40, 10:70
Academic duties, 20:20, 20:50
Academic freedom, 17:482
Academic records, 7:270, 7:350
Academic standards,
　　graduation requirements, 10:30
　　IHSA, 27:220
　　no pass, no play, 11:405
　　school board, 10:10
　　state, 1:300
　　testing, *see Testing, academic*
Academic watch list, 1:320
Access, equal, 14:140
Access, police, *see Police*

Access to education, 12:80
Access to facilities, 9:430
Accessibility, *see Handicapped accessibility*
Accounts and accounting, 25:50, 25:200
Accrual accounting, 25:50
Acquisition of tenure, 16:50
　　maximum time for, 15:250,
　　federal programs, 16:120
Act of God, 24:150
　　effect on athletics, 27:100
Activities accounts, *see Funds*
Activities, employees,
　　moonlighting, 17:640
　　political, 17:460
Activities, extra-curricular, *see Activities, student*
Activities, fees, 11:260,
　　see also Fees
Activities, insurance, 11:280
Activities, off-campus,
　　in loco parentis, 22:140
　　loitering, 12:35
　　student disciplinary, 12:30
　　teacher disciplinary 18:160
Activities, political, *see Political activities*
Activities, student,
　　academic eligibility, 11:405
　　accident insurance, 11:280
　　creation of, 21:166
　　fees, 11:260

interscholastic, 27:10
  cooperative programs, 27:60
  rules, 27:30
  non-teacher supervisors for, 20:50
  no pass, no play, 11:405
  protection from suit, 22:140
  record of, 7:260
  rules of conduct, 12:40
  IHSA, 27:110
  spectators, 12:40
  supervision of extra-curricular
    activities, 18:170
  student selection for clubs, 11:400
  supervision of,
    chaperons, 20:50
    dismissal of teacher, 18:170
  in loco parentis, 22:140
  suspension or expulsion from,
    12:495
  teacher assignments,
    generally, 15:230
  tenure, 16:130
  transportation, 11:394, 25:110
ADA, see Americans with
    Disabilities Act
ADA, see Average daily attendance
Adjournment, see Meetings
Administration, school, 19:10
Administrative Code,
    Illinois, 1:40
Administrative expenditure
    limitation, 25:25
Administrative meetings, 6:40
Administrative procedures, 2:167
Administrative review,
    detachment, annexation,
      8:280, 8:340
    Freedom of Information Act,
      7:520
    grievance arbitration, 21:542
    property assessments, 23:70
    student expulsion, 12:480
    student transportation, 11:380
    teacher dismissal hearing, 18:320,
      18:360
Administrator certification,
    19:60, 19:75
  alternative route, 19:80
Administrator contracts,
    length, 19:93
    multi-year, see Multi-year
      contract
    oral, 19:94
    performance, 19:102

rollover, 19:100
  survival of a rollover, 19:102
  tenure, 19:110
  who may be given multi-year
    contracts, 19:92
Administrator, department
    chairs, 19:75
Administrator dismissal, 19:160
Administrator duties,
  adoption of rules, 2:167
  economic interest statement
    notice, 3:115
  principal's duties, 19:20
  records appeal, 7:500
  report of attacks, 17:660
  superintendent's duties, 19:10
Administrator, filing of economic
    interest statement, 3:90
Administrator, principal, 19:20
Administrator salaries,
  use of tort fund to pay, 23:221
Administrator, superintendent,
    19:10
Administrator, tenure, 19:110
Adult education, 10:62, 10:190
Advertising, 12:135
Advisory committee, student
    disciplinary 12:60
Advisory referendum, see
    Referendum
Advocate, special education,
    13:565
Affirmative action,
  admission to school programs
    14:420
  hiring to remedy discrimination
    14:530
  reduction in force, 20:180
Affirmative defense,
  employee sexual harassment,
    17:505
After school programs,
  prayer meetings, 14:150
  day care, 10:170
Age, compulsory school, 11:10
Age discrimination,
  athletic eligibility, 27:262
  retirement age, 17:630
  salary schedule credit, 15:420
Age, interscholastic sports, 27:260
Age, retirement, 17:630
Age, special education services,
    13:40

Agency,
  employee sexual harassment,
    17:504
  student sexual harassment,
    11:417
Agency shop, 21:330
Agenda, *see Meetings*
Agreement, collective bargaining,
    see Collective bargaining
Agreement, cooperative
    (intergovernmental),
  charter school, 1:560
  units of local government, 1:270
  with other school districts, 10:210
Agreement, joint,
  annexing districts, 8:140
  building site, 9:80
  collective bargaining, 21:70
  general authority to form, 10:210
  special education, 13:430
  teacher strike, 13:310
  teacher tenure, 16:90, 16:100
Agreement, last chance, 17:710
Aggregate tax levy, *see Tax levy*
Aide, teacher, *see Teacher*
AIDS, 13:100
Alcohol abuse, *see Drugs and*
    alcohol
Alternative certification,
  for administrators, 19:80
  for teachers, 15:27
Alternative educational setting,
    see Special Education
Alternative education plan,
    see Alternative school
Alternative school (Safe
    Schools Law),
  alternative education plan, 12:550
  collective bargaining, 21:74
  defined, 12:500
  disruptive student defined, 12:530
  education plan, 12:550
  employer, 21:75
  establishment of, 12:510
  establishing additional, 12:520
  objection to removal, 12:560
  special education, 12:540
American Arbitration
    Association, 21:470
Americans with Disabilities Act,
    13:30, 17:350
  athletics, 27:262

  employment, 17:350
    disability defined, 17:355,
      17:362
    employer duty of care, 17:384
    information requested, 17:390
    offer of accommodation, 17:400
    reasonable accommodation,
      17:360
    undue hardship, 17:370
Annexation, *also see New*
    school district
  boundary change, 8:80, 8:100
  charter district, 8:300
  non-charter district, 8:110
  withdrawal of petition, 9:165
Annual report, 25:190
Anticipation, state aid, 26:110,
    26:175
Anticipation, tax,
  financial difficulty, 26:280
  interfund loans, 26:40
  short term debt, 26:110
  tax anticipation notes, 26:150
Appeals, *see Tax appeals; see*
    Administrative review;
    see Challenge
Application for recognition, 1:210
Arbitrage, 24:188
Arbitration award, 21:390, 21:542
  appeal of, 21:540
Arbitration, closed meetings,
  as a reason for closed session,
    6:170
  exception to Open Meetings Act,
    21:60
  in general, 6:10
Arbitration defined, 21:450
Arbitration, grievance, 21:520
Arbitration, interest, 21:460,
    21:490, 21:530
Arbitrator,
  mediation, fact finding and
    arbitration 21:450
  in general, 21:460
  teacher dismissal case, 18:280
Architect,
  condemnation of buildings, 9:350
  Freedom of Information Act,
    7:450
  selection of, 25:225
  site and construction fund, 25:140
Arrest, employee, 17:680
Arrest, student, 12:300, 12:340

Asbestos,
Asbestos Abatement Act, 9:410
injury, 22:190
safety in general, 9:320, 22:190
sale of property, 9:145
Assessed valuation,
amendment of levy, 23:130
certificate of tax levy, 23:80
consolidation of districts, 8:10
failure to adopt a budget, 25:35
general state aid computation,
24:100
tax rate in general, 23:175
Assessment,
general state aid, 24:100
kindergarten readiness 11:20
property tax, , 23:40
special education, 13:190
student, 10:300
under assessment of property,
23:70
Assessor,
property, 23:40
school income generally, 24:30
Assets,
consolidation of districts, 8:140
school district generally, 24:20
Assignment, teacher,
extra duties, 15:230
teacher transfers, 15:160
tenure
extra duty, 16:130
in position, 16:55
At-will employment, 20:142
Athletic fields,
acquisition, 9:70
construction, 9:220
financing, 26:210
Athletics, *also see Illinois High
School Association*
daily physical education, 10:120
drug testing, 12:234
eligibility,
absence of constitutional right,
11:400, 27:130
academic requirements,
11:405, 27:220
age limitations, 27:260
attendance requirements,
27:190
authority of IHSA, 27:30
no pass, no play, 11:405
physical examination, 27:170

residence requirements,
27:240
transfers, 27:250
insurance, 11:280
prayer, 14:55
regulation of, 27:30
revenues, 25:80, 25:170
rules of conduct, 12:40
student records, 7:260, 7:300
At-large school board member,
2:10, 2:27, 2:30
Attacks on school personnel,
17:660
Attacks on students,
child abuse, 11:310
corporal punishment, 12:90
sexual harassment, 11:410
Attendance,
centers, boundaries, 11:120
part time, 13:110
requiring employees to work,
17:140
Saturday duties, 15:220
state aid computation, 24:100
student, *see Student attendance*
teacher, 15:210, 15:370
zones, 11:120
Attorney, communications with,
7:450
Attorney fees, *see Fees*
Attorney General,
incompatible offices, 3:40
Attorney, right to legal counsel,
expulsion hearing, 12:380
reclassification of principal,
19:140
special education, 13:530
tenured teacher dismissal
hearing, 18:270
Auction, 9:140, 24:300
Audit,
failure to file, 2:190
Freedom of Information Act,
7:450
revolving fund, 25:170
tort fund expenditures, 23:221
Authority,
city and county, 1:260
election, *see Election authority*
federal, 1:10
health and safety, 9:345
regional trustees, *see Regional
Board of School Trustees*

school board authority,
    curriculum, 10:10
    delegation of, 2:163
    generally, 1:100
    non-delegable, 2:163, 2:210
    powers and duties, 2:130
    school board member, 2:135
    school board member acting
        outside scope, 2:144, 22:75
    State Board of Education, 1:130
    State Superintendent, 1:200
    student grades, 10:320
    teacher, 12:10
    textbooks, 10:350
Average daily attendance,
    Capital Development Board,
        9:260
    consolidation incentives, 8:70
    state aid, 24:100
    tuition, 11:200
Awards, student, 27:570

- B -

Baccalaureate, 14:62
    use of facilities for, 14:145
Back door referendum,
    bonds, 26:190
    generally, 23:240
    notice, 4:313
    number of issues, 4:300
    public policy issues, 4:50
    working cash fund, 26:240
Background checks, see Criminal
        background check
Ballot,
    bargaining unit election, 21:260
    school election, 4:40, 4:110, 4:200,
        4:250
Bargaining, see Collective
        bargaining
Bargaining unit, see Collective
        bargaining unit
Battery, 17:660
Beepers, 12:165
**Benefits, discrimination against
        teacher certificate
        holders,** 15:28
Benefit-detriment analysis,
        8:250, 8:330
Bids and bidding requirements,
    architectural and engineering
        services, 25:225
    bidding generally, 25:220
    bid rigging, 25:270

insurance and self insurance,
        25:223
    local bidders, 25:260, 25:261
    negotiating with low bidders,
        25:222
    prevailing wages, 9:300
    real estate, 9:140
    records disclosure, 7:450
    rejection of bids, 25:250
    responsible bidder, 25:230
    transportation contracts, 25:115
    unsuccessful low bidder, 25:240
Bilingual education,
    generally, 10:140, 10:305
    state aid, 24:80
Bill of particulars, 18:90, 18:350
Board of Education, State,
        see Education, State Board of
Board of Elections, State,
        see Elections, State Board of
Boards of education, see
        School boards
Boards of school directors,
        see School boards
**Bona fide occupational
        qualification,** 17:620, 17:630
Bonded, see Performance bond
Bond and interest fund,
    construction debt service grant,
        9:255
    generally, 25:120
Bonds and bond issues,
    authority for, 26:190
    buildings,
        generally, 9:200
        site and construction fund,
            25:140
    consolidated districts, see Debt,
        consolidated districts
    debt limit, 26:100
    debt service grant, 9:255
    generally, 26:190
    printing of, 25:220
    real estate or improvements,
        26:210
    referendum, 4:40
    retirement of, 23:195
    tort judgment, 23:220, 26:250
    types and purposes, 26:190
    working cash fund 26:50, 26:240
Books, also see Textbooks
    financial, failure to report, 2:190
    funds generally, 25:60
    objections to, see Censorship

revolving funds, 25:170
textbooks, 10:380
Booster groups, 27:410, 27:500
Borrowing, school district,
  also see Debt
  investment of borrowed funds,
    24:188
  fund to fund loans, 26:10
  purchase of school bus, 25:280
Boundaries, district,
  changes in, 8:80, 8:110, 8:150
  property outside of, 9:80
  taxable property, 23:10, 23:50
Boundaries, school attendance,
  11:120
Breach of contract,
  administrator, 19:160
  dismissal of probationary teacher,
    18:40
  teacher resignation, 15:70
Bribery, *see Illegal acts*
Budget,
  administrative expenditures,
    25:25
  adoption of, 25:10
  amendment of, 25:30
    after referendum, 23:134
  basis for tax levy, 23:100
  failure to adopt a budget, 25:35
  file with county clerk, 25:10
  financial difficulty, 26:280
  purchasing, 25:210, 25:280
Building and school site bonds,
  see Bonds and bond issues
Buildings, *see Facilities*
Buildings, access, *see Handicapped*
  accessibility
Bumping,
  administrators, 19:120, 19:170
  noncertificated employees, 20:180
  teachers, 16:235, 16:320
Burden of proof,
  boundary change petition, 8:210
  employee dismissal,
    charges, 17:680
    generally, 18:340
    irremediable conduct, 18:200
Bus driver, 20:210
Bus, discipline on, 12:380
Buses, *see Transportation*
Bussing for integration, 14:480

- C -

Cafeteria supervisor, 20:30

Cafeterias,
  inspection, 9:345
  funds, 25:170
Calendar, school, *see School term*
Campaign financing,
  candidate disclosure, 3:120
  expenditure of public funds to
    influence election, 4:340
Campaign literature, *see Election*
  literature
Candidates, school board,
  board secretary's duties, 4:80
  campaign expenditures, 3:120
  nominating procedures, 4:110
  withdrawal, 4:200
  write-ins, 4:280, 4:410
Canvass of votes, 4:400
  duties generally, 4:70
Capital Development Board
  (CDB),
  construction project, 9:266
  generally, 9:230
  maintenance project, 9:267
  rent fund, 25.150
Capital improvements, 25:160
Career education, 15:20
Cash accounting, 25:50
Categorical state aid, *see State aid*
Causes for dismissal,
  administrator, 19:160
  noncertificated, 20:140
  teacher, 18:10, 18:100
Cellular telephones, 12:165
Censorship, 10:400
  curriculum, 17:482
Censure of board member, 6:227
Census, 1:120, 2:45
Certificate of tax levy, 23:80,
  23:120,
Certification, administrative,
  19:60, 19:75, 19:110
  alternative route, 19:80
Certification of candidates, *see*
  Election certification
Certification, teacher,
  alternative route, 15:27
  discrimination against initial,
    15:28
  discrimination against provisional
    alternative, 15:28
  generally, 15:10
  home school, 11:42
  initial, 15:25
  master, 15:25

nurse, 15:45
provisional alternative, 15:27
renewal of, 15:80
standard, 15:25
teacher certificate, 15:40
tenure, 16:60
valid and active, 15:23
working as an aide, 16:110
Challenge (objection),
detachment, annexation petition,
8:200, 8:280, 8:310
nominating petition, 4:220
personnel records, 7:150
student records, 7:350
voter petition, 4:315
right to hold office, 3:196
Chaperons, 20:50
Charter school district,
board of education, 2:10
detachment-annexation, 8:105,
8:300
elections, 4:30
generally, 1:70
Charter school,
appeal of denial, 1:520
creation of, 1:510
defined, 1:500
employees of, 1:590
number of, 1:540
private schools, 1:550
proposal, 1:510, 1:600
requirements, 1:530
teachers, 1:590
leave of absence, 1:640
qualifications, 1:620
term of charter, 1:610
Child abuse,
failure to report, 11:330
teacher certificate revocation,
15:60
false report, 11:350
generally, 11:310
superintendent of schools,
reporting, 19:10
Child labor law,
attendance at school, 11:40
work permits, 10:150
**Children and Family Services,
Department of,**
employee personnel files, 7:140
reporting child abuse, 11:330
truancy, 11:80
Children with disabilities, *see*
Special education

Christmas programs, 14:123,
14:225
Citizens advisory committee, *see*
Advisory committee
Civil rights, *also see Constitutional
issues*
attorney fees, 22:240
special education, 13:530
employee speech, 17:450, 17:482
employment discrimination,
14:510
good faith defense, 22:30
indemnity and immunity, 22:60
racial issues,
desegregation of schools,
14:400
employment, 14:510
students,
dress code, 12:125
due process, 12:70,
political expression, 12:120
searches, 12:230,
suspension and expulsion,
12:300
violation of, 22:30,
Class I and Class II, *see*
County school units
Class size,
generally, 10:20
special education, 13:180
Clerk, county, *see County clerk*
Clerk, school board, *see Secretary*
Closed meeting, *see Meetings*
Clubs and Activities,
pregnancy 11:403
selection process, 11:400
Coaching requirements, *see*
*Illinois High School
Association*
Collective bargaining, 21:10,
also see Negotiations
**Collective bargaining
agreements,**
class size, 10:20
election of remedies, 21:206
evaluations, 15:380
extra duties,
assignment of, 15:230
creation of, 21:166
tenure, 16:130
fair share, 17:100

just cause discipline or dismissal,
see *Just cause*
last chance agreement, 17:710
recall, 16:340
salary freeze, see *Salary*
school year, 10:230
staff reduction, 16:220
work assignments, 15:180, 15:230
**Collective bargaining
alternatives,** 21:145
**Collective bargaining,
alternative schools,** 21:74
Collective bargaining election,
21:250 *See also Representation*
Collective bargaining meetings,
application of Open Meetings Act,
6:10, 21:60
closed sessions 6:170
**Collective bargaining
representative,** 21:240,
21:320, 21:430
Professional Development
Committee, 15:85
Collective bargaining unit,
21:210, 21:280, 21:320
Combined school districts,
generally, 8:10
incentives, 8:70
tax levy, see *Tax Levy*
Commencement, see *Graduation*
Committee, advisory, see
Advisory committee
Committee of ten, 8:15, 8:165,
8:295
Committees, school board,
application of Open Meetings Act,
6:35
power to appoint, 2:210
Common school fund,
delivery to school districts, 24:160
source of state aid, 24:90
Common school land, 9:10
Common schools, 1:50
Community college,
high school graduation
requirements, 10:30
teacher certification, 15:20
Community service requirement,
10:34
Compatibility, see *Incompatible
offices*
Compensation, board members,
school boards, 3:50
State Board of Education, 1:160

Compensation, employee,
Fair Labor Standards Act
generally, 17:60
hours and overtime, 20:70
minimum salary, 15:400
requirement to work on holidays,
17:140
salaries, see *Salaries*
Compensation for damages,
punitive damages, 22:12
tort judgment bonds, 26:250
**Compensation, school board
secretary,** 3:50, 5:50
Compensation, teacher,
see *Salaries*
Compensation, treasurer,
5:90, 5:120
Compensation, Workers',
employee right to sue, 22:80
tort judgment bonds, 26:250
Competency testing, see
Testing, academic
Complaints against employees,
6:225
Compulsory school attendance,
generally, 11:10
kindergarten, 11:30
religion, 14:30
truancy, 11:70, 11:90
Computers,
employee use, 17:475
student use, 12:122
Computers, purchase of,
financing, 23:207
leases, 23:207
State Board of Education loans,
25:295
Condemnation, 9:40, 9:350
Condoms distribution, 10:95
Confidential communication, see
Privileged communication
Confidential employee, 21:110
**Confidential information,
disclosure,** 6:227
Confidential records,
closed meetings, 6:170, 6:320
employees, 7:80
Freedom of Information Act,
7:450
students, 7:200, 7:320
Confirmation class,
exemption from compulsory
attendance, 11:40

release for religious instruction,
14:35
Conflict of interest, 3:130, 3:150
Conflicting offices, *see*
Incompatible offices
Consent to sexual harassment,
11:416
Consolidation of schools,
administrator contract
implications, 19:105
debt, *see Debt*
generally, 8:60
incentives, 8:70, 8:145
tax levy, *see Tax Levy*
tenure implications, 16:150
Constitutional issues,
censorship, *see Censorship*
church and state, 14:10
civil rights violations and
defenses, *see Civil rights*
community service requirement,
10:34
desegregation, 14:400
dress codes, 12:125, 17:455
due process, *see Due process*
duty to protect, 11:430
eminent domain, 9:50
employees,
drug testing, 17:730
private conduct, 18:160
property right, 18:40,
liberty interests, 6:226, 18:60
search, 17:730
sexual orientation, 17:570
speech, 17:450, 17:480
extra-curricular activities,
clubs, 11:400
athletics 27:130
immorality, dismissal for, 18:140
incompatibility of offices, 3:40
intergovernmental agreements,
1:270
liberty interests,
disclosure of causes for
dismissal, 6:226
infringement of, 18:60
local government, 1:260
loitering, 12:35
loyalty oath, 4:180
minority employment, 14:510
police powers, 12:300
political literature, 4:380
political speech,
employee, 17:450, 17:470
student, 12:120

prayer meetings, 14:150
property interests,
extra-curricular activities,
11:400, 27:140
probationary teacher midterm,
18:40
support personnel, 20:140
tenure, 17:600; *also see Tenure*
racial discrimination, 14:400
religious instruction, 14:35,
14:200
school board powers, 1:90
State Board of Education, 1:130
students,
fees, 11:260
organizations, 11:400
searches, 12:230
seizure, 12:250
speech, 12:120
suspension, 12:300
use of school facilities,
generally, 9:432
religious groups, 14:120
Construction,
construction project, 9:266
maintenance project, 9:267
Construction fund, 25:140
Construction grants, 9:250, 9:265
Construction of schools,
authority for, 9:200
financing,
assistance, 9:230
bond issues, 26:190
construction grants, 9:230
debt service grants, 9:265
site and construction fund,
25:140
special education facilities,
23:200
safety standards, 9:320
Consulting teacher, 15:380
Consumer education, 10:50
Continuing education, 19:70
Contract, administrator,
see Administrator
Contract, collective bargaining,
see Collective bargaining
Contract for deed, 9:44, 9:110
Contract, installment purchases,
25:280
Contractor,
bidding requirements, *see Bids*
and bidding
economic interest statements,
3:90

employees of,
  bargaining obligations, 21:120
  criminal background check,
    17:30
  prevailing wage, 9:300
  Freedom of Information Act,
    7:400
  minority contractors, 14:540
  performance bond, 9:305
  transportation, 25:285
Contract, teacher, see Teacher
Contractual continued service,
  see Tenure
Control of students, 12:30
Convenience accounts, 25:175
Cooperative agreement, see
  Agreement
Corporal punishment, 12:190
  child abuse report, 11:310
Corporate replacement tax, see
  Personal property
  replacement tax
Corrupt Practices Act, 3:130
Cost of living adjustment
  (COLA), 21:580
Counsel, legal, see Attorney
County board, 11:110
County Board of Review,
  property tax assessment, 23:40
  school board intervention for
    under assessment, 23:70
County clerk,
  canvass of election, 4:400
  economic interest statement, 3:90,
    3:115
  election authority, 4:60,
  local political committee 4:370
  tax anticipation, 26:150
  tax levies, 23:50, 23:80, 23:110,
    25:10
County health department, 9:345
County school units, 1:60,
  filing of reports, 2:190
  title to property, 9:20
  treasurer, 5:90, 5:110
County treasurer, 5:100
Creationism, 14:200, 14:210, 14:230
Creation science, 14:231
Crime, infamous, see Infamous
  crime
Criminal acts generally, see
  Illegal acts

Criminal acts, student
  cooperation with police, 12:360
  guns, 12:156
  reporting, 12:350
Criminal background check,
  17:20,
  independent contractor, 17:30
  bus driver, 20:214
  liability for failure to check, 17:33
Criminal conviction,
  board members, 2:70
  employees generally, 17:690
  liability for obscuring, 17:35
  teachers, 15:63
Cross examination,
  expulsion, 12:477
Crossing guards, 9:380
Cruelty, 18:100, 18:120
Curriculum,
  freedom of speech, 17:470, 17:482
  generally, 10:10
  objections, 14:210
  principal's duties, 19:20
  regulation of publications, 12:130
  religion in, 14:200
  Religious Freedom Restoration
    Act, 14:210
  school board authority, 10:10
  secular nature, 14:30
Curriculum-related
  organizations, 14:140
Custody,
  student, 11:190, 11:220
  student-athlete, 27:252

- D -

Damages, 11:417; also see
  Punitive damages
Dangerous student, 13:370
Day care center, 10:170
Day, school (clock hours),
  see School Day
DCFS, see Children and Family
  Services, Department of
Deactivation of high school, 9:120
Deaf student, 13:160
Debt,
  consolidated districts, 8:45
  dissolved districts, 8:140
  intergovernmental agreements,
    1:270
  limits, 26:100, 26:150, 26:175,
    26:270

long-term, 26:190
short-term, 26:110
Debt service grant, 9:255
**Decertification of bargaining
    unit,** 21:280
Delayed state aid payment,
    1991 legislation, 24:175
    state aid anticipation, 26:175
Delegation of power, 2:163
Demotion of principal, 19:140
**Department of Children and
    Family Services,** *see
    Children and Family Services,
    Department of*
Department of Education, *see
    Education, U.S. Department of*
Department of Labor, *see Labor,
    Department of*
Department of Public Health, *see
    Public Health, Department of*
Department of Revenue, *see
    Revenue, Department of*
Depositary, 24:180
Desegregation,
    court order, 14:450
    generally, 14:400
    multi-district plan, 14:490
    plan, 14:460
    relief from court order, 14:500
Detachment, *see Annexation*
Detention, student, 12:45
Developer, *see Residential developer*
Diagnostic services,
    children with disabilities, 13:120,
        13:140, 13:220
    parochial school students, 14:100
Diploma, *see Graduation*
Disability, employee,
    defined, 17:355
    dismissal due to, 17:410
    pregnancy, 17:170, 17:200
    use of sick leave, 15:580
    worker compensation, 17:240
    *also see Americans with
        Disabilities Act*
Disability, public official,
    1:170, 2:70
Disability, student with, *see
    Special education*
Disciplinary records,
    employee, 7:90, 7:130
    Freedom of Information Act,
        7:450
    student, 7:270

Discipline, employee,
    closed meeting, 6:170
    for public speech, 17:450
    just cause, 15:235
    remediability, 18:190
Discipline, student, *see Student
    discipline*
Disclosure, economic, 3:80
Discrimination,
    age, 17:620, 15:420
    contractors, 15:540
    employment, 14:510
    Equal Pay Act, 17:70,
    marital, 17:47
    pregnancy,
        employee 17:220
        student 11:403
    racial, 14:400
    religious, 14:10, 14:25
    sex,
        compensation, 17:70
        maternity, 17:220
        interscholastic teams, 27:300
        rule classifications, 27:300
        title IX, 11:150
Disease, communicable, 11:240,
    17:10
Disease, instruction, 10:100
Dismissal for cause,
    administrator, 19:160
    employee
        criminal conduct, 17:680
        damage to reputation, 18:175
        generally, 17:600
        insubordination, 17:720,
            18:150
        speech, 17:450
    noncertificated, 20:140
    grievances, 18:25
    teacher,
        probationary, 18:10
        tenured, 16:20, 18:100
Dismissal hearing,
    appointment of hearing officer,
        18:305
    noncertificated employee, 20:140
    probationary teacher, 18:50
    superintendent, 19:170
    tenured teacher, 18:250
Dismissal notice, *see Notice*
Dismissal, teacher,
    causes,
        damage to reputation, 18:175
        just cause, 18:25

public disclosure, 6:226
tenured teacher dismissal
    causes, 18:100
    third year probation, 15:280
extra duties, 15:235
layoff, 16:190
procedures,
    probationary teacher, 18:10
    tenured teacher, 16:20, 18:70,
        18:250
Disruptive student, see *Alternative
    school*
Dissolution of school district,
generally, 8:80
survival of administrator's
    contract, 19:105
Distribution of condoms, 10:95
Divorce,
report of records to parents, 10:340
residence after divorce, 11:180
**Doctor's certification, physical
    education,** 10:120
Doctor's certification, sick leave,
    17:160, 17:170, 17:210
Dog search, 12:310
Donations,
acquisition of property, 9:40
defined, 24:190
Dress code,
student, 12.125
employee, 17:455
Driver education,
drop-outs, 10:64
fees, 11:270
non-students, 10:62
proficiency, 10:60
Driving to school,
drug tests, 12:235
Drop-outs, 10:64, 10:82
re-enrollment, 11:41
Drugs and alcohol,
bus driver, 20:230
drug dealers, 12:110
reporting student possession,
    12:156
revocation of teaching certificate,
    15:60
student dependence, 11:225
Drug testing,
athletes, 12:234
bus drivers, 20:230
employees, 17:730
extra-curricular activities, 12:235
student drivers, 12:235

Dual school district, 1:70, 8:36,
    23:180
Due process,
administrator, 19:160
criminal charges, 17:680
defined, 12:70
noncertificated employee, 20:140
procedural,
    administrator, 19:75
    non-tenured teacher, 18:40
    tenured teacher, 18:70, 18:100,
    special education, 13:230, 13:340,
        13:500
    student discipline, 12:390, 12:475
    athletics and extra curricular
        activities, 12:495
    special education, 13:360
substantive, 12:70
Dues deduction, 17:100
Dues, membership, 2:200
Duties of administrators, see
    Administrators
Duties of school boards, see
    School boards
Duty free lunch, 15:200
Duty of care,
duty to protect, 9:320, 11:430
in general, 22:200
invitees, 22:210
school busses, 22:145
students, 11:417
Duty to defend, 11:435
Duty of fair representation,
    21:320
Duty to bargain, 21:130, 21:202

- E -

Early childhood programs, 13:96,
    13:180
EAV, see *Assessed valuation*
Economic development, 23:60,
    23:270
Economic interest statement, see
    Statement of economic interest
Educational fund,
amended budget, 25:40
borrowing, 26:10, 26:70
tax levy, 23:170, 23:250
uses of, 25:80, 25:140
**Educational Labor Relations
    Act,** 21:10
**Educational Labor Relations
    Board,** 21:30
Educational malpractice, 22:170

Educational materials, 10:350
    financial interest in, 3:170
Educational service region, 1:220,
    also see Regional
    superintendent
Educational support personnel,
    see Noncertificated employees
Education of All Handicapped
    Children Act, *see Individuals*
    with Disabilities Education Act
Education Officers Electoral
    Board, 4:230, 4:240
Education, State Board of,
    academic standards,
        minimum school day, 10:270
        performance testing, 10:300
        proficiency exams, 10:50
        recognition of schools, 1:310
        summer school, 10:130
        also see Quality review; School
        improvement; Watch list
    assistance to schools, 8:60
    capital grants, 9:240
    charter school proposals, 1:510
    creation of, 1:130
    enforcement,
        civil rights, 14:410
        Student Records Act, 7:390
    incompatibility of offices, 3:40
    prohibited interest, 3:170
    safety regulations,
        fire, 9:360
        generally, 22:190
        school property, 9:320
    school finance,
        accounting, 25:50
        budget, 25:20
        debt, 26:270
        delivery of state aid, 24:160
        failure to budget, 25:35
        payment for purchases, 25:210
        revolving funds, 25:170
        state aid, 24:100
    special education, 13:120, 13:170,
        13:200, 13:260, 13:505
    student discipline, 12:90
    teacher certification,
        certified-qualified, 16:300
        endorsement, 15:40
        substitutes, 15:300
    teacher dismissal, 18:270, 18:310
    teacher evaluation, 15:350, 15:380
        by administrators, 19:70
    teacher workload, 15:180

Education, State
    Superintendent of,
    act of God, 24:150
    duties, 1:200
    qualifications, 1:190
    school district organization, 8:10,
        8:40, 8:295
    teacher certification, 15:60
    withhold general state aid, 25:27
Education, U.S. Department of,
    1:20
Ejection from game,
    coach, 27:124
    player, 27:122
Election,
    authority, 4:60, 4:250, 4:280,
        4:330, 4:390
    bond issue, *see Bond issue election*
    certification of ballot, 4:80, 4:250,
        4:290, 4:330
    Code, 4:40, 4:80, 4:180, 4:360,
        4:380
    dates of, 4:30, 4:31, 4:50
    duties, 4:60
    emergency, *see Emergency election*
    employee representation, *see*
        Collective bargaining election
    expiration of term, 4:31
    federal employees, *see Federal*
        employees
    literature, 4:340, 4:380
    notice, *see Notices*
    official, local, 4:80
    school board members, 4:20, 4:90
    tax rate, *see Tax rate election*
    term of office, 4:31
    territorial representation, 2:25
Election of benefits, 17:270
Election of officers, 5:10
Electioneering, 4:340
Elections, State Board of, 4:60,
    4:370, 4:400
Electronic paging devices, 12:165
E-mail,
    student, 12:122
Emancipated minor,
    defined, 11:290,
    financial responsibility, 9:420
    records, 7:210
    request for hearing, 13:525
    residence, 13:72
    athletic eligibility, 27:252
Emergency, child with disability,
    13:510

Emergency days, 10:230
Emergency election
  (referendum), 4:50, 4:320
Emergency expenditures,
  bidding, 25:220,
  borrowing, 26:100
Emergency, medical, 22:150
Emergency meetings, see *Meetings*
Emergency work, 17:140
Eminent domain, 9:50
Employee benefits,
  noncertificated employees, 20:120
  teachers, 15:500, 15:540
Employees,
  disciplinary representation,
    17:740
  dismissal, see *Dismissal*
  suspension, see *Suspension*
Employment discrimination,
  14:510
Employment history,
  investigation, 17:33
  obscuring of, 17:35
Employment of board member's
  spouse, 3:160
Employment of student, 10:150
  student training for, 13:165
Energy expenditures, 25:135,
  25:300
  bonds, 26:190
Energy savings contracts, 25:300
Enrollment, see *Student enrollment*
Equal Access Act, 14:140
Equal funding of education,
  24:62
Equal Pay Act, 17:70
Equalization, 23:40, 23:130
Equalized assessed valuation, see
  Assessed valuation
Equipment, see *Personal property*
ESR, see *Educational Service Region*
Ethics statement, see *Statement of*
  economic interest
Evaluation of teachers, 15:350
Evolution, teaching of, 14:230
Exams, see *Testing*
Exclusionary rule, 12:300
Exclusive bargaining
  representative, see *Collective*
  bargaining representative
Executive session, see *Meetings,*
  closed
Expedited hearing (special
  education), 13:373

Expenditures, administrative,
  23:221, 25:25
Expenses of board members,
  newly elected school board
    members, 3:61
  school board members, 3:50
  State Board of Education, 1:160
Expert witness, 13:570, 22:240
Expression, see *First Amendment*
Expulsion, student,
  appeals, 12:480
  attempt to enroll in another
    school district, 12:490
  authority to expel, 12:450
  due process, 12:475
  generally, 12:170, 12:440
  procedures, 12:470
  right to confront an accuser,
    12.477
  special education student, 13:370,
    13:520
  transcript of hearing, 12:478
Extending probation, 15:260
Extra-curricular activities, see
  Activities, student
Extra duties, teacher,
  assignment to, 15:230
  creation of, 21:166
  dismissal for just cause, 15:235
  rights of tenure, 16:130

- F -

Facilities, school,
  Capital Development Board,
    9:260
  condemnation, 9:350
  distribution of religious literature,
    14:120
  financial aid, 9:230
  maintenance, 22:190
  maintenance fund, 25:90
  maintenance grants, 9:267, 9:268
  special education, 13:410
Facilities, use of,
  baccalaureate ceremonies, 14:145
  outside organizations, 9:430
  religious groups, 14:130
Fact-finder, 21:450
Fair Labor Standards Act,
  application to schools, 17:60
  wage and hour provisions, 20:70
Fair market value,
  eminent domain, 9:60
  property assessments, 23:40

Fair representation, duty of,
21:230
Fair share deduction,
defined, 17:110
mandatory, 21:310, 21:330
Family Educational Rights and
Privacy Act, 7:10, 7:190
Federal employees, 3:15
Federal Mediation and
Conciliation Service, 21:470
Fees, *also see Tuition*
adult education, 10:190
attorney fees,
civil rights generally, 22:240
Open Meetings Act, 6:60
Parental Right of Recovery
Act, 12:110
special education, 13:530
Student Records Act, 7:390
copying of records, 7:430
distinguished from tuition, 11:260
driver education, 11:270
fair share, 21:330
mediators, 21:470
parental institute, 10:245
school income, 24:10
special education,
advocate, 13:565
expert witness, 13:570
state income, 24:90
students, 11:260
textbooks, 10:370
transportation, 11:390
use of facilities, 9:220, 9:440
waiver of,
generally, 11:260
textbooks, 10:390
Field trip, 22:160
Filing requirements,
bargaining unit petition, 21:250
detachment petition, 8:180
economic interest statement, 3:90,
3:170
financial report, 25:190
joint agreement, 13:440
meeting notice, 6:140
rules and regulations, 2:130
school board candidacy, 4:110
tax levy, 23:90
textbooks adopted, 10:350
unfair labor practice charge,
21:360
Financial difficulty, 26:270
recovery from, 26:300

Financial institutions, 24:180
Financial reports,
failure to provide, 2:190
Freedom of Information Act,
7:400
Local Records Act, 7:20
school districts, 25:190
student organizations, 25:180
tax increment financing district,
23:65
Firearms, 12:160
Fire marshal, 9:330, 9:350
Fire safety and protection,
buildings, 9:340, 9:360
fire protection service, 1:280
funds, 25:135, 26:190
First amendment,
access to facilities,
generally, 9:432
religious, 14:130
employee association and
expression,
curriculum, 14:230
keeping of records, 7:120
private speech, 17:470
school speech, 17:480
political communication,
campaign committee, 4:380
employee speech, 17:450
religion, 14:10
student expression (speech),
12:120
religious topic, 14:220
Fiscal year, 25:205
FMCS, *see Federal Mediation and*
Conciliation Service
Foreign language, 10:30, 10:70
Forfeiture of office or removal,
see Removal from office
Formation of school districts,
also see New school district
by combination, 8:10
origin of, 1:60
Foundations, educational, 24:200
Fraternities and sororities,
12:170
Frauds, statute of, 19:94
Free appropriate public
education,
special education implications,
13:20
student fees, 11:260
Free schools, 1:50
Free speech, *see First amendment*

Free textbooks, 10:380
Freedom of Information Act,
    defined, 7:390
    exemptions, 7:450
    generally, 7:10
    meeting minutes, 6:315
    student records, 7:320
Freeze, salary, see Salary
Fringe benefits, see Employee
    benefits
Full recognition, 1:210
Full-time temporary teacher,
    15:320
Fundamental right, education as,
    24:62
Funding bonds,
    back door referendum, 23:250
    generally, 26:190
Funding education, equality of,
    24:62
Funds,
    accounting, 25:60, 26:10
    activities accounts, 25:175
    bond and interest fund,
        generally, 25:120
        levy for, 23:195
    building construction,
        accumulation of funds for,
            9:210
        site and construction fund,
            25:140
        special education, 13:410
    capital improvement fund, 25:160
    educational fund, 25:80
    insufficient,
        debt limit, 26:270
        payment of teachers, 15:470
    invested, 24:186
    municipal retirement fund, 25:130
    operations and maintenance fund,
        25:90
    payment of, 25:210
    public, 4:340, 14:35
    rent fund, 25:150
    revolving funds, 25:170
    site and construction fund, 25:140
    state aid, 24:90
    summer school, 10:130
    tax rates, 23:170
    transfers, see Interfund loans and
        transfers
    transportation fund, 25:110
Fund raising, 24:200

- G -

Gangs, 12:18
Gays, see Homosexuality
GED, see High school equivalency
Gender equity, see Sex
    discrimination
General election,
    cost, 23:160
    consolidation, annexation,
        detachment, 8:120
    dates, 4:50
    laws, 4:20, 4:330
General state aid, see State aid
Gift Ban Act,
    application of, 3:300
    employees, 17:750
    generally, 3:300
    gift defined, 3:310
    gift giver defined, 3:320
    gifts permitted, 3:330
    penalties, 3:340
Gifted and talented,
    defined, 10:105
    levy for, 23:205
    state aid, 24:80
Gifts, see Donations
God, acts of, see Acts of God
Good faith bargaining,
    defined, 21:350
    impasse 21:440
    unfair labor practices, 21:390
Grade levels, 11:240, 15:30
Grade level weighting, 24:110
Grade reduction, 10:330
Grades and grading, 10:320, 11:405
Graduation,
    community service requirement,
        10:34
    prayer at, 14:60
    requirements for, 10:30, 10:303
    special education, 13:290, 13:505
    student records, 7:170, 7:210
Grants,
    acceptance of, 24:190
    construction, 9:250,
    legality of receipt, 24:10
    maintenance project, 9:268
    types of, 24:80
Grievance, dismissal, 18:25
Grievance procedure, 21:460,
    21:510
    work-related injury, 22:80
Guardianship, 13:71

Guns,
    defined, 12:156
    on school property, 12:150
    reporting, 12:156

- H -

Handicap, see Disability
Handicapped accessibility,
    defined, 9:215
    special education accessibility
        13:30
Handicapped student, see Special
    education
Harassment, see Sexual harassment
Hazardous materials,
    safety requirements, 22:180, also
        see Asbestos
    sale of property, 9:145,
Health, Department of Public, see
    Public Health
Health and safety,
    act of God, 24:150
    fire inspections, 9:370
    generally, 22:190
    inspection of cafeterias, 9:345
    transportation, 11:380
Health and Safety Act, 9:370
**Health examinations and
    immunizations,**
    employee, 17:10
    student, 11:240
    teacher, mental fitness, 15:100
Health insurance,
    bidding, 25:223
    maternity coverage, 17:220
    self-insurance, 25:223
    student athletes, 11:280
    Teachers Health Insurance
        Security Fund, 15:530
Hearing,
    certification revocation, 15:60
    detachment and annexation,
        8:200, 8:320
    dismissal, see Dismissal hearing
    expedited (special education),
        13:373
    expulsion, see Expulsion
    joint agreement withdrawal,
        13:460
    pre-termination, 20:140
    public, see Public hearing
    reduction in force, 16:280
    special education, see Special
        education

    tax levy, 23:140
**Hearing officer, special
    education,** see Special
    education
Hearing officer, tenure dismissal,
    appointment of, 18:305
    pre-hearing, 18:250
    remediability determination,
        18:190
High school equivalency (GED),
    10:64, 10:80
    denial of enrollment, 11:41
Hold harmless,
    individual liability, 22:60
    state aid, 24:70
Holidays,
    employees working on, 17:140
    hourly employees, 17:142
    meetings on, 6:90
    pay for, 17:142
    Saturdays, 15:220
Homeless child,
    resident district, 11:230
    special education, 13:72
    transportation, 11:235
Home rule, 24:120
Home schooling, 11:42
    extra-curricular activities, 11:45
    part-time enrollment of student,
        11:44
Homosexuality,
    assignment, 17:571
    employee, 17:570
    speech, 17:571
    student, 11:428
Honorable dismissal,
    reduction in force,
        teachers, 16:270
        support staff, 20:180
Hostile environment, 17:510
Hourly employees, 17:142
Human Rights Act,
    marital discrimination, 17:47
    sexual harassment,
        of students, 11:410
        of employees, 17:530
    work-related injury, 22:80

- I -

IDEA, see Individuals with
    Disabilities Education Act
IELRB, see Educational Labor
    Relations Board
IEP, see Individual education plan
IGAP testing, 10:300

IHSA, *see Illinois High School Association*

Illegal acts,
bid rigging, 25:270
bribery, 3:130
child abuse, *see Child abuse*
conflict of interest, 3:110, 3:130
criminal misconduct, 17:35
drug sales to minors, 12:110
false residency information, 11:210
falsified employment application, 15:65
felonies,
conviction of, 15:63
discipline for, 17:680
gang recruitment, 12:180
Gift Ban Act violations, 3:300, 3:340
infamous crimes, *see Infamous crimes*
letting of contracts, 25:270
official misconduct, 3:200
Open Meetings Act, 6:60
political literature, 4:38
punitive damages, 22:12, 22:70
sale of firearms, 12:160
sale of illegal drugs, 12:110
Student Records Act, 7:390
truancy, 11:70
union shop, 21:330
weapons on school grounds 12:150, 12:160
reporting, 12:156
working cash fund, 3:210
Illinois Constitution, 1:30, 1:90
Illinois Department of Labor, *see Labor*
Illinois Department of Revenue, *see Revenue*
Illinois High School Association (IHSA), 27:10
academic requirements, 27:220
age limitations, 27:260
attendance requirements, 27:190
awards, athletic, 27: 570
booster groups, 27:410, 27:500
coaching requirements, 27:350
cooperative activity programs, 27:60
court intervention, 27:35
custody of student athlete, 27:252
eligibility, 27:130
foreign exchange student, 27:246

gender-based rules, 27:300
governance of, 27:20
home-schooled students, 11:45
music programs, interscholastic, 27:200
non-boundaried schools, 27:244
non-school teams, 27:400, 27:520
open gym policy, 27:380
penalties, 27:35, 27:110, 27:460
physical examinations, 27:170
practice sessions, 27:100, 27:430
private and parochial schools, 27:50, 27:242
recruiting, academic, 27:470
recruiting, athletic, 27:450
residence requirements, 27:240
sex equity, 27:300
size classification system, 27:40
special education student, 27:248
sports camp (summer camp), 27:370, 27:420
sportsmanship, 27:110
teachers strike, 27:100
tournaments, 27:80, 27:310
transfers, student 27:250
unsportsmanlike conduct, 27:120
vocational education student, 27:248
waivers, *see Waivers, student*
Illinois Human Rights Act, *see Human Rights Act*
Illinois Municipal Retirement Fund (IMRF), *see Municipal retirement*
Immorality, 18:140
Immunity, tort, *see Tort immunity*
Immunization,
date of, 11:252
exclusion of student, 11:250
exemption from, 11:255
generally, 11:240
Impact bargaining, 21:160
Impasse, 21:430
Implied consent, 20:240
IMRF, *see Municipal retirement*
Incentives, *see Consolidation of schools*
Inclusion, *see Special education*
Incompatible offices, 3:40
Incompetency,
certification, 15:60
dismissal, 18:100

Indemnification,
  employee sexual misconduct,
    11:435
  generally, 22:60
Independent contractor, *see*
  Contractor
Individualized education plan
  (IEP),
  gifted students, 10:106
  students with disabilities, *see*
    Special education
Individuals with Disabilities
  Education Act (IDEA),
  children with disabilities, 13:95
  conflict with Gun-Free Schools
    Act, 12:155
  evaluation and placement, 13:190
  generally, 13:10
  programs and services, 13:120
Infamous crime,
  conviction of, school board
    vacancy, 2:70
  conviction of, State Board of
    Education vacancy, 1:170
  definition of, 2:74
  restoration to office, 2:80
Information, collection of, 1:310;
    also see Freedom of
    Information Act
Inherent managerial policies,
    21:140
Injuries, 22:80, 22:100; *also see*
    Student injury
In loco parentis,
  defined, 12:20
  immunities, 22:200
  noncertificated employees, 20:60
  negligence and, 22:100
  teachers, 22:140
  also see Willful and wanton
    misconduct
Inspection of instructional
  materials, 10:360
Inspection of textbooks, 10:360
Inspection, *see Public inspection*
Inspections, safety, *see Safety*
    inspections
Installment contracts, 25:280
Institute days, 10:230, 10:250
Instruction, student,
  bilingual, 10:140
  children with disabilities, *see*
    Special education

compulsory attendance
  alternatives, 11:40, 14:30
  costs of, 25:80
  disease, 10:100
  drivers education, 10:190
  handicapped student, *see Special*
    education
  high school requirements, 10:30
  materials, 10:350
  pregnant student, 11:160
  principal's duties, 19:20
  qualifications required,
    noncertificated, 20:20
  teachers, 15:20
religion,
  by outsiders in public school,
    14:95
  in the curriculum, 14:200
  released time for, 14:35
  Religious Freedom Restoration
    Act, 14:210
special education,
  class size, 13:180
  due process, 13:505
  facilities and services, 13:120
  generally, 13:10
  residential facilities, 13:220
Instructional materials, *see*
    Materials; also see Textbooks
Insubordination, 17:720, 18:150
Insurance,
  bidding, 25:223
  claims, 6:170
  fidelity, 25:140
  health, *see Health insurance*
  maternity coverage, 17:220
  premiums, 25:90
  self-insurance, 25:223
  student, 11:280
  Teachers Health Insurance
    Security Fund, 15:530
  tort fund levy, *see Tort fund levy*
  unemployment, 17:280
  Workers' compensation, 17:240,
    26:250
Integration, *see Desegregation*
Intelligent design, 14:231
Intentional infliction of
  emotional distress, 22:18
Inter-district desegregation
  order, *see Multi-district*
    segregation
Interest, prohibited, *see Conflict*
    of interest

Interest earnings, 24:186, 26:24
Interest rates, 26:220
Interfund loans and transfers,
  in general, 26:10, 23:222
  interest transfer, 24:186, 26:24
  interest transfer prohibited, 26:25
  line items within a fund, 26:30
  loans, 26:40
  permissible transfers, 26:20
  working cash, 26:70
Intergovernmental cooperation,
  see Agreement
Interim bargaining, 21:190
Internal Revenue Code, 20:120
Internal Revenue Service, 24:188,
  24.200
Internet,
  use by students, 12:122
Interscholastic programs, 27:10
Investments,
  depositary, 24:180
  generally, 24:184
  policy requirements, 24:182
  school treasurer, 5:80
Irremediable conduct, see
  Remediable conduct; also see
  Dismissal for cause

- J - K - L -

Job description, administrator,
  19:20
Joint agreement, see Agreement
**Just cause discipline or
  dismissal,**
  defined, 21:565
  extra-duty assignment, 15:235
  non-certificated employee, 20:143
  notice to remedy, 18:235
  probationary teacher, 18:25
Juvenile Court Act
  cooperation with police, 12:360
  guns, 12:156
  reporting, 12:350
Kindergarten,
  full day, 10:160
  immunizations, 11:240
  minimum age, 11:20
  school day, 10:280
  state aid, 24:100
Labor, Illinois Department of,
  9:370
Labor Board, see Educational
  Labor Relations Board

Labor law, Illinois, see Educational
  Labor Relations Act
Last chance agreement, see
  Agreement
**Law enforcement, cooperation
  with school officials,** 12:350
Law enforcement officer,
  see Police
Learning disabilities, see Special
  Education
Leases and leasing,
  closed meeting discussion, 6:170
  computers, 23:207
  school board authority,
    acquisition of property, 9:40
    from Capital Development
      Board, 9:280
  school busses, 25:280
  to a third party, 9:190
  vote required,
    generally, 6:280,
    personal property, 25:290
    real property, 9:46
    to a third party, 9:190
Lease-purchase agreements,
  personal property, 25:290
  real estate, 9:46
Least restrictive environment,
  13:50
Leave of absence,
  military, 17:230
  pregnancy, 17.200
  sabbatical, 15:540
  teacher replacing a teacher on,
    16:80
Leave, maternity, see Maternity
  leave
Leave, military, see Military leave
Leave, personal and professional,
  15:550
Leave, sabbatical, see Sabbatical
  leave
Leave, sick, see Sick Leave
Legal counsel, see Attorney
Legal holidays, see Holidays
Legal notice, see Notice, public
Length of work day, 15:210
Letters of credit, 9:305
Levy, see Tax levy
Liability,
  acts of employees,
    criminal misconduct, 17:35

in general, 22:60, 22:100
in loco parentis, 12:20
noncertificated, 20:60
sexual harassment, 11:415
duty of care, *see Duty of care*
duty to defend,
　generally, 22:60
　sexual harassment case,
　　11:435
employee background
　investigation, 17:33
notification of misconduct, 17:35
personnel records, 7:60, 7:100
placement costs, 13:350
punitive damages, 22:50
sale of illegal drugs, 12:110
school board member, 22:60
defamation, 2:144
tort immunity, *see Tort
　liability/immunity*
unsafe buildings, 22:200
waiver of, 22:164
Libel, school board member, 2:144
Liberty interest, *see Constitutional
　issues*
Library, 10:400
Life-Safety bonds, 26:190
Life-Safety Code, 22:190
Life-Safety deficiencies, 9:355
Life-safety inspection, *see
　Safety inspection*
Life-Safety tax levy, 25:135
Limitations period
　sexual harassment, 11:440
　special education, 13:64
Limited public forum, 12:133
Local bidders, 25:260
**Local Government Employees
　Political Rights Act,** 17:470
Local Records Act, 7:10, 7:20
Locker search, 12:240
Loitering, 12:35
Long-term debt, *see Debt*
Lost state aid payment, *see
　Delayed state aid payment*
Lottery, election,
　order on ballot, 4:80, 4:270
　tie vote, 4:415
Lottery, state, 24:90
Lowest bidder, *see Bids and
　bidding*
Low-income pupils, 24:110
Loyalty oath, 4:180

- M -

Mailing list,
　minutes of meetings, 6:305, 6:315
Mainstreaming (inclusion), *see
　Special education*
Maintenance of facilities, *see
　Facilities*
Majority of a quorum, 6:10, 6:250
Majority vote, 6:235; *also see Votes
　required for adoption*
Malice, 7:390
Malpractice, educational, 22:170
Management rights, 21:150
Managerial employee, 21:100
Mandates, 24:40
Mandatory retirement, 17:630
Mandatory subject of bargaining,
　defined, 21:140
　military leave, 17:230
　seniority, 16:315
　sick leave, 15:570
Married student, 11:290
Master teacher, 15:25
Materials, educational, *also see
　Textbooks*
　employee or board member
　　interest in, 3:170
　objections to, *see Censorship*
　school board authority to adopt,
　　10:350
Maternity leave, 17:180
Maximum tax rates, *see Tax rates*
Mechanic's lien, 9:310
Mediation, 21:450
Medical emergency, 22:150
Medical records, 7:450
Medicare, 15:500
Medication,
　administration by
　　employees,17:670
　refusal to administer, 17:672
Meetings, adjournment,
　to another meeting, 6:130,
　without a quorum present, 6:260
Meetings, agenda,
　closed meeting, 6:104
　conduct of business not on
　　agenda, 6:165
　posting of, 6:102, 6:140
　special meeting, 6:120
　with public notice, 6:140

Meetings, closed,
allowable exceptions for, 6:170
collective negotiations and
grievances, 21:60
disclosure of information, 6:226,
6:227
hearing complaints, 6:225
no agenda, 6:104
Meetings, committee, 6:35
Meetings, emergency, 6:140
Meetings, minutes, 6:300,
closed meetings
confidentiality of, 6:330
Freedom of Information Act,
7:450
procedure for closing, 6:200
record of, 6:320
minutes in general, 6:300
payment of bills, 25:210
public inspection, 6:315
Meetings, motions,
recording, 6:300
teacher dismissal, 18:270
voting by officers, 6:270
Meetings, negotiating,
application of Open Meetings Act,
21:60
closed session for, 6:10
Meetings, new board members,
6:37
Meetings, public, see Open
Meetings Act
Meetings, public comment,
6:225, 6:240
Meetings, public notice, see
Notice, public
Meetings, quorum, 6:10, 6:250
Meetings, regular, 6:80
Meetings, rules of procedure,
6:230
Meetings, special,
agenda, 6:160
closed session, 6:210
generally, 6:120
scheduling, 6:90
Meetings via telephone, 6:297
Meetings, votes and voting,
abstain from voting, see Abstain
from voting
board officers, 6:270
closing a meeting, 6:200
electing officers, 5:20
final actions in public, 6:170
record of, 6:300, 7:400

also see Majority vote
also see Votes required for
adoption
Membership dues, 2:200
Metal detectors,
generally, 12:315
required searches, 12:317
Midterm bargaining, see Interim
bargaining
Military leave, 17:230
Minimum (clock) hours, see
School day
Minimum competency test,
generally, 10:290
students with disabilities, 13:300
Minimum salary, 15:320, 15:400
Minimum school term, see
School term
Minimum wage,
Fair Labor Standards Act, hours,
20:70
Fair Labor Standards Act, wages,
17:60
Minorities,
attendance boundaries, 11:120
racial issues generally, 14:400,
also see Discrimination
Minors,
drug sales to, 12:110
emancipated defined, 11:290,
special education, 13.72
labor laws, 10:150, 11:40
parental responsibility, 9:420
purchase of tobacco, 11:300
search consent, 12:320
waiver of liability, 22:164
Minutes, see Meetings
Moonlighting, 17:640
Motions, see Meetings
Multi-disciplinary conference,
eligibility for special education,
13:80
evaluation, 13:190
expulsion, 13:370
parental challenge, 13:260
records, 7:270
Multi-district segregation, 14:490
Multi-year employment contract,
administrators generally, 19:90
application of tenure, 19:130
dismissal, 19:170
Municipal authority,
fire protection, 1:280

real estate, 9:90
tax increment financing, 23:60
Municipal retirement (IMRF),
generally, 20:120
municipal retirement fund, 25:130
Music programs, interscholastic,
27:200

- N -

**National Collegiate Athletic
Association (NCAA),** 27:140
**National Labor Relations Board
(NLRB),** 21:20
Neglected child,
defined, 11:320
revocation of teacher certificate,
15:60
superintendent reporting, 19:10
Negligence,
defined, 18:130
injuries due to, 22:100
in loco parentis protection, 12:20
negligence and willful misconduct
compared, 22:15
non-certificated employees, 20:60
supervision of students, 22:22
teacher dismissal for, 18:10
also see Tort liability / immunity
Negotiations,
application of Open Meetings Act
to, 21:60
closed sessions, 6:170
Freedom of Information Act,
7:450
impasse, 21:440
meetings, 6:10
also see Collective bargaining
Nepotism,
board members, 3:160
generally, 17:47
New employees,
criminal background check, 17:20
duty to bargain, 21:150
employment standards, 17:10
freedom from disease, 17:10
probationary period, teacher,
15:250
refusal to honor contract, 15:70
New school district,
combination, 8:10
consolidation, 4:90
employee rights,
administrators, 19:105
teachers, 16:150

sick leave, 15:590
tax levy, 23:115
Newspaper, student, *see Student
publications*
Nominating petitions,
duties of school board, 4:70
duties of secretary, 4:80
filing, 4:140
withdrawal, 4:190
Noncertificated employees,
defined, 20:10
in loco parentis, 22:110
just cause for discipline, 20:143
part-time, 20:160
reduction in force, 20:150, 20:180
seniority, 20:150
state incentives after annexation,
8:145
temporary or substitute, 20:183
union recognition, 21:120
wall-to-wall bargaining, 21:220
Nonpublic forum, 12:133
Nonpublic schools,
compulsory attendance, 14:30
IHSA, 27:50, 27:242
placement of special education
students in, 13:330
qualification for State Board of
Education, 1:150
special education, 13:70, 13:110
transportation to, 14:80
also see Parochial schools
Non-recognition of schools,,
minimum school year, 24:140
types of recognition, 1:210
watch list penalties, 1:370
Non-resident,
residence, 11:180
special education, 13:320
tuition, 11:195, 11:200
Non-school teams, 27:400, 27:520
Non-teaching duties, 20:20
Non-tenured teachers, *see
Probationary teachers*
Non-union employees, 21:310
No pass, no play, 11:405
Notice, dismissal
noncertificated employee, 20:140,
20:180
probationary teacher,
acquisition of tenure, 16:70
generally, 18:10

reduction in force,
    non-certificated employees,
        20:180
    teachers, 16:270
    superintendent, 19:170
    tenured teacher,
        causes, 18:90
        procedures, 18:250
Notice, employment,
    principal reclassification, 19:140
    superintendent, non-renewal,
        19:100
    teacher, probationary, 15:260
    teacher, tenured,
        dismissal hearing, 18:270
        hearing officer, 18:310
        notice to remedy, 19.25
        reduction from extended
            contract, 16:230
        remediation, 18:210
        tenure, 16:20
Notice, public,
    back door referendum, 4:313
    elections,
        ballot, 4:330
        conduct of, 4:60
        school board secretary, 4:80
    Freedom of Information Act,
        7:430
    Health and Safety Act, 9:370
    meetings,
        closed session, 6:104, 6:210
        collective negotiations and
            grievance arbitration, 21:60
        date, time and place, 6:90
        emergency meeting, 6:150
        generally, 6:130, 6:140
        special meeting, 6:120
    rights of children with
        disabilities, 13:230
    Truth in Taxation hearing, 23:140
Notice, student discipline, 12:390,
    12:470
Notice to remedy,
    authority to issue, 19:25
    grievability, 18:235
    nontenured teacher, 18:30
    tenured teacher, 18:210
Notices, miscellaneous,
    ballot order lottery, 4:275
    bargaining unit representation,
        21:250, 21:270
    bids and bid opening, 25:220
    denial of records request, 7:500

detachment petition, 8:200
failure to file budget documents,
    budget in general, 25:10
    effect on tax receipts, 23:110
failure to file economic interest
    statement, 3:110
hearing on election objector's
    petition, 4:240
intent to strike, 21:490
Juvenile Court Act, 12:350
personnel records, 7:90
rules violations, 12:40
special education due process
    hearing request, 13:525
student directory information,
    7.300
student records challenge, 7:360
teacher resignation, 15:600
Nursery school, 10:200, 11:240
Nurse,
    administration of medication,
        17:670
    certification, 15:45
    services to special education
        students, 13:150

- O -

Objection, legal, see *Challenge*
Obscene expression, 12:120,
    12:128
Occupational diseases,
    Occupational Disease Act, 17:240
    tort judgment bonds, 26:250
Occupational qualification,
    age, 17:620
    mandatory retirement, 17:630
**Occupational Safety and Health
    Act (OSHA),** 22:90
Officers of school board, see
    School board officers
**Older Workers Benefit
    Protection Act,** 17:635
Open enrollment, 14:470
Open gym policy, 27:380
Open Meetings Act,
    collective negotiations and
        grievance arbitration, 21:60
    election of board officers, 5:20
    Freedom of Information Act
        application, 7:450
    generally, 6:10
    new board members, 6:37

Operating funds,
  construction of building, 9:210
  defined, 25:60, 25:80
  tax anticipation notes, 26:150
Operating tax rate,
  amendment of, 23:130
  computation of state aid, 24:100,
    also see Tax rate
**Operations and maintenance
  fund,**
  tax rate,
    amendment, 25:40
    back door referendum, 23:250
    levy, 23:170
    maximum, 23:230
  transfer of funds, *see Interfund
    loans and transfers*
  use of,
    accumulation of funds, 9:210
    defined, 25:90
    distributions, 25:100
Orders, teachers', *see Teachers'
  orders*
Ordinance, land development,
  9:100
Organizations,
  non-school groups, 9:430
  religious groups, 14:130
  student groups, *see Students*
OSHA, *see Occupational Safety and
  Health Act*
Outside employment, *see
  Moonlighting*
Out-of-state field trip, 22:160
Overtime,
  application of Fair Labor
    Standards Act, 17:60
  generally, 20:70
  leaves, 20:102

- P -

PAC, see *Political action committee*
Paraprofessionals, 16:110
Parental institute day, 10:245
Parental Responsibility Act, 9:420
Parental Right of Recovery Act,
  12:110
Parental rights,
  discipline notice, 12:400, 12:470
  discipline policies, 12:60
  fee waivers, 10:390
  school reports,
    notification of student absence,
      11:60

  state report card, 10:310
  student report card to divorced
    parent, 10:340
  student records, 7:160, 7:330
Parents,
  children with disabilities,
    due process, 13:505
    IEP, 13:40
    referral, 13:200
    special education generally,
      13:10
    tuition, 13:330
  consent,
    attendance centers, 11:120
    immunizations and
      examinations, 11:255
    safety patrol, 9:390
    sex education, 10:90
  control of student,
    emancipation, 11:290
    in loco parentis, 12:20
  preference of,
    detachment and annexation,
      8:260
    kindergarten, 10:160
  residence of,
    for special education defined,
      13:71
    payment for special education,
      13:325
  tuition, 11:180
Parent Teacher Association,
  see PTA
Parent-teacher conferences,
  10:280
Park district, 10:220
Parking lots,
  searches, 12:310
  site and construction fund, 25:140
Parochial schools, *also see
  Nonpublic schools*
  compulsory attendance, 14:30
  IHSA, 27:50
  public school teachers in, 13:114,
    14:90
  transportation, 11:360, 14:80
**Part time employee,
  noncertificated,** 20:160
Part time teacher,
  benefits, 15:570
  reduction in force, 16:230
  tenure, 16:160
Paternity leave, 17:180

Patrol, school safety, see *Safety patrol*

Payroll,
teachers orders, 26:180
union dues, 17:100

Payroll deductions, 17:100

Penalties,
bid rigging, 25:270
disclosure of economic interest, 3:110
encouraging truancy, 11:70
Gift Ban Act violations, 3:340
IHSA, 27:35, 27:110, 27:560
improper teacher resignation, 15:600
Open Meetings Act, 6:60
street gangs, 12:180
Student Records Act, 7:390
weapons on school grounds, 12:150
working cash fund, 3:210
also see Academic; also see Removal from office; also see State aid

Pension,
Illinois Municipal Retirement Fund, 20:120
Teacher Retirement System, 15:510

Performance bond,
building contractor, 9:300, 9:305
regional superintendent, 1:250
responsible bidder, 25:230
revolving funds, 25:170

Performance contract,
administrator, 19:91
energy savings, 25:300

Period of silence, 14:50

Permission slips, see *Waivers, student*

Personal leave, 15:550

Personal property, see *Property*

Personal property replacement tax,
bonds, 26:190
borrowing against, 26:110
corporate personal property replacement tax notes, 26:170

Personal property tax,
levy, 23:30
replacement, 26:170

Personnel Records Act, 7:10, 7:40

Petition,
emergency election, 4:320
detachment and annexation, filing of, 8:150
withdrawal of, 8:165
financial watch list, 26:290
nominating, see *Nominating petition*
signatures, see *Signatures*
voters, see *Voter petition*

Physical education, 10:120

Physical examinations, see *Health examinations*

Physical fitness,
bus drivers, 20:210
employees generally, 17:10

Physical restraints, 12:195

Picketing, 21:500

Piercing, body, 12:127

Placement, student,
change in, 13:505
class size, 13:180
mainstreaming, 13:50
new placement, 13:520
parental challenge, 13:260, 13:510
records, 7:270
reevaluation, 13:210
residential, 13:325
stay put, 13:520
unilateral, 13:340

Playgrounds,
acquisition of property for, 9:70
borrowing for, 26:210
injury on, 22:167
supervisors, 20:30

Pledge of Allegiance, 14:53

Police,
access to student records, 7:204
cooperation with school officials, 12:360
records, 7:172

Police investigations,
interrogation of students, 12:340
prosecution of students, 12:360
records, 7:172
searches, 12:300

Police, Illinois State, 12:156, 17:660, 20:214

Police, reports to, 12:156, 17:660

Policy, 2:165
see also School board policies; Rules and regulations

Political action committee (PAC), 4:360

Political activities,
campaigns, 4:340

discrimination for, 17:460
personnel records, 7:100
Political buttons, 12:123
Political expression,
employee, 17:450
student, 12:120
Political party affiliation,
elections, 4:170
employees, 17:470
Population, changes in, 2:26, 2:45
Postal employee, 3:15
Powers, *see Authority*
Prairie State Achievement Test,
10:302
requirement for graduation,
10:303
special education, 10:304
Prayer,
at school board meetings, 14:70
at graduation, 14:60
by coach, 14:55
by students, 14:40
by teachers, 14:150
moment of silence, 14:50
Pregnancy, employee, 17:170,
17:200
Pregnancy, student,
attendance, 11:160
clubs and activities, 11:403
Preponderance of evidence,
teacher dismissal, 18:340
Preschool, 13:20
President, school board,
absence, 5:40
duties,
Education Officers Electoral
Board, 4:230
inspection and copying of
records, 7:500
minutes, 6:300
voting, 6:270
election of, 5:10
special meetings, 6:90, 6:120
Press, student, *see Student
publications*
Pre-termination hearing,
see Hearing
Prevailing wage, 9:300
Principal and interest,
bond and interest fund, 25:120
bonds, 26:200
levy, 23:160
sale of school property, 9:180

tort settlement or judgment,
22:230, 23:220
**Principal, employment and
duties,** 19:20
qualifications, 19:65
Prior experience credit, 15:400,
15:420
Private schools, *see Nonpublic
schools*
Privileged communication,
guidance counselor, 12:100
student records, 7:230
Probable cause, 12:232
Probate Act, 1:170
**Probationary employment,
noncertificated,** 20:150,
20:170
**Probationary recognition of
schools,** 1:210
Probationary teacher,
defined, 16:10
dismissal grievance, 18:25
non-renewal, 18:10
probationary period, 15:250
recall, 16:350
reduction in force, 16:260
seniority, 16:190
Probation, extension of, 15:250
Procedural due process, *see Due
process*
Professional development,
activities, 15:92
certificate renewal plans, 15:80,
15:88, 15:110
Committee, 15:84
Professional growth, 15:110
Professional leave, 15:550
Proficiency examination, 10:40,
10:60
Promotion, student, 10:320
special education, 13:300
Proof, burden of, *see Burden of
proof*
Proof of immunization, *see
Immunization*
Property interest, *see
Constitutional issues*
Property, personal,
acquisition of, 25:290
sale of, 24:300
teacher protection of, 15:460
also see Personal property tax
Property, real,
acquisition of, 9:40

contract for deed, 9:44
damage to, 9:420
disposal of, 9:110, 13:420, *also see*
  Sale of property
lease; lease-purchase, 9:46
protection of,
  loitering, 12:35
  tort immunity levy, 23:220
title to, 9:20
Property tax, 23:10
appeals, *see Tax appeals*
levy, *see Tax levy*
multiplier, 23:40, 23:130
tax cap (PTELL; Extension
  Limitation Law), 23:170,
  23:235
valuation, *see Assessed valuation*
Protection from suit, 22:60
Proxy, voting by, 6:295
Psychological records, 7:270,
  7:340
Psychiatric testing, 13:90, 13:120
PTA,
use of facilities, 9:440
worker compensation, 17:250
PTELL, *see Property tax*
Publications, election, *see*
  Election literature
Publications, student, *see*
  Student publications
Public forums, *also see Facilities,*
  use of
forum analysis, 12:133
student publications, 12:130
teacher speech, 17:480
Public Health, Department of,
  9:330, 9:350
Public hearing,
budget, 25:10
principal reclassification, 19:140
reduction in force, 16:280
tax increment financing district,
  23:61
tax levy, 23:140
truth in taxation, 23:140
waiver request, 1:384
Public inspection,
budget, 25:10
financial records, 7:20
Freedom of Information Act,
  7:400
minutes of meetings, 6:315
nominating petitions, 4:220

Public meetings, *see Open*
  Meetings Act
Public notice, *see Notices*
Public policy question, 4:40,
  4:300, 4:340
Public records, 7:400
Punitive damages,
defined, 22:12
drug dealers, 12:110
school officials, 22:50, 22:70
Pupils, *see Students*
Purchases and purchasing,
bidding, *see Bids and bidding*
  requirements
installment purchases, 25:280
insurance and insurance pools,
  25:223
penalties for bid rigging, 25:270
purchase of land, buildings, 9:40
bonds, 26:210
contract for deed, 9:44
lease-purchase, 9:46
release of payment, 25:210
sale of land, 9:130
school board member interest in
  contracts, 3:140

- Q - R -

Qualifications,
principal, 19:65
regional superintendent, 1:250
school board member,
  generally, 3:10
  vacancies, 2:70, 2:110
State Board of Education, 1:150
State Superintendent, 1:190
superintendent of schools, 19:60
teacher, 15:10
treasurer, 5:95
voter, 4:500
Quality review, 1:335
Quorum,
defined, 6:250
illegal meeting, 6:30
meeting defined, 6:10
number of votes necessary to
  carry, 6:280
required for action, 2:140, 6:90
Quota employment, 14:530

Racial classifications, 14:420,
  14:530

Racial discrimination,
employment, 14:510
school segregation, desegregation,
14:400
segregation remedies, 14:440
Real property, *see Property*
**Real Property Tax Increment
Allocation Development
Act,** *see Tax increment
financing district*
Reasonable cause,
exclusionary rule, 12:300
representation election, 21:250
student search, 12:240
Reasonable suspicion, 12:238,
12:300
Reasons for dismissal, *see
Dismissal*
Recall,
noncertificated employee, 20:190
teacher, 16:340
Recall election, 3:195
Reclassification of principal,
19:130
Recognition of bargaining unit,
appropriateness, 21:230
defined, 21:210
noncertificated employees, 21:120
procedure, 21:250
Recognition of schools,
generally, 1:210
penalties for failure to have full
calendar, 24:140
standards for, 1:300
Reconsideration of board action,
generally, 2:170
minutes, 6:310
Records,
access to student records by
state's attorney or police, 7:204
appeals, 7:360, 7:500. 7:520
custodian, 7:180, 7:200, 7:220
electronically stored, 7:435
exempt from inspection, 7:450
lists of, 7:435
local, *see Local Records Act*
personnel, 7:10, 7:40
police, 7:172
public, 7:400
salaries, 7:470
school board member, 7:415
school district, 7:10
state aid, 7:30
student, 7:160

Recreational programs,
acquisition of property, 9:70
borrowing for, 26:210
joint recreational programs,
10:220
student organizations 25:180
Recruiting, student, 27:450
Reduction in force (RIF),
bumping, 16:320
defined, 16:200,
hearings for, 16:280
order of, 16:260,
payment of earnings, 15:450
Reduction in salary,
in reduction in force, 16:230
principal reclassification, 19:140
Referendum, advisory, 4:10, 4:55
Referendum, back door, *see Back
door referendum*
Referendum, bond issue, *see Bond
issue election*
Referendum, emergency, *see
Emergency election*
Referendum, free textbooks,
10:380
**Referendum, tax extension
limitation,** 23:235
Referendum, tax rate, *see Tax
rate election*
Refunding bonds, 26:190
**Regional Board of School
Trustees,**
alternative school employer, 21:75
amendment of petition, 8:170
detachment and annexation,
8:120
dissolution, 8:90
filing of petition, 8:200
rulings, 8:220, 8:260
title to property, 9:20
withdrawal from special
education cooperatives, 13:460
Regional superintendent,
adoption of textbooks, 10:350
alternative schools, 12:510
district organization,
detachment, annexation, 8:10
voter initiated, 1:120
election of, 1:230
equivalency examinations, 10:80
governance, 1:220
length of school day, 10:280
parental institutes, 10:240
qualifications, 1:250, 3:40

receiving reports, 2:190
removal of school board member,
  3:190
school board election, 4:100
school board vacancy, 2:90
school buildings,
  handicapped accessibility,
    13:30
  Life Safety Code, 9:340
  safety survey report, 9:337
school employees,
  strikes, 21:490
  substitute teachers, 15:300
  teacher certification, 15:60,
    15:84
school finance,
  audits, 25:200
  delivery of funds, 24:160
student records, 7:360
students, 11:40
students, disruptive, *see*
  Alternative school
treasurer's books, 5:130
truancy, 11:80, 11:110
Regular meeting, school board,
  see Meetings
Rehabilitation Act, 13:30
  athletics, 27:262
Rehiring, support personnel,
  20:190
Rehiring, teacher, 16:340
Reinstatement,
  after loss of school board seat,
    2:80
  completion of remediation period,
    15:380
  suspension without pay, 18:370
Related services,
  children with disabilities defined,
    13:60
  due process, 13:505
  evaluation, 13:190
  services defined, 13:140
  services provided, 13:120
Religion, *also see Prayer*
  Christmas programs, 14:123,
    14:225
  compulsory attendance, 11:40
  curriculum, 14:200
  curriculum objections, 14:210
  evolution, teaching of, 14:230
  generally, 14:10
  immunizations and health
    examinations, 11:255

instruction, 14:35
records of employees, 7:120
religious instruction during school
  day, 14:95
school assignments, 14:220
student testing objections, 10:315
Religious Freedom Restoration
  Act, 14:25
Religious groups,
  student groups, 14:140
  use of facilities, 9:430, 14:130
Religious instruction, 14:35,
  14:200
Religious literature, 14:120
Remediable conduct,
  extra-curricular activities, 18:170
  incompetency defined, 18:110
  insubordination defined, 17:720,
    18:150
  probationary teacher, 18:30
  remediability, 18:180
  remediation plan, 15:380
  time to correct, 18:240
Remedial warning, *see Notice to*
  remedy
Remediation plan,
  causes for dismissal, 18:100
  conflicting bargaining agreement,
    15:384
  construction of, 15:380
  length of remediation, 15:382
  notice to remedy, 18:30
Remedy, notice to, *see Notice to*
  remedy
Removal from office or
  forfeiture,
  Educational Labor Relations
    Board member, 21:40
  failure to file economic interest
    statement, 3:110
  school board member,
    academic watch list, 1:370
    by regional superintendent,
      3:190
    vacancy defined, 2:70
  school board officer, 5:75
  State Board of Education
    member, 1:180
  treasurer, 5:140
Renewal of teaching certificate,
  15:80
Rent fund, 9:46, 25:150
Reorganization, school district,
  authority for, 4:40,

effect on school board members,
   4:90
generally, 8:10
Report, student arrest, 12:350
Report card, district, 10:310
Report card, student,
   disciplinary measures, 7:240
   grades, 10:320
   non-custodial parent, 10:340
Report, financial, *see Financial
   reports*
Representation, union, 17:740
Representation election, 21:250
   ballots, 21:260
   challenges, 21:290
   conduct of, 21:270
   decertification, 21:280
   decertification inquiries by
      employees, 21:282
   recognition, 21:260
   voter eligibility lists, 21:274
**Representation, territorial
   changes,** 2:26
Rescind previous action, *see
   Reconsideration*
Residence,
   picketing, 21:500
   school board member,
      defined, 3:20
      names on ballot, 4:270
      petition for candidacy, 4:150
   student,
      change in custody, 11:220,
         27:252
      custody, 11:190, 11:220
      defined, 11:185
      emancipated minor, 11:295
      foreign exchange, 27:246
      homeless, 11:230
      IHSA, 27:240
      move from district, 11:215,
         27:247
      penalty for providing false
         information regarding,
         11:210
      private school, 27:242
      removal from school, 11:205
      right to attend school, 11:180
      special education, 13:71,
         13:216
Residency requirements,
   access to records, 7:420
   administrators, 19:96

employees, 17:44
   pollwatcher, 4:390
   school board,
      canvass, 4:405
      defined, 3:10
      qualifications, 2:110
      territorial representation, 2:25
      vacancy defined, 2:70
   State Board of Education, 1:140
   voters, 4:500
Residential developer, 9:100
Residential facility,
   payment for, 13:325
   placement in, 13:220
Resignation, board member,
   date effective, 3:180
   incompatibility, 3:30
   vacancy defined, 2:70
Resignation, employee,
   tenured teacher, 15:600
   unemployment compensation,
      17:290
Responsible bidder, 25:220
**Retailers' Occupation and Use
   Tax,** 24:90
Retirement age, 17:630
**Retirement, noncertificated
   staff,** 25:130
Retirement, teacher, 15:500
Revenue bonds, 9:220
Revenue Code, 20:120
Revenue, Illinois Department of,
   assessments, 23:40
   levy, 23:130
   state aid, 24:120
   tax rates, 23:180
Revenue sources, school, 24:10
Review, administrative, *see
   Administrative review*
Revocation of certificate, 15:60
Revolving fund, 25:170
RIF, *see Reduction in force*
Risk care management,
   levy for, 23:220
   tort immunity fund, 23:220
   use of tort fund for, 23:221
Rollover, 19:100, 19:102
Role model, teacher, 18:175
Rules and regulations, *also see
   Authority*
   Educational Labor Relations
      Board, 21:270, 21:390

school boards,
administrative, 2:165, 2:167
generally, 2:130
home schools, 11:42
inherent powers, 1:100
policy, 2:165
Rules of evidence, 18:330
Rules of procedure, see Meetings

- S -

Sabbatical leave,
generally, 15:540
unemployment compensation,
17:300
Safe Schools Law, see Alternative
schools
Safety,
Act of God,
generally, 24:150
IHSA, 27:100
bus construction, 22:193
costs,
fire, safety, environmental and
energy fund, 25:135
long term debt, 26:190
tort levy, 23:220
dangerous student, 13:370
disruptive student, see Alternative
schools
employees,
Health and Safety Act, 9:370
OSHA, 22:90
inspections,
deficiencies, 9:355
Life-Safety Code, 9:340
State Fire Marshall, 9:360
ordinary care, 22:14
reasonable force, 12:190
safety patrol, 9:390
school property, 9:320
fire prevention, 9:360
safety requirements, 22:180
standard of care, 22:210
student dress, 12:125
student suspension,
buses, 12:380
generally, 12:410
visitors, 22:180, 22:210
Safety Survey Report, 9:337
Salaries, teacher,
consolidation of districts, 8:70
cost of living adjustment, 21:580
extra duties, 15:230
freeze, 15:432

minimum, 15:400
prior experience credit, 15:420
substitute, 15:320
suspension without pay, 18:370
Teacher Retirement System,
15:520
Salary schedule,
advancement on, 15:430
consolidation of districts, 8:70
discrimination against certain
certificates, 15:28
extra duties, 15:230
minimum, 15:400
prior experience credit, 15:420
Sale of property,
historically, 9:10
means of sale, 9:140
personal property, 24:300
proceeds of sale, 9:180
real property, 9:140
votes needed for, 6:280, 9:110
Sales tax, 24:90
Saturday, 12.45, 15:220, 17:140
School board,
authority (powers), see Authority
board of education, 1:80, 1:110
board of school directors, 1:80,
1:110
committees, see Committees
duties,
elections, 4:70
removal from office, 3:190
rules and regulations, 2:130
election of,
generally, 4:20
nominating petitions, 4:160
general powers, 1:100
meetings, 6:10
membership, 2:10
officers,
required, 5:10
votes of, 6:270
policies,
distribution of religious
literature, 14:120
employment rights, 17:600
nepotism, 17:47
rules, see Rules and regulations
vacancy, see Vacancy in office
School board member,
appointment of, 2:90
authority, see Authority
censure of, 6:227
districts, 2:30, 4:500

election of, 4:20
expenses, 3:50
liability, see Liability
qualifications, 3:10
records, see Records
removal, 3:190
unseated, 3:61
School board officers,
absence of at meeting, 5:40
compensation, 5:50
election of, 5:20
removal, 5:75
required, 5:10
terms, 5:30, 5:90
treasurer, 5:90
vacancy, 5:110
votes of, 6:270
School board president, see
President
School board secretary, see
Secretary
School Building Code, see
Life-Safety Code
School construction, see
Construction
School day,
minimum, 10:270
kindergarten, 10:280
substitute teacher, 15:310
School districts, see Formation of
school districts
School district records,
see Records
School district report card,
see Report card
School facilities, see Facilities
School improvement plans,
academic watch list, 1:330, 1:360
exemption, 1:335
School term,
Act of God, 24:150
institute days, 10:250
minimum, 10:230
Search, 12:230, 12:238
consent, 12:320
dogs, 12:310
employee, 17:730
exclusionary rule, 12:300
metal detectors, 12:315
police, 12:300
school grounds, 12:242
strip, 12:231
warrant, 12:300

Secretary, school board,
absence, 5:70
compensation, 3:50, 5:50
duties,
ballot, 4:270
canvass, 4:400
certificate of tax levy, 23:80
economic interest statements,
3:90
elections, 4:70
financial interest in books or
equipment, 3:170
minutes, 6:300
nominating petitions, 4:140,
4:210
notice of election, 4:330
public policy referenda, 4:290
reorganization, 4:100
resignation of board member,
creation of vacancy, 2:70
effective date of, 3:180
resignation of employee,
15:600
voter initiated petitions, 4:310
voting by, 6:270
election of, 5:10
Secretary of State, 20:214, 20:220,
24:210
Secret organizations, 12:170
Secret voting, 5:20, 6:180
Segregation, also see Desegregation
complaints, 14:410
court order, 14:450
generally, 14:400
remedies, 14:440
school attendance boundaries,
11:120
Seizure (Fourth Amendment),
generally, 12:250
required searches, 12:317
Self insurance, 6:170, 25:223
Seniority, also see Bumping
equal pay, 17:70
list, 16:310
noncertificated employees, 20:150,
20:200
teachers, probationary, 16:190
teachers, tenured, 16:20, 16:220
Sex discrimination,
Equal Pay Act, 17:70
suspect classification, 27:300
title IX, 11:150
Sex education, 10:90
Sexually explicit material, 11:450

Sexual harassment,
affirmative defense to employee
harassment, 17:505
agency, employee, 17:504
agency, student, 11:417
consent by student, 11:416
constructive notice, employee,
17:504
constructive notice, student,
11:417
damages, employees, 17:520
defense to employee harassment,
17:505
defined, employee, 17:500
defined, student, 11:415, 11:420
duty to defend, 11:435
hostile environment, employees,
17:510
hostile environment, students,
11:422
statute of limitations, 11:440
students, 11:410
liability for, 11:415, 11:430
damages, 11:417, 11:420,
11:440
Sexual misconduct, 11:435
Sexual orientation, *see*
Homosexuality
Short-term debt, *see Debt*
Short-term employee, 21:115
Sick leave,
defined, 17:150
non-certificated employees, 20:130
pregnancy, 17:210
worker compensation, 17:270
Signatures, number required,
advisory referendum, 4:55
at-large school board, 2:27
backdoor referendum, 4:313
creation of unit district, 8:40
detachment, 8:300
nominating petition, 4:160, 4:210
representative districts, 2:30
Simultaneous filings, 4:270
Site and construction fund,
25:140
Slander, school board member,
2:144
Smoking, 9:375, 11:300
Social Security, 15:500, 25:130
Special education, 13:10
administrative remedies, 13:510
alternative educational setting,
13:371

appeals, 13:270, 13:515, 13:562
assessment, 10:300
building bonds, 26:190
children with disabilities, 13:95
class size, 10:20, 13:180
cooperative,
acquisition of tenure, 16:90
maintenance of facilities,
13:430
taxes, 23:20
dangerous student, 13:515
discipline,
alternative educational
setting, 13:371
expedited hearing, 13:373
expulsion, 13:370
factors to consider, 13:375
generally, 12:300
suspension, 13:360
drop-out, 11:41
due process, 13:370, 13:500
eligibility, 13:60
facilities,
construction of, 13:410
disposal of, 13:420
tax, 23:200
grading, 10:320
graduation, 13:290, 13:505
guardianship, 13:71
hearing (due process), 13:370,
13:500
appeal of decision, 13:562
evidence presented, 13:547
hearing officer selection,
13:535
notice of, 13:525
open or closed meeting, 13:538
pre-hearing conference, 13:543
record of hearing, 13:552
request for, 13:525
right to counsel, 13:530,
13:552
time and place, 13:540
written decision, 13:552
inclusion (mainstreaming), 13:50,
13:145
individualized education plan
(IEP), 13:40, 13:160, 13:280,
13:520
interscholastic activities, 27:248
joint agreement, *see cooperative*
learning disabilities defined,
13:90

limitations period for provision of
   services, 13:64
new placement, 13:520
notice, 13:230, 13:525
parental consent, 13:240
placement, *see Placement, student*
Prairie State Achievement Test,
   10:304
pre-hearing conference, 13:543
pre-school, 24:120
private facilities, 13:220, 13:330
provision of services in parochial
   schools, 13:114, 14:90
programs,
   eligibility 13:80,
   for non-public school students,
      13:110
   during a strike, 13:310
   tax for, 23:200
records, 7:270
residency, 13:71, 13:325
right to sue, 13:510
services,
   free and appropriate, 13:25
   medical, 13:150
   non-public school students,
      14:100
standards, 13:25
state aid, 24:80
stay put, 13:520
supplementary aids, 13:145
tax rate, 23:200
transition services, 13:165
transportation, 11:360
Special meetings, *see Meetings*
Speech, protected, *see Political
   expression; also see Political
   buttons; also see First
   amendment*
Spectators, *see Visitors*
Sports, *see Athletics; also see Illinois
   High School Association*
Sports camp, *see Summer camp*
Sportsmanship, 27:110
Spouse, employment of, *see
   Nepotism*
Sprinkler systems, 9:365
State aid, 24:70
   borrowing against, 26:110, 26:175
   categorical aid, 24:10, 24:70
   general aid, 24:70, 24:175, 25:70
   penalties, 1:360, 24:140, 25:27
   recomputation, 24:105
   records, 7:30

reorganization incentives, 8:70
standards, 10:270
tax effort, 23:130
wealth basis, 23:40
State aid anticipation, *see
   Anticipation*
State Board of Education, *see
   Education, State Board of*
State Board of Elections, *see
   Elections, State Board of*
State Department of Labor, *see
   Labor*
**State Department of Public
   Health,** *see Public Health*
State Department of Revenue,
   see Revenue
State Fire Marshal, *see Fire
   Marshal*
State Mandates Act, *see Mandates*
State Police, *see Police*
State Tax Appeals Board, 23:70
State recognition standards, *see
   Recognition of schools; also see
   Academic standards*
**State Superintendent of
   Education,** *see Education,
   State Superintendent*
State's attorney, access to student
   records, 7:204
Statement of economic interests,
   regional superintendent, 1:250
   school board member,
      nominating papers, 4:150,
         4:210
      notice of failure to file, 3:115
      requirement to file, 3:90
   school employee, 3:90, 3:115
   write-in candidate, 4:410
Statement of financial condition,
   25:190
Status quo bargaining, 15:432,
   21:590
Statute of frauds, 19:94
Statute of limitations, *see Sexual
   harassment*
Stay put, *see Special education*
Straw vote, 6:190
Street gangs, 12:180
Strikes,
   no-strike clause, 21:480
   permissible conditions, 21:490
   picketing, 21:500
   special education, 13:310
Strip search, *see Searches*

Student absences, see Truancy
Student activities, see Activities
Student athlete,
  discipline, 12:495
  drug testing of, 12:234
  health insurance for, 11:280
  right to participate, 27:130
Student attendance,
  athletic eligibility, 27:190
  compulsory, 11:10, 14:30
  minimum days, 10:230
  minimum hours, 10:270
  state aid, 24:100, 24:140
Student discipline,
  alternative schools, 12:500
  athletics and extracurricular
    activities, 12:495
  authority for, 12:10
  closed meetings for, 6:170
  committee for, 12:60
  corporal punishment, 12:190
  dangerous student, 13:370
  detention, 12:45
  disruptive student, 12:530
  dress, 12:125
  expression, 12:120
  expulsion, 12:440
  extra-curricular, 12:40
  firearms, 12:150
  gangs, 12:180
  generally, 12:10
  in loco parentis, 12:20
  loitering, 12:35
  off school grounds, 12:30
  organizations,
    control of funds, 25:180
    discipline, 12:495
    fraternities, sororities, 12:170
    religious groups, 14:140
  physical restraint, 12:195
  prohibited behaviors, 12:150
  publications, 12:130
  searches, 12:230
  special education,
    expulsion, 13:370
    factors to consider, 13:375
    suspension, 13:360
    weapons, 12:155
  suspension, 12:380, 12:475,
    12:530
    special education, 13:360
  time out, 12:195
  transportation, 12:46, 12:380
  weapons or drugs, 13:371

Student enrollment, 24:30; also see
  Average daily attendance
  after expulsion from another
    district, 12:490
  removal of non-resident pupil
    from school, 11:205
Student fees, see Fees
Student injury,
  liability, 11:430
  also see Emergency, medical
  also see Tort liability/immunity
Student, nonpublic school; also
  see Illinois High School
    Association
  compulsory attendance, 11:40
  driver education, 10:62
  special education, 13:70
  transportation, 11:360, 14:80
  tuition, 13:330
Student organizations,
  access by religious groups, 14:140
  discipline, 12:495
  funds, 25:180
  membership, 11:400
  secret organizations, 12:170
Student piercing, 12:127
Student publications,
  content regulation, 12:130
  distribution, 14:120
Student Records Act,
  generally, 7:160
  maintenance of records, 7:370
  notification, 7:250, 7:310
  penalties, 7:390
Student tattoos, see Tattoos
Student teacher, 22:60
Student transportation, see
  Transportation
Study hall monitor, 20:30
Subcontractor, 21:180
Subpoena, 18:270
Substantive due process, see
  Due process
Substitute teacher,
  assignment of aide, 20:40
  certification, 15:300
  compensation, 15:320
  conflict of interest, 3:145
  full-time, temporary, 15:320
  limitation on work year, 15:310
  part-time, 16:160
  qualifications, 15:300
  seniority, 16:190
  tenure, 16:80

Summer camp,
athletic eligibility, 27:370
coach, 27:420
Summer school,
generally, 10:130
minimum salary, 15:410
tax levy, 23:210
transportation, 11:390
Sunday, 9:430
Super-tenure, 16:90
Superintendent
dismissal, 19:160
dual role as principal, 19:30
multi-year contract, *see
Multi-year contract*
qualifications, 19:60
regional, *see Regional
Superintendent*
State, *see Education, State
Superintendent*
tenure, 19:110
**Supervision of students, liability
for,** 22:22
Supervisory employee, 21:90
Supplemental budget, 25:40
Suspension, bus driver permit,
20:220
Suspension, employee, 17:685
noncertificated, 20:140
teacher, 18:370
**Suspension, special education
student,** 12:410, 13:360
Suspension, student, *see Student
discipline*
Suspension, teaching certificate,
15:60, 15:600

- T -

Talented student, *see Gifted*
Tattoos, student, 12:127
Taxable property,
assessment intervention, 23:70
borrowing, 26:100
estimation of aggregate tax levy,
23:150
information about, 23:50
levy generally, 23:10
tax rates, 23:180,
also see Property tax
Tax abatement,
generally, 23:270
state aid generally, 24:100
**Tax anticipation notes and
warrants,** *see Anticipation*

Tax appeals,
assessment generally, 23:40
assessment intervention, 23:70
Tax cap, *see Property tax*
Tax exempt,
foundation, 24:200
investments, 24:188
**Tax increment financing district
(TIF),**
creation of, 23:61
failure to develop, 23:68
financial information, 23:65
state aid computations, 24:100
value of property, 23:60
Tax levy,
aggregate, 23:140
amended, 23:130, 23:134
budget, 25:10
certificate of, 23:80
deadline, 23:90, 23:136
failure to adopt a budget, 25:35
new school district, 23:115
special education buildings,
13:410
transportation, 25:110
Tax limitation law, *see Property tax*
Tax rate defined, 23:175
Tax rate election, procedures,
certification of resolution, 4:290
governing laws, 4:40
information required, 4:330
Tax rate election, purposes,
amendment of budget after
election, 25:40
excess of maximum rate, 23:230
income generally, 24:30
Tax rate increase,
additional levy after election,
23:134
amendment of budget after
election, 25:40
excess of maximum rate, 23:230
laws governing election, 4:40
notice of election, 4:330
temporary, 23:232
Tax rate, special education,
23:200
Tax rates, maximum, 23:230
Tax rates, property,
amendment of levy, 23:130
bond rate, 23:195
excess of maximum rate, 23:230
generally, 23:170
income generally, 24:30

rent, 9:46
state aid computation, 24:100
Teacher aide,
generally, 20:20
teaching, 20:40
Teacher assignment and
transfer, see Assignment
Teacher certification, see
Certification
renewal of, 15:80
Teacher Certification Board,
revocation of teaching certificate,
15:60
use of noncertificated personnel,
20:20
Teacher, conflict of interest,
3:170
Teacher contracts,
extra duty, 15:230
part time, 16:160
probationary, 15.250
temporary, 15:320
tenured, 16:50
Teacher, duties of,
economic interest statement, 3:90
reporting child abuse, 11:330
Saturday duties, 12:45
transfer, 15:160
Teacher qualifications,
criminal background check, 17:20
generally, 15:10
reduction in force, 16:290
role model, 18:175
Teacher Retirement System
(TRS), 15:500
Teachers Health Insurance
Security Fund (THIS),
15:530
Teachers institute days, 10:230
Teachers orders,
debt limit, 26:270
generally, 15:470
orders, 26:180
short term borrowing, 26:110
Teacher, substitute, see Substitute
teacher
Teaching load, 15:180
Technical foul,
coach, 27:124
player, 27:122
Telephones, cellular, 12:165
Telephones, meetings via, 6:297
Temporary tax rate increase,
23:232

Temporary teacher, 15:320; also
see Short-term employee
Ten Commandments, 14:124
Tenure, administrator, 19:110
Tenure, teacher,
acquisition, 16:70
causes for dismissal, 18:100
creation of tenure rights by school
board, 17:600
defined, 16:20
dismissal of, 18:70, 18:250
repeal of, 18:72
sabbatical leave, 15:540
Term, school, see School term
Term of office,
Educational Labor Relations
Board, 21:40
school board, 2:50, 4:31
State Board of Education, 1:140
Territorial representation on
school boards,
canvass of election results, 4:405
eligibility to vote, 4:500
generally, 2:25
vacancies, 2:115
Testing, academic,
competency testing generally,
10:290
competency testing of students
with disabilities, 13:300,
10:303
excuse of student from, 10:315
Prairie State Achievement test,
10:302
proficiency exams, 10:40
required by law, 10:300
special education, 13:300
state authority, 1:300
Testing, drug, 20:230
Testing, employment, 14:520
Testing, GED, see High school
equivalency
Textbooks, also see Materials
adoption of, 10:350
fees, 10:370
funds for and from, 25:80
Tie vote, 4:415
TIF, see Tax increment financing
Time out, 12:195
Title IX,
generally, 11:150
sexual harassment, 11:410
suit by student against employee,
11:417

Title to school property, 9:20
Tobacco,
  on school property, 9:375
  purchase by minors, *see Minors*
Tort fund levy,
  defense costs and judgments,
    22:230
  tort immunity fund, 22:250,
    23:220
  tort judgment bonds, 26:250
  use of tort fund for risk
    management, 23:221
Tort judgment bonds,
  levy, 23:220
  generally, 26:250
Torts and tort immunity,
  closed meetings, 6:170
  duty of care, *see Duty of care*
  injuries to students, 22:100
  in loco parentis, 12:20, 22:100
  intentional infliction of emotional
    distress, 22:18
  invitees (visitors), 22:210
  negligence, 22:100
  negligent supervision, 22:22
  noncertificated employees, 20:60
  out-of-state trip, 22:160
  playgrounds, 22:167
  punitive damages, 22:12, 22:70
  qualified immunity, 22:64
  school boards generally, 22:20
  school bus, 22:145
  waiver, 22:164
  willful and wanton misconduct,
    22:14
Township, congressional,
  ballot position, 4:260
  historically, 9:10
  membership on school board, 2:10
  territorial requirements, 2:25
  vacancies on school board, 2:115
Township school trustees,
  appointment of treasurer, 5:90
  compatibility of office, 3:40
  title to property, 9:20
Township treasurer, *see Treasurer*
Traffic safety,
  crossing guards, 9:380
  generally, 9:320
  other safety requirements, 22:190
  traffic signals, 9:400
Transcript,
  expulsion hearing, 12:478

Transfer of funds, *see Interfund
    loans and transfers*
Transfer of power, 1:270
Transfer of teachers, 15:160
Transfer of employment rights,
  administrator, 19:105
  combination of districts, 16:150
  sick leave, 15:590
  super tenure, 16:90
  tenured teacher, 16:150
Transfers, student
  attempt to enroll after expulsion,
    12:490
  generally, 27:250
Transitional bilingual education,
    see Bilingual education
Transportation, 11:360
  after school detention, 12:46
  borrowing, 25:280
  bus construction, 22:193
  day care, 10:180
  extra-curricular activities, 11:394
  general requirements, 11:360
  homeless student, 11:235
  parochial school students, 14:80
  pick-up, drop-off points, 11:365
  private carrier, 25:285
  purchase or lease of bus, 25:280
  safety, 22:145
    construction of buses, 22:193
  special education student,
    private schools, 13:110
    related services, 13:140
    summer school, 11:390
  vans, 22:196
  also see Bus driver
Transportation fund,
  bidding, 25:220
  excess of maximum tax rate,
    23:230
  generally, 25:110
  interfund loans, 26:40
  tax anticipation warrants, 26:130
  tax levy, 23:170,
Treasurer, school,
  appointment or election, 5:80
  county school units, 1:60
  incompatible offices,
    generally, 3:40
    qualifications of school board
      member, 3:10
  vacancies, 2:110
  qualifications, 5:95

receipt of revenue,
  dates for property tax, 23:100
  delivery of state aid, 24:160
  depositaries, 24:180
  release of payments, 25:210
  revolving funds, 25:170
  teachers orders, 15:470
TRS, see *Teachers Retirement System*
Truancy, 11:50, 11:70,
Truant officer, 11:80, 11:110
Trustees, school, see *Regional
  Board of School Trustees; also
  see Township school trustees*
Truth in taxation, 23:140
T-shirts, 12:128
Tuberculosis examination,
  11:250, 17:10
Tuition, *also see Fees*
  adult education, 10.190
  deactivated high school, 9:120
  distinguished from fees, 11:260
  entire school, 8:165
  non-high school district, 23:250
  procedure to require
    non-residents to pay, 11:205
  residents and non-residents,
    11:180, 11:200
  special education students, 13:330
  summer school, 10:130
  waiver of, 11:195

▪ U - V - W - X - Y - Z -

Unemployment insurance,
  eligibility, 17:280, 20:140
  tort judgment bonds, 26:250
Unexcused absence, 11:60
Unfair labor practice,
  bargaining in good faith, 21:360
  communication with employee,
    21:166, 21:282
  status quo, 21:590
  union representation, 21:282,
    21:340
  vacating arbitration awards,
    21:540
  waiver of additional bargaining,
    21:202
Uniforms, student, 12:126
**Union certification/
  decertification,** 21:270
Union shop, 21:310
Unit school district,
  creation, 8:33

tax rates, 23:180
types of districts, 1:70
Unsatisfactory rating, 15:370
Unsportsmanlike conduct, *see
  Sportsmanship*
Vacancy in office,
  candidates to fill,
  closed meeting discussion,
    6:170
  petition, 4:150
  running for two offices, 4:190
  school board,
    creation of, 2:70, 3:190, 3:196
    resignation, 3:180
    filling of, 2:90
  State Board of Education, 1:170
Vacation pay, 15:440
Vandalism, 9:420
Vans, 22:196
Veterans, 17:40
Vice president, school board,
  absence from meeting, 5:40
  officers generally, 5:10
  voting, 6:270
Visitors and spectators,
  bargaining representative, 21:430
  extra-curricular events, 12:40
  safety of, 22:180, 22:210
  school board member, 2:150
Vocational education,
  cooperative,
    debt, 26:190
    joint agreements, 10:210
    tax levy, 23:20
  graduation requirements, 10:30
  interscholastic activities, 27:248
  real property, 9:20
  required, 10:155
  special education, 13:165
  state aid, 24:80
  teachers,
    certification, 15:20
    tenure, 16:100
Voluntary recognition, 21:130
Volunteer,
  liability for negligence, 22:60
  punitive damages, 22:70
  supervision of students, 20:20
  worker compensation, 17:260
Voter approval,
  bond issue, 26:190
  construction of building, 9:200
  deactivate high school, 9:120
  district organization, 8:10, 8:40

elections, 4:290
free textbooks, 10:380
school board type, 1:110
tax limitation increase, 23:235
tax rate increase,
     by referendum, 23:230
     capital improvement fund,
          25:160
     effect on income, 24:30
     temporary increase, 23:232
Voter petitions,
district reorganization,
     boundary changes, 8:80
     unit district, 8:40
filing, 4:80, 4:310
free textbooks, 10:380
objections to, 4:70, 4:315
sale of school land, 9:150
school board representation, 2:27
school board type, 1:120
Voter qualifications, *see
Qualifications*
Votes required for adoption,
dismissal of teacher, 18:80
emergency election petition, 4:320
exchange of school property, 9:170
lease of property,
     personal property, 25:290
     real property, 9:46
     real property, to a third party,
          9:190
reduction in force, 16:280
sale of school site, 9:110
supplemental budget, 25:40
waiver of administrative
     expenditure limit, 25:25
withdrawal from joint agreement,
     13:46
Voting, school board, *see Meetings*
Wages and hours,
Fair Labor Standards Act, 20:70
minimum salary, 15:400
reduction in force, 20:182
Waiver of bargaining right,
     21:145, *also see Zipper clause*
Waiver of meeting notice, 6:150
Waiver of state rules, statutes,
     1:380
approval of, 1:386
charter schools, 1:500
denial of, 1:382
length of, 1:388
procedure for, 1:384
Waivers, employee, 7:90

Waivers, fee,
parent institute, 10:245
student fees, 11:260
textbooks, 10:390
tuition, 11:195
Waivers, student,
IHSA rules, 27:90, 27:190
liability for injury, 22:164
records, 7:230
Wall-to-wall bargaining unit,
     21:220
Watch list, academic, 1:320
removal from, 1:340
Watch list, financial, 26:280
removal from, 26:300
Weapons,
discipline of students for, 12:155
defined, 12:157, 13:371
generally, 12:150
reporting, 12:156
Weighted grades, 24:110
Weingarten rights, 17:740
Whole child test, 8:240
Willful and wanton misconduct,
generally, 22:14
in loco parentis, 12:20
Witness fees, 13:570, 22:240
Work experience programs,
generally, 10:150
required, 10:155
Work load, *see Teaching load*
Workers' compensation,
application to school employees,
     17:240
borrowing for, 26:250
Working cash fund,
abolishing, 26:70, 26:240
bonds,
     abolishing working cash fund
          to issue, 26:240
     back door referendum, 23:250
     elections, 4:40
     generally 26:190
creation of, 26:50
loans from, 26:40
misuse of, 3:200, 3:210
state aid and, 25:70
Work rules, 17:720
Write-in candidates, 4:280
Zipper clause, 21:190, 21:200,
     21:202
Zones, *see Attendance zones*